Regional and Ethnic Conflicts

Perspectives from the Front Lines

JUDY CARTER

Royal Roads University

GEORGE IRANI

Toledo International Center for Peace

VAMIK D. VOLKAN

University of Virginia

PEARSON

Prentice Hall

Upper Saddle River, New Jersey 07458

Library of Congress Cataloging-in-Publication Data

Regional and ethnic conflicts : perspectives from the front lines /[edited by] Judy Carter,
George Irani, Vamik D. Volkan.
    p. cm.
    ISBN 0-13-189428-5
    1. Ethnic conflict—Case studies.   2. Conflict management—Case studies.   I. Carter, Judy.
II. Irani, George.   III. Volkan, Vamik D.
    HM1121.R44 2008
    305.8—dc22

                                          2007051142

Editor-in-Chief: Yolanda de Rooy
Executive Editor: Dickson Musselwhite
Associate Editor: Rob De George
Editorial Assistant: Synamin Ballatt
Senior Marketing Manager: Kate Mitchell
Managing Editor: Joanne Riker
Manufacturing Project Manager: Wanda Rockwell
Creative Director: Jayne Conte
Cover Design: Jonathan Boylan
Full-Service Project Management/Composition: Aptara, Inc.
Printer/Binder: R. R. Donnelly/Harrisonburg

Credits and acknowledgments borrowed from other sources and reproduced, with permission, in this textbook
appear on appropriate page within text.

Pearson Education LTD.
Pearson Education Australia PTY, Limited
Pearson Education Singapore, Pte. Ltd
Pearson Education North Asia Ltd

Pearson Education, Canada, Ltd
Pearson Educación de Mexico, S.A. de C.V.
Pearson Education–Japan
Pearson Education Malaysia, Pte. Ltd

10 9 8 7 6 5 4 3 2 1
ISBN-13: 978-0-13-189428-0
ISBN-10:   0-13-189428-5

Contents

Acknowledgments

The editors of this book would like to extend their warm appreciation to Amelie Gauthier and Joumana Yahchouchi for their assistance. We also wish to thank Judy Barsalou and Joe Klaits from USIP and Vern Redekop from St. Paul University in Ottawa, who helped us identify the authors of some of the readings.

We also wish to thank the following reviewers for their valuable suggestions: Stephan L. Rozman, Tougaloo College; Timothy J. Schorn, University of South Dakota; Marc V. Simon, Bowling Green State University; Timothy D. Sisk, University of Denver; Stephen J. Spielman, Webster University in Thailand; and Frank Wilmer, Montana State University.

1

Ethnopolitical Conflict in Perspective

Judy Carter, George E. Irani, and Vamik Volkan

Ethnopolitical conflicts are a leading cause of violence, suffering, and instability around the world. The end of the Cold War failed to produce stability and peace. Some interstate conflicts abated, but intrastate conflicts escalated sharply, both in number and deadliness. Many of the world's most intractable conflicts involve age-old cycles of oppression, victimization, and revenge. Violence, war, and "ethnic cleansing" are among the most dramatic manifestations of this cycle. From Sri Lanka to Cyprus, from Nigeria to Northern Ireland, and from Rwanda to Kashmir, the recurrent, intractable nature of ethnopolitical conflicts is evident in the cases discussed in this book.

While researchers' understanding of and ability to manage conflict have increased during the past two decades, ethnopolitical conflicts remain difficult to understand and mitigate. Ethnopolitical conflicts are especially complex and multi-causal. As well, the forces and factors at play are different, steeped in history, and in some ways alien to those at play in other contemporary conflicts. One salient feature that distinguishes ethnopolitical conflict is the role that ethnicity plays. Ethnopolitical conflicts occur when some aspect of a group's ethnicity becomes politicized. Groups may define themselves or be defined by others using ethnic criteria. They may allege that their collective interests are being threatened or thwarted by internal (national or state government) or external (political or economic) forces.

Alternatively, ethnicity may be advanced as the reason for attacking or even trying to exterminate a group. Ethnicity, in many cases, plays a key role in disputing parties' sense of identity, which explains why threats to culture, beliefs, and values sometimes result in virulent ethnopolitical conflict.

Looking ahead, ethnopolitical conflicts are forecast to be a leading cause of violence and war in the twenty-first century. Conventional efforts to mitigate ethnopolitical conflict are slow, can be ineffective, and are sometimes inappropriate. Consequently, economic, social, political, ecological, and human costs associated with ethnopolitical conflict are continuing to accrue.

Humanity's failure to prevent, mitigate, and resolve intractable interstate and intrastate ethnopolitical conflicts suggests that those seeking to end them may be missing certain insights or new, alternative perspectives into the parties, issues, and dynamics involved in these deadly, tragic conflicts. The urgency with which new insights, deeper understanding, and more effective approaches to ethnopolitical conflict must be sought continues to be driven home by nightly news headlines of violence, war, and suffering. Terrorist attacks on centers of political and economic power and the targeting of civilians underscore developed countries' inability to shield citizens from ethnopolitical conflicts occurring elsewhere in the world and the violent tactics that desperate disputing parties employ.

Perspectives from the Front Lines aims to provide an alternative vantage point, one that offers new perspectives to the study of ethnopolitical conflict. *Perspectives from the Front Lines* endeavors to deepen and broaden the global community's understanding of ethnopolitical conflict. Two key features distinguish this text.

First and foremost, chapters comprising this book have been contributed by people who have lived or worked in regions afflicted by ethnopolitical conflict. *Perspectives from the Front Lines* gives readers alternative, firsthand, front-line perspectives and insights on some of the major ethnopolitical conflicts plaguing the planet. It also gives people who have lived on the front lines an opportunity to tell their stories in their words, thereby humanizing their plight. Contributors describe and explain the factors and forces that have instigated and perpetuated the conflict in which they, their compatriots, and their enemies are ensnared. Contributors' chapters provide front-line accounts of the realities and complexities of ethnopolitical conflict. In addition, they note the clear and present danger that ethnopolitical conflicts pose to global security.

The second distinguishing feature of this book is its multidisciplinarity. Contributors come from several fields, including international relations, conflict management, government, nongovernmental organizations, military, diplomatic service, law, political science, sociology, psychology, anthropology, psychiatry, engineering, and project management. In an effort to contribute new insights to a sometimes overlooked aspect of ethnopolitical conflict, special attention is paid to its socio-psychological dimensions. Purposely inviting contributors from diverse fields and perspectives to share their views succeeds in illustrating the many perspectives from which ethnopolitical conflicts can be viewed. Chapters are, in some cases, presented in pairs so that readers can study disputing sides' views and reflect on their differing perspectives of the same conflict. Especially noteworthy is the chapter on the Israeli/Palestinian conflict. By co-writing this chapter, its authors exemplify how parties with differing perspectives can respect each others' views and work together.

Perspectives from the Front Lines aims to broaden the discussion and go beyond the usual single-discipline view presented in most academic texts. Rather than focusing on a specific conflict resolution theory or intervention strategy, this text encourages readers to inventory, weigh, and contemplate the interplay between the many forces and factors involved in these intractable, violent conflicts.[1] It encourages readers to consider the multi-dimensionality of ethnopolitical conflict, its many intertwined causes, and the multi-pronged approaches needed to effect enduring, systemic change. By inviting front-line observers to share their stories, it is hoped that their passion and depth of expression will convey the complexity of these conflicts and the challenges that must be surmounted to resolve them and achieve lasting peace.

While contributors' chapters demonstrate how different disputants' interpretations of the conflict in which they are mired can be, they also reveal striking similarities. Chapters in this book make it possible for readers to see how old conflicts, as well as previous peacemaking efforts, are impacting current events. They illustrate how, after several generations, conflict can become embedded in group identity, such that disputing parties define themselves in terms of their fight with one another. They show, too, the tragedies that unresolved ethnopolitical conflicts cause.

Equally, if not more, important, contributors propose recommendations for action. They flag those aspects of the conflict they are analyzing that are most volatile and potentially deadly. They propose interventions and initiatives they believe will reduce and resolve tensions and promote peace. Contributors' recommendations are synthesized, and guidelines for action are presented in the concluding chapter.

Ethnopolitical conflicts discussed in *Perspectives from the Front Lines* include those in Northern Ireland, Cyprus, Rwanda, Nigeria, and Sri Lanka, as well as those between Israel and Palestine, Turkey and Greece, Croatia and Serbia, Macedonia and Albania, and India and Pakistan. In the cases presented, contributors go beyond conventional "real politik" analyses of ethnopolitical conflict. They look behind facts, figures, dates, and names. They discuss how history, politics, geography, economic development, and psychosocial factors such as identity, culture, beliefs, and values can contribute to ethnopolitical conflict. Contributors write candidly about international intervention and show how it can cause or aggravate ethnopolitical conflict. Some reveal the effects of globalization and explain how it and modernization actually exacerbate ethnopolitical conflict. Others show how the uneven distribution of power and wealth, injustice, oppression, inequity, poverty and hopelessness can precipitate violence and terrorism.

By taking a case analysis approach, this book answers calls from within the conflict management field for less state-centric and more humanistic approaches to both conflict analysis and intervention. In addition, this text showcases the power of disputants' personal narratives to articulate what is at issue in a given conflict. It also reveals disputants' ability to propose solutions that will resonate with and receive popular support from those who see aggression and even terrorism as the only effective ways of achieving their aspirations.

Contributors were invited to discuss the following aspects of the conflict afflicting their homeland:

- The history of the conflict
- The parties and issues involved in the conflict
- The way in which group identity, beliefs, values, sense of belonging, and security are impacted or threatened by the conflict
- Past glories, traumas, and events that sparked the conflict or are contributing to its persistence
- The way in which one group perceives "the enemy"
- Efforts that have been made to resolve the conflict and reasons for their success or failure
- Future predictions and recommendations on how best to promote peace

Each author chose how to best share his or her story and insights. Chapters are, as a consequence, wonderfully diverse. Each provides a snapshot of a dynamic conflict, details of which will likely have changed and continue to change. To gain a fuller understanding of the conflicts included in this text, readers are encouraged to seek additional and updated information.

Broadly speaking, contributors look to the past to explain how previous conflicts that were not satisfactorily resolved are impacting contemporary conflicts. They show how current conflicts open old wounds and reactivate old hurts and grudges. They demonstrate how conflict can be time-collapsed, resulting in centuries-old issues influencing contemporary conflicts. They demonstrate how a seemingly small incident or "chosen trauma" can become a lightning rod. In detailing disputing parties' divergent perspectives and concerns, they make plain the improbability of achieving a single, consensual truth about the past. They show, too, that when conflict becomes a defining aspect of group identity, disputes are inclined toward intractability and recurrence.

Contributors analyze the present. They delve behind the headlines and investigate the forces and factors contributing to the conflict plaguing their community. They describe the tangled web of political, historical, socio-cultural, military, legal, economic, psychological, ecological, and other factors contributing to most ethnopolitical conflicts. They explain how differing beliefs and values, large group identity and threats to it, and the role that political and community leaders play can influence ethnopolitical conflict. In explaining these intangible aspects of ethnopolitical conflict, contributors call into question, albeit unintentionally, the prevailing ethnocentric tenet that if disputing parties' underlying interests are addressed, their conflict can be resolved.

Contributors also look at the future. After summarizing efforts to resolve the conflict plaguing their community and reasons for their success or failure, contributors proffer their suggestions for reducing and hopefully ending ethnopolitical violence and discord.

Perspectives from the Front Lines is intended for use by concerned thinkers interested in deepening their understanding of ethnopolitical conflict and learning how the suffering it inflicts can be reduced or prevented. This book is intentionally accessible to a wide range of readers. It is not for experts and pundits alone. It is meant to serve as a forum to stimulate thought, dialogue, and change.

This book is for college and university students. Student's gain interest and insights into how complex ethnopolitical conflicts can be mitigated, resolved, and prevented, and this gives hope to the future. *Perspectives from the Front Lines* is meant to complement other texts. It can serve as a reader for undergraduate and graduate students. It is designed for use in a range of disciplines, including, but not limited to, peace and conflict studies, international relations, political science, history, sociology, public administration, and anthropology.

From a pedagogical perspective, this text is designed to expose students to alternative perspectives. It is intended to add realism and insight to students' understanding of distant ethnopolitical conflicts. Contributors were purposely asked to discuss a range of factors to bring to light the complexity of ethnopolitical conflict. Their chapters are meant to prod students to internalize the importance of analyzing and understanding ethnopolitical conflicts from multiple perspectives.

In addition to students, this book is for professionals working in the fields concerned with ethnopolitical conflict. It is for academics, practitioners, researchers, business leaders, and policy makers alike. The perspectives it presents and insights it offers are equally pertinent for diplomats, negotiators, legal professionals, and members of the media wanting to learn more about ethnopolitical conflict.

Perspectives from the Front Lines aims to foster deeper understanding of the issues involved in ethnopolitical conflict. Cases constituting this text bring to light the common characteristics of the ethnopolitical conflict and illustrate why complex ethnopolitical conflicts do not lend themselves to simple solutions. Contributors' stories give readers a front-line view of the tragedy ethnopolitical conflict causes and underscore the need to develop new, alternative approaches.

With regard to public policy and action, *Perspectives from the Front Lines* aims to provoke vigorous, thoughtful debate. It endeavors to challenge readers' perceptions and beliefs. It urges them to think more deeply and broadly about ethnopolitical conflict around the world. It asks them to think critically and reflectively about prevailing ethnocentric views of ethnopolitical conflict and the policies they engender. At the same time, this volume endeavors to foster and contribute positively to improved global ethnocultural understanding. It encourages and enables students, academics, decision makers, political leaders, and civic activists to become better informed. It urges them to take history, identity, and culture, as well as beliefs and values, into account so they can make wise, well-informed, culturally appropriate, pacific choices.

In summary, *Perspectives from the Front Lines* aims to promote the development and implementation of policies and initiatives that effectively decrease the incidence of ethnopolitical conflict and violence. It aims to contribute to the cultivation of a global culture of conflict prevention and peace promotion. It advances the notion that education, because of the understanding it engenders, is a portal, if not the key portal, to peace.

ENDNOTE

1. Owing to their multicausality, it is difficult to do justice to the many factors that cause and exacerbate ethnopolitical conflicts. In additional to those discussed in this text, forces and factors that students wanting to fully understand ethnopolitical conflicts should consider include economic welfare and development, the long-term effects of colonial government's "divide and rule" policies, religion, globalization and democratization, the availability of cheap and deadly weapons, socioeconomic inequality, stratification and its consequences, political and economic instability, impunity, and the lack of legal and moral accountability.

REFERENCES

Carnegie Commission on Preventing Deadly Conflict. Final Report. Washington, DC: Carnegie Corporation of New York, 1997.

Gurr, Ted Robert. "Peoples Against States: Ethnopolitical Conflict and the Changing World System: Presidential Address to the International Studies Association Annual Meeting," April 1, 1994, Washington, DC. http://www.csis-scrs.gc.ca/en/publications/commentary/com50.asp (accessed September 5, 2007).

Irani, George. "Mediating Middle East Conflicts: An Alternative Approach." In *Revolutionaries and Reformers: Contemporary Islamist Movements in the Middle East*, edited by Barry Rubin (Lanham, MD: University Press of America, 2000).

Irani, George, and Nathan Funk, "Rituals of Reconciliation: Arab-Islamic Perspectives." In *Peace and Conflict Resolution in Islam: Precept and Practice*, edited by Abdul Aziz Said, Nathan C. Funk, and Ayse S. Kadayifci (Lanham, MD: University Press of America, 2000).

Julius, Demetrios A. "The Genesis and Perpetuation of Aggression in International Conflicts." In *The Psychodynamics of International Relationships, Volume I: Concepts and Theories*, edited by Vamik D. Volkan, Demetrios A. Julius, and Joseph Montville (Lexington, MA: Lexington Books, 1990).

Lund, Michael. *Preventing Violent Conflicts: A Strategy for Preventative Diplomacy*. Washington, DC: United States Institute of Peace Press, 1996.

Montville, Joseph V. "Psychoanalytic Enlightenment and the Greening of Diplomacy." In *The Psychodynamics of International Relationships, Volume II: Unofficial Diplomacy at Work*, edited by Vamik D. Volkan, Demetrios A. Julius, and Joseph Montville (Lexington, MA: Lexington Books, 1991).

Rasmussen, J. Lewis. "Peacemaking in the Twenty-First Century." In *Peacemaking in International Conflict: Methods and Techniques*, edited by William J. Zartman and J. Lewis Rasmussen (Washington, DC: United States of Peace, 1997).

Ropers, Norbert. "Peaceful Intervention: Structures, Processes and Strategies for the Constructive Regulation of Ethnopolitical Conflicts." Berlin: Berghof Center, 1995. http://www.berghof-center.org/uploads/download/br1e.pdf (accessed September 5, 2007).

Volkan, Vamik, *Bloodlines: From Ethnic Pride to Ethnic Terrorism*. New York: Farrar, Straus & Giroux, 1997.

Volkan, Vamik D., Demetrios A. Julius, and Joseph V. Montville, eds., *The Psychodynamics of International Relationships, Volume I: Concept and Theories*. Lexington, MA: Lexington Books, 1990.

Volkan, Vamik D. *Blind Trust: Large Groups and Their Leader in Time of Crisis and Terror*. Charlottesville, VA Pitchstone Publishing, 2004.

2

Macedonia

Macedonia gained its independence peacefully from Yugoslavia in 1991, after holding a national referendum on the issue. Greece objected to the new state's use of what it considered to be a Hellenic name and symbol, so it delayed international recognition of Macedonia, which finally occurred with the provisional designation of the Former Yugoslav Republic of Macedonia (FYROM) in 1995. Macedonia became a member of the United Nations in May 1992, and subsequently became a member of other international organizations, under the FYROM provisional name. President Kiro Gligorov, leader of the Social Democratic Party (SDSM), who ruled the country between 1991 and 1999, managed to keep Macedonia independent of the conflicts occurring in the rest of the former Yugoslav states, during which period Macedonia also gained its international recognition.

Macedonia is a small inland country that has borders with Greece, Bulgaria, Albania, Serbia, and Montenegro (part of the border is with Kosovo). Macedonia has a population of two million people composed in majority by Slav Macedonians (64 percent), followed by Albanians (25 percent). Turks, Roma, Serbs, and Vlachs living in Macedonia account for about 8 percent. Religion is an important factor that differentiates ethnic Albanians from Macedonian Slavs. The majority of Macedonians are Orthodox Christians, in contrast with the majority of Albanians, who are Muslims. Furthermore, language is a factor that differentiates the Macedonians and the Albanians, as well as the Turks, Serbs, and Roma. Ever since the referendum in 1991 and the adoption of the new constitution, relations between the two major ethnic groups have remained tense, and Macedonia has remained a segregated country.

Ethnic Albanians in Macedonia have demanded greater cultural and educational rights, the most important being the recognition of Albanian as an official language. They have also sought greater representation in the government and other governmental bodies, such as the ministries, armed forces, and police. Furthermore, the 1991 constitution fully guarantees the right for ethnic Albanians to be represented in the government and parliament. Macedonians argue that ethnic Albanians enjoy sufficient rights. Macedonia is reluctant to give further rights to Albanians because they fear the Albanians will pursue autonomy and secession on part of its territory. Macedonia also cites the evidence that Albanians already have a state of their own, while Macedonians fought to be independent and recognized as a state.

During 1999, the SDSM was defeated and shifted to a government supported by Albanians, while at the same time Macedonia opened its borders to receive Kosovar Albanians seeking refuge from the crisis occurring in Kosovo. Some 300,000 refugees fled to the north of Macedonia during the height of the crisis, settling in with the rest of the Albanians. At the end of 2000 and beginning of 2001, tensions between both groups grew more intense, and as a result attacks exploded in the north of Macedonia, where it is claimed that Albanian guerrillas assaulted security forces and police, and vice versa. The Albanian guerrillas claimed that the rebels' main objective was to protect and improve the rights of the Albanian community in Macedonia. They appealed for international mediation to resolve their differences with the Macedonian Slav majority, and they demanded modification of the Macedonian constitution to recognize Albanians as constituent people. Attacks continued for months, rebels advanced near the capital Skopje, the Macedonian forces increased, and various truces were declared from both sides, only so they could replenish weapons supplies and regroup

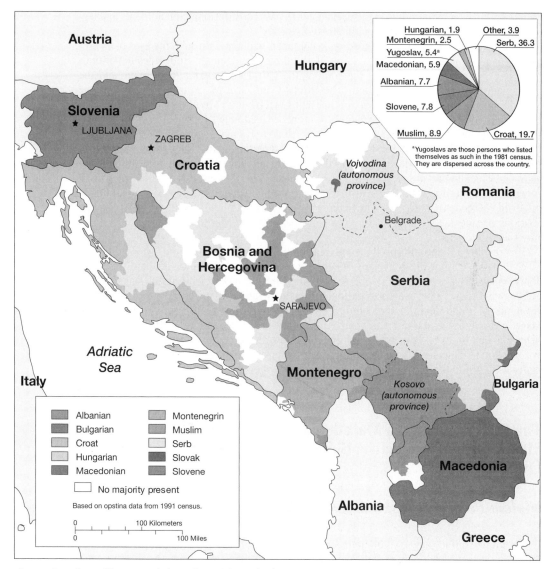

Hungarian, 1.9   Other, 3.9
Montenegrin, 2.5   Serb, 36.3
Yugoslav, 5.4[a]
Macedonian, 5.9
Albanian, 7.7
Slovene, 7.8
Muslim, 8.9   Croat, 19.7

[a]Yugoslavs are those persons who listed
themselves as such in the 1981 census.
They are dispersed across the country.

Legend:
- Albanian
- Bulgarian
- Croat
- Hungarian
- Macedonian
- Montenegrin
- Muslim
- Serb
- Slovak
- Slovene
- No majority present

Based on opstina data from 1991 census.

0   100 Kilometers
0   100 Miles

Source: http://www.lib.utexas.edu/maps/europe/yugoslav.jpg

forces. Violence increased continuously; the rebels called on all ethnic Albanians to join the ranks and for Albanians worldwide to support the movement morally and financially.

At the same time attacks were taking place, peace talks were also initiated between the National Liberation Army (NLA) and the government, with international mediators from the United States and Europe. NATO also played a central role during the peace talks, securing agreement and ensuring weapons collection.

After several months of deliberations, negotiations, and deadlocks, the parties finally agreed to sign the Ohrid Framework Agreement in Skopje on August 13, 2001. On August 15, the Macedonian government formally approved the deployment of a NATO force to collect weapons. The agreement required the parliament to pass constitutional amendments and legislation implementing the reforms within forty-five days.

In the following chapters, the Macedonian conflict is explained through the eyes of an ethnic Albanian, contrasting with the version of an ethnic Macedonian. Both sides detail their views in reference to the origin of the conflict, the Ohrid Framework Agreement, and the consequences. In the reading entitled "The Ethnic Conflict in Macedonia from the Ethnic Macedonians' Perspective: Being Victims in Their Own Country" by Violeta Petroska-Beška and Nicolina Kenig, the authors explain how ethnic Macedonians feel pressured by Albanians in "their" own land, how the use of force by Albania has managed to attract the international community's support for their demands for greater rights. The Ohrid Framework Agreement is seen by the Macedonians as the ultimate defeat in their battle against the Albanians. They feel it gives more power to the Albanians to remain segregated while penetrating government institutions, and they fear that in the future Albanians will demand secession and will divide Macedonian territory. The reading also refers to ethnic Albanian and Macedonian relations decades ago, exposing the views and feelings the Macedonians have developed about the Albanians.

The reading "Relationships Between Macedonians and Albanians in the Republic of Macedonia" by Fatmir Musa explains the discrimination directed at the Albanians in Macedonia, especially after passage of the referendum and the new constitution. Language has been an important factor in discrimination, employment, and the concentration of the Albanian minority in the north of the country. Violence against Albanians was escalated by the Macedonian police, and as a result many Albanians joined the fighting for the sole objective of having their humans rights protected. The Albanians see the Ohrid Framework Agreement as a solution to the conflict with the support of the international community and, most important, a way to stop the violence.

The Ethnic Conflict in Macedonia from the Ethnic Macedonians' Perspective: Being Victims in Their Own Country

Violeta Petroska-Beška and Nikolina Kenig

Every ethnic conflict has as many perspectives as there are parties. Macedonia's ethnic conflict is no exception. Ethnic Macedonians and ethnic Albanians who are the major players in the conflict hold opposite and evenly ethnocentric views of each other and of the causes and the consequences of the armed conflict. This chapter deliberately presents only the mainstream perspective of the community of ethnic Macedonians in its (as much as possible) authentic wordings and discourses.

Belonging to the ethnic group whose perspectives have to be presented has its advantage, but it poses a disadvantage, too. The advantage is that the presenter has easy access and genuine insight into his or her ethnic group's mainstream opinions. Most often it is enough to sit in a café and listen to others (all members of the same ethnic group) discussing their favorite topic: what innocent victims *we* are and what merciless perpetrators *they* are. The disadvantage is that such widespread conversations often take a direction that triggers a feeling of unease in us as observers.

This is exactly the case here. The pieces of the mosaic we present were gathered mainly by asking casual questions and listening to informal conversations, although we formally interviewed prominent historians, consulted history textbooks, and observed the media. In addition, one of us has personal experience facilitating a workshop in which both Macedonians' and Albanians' views of the armed conflict were openly presented and discussed.[1] The authors believe that this text strikes a good balance in integrating the voice of both "ordinary" people and intellectuals, as well as those who are liberal, moderate, and radical.

Therefore, the presented view is by no means a personal perspective of the authors. On the contrary, restraining from presenting our own comments and standpoints was one of the most difficult challenges we ever faced. What follows, then, is a summary of views of the common man and woman in present-day Macedonia, in which common, everyday observations are idealized, summarized, and presented.

THE CONFLICT AND ITS ESCALATION: OUR INNOCENCE AND THEIR UNSCRUPULOUSNESS

The modern-day state of Macedonia was created in mid-1944 on the eve of complete liberation from fascist occupation. Macedonia was constituted as a member state of the Yugoslav federation, making it an equal partner with Serbia, Croatia, Slovenia, Bosnia and Herzegovina, and Montenegro. The establishment of Macedonia was an outcome of the national liberation struggle of ethnic Macedonians and their centuries-long aspirations for national freedom and independence and a state of their own.

In September 1991, Macedonia seceded from Yugoslavia in a peaceful, democratic, and legal way. It was proclaimed a sovereign and independent state after a referendum in which 98 percent of those who voted were in favor of separation. Under the name Republic of Macedonia, it remained a state of the Macedonian people (ethnic Macedonians) who constitute two-thirds of the country's population of two million. Other ethnicities in Macedonia include ethnic Albanians, who account for one-quarter of the population, and ethnic Turks, Roma, Serbs, Vlachs, and others who account for the remaining 10 percent.

From ethnic Macedonians' perspective, the Albanian minority in Macedonia has been a source of persistent internal tensions ever since sovereignty and independence were proclaimed. Concentrated in the northwest part of the country that borders Albania and Kosovo, where over 90 percent of the population is ethnic Albanian, Macedonia's Albanians have resented and resisted what they regard as inferior status and discrimination while openly demonstrating greater loyalty to Kosovo and Albania than to Macedonia. They have used the Albanian state flag and anthem in all their official events and private gatherings, refusing to acknowledge Macedonia's official state insignia.

Whenever ethnic Albanians (who are predominantly Muslims) talk about inferior status, ethnic Macedonians (primarily Orthodox Christians) point to the differences in the socioeconomic status of the two ethnic communities, which they see as an outcome of unequal emancipation due to the religious traditionalism of the Albanian Muslim community. Ethnic Albanians and their deeply rooted patriarchal conservatism are, therefore, held responsible for their lower level of education and their commitment to remain impenetrable to outgroup influences and resistant to broader social integration. For ethnic Macedonians, Albanians' choices are not perceived as an obstacle to their coexistence with their Albanian countrymen.

Ethnic Macedonians tend to believe that the radical ethnic Albanian political elite was the major player in creating interethnic tensions and disrupting Macedonian–Albanian coexistence within Macedonia. Radical political elites were held accountable for preventing ethnic Albanians from voting in the referendum for the independence of Macedonia. They are also considered responsible for imposing a referendum that created an illegal, autonomous Albanian territory within Macedonia. In addition, ethnic Albanian political representatives refused to vote for the Constitution of 1991 even though it guaranteed equal rights and freedoms to all Macedonia's citizens and granted additional cultural, educational, and language rights to ethnic minorities, which exceed the rights granted to ethnic minorities in most of the countries inside and outside of Europe. Albanian leaders forced the Albanian ethnic community to boycott a national census, claiming that the government had a hidden agenda and intended to falsify the figures by reducing the reported number of ethnic Albanians living in Macedonia.

Ethnic Macedonians are convinced that the violence that broke out between Serbian police and ethnic Albanian separatists in the neighboring Serbian province of Kosovo in 1998 deeply affected the interethnic relations in their country. The engagement of the international community, especially the United States campaign against Serbia for the stated purpose of protecting Kosovo Albanians from severe violation of human rights, convinced ethnic Albanians in the region that they had the world's most powerful allies on their side. International intervention encouraged Albanians to renew their long-standing bid to create "Greater Albania." It was not enough that Macedonia hosted more than 300,000 Albanian refugees who fled Kosovo during the NATO air strikes against Serbia in 1999; two years later, the Albanian separatists who fought for an independent Kosovo started the same terrorist strategy in an attempt to launch a new war, this time in Macedonia.

The armed conflict in Macedonia began in February 2001, when a group of Albanian extremists operating from Kosovo directly attacked Macedonia's security forces near the border. They called themselves the National Liberation Army but were using the same acronym (UÇK) as the Kosovo Liberation Army. When military officials set up posts aimed at preventing the spread of terrorist activities into a larger territory, extremists started ambushing and murdering members of the security forces. They expanded their attacks to civilian targets and began kidnapping innocent people, and they destroyed houses and religious buildings by robbing them, setting them on fire, and/or bombing them with mortars and grenades. Ethnic Macedonians and the other non-Albanians from the areas directly affected by the armed conflict were expelled from their homes.

At first, Macedonia's Albanians and their political representatives were against these terrorists. Later, they were forcefully driven into the conflict—they had to support the terrorists, either financially, by joining the fighting, or by serving as shelters or human shields to protect the terrorists from security forces. The Albanian political representatives (especially those who were part of the government) openly condemned the ongoing terrorist acts at first but later, to preserve their political power, they switched sides and justified the terrorists' cause, which added fuel to the fire.

Ethnic Macedonians blame the international community (the United States and the European Union) for preventing Macedonia's security forces from acting promptly and efficiently when the first terrorists' attacks started. Although the United States and the European Union condemned the terrorists and their actions at first, by switching from the word *terrorists* to *rebels,* they contributed to the later development of the conflict.

Macedonians blame the United States and the European Union for several reasons. First, the international community stands accused of doing nothing to prevent the flow of arms and fighters into Macedonia from Kosovo, even though Kosovo was (and still is) officially a protectorate under international control. Second, by urging the government to use "appropriate" force against Albanian terrorists instead of all possible means to destroy them, they allowed the armed conflict to spread to a larger territory and encouraged more Albanians living in those regions to join the fight. Third, Macedonians believe that by insisting on a peaceful settlement of the conflict, the international community approved violence and justified the Albanian terrorists' cause.

Ethnic Macedonians have never agreed with the ethnic Albanians' grievances, and they see their complaints as an excuse to take up weapons against the Macedonian government. They consider completely absurd ethnic Albanians' claim that in Macedonia they are treated as "second-class" citizens and deprived of basic human rights. Ethnic Macedonians are convinced that Macedonia's record on democracy, which used to be praised in numerous evaluations done by the international community, by far surpasses the records of other countries, not only in the Balkans but also in Europe, since no other minorities in the world enjoy all the rights to which ethnic Albanians in Macedonia are entitled. Ironically, Macedonian minorities in neighboring European countries (especially Greece) are left without even basic human rights.

On the other hand, the very same complaints lodged by ethnic Albanians regarding the way they are treated in Macedonia apply straightforwardly to the way in which Albanian men treat Albanian women. Albanian women are deprived of basic human rights and are discriminated against within the Albanian community in all spheres of life. For Albanian women in Macedonia, home is a prison. Albanian women live in a house surrounded by tall walls. They are never allowed to leave home without a man accompanying them and without a scarf covering their head and a long coat covering their body. Albanian women in Macedonia are rarely permitted to study or work or earn a living. Their status depends on the number of sons they give birth to and their obedience to male members of their extended family.

In addition to the general rights and freedoms that are equally guaranteed to all Macedonia's citizens, the constitution that was adopted in the parliament in 1991 provides special rights to ethnic minorities. According to the constitution, ethnic Albanians enjoy the right to express their ethnic/cultural identity on individual and institutional levels. In reality, many radio and TV stations, including the state-funded network, broadcast full programming in Albanian. Numerous private and state-funded daily newspapers, magazines, and other publications are written exclusively in Albanian, and a state-funded theater performs plays in Albanian.

With regard to education, minority rights in Macedonia are extended to the maximum. Consequently, ethnic Albanians can be educated in their mother tongue up to and even including university. In addition to the numerous elementary and high schools in which Albanian is the language of instruction, both state-funded universities in Macedonia have positive discrimination policies designed to favor ethnic Albanians and other ethnic minorities. One university even provides preservice training for preschool and primary school teachers completely in Albanian and has a well-established department of Albanian language and literature. In 2000, the government adopted legislation permitting the founding of private higher education institutions devoted to addressing Albanian demands for university-level education.

Albanian political parties have had representatives in parliament and have participated in every coalition government in the Republic of Macedonia. When the armed conflict began, ethnic Albanians held six out of eighteen ministerial postings in the government and accounted for 25 out of 120 members of the parliament. Whether they belong to the ruling coalition or are the opposition, Albanian politicians have focused primarily on issues that are of concern to ethnic Albanians only. Ethnic Albanians in Macedonia also have held high-ranking executive positions in public institutions, the army, the police, and local governments. Through the engagement and efforts of Albanian political representatives, many Albanian grievances and demands have already been addressed and numerous concessions have been made by Macedonian government leaders.

In the context of such circumstances, the first question that ethnic Macedonians often raise is this: *Is there a justification for taking up arms and using violence and terror to acquire political aims in a country with well-established and functioning political and media channels for expressing and tackling grievances?* The second question asks this: *Why is a fight for the protection of human rights being pursued by destroying other people's lives and property?* In the view of ethnic Macedonians, the answers to these two questions reveal the real nature of the so-called Albanian "freedom fighters" and the genuine cause of their fight. To ethnic Macedonians, Albanians are nothing but terrorists who fight for territorial autonomy and even secession and want either to change the borders and create an ethnically pure "greater Albania" (or at least "Greater Kosovo") or to control the region for the benefit of their highly organized criminal activities, which include smuggling narcotics and weapons and people trafficking.

TOWARD RESOLUTION OF THE CONFLICT: THE REWARDS OF VIOLENCE

Violent confrontation between the Albanian terrorists and Macedonia's security forces ended with the signing of the Ohrid Framework Agreement in August 2001. It was an agreement between the four largest political parties in the country (two Macedonian and two Albanian). The agreement stipulated the political and constitutional reforms required to improve the status of ethnic Albanians in the Republic of Macedonia.

The Macedonian ethnic community received this agreement as the ultimate defeat in the battle against Albanian extremism. The agreement was enforced by the international community, primarily the United States and the European Union, which pushed the Macedonian government to negotiate with terrorists who had killed innocent people sent by the very same government to protect the country. The international community took sides and directly supported Albanians' demands, neglecting or refusing to see the terrorists' real agenda hidden behind their struggle for equality: a battle for territory and power.

In general, the Ohrid Framework Agreement made the Albanian terrorists and ethnic Albanians appear as winners and the ethnic Macedonians as losers. Ethnic Macedonians do not see the agreement as a foundation for securing the future of Macedonia's democracy and improving interethnic relations in the country. Most of the Albanians' demands that are included in the agreement are perceived as factors that will contribute to disintegration instead of integration, the latter being what they are meant to encourage. Ethnic Macedonians present many arguments to support their view, including the following:

1. The Ohrid Framework Agreement met Albanian demands with regard to the establishment of official status for the Albanian language. Since it is spoken by more than 20 percent of the population, the Albanian language is to become the country's second official language. Its use will be required in all official business conducted at the republic government level, as well as in municipalities with more than 20 percent ethnic Albanians. Ethnic Macedonians see this as an official encouragement of ethnic Albanians' reluctance to learn Macedonian, as well as a clear signal for ethnic Macedonians in ethnically mixed (especially Albanian-dominated) municipalities to sacrifice their mother tongue in order to communicate with their Albanian neighbors.

2. The language issue is very closely connected with the required revision of the municipal boundaries to those that existed in the time of the violent conflict. It is obvious for ethnic Macedonians that the draft law on new territorial organization that is being offered to satisfy the obligations of the agreement is being strongly influenced by ethnic Albanians' desire to make the Albanian language the official language in as many municipalities as possible. Likewise, ethnic Macedonians are afraid that the territory will be tailored in such a way as to create as many Albanian-dominated municipalities as possible. That was made possible by the adoption of a policy (imposed by the agreement) that no decision in the parliament that affects the nonethnic Macedonian communities can be reached without an approval from the majority of the non-Macedonian representatives.

3. The agreement calls for administrative decentralization. The central government is to transfer significantly more responsibilities to local self-governments: each municipality is to have a stronger and more efficient local self-government and be responsible for managing its own financial affairs. Ethnic Macedonians are convinced that by permitting this kind of independence to the Albanian-dominated municipalities, the government will lose control over the western part of Macedonia's territory. They see the decentralization combined with the new territorial organization (ethnically defined municipal boundaries) as a step toward federalization of the country and possible secession of an "Albanian territory."

4. The agreement includes a commitment to satisfy ethnic Albanians' demand to have the government provide university education in the Albanian language first among all privileges accorded Albanian students at all levels of education. In other words, the government should finance the illegal Tetovo University—an Albanian-language university founded some years before the armed conflict. Ethnic Macedonians see this request as evidence that ethnic Albanians have no intention of integrating into a shared society with them. They see it as evidence that they intend to foster a separate Albanian society within Macedonia. Since international observers have described Tetovo University's curriculum as highly ideological and nationalistic, ethnic Macedonians have no doubts that the previous experience with the Albanian-language university in Kosovo, which had become a center of demands for the secession of Kosovo from Serbia, will soon be repeated in Macedonia. Tetovo University was also assessed as being below standard in terms of curricula and the qualifications of personnel, which leads ethnic Macedonians to the conclusion that Albanian nationalist leaders are more determined to provide "Albanian education" than to provide "good education" to their children.

5. The agreement set up the principles of nondiscrimination and equitable representation of ethnic minorities in the public sector, requiring increased representation of ethnic Albanians in public institutions. Due to the internationally imposed economic reforms that call for a reduction of the number of citizens employed in public administration, ethnic Macedonians stand to lose their jobs and be replaced by ethnic Albanians who are, most of the time, underqualified or less qualified. Such job losses add an additional burden to the ethnic Macedonian community. Since Macedonia has been going through a transitional process of privatization, a huge number of ethnic Macedonians who used to work in big companies have lost their jobs. Given that Macedonia is a very poor country with an exceptionally high level of unemployment (almost 40 percent), ethnic Macedonians feel as if the ethnic Albanians' grievances are being solved at the expense of the ethnic Macedonians' everyday survival.

6. The principles of nondiscrimination and equitable representation call for increased representation of ethnic Albanians in the police service, too. Ethnic Macedonians regard this as an unfair solution for two reasons. To become police, ethnic Macedonians have to go through at least four years of training. In contrast, ethnic Albanians now go through only several weeks of training before they put on a police uniform. Even more offensive to ethnic Macedonians is the fact that former UÇK members, who used to kill and massacre Macedonian police during the armed conflict, are now being recruited to serve as police after being granted amnesty under the terms of the agreement. At the same time, most of the Macedonian police reservists who were fighting against the terrorists, trying to defend their country, are left jobless and out of the regular police forces. This situation in very beneficial to the ethnic Albanians living in the areas affected by the armed conflict, who pay neither income taxes nor utility bills but use public health and social services, all at the expense of the ethnic Macedonian population.[2] Bill collectors are afraid to enter the territories that are not controlled by the police, and to prevent unrest company officials do not dare to cut off utilities. State officials also avoid sending tax police to companies owned by ethnic Albanians because such actions can easily be used as to rationalize alleged ethnic discrimination.

Conducting a new census was one of the demands that ethnic Albanians made. They want to prove that they represent more than one-third of the population in Macedonia (even though the figure of 22.9 percent was registered in the previous census of 1994). A new census, conducted in 2002 under international monitoring, confirmed the proportion of Albanians to be 27.2 percent, with the increase due to a high birthrate and illegal immigration from Kosovo and Albania. To ethnic Macedonians, this is just more evidence that ethnic Albanians are using all means to achieve their goal of creating "Greater Albania."

Although implementation of the agreement is imminent, the security forces do not yet have control over the whole territory of the Republic of Macedonia. A large portion of the territory that was directly affected by the armed conflict is still under the control of Albanian terrorists, who can freely engage in criminal activities. Regardless of the fact that the official UÇK leaders now hold government positions and that many UÇK members are in police service, they do nothing to facilitate the return of this territory to the control of the government and provide safety and security to the non-Albanian people who used to live there.[3]

The purpose of the Ohrid Framework Agreement was to offer a solution to the ethnic conflict in Macedonia by satisfying ethnic Albanians' demands. However, ethnic Macedonians do not see any benefits from its implementation. On the contrary, they see how damaging it is to Macedonian–Albanian interethnic relations. For the time being, ethnic Macedonians see the agreement as a factor that deepens the divide between the Macedonian and Albanian populations in Macedonia, instead of a source that contributes to improved social cohesion. This is not surprising when the agreement itself (and the Macedonian–Albanian propaganda around it) makes ethnic Macedonians see themselves as losers, and perceive ethnic Albanians as winners.

AWAKENED TRAUMAS: WILL THE UNJUST HISTORY BE REPEATED?

Macedonia is known as an "apple of discord" throughout the Balkans. It has been a target of neighboring countries (Bulgaria, Greece, and Serbia), which despite their bitter disputes over the territory agreed how to divide it before they jointly defeated the Ottomans at the end of the first Balkan War. Soon after that, however, it became apparent that more of the cake was expected, and eventually the second Balkan War—in which Greece allied itself with Serbia and fought against Bulgaria—broke out.

In the August 1913 Treaty of Bucharest, Macedonia's partition was signed and heavily supported by the Great Powers. The smallest part was given to Bulgaria (to its great disappointment), and the rest was divided between Serbia and Greece. The state policies in all three countries sought to create a variety of strategies aimed at ethnic purging and assimilation, which caused unspeakable terror among the local ethnic Macedonian population. That situation worsened at the end of World War I when the superpowers at the Paris Peace Conference ratified the Treaty of Bucharest, leaving the Macedonian territory partitioned to this day.[4]

Although the history of ethnic Macedonians from Vardar Macedonia (the ex-Serbian part) might be considered to be most fortunate—taking into account that they eventually acquired their rights to national identity and autonomy—their victory was not without bloodshed and grief.

During World War II, ethnic Macedonians reacted to the Nazi occupation by organizing an insurrection and seeking liberation. The occupational forces split the territory of Vardar Macedonia. While the central and the eastern parts were under the occupation of Bulgaria, the western portion was incorporated into Greater Albania, which was under Italian control. The life of ethnic Macedonians that inhabited this area became unbearable under the constant terror of the Albanian fascists called *balisti* and the uncontrolled Albanian gangs of *kachaci*.[5] Ethnic Macedonians were systematically impoverished by violent robberies and enormous taxes. The agenda became more than clear: it was to expel ethnic Macedonians from their homes and change the ethnic composition of the territory.

The clashes of 2001, and especially the behavior of the European Union and the United States, pulled the metaphorical trigger. Stories that had almost been forgotten over the past fifty years became vivid again. Macedonians once again had to ask themselves, *Is the land going to be torn up again to satiate the appetite of Albanians wanting to create Greater Albania? Is it possible that the powerful West will again overlook ethnic Macedonians' right to keep their country whole? Will hundreds of ethnic Macedonians who live in the northwest part of the country be forced to migrate, under the threat of terror, leaving space for another demographic alteration?*

THE CHAIN REACTION: FROM OUR GRIEVANCES TO OUR HELPLESSNESS

Ethnic Macedonians have only one homeland, and they would like their own country to belong to them. The territory symbolically embodies the struggles and sufferings of several ancestral generations striving to live free from oppression. After centuries of slavery, just when ethnic Macedonians thought they would be able to enjoy the right to express their own ethnic identity and nourish their own cultural values, the demands of ethnic Albanians dashed their hopes and provoked deep fears of another forceful and unnatural division of the land. Ethnic Macedonians are quick to point out that they already have their own mother state (Albania) with another on its way (Kosovo) and that they can enjoy the advantages of being the dominant group there.

The anxiety of losing their homeland is exacerbated by the fact that the very existence of Macedonian identity has been questioned and denied for a long time. Ethnic Macedonians are seen in mainstream Bulgarian politics and "science" as Bulgarians with repressed memory. Even more vexing, Greece has banned the use of the term *Macedonians* and the name *Macedonia* in its international communication, claiming that the name belongs to Greece exclusively, despite the fact that for generations these were words designating the identity of people who lived in the Macedonian territory.

In such aggravating circumstances, ethnic Albanians' political and intellectual elites came up with another line of attack. To stress their historical "right" over the territory, they constructed a theory of indigenousness and claim it applies to all Albanian people in the Balkans. They also maliciously deny the cultural and ethnic distinctiveness of ethnic Macedonians and derogatorily call them *Slavs*.[6] Unfortunately, this discourse was accepted internationally, causing fury among ethnic Macedonians who feel they are being wiped off the world ethnic map.

However, ethnic Albanians could not care less for the patriotic feelings of ethnic Macedonians and their need to maintain their identity (which is constantly denied by neighboring countries) by preserving the country as their own. On the contrary, ethnic Albanians use every opportunity to menace the country's integrity and confirm their disloyalty. The list of ways in which they do this is very long. At the very beginning of the history of the Republic of Macedonia as a sovereign state, ethnic Albanians were showing their animosity by openly abstaining from the 1991 Macedonian Referendum for Independence and by withdrawing from parliament when the first Constitution of Independent Republic of Macedonia was voted on. Ethnic Albanians disobey the duty to serve in the national army but will attend massive gatherings to hear fiery speeches in support of Kosovo's independence. They pledge readiness to sacrifice lives for that cause. There was no occasion when ethnic Albanians failed to fly the national flag of Albania *exclusively* and to sing its anthem *exclusively* on the territory of the Macedonian sovereign state, despite the clear regulations about how both are to be respected. In addition, Albanians attacked the holy core of Macedonian collective identity by desecrating and demolishing centuries-old churches and monasteries during the violent clashes.

Another legitimate fear that evolves gradually among ethnic Macedonians is that they might very soon find themselves in a position of being a minority in their own (one and only) country. The strategy of ethnic Albanian authorities—namely politicians and religious figures—that has stimulated an enormous increase in the birthrate among ethnic Albanians, combined with the state's indolence in creating appropriate population policies, portend future problems.

The frustration felt by Macedonians are not only at the level of wounded national feelings. They also worry about their everyday security. Flourishing crimes commited by bosses of the ethnic Albanian mafia are easily ignored by the security forces that sometimes share the interest and sometimes are scared to confront them. Not only are ethnic Macedonians insecure in conditions like these, but they also find themselves in the paradoxical position of being discriminated against for being good citizens.

Disappointed by the weakness of their politicians to protect their interests and dignity and betrayed by the double standards of the international community and by Albanian intellectuals who express disapproval over the violence but justify it as the only means to any end, ethnic Macedonians feel deprived of their rights to survive and disillusioned about non-violence paying off. The situation, they say, brings about nothing but anger, shame, and humiliation.

Ethnic Macedonians have a deep feeling of helplessness. Unable to control events in their country, betrayed both by domestic politicians and Western superpowers, they have no other option but to face the disgrace of being unable to protect their offspring and future generations.

THE FACE OF THE ENEMY: THE CRUEL COWARD

The wide us-against-them gap decisively shapes the perceptions of ethnic Macedonians who see ethnic Albanians as being an almost unnaturally compact and homogenous group.[7] In everyday discourse, the most widespread complaint one can hear from Macedonians is that "they suffer primarily because they did not learn how to stick to each other as ethnic Albanians do." In the imaginations of ethnic Macedonians, an Albanian would never oppose his or her in-group, let alone the leader. The enemy is, in Macedonians' mind, a bigot ready to make all kinds of sacrifices for the cause and to blindly obey the orders of ethnic leaders with no questioning whatsoever. No member of the ethnic Albanian community can be an individual in his or her own right but only a part of the monstrous (mysterious) collectivistic machine.[8]

In the eyes of ethnic Macedonians, the most commonly shared view of ethnic Albanians is that they are active and dangerous.[9] Some see the danger in their primitivism; some see it in their culturally inculcated worship of weapons; others see it in Albanians' agenda to take "everything that belongs to Macedonians," including part of the country. The danger ascribed to the enemy comes not only from the brutality of unspeakable cruelties but also from Albanians' deceptiveness.[10] There is a saying, especially widespread in the western part of the country, that expresses this fear clearly: *You should never trust a dog or an Albanian.* A dog can pretend to be your best friend. It can lick your hand, but you never know when it will attack you aggressively. An ethnic Albanian can pretend to be your friend but will easily betray you behind your back. On a larger scale, this tendency means that a supposedly naïve illiterate peasant, who does not understand or know anything, can turn into a terrorist overnight. Even more, being by definition predisposed to manipulation by and submission to their leaders, ethnic

Albanians are able to repeatedly fake mass sickness for the sake of creating an image of themselves as victims.[11]

The immense might of the enemy is seen to be due to its duplicity and disloyalty. In the realm of politics, the enemy can smile and talk about human rights. The enemy can appear to care for the country and its security, then suddenly change its statements or perform acts that are the exact opposite of what has been said. The attacks, however, are always craven and behind the back. In everyday life, the enemy is seen as skillfully manipulating perceptions with its twofold face. It pretends to be poor and disadvantaged but actually has a lot of money earned in illegal ways. It acts as if it is helpless but in reality gets better status than what is deserved.

Another view of the enemy focuses on its insatiable greediness. *"Give him a finger, and he will ask for the whole hand,"* say ethnic Macedonians when they describe the behavior of ethnic Albanians. The logic behind this stereotype is the step-by step political strategies used by political elites, which make Macedonians feel that there will never be an end to the demands that they must meet at their own cost.

The list is not complete without mentioning the primitive and animalistic side of the portrait, usually discussed more privately than publicly. This enemy, as every other created in collective fear, is not only warlike and predatory but also uncivilized, uneducated, and therefore a threat to everything that the country considers to be part of its cultural heritage. Perhaps the most offensive aspect of the enemy is acts in which it is both a lawbreaker and rapist. The enemy sees only non-Albanian women as sexual targets, while preserving Albanian women's purity and converting them to "birth-giving machines."

In this particular conflict, perhaps the most frightening potential of the enemy is its ability to manipulate the international community and succeed in getting sympathy from Western countries. Without "the little help from these friends," the terrorists would not be able to present themselves as martyrs or heroes, let alone tailor the politics of the country according to their own interests. Since the friend of my enemy is my enemy, too, the superpowers constitute another not quite so horrifying enemy.[12] Ethnic Macedonians' feelings toward this enemy, however, are very ambivalent. In the eyes of ethnic Macedonians, the West is unjust, decadent, conspiring, and selfish. It is interested in pursuing its own goals while "promoting" ideas of democracy and peace. Ironically, the West intervenes in Macedonia's sovereign affairs for the purpose of weakening precisely the same principles the West is striving to uphold and advance. Despite their anger, ethnic Macedonians admit they wish to be a part of wider pro-Western community.

WHAT CAN BE DONE: ONLY IF THERE WERE JUSTICE

Ethnic Macedonians blame the international community for their suffering in the Macedonian–Albanian ethnic conflict. The European Union and the United States approved Albanians' grievances and demands. They justified the violence committed by Albanian terrorists. Now ethnic Macedonians would like to see open and clear signals from the international community that it recognizes their grievances, praises them for their heroic tolerance toward ethnic Albanians, and consistently supports punishment of violence committed by ethnic Albanians inside and outside Macedonia.

The solution to the conflict as envisioned by ethnic Macedonians depends on the behavior of the ethnic Albanians and the government. Ethnic Macedonians want an end to the provocations that constantly shake ethnic Macedonians' tolerance. They want ethnic Albanians to start showing loyalty to Macedonia and its democratically established institutions. In other words, ethnic Albanians should insist less on preserving their ethnic identity and more on nurturing a broader civic identity. Ethnic Macedonians want the government to switch its attention to resolving social and economic problems instead of aggravating them on behalf of ethnic issues.

Nevertheless, the most important condition for a permanent solution to the conflict is a firm guarantee of sovereignty and territorial integrity for Macedonia from the international community, Albanian political elites, and the government itself.[13] According to ethnic Macedonians, the unitary character of the state can be preserved only if ethnic Macedonians are accepted as being the majority and the Macedonian language is spoken in the whole territory by all Macedonia's citizens.

Acceptance of Macedonia in the European Union and NATO is definitely seen as the best overall solution to all the problems affecting Macedonia, including ethnic conflict. Ethnic Macedonians believe that by becoming a member of the European Union and NATO, most of the socioeconomic problems will be solved and most of the reasons for the ethnic conflict will be abolished.

WAITING FOR THE FUTURE TO COME: CAN LOSERS LIVE IN PEACE WITH WINNERS?

The Macedonian–Albanian conflict is settled but not resolved. The violent attack on the state, presented as a "justifiable struggle for rights," ended as a triumph that brought privileges to the perpetrators. Contrary to what might be expected in such a situation, it did not raise the loyalty of the ethnic Albanians toward Macedonia or create a feeling of gratitude toward ethnic Macedonians. Ethnic Alba-

nians continue to neglect their basic obligations as Macedonia's citizens. They continue living at the expense of ethnic Macedonians and persist in fostering ongoing separation along ethnic lines.

The Ohrid Framework Agreement produced winners and losers. On one hand, ethnic Macedonians feel degraded by the international community, humiliated by their Albanian countrymen, and betrayed by their own government. On the other hand, ethnic Albanians celebrate the glory of their victory, convinced that the language of arms is not only the most efficient but also the most valued way of getting their own way. These recent and current circumstances have generated and perpetuate a psychological basis for maintaining tense interethnic relations, which—if unresolved—are likely to launch a whole new cycle of ethnic conflict.

ENDNOTES

1. V. Petroska-Beška and M. Najcevska. *Macedonia: Understanding History, Preventing Future Conflict, Special Report 115.* Washington, DC: United States Institute of Peace, 2000. http:// www.usip.org/pubs/specialreports/sr115.html (accessed September 5, 2007).
2. The budget for public health and social services is provided through income taxes that are collected on a monthly basis as part of employees' salaries. As in most transitional economies, people have many ways to avoid paying taxes.
3. After official amnesty was granted to all UÇK members who were not indicted for genocide, the official UÇK leader founded a political party that after the election in 2002 gained the majority of Albanian seats in the parliament and became a coalition partner in the government.
4. The contemporary Republic of Macedonia is actually the part that was given to Serbia by the Bucharest Treaty, known as *Vardar Macedonia.* The country acquired its autonomy by the end of World War II as one of the six republics within the Yugoslav federation.
5. The terror of Albanian *balisti* and *kachaci* is emphasized in all history textbooks intended for ethnic Macedonian students. It has become a major theme of the collective MacEdonian narratives that are connected with Macedonian–Albanian interethnic relations.
6. For instance, Russians, Bulgarians, Serbs, Croats, Slovenians, Czechs, Slovaks, Poles (and others) are also Slavs, but nobody refers to them under that name. Likewise, French, Italians, Spaniards, and others belong to the Romance group of peoples but are not called Romance when a distinctive nation is designated.
7. Whenever a non-Albanian threatens an Albanian, Albanians will support him or her without taking into account whether he or she is right or wrong.
8. Along these lines, the major disappointment, especially stressed by Macedonian intellectuals during the armed

conflict, was that not a single soul among Albanians has ever publicly opposed the mainstream claims and statements made by the Albanian political elites. They were voiceless to condemn even the brutal violent acts against Macedonian civilians or monuments.
9. V. Petroska-Beška, and N. Kenning, "The Self-Group and the Other-Group Images Held by Ethnic Macedonian and Ethnic Albanian Students at the Teachers College in Skopje, *Annual of the Faculty of Philosophy* 55 (2002): 105–24. A longitudinal research study was conducted in 1996, 1998, 2000, and 2002, after events that produced major crisis in interethnic relations. It was intended to reveal ethnic stereotypes among future preschool and primary school teachers. The results have shown that ethnic Macedonians tend to perceive ethnic Albanians as becoming increasingly active and stronger over time.
10. A frightful image that was frequently brought into play in media during the war were the backs of five ethnic Macedonian road workers, with letters carved by knife. This sadistic abuse, perpetrated by NLA fighters who appeared from the nearby woods, started with severe beatings and continued with anal raping and other horrifying humiliations (for illustration see http://www.hrw.org/press/2001/08/macedonia-0811.htm).
11. There were three incidents (1995, 1996, and 2002) of alleged group poisoning among Albanian adolescents, who claimed to be a target of ethnic hatred. Since a number of medical examinations have failed to pinpoint the cause, the incidents were reported in the Macedonian media as cases of collective delusion tailored by Albanian leaders with the aim of presenting the Macedonian state as conducting discriminatory policy against Albanians.
12. N. Kenig, "Assessment of Macedonians' and Albanians' Ethnic Identity with Identity Structural Analysis" (unpublished master's thesis, University of Skopje, 2000). Ethnic

Macedonians tend to perceive Western countries as allies to Albanians who live in Macedonia, but at the same time they identify themselves with some aspects of what they imagine to be Western. In other words, the perception of the Western powers is a source of conflicting identification in ethnic Macedonians' group identity.

13. In their daydreaming little talks, ethnic Macedonians frequently come up with ideas for dividing the country through an exchange of territories and populations between ethnic Macedonians and ethnic Albanians. They see such a swap as being the best logical solution to their interethnic problem. The same idea was uttered as a possible solution by a small number of radicals among the political elites. However, this option is rarely considered seriously, for in the eyes of Macedonians it favors Albanian extremists' quest to create "Greater Albania."

ABOUT THE AUTHORS

Violeta Petroska-Beška is a professor of psychology at the University of Skopje. She holds a B.A. in psychology from the University of Skopje in the Republic of Macedonia, an M.A. in psychology from Columbia University in New York, and a Ph.D. in psychology from the University of Belgrade in Yugoslavia.

In January 1994, Petroska-Beška founded the Ethnic Conflict Resolution Project, which was dedicated to mobilizing Macedonian citizens to assume an active role in the resolution of seemingly intractable ethnic conflicts. Since November 2001, she has been a co-director of the Center for Human Rights and Conflict Resolution, a research and training institution based at the University of Skopje.

Petroska-Beška is the author of several conflict resolution and peace education programs and manuals, as well as the author of the first book and thus far the only conflict-resolution primer prepared by a Macedonian professional for a domestic audience, *Conflicts: Their Nature and Ways of Resolving Them*. She has participated in many international conferences in the field of peace and conflict resolution and has given lectures on the ethnic conflict in the Republic of Macedonia at several universities around the world. Many of her articles have been published in local and international journals.

Nikolina Kenig works at the Institute of Psychology at the University of Ss. Cyril and Methodius in Skopje. She received an M.A. in international peace studies from the University of Notre Dame in Indiana in 1994 and completed graduate studies in social psychology at the University of Ss. Cyril and Methodius six years later. Currently she is working on her doctoral dissertation on culture dimensions. Her main research interests center on issues of ethnic identity, social categorization, and gender.

Since 1996, Kenig has worked as a research assistant at the Center for Human Rights and Conflict Resolution at the Institute for Sociological Political and Juridical Research. She has participated in numerous conferences on peace and conflict resolution and has been engaged as a guest lecturer abroad and in Macedonia. She is author or co-author of more than twenty scholarly papers on ethic and gender identity, as well as ethnic stereotypes and nationalism, all of which have been published in local journals.

Relationships Between Macedonians and Albanians in the Republic of Macedonia

Fatmir Musa

The Republic of Macedonia is a small state located in the Balkan peninsula. It is a country with a population of two million. The population is mixed; the majority are Macedonians, followed by Albanians, Turks, Roma, Serbs, Vlachs, Bosnians, and other ethnic groups. Macedonia is a multireligious state; orthodox Muslims and Catholics are represented, as are some other minor religious groups.

The Republic of Macedonia, officially recognized by the international community and United Nations as the Former Yugoslav Republic of Macedonia (FYROM) since 1995, was previously one of the six republics of the former Yugoslavia. After the Second World War, Macedonia became one of the equal republics that constituted the federation of Yugoslavia, along with Slovenia, Croatia, and

Bosnia and Hercegovina. Macedonia and Serbia were included as republics, and two entities, Kosova and Vojvodina, were granted special status and administrative autonomy.

As part of the former Yugoslavia, Macedonia as a region was less developed than the other republics and regions in every aspect of life. Often people who came to Macedonia were surprised by the differences between the region and other parts of the former Yugoslavia. Reasons for the regional disparity generated much discussion, but the reality on the ground remained unchanged.

Albanians were part of the Yugoslavian federation. Most of them lived in Kosova and dominated its population. Albanians were the second-largest ethnic group in Macedonia, not many fewer than the total number of Macedonians. Albanians also dominated south Serbia and Montenegro.

Albanians were all connected through their geographic position, symbols, culture, customs, and perhaps most importantly through marriage and close relationships. During the 1950s, when the communist regime was in power, many Albanians were deported to Turkey. They were pressured in different ways by Yugoslavian official authorities. The exodus included Albanians from Kosova and Macedonia and a small number of Albanians who were living in Montenegro and south Serbia. According to some statistics, more than one million Albanians currently live in Turkey. Ethnopolitical tensions and official pressures continued in the years that followed, and in 1968 huge protests were held, especially in Kosova. They were supported by Albanians in Macedonia and elsewhere. Protesters' goal and request was for the Albanian flag to be displayed in public in regions in which Albanians were a majority. Albanians in the federation supported this goal. During those protests, many Albanians were interrogated, imprisoned, and mistreated in all parts of Yugoslavia. Many Albanians were convicted, tortured, injured, or disappeared. As a consequence, Albanians were forced to find new solutions to survive the bitter realities of their situation. Many of those who were persecuted or mistreated decided to escape from Yugoslavia. The majority of migrants went to western Europe to work and live. They now reside in Switzerland, Germany, Austria, Belgium, Holland, France, Italy, and Great Britain, as well as the United States and Canada.

During the 1970s, Albanians were accused of being the group wanting to destroy the federation of Yugoslavia. This discrimination was felt on many levels in every aspect of life, including education, administration, culture, and economic development. In 1974 Yugoslavia adopted a new constitution, which gave more rights to Albanians and treated them more respectfully than in the past. Albanians won the right to use the Albanian language, which was accorded official status. They won the right to superior education in their own university. The Macedonian government promised it would employ a larger percentage of Albanians in governmental administration. Many Albanians who were living outside of Kosova were educated in Prishtina, the capital of Kosova. As a result, relationships were strong. By the late 1970s, Albanians were more united than before. Huge demonstrations took place in 1981. Albanians demanded that the human rights of Albanians living in Kosova be respected. Smaller demonstrations took place in Macedonia, where Albanians were the majority. Once again, many Albanians were mistreated, killed, injured, persecuted, or disappeared without a trace. In many cases, Macedonian police and army personnel were held responsible. Once again, Albanians were accused of trying to destroy the Yugoslavian federation—even though their legal and human rights were being violated.

At the beginning of the 1990s the federation of Yugoslavia started to fall apart, in large measure because it was a country without respect for human rights, it had no rule of law, and many instances of discrimination and fighting were used to dominate others. It was a country in which the Albanians were blamed for any problem.

In 1990, Macedonia held, for the first time in its history, pluralistic parliamentary elections. This was the first time a race was run among many political parties for seats in the parliament. The parties were all ethnically based, and none had any civilian political background. For the first time an Albanian political party was founded. The Partia per Prosperitet Demokratik (Party for Democratic Prosperity, PPD) was founded in Tetovo, one of the biggest cities in Macedonia, where Albanians constituted the majority. By participating in those elections, Albanians in Macedonia won their own official representatives in the Parliament of the Republic of Macedonia, the highest republican institution in the republic. After the election, the next step for Macedonia was to decide on the future of the Yugoslavian federation. After the separation of Slovenia and Croatia, the Macedonian parliament decided to conduct a referendum regarding the future status of Macedonia. In the September 1991 referendum, the citizens of the Republic of Macedonia decided that Macedonia should be an independent state, separate from the federation. From that day forward, Macedonia was a country responsible to its citizens.

After the proclamation of Macedonia's independence, the next big step—and I would say the most important one—was the adoption of the new constitution. A group of experts worked on a draft of the new constitution; no Albanian was part of the group. This exclusion was a crucial factor in the development of Macedonia in every aspect. Perhaps this was the point when everything started to go wrong. All Albanian political representatives were saying that exclusion was wrong. They argued that Albanians needed to be included in such important processes, but no one listened or cared about it. No one foresaw that these issues would cause the tensions they did and that they would still need to be redressed years into the future.

On November 17, 1991, Macedonia's parliament declared the new constitution. It was not supported by Albanian members of the parliament, since it did not recognize Albanians as a constitutional national entity within Macedonia. (This was later changed with revisions to the constitution in 2001, which were enacted as a result of the Ohrid Framework Agreement.) Albanian parliamentary representatives tried to explain to the Macedonian majority why the constitution harmed Albanians and other ethnic minorities. Their suggestions and arguments were not considered, although it was very obvious that the constitution was discriminatory. Many Albanians' rights guaranteed under the 1974 constitution were repealed, so Albanians had fewer rights than they had under the constitution of the former federation of Yugoslavia. However, the majority made its biggest mistake when it officially adopted the constitution without the support of the Albanians, the second-largest ethnic group in Macedonia. The fatefulness of this decision was demonstrated by events, which ensued immediately after the constitution's official enactment. The constitution became the source of all the conflicts that currently afflict Macedonia. Instead of

moving toward prosperity and further economic development, the Macedonian-dominated majority decided to withdraw from twentieth-century modernization trends and continue its discriminatory politics against Albanians. No dialogue or consensus occurred regarding this crucial decision. The position of the majority was clear: we are a majority, this is our state, so we will rule it as we want. It was a situation in which Albanians were treated like someone forced to pay rent for living in their own home. While this discrimination continued, Albanians were forced to pay taxes and serve in the army, and but they could not officially use their own language, gain access to higher education in their mother tongue, or take part in discussions regarding important decisions.

During those years, a coalition government was in place. The Albanian political party was included in the government, but its members were not given any real power or prestige in the prime minister's cabinet. Albanians were assigned to head departments that were unimportant, their authorities were limited, and they could make no decisions without the permission of the political party that was the majority. Albanians were just figureheads in a big picture, with no power or value. Some of them expended more energy looking after their personal interests than after the interests of Albanians who were living in Macedonia.

During the late 1980s and early 1990s many secondary schools, in which courses were taught in the Albanian language, were closed in Struga, Kicevo, and Kumanovo. In other places that offered a secondary education in the Albanian language, the number of classes was limited. As a result, Albanians who finished elementary school did not have adequate access to secondary school education. At the same time, in several cases (in the cities of Veles, Prilep, etc.) where Albanians were a minority, education from grades 5 through 8 was only available in the Macedonian language. Even though Albanian pupils wanted to study in their mother tongue—a right that was guaranteed under the constitution of the Republic of Macedonia—they could not. These and other forms of discrimination heightened ethnic tensions and contributed to conflict in Macedonia.

Pursuing the policy of the former Yugoslavia, the Macedonian government continued to blame Albanians for everything that went wrong in the state. Albanians were excluded from the state administration. They had very limited access to governmental administration, jobs, and services. The number of Albanians employed by the government was less than 3 percent. Most Albanians were employed in the Ministry of Education, not as administrators but as teachers and professors who were teaching in Albanian in primary and secondary schools. Comparing this with other ministries, where the representation of Albanians was about 1 percent of employees, gives a clear picture of the breadth of discrimination in Macedonia.

The conditions in schools are another concern. In the schools where Macedonians study, conditions are excellent, with many cabinets that contain all the necessary equipment, computers, and so forth. In some cases, the schools in which Albanians study do not even have a roof above students' heads; sometimes basic supplies like chalk and a blackboard are missing. These things irritate Albanians because they pay the same taxes as the Macedonians do but do not have the same facilities.

According to Macedonians, Albanians are the ones dealing in all the bad things, such as weapons, drugs, and contraband. The stories Albanians have lived through are not widely reported, especially not outside Macedonia. I will mention a few cases, that stand out for Albanians because of their importance, both actual and symbolic.

Bit Pazar in Skopje, also known as the Old Bazaar, was built during the Ottoman Empire. It is an interesting place for foreigners because of its unique architecture and well-known restaurants. In the green market nearby, the police caught a ten-year-old Albanian child selling chocolates and candy to feed his family. The police beat him in front of all the other people, many of whom were Albanians. A crowd was present, and the special forces of the Ministry of Interior Affairs took the situation into their own hands. In the end, three Albanians were killed, many were wounded, and several were injured and beaten. After that action, many Albanians were prosecuted and convicted. Several Albanians were invited to "informative inquiries" by the police, where they were brutally tortured. There were stories about this case in the newspapers and on Albanian-language television, but official representatives censored them.

Another example is the case of the village named Ladorishta, which is near Struga in the southwest of Macedonia. The village is near the border between Macedonia and Albania and is inhabited 100 percent by Albanians. In the early 1990s the police, comprised of ethnic Macedonians (with no Albanians), surrounded the village on the pretext that they were searching for illegal weapons. They destroyed several houses, arrested many people, tortured local citizens, and invited many of them to "informative inquiries."

In 1994, three municipalities with dominant Albanian populations (Tetovo, Gostivar, and Debar) decided to form a new private university, based in Tetovo, in which education would be provided in Albanian. The municipalities' intention was to finance the university with funds from the government's budget. The government was strongly opposed to their idea and refused to talk about it. The concept was supported by Albanians in Macedonia. There was support from Albanian members of the parliament, as well. On the day of the official creation of the university in Tetovo, several thousand Albanians attended the ceremony, along with guests from outside Macedonia. The special forces of the Ministry of Interior Affairs mounted an action against the institution and the people who were in attendance. One person was killed; several others were wounded; many more were injured, beaten, or tortured; and others were mistreated in the police stations. Despite this, Tetovo University has continued to function illegally in private homes and is financed by Albanian immigrants living outside the country.

Another incident occurred in 1997 in Gostivar, a city where the majority of citizens are Albanians. According to the law of that time, in the front of the municipal headquarters of Tetovo, Gostivar and Debar, the flags of Albanians and Turks were flying. The constitutional court of Macedonia decided municipal practices were anti-constitutional and ordered the other flags removed from the front of official buildings. The representatives of the local authorities opposed the edict and refused to remove the Albanian and Turkish flags. The very next day, police forces removed the flags in all three cities. A constantly increasing crowd gathered in Gostivar to protest the government's decision. The police attacked, and the situation became chaotic. During this incident three people were killed, many and others were mistreated, tortured, and injured—even children and elderly people in their homes. The police action continued for the whole day. Although no people remained on the streets, the special police forces searched people's homes. When they found people they beat them. Many people were arrested, one of whom died because of injuries received at the police station. Albanian people said they saw hell with their own eyes.

That same day, the mayor of Gostivar, Rufi Osmani, was arrested. He enjoyed the respect of Albanians not only in Macedonia but worldwide. The president of the municipal council of Gostivar and his colleague from Tetovo also were arrested. The court sentences were draconian. Rufi Osmani was sentenced to thirteen years and eight months; the appeals court reduced his sentence to seven years imprisonment. He served his time until 1999, when an amnesty for all political prisoners was declared. Worst of all was the position of the government, which tried to hide this case. The very same day the national currency was devalued. This action was clearly taken to focus attention on issues other than the Gostivar case. Also at this time, the prime minister, Branko Crvenkovski (who later became president of Macedonia), congratulated the police forces for a successful action. It is a strange behavior to be satisfied by the torture of your own citizens. (After many years, Crvenkovski acknowledged that the action in Gostivar was a mistake and should not have happened.) President Kiro Gligorov was in a similar position. The people who elected him were killed in Gostivar. Gligorov became president in the 1994 election thanks to Albanian votes. His election was a protest vote against the opposition party and its political platform, which boiled down to "We know how to handle Albanians!"

Many other minor incidents have occurred, including a case in which the pedagogic faculty in Skopje was penalized for using the Albanian language and incidents along the border with Albania, all of which have contributed to tensions and cannot be forgotten by Albanians in Macedonia. It is possible that the crisis in 2001 was a result of all these developments, as well as government repression, the government's politics, and frustration over the fact that the government did not have a clear position about what it should do. Albanians often asked if their houses were the only ones that should be searched, if they should always be the only ones to be blamed, if they were the only ones

who committed crimes or possessed weapons. The point of these activities was to portray Albanians to the international community as the only ones not respecting Macedonia's laws and to intimate that Albanians were guilty for whatever happened, even though newspapers reported many crimes that were committed in places populated exclusively by Macedonians. Some of the questions Albanians kept asking were, Why isn't there anyone who speaks about that? Why are there no raids for illegal possession of weapons in central and east Macedonia? Albanians never got any answers.

After all the developments in the 1990s, the 2001 conflict was the worst thing that could have happened in Macedonia. Many people still do not know what to call it: a crisis, armed conflict, war, or something completely different. Historically, no armed conflicts ever occurred between Macedonians and Albanians, but this cannot be said after 2001. Many people were killed, kidnapped, and disappeared then. Many houses were destroyed, as were mosques, churches, and shops owned by Albanians. Worst of all were the bombing and killing of civilians because they created a huge gap between the two parties involved in the conflict. The government did not have a clear vision. It did not plan to solve the problem through negotiations. Instead it decided to use force to handle the situation. The Albanian party, which was in power, did not have enough influence, and its members were very shocked by the situation. At the beginning of the conflict in February 2001, citizens heard many contradictory statements, which did not succeed in calming the situation. The prime minister and the minister of Interior Affairs were leading with claims that their opponents were terrorists who wanted to separate Macedonia and should, therefore, be eliminated. After the 2001 conflict, the Macedonian prime minister at that time, Ljubco Georgievski, and officials of the Macedonian Academy of Arts and Sciences offered an "exchange of territory and population" with Albania. They had probably forgotten that members of the National Liberation Army (NLA) were ordinary citizens of Macedonia and that discussion to advance the rights of Albanians in Macedonia was needed. Events in Macedonia clearly illustrated how, if the authorities had pursued negotiation from the beginning, the crisis could have been ended earlier without so many casualties and the mutual trust that previously existed between the two communities could have been preserved. The government chose the wrong approach, with many catastrophic consequences that made matters even worse.

The situation began to unravel, beginning with the village of Tanushevc, which is near the border with Kosova. The people who live in this mountainous village, which is in the territory of the Republic of Macedonia, were treated very badly by the authorities. More than 200 newborn infants were not registered (officially they do not exist), so they have no citizenship, which means they cannot obtain documentation for identification and is the reason why they were treated badly by the police and army. Villagers did not have the basic conditions they needed to live decently: they had no roads, no telephone lines, no school premises (the school looked as if it had been bombed). The state did not show any interest at all. As a result, the entire situation was fragile, and small issues created large consequences. The story started there and continued. The army and police surrounded the village, without trying to negotiate or speak with local citizens, and the situation deteriorated rapidly.

People who were part of the NLA started to issue official statements, claiming to be representatives of the Albanian people in Macedonia. They said their goal was to improve the position of Albanians in Macedonia while developing and protecting human rights. During March 2001, a big protest took place in Tetovo (one of the biggest cities in Macedonia, with an Albanian majority), during which many people showed their support for the NLA fighters. The same day the conflict enlarged to encompass the region around Tetovo. Later the conflict became even larger. Crises occurred in Kumanovo and Gostivar. The conflict continued to expand to other regions. In the Skopje region, villages such as Aracinovo and Radusha (which belong to the municipality of Skopje) were hit by violence.

During the conflict more than 140 people were killed. Casualties were suffered by both sides. Army and police forces and NLA fighters were killed. Some civilians (all Albanians) were killed. At the same time, some people (Albanians and Macedonians) were kidnapped. Some of them were killed. A lot of people were displaced from their homes. Many houses were burned or destroyed. (With the help of different international agencies, many houses have since been rebuilt.)

Some people who were part of the government were more interested in war profiteering. Tensions increased and decreased, and it was very difficult to find a solution. Realizing that the Macedonians and Albanians could not find a solution, the international community became involved in searching for a compromise.

At the same time, many people who had lost their homes started to seek refuge elsewhere. Some people are still counted as Internally Displaced People, since they fear going back to their homes, which in many cases have been destroyed and rebuilt. The bombing and killing of civilians was another big mistake. Some of these cases may appear before the International Criminal Tribunal for the Former Yugoslavia, which is located in The Hague. It seems that some people completely forgot that after every war negotiations must be conducted to find a resolution to the crisis.

The discourse of the Macedonian polity was wrong as well. The government wanted to show the international community that the armed Albanians were terrorists and not fighters demanding their human rights. This was very contradictory because in official declarations in the parliament of the Republic of Macedonia these fighters were named "armed groups." Logically, the word *terrorist* cannot be used because no one was attacking Macedonia from outside. The fighters were citizens of Macedonia, people who quit their jobs and went to fight for their human rights. If we analyze the official statements of the NLA, we will see that these fighters never claimed to be against Macedonia or demanded separation from Macedonia. I think that the problem was the lack of skills for solving the crisis without a conflict. However, it seems that personal interests combined with lack of skills and will to solve the crisis were reasons the conflict continued.

After people's homes were destroyed and lives were lost, the chances for cooperation decreased. After the burning of houses, which were not in the conflict area (Bitola, Prilep, Veles), the burning of mosques (where Albanians were the minority), and the killing of civilians in Luboten and Sllupcan, life became harder and relationships dipped to a very low level. Under pressure from the international community, the parties were invited to start a dialogue, which was held in Ohrid. In the meetings, which lasted more than two weeks, the biggest political parties were present. The president of Macedonia led the dialogue. Representatives of the United States and the European Union were present as well. Finally, on August 13, 2001, the parties agreed to sign the Ohrid Framework Agreement, which was aimed at charting a new future for Macedonia.

The Ohrid agreement was reached by consensus, which did not satisfy any of the parties. It was, however, the only way to stop the war in Macedonia and achieve peace. The framework itself contains many provisions, which should be changed. However, it is a document that aims to achieve the equal treatment of everyone at all levels of life in the Republic of Macedonia. It is a document intended for a better future.

Regarding the identity of Albanians in Macedonia, I think that the problem Macedonians have is that they perceive Albanians to be incomers from Albania and not ethnic Albanians who are citizens of the Republic of Macedonia. They perceive them as a group of people who are against Macedonia, instead of seeing them as people with whom they could live and who respect the obligations and the laws of Macedonia, even though no one asked ethnic Albanians about changing the flag or the name of the Republic of Macedonia, which Macedonia agreed to under pressure from Greece. Maybe if both sides tried to work together, the situation would be much better. Certain groups still have an aversion to cooperation and working together to develop a solution that would be acceptable to both sides.

The traumas of the war in Kosova (1999) are another issue that affects the lives of Albanians in Macedonia. Being connected and related to each other, the traumas that Kosovars suffered were transmitted to their relatives and friends living in Macedonia. They feared that the same thing would happen to Albanians in Macedonia. Another fear was that a violent exodus of Albanians would occur. No one wanted to see these fears come true. Albanians were doubly afraid because they did not have the means to protect themselves. The majority (ethnic Macedonians) and those leading state institutions did not care. For Albanians, memories of the Blace border point—an exodus of Albanians who were deported by force by the Serbian police and military forces—were still fresh. Although they had signed all the conventions promising to protect the refugees, which means that the refugees are part of Macedonian national jurisdiction, the Macedonian authorities at first did not allow refugees to enter Macedonia. Several people died in Blace from starvation and illnesses. The explanation Macedonians offered for their refusal to admit refugees was that the huge number of Kosovars who entered Macedonia (300,000 to 350,000 Albanians from Kosova) was going to change the demographic structure of the population in Macedonia and jeopardize Macedonia. They were wrong once more, since immediately after NATO forces entered Kosova all the refugees returned home. Upon departing, the Kosovars thanked Macedonians for their help but also criticized them for not saving more lives when they easily could have.

Talking about past glories, I can say that the only thing that the Albanians were demanding was to have their rights, which they got with the constitution of 1974 and then lost with the first constitution of the republic (1991). The word *demand* irritates Albanians because Macedonia is our common state and all of us must be equal. Instead of working for the further development of Macedonia, we were and are arguing about which rights Albanians should have. The fact that Albanians have always had to make demands before getting what rightly belongs to them anyway is annoying. All the rights the Albanians wanted were something that they deserved to have, not because they were good or bad but because they are citizens of Macedonia, an independent state that is obligated to provide for them, without any kind of discrimination.

In response to all the developments in previous years, contact between ethnic Macedonians and Albanians is less frequent than before. Even though no open conflict or violence in the streets or within institutions occurred after 2001, relationships between Macedonians and Albanians are at a very low level. Some efforts are aimed at connecting people from these two communities, but the results are not sufficient. I think that we should work harder to bring younger generations closer to each other, instead of having them in ethnically divided schools. Instead of separating youths at an early age, which continues and later becomes an even bigger divide, reintegration would bring them closer together. They could work together on projects that would help them feel that they can do something together. That would be useful for them as individuals and for the community. Finding common interests is the key to solving all conflicts that may arise. It is a kind of prevention, and it is always better to prevent problems before they happen or get big and become harder to resolve. In the latter cases, emotions overpower reason. Instead of using their intellect, people react out of patriotic reflex, without strong arguments for the issue being discussed.

After the conflict in 2001, relations worsened, especially after the bombardment of some villages, including Luboten, where several Albanian civilians were killed by the police. Mutual trust is at a very low level, and the other side is often seen as an enemy. Such perceptions and feelings are even more visible among Macedonians because they cannot accept Albanians as equal partners in daily life. For instance, if you take the regular coach from Skopje to Tetovo, in which the majority of the passengers by default are Albanians, the music you will hear on the coach will be Macedonian or Serbian. Probably no one will answer the question which people often ask: Why can we not listen to Albanian music, too, since we have listened to songs in other languages? Albanians can and do listen to Macedonian and Serbian music, which shows their willingness to live together and be part of the same team. Maybe now Macedonians can perceive this as an advantage, not a danger.

Respect and values are very important principles for each community. Respecting the other community is like opening a door that has been closed for several years—a door that is very heavy—and if no one opens it, nobody will benefit from the "treasure" inside. When tolerance and understanding are the most important values of each community, the door opens wide. Doing this will build a very strong base for further cooperation and development, without any obstacles or humiliation. Whenever a problem arises, there is no need to rush, to accuse and blame the other side, without evidence. The worst that can happen is the division between *us* and *them*. We should always look first at ourselves and see what we have done, what our mistakes might be, and what if anything we can do ourselves before casting blame. Even if someone is guilty of a wrongdoing, that person must have a fair trial, without any prejudices or stereotypes. In the past, those accused of crimes often were convicted before the judicial process even started. If there is no justice, there will be no equality and no democracy. So, if the constitution stipulates that all citizens are equal in front of the law, then everyone

should be treated in the same manner and have a chance to defend himself or herself. The duty of the judge is to decide, based on the content of the trial. Judges should not listen to state authorities, the media, or public pressure. Evidence pertinent to the case is all that should be valid, and it must be relevant and not fictitious.

In reviewing the efforts made to resolve the conflict in 2001, I say that the biggest credit for the agreement goes to the international community, especially the United States, the European Union, and NATO. However, for some Macedonians, the people who represented these institutions during their mission in Macedonia are seen as betrayers and not as the people who helped to stop the war, or the people who actually preserved the unity of Macedonia. On this matter, the view of Albanians is completely the opposite. Albanians share the opinion that the international community was crucial in ending the conflict and proposing a solution. Maybe it was not the best solution and not acceptable for many people, but the same agreement stopped the killing and the violence. It was a compromise that saved many lives and stopped the growing gap between Albanians and Macedonians. In 2007, we can see in hindsight that the situation was very bad and that it is very difficult to go back and rebuild everything that disappeared during the crisis in 2001.

I do not know what would have happened if there had been no help, influence, and pressure from the international community, whose biggest contribution was that it guaranteed the implementation of the Ohrid Framework Agreement. Without that international presence, I would say that nothing that was agreed to in Ohrid would have been implemented. I doubt that everyone was interested and ready to move matters forward. This is especially true of some Macedonian politicians, who after signing the agreement started to create obstacles and minimize the value of that document. One such person was the president of the Macedonian parliament in 2001, who paid more attention to his personal adventures and thereby harmed the implementation of the Ohrid agreement. I say that all his demands in parliamentary debate were stupid and that his only aim was to gain more attention and to disseminate propaganda before the elections. The citizens noticed these tactics and abandoned Stojan Andov. When he realized it, it was already too late for him.

However, Macedonian and Albanian citizens are still divided over the role of the international community in 2001. Macedonians think it had a negative impact. This is the opposite of what Albanians think: they say that the international community saved Macedonia. Now it is our duty to keep and develop the peace the agreement created, and to start to see our common future without any discrimination. All we can do is thank the international community and hope that in the future its members will help Macedonia in the areas of economic development, education, and other initiatives that will benefit the citizens of Macedonia.

This reading would be incomplete without mentioning the damaging role of the media. In my opinion, during the years following independence the media (including TV and different newspapers) has had a negative effect on Albanians and all their initiatives. From the start, their ideas were dismissed without any further analysis. Whatever came from Albanians was presented by the media as something negative that did not deserve attention. The Macedonian media have many prejudices and biases, which are reflected in their work. None of the media wanted to explore the issues or to inquire into the ideas and demands of Albanians. Although in some cases journalists were objective (like the journalists of TV A1), most were perceived as betrayers of the Macedonian nation.

The role the media played during the 2001 crisis was even worse and complicated the situation even more. Publishing and broadcasting news, which reflected only one side of the conflict, forced citizens to believe that Albanians were guilty for the situation. There was no airing of Albanians' point of view. The most notorious case occurred when a journalist from Macedonia's TV Channel 5 took control of a cannon and shot it at Albanian civilians' houses. This was shown on the central TV news. To make things worse, the bomb was shot by a woman who was a patriot attempting to kill civilians! I think that the people who work in media should be very careful about both the manner in which they present the news and the reliability of their resources. They should be objective. They should be protected from different kinds of pressure that come from the authorities or other sources of influence. At the same time, there must be a code that guides their actions and how they present the news. Journalists must bear in mind

that the way they present the news has an enormous influence on people's perceptions. The media have a big responsibility and can play a key role in efforts to solve the issues—or can make them look worse.

The coverage provided by national TV and radio news outlets during the 2001 conflict was very strange. National media outlets are supposed to be institutions for all citizens because they are financed by the taxes that everyone pays. Anyone who listened to the news in Macedonian and Albanian noticed a big difference in the way the news was presented. The national TV and radio outlets are named "Macedonian TV and Radio." They are not seen as or called "Radio and TV of Macedonia," as they should be because they belong to everyone and not exclusively to Macedonians. One can understand the position of the "independent" and private media that make policies based on their interests, but the position of national TV and radio is both strange and symptomatic of what is wrong in Macedonia. Both media should change some things and provide real services to the citizens of Macedonia. If you listen to national TV, which is controlled by the parties in power, and compare it to private TV stations, which are more or less independent, you will notice a huge gap. From the national media outlets, you will get the impression that citizens of Macedonia live in a very wealthy and peaceful country. From the other media, you will get the impression that Macedonia is the worst and poorest country. Such discrepancies make it hard for outside viewers and listeners to know how to react.

After all of this, the question that remains is, What is the best way to avoid further conflicts in the Republic of Macedonia, especially between Macedonians and Albanians? In my view, the full implementation of the Ohrid agreement is the key to peace and relaxed relationships. The Ohrid Framework Agreement is the only way to correct the mistakes committed in 1991, when the constitution of Macedonia—which became the main reason for all the conflicts—was passed. The same mistake cannot and should not be repeated. Future generations will judge all those who had the chance to correct past mistakes and did not. The implementation of the Ohrid agreement must happen without any delays or changes. Any intention to change that which was agreed on, or to create obstacles to its implementation, could cause many problems and generate other conflicts. I think we learned that conflict does not solve problems. Instead, it is negotiation and discussion that lead us to solutions to problems. Other attempts to derail implementation of the Ohrid agreement must be dismissed, or Macedonia will not find peace. It may be human nature to make mistakes, but it is also up to those who make mistakes to strive to fix them. Now it is up to Macedonia to undo the mistakes of the recent past.

The economic development of Macedonia is another important issue. At the moment, Macedonia has more than 400,000 unemployed citizens. These people are a potential "social bomb" for Macedonia, and I think the government of Macedonia should pay more attention to this issue, rather than to some of the political games being played. In addition, terms of employment must be the same for all citizens, and everyone must have an equal chance to find employment in all levels of government institutions. Employment inequity could cause another big conflict with long-term repercussions. The government of Macedonia has a lot of work to do on this and should start as soon as possible.

As in the past, the support and monitoring provided by the international community are very important for Macedonia. To rebuild, Macedonia now needs help in all areas of life. The international community should serve in a corrective role when political discourse in Macedonia starts to go away. By combining support and monitoring, there is no doubt that Macedonia will walk faster toward NATO and EU integration.

The final status of Kosova is another issue that is very important for the future of Macedonia. Even though some politicians say this issue has nothing to do with Macedonia (which is partially true, since Macedonia does not have authority to solve this problem), I say that the sooner the status of Kosova is defined, the sooner stability is going to come to Macedonia. Macedonia as a country will benefit if the final status of Kosova is decided in the near future.

People often ask me if there is a future for Macedonia as it is now. When I reply, people look at me doubtfully. In that moment, I can see fear and lack of trust in their eyes, a response based on all the developments of the past fourteen years. Perhaps they are right, remembering all the events and the limited skills of leaders who led this country in recent years. People in senior positions in the leading institutions should spend more time on the ground and try to figure out what is best for citizens, not for themselves.

The two biggest communities (Macedonians and Albanians) comprise the base of the Republic of Macedonia as a society and a country. (This is not to underestimate the other communities that live in Macedonia, who have their own values and traditions and the same needs to be protected, respected, and developed as much as possible.) The progress of Macedonia depends on the development of the relationships between these two communities. Ethnic Macedonians must understand that ethnic Albanians are their best partners, with whom they can build a great future. The same can be said in regard to the political positions of Macedonia's neighbors, who do not regard Macedonia as a bona fide state. Greece did not recognize the name Macedonia, so Macedonia changed its name under that pressure. The same happened with the flag, and now we are officially known as FYROM, not as the Republic of Macedonia, which is our constitutional name. Bulgaria does not recognize the Macedonian nation and in certain cases does not recognize the existence of the Macedonian language. Serbia does not recognize the Macedonian Orthodox Church. The Republic of Albania is the only neighboring nation that does not contest any aspect of the existence of the Republic of Macedonia. In addition, the Republic of Albania was one of the first countries to recognize the independence of Macedonia and its constitutional name.

After the 2001 conflict, several constitutional amendments were adopted and many things have changed. There is positive movement, but the process is going very slowly (Macedonians see the slowness as a ruse whereby Albanians will try to get more rights than they deserve). In order to not create further doubts about the situation, all the obligations agreed to in the Ohrid Framework must be fulfilled promptly, without any changes and delays. Failure to do so will harm the process and show our capability in a bad light. Macedonians are faced with a new global reality and must accept it. It is in all of Macedonia's best interest to work toward NATO and EU integration, and at the same time to show our desire to live and work together.

With the implementation of the Ohrid agreement, the population will be more relaxed and there will be less chance for unpleasant surprises, which could damage the process. Several positive steps were taken in this direction recently, including the legalization of the University of Tetovo and provisions for equal representation in government administration, police, and the army, which is very important for trust building. All these positive movements need to continue. The same approach needs to be taken on matters concerning economic development, since living conditions in Macedonia are very bad. If economic development is not made a priority, the fragile peace that exists could be shattered, which would be very disappointing after all our efforts.

Looking ahead, one of the last challenges Macedonia faces is the decentralization of power, which is the main subject of the Ohrid agreement. Many matters were clarified in the November 2004 referendum. The success or failure of the referendum will determine whether there will be space for the implementation of the Ohrid Framework Agreement. I hope that Macedonians made the right decision and begin figuring out the best solution for Macedonia. If Macedonians pass this exam, the doors will be opened and the nation will be able to go on to the next issue on Macedonia's agenda. No one dares to think what could happen if things start to move in the wrong direction. Hopefully, the worst will not happen and the 2001 conflict and its bitter history can be set aside. All of us may remember the past, but now it is important to look forward and seek a brighter future.

Regardless of the referendum's outcome, Macedonia is still obligated to respect the basic precepts of international law. There must be rule of law in Macedonia (equality for all citizens). Democracy must be developed in every aspect of society and at all levels. The corruption that touches all levels of Macedonia's institutions must be destroyed. Efforts to combat criminal activities must be given greater attention. The judicial system must be reformed. Conditions that attract foreign investments must be created. The government administration must become more efficient. The brain drain must stop. There must be more transparency in the work of the government. All these will give Macedonians a fresh, new start and maybe a great finish.

In regard to the relationships between Macedonians and Albanians, I say that Macedonia will have a good future if only we follow democratic principles and find common solutions to each problem. The use of force never brings peace. It is diplomacy that creates peace and prosperity. An overall consensus satisfying all parties' interests is the best way. If Macedonians do not achieve consensus its leaders have to continue to negotiate, analyze, and discuss options further. In the end, there should be a decision that is accepted by both parties. Any other way is the wrong way, and no one should take a step in that direction.

Macedonians have a long journey ahead of them, but every journey starts with a single step. The Albanians in Macedonia took the first step, and now it is Macedonians' turn to take their first step—to start the journey together. I hope they make the right decision. I hope that I will soon be able write about my first trip to Europe without a visa instead of writing about conflict. Hope is always present in my mind, and I hope that I will be able to offer positive energy that benefits all citizens of the Republic of Macedonia.

ABOUT THE AUTHOR

Fatmir Musa is an Albanian from the Republic of Macedonia. He graduated from the faculty of law in Skopje in 2001 and immediately started postgraduate studies in international law. While studying international law, he was involved in several different projects. He is a debate skills coach and has completed several mediation and conflict resolution training programs. Since 2001, he has worked with teachers and facilitators from various international backgrounds. He is a consultant for Conflict Management Group in Cambridge, Massachusetts. He has worked for the Open Society Institute (Soros Foundation). He previously worked at the parliament of the Republic of Macedonia. He also has been a member of the executive board of the Helsinki Committee for Human Rights in Macedonia.

Musa is one of the coauthors of a trilingual dictionary of legal terms (Macedonian–Albanian–English), the first such reference book for the Balkans. He speaks five languages and has often worked as a translator for such organizations as the Council of Europe, the Catholic Relief Center, and the Youth Children Theatre. Musa is staff member of SEEYLI (South East European Youth Leadership Institute), which has run a youth leadership program in the United States each July since 2001.

Musa has been involved in several roundtables, seminars, and workshops on different topics, while writing many articles about human rights, democracy, ethnic conflicts, youth, and other topics. He is actively involved in different nongovernmental organizations (NGOs) and takes an active role in discussions about society. He has taught and lectured in the United States, Albania, Macedonia, Kosova, Croatia, and elsewhere. Currently he is finishing his postgraduate studies.

3

Kashmir

The Kashmir Valley is a mountainous region located in the northern part of India and divided to form part of India and part of Pakistan. Kashmir has been at the heart of a territorial dispute between India and Pakistan since the two nations gained their independence in 1947. Still, as of today, both India and Pakistan wish to control this region, which represents a strategic territory that also holds religious sites.

This fertile region was ruled by several local dynasties before being invaded by the Moghuls who incorporated the region into their vast empire in the sixteenth century. The British occupied the region in the nineteenth century, and in 1846 they sold the entire region to Maharaja Dogra Hindu chief the Gulab Singh. For the next hundred years, Kashmir became part of an entity called the "State of Jammu and Kashmir," which belonged to the Dogra dynasty. The latter was an unrepresentative and autocratic rule and was led by Hindus. This context created a feeling of exclusion in the preeminently Muslim population of Kashmir. This bitterness was later fueled by the process of decolonization and the concepts of self-determination and nationalism that followed.

Those new ideas created a rising political consciousness in the region. The first clashes observed dated from 1931. At that time, massive protests against the Dogra rule took place. In 1932, Sheikh Abdullah, a Kashmir nationalist, formed the region's first political party, forcing the maharaja to allow a limited democracy. Under pressure, the latter agreed to create a legislative assembly in 1932. However, the Kashmir conflict finds its origin in the partition by the British Empire of the Indies, in August 1947, between India and Pakistan. This treaty implied that the country would be divided into two separate entities: India and Pakistan. The ruler of Jammu and Kashmir, whose state was situated between the two new countries, could not decide which country to join. According to the paper, Kashmir legally belonged to India, but the predominantly Muslim population (78 percent) did not agree with its Hindu ruler and his plan to join his southern neighbors. Instead, it would have preferred to join Pakistan and felt that India had violated its right of self-determination. The Indians used the situation to their advantage by sending in Indian forces to occupy Kashmir.

Two other wars took place in 1965 and 1971 and resulted in United Nations Security Council resolutions which remained largely unimplemented. Pakistan affirmed that the Muslim majority of Kashmir was in favor of being part of Pakistan but that India occupied the territory by trick and force. The Jammu and Kashmir was a "disputed" territory. Islamabad calls, in addition, for the application of U.N. resolutions particularly concerning a referendum. For India, the situation didn't cause any judicial or constitutional discussion.

This unfortunate situation also created a cross-border form of terrorism that has been regularly striking the region since 1989. In the past fifteen years, the Kashmir insurgency has been fueled by massive weapons transfers, financial and training support (from Pakistan), and religious extremism. Thus, this region has been a major source of conflict between the two nuclear-armed nations. These factors created a climate of extreme violence and terrorism. What began mainly as a local movement became a larger issue, involving outside forces who supplied and indoctrinated the insurgents. Islamabad is claiming that the disputed territory should become a part of Pakistan because of the Muslim majority who lives there. Pakistan is also pushing for a Kashmir referendum so that the population gets the opportunity to choose

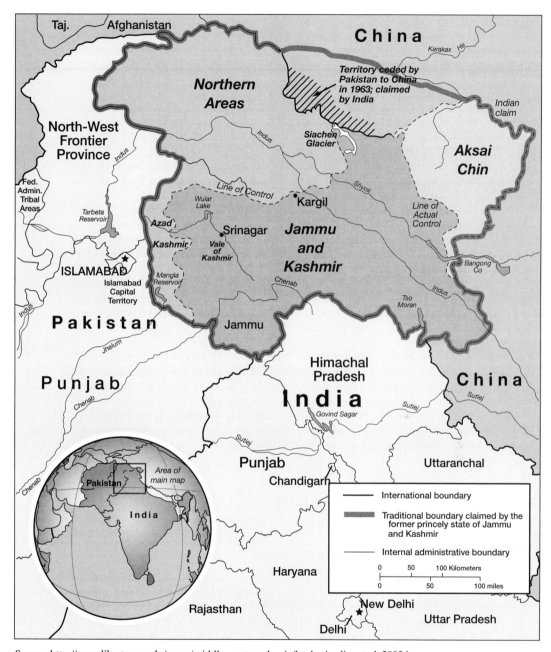

Source: http://www.lib.utexas.edu/maps/middle_east_and_asia/kashmir_disputed_2003.jpg

its own fate. However, India refuses to hear anything about those ideas. Moreover, the post 9/11 area clearly demonstrated the clear link between al-Qaeda and terrorism in Kashmir.

The positions of India and Pakistan have adapted in recent times in response to international opinions. Pakistan used to promote the view that Kashmir should be part of Pakistan.

To gain U.N. support, Pakistan has been promoting national self-determination, the process by which a country gains independence, which is a fundamental right according to the U.N. charter. On the contrary, India believes that Kashmir is unequivocally part of India and its contemporary opinion is that cross-border terrorism must stop before it can negotiate with Pakistan regarding various issues, including periodic skirmishes along the line of control separating India and Pakistan in Kashmir.

In summary, Kashmir is entangled in a complicated blend of geopolitical, historical, ethnic, identity, and strategic issues that have to be resolved if a new war between the two rivals is to be avoided. A closer look at Kashmir's dangerous network support is also needed. Countries such as Pakistan and Afghanistan are suspected of providing tools to the insurgents so that they can radicalize their movement and create an atmosphere of violence and terror in the region. What originally started as a bilateral problem has become a global issue with potentially disastrous consequences.

The following two essays try to explain the causes of the conflict. The first essay, "Jammu and Kashmir: An Indian View," written by Dipankar Banerjee, presents the historical background of this issue and narrates the first war (1947–1948), its causes, and factors contributing to the persistence of this war, which ended with a U.N. Security Council resolution, asking for a cease-fire between the two forces and a withdrawal of both countries' troops from Kashmir. The text also outlines the numerous efforts made by the U.N. from 1948 to 1989, to resolve this conflict. Another bloody war erupted during this period, in 1965. Following the elaboration of a series of scenarios discussed to solve this conflict, the author indicates that the international community must keep up the pressure on both governments so that they can find a reasonable compromise.

The second essay, entitled "Kashmir Dispute" and written by Touqir Hussain, also provides a chronological report of the events and outlines the efforts that have been made to resolve the dispute. It also highlights the issues of cross-border infiltration, used by India to deligitimize the Kashmiri resistance by redefining the Kashmir issue in terms of international terrorism, and external influences on the region. The author also reveals the impact of the dispute on Pakistan's identity, beliefs, values, sense of belonging, and security, which influence undoubtedly the vision that they have developed of their rival.

Jammu and Kashmir: An Indian View

Dipankar Banerjee

HISTORICAL BACKGROUND

The genesis of the current Kashmir problem can be traced to 1846 if you are willing to look back that far. The battle of Sobraon in the Punjab fought in February that year ended Sikh rule in north India and allowed the British to consolidate their empire in India. Maharaja Gulab Singh, then the Dogra ruler of Jammu and an ally of the Sikhs, was persuaded by the British to remain neutral. At the Treaty of Amritsar signed following the battle, Kashmir was sold to him for a paltry sum of seven and a half million rupees. This deal provided a valuable buffer for the British against a possible Russian advance in the north. It also led to a hodgepodge of a kingdom, ruled now by the Hindu Dogras inhabiting mainly the south of the province, with a sizable Sikh population, but a large majority of Muslims of different sects and ethnic groups in its many valleys and plains, as well as the high-altitude terrain of Baltistan. The largely Buddhist-occupied and mountainous desert of Ladakh in the east, adjacent to Tibet, was added a few years later. The Kingdom was larger than France, although it had a population of about four million in 1941.

The curtain next rises at the breakup of the subcontinent, when under the Indian Independence Act passed by the British parliament in 1947, two separate countries came into existence: India and Pakistan. Five hundred and sixty-two "independent" kingdoms in united India now had to be incorporated into either the new India or Pakistan. Some kingdoms were very large, such as Jammu and Kashmir. (This is the Indian government's official name for the "Kashmir" province and is used here to reflect that political reality). Some kingdom rulers dreamed of an independent royal existence. This option was firmly ruled out under the act. The choice was to merge with either of the two nations. Geographic contiguity would be important, as well as the subjects' religious beliefs, for that was the basis of partition. Under the act, the choice was left to each king or maharajah, to be exercised with due caution. Hyderabad, a large province populated largely by Hindus in the heart of India, was ruled by a Muslim who toyed with the idea of joining Pakistan and encouraged an armed rebellion in an effort to achieve this conjunction. This movement was quickly scotched through a swift Indian military operation. Junagadh was a tiny principality in western India but not contiguous to Pakistan. It was ruled by a Muslim, though its population was overwhelmingly Hindu. The ruler acceded to Pakistan, but when faced with some reluctance there and growing discontent within, he quickly fled the country, taking many of his pet dogs along but leaving most wives behind.[1]

Accessions of these kingdoms were obtained swiftly in most cases and without acrimony, a remarkable piece of diplomacy. This was through the rulers signing the Instrument of Accession, perhaps with a degree of persuasion as well as coercion present but largely peacefully. The exception was Jammu and Kashmir. Maharaja Hari Singh dithered. He nursed ambitions of grandeur, no doubt, but he was also seriously concerned with divisions within and among his people. Perhaps he feared trouble breaking out, for revolt was in the air. He wanted time to consider before deciding. On August 12, 1947, the maharaja asked for a standstill agreement from both India and Pakistan, whereby "existing arrangements should continue pending settlement of details."[2] Pakistan agreed, but India sought additional clarifications.

Cut off largely from the rest of India, winds of democracy had nevertheless come to the kingdom. In 1932 Sheikh Abdullah, a charismatic Kashmiri leader, organized the All Jammu and Kashmir Muslim Conference. Abdullah understood the diversity of the people and the genuine secular sentiment of Muslims in Kashmir—influenced by Sufism and a tolerant view of Islam. His contact with Jawaharlal Nehru and the Congress Party, with its secular and more egalitarian socioeconomic policies, convinced him that his people's interests would be better served by aligning with India rather than the feudal Muslim League. In 1939 he renamed his party the National Conference and gave it a secular character that represented all the people of Jammu and Kashmir.[3] A faction of the party, under Ghulam Abbas and Yusuf Shah, moved toward the Muslim League. The latter's support was mainly confined to western Kashmir in Poonch and Mendhar.[4]

THE ACCESSION AND THE FIRST WAR: 1947–1948

Even as the maharaja was making up his mind, the situation changed rapidly. Thousands of tribesmen from the northwest frontiers of Pakistan suddenly materialized on his borders on October 21. They were heavily armed, in commandeered trucks, and led by junior officers from the Pakistan Army on leave or recently discharged after the end of the Second World War. This was a formidable force advancing along several routes both toward Jammu in the south and to the summer capital Srinagar in the Kashmir Valley. Another smaller force also moved toward Ladakh.

If Srinagar could be captured, the kingdom would stand annexed. A respite was provided when the raiders suddenly stopped at Baramula—barely sixty kilometers from Srinagar along an open and undefended road—to pillage, rape, and loot. Throughout several centuries of aggression by the tribal forces from the time of Genghis Khan, this has been the principal enticement for recruitment. It was no different now and the tribesmen would not be denied. It led to two days delay, and this would ultimately save the kingdom.

Maharaja Hari Singh urgently sought help from India. Lord Mountbatten, the last British viceroy and then the governor general of independent India, also headed the Defense Committee of the cabinet. Under his chairmanship the committee met on October 25, 1947, and decided that Indian troops would be sent only after the maharaja had acceded to India. The maharaja signed the Instrument of Accession on October 25, and Mountbatten accepted it on October 27.[5] In his reply to Hari Singh's letter, Mountbatten promised that "when order had been restored in Kashmir and her soil cleared of the invader, the question of the State's accession should be settled by a reference to the people."[6]

Indian forces landed on the dirt airstrip at Srinagar immediately afterward. Additional troops flew in on subsequent days, saving the state capital from capture. This response would not have been easy, or even possible, without the full support of Sheikh Abdullah and the National Conference cadres, who mobilized the entire Kashmir Valley behind them.[7]

The Kashmir Valley was cleared of the invaders by the end of 1947.[8] Battles continued elsewhere in the province through the winter and into the next year. In early 1948, the Pakistan army intervened directly. With mountains favoring defense, the front stabilized by midyear.

Indian Prime Minister Jawaharlal Nehru was keen to exhaust all peaceful options before countering Pakistan militarily. Accordingly, he referred the matter to the U.N. Security Council on December 20, 1947, and lodged a complaint with it on January 1, 1948.[9] Mountbatten too advised in favor of referring the matter to the United Nations. The Indian government's expectation was that in this clear case of aggression the Security Council would promptly direct Pakistan to withdraw its forces and the fighting between the two newly emerged states would stop.[10]

The Security Council Resolution of August 13, 1948, called for the following:

- A cease-fire to come into effect between Indian and Pakistani forces
- Complete withdrawal of Pakistani troops from the disputed territory
- The subsequent withdrawal of Indian troops from Kashmir except for a minimum force required to maintain law and order
- The future of Kashmir to be determined "in accordance with the will of the people"[11]

Both countries accepted these terms, and a cease-fire came into effect at midnight on December 31,

1948, and a Cease Fire Line (CFL) agreed to in Karachi by both sides, separated the two armies. India's expectation that Pakistan would be declared an aggressor was not fulfilled, and the Kashmir question was viewed by the U.N. as a dispute rather than an act of aggression by Pakistan.

Pakistani soldiers never withdrew from Jammu and Kashmir. India held that unless this happened and all aggressive forces were vacated from the state, there could be no plebiscite. Besides, the option of plebiscite soon became obsolete. In the trauma of partition, large numbers of people had crossed borders and the demographic profile had changed. In March 2003, the Indian external affairs minister, Yashwant Sinha, stated that the U.N. resolution on Kashmir was "irrelevant and incapable of implementation, as Pakistan has failed to fulfil the conditions attached to it." Moreover, the minister stated that "self determination" in a pluralistic society like India could only mean "internal self-governance within the overall constitutional framework."[12]

Elections to a constituent assembly were held in 1951, and the National Conference swept the polls. A few years later a state constitution was adopted. Jammu and Kashmir has since been governed by its people's representatives, except for brief periods when terrorism prevented the possibility of rule by an elected government. The province's constitution precludes the possibility of outsiders contesting elections in the state, but elections in Jammu and Kashmir were seldom entirely free, thus blotting India's case. The area of Kashmir under Pakistan, however, has seen much less democracy. The northern areas remain in political limbo with no constitution or democratic representation at all and are directly administered bureaucratically from Islamabad. The rest of Pakistan Occupied Kashmir (POK) has had occasional elections, but real power and executive authority remain in the control of a fairly low-level government bureaucrat in Islamabad.

THE PERIOD FROM 1948–1989

Efforts were made by the U.N. in the 1950s to find a solution. All attempts failed. When Pakistan joined the western military alliances, first the Central Treaty Organization or the Baghdad Pact (CENTO) in the mid 1950s and later the Southeast

Asia Treaty Organization (SEATO), the basis for a mutual settlement was undermined in India's view. With its belief in nonalignment, India saw these military alliances as possibly coercive mechanisms that potentially could threaten its independence. From the perspective of Delhi these new alignments by Pakistan put it firmly in a hostile camp, precluding the possibility of a negotiated settlement.

One major war in 1965 and several serious skirmishes were fought over Jammu and Kashmir in this period. Sensing that the balance was shifting in India's favor, after the Chinese attack on India in 1962 resulted in the West coming to India's help, Field Marshal Mohammad Ayoob Khan framed a plan of attack on Jammu and Kashmir. It was based on the advance of multiple armed guerrilla columns from the regular army of Pakistan specially trained for the purpose of advancing along several axes. The expectation was that this would lead to a general uprising within Jammu and Kashmir, particularly in the Kashmir Valley. This would then be followed by a major conventional attack by Pakistan from across the international border and the CFL in Jammu and Kashmir. By winter, the entire province was expected to fall to Pakistan. The basic premise proved wrong. Instead of supporting the guerrillas, the locals provided information and guides to the Indian army, which promptly defeated and threw back the columns. Pakistan did launch a conventional attack in the Chhamb sector in the south, but here too it failed in its mission. Instead, the Indians took the war into the Pakistani heartland near Lahore and Sialkot. The war changed nothing in Jammu and Kashmir except for altering the CFL a little.

Again in 1971, Jammu and Kashmir was dragged into the larger conflict that resulted in the independence of Bangladesh. Skirmishes took place along the CFL and some territory changed hands, overall favoring India. The larger consequence was that about 93,000 Pakistani soldiers and civilians became Indian prisoners of war in Bangladesh. This was a major embarrassment to both countries but understandably perhaps more so to Pakistan. The issue was finally resolved at the summit meeting at Shimla, in June 1972, between prime ministers Indira Gandhi and Zulfiqar Ali Bhutto. Under the agreement signed there, both sides agreed to maintain the status quo on the border and resolved to settle the issue bilaterally through dialogue. A new line on the border was to be demarcated by senior military commanders after detailed reconnaissance. This was done through intense work over six months, and maps were signed and exchanged. The new line was called the Line of Control (LoC). The prisoners returned to Pakistan soon after the LoC was finalized. The Indian view since then has been that with the line having changed, the old U.N. arrangement had ended. The U.N. forces monitoring the old CFL now had no locus, and the issue of Jammu and Kashmir was to be resolved in the future through mutual dialogue, as agreed by both countries.

Jammu and Kashmir remained entirely peaceful for over a decade and a half following the Shimla agreement. There were, of course, political changes. The state was integrated more fully with the rest of India, though it retained some of the special provisions granted to it under Article 370 of the Indian constitution. Sheikh Abdullah was interned by the Indian government under different circumstances more or less continuously beginning in 1953 for what were alleged to be his anti-India and secessionist policies, though he was neither charged nor was any case proved against him. In 1975 he signed an agreement with Delhi accepting Jammu and Kashmir's position under the constitution of India and became the chief minister of the province until his death in 1982. His son Faroukh Abdullah succeeded him in the party and was elected to the office of chief minister soon afterward. Disaffection arose within the National Conference over the succession. Through biased manipulation by the state governor, Jag Mohan Malhotra, Faroukh Abdullah was ousted in 1984. This created severe political instability, and when elections were held again in 1987 a coalition of the National Conference under Abdullah and the congress came to power. The elections, it appears, were blatantly rigged and led to severe alienation among the people.

This new alienation combined with demographic explosion, severe unemployment, the rise of extremist Islamist influence in the province, poor governance, larger global geopolitical changes in eastern Europe, the fallout of the Afghan War, and overt Pakistani support to potential insurgents in Jammu and Kashmir, all proved to be powerful negative forces. Separatist groups now found support among the people, and the Jammu and Kashmir Liberation Front and Hizbul Mujahideen emerged as major terrorist organizations ready to use force against the state. Isolated violence broke out often in the Kashmir Valley during 1988 and 1989. The situation exploded suddenly in December 1989.

THE KASHMIR JIHAD: 1989–2004

Elections to the central parliament in India in 1989 saw a change of government in Delhi. A new minister was sworn in soon after with a Muslim from the Kashmir Valley, Mufti Mohammad Sayyid, appointed for the first time to the powerful position of the home (interior) minister in Delhi. Within a week his daughter, a young medical doctor in Srinagar, was abducted by Kashmiri militants. They demanded the release from custody of five militants charged with heinous crimes. In a curious collapse of governance, which can only be explained by the utter inexperience of a new set of political leaders, the government succumbed entirely.

This seemed to give the impression in the valley that the central government in Delhi had abdicated its responsibility over the state. In turn this led to an immediate breakdown of order and ushered in a strong secessionist movement in the Kashmir Valley. Strong countermeasures had to be taken to restore order, which at times went out of hand and often provoked by the terrorists. The small contingents of police and paramilitary forces found themselves outnumbered and threatened and responded in self-defense, leading to further deaths in clashes. Many mistakes were made and hundreds of innocent lives were lost in those years, both due to insurgent attacks and counterviolence by the forces of the state. The armed insurgency that began in 1989 has persisted and is seen particularly by the Islamist forces as a kind of jihad.

The Kashmir Valley is among the most beautiful and bountiful places in the world. Some of the prettiest flowers and tastiest fruits, envied around the world, grow there. But its soil does not grow arms or ammunition, and its people by nature abhor violence. Thus, a sudden rise of militant extremism seemed unreal. This happened because of the induction of an enormous quantity of weapons, ammunition, and explosives across the LoC from Pakistan and intense terrorist training from outside the state. Massive quantities of weapons and am-

munition were supplied by funds from the United States and western Asia, first to the Afghan War and simultaneously diverted into India by Pakistan's Inter Service Intelligence, which controlled the Afghan operations. Matching funds provided by Saudi Arabia were also diverted to Jammu and Kashmir. Large numbers of madrasas were established earlier in the Kashmir Valley through generous religious grants from western Asia, which slowly converted the Sufi version of tolerant Islam prevailing there to the more extremist version of Wahabi Islam practiced in Saudi Arabia. These armaments were diverted to India first in Eastern Punjab to stir up Sikh militancy in the 1980s and 1990s. Since 1987 a huge quantity of arms have been diverted to Jammu and Kashmir. Of course, a large proportion of these weapons ultimately went to al-Qaeda and the Taliban in later years and continue to circle the world among numerous international terrorist organizations.

It was this massive weapons transfer, along with financial and training support combined with religious extremism, that fueled the insurgency in Jammu and Kashmir. A political discontent that was widespread, which would under normal conditions have found expression through peaceful political protest and been accommodated under the rule of law in India, as happened elsewhere in the country, now found expression through extreme violence and terrorism. This was possible only because of the widespread network of support and weapons provided to the terrorists from Pakistan.

A quick summary of major developments during the last fifteen years highlights key events in the story to date:

- The insurgency began mainly as an indigenous movement, though insurgents were supplied, trained, and indoctrinated by outside forces. This remained the case until about 1995. When insurgents failed to make any advance and armed violence in Jammu and Kashmir appeared to peter out, international jihadists were introduced into the insurgents' ranks in larger numbers. Initially, they came from the Pakistani side of the LoC; then they came from Pakistan and later from around the world. According to Indian intelligence in 2003, some 60 percent of the terrorists in the Kashmir Valley were now from outside Kashmir. Most came on a two-year contract and were very well paid, with additional monetary incentives for terrorist acts and compensation to their families in case of death.

- Training was provided across the LoC in selected camps. Major training in explosives, commando operations, and collective terrorist activities was provided in Afghanistan in al-Qaeda training camps.
- Indian forces were stretched in 1990 and took time to respond to the situation in Jammu and Kashmir. Four divisions of the army returned from peacekeeping in Sri Lanka in April 1990 and needed rest. Major forces were operating in support of the police to counter Sikh terrorism in the Punjab until 1992. Additional forces had to be raised, trained, and then deployed in Jammu and Kashmir, which could happen only by 1995, and the situation was gradually brought under greater control. Local militant groups were by now disenchanted with the foreign militants, who were arrogant, highly demanding, and often exploited the local people. Many local Kashmiri youth who had earlier turned against the state now turned against the militants and helped the security forces counter them.
- Until 1993 militancy was restricted entirely to the Kashmir Valley. From then on, helped by Pakistan, it spread gradually to the rest of the state, stretching security forces considerably. The intensity of violence still remains the highest in the Kashmir Valley and in the southwestern part of the province adjacent to Pakistan.
- By 1996 the situation had changed for the better to such an extent that elections were held throughout the state, along with the rest of the nation, for the central parliament at Delhi. In spite of terrorist violence, these elections were successfully conducted even though some coercion to vote cannot be ruled out. In 1997 elections were held again for the state assembly, and popular government was reestablished in the province, with the National Conference under Faroukh Abdullah returning to power.
- Nuclear tests in 1998 by both India and Pakistan exacerbated the tension between the two countries, and the level of violence rose.
- A pathbreaking attempt at peace was made when Atal Behari Vajpayee, the Indian prime minister, traveled to Lahore by bus in February 1999. He met there with Prime Minister Nawaz Sharif of Pakistan, and they signed a historic agreement opening up serious prospects for peace in the subcontinent. This hope would be shattered in a few months with an outbreak of conflict in the frozen heights of Kargil. Pakistani soldiers had already transgressed deeply into Indian territory even as the Lahore agreement was being signed. Another attempt was made to resume the dialogue in Agra in mid-2001 but proved abortive.
- Following Pakistani intrusions in Kargil, which were detected in May 1999, a strong border skirmish broke out when the two armed forces confronted each other in a series of high-altitude battles. By late July, the intruders were driven back. The United States put direct pressure on the Pakistan government to withdraw, which it did.
- Taliban and al-Qaeda links to terrorism in Jammu and Kashmir were demonstrated dramatically at the end of the millennium. In late December 1999, an Indian Airlines aircraft on a routine flight from Kathmandu in Nepal to Delhi was hijacked. It landed in Amritsar, Dubai, and went on finally to Kandahar, Afghanistan, as demanded by the hijackers who turned out to be Islamic terrorists. In another instance of shameful capitulation, the government of India accepted the slightly pruned demands terrorists negotiated with the Taliban foreign minister of Afghanistan. Three leading terrorists, undergoing long prison terms in Indian custody, were released and taken to Kandahar accompanied by the Indian foreign minister. The hijackers vanished soon after and are said to have found shelter immediately in Pakistan, where they are still living. The released terrorists, emboldened by their recent success, soon resumed their terrorist activities in Pakistan.
- The terrorist attacks on the United States on September 11, 2001, impacted Jammu and Kashmir directly. The attacks were traced to al-Qaeda, which was sheltered by the Taliban in Afghanistan, which was itself founded and supported by Pakistan, one of only three governments in the world that recognized it. Under pressure from the United States, Islamabad turned its policy around and joined the U.S.-led "War on Terrorism" against al-Qaeda. Support to the Kashmiri terrorists continued. On October 30 and December 13, 2001, the terrorists struck the state parliament in Jammu and Kashmir and the central parliament in Delhi, respectively, killing a large number of innocent civilians. The latter attack, in particular, came close to success, which would have wiped out the entire political leadership of India. New Delhi was compelled to respond and deployed its regular army on the border for ten months until October 2002, poised to strike at Pakistan. The possibility of an outbreak of war between two nuclear rivals was real and imminent on at least two occasions over that year.
- Serious attempts toward peace were made again in 2003, first by Vajpayee in April and later by the Indian government in October. These overtures were received well by Pakistan, which responded with positive counterproposals. By November, substantial confidence-building measures had been proposed and

were being implemented. A cease-fire across the LoC came into effect in December 2003. A summit meeting took place along with the annual South Asian Association for Regional Cooperation (SAARC) heads of government meeting in January 2004 in Islamabad, at which it was announced that dialogue between the two governments would be resumed.

Violence has taken a serious toll in the province. Casualties, incidents, and seizures of weapons acts are summarized in Table 3.1.

Post-9/11 Scenario. What until then had been a bilateral affair between two nations in south Asia, where cross-border violence merited little acknowledgment in the West, was suddenly catapulted onto center stage in world affairs on September 11, 2001. The infrastructure, money supply, training bases, and motivation of all these jihadi organizations were the same and closely interlinked. One could not be dismantled without the other, and if one remained the other would continue to prosper. This belated realization may well shape future policy; for the present it has led to considerable international pressure on Pakistan and India to resolve their outstanding dispute over Jammu and Kashmir.

Several factors have contributed to the region's willingness to discuss peace. The cease-fire at the LoC since December 2003 ended the firing along the border and generated hope of a new beginning. The summit at Islamabad in January 2004 consolidated the parties' position regarding peace

TABLE 3.1   Data on Casualties, Incidents, and Weapons Seizures in Jammu and Kashmir 1988-2004 (June)[1]

	Incidents	Terrorists Killed	Civilians Died	Security Force Personnel Died	Seizures of AK-Series Rifles Only	Total Casualties Dead
1988	390	1	29	1	n/a	31
1989	2,154	0	79	13	n/a	92
1990	3,905	183	862	132	1,240	1,177
1991	3,122	614	594	185	2,320	1,393
1992	4,971	873	859	177	3,504	1,909
1993	4,457	1,328	1,023	216	2,209	2,567
1994	4,484	1,651	1,012	236	2,196	2,899
1995	4,479	1,338	1,161	297	2,055	2,796
1996	4,224	1,194	1,333	376	2,150	2,903
1997	3,004	1,177	840	355	1,725	2,372
1998	2,993	1,045	877	339	1,520	2,261
1999	2,938	1,184	799	555	1,244	2,538
2000	2,835	1,808	842	638	1,405	3,288
2001	3,278	2,850	1,067	590	1,646	4,507
2002	n/a	1,714	839	469	1,571	3,022
2003	n/a	1,546	658	338	1,440	2,542
2004 (June)	n/a	483	295	159	396[2]	937
Total	**47,234**	**20,640**	**13,169**	**5,076**	**26,621**	**37,234**

[1]"Annual Casualties in Terrorist Violence in Jammu and Kashmir," http://www.satp.org/satporgtp.countries/india/states/jandk/data_sheets/annual_casualties.htm (accessed July 19, 2004). "Recovery of Weapons in Jammu and Kashmir," http://www.satp.org/satporgtp/countries/india/states/jandk/data_sheets/recovery_of_weapons_jan1990_to_15_Nov_2000.htm (accessed July 19, 2004).

[2]Data for recovery of AK rifles available up to May 31, 2004.

and put an official stamp on it. The cricket matches that followed in March/April 2004 in Pakistan saw hordes of Indians traveling there and receiving a cordial welcome. This has provided a proper environment for a constructive dialogue, and preliminary rounds since then have been positive. Foreign secretary–level talks and a foreign ministers meeting scheduled for mid-2004 are expected to be exploratory rather than substantial, and much more preparation is needed before any breakthrough can realistically be expected. Still, the talks provide an excellent opportunity to examine both cases and attitudes on Kashmir. The remainder of this paper summarizes Pakistan's case in outline and India's position in more detail.

THE PAKISTAN CASE

Pakistan's official case is borne on three pillars, which are often articulated in different forms:[13]

- Jammu and Kashmir is disputed territory. As parties to the dispute, both India and Pakistan have equal status and the same rights and obligations in Kashmir.
- The accession of the state to India was illegal, and hence India is in illegal possession of the state.
- U.N. resolutions allow Kashmiris to determine their future through plebiscite to accede to either India or Pakistan.[14]

The real reasons go deeper. The conflict rests on questions about the legitimacy of the state of Pakistan and its need to define its nationalism vis-à-vis India. Kashmir provides a focus. It legitimizes a role for the Pakistan military and its intelligence organizations, the only institutions of consequence in the country, and which continue to dominate politics and governance in Pakistan. They secure their existence and influence by keeping the Kashmir issue alive.

Therefore, Pakistan's policy toward Kashmir is shaped by its own perception of the Indian threat and by its domestic imperatives. When relations improve and a civilian government in Islamabad feels secure, or when other conditions dominate, Kashmir is placed on the back burner. In times of internal crisis, when guided by extremist sentiments and under an insecure military rule, the issue is resurrected.

Due to its comparative inferior power vis-à-vis India, Pakistan's policy has always been to try and internationalize the Jammu and Kashmir question and to entice outside powers, particularly the United States, to intervene. In this endeavor it also attempts to get the U.N. involved in the process. This policy has detracted from the real possibility of a bilateral negotiated settlement of the problem with India.

THE INDIAN CASE

The Indian case on Jammu and Kashmir adheres to the following:

- The entire kingdom of Jammu and Kashmir acceded to India under the Indian Independence Act prior to independence and, therefore, all of it legally belongs to India. Pakistan is in illegal possession of the territory it still holds, which is a result of aggression.
- The dispute over Jammu and Kashmir is clearly one of aggression by Pakistan, and the question is how the territory under its illegal occupation should be vacated.
- The promise made by Nehru of asserting the people's views on accession could not be kept as Pakistan never vacated the territory and, therefore, its aggression is yet to end. The U.N. resolution clearly prioritizes the actions to be taken, and Pakistan's continued occupation does not allow action on subsequent steps to be taken. At this late stage, a plebiscite is impractical.
- Therefore, converting the LoC into an international border is the only pragmatic option. Meanwhile Srinagar may still be provided maximum autonomy for political purposes, but this will have to be in consonance with the need of the state's full integration into the Indian state and to meet its legitimate developmental needs.

Within the preceding consensus are several nuances. Most Indians accept that Kashmir is entwined in a complex mix of historical, communal, ethnic, identity, geopolitical, and strategic factors. Therefore, any sudden unraveling of the situation could cause many reverberations around the subcontinent, which is in the interest of neither India nor Pakistan.

Nevertheless, Kashmir is central to India's perception both of its internal and external security for several reasons. First, Jammu and Kashmir has been either the cause of major conflicts between India and Pakistan or the theater of one on other occasions. Ongoing cross-border terrorism since 1989 also makes it a more likely source of future conflict between these two nuclear-armed nations.

Second, a part of Jammu and Kashmir under Pakistani occupation has been ceded to China illegally (though subject to final settlement of the Jammu and Kashmir issue) making it a trilateral issue between India, China, and Pakistan. The eastern border of Jammu and Kashmir is shared with China. Beijing launched an attack on India in 1962, and large areas remain disputed and under China's possession.

Third, apart from the territorial questions, there are major differences over the sharing of river waters, a vital lifeline in the subcontinent. Though this issue was satisfactorily addressed under the World Bank negotiated Indus Water Treaty, residual problems remain over the Wular Barrage/Tulbul Navigation Project and other prospective projects involving power generation and navigation on rivers. The Siachen glacier region question is also outstanding. In this inaccessible high-altitude terrain north of the LoC in an undemarcated area of the state, artillery fire was exchanged for almost two decades until the cease-fire in December 2003.

Fourth, cross-border terrorism in the state has security implications well beyond Jammu and Kashmir and has to be addressed. According to the *Annual Report of the Indian Home Ministry* in 2002, between 60 and 70 percent of the terrorists in Kashmir come from outside the state and are "under the direct control of Pakistan's Inter Services Intelligence Directorate.[15] These terrorists often find their way to the rest of India and commit terrorist acts there.

CONCLUSION

Though these differences remain and need to be understood, they also need resolution. Two developing countries deeply concerned about the welfare of their people can no longer continue to spend enormous amounts of money on armaments and terrorist and counterterrorist operations. The core issue in the world today has become international terrorism, and this has to be addressed jointly by both nations separately and in conjunction with the international community. The promising signs in 2004 need to developed further through coordinated and resolute actions toward peace.

ENDNOTES

1. C. Dasgupta, *War and Diplomacy in Kashmir 1947–48* (New Delhi: Sage Publications, 2002), 20–33.
2. "Standstill Agreement with India and Pakistan," in *The Story of Kashmir: Yesterday and Today,* vol. III, ed. Verinder Grover (New Delhi: Deep and Deep Publications), 106.
3. Dasgupta, *War and Diplomacy in Kashmir,* 35.
4. Ibid.
5. Ibid., 36–41.
6. Grover, *Story of Kashmir,* 108. For another view of the accession favoring Pakistan, see Alastair Lamb, *Kashmir: A Disputed Legacy, 1846–1990* (London: Oxford University Press, 1991).
7. L. P. Sen, *Slender was the Thread* (New Delhi: Orient Longman, 1961).
8. Ibid.
9. Dasgupta, *War and Diplomacy in Kashmir,* 100.
10. "Kashmir: the view from New Delhi" ICG Asia Report No. 69 P. R. Chari and Suba Chandran, New Delhi/Brussels, December 4, 2003, 4.
11. P. R. Chari and Suba Chandran, eds. *Kashmir: The Road Ahead,* IPCS Topical Series 2 (New Delhi: Institute of Peace and Conflict Studies, 2001), 113–115.
12. "Pak Wrecked Plebiscite Prospects: Sinha," *The Times of India,* March 16, 2003.
13. "Kashmir: The View from Islamabad," ICG Asia Report No. 68 Islamabad/Brussels, December 4, 2003.
14. Ibid., 4.
15. "Threat of Internal Security: Report," *The Hindu,* April 20, 2003.

ABOUT THE AUTHOR

Major General (Retd) Dipankar Banerjee was commissioned into the 1st Gorkha Rifles of the Indian Army and retired in August 1996 after thirty-six years of active service. He has commanded troops from a platoon to a division, the last of which was in counterinsurgency operations in Jammu and Kashmir (J&K), for which he was awarded the Exceptional Distinguished Services Medal in 1991.

He is presently the Director of Institute of Peace and Conflict Studies, an autonomous think tank in Delhi. From 2002–2003, Banerjee was a Jennings Randolph Fellow at the U.S. Institute of Peace, a leading congressionally funded think tank in the United States. Previously, he was the executive director of the only regional think tank in south Asia, the Regional Centre for Strategic Studies, based in Colombo from 1999 to 2002. Before that he worked for many years at the Indian government's security think tank, the Institute for Defence Studies and Analyses, as a senior fellow and later as the deputy director.

Banerjee has authored and coauthored six books, edited fourteen books, written over thirty chapters in different books, and published over eighty articles in journals and numerous op-ed pieces in various newspapers and magazines in India and abroad. He lectures extensively at defense institutions in India, south Asia, and leading international institutions.

Banerjee has been active in a number of NGO efforts in banning antipersonnel land mines, small arms, and light weapons and has been involved in several peace mediation efforts. Banerjee was a consultant to the United Nations Group of Governmental Experts reviewing the Conventional Arms Register in 2000. Banerjee was an international advisor with the ICRC at Geneva from 2000 to 2003. He is a member of boards and advisory committees for several international institutions and think tanks.

Kashmir Dispute

Touqir Hussain

Kashmir is no ordinary dispute. It is about a territory, its people, and the dynamics of their history, culture, and aspirations for freedom—and it is about the ethics of international politics. The dispute affects and reflects the tensions between the national identities, political ambitions, and contrasting views of history of the two disputants, India and Pakistan. It is truly the friction of these moving parts, which has defied all attempts to resolve the conflict and tests the limits of diplomacy as much as of force of arms.

Yet, these challenges also stimulate the search for a solution. After all, there have been three wars over the dispute, not to mention the long and dark shadow it has cast on the national development in a region that is home to more than a billion people. In addition, there is the potential for a nuclear war and for radiating radical impulses in the region and beyond. It also threatens international security and stability.

INDIA–PAKISTAN HISTORY

A brief history of the subcontinent is a good point to begin the story of the Kashmir dispute. Here, the names are confusing. The name *India* signifies a territorial entity that has long existed in history, predating the modern concept of a nation-state.

That India has been, for much of its history, an assortment of kingdoms, principalities, fiefdoms, satrapies, vassal states, and autonomous territories. Though it was the seat of one of the oldest civilizations, the Indus Valley, India's enduring contribution to human civilization in thought, language, and culture was not to come until after the Aryan invasions. Its core was a great religion and culture, namely Hinduism, but even this great idea could not unite the territorial India into a single political institution. The Indian unity, when it happened a little more than two millennia ago, was an empire. Nonetheless, a distinct Indian civilization was in the making, and as in Europe it lacked a national idea whose time was still to come.

Waves of further conquests by the Greeks, Arabs, Central Asians, and Mughals unrolled, irrigating Indian civilization. Further empires were to follow. One of the most enduring was led by the Muslims, who gave India a long and uninterrupted stretch of political life, but at its greatest extent, like its predecessors it could neither embrace the whole of India nor give it more than a military and administrative unity that found its most efficient expression only later under the British Raj.

Indeed the British rule gave India more than an administrative unity. It introduced modern political ideas whose interplay with the native culture and traditional institutions exposed the Indians to such European concepts as nationalism. This happened in a land where religion had always been central to the culture, and where culture, religion, and language, which defined an ordinary Indian's life, could only find a regional, not a national, focus.

In this environment the first stirrings of nationalism, therefore, naturally followed regional and communal fault lines, sharpening the polarity between Hindus and Muslims. Religion tends to reinterpret history, and the two communities found in the history of their collision and coexistence in the subcontinent enough mythology to shape their national identities along religious lines.

With the introduction of reforms by the British, who implanted a representative political process in India, these different identities became distinct. As they sought political expression, they came increasingly to define themselves in opposition to each other. Hindu leaders were resting their conception of free India on one nation encapsulating a civilization whose substance was Hinduism. The Muslims saw in this singularity of view the first signs of the majority Hindu community's aspirations to be the masters of a united India and began thinking of going their own separate way.

Indeed the idea of a civilization lacking a linguistic and cultural unity and a collective and integrative historical experience forming the basis of nationalism ran up against historical facts. Other civilizations, Europeans' for example, expressed themselves through myriad nation-states. Rather than accepting Pakistan's nationalism, many in India—the broad spectrum of leadership in the early years of independence and nationalist extremists since then—have looked upon Pakistan as a breakaway part of modern-day India, and by the same token they regarded Kashmir as its integral part in "the nationalist belief that Indians were all one people, whose varying faiths and practices enriched a common culture.[1]

When the idea of a separate homeland for the Indian Muslims gained ground, Hindu leaders tried to weaken its appeal by claiming secularism to be the core idea of its nationalism and thus a rationale for greater India. But secularism does not define nationalism; it is a social institution and a concept of governance. It thus found few converts among the Muslims.

This is where reference to the historical origins must end, and the story of Kashmir begins. The conflict runs deep into the raison d'être of the two states.

HISTORY OF THE CONFLICT, ITS CAUSES, AND FACTORS CONTRIBUTING TO ITS PERSISTENCE

First, let us begin with a brief historical background of Kashmir itself. Beginning with the Maurya empire in India, Kashmir was ruled by various dynasties of local and nonindigenous origins until the Moghul emperor Akbar conquered it in the sixteenth century. In 1757, Kashmir was invaded by an Afghan warrior, Ahmed Shah Durrani, and became part of Afghanistan but was conquered before long by the Sikhs, who in turn were defeated by the British in 1846. The British, however, did not bring Kashmir under their direct administrative control. They sold it for a certain sum to one Gulab Singh, a warrior from Jammu who under a treaty with them acquired the status of maharaja, a princely ruler. Gulab Singh soon added Ladakh to his domain.

For the next almost hundred years, it was this Dogra dynasty that ruled what came to be known as the State of Jammu and Kashmir. Like other princely rules in India, it was unrepresentative, autocratic, and colonial in substance. The fact that the population was predominantly Muslim while the ruling dynasty was Hindu reinforced the majority's feelings of exclusion from self-rule.

As the idea of decolonization of British India advanced, it stirred the Muslim political consciousness in Kashmir, as it did in the rest of India. In 1931, massive protests, which were put down ruthlessly, were conducted by the Muslim population against the Dogra rule. In 1932 Sheikh Abdullah, a Kashmiri nationalist, formed Kashmir's first political party: All Jammu and Kashmir Muslim Conference (renamed as the National Conference in 1939). Under pressure, the maharaja allowed limited democracy in the form of a legislative assembly in 1934, but it did little to ease Muslim alienation.

The decolonization of British India in 1947 was based on the principle that the territories under the direct administrative control of the British were to be divided into two separate states—areas where

Muslims were in majority were to become Pakistan, and the rest was to constitute India. There were, however, several hundred principalities and small states—in fact, 565 of them, headed by princely rulers (maharajas and nawabs)—that enjoyed a substantial degree of local autonomy under the overall British paramountcy. The British advised these rulers to join either India or Pakistan, keeping in view each state's geographical location, economic and commercial interests and linkages, and the religious and cultural complexion of the population.

On the basis of contiguity to one or the other country, the economic ties, and above all the wishes of their people, many states joined India and some joined Pakistan. Their choice was obvious. Most of them were already embedded in the country of their choosing, and the ruler and the population had a similar view. But problems arose in three states, including two of the largest—Hyderabad and Kashmir—and Junagadh, where in each case there was a conflict of choice between the ruling dynasty and the population.

In Hyderabad, a Hindu majority state, the Muslim ruler aspired to independent status. India responded by invading and annexing the state, claiming that it had acted in accordance with the wishes of the population to join India. The same action and argument were replicated by India to annex Junagadh, another state with a predominantly Hindu population but a Muslim ruler who in fact had already acceded to Pakistan.

In Jammu and Kashmir, the situation was the reverse. The ruler of the state was a Hindu, while the population was overwhelmingly Muslim and wished to join Pakistan. When Jammu and Kashmir achieved its 1947 boundaries, the Muslims constituted 78 percent of the population of the entire state. This percentage rose to 93 percent in the Kashmir Valley, the largest of all the regions in terms of population. Here again, the fate of the state was preempted by India's territorial ambitions. India went against the wishes of the Kashmiri people in violation of the very idea of self-determination it had invoked in occupying the other two states.

Here the chronology of events is important. The Hindu ruler of Kashmir was undecided about accession, though he was under pressure from his population to join Pakistan. The delay over accession detonated a popular uprising in parts of the state, especially in Jammu and the Poonch area,

which was joined by Pakistani tribesmen following inflammatory reports of communal violence against Muslims. The rebels, who faced no resistance from the predominantly Muslim security forces, many of whom in fact changed sides, reached within thirty miles of the capital Srinagar, forcing the maharaja to flee. The Kashmiri rebels formed their own government on October 24, 1947.

The maharaja asked India for military assistance but was pressured to sign the instrument of accession before such aid could arrive. The Indians claim that he acceded to India on October 26. However, serious doubts remain whether an instrument of accession was ever signed and, if so, when British historians, specifically Alastair Lamb (in his book *Kashmir: A Disputed Legacy, 1846–1990*) point out that the Instrument of Accession could not have been signed by the maharaja on October 26 as he was traveling by road to Jammu (a distance of over 350 kilometers). There is no evidence to suggest that a meeting or communication of any kind took place on October 26, 1947, between him and the Indian emissaries. In fact, he could not have signed the Instrument of Accession, if at all he did, until October 27, 1947. Meanwhile, units of the Indian army had already arrived and secured Srinagar airfield during the middle of October 1947. On October 26, 1947, a further massive airlift brought in thousands more Indian troops to Kashmir—which is still before any possible signing of the Instrument of Accession. The implication is that if an instrument of accession was indeed signed, it may have been done under duress.

Whatever the true facts are about the signing of the Instrument of Accession, India's leaders—including Prime Minister Nehru and Lord Mountbatten, then the governor general of India—affirmed that the final status of Jammu and Kashmir would be decided by the people of the state. This was spelled out in a letter from Lord Mountbatten to the maharaja on October 27, 1947. Accepting the accession, Mountbatten made it clear that the state would only be incorporated into the Indian Union after a reference had been made to the people of Kashmir. Prime Minister Nehru had also accepted this principle earlier in a letter to the British prime minister on October 25, 1947, in which he stated "our view, which we have repeatedly made public, is that the question of accession in any disputed territory must be decided in accordance with the wishes of the people and we adhere to this view."

On October 30, 1947, Prime Minister Nehru addressed a telegram to Pakistani Prime Minister Liaquat Ali Khan, saying, "Our assurance that we shall withdraw our troops from Kashmir as soon as peace and order are restored and leave the decision about the future of the State to the people of the State is not merely a pledge to your Government but also to the people of Kashmir and to the world."

Pakistan immediately contested the accession, questioning its legitimacy on several grounds. It suggested that the accession document was fraudulent. It further argued that in any case the maharaja had no right to sign an agreement with India when he had fled from the Kashmir Valley and was not in control of the state and, therefore, not in a position to make a decision on behalf of the people. No original or authentic Instrument of Accession has ever been produced in an international forum or presented to Pakistan or to the United Nations. (In the summer of 1995, Indian authorities reported the original document as lost or stolen, thus reinforcing doubts about its existence in the first place.)

Heavy fighting took place in 1947–48 between Indian forces and the rebels, helped first by Pakistan's logistical support and irregular forces and later joined in by units of the Pakistan army. On January 1, 1949, the U.N. Security Council arranged a cease-fire after having adopted resolutions providing for the holding of a fair and impartial plebiscite in the State of Jammu and Kashmir under U.N. auspices to enable the Kashmiri people to exercise their right of self-determination and join either Pakistan or India.[2]

The cease-fire left Pakistan in control of about one-third of the state, comprising a strip of land west of the Indian-controlled area, called Azad Kashmir (meaning "liberated Kashmir") and the Northern Areas, comprising Gilgit, Hunza, and Baltistan. Azad Kashmir enjoys a measure of autonomy, has its own president, prime minister, parliament, and supreme court. Pakistan is responsible for defense and foreign affairs. The Northern Areas, which were once under the nominal suzerainty of the maharaja of Jammu and Kashmir, but were being ruled directly by the British in the years leading up to the independence of British India, had declared their allegiance to Pakistan in 1947 and were being administered directly by it.

India has thwarted all attempts by the United Nations to organize a plebiscite. While frustrating the implementation of the U.N. resolutions and thus hoping to erode their relevance, if not validity, over a period of time, India went about creating new ground realities by pressing for a political process inside Kashmir that could give its occupation and Kashmir's controversial accession to India a semblance of legitimacy. The strategy focused on a dual process, constitutional and political.

The Indian constitution affirmed Kashmir as an integral part of the union but under Article 370 temporarily gave the state a special status restricting the power of the Indian parliament to legislate for Kashmir only on the subjects of defense, foreign affairs, and communications. This helped India to get the support of some of the nationalist leaders, such as Sheikh Abdullah. Convinced that India might never agree to the state's accession to Pakistan, and concerned that their own personal political statures might be diminished by a merger with Pakistan, these leaders settled for what they thought was the next-best option at the time—a special status—hoping perhaps that Kashmiris might be able to break free of these ties on a distant day.

As part of this process, Sheikh Abdullah, who remained popular, collaborated with India in rigging the elections to the constituent assembly of the state in 1951 but felt betrayed as the Indian designs became apparent. Sheikh Abdullah and his associates had thought they were signing up for autonomy but soon realized that they had instead ended up as collaborators in instituting an insidious political process intended to absorb the state into the union of India. This process was to be facilitated by the cooperation of popular Kashmiri leaders who, after serving their purpose, were discarded in favor of a pliant leadership that would do India's bidding. Sheikh Abdullah was dismissed in 1953 and spent most of the next twenty-two years rotating in and out of jail, during which time he came out openly against the accession and founded the Plebiscite Front, a political party dedicated to asserting and achieving Kashmiris' right of self-determination.

The assemblage of opportunistic and discredited leadership in the constituent assembly went on to ratify the accession of Kashmir to India on February 6, 1954. They did so in contravention of U.N.

Resolution 91 (March 30, 1951), which specified that any such determination by the constituent assembly would be in violation of the U.N. resolutions affirming that the final determination of the state should "be made in accordance with the will of the people expressed through the democratic method of a free and impartial plebiscite conducted under the auspices of the United Nations."

On January 26, 1957, India further violated the sovereignty of Kashmir by adopting a new state constitution that effectively incorporated the state into the Indian Union, again in the face of fierce protests from the Kashmiri people, Pakistan, and the U.N. (Resolution 122, 1957). The document declared that "the state of Jammu and Kashmir is and shall be an integral part of the Union of India." This was not only in direct contravention of the standing U.N. resolutions but also the conditions of the Instrument of Accession, according to which India's jurisdiction was to extend only to external affairs, defense, and communications.

In ensuring years, the provisions of special status were systematically whittled down by the extension of various pieces of Indian legislation to the state. Pakistan's defeat in 1971 had virtually counted it out as a player in Kashmir, thus weakening the morale of the nationalist political leadership in Kashmir. This gave India the license to rig the political process further and remove any vestigial constitutional concessions to the state.

Elections continued to be flawed and manipulated and a succession of Indian-sponsored governments handed a rank misrule to the state, alienating and despairing the population, an ideal environment for people to resort to radical solutions. Even Sheikh Abdullah, who returned to power in 1977, after an agreement with India compromising much that he had stood for, was a disappointment. His five-year rule was authoritarian and focused largely on dynasty building.

When the time-honored tradition of electoral fraud was repeated in 1987, perhaps ever more blatantly, India overplayed its hand, but events came at an inopportune moment for India. The mantle of leadership in the state was passing to a younger generation, which had become desperate and radicalized by decades of political manipulation by India, misgovernance and corruption, denial of social justice and economic opportunities, and systematic abuse of personal liberties and human

rights by wide-ranging draconian laws. The late 1980s also saw the unrolling of new historical forces, with the defeat of Soviet occupation forces in Afghanistan, the beginning of the end of the Soviet empire in Central Asia, and the gathering winds of freedom and self-determination in the world that imparted hope and strength to the Kashmiri struggle to overthrow the Indian tutelage.

Thus began a Kashmiri intifada, which soon came to be supported at the political level by a broad coalition, set up in 1993, of secularists, moderate liberals, traditional politicians, and elements attracted by the force of religiously inspired nationalism, a rising political force in the Islamic world that appealed to the wider population. Named the All Parties Hurriyat Conference (APHC), its objective was *azadi* (freedom). Azadi, however, remained undefined but certainly meant rejection of Indian dominance.

India sought to suppress the resistance with a massive use of force, killing hundreds of innocent men, women, and children in the year it began, 1989. The continued repression led Kashmiri youth to militancy. Jihadi forces in the region, already in battle harness and looking for new challenges, may have provided a helping hand, but the movement has essentially remained indigenous and homegrown. The resistance was not created de novo by outsiders, nor did its continuation depend on their support.

According to official Pakistan government sources more than 60,000 Kashmiris have been killed since 1989 directly at the hands of over 600,000 Indian troops or in hostilities undertaken on their behalf by the state security apparatus and renegade militants.[3] Thousands continue to languish in Indian jails, where they are subjected to torture and custodial deaths. There have been frequent reports of gang rapes of Kashmiri women by the Indian forces and deliberate burning down of entire localities and villages.

A number of laws dating back to the 1970s have severely restricted human rights and civil liberties in Kashmir. Examples include the Jammu and Kashmir Public Safety Act of 1979, Terrorist and Disruptive Activities Act (TADA) of 1987, and Armed Forces Special Powers Act of 1990, to mention just a few. The state has also been under presidential rule for a prolonged period of time, transferring the Kashmir legislature's parliamentary powers to the president of India. Its judicial system has been utterly dysfunctional. The fact is, since 1989 the Kashmiri population is so alienated that India has not enjoyed a shred of support in the state.

Writing for the Carnegie Endowment for International Peace, Paula Newburg explained that "since 1989, the number of dead (in Srinagar) has reached tens of thousands, the exact number unknown. Mostly boys and men, they have died for their religious beliefs, their political beliefs or because they were in the way. The circumstances of birth have become the accidents of death."[4]

Indeed, the scale and horror of violence have been well documented by international and even Indian human rights organizations. Several reports of such organizations as Amnesty International, Human Rights Watch, and the International Commission of Jurists have extensively documented the gross and systematic violation of human rights of the Kashmiri people by Indian military and paramilitary forces.[5] Extrajudicial killings, involuntary disappearances, arbitrary detentions, rapes, and torture continue to be reported on a large scale.

HISTORY OF EFFORTS TO RESOLVE THE DISPUTE

Efforts to resolve the dispute have focused on the U.N. and bilateral dialogue between India and Pakistan, with or without big power involvement. Such efforts have been alternated by armed conflicts in 1947–1948, 1965, 1971, and 1999. Since the late 1990s, the dispute has also raised cross-border tensions along the Line of Control (LoC), causing broader military and diplomatic strains between the two nuclear-capable countries and heightening international concerns about Kashmir.

The U.N. Security Council has adopted eighteen resolutions so far directly or indirectly dealing with the Kashmir dispute, beginning with Resolution 47 (1948), later reaffirmed by Resolutions 51 (1948), 80 (1950), 91 (1951), and 122 (1957). All affirm that the final disposition of Jammu and Kashmir should be made in accordance with the will of the people expressed through a U.N.-supervised plebiscite. The most recent was Resolution 1172, adopted in 1998, which while addressing the then recent nuclear tests in South Asia urged both Pakistan and India to find mutually acceptable solutions that address

the root causes of tensions between them, including Kashmir.

Resolution 47 of the U.N. Security Council (April 21, 1948) is the most important of the U.N. documents on the dispute. It called for the withdrawal from Jammu and Kashmir of the tribesmen and Pakistani irregular and regular forces and the reduction of Indian forces in the state to "minimum strength required" in order to facilitate a plebiscite. However, both Pakistan and India had reservations regarding the extent and mechanism of withdrawal of forces. The Security Council amended this item through Resolution 98 of December 23, 1952, providing for a synchronized reduction of troops on both sides of the cease-fire line to 3,000 to 6,000 on the Pakistani side and 12,000 to 18,000 on the Indian side. Pakistan agreed to the proposal, but India did not. The problem was that India did not want to cede control of the state.

India's reluctance to demilitarize the state was confirmed by Sir Owen Dixon, Head of the U.N. Commission for India and Pakistan (UNCIP), in his report to the Security Council on September 15, 1950. He stated, "In the end I became convinced that India's agreement would never be obtained to demilitarization in any form or to provisions governing the period of plebiscite of any such character, as would in my opinion, permit the plebiscite being conducted in conditions sufficiently guarding against intimidation and other forms of influence and abuse by which freedom and fairness of the plebiscite might be imperiled." Indeed successive attempts by the U.N. to hold a plebiscite foundered on India's reluctance to let the plebiscite be organized in the presence of only a limited number of Indian forces and under the auspices of the U.N. as the resolutions prescribed. India was simply not willing to relinquish the control over the administration of the state.[6]

India has always resisted a serious dialogue on Kashmir, claiming the territory to be an integral part of India and thus nonnegotiable. From time to time, however, either pushed by some military crisis on its borders or propelled by the need to seek some tactical advantage within Kashmir or internationally, India has agreed to talk either on its own initiative or on the urging of big powers concerned about the regional stability and their own strategic and economic interests. However, its commitment to dialogue has waned as soon as the tensions subsided or the big power attention shifted elsewhere, so the dialogue could never mature to a higher plane or achieve a sustainable level.

During the 1962–1963 urging of the United States, the Indians opened an extended dialogue on Kashmir. At the time as the Sino–Indian war, India found it necessary to protect its western flank with Pakistan. The talks were conducted between the foreign ministers of India and Pakistan, Swaran Singh and Zulfikar Bhutto, and came to be known as the Swaran–Bhutto talks. Nothing came of the talks.

In 1965, following the eruption of a civil disobedience movement and widespread disturbances in Kashmir triggered by the rearrest of Sheikh Abdullah, the government of Pakistan thought the moment might be ripe for a Kashmiri uprising. Though it was never officially acknowledged by Pakistan, it is an accepted fact that thousands of irregulars had infiltrated from Azad Kashmir into the Indian-held Kashmir during the summer of 1965 to help a revolt against the Indian occupation. The Indian army came down heavily on the developing insurrection. Pakistan committed its regular troops to the conflict, to which India responded by attacking Pakistan across the international border, leading to a broader conflict. The seventeen-day war, which neither side won conclusively, was brought to an end by the U.N. Later, at a summit in Tashkent, arranged through the good offices of the Soviet Union, the leaders of Pakistan and India agreed on a cease-fire and withdrawal to the prewar boundaries in Kashmir and the international border, without however addressing the Kashmir dispute. Though the revolt failed, the agitation continued in Kashmir.

In 1971, India and Pakistan went to war a third time. It was not over Kashmir but about East Pakistan, but Kashmir did get entangled with the conflict. The military engagement in Kashmir remained inconclusive, but an agreement signed by the leaders of India and Pakistan on June 28, 1972, in Simla, India, to resolve the overall issues arising from the 1971 conflict had two paragraphs on the Kashmir dispute that each side has since found to be of some significance in supporting its respective case.

Pakistan's position is that the Simla Agreement recognizes Kashmir as a dispute requiring settlement. India does not oppose this view but interprets the agreement to have implied that the dispute would be settled only bilaterally without reference to a third party such as the U.N. or international mediation, a position contested by Pakistan. Another problem with the agreement is that the people of the state were not a party to it. These flaws and the fact that no meaningful bilateral negotiations have taken place between India and Pakistan under its aegis have virtually sidelined the agreement.

Between 1990–94, India was once again hard pressed for a dialogue to deflect international criticism following the start of the Kashmiri uprising in 1989. Facilitated by the mission to the region of the U.S. president's special envoy, Robert Gates, India engaged in seven rounds of talks with Pakistan at the foreign secretary level. It was no surprise that the process broke down due to the known India intransigence on one hand and lack of new ideas on the part of weak political governments in Pakistan.

The talks were resumed at Pakistan's initiative in March 1997. Following the foreign secretary–level talks in June 1997, an agreed agenda was adopted that specifically included Kashmir. As the first round of talks on Kashmir was held in October 1998 between the two foreign secretaries, as had been agreed earlier, it became evident there was little give in the Indian position. India rejected Pakistan's framework proposal for a structured and substantive dialogue on Kashmir, maintaining its traditional stance that the status of Kashmir was not open for discussion, much less negotiation.

At Prime Minister Vajpayee's initiative, a much heralded summit took place in Lahore in February 1999. The Lahore Declaration committed both sides to intensify efforts to resolve the Kashmir dispute. The summit was important not so much for laying any groundwork for the settlement of the dispute but for trying a landmark new approach in which the two countries sought the normalization of a broad range of bilateral ties parallel to their search for a lasting solution for Kashmir. The approach essentially synthesized two opposing approaches: Pakistan's emphasis on Kashmir's centrality to the relationship and India's insistence on normalizing the relationship before addressing this dispute.

It looked as if India and Pakistan were about to turn a new leaf in their history. However, before the sincerity of their commitment could be tested the two countries became embroiled in a military operation at Kargil on the LoC, blighting hopes for a diplomatic breakthrough. It took the intervention of President Bill Clinton to defuse the crisis.

While the Lahore Summit of 1999 failed largely because of lack of consensus in Pakistan, the leadership of the two countries met again in Agra in July 2001 to give diplomacy another chance. This time the consensus failed on the Indian side more than on the part of Pakistan. Both Lahore and Agra thus fell victim to the politics of respective hardliners. In Pakistan, the army did not appear to have been taken into confidence about the new moves by the political leadership. It proved again that long-running disputes, embedded in bitter history, chained to domestic political weaknesses and burdened by an all-pervasive sense of righteousness, are not susceptible to sudden breakthroughs. Consensus among key centers of power is an important requisite to any major initiative for change.

CROSS-BORDER INFILTRATION

In recent years, by taking advantage of the growing global anxiety about Islamic fundamentalism and religious extremism and militancy, India has tried to delegitimize the Kashmiri resistance by redefining the Kashmir issue in terms of international terrorism. There is little doubt that some of the overzealous militant elements (jihadis), after having helped the U.S.-sponsored mission of defeating the Soviets in Afghanistan, have joined the battle in Kashmir, especially in training the youth, but the fuller truth is that the substance of Kashmiri resistance has remained indigenous. "No external influence could have persuaded the Kashmiri people to sustain their struggle for so long in the face of India's brutal military repression. It is only [a] genuine and popular quest for freedom which evokes such monumental sacrifices."[7]

If there was an infiltration from across the LoC, as alleged by India, Pakistan has no doubt facilitated or tolerated it. The government of Pakistan, however, continues to deny any official sponsorship. It has always condemned terrorist attacks against innocent civilians and proposed an impartial and independent mechanism to verify India's allegations regarding cross-border infiltration. To this end Pakistan has already agreed to various concepts, such as the strengthening of the United Nations Military Observers Group for India and Pakistan (UNMOGIP), which continues to observe

and monitor the cease-fire arranged by the U.N. Security Council in 1949, or alternatively the stationing of 300 helicopter-borne monitors, or a multinational force across the LoC. India did not agree and instead proposed joint patrolling as an alternative, a proposal it quickly withdrew.[8]

Pakistan feels that India has not agreed to the monitoring of the LoC because it has suited her to make unsubstantiated allegations about what it has called "cross-border" terrorism. From Pakistan's point of view, India has used this powerful propaganda tool to win international sympathy and support by portraying itself as a victim of terrorism and at the same time tarnishing the Kashmiri resistance, as well as isolating Pakistan diplomatically. "India is thus acting as accuser, judge and executioner."

The dialogue process was renewed in late 2003 and culminated in a summit meeting on January 6, 2004, in Islamabad with Pakistan's President Pervez Musharraf and India's Prime Minister Vajpayee committing themselves to a dialogue covering all issues between the two countries, including Kashmir. Leading up to the summit, President Musharraf said that he was prepared to "put aside" the U.N. resolutions and also gave an assurance that he would not allow Pakistan-controlled territory to be used to support terrorism. In addition, the Pakistani and Indian armies observed a cease-fire along the LoC. At the date of this writing, the schedule of talks was being observed. Indications were that the new congress-led government in India would honor the commitment to dialogue.

THE IMPACT OF THE DISPUTE ON PAKISTAN'S IDENTITY, BELIEFS, VALUES, SENSE OF BELONGINGNESS, AND SECURITY

Pakistan sees Kashmir as more than an unfinished agenda of the decolonization of British India or an unfulfilled dream for a separate homeland for the Muslims. The Indian occupation of Kashmir in 1947 sent a powerful message confirming Pakistan's lurking suspicions that India was intent on keeping Pakistan incomplete and weak and wished her ill. It was a symbol of Indian denial of Pakistan's identity and destiny as a nation. If any proof of Indian designs to undo Pakistan's territorial integrity and sovereignty was needed, it came in 1971 when India helped to dismember Pakistan.

Military establishment in Pakistan, stung after the 1971 defeat and loss of half of the country, has come to consider Kashmir, more than ever before, to be of vital strategic value to the country's security. The Indian military presence in Kashmir exposes Pakistan's vulnerability to an attack across the Jhelum River, which is especially of concern because it faces an unstable Afghanistan on its western flank. Another point worth noting is that Kashmir is the source of Pakistan's rivers.

Pakistan's deep concern about security, to which Indian actions in Kashmir have made a seminal contribution, raised the profile of the military establishment and led Pakistan to an alliance with the United States, whose military assistance gave the armed forces a dominant voice in conceiving the country's security and Kashmir's centrality to it. In the end, this dominant influence came to strengthen the military's role in the country's political life and, indeed, in its foreign policy. Security, nationalism, and Kashmir became synonymous.

The important question remains this: Do any flaws in Pakistan's approach to Kashmir justify India's repression or, more important, detract from the Kashmiris' right of self-determination. The answer is obviously "no."

PAKISTAN'S PERCEPTION OF THE INDIAN VIEW OF THE CONFLICT

Pakistan sees all Indian arguments that regard Kashmir as being critical to India's secular status as disingenuous rationalizations made to support an expansive nationalism and an attempt to make its Muslim population hostages to Pakistan's demands on Kashmir. In fact, long before the British left and the Kashmir issue arose, the Indian political leaders were expressing the view that partition would be a tragedy. Now they say it would be a tragedy to let Kashmir go as it would weaken India's cohesion, be a blow to its secularism, and produce a backlash against its Muslim population. If, in fact, India's secularism faces any threat, it is from the rising Hindu fundamentalist nationalism, not from the fate of the Kashmir dispute. As for the argument that letting Kashmir go will negatively impact India's cohesion, one can perhaps ask, Is the Indian unity too fragile to absorb the effects of releasing a territory under

wrongful occupation, should it not raise questions directed at the very foundations of the idea of Indian nationhood?

Other Indian arguments, advanced at various times, are equally false and unconvincing. An example is the argument advanced in the 1950s and 1960s that since Pakistan had allied itself with the United States and thus introduced superpower rivalry in the region, it had made it difficult for India to accept any change in the status of Kashmir.

India has also been saying that with the passage of time the U.N. resolutions on Kashmir have lost their relevance. Legally and politically, this claim is not correct. No U.N. Security Council resolution can lose its relevance unless the council adopts another resolution calling for its supercession for whatever reasons. This has been confirmed by the U.N. secretary general in a statement on January 6, 1994.

India has also argued that the Kashmiris have spoken about their accession to India through various elections. Pakistan's position, and that of the U.N., is that elections and decisions such as those of the constituent assembly are not a substitute for a U.N.-prescribed plebiscite for the simple reason that they presuppose the allegiance of Kashmiris to the Indian constitution. Besides, almost every election has been rigged or accompanied by widespread fraud and use of force, a fact acknowledged by the Indian media itself.

India also claims that the Simla Agreement excluded the mediation of the U.N. in the Kashmir dispute and that U.N. resolutions consequently have been sidestepped and cannot provide a basis for settlement. No bilateral agreement between India and Pakistan has changed the relevance of U.N. resolutions. India based this argument on Article II of the Simla Agreement, which says that the two countries "are resolved to settle their differences by peaceful means through bilateral negotiations." Pakistan's view is that, coming as it did after a war, the Simla Agreement merely emphasized the two countries' commitment to opt for peaceful means—bilateral negotiations, for one—instead of resorting to force of arms. It did not expressly exclude other means, such as the U.N. On the contrary, the agreement specifically provides that "the principles and purposes of the Charter of the United Nations shall govern the relations between the two countries."

ACTIONS AND/OR POLICIES TO SOLVE THE DISPUTE

Ideally, Pakistan would like Kashmiris to be allowed to exercise the right of self-determination. Whether this right had been acquired by the population of Jammu and Kashmir at the time of partition of British India in 1947 is a question that has been fully examined by the International Commission of Jurists (ICJ) report of 1995 in the light of available literature on the subject, historical facts, and the findings of their mission to Kashmir. Page 98 of their report sums up the commission's conclusions by saying that the state did acquire the right of self-determination in 1947, and, as a result, it remains to be exercised and should not be "affected by acts of the Government of Pakistan" including the presence of its forces in the state.

The ICJ mission was also of the view that though it is true that the decision on accession was given by the British to the princes rather than to the people, "This should not be regarded as giving the rulers the right to override the wishes of their people." "This was indeed the view that was adopted by the Indian government in justifying its actions in Junagadh and Hyderabad." The report goes on to say that "If, as the ICJ mission has concluded, the people of Kashmir have a right of self-determination, it follows that their insurgency is legitimate" even if Pakistan has no right to support it.

Of course, as the ICJ has acknowledged in its report, the state is not homogenous in language, religion, and culture, which presents difficulties organizing a single plebiscite within its 1947 boundaries, but that does not mean the right of self-determination can only be exercised in this manner. Each constituent unit can exercise the right separately.

Pakistan has not addressed the idea of separate plebiscites because India has never come around to validating Kashmiris' right of self-determination in the first place. Though Pakistan is morally and politically committed to plebiscite in the whole of Jammu and Kashmir, Pakistan's main interest has been in the Kashmir Valley, which has been the focus of resistance against Indian rule and victim of violence and repression. It is this area that has to be the core of any future settlement. Perhaps the two sides should explore the solution along

these lines, even though it may lead to an imperfect solution, which would still be better than an inconclusive conflict.

Pakistan, however, will not accept a settlement that simply freezes the status quo by turning the LoC into an international border, thus letting down both the Kashmiri population and the Pakistani public. No strategic prize, including the promise of a better relationship with India and the peace and stability of the region, would compensate the sense of betrayal of over half a century of strategic commitment to the Kashmir cause and the supreme sacrifices of generations of the Kashmiri population. Any improved relationship built on this moral wreckage will soon be blown away like a house of cards.

PROPOSED SOLUTIONS

Various solutions to the Kashmir dilemma have been discussed. The BBC summed up the alternatives well, along with the likely responses of India and Pakistan.[9] A brief summary follows.

Scenario One: Status quo. The LoC becomes the international boundary dividing the region in two, with one part administered by India and one by Pakistan. India would accept this solution, but Pakistan will not.

Scenario Two: Kashmir joins Pakistan. Historically, Pakistan has advocated this as the best solution and believes that the state's majority Muslim population would guarantee a vote for Pakistan in a plebiscite. However a single plebiscite held in the state comprising people that are culturally, religiously, and ethnically diverse, could create disaffected minorities. Besides, India would not accept this option.

Scenario Three: Kashmir joins India. Pakistan would not accept this, nor would the people of Pakistani-administered Azad Kashmir, and the Northern Areas, which historically had only tenuous cultural and political ties with the maharaja's Kashmir. The Kashmir Valley would also reject this option.

Scenario Four: Independent Kashmir. This would require both India and Pakistan to relinquish territory, which they may not be willing to do. It may also be unacceptable to minorities, which are content with their present status.

Scenario Five: A smaller independent Kashmir. An independent Kashmir could be created in the Kashmir Valley and Azad Kashmir. This would leave the strategically important regions of the Northern Areas and Ladakh, bordering China, under the control of Pakistan and India, respectively.

Scenario Six: Independent Kashmir Valley. Kashmir Valley, which has been at the heart of the resistance against the Indian government, could become independent.

Scenario 7: Divided Kashmir. This plan would see Kashmir divided along the line of the Chenab River. This would give Pakistan the entire valley, with its Muslim majority population, as well as the Muslim majority areas of Jammu.

In their publicly stated positions neither India nor Pakistan would like to entertain the notions of scenarios five, six, and seven. However, as and when they are ready for solution of the dispute and a change in the present status quo, these scenarios—as well as a plan developed by the Kashmir Study Group, (see the following section)—could form the basis of their search for a mutually acceptable formula.

A WAY FORWARD: A PROPOSAL BY THE KASHMIR STUDY GROUP

The following proposal was developed by members of the Kashmir Study Group, composed of eminent members of the U.S. strategic community, in consultation with several Indians and Pakistanis, and can be accessed on the group's Web site.[10] The proposed solution "recommends that part of [the] State of Jammu and Kashmir be reconstituted as a sovereign entity (but one without an international personality) enjoying free access to and from both India and Pakistan which would guarantee its sovereignty." Its boundaries shall be determined through an internationally supervised plebiscite on either side of the LoC. The new entity would legislate on all matters other than defense and foreign affairs. India and Pakistan would be responsible for the defense of the Kashmiri entity, which would itself maintain police and gendarme forces for internal law-and-order purposes. India and Pakistan would be expected to work out financial arrangements for the Kashmiri entity, which could include a currency of its own. "Kashmiri citizenship would also entitle such citizens to acquire Indian or Pakistani passports (depending on which side of the

Line of Control they live on). The borders of Kashmir with India and Pakistan would remain open for the free transit of people, goods, and services in accordance with arrangements to be worked out between India, Pakistan, and the Kashmiri entity."

FUTURE OF THE CONFLICT

Pakistan sees the Kashmir dispute at several levels: as a moral issue going to the heart of the political aspirations of the Muslims of British India for a separate homeland, as an act of bad faith by India in denying the accession of the state to Pakistan, and as a symbol of India's rejection of the very idea of Pakistan.

Over time the dispute has come to amass a much larger identity, fed by the two sides' hardening of historical attitudes, as well as contrasting paths to political development and foreign and security policies that put them at the center of each other's national aims. These aims came to focus very much on Kashmir. Both Pakistan and India have failed to settle on a well-defined view of each other, and Kashmir has become a theater in which they have tested each other's will for hegemony or survival.

Pakistan's case has rested essentially on the illegality of Kashmir's accession to India and its rejection by the Kashmiris, as well as on the sanctity of U.N. resolutions calling for a fair and independent plebiscite that would allow the Kashmiris the opportunity to exercise their right of self-determination. While Pakistan as a weaker party has invoked the concepts of legitimacy, morality, and justice, backed by a modicum of force, India has practiced cold-blooded power politics to back up a claim to sovereignty that rests simply on a legal document—and a controversial one at that. With force of arms, India has on one hand tried to sustain a sham political process and on the other kept up an unrelenting repression of the resistance aimed at breaking the will of the people, all at great human expense. It has not worked. As a U.S. Institute of Peace report on Kashmir observes, "Whatever the legal right, the Accession was more than 50 years ago. Does that right still hold through all that has happened since? Nations, much less democratic nations, may be created but not built as a result of legal decree alone. Military strength in itself can secure only a transient unity. The will of the people, or at the very least their willing acceptance, must be the binding force of a nation, particularly one that aspires to freedom. When that will erodes, mighty empires will fall."[11]

There is enough blame to go around, but India must bear major responsibility for causing this tragedy, which in recent years has merged indistinguishably with a broader India–Pakistan conflict. Paradoxically this merger may contain the seeds of resolution of the dispute, as by reaching the brink it has raised global alarms, especially after 9/11.

Favorable and reciprocal changes in multiple contexts—domestic, bilateral, and international—that host long-standing conflicts, especially ones entangled with larger issues such as religion and nationalism, are requisite to their resolution. In that sense a critical mass for the resolution of this conflict may indeed be approaching.

South Asia in recent years has come to present new dangers and incentives. It is a far more dangerous place, a threat to itself and the world. The extremism swirling in and around the region destabilizes it, and the tensions springing from Kashmir lower the threshold for a nuclear war. A resurgence in China's strategic shadow also looms large over the region. On the other hand, globalization enhances the region's economic potential and offers attractive new incentives. This especially impacts, in the long term, the strategic and economic interests of the United States, the country with the most influence and stake in both India and Pakistan.

All this has stimulated or forced new strategic choices on the United States and on the leadership of Pakistan and India—domestically, in Kashmir, and in bilateral relations. So far, whether through dialogue or force, the disputants have sought only victory, not solution, each hoping that time was on its side, but time has only invalidated their calculations.

The picture is indeed changing in India and Pakistan. In India, a shift in national priorities relating to the rise of China and the urge to compete with it; the information technology (IT) revolution; the rise of India's enterpreneurial class, especially its expatriate community in the West; and, of course, nuclear capability have brought the country closer to the United States. A corollary to these changes was the search by India and Pakistan for a new relationship between themselves. India recognizes that in the interest of her own economic aspirations

and "big power" ambitions, in which the United States can contribute enormously, with investment, trade, technology, and security assistance, it has to accommodate U.S. priorities that include a stable Pakistan and a reduction of tensions in the region. Thus, peace with Pakistan may have become a strategic imperative for India.

Pakistan, too, is slowly changing its external behavior to strengthen its internal order, rather than pursuing external goals at the expense of its internal stability. A catalyst in spurring the necessary changes has been 9/11, especially in setting a new direction in Pakistan. That catastrophic event necessitated closer relations with the United States.

Pakistan finally may be realizing that it overstretched strategically by following a forward foreign policy in the region for which Pakistan, and indeed the world, have paid a heavy price. It placed an unsustainable burden on its economy, undermined its security, and caused diplomatic isolation.

Economics poses a stark choice: either prosper or be relegated to a subservient status to a shining India. Thus, peace with India has become critical to Pakistan's economic survival, national security, and safeguarding of its national honor.

As for the United States, it too now recognizes that the totality of its current and future interests in the region will not be served if the Kashmir dispute and relations between India and Pakistan are not addressed. The United States needs both India and Pakistan to achieve their objectives in the region, especially in the war against terrorism, and it cannot do so without the normalization of relations. India, Pakistan, and the United States, therefore, may now have interlocking interests.

The people of the subcontinent and the international community can only hope that with these changes in perceptions and policies a defining moment may have arrived in the history of the dispute. The two countries' leaders realize this and in recent years have been seeking a negotiated solution to the dispute. President Pervez Musharraf and Indian Prime Minister Manmohan Singh had their first formal talks in October 2004 when they were attending a U.N. General Assembly session. The talks were very purposeful. The two leaders discussed various "options" for solving the Kashmir dispute. Later, President Musharraf made some of these proposals public, including the idea of demilitarizing and jointly governing the disputed territory. He also offered to withdraw Pakistan's demand about the plebiscite. India was not receptive to the proposals but did respond by withdrawing some of its troops from Indian-administered Kashmir.

In February 2005 the two countries agreed to launch a bus service across the Line of Control, providing historical opportunity to divided families to reunite. Later, in a major earthquake that hit a part of Kashmir administered by Pakistan, the two governments cooperated in the relief effort. However, except for these two developments the peace process has had nothing much to show and Pakistanis have been feeling a little frustrated. President Musharraf has kept repeating his different peace initiatives publicly but apparently with little reciprocity from India. Lately, with Pakistan becoming heavily involved in its internal issues, especially the transition in the 2007–2008 elections from a military-dominated regime to a civilian democratic system, India is playing a waiting game. Yet there are reports that back-channel diplomacy is at work and that the two countries are much closer to the resolution of the dispute than they to be appear in public. If true, this is good news.

Both India and Pakistan are integrating into a wider world. The younger generation in both countries sees the relationship in terms of connectivity to the outside world and look upon each other as partners in economic progress and builders of the respective futures of their countries. This provides a good opening for India to sustain this emerging outlook in Pakistan—and to soften its approach to Pakistan, and especially to Kashmir. It is important to maintain dialogue with the Kashmiris, and conciliating them will contribute more than anything else to moderating Pakistan's position on Kashmir. On his own, President Musharraf cannot succeed in moderating Pakistan as that country is caught up in global Islamic revivalism. Pakistanis need to have a different vision of their country, and India can help in providing them an alternative vision.

Kashmiri leaders may also be thinking that, in effect, India holds most of the power. The connection with Pakistan has, of course, helped the Kashmiri resistance, but it can only take that so far. Meanwhile, the military runs the risk of turning on

itself and becoming its own reward, as well as an end in itself.

Yet there remains a view in Pakistan that India may just be leading Pakistan up the proverbial garden path, hoping that in time the so-called "confidence building measures" (CBMs) between the two countries will become their own reward and that, perhaps with increased economic and commercial exchanges, cultural interplay, and trends toward moderation in Pakistan, Pakistanis will develop a different perception of India and Kashmir. It is also hoped that other critical issues, such as energy, sharing of water resources, security, and good neighborly relations, may eventually take precedence over Kashmir in defining the countries' relationship, freeing India to find an internal solution to the dispute, facilitated by Pakistan's diminished leverage and unforced concessions. If true this would be a short-sighted view on the part of India. The stakes are much higher and the two countries need to seize the moment.

While in Pakistan awareness is growing that victory remains elusive, the feeling that defeat is not an option is also on the rise. India must recognize that. Thus, any Kashmir settlement must be such that it does not tarnish as defeated any side in the dispute. India will not accept a settlement that degrades its territorial integrity. Pakistan will not accept an agreement that is unacceptable to the Kashmiris who will not settle for anything less than internal self-rule. Consequently, the settlement may have to be political more than territorial, and the changes may come to focus on the Kashmir Valley of Kashmir (including parts of Jammu) and the relationship of this predominantly Muslim region with the Azad Kashmir.

This may make for dissatisfied parties, but seen in a larger context this could be a win–win situation for all. The gains will manifest themselves in lasting prospects of peace and stability, within Kashmir and between India and Pakistan, and in staving off risks of a nuclear war, and they will enhance the potential for economic cooperation leading to the emergence of an integrated regional market. It will also undercut forces of extremism, help stabilize an insecure Pakistan uncertain of its future and place in the world, and advance India's ambitions for "big power" status. All this will be beneficial not just to India, Pakistan, and Kashmir but also to the international community.

ENDNOTES

1. Shankar Bajpai, former Indian Ambassador to Pakistan, China, and United States, *Foreign Affairs*, May 2003.
2. Whenever the words the "State of Jammu and Kashmir" or "Kashmir" appear in this writing they are interchangeable and signify the territory in its 1947 boundaries and as referred to by the U.N. This is without prejudice to the recognized positions of both India and Pakistan.
3. http://www.mofa.gov.pk/Pages/Brief.htm
4. Additional information about Pakistan's Permanent Mission to the U.N. can be found at the following Web site: http://www.pakun.org
5. In 1995, the International Commission of Jurists published a report entitled "Human Rights in Kashmir."
6. For one of the most objective and scholarly accounts of the origins of the dispute and the initial history of the

U.N. involvement please, see S. M. Burke, *Foreign Policy of Pakistan—An Historical Analysis.*
7. Quoted from official sources of government of Pakistan.
8. Quoted from official sources of government of Pakistan.
9. BBC Web site Kashmir Flashpoint http://news.bbc.co.uk/2/shared/spl/hi/south_asia/03/kashmir_future/html/default.stm
10. Based on information at the Web site of the Kashmiri Study Group (accessed September 12, 2007). http://www.kashmirstudygroup.com
11. Wajahat Habibullah, "The Problem of Kashmir and Its Resolution," U.S. Institute of Peace Special Project Report 2003–04.

ABOUT THE AUTHOR

Ambassador Touqir Hussain is a former career diplomat from Pakistan who served in several high-ranking and key positions before retiring in 2006. Hussain joined the Foreign Service in 1966 and held varied diplomatic assignments both abroad and at the Foreign Office. He served as ambassador to Japan from 1998 to 2003. Earlier he served as ambassador to Spain and to Brazil. He also held senior positions in the Pakistan Foreign Office, including that of additional foreign secretary. From 1996 to 1998, he served as the diplomatic adviser to the prime minister of Pakistan.

Though most of Ambassador Hussain's diplomatic experience had focused on U.S. relations with South Asia, in the prime minister's office he had the opportunity to work with a much wider range of issues, including India, the nuclear question, and Afghanistan. In that capacity he attended two summit meetings between the prime ministers of Pakistan and India. He was also a member of the Pakistan delegation at an earlier round of talks between the two prime ministers in 1992 at the Rio Earth Summit. As diplomatic advisor to the prime minister of Pakistan, Hussain was a member of the Pakistan delegation at several international conferences.

Hussain has been writing in the op-ed pages of U.S. and Pakistani newspapers on the subjects of Pakistan–India and Pakistan–U.S. relations, the Kashmir dispute, political Islam, terrorism, and issues that the United States has with the Islamic world. His articles can be found on his Web site (http://touqirhussain.com). The Web site also contains his speeches and media interviews on major international issues.

Ambassador Hussain is a recipient from the government of Brazil of the highest civil award for foreign nationals.

After his diplomatic service, Ambassador Hussain began pursuing an academic career in the United States. He was a Senior Fellow at the U.S. Institute of Peace in 2004–2005, and since then he has been a Research Fellow at the Center for the Study of Globalization of George Washington University. He is currently an adjunct professor in the Woodrow Wilson Department of Politics at the University of Virginia, Charlottesville, and at the School of Foreign Service at Georgetown University. He has been a guest speaker at several universities and also has appeared on the *PBS News Hour*, *Voice of America*, and GEO (a Pakistani channel).

Mr. Huissain lives in Chevy Chase, Maryland. You may reach him at thussain@gwu.edu.

SUGGESTED READING

Bajpai, Kanti. "Diversity, Democracy & Devolution in India." In *Government Policies and Ethnic Relations in Asia and the Pacific,* edited by Michael E. Brown and Sumit Ganguly. Cambridge, MA: Center for Science and International Affairs, Kennedy School of Government, 1997.

Burke, S. M. *Pakistan's Foreign Policy: An Historical Analysis.* London: Oxford University, 1972.

Cheema, Pervaiz, "Parkistan, India, and Kashmir: A Historical Review." In *Perspectives on Kashmir: The Roots of Conflict in South Asia,* edited by Raju Thomas. Boulder, CO: Westview Press, 1992.

Cohen, Steve. *India Rising.* Washington, DC: Brookings Institution Press, 2001.

_____. The Pakistan Army. New York: Oxford University Press, 1998.

"Human Rights in Kashmir: Reports of a Mission." Geneva: International Commission of Jurists, 1995.

Lamb, Alastair. *Kashmir: A Disputed Legacy, 1846–1990.* Hertingfordbury: Roxford Books, 1991.

Schofield, Victoria. *Kashmir in the Crossfire.* London: I. B. Tauris Publishers, 2002.

Web site of the Ministry of Foreign Affairs, Pakistan, at http://www.mofa.gov.pk.

Web site of the Pakistan Mission to the United Nations (New York), at http://www.pakun.org.

4

Cyprus

The Island of Cyprus has been part of many empires—Egyptian, Phoenician, Roman, Byzantine, Ottoman, and others—because of its strategic location in the Mediterranean Sea. Today the island is divided into four areas: Republic of Cyprus (the Greek Southern Cyprus, unrecognized by Turkey), Turkish Republic of Northern Cyprus (recognized by Turkey), United Nations–controlled Green Line separating the territories, and two British Base Areas. The population of Cyprus, nearly 880,000, is mostly Greek Cypriots, 77 percent, and Turkish Cypriots, 21 percent. The religious groups reflect perfectly the ethnic division, with 78 percent of the population Greek Orthodox and 21 percent Muslim. Despite the convivial relations that existed between both ethnic groups for centuries, Turkish and Greek Cypriots have been disputing the control of the island especially since 1950s.

In 1571, the Ottoman Turks conquered Cyprus and the island became part of the Ottoman Empire. Prior to Ottoman rule, the Venetians ruled the island from 1489 to 1571. Since the Catholic Venetians had oppressed Greek Cypriots, the latter celebrated the conquest of the island by the Ottomans. For three centuries, Greek Cypriots were free to engage in their religious, economic, and cultural activities. The Greek Cypriots supported Greek independence from the Ottomans in 1821 and, further, wished to unite with Greece, giving birth to the *enosis* movement (union with Greece). In spite of the Cypriot Greek uprisings for *enosis,* which were quelled, Cypriot Greeks were allowed to continue their religious, economic, and cultural activities.

In 1878, the United Kingdom and the Ottoman Empire secretly negotiated and signed the Cyprus Convention, granting control of Cyprus to the United Kingdom in exchange for supporting the Ottomans against the Russians. The territory remained in the hands of the

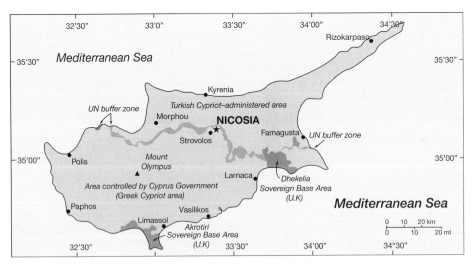

Source: https://www.cia.gov/library/publications/the-world-factbook/geos/cy.html

Ottoman Empire up to 1914, when it was annexed by Britain. Cyprus had become an important and strategic British naval base, from which the United Kingdom exercised a certain control of the Suez Canal and commercial routes. Furthermore, the Lausanne Treaty of 1923, signed by the Allied powers (United Kingdom, France, and Russia) and the newly founded Republic of Turkey, formally recognized Britain's ownership of Cyprus and its right to claim the island. In 1925, the island's status changed to Crown Colony.

From the 1920s through the 1950s, tensions recurred between the two ethnic groups on the island. The Greek Cypriots rebelled against British rule as their fervor for *enosis* grew stronger. In 1931, Greek Cypriots rioted against the British, resulting in a few deaths and burning of the British governor's palace. The British then imposed a repressive regime on both Greek and Turkish Cypriots and rejected the idea of the union of Cyprus with Greece. The Turkish Cypriots strongly rejected *enosis*. Facing the growing Greek Cypriot sentiment for enosis, the Turkish Cypriots could not conceive that Cyprus be annexed to Greece and began feeding a national movement. A large majority of Greek Cypriots were determined to unite with Greece, and when their demand of self-determination was rejected by the U.N. in 1954, it led to a preamble to the creation of the terrorist group National Organization of Cypriot Fighters (EOKA), which became very active from 1955, assaulting Turkish Cypriot inhabitants, villages, and anything Turkish.

By the 1960s, Cyprus had become an independent binational state. Britain and the two "motherlands," Greece and Turkey, signed the Treaty of Guarantee, which established an independent Cypriot state with the Commonwealth nations and Britain retaining two sovereign areas with military bases. The treaty also established the right of each power to take military action in the face of any threat to the constitution. A new government was established, and a constitution was drafted. The state was to be headed by a Greek Cypriot president and a Turkish Cypriot would take office as vice president, both with a veto power. The year following the independence of Cyprus, Greek Cypriots deemed the new constitution inappropriate and wished to eliminate clauses referring to veto powers and ethnic issues. In 1963, the Greek Cypriots presented new amendments to the constitution to reflect their new demands, which were rejected by the Turkish Cypriots. Later that same year, the Greek Cypriots expelled the Turkish Cypriots from the government, forcing them to live in enclaves and as refugees for the following decade. Even though the U.N. sent a peace-keeping mission in 1964, violence continued between both groups.

In 1974, the Greek military government ordered a coup d'état to remove the president of Cyprus, the Greek Cypriot Archbishop Makarios, who was forced to flee. A transitional regime was installed, with the intention of proclaiming enosis. Turkey, aware of the intention of the transitional government, five days later intervened militarily and took control of 35 percent of the northern part of the island using its right under the Treaty of Guarantee. Greek Cypriots living in the north moved to the Greek-controlled southern part of the island, and the Turkish Cypriots living in the south moved to the Turkish-controlled northern part of the Island. Makarios was brought back in December 1974. The Turkish Cypriots declared a Federated State, and in 1983 they proclaimed the Turkish Republic of Northern Cyprus, which is only recognized by Turkey. In 1985, a new constitution was enacted for the Turkish Republic of Northern Cyprus.

Efforts to solve the conflict initially were begun in 1968, and respective community leaders have met many times over the last thirty-eight years. The U.N. and the international community have long been involved in the resolution elaborating a settlement plan for a bicommunal, bizonal state, giving equal political rights to both groups. In 2004 a referendum was voted on the issue; while the Turkish Cypriots support the settlement plan, the Greek Cypriots voted against.

Caesar V. Mavratsas describes in the following reading, *The Cyprus Conflict,* the evolution of the relations between the Greek and Turkish Cypriots through historical periods. An examination of key events provides a more objective panorama, though he describes the conflict through a Greek nationalist perspective. Kenan Atakol, in the reading entitled *Turkish and Greek Cypriots in Conflict,* explains the conflict from the Turkish point of view, emphasizing the discrimination suffered and the consequences of the partition of the island for the Turkish Cypriots, which never gained international recognition. Both readings examine the future of reconciliation, as well as the differential status given by the European Union (EU) to the Greek and Turkish Cypriots.

The Cyprus Conflict: National Mythologies and Real Tragedies

Caesar V. Mavratsas

The aim of this chapter is to provide a historical overview of the Cyprus conflict and to analyze its main social and political dimensions. My perspective is that of a Greek-Cypriot sociologist, who focuses on developments in the Greek-Cypriot community. Whereas there is a vast literature on the so-called Cyprus problem, most of it is written from a nationalist angle and is emotionally and politically charged. I seek, above all else, to be objective, and, given my emphasis upon the Greek Cypriot side, it may appear that I place most of the blame for the dispute upon the Greeks of the island. I can only say that this is by no means my intention, and that my focus on one side of the dispute is simply a matter of analytic interest.

The Cyprus conflict in its modern form dates back to the 1950s, when the confrontation between the Greeks and the Turks of the island began to assume a violent character. The Greek Cypriots are Christian and believe themselves to be descendants of Greeks who came to the island around 3,000 years ago. They comprise about 80 percent of the population, whereas the Turkish Cypriots, who are Muslim and believe themselves to be descendants of the Ottoman Turks who conquered Cyprus in 1571 and ruled the island until 1878, comprise about 18 percent of the island's population. Small Armenian, Maronite, Latin, and Roma communities also live in Cyprus, but their role in the political history of the island has been and remains marginal. Greek and Turkish Cypriots began negotiating a "solution" to the Cyprus prob-

lem in 1968. Glafcos Clerides, who represented the Greek Cypriots, and Rauf Denktash, who represented the Turkish Cypriots, have met innumerable times over the last thirty-five years. Trying to solve the Cyprus problem has become synonymous with an exercise in futility and frustration. At the beginning of 2003, Clerides and Denktash were still the leaders of their communities and were still negotiating.

In November 2002, Kofi Annan, then Secretary-General of the United Nations, submitted a detailed plan for a comprehensive settlement of the dispute based on the idea of a bicommunal and bizonal federation—an idea that was officially accepted by both sides in the so-called High Level Agreements of 1977 and 1979. The former agreement was signed by Makarios, archbishop and first president of the Republic of Cyprus, and Turkish Cypriot leader Rauf Denktash. The latter agreement was signed by Spyros Kyprianou, then president of the Republic of Cyprus, and Denktash. The proposed state was envisioned in successive U.N. Security Council resolutions to have "a single sovereignty, international personality and citizenship . . . comprising two politically equal communities" (U.N. Security Council Resolution 1251/1999). The international community appeared determined to settle the dispute, and that commitment certainly represented the best opportunity for settlement that Cyprus had seen in years. The United Nations, the European Union, the United States, Greece, and Turkey all supported the secretary general's plan. The prospect of Cyprus's entry into the European Union on May 1, 2004, put pressure on both the Greek and Turkish communities of Cyprus to iron out their differences. Still, the history of the Cyprus problem has rightfully been described as a history of missed opportunities, and no one ought to be surprised that this opportunity was also lost.

April 24, 2004, was a truly historic moment and a real turning point in the modern history of Cyprus. For the first time in their centuries-long co-existence on the island, the Greeks and Turks of Cyprus were called to decide through popular vote on the same question concerning the political future of their homeland—if, that is, they were willing to accept both a solution to the Cyprus dispute on the basis of the Annan plan and the entry of a re-united Cyprus into the European Union. While 76 percent of Greek Cypriots voted "no" to the proposed settlement, 65 percent of Turkish Cypriots voiced their support for it. Whereas it lavishly praised the Turkish Cypriot community for its decision in the April 24, 2004, referendum (making it clear that the Turkish Cypriots are no longer to blame for the Cyprus stalemate, and that they should now be rewarded for their courageous stance with a gradual ending to their economic and political isolation), the international community expressed its deep disappointment over the decision of the Greek Cypriots to reject what many international leaders considered a historic opportunity to solve the Cyprus problem. The results of the referendum came as a shock to the international community, but, as I will argue in this essay, they seemed quite logical and predictable to any objective analyst who has studied the modern political history of Cyprus and the clash between Greek and Turkish nationalism on the island.

THE CLASH BETWEEN GREEK AND TURKISH NATIONALISM IN CYPRUS

Greek Cypriots and Turkish Cypriots have different interpretations both of the Cyprus problem and its possible solutions. The intractability of the conflict points precisely to the fact that the Cyprus problem has always been, above all else, an internal dispute—between the two communities and, perhaps equally importantly, within each

of them. Greek Cypriots often like to stress the role of foreign powers and interests, claiming that the Cyprus conflict is first and foremost a creation of conspiracies plotted outside the island, but the real picture is very different. Notwithstanding its undeniable complexity, the Cyprus problem is a classic case of a clash of two competing ethnic nationalisms. Although no one can deny that the dispute has acquired an international dimension, nationalism is the key force in the political history of the island. Greek and Turkish nationalists cannot think of the world without the Cyprus problem, and thus it is simply impossible to reach a solution as long as nationalism sets the parameters of ideological orthodoxy on the island.

To understand the complexity and entrenchment of each group's thinking, it is important to understand the modern political history of the island.

THE PERIOD OF BRITISH RULE: 1878–1960

In Ottoman Cyprus, ethnically Greek Christians and ethnically Turkish Muslims coexisted peacefully. Although there was very little intermarriage—the strongest sociological index of assimilation—the two communities maintained good relations and even, at times, joined forces in uprisings against the Ottoman administration and the Orthodox church. In this prenational setting, religion was the main factor separating the two communities. Nevertheless, they certainly developed some sense of commonality or shared localism.

With the advent of British colonialism in 1878, Greek Cypriot irredentist nationalism, in the form of the demand for *enosis* (union) with Greece began to be transformed into a mass movement. In response to this movement, there gradually arose an opposing Turkish Cypriot nationalism, calling for *taksim*, the partition of Cyprus along ethnic lines. Greek Cypriot nationalism must be understood as part of Greek irredentism, the prevailing ideology of the Greek state from the 1850s to the 1920s, which was aimed at the creation of a "Great Greece" that would have incorporated all Greek-speaking people living in the disintegrating Ottoman Empire. Given the social and cultural dominance of the island's Greek-speaking population, Cyprus proved to be especially fertile ground for the transplantation of Greek irredentism. The Greek-speaking Christians gradually but firmly began to imagine themselves as part of the greater political community of the Greek nation and to demand union with their "motherland." Ethnicity, thus, began to be politicized and to replace religion as the main identifying attribute. As in so many other areas in the Balkans and the Middle East, nationalism was soon to undermine the peaceful coexistence of different ethnic groups in traditional society.

Under the relative tolerance of the new British administration, the construction of Greek nationalist identity in Cyprus accelerated. The main mechanisms of nation building were the educational system (which was in the hands of the Orthodox church), the activities of voluntary associations formed by intellectuals educated in Greece, and the Greek consulate. The ethnic predominance of Greeks on the island and the tremendous success of the spread of nationalist irredentist ideology "resulted in an oversight, even oblivion of the existence of the Muslim community in the island and a concomitant loss of the sense of importance of neighboring Turkey"[1]. The Greek Cypriot leadership began to act as if it could decide the political future of the island without consulting with or considering the Turkish Cypriots.

In the period before the 1950s, Greek Cypriot nationalism was a pervasive sentimental ideology, which aimed at union with Greece on the basis for the most part of spontaneous feelings and deliberations. The emotional appeal of Greek nationalism was tremendous, and in a 1950 plebiscite more than 95 percent of the Greek Cypriots voted in favor of unification with Greece. However, on the level of practical politics and philosophy, the ideology was rather crude and naïve. It ignored not only the presence and interests of the Turkish Cypriot community but also the political balances within the Greek Cypriot community—and the effects upon it that union with Greece would have had. It should not be forgotten, for example, that in Cyprus the political left developed with relative freedom, while in Greece the left did not begin to function freely until after 1974.

It was in light of these developments that an antagonistic Turkish Cypriot nationalism began to form in reaction to the Greek nationalism trans-planted to the island more than half a century earlier. The role of the British colonial administration in fostering Turkish Cypriot nationalism and preparing its eventual collision with its Greek Cypriot counterpart was of great significance. The opposition between the two communities was essentially institutionalized by British manipulation of local politics and British officials' conscious effort to use Turkish Cypriots to oppose the aspiration of Greek Cypriots for union with Greece. Turkish Cypriots were, as a result, overrepresented in the colonial administration and the police and often formed political alliances with the British—for example, in the legislative council that was set up by the colonial administration—in order to thwart Greek Cypriot demands.

By the late 1940s, Turkish Cypriot nationalist consciousness was forming rapidly. Internal developments in Turkey led to an increase in the power of extreme right-wing views and religious fundamentalism. Turkish nationalist ideology, imported from the mainland through mechanisms similar to those employed by Greek nationalism, had already begun to move away from the progressive elements of Kemalism toward an increasingly reactionary and intolerant orientation. Thus, the leadership of the Turkish Cypriot community fell in the hands of extremists who were directly linked to conservative reactionary forces in mainland Turkey and were promoting the idea of the partition of Cyprus. British and Turkish governments naturally viewed partition favorably as it would support their efforts to frustrate the aspirations of the Greek majority of the island.

By the early 1950s, the Greeks and Turks of Cyprus began to see each other as enemies. The two nationalisms reinforced each other, and their collision was violent. The clash between the two communities took place at the time when the nationalist armed anticolonial struggle of the Greek Cypriots had escalated. In 1952, the struggle was institutionalized through the formation of the National Organization of Cypriot Fighters (EOKA), which was soon to begin guerrilla action against the British with the aim of achieving union with Greece. The colonial rulers, however, were not EOKA's only enemies. The organization, led by a reactionary ex-officer of the Greek army who had formed a fascist paramilitary group during the Greek Civil War in the 1940s, Georgios Grivas, also turned against

Greek Cypriot leftists and, as one could expect, against the Turks of the island. In reaction to EOKA, the Turkish Organization of Defense (TMT) was founded in 1956 and openly demanded the partition of the island between Greece and Turkey.

An issue that is often overlooked in conventional historiographies of the Cyprus conflict is that the escalation of the Greek Cypriot enosis movement in the mid-1950s was largely the result of the conflict between the political left and right within the Greek Cypriot community. In an effort to control the increasing power of the left in the 1940s (when the communists won the municipal elections in major towns of the island), the conservative elites, representing the traditional right and the Orthodox church, used the intensification of nationalist agitation to outbid the leftist opposition and protect their interests. Greek nationalism thus acquired a militant anti-Left and essentially reactionary orientation. The EOKA struggle against colonial rule was perhaps the only anti-colonial movement worldwide that lacked any substantive social program or agenda. "Union and only union" is what the Greek Cypriots demanded, thereby accepting the dominance of their entrenched elites and essentially ignoring the interests of the Turkish Cypriot population. History, of course, rarely proceeds according to people's wishes, and the case of Cyprus was no exception. Even before the end of the EOKA struggle in 1959, it was becoming clear that the Greek Cypriot demand for enosis would almost certainly meet with Turkish interference and would perhaps even lead to the partition of the island. The latter would, of course, disrupt the centuries-old demographic pattern of the island and result in the uprooting of a considerable number of Greek and Turkish Cypriots. It was in these circumstances that the idea of an independent Cyprus appeared as a compromise solution.

FROM INDEPENDENCE TO PARTITION: 1960–1974

The agreement reached among Greece, Turkey, and Britain through the treaties of Zurich and London (1959) provided for the establishment of a binational or bicommunal republic with a constitution with the following basic terms. There was to be a Greek Cypriot president and a Turkish Cypriot vice president, and Greece, Turkey, and Britain were guarantor powers. Britain was allowed to maintain sovereign military bases on the island, and there was provision for small Greek and Turkish military contingents. Turkish Cypriots were afforded a 30 percent representation in the state sector, as well as extensive veto rights. Each community had its own Communal Chamber, which was responsible for educational, cultural, and religious matters. The Republic of Cyprus could be thought of as a functional federation, based on the political equality of the two communities, and it did not disrupt the geographical dispersion of both ethnic groups across the entire island. The 1960 arrangement was perhaps the most important missed opportunity in the history of the Cyprus conflict.

In the new realities of independence, and given the perceived dangers of enosis, a Cypriotist political consciousness began to emerge in the Greek Cypriot community—revolving around the idea that the Greek Cypriots could still be Greek in an independent Cyprus and actually enjoy more benefits (social, political, and economic) than if Cyprus were to become a province of Greece. However, Cypriot independence was never ideologically legitimated. Given the continued political attachment of the two Cypriot communities to their respective motherlands, the new, unexpected, and certainly unorthodox solution of the independent Republic of Cyprus was, not surprisingly, only halfheartedly supported, and even explicitly undermined, by both Greeks and Turks on the island. Added to this, the interference (not always official) of Greece and Turkey continued to be a critical factor. It soon became evident that the London–Zurich agreements could not reverse the "dialectic of intolerance," to use P. Kitromilides's (1979) apt characterization of the clash between the two communities, which had gradually but firmly been set in motion.

The culmination of this intolerance was the intercommunal violence that broke out in December 1963, following Makarios's proposals to amend the 1960 constitution. Both sides had been secretly arming themselves in anticipation of trouble, and the 1960 solution of the Cyprus dispute collapsed in a few days. The Turkish Cypriots withdrew their representatives from the government and the parliament, and large numbers moved into isolated enclaves formed around the Turkish quarters of towns and Turkish Cypriot villages. In early 1964, the United Nations sent a peacekeeping force to the island and established the so-called Green Line, firmly separating the two sides. Since 1963, the internationally recognized Republic of Cyprus has essentially functioned as a Greek Cypriot polity. The Turkish Cypriots have formed their own political institutions, still unrecognized by the international community, and have lived in a state of marginality and isolation.

In 1968, as a result of international pressure, the climate between the two communities began to improve and bicommunal negotiations to solve the Cyprus problem began. The two sides came very close to reaching an agreement in 1972, but the effort collapsed because of Makarios's intransigence. In the words of the Greek Cypriot negotiator Glafkos Clerides:

> In 1972, we could have had a solution to our problem based on a much improved constitution than the Zurich one....We rejected it because it did not give us the maximum of our aims, i.e., Cyprus, a Greek Cypriot island ruled by the Greek Cypriot majority.[2]

As mentioned, the Cyprus conflict also has an intracommunal dimension, and this became clear and proved to be catastrophic in the early 1970s. Armed clashes started to break out within the Greek Cypriot community between followers of General George Grivas, the EOKA military leader, who also served as chief of the Cypriot National Guard, and followers of Archbishop Makarios. The supporters of Grivas insisted the demand for enosis be advanced and considered Makarios a national traitor. The enosists were supported by the Greek military government (1967–1974). The Cypriot National Guard, controlled by the Athens regime, was essentially undermining Makarios. The Cypriot president spoke out against the Greek government, demanding the withdrawal of its military contingent from the island. The Greek colonels responded by staging a coup against Makarios on July 15, 1974. Makarios was overthrown, and notorious nationalist Nicos Sampson, who had played a leading role in the intercommunal violence of the 1960s, was installed as president of the Republic of

Cyprus. This gave Turkey a pretext for invading the island five days later (July 20, 1974) and occupying about one-third of its territory.

The basic question concerning the period from 1960–74 is formulated succinctly by M. Attalides: "Why did the apparently suicidal slogan of enosis continue to be an expression of political orthodoxy?"[3] Why, in other words, did Greek Cypriot nationalism fail to adjust to the new situation and challenges that were created with the establishment of the independent Republic of Cyprus in 1960? To answer this question, one would have to examine not only the continued emotional appeal of enosis and the internal dynamics of Greek Cypriot society but also the role of foreign interests and interference. By 1967, with the rise to power of the Greek colonels who were eager to "settle" the Cyprus problem through the division of the island between Greece and Turkey, the partitionist implications of enosis were clear to all but a very thin minority of nationalist extremists. The partition of the island between Greece and Turkey, it is important to stress, was also the settlement of the Cyprus problem most favored by the West. President Makarios's policy of nonalignment and strong ties with the Socialist bloc had nothing whatsoever to do with any socialist inclinations on his part or any real possibility of a Communist takeover of the island. It was merely an effort to achieve diplomatic support in the United Nations and to prevent the imposition of a settlement, which would essentially divide the island into two ethnic provinces. In the eyes of the West, however, Makarios's foreign policy appeared threatening, and there can be no doubt that the partition of the island was certainly more preferable to an independent and nonaligned Cyprus. In 1968, President Makarios made it officially clear that enosis was no longer a realistic goal, precisely because its consequences would be catastrophic for the Cypriot people, and pledged his support to a policy of independence.

What is intriguing, however, is that for Makarios, and even the Progressive Party of the Working People (AKEL), the Communist Party that had traditionally stressed the need for cooperation with the Turkish Cypriots, *enosis* continued to define the desirable state of affairs—and to be seen as a goal that could again be pursued in the future under more favorable conditions. Even in the context of an independent Cypriot state, the Greek Cypriots felt they could continue to completely disregard the interests of the Turkish Cypriots. With the Turkish Cypriots isolated in enclaves on 3 percent of the island, Makarios felt no urgency to restore the 1960 constitution and reincorporate the Turkish Cypriots into mainstream institutions.

The picture is more complex than it may initially appear, and analysts do not explain much by simply attributing the reluctance to reject the claim for *enosis* to nationalist sentiments. While the most radical nationalists demanded "enosis and only enosis," continuing the rhetoric of the 1950s, it is clear that in the eyes of Makarios and the more moderate Greek Cypriot elements after 1963, and especially after 1968, the demand for "genuine" *enosis* "in the distant future" no longer signified a concrete political aim. Given the continued emotional appeal of *enosis*—one must not forget that in the 1950s it had "acquired . . . the socially detached, messianic character of a religious symbol"—the outright renunciation of nationalist symbolism would not only have meant the loss of electoral support, especially on the part of AKEL, but also posed a serious threat to Greek-Cypriot unity.[4] In light of the repeated Turkish threats of invasion, the presentation of a united Greek Cypriot front was deemed essential, even if it implied the burial of fundamental differences and the prolongation of an utterly unrealistic rhetoric. Given the Turkish threat, "enosis symbolized a claim on the part of the Greek Cypriots to be entitled to defense by the Greek armed forces in the case of an attack by Turkey."[5] Makarios had made it clear that what was desired was a pure form of enosis—that is, one that would not compromise any of the interests of the Greek Cypriot majority of the island by, for example, leading to the partition of the island between Greece and Turkey or, minimally, allowing Turkey to have a military presence on Cyprus. With the exception of some hard-core nationalists, it was clear that this form of enosis was not possible—even in the "distant future." After 1967, enosis clearly began to lose its mass appeal, and "the enosis movement in Cyprus was basically maintained through the terrorism of the Greek junta, its officers in Cyprus and the small group of Greek Cypriots who supported them."[6]

Despite losing its power on the level of political praxis, enosis continued to have an ideological hold on the Greek Cypriots. It is this ideological spell, one may say, that allowed a small group of intolerant fanatics to strike a fatal blow to the Republic of Cyprus. One might expect that the overwhelming majority of the Greek Cypriots who supported Makarios and his pragmatic pro-independence policy would have reacted more strongly and would not have allowed the Greek junta to act in the manner that it did. One might expect that Makarios would have managed to mobilize this silent majority in support of his policies and would have controlled the enosist fanatics more effectively. Tragically, however, these scenarios did not materialize, and the hesitant Republic of Cyprus proved, once again, to be too fragile a political entity.

It is clear that as far as the mainstream political culture of the Greek Cypriots was concerned, the independence of 1960 was essentially considered a temporary state of affairs, and one that would eventually lead to union with Greece. The Turkish Cypriots perceived the Greek Cypriot position as utterly threatening to their interests and security. They clearly considered the Zurich and London agreements a victory—one that would have to be defended at all costs, even if this meant the virtual paralysis of the newly formed state. While the political climate of the young republic proved to be conducive to economic development—at least among the Greek Cypriots—one may indeed talk about a failure of politics in Cyprus. This failure stemmed from the inability to construct a functional framework for the peaceful coexistence of the two communities. This political deficiency is by no means solely the responsibility of the Greek Cypriots and the Turkish Cypriots, even though both communities made mistakes and miscalculations—one of the most serious being the nationalist illusion that each community can exist independently from, or ignore, the other.

THE PERIOD OF TOTAL SEPARATION: 1974–2004

Following the events of the summer of 1974, Cyprus became a divided island, having experienced "ethnic cleansing" long before it became a way of "solving" ethnic differences in the republics of the former Yugoslavia. As a result of intercommunal strife in the

1960s and in the war of 1974, both sides suffered. Exact casualty and fatality counts remain sketchy, but both sides continue to have numbers of people missing, from either the pre-1974 intercommunal fighting or the 1974 war. After the Turkish occupation, about 170,000 Greek Cypriots were displaced in their own country and most Turkish Cypriots moved to the areas controlled by the Turkish army. Since 1974, a cease-fire zone has separated the two communities, with the Greek Cypriots living in the south and the Turkish Cypriots living in the north. In 1983, the Turkish Cypriots declared the occupied north to be the Turkish Republic of Northern Cyprus, which is still not recognized by the international community.

The immediate consequence of the Turkish invasion upon Greek Cypriot political culture was the temporary marginalization of nationalist ideology and the parallel rise of a "Cypriotist" one. As reunification of the island became the main political priority, the emphasis shifted to the independence of the island—precisely because the latter was considered a sine qua non for the achievement of a settlement that would reunify the island. The symbol of enosis was naturally associated with the events that made up the disaster of 1974: Terrorism, fascist authoritarianism and the overthrow of democracy, foreign invasion and occupation, and violent displacement. At the same time, the Greek Cypriots began to consciously differentiate their political fate from that of Greece.

The emphasis on Cypriot independence led to significant shifts in Greek Cypriot official historiography and to the reinterpretation of certain aspects of the island's recent political past. The EOKA movement (1955–59), for example, began to be seen as an anticolonial independence struggle rather than as a movement aiming at union with Greece. EOKA was presented as a mass movement of all Greek Cypriots demanding the liberation of the island—a liberation, it was implied, that was to benefit not only the Greeks but also the Turks of Cyprus. It is not surprising, therefore, that since 1974 there has been an increasing emphasis upon the official symbolism, as well as the commemoration, of the independence of the island. Whereas Cypriot Independence Day (October 1) was hardly celebrated before 1974—when the stress was upon Greek national commemorations (October 28 and March 25)—it started to be officially seen as the most important commemora-

tive ritual in Greek Cypriot political culture. For the first time since 1960, the Cypriot flag began to be publicly displayed on a large scale and to sometimes displace (or at least be placed aside) the Greek flag, which had, until 1974, expressed the attachment of the Greek Cypriots to the mainland and simultaneously their ambivalence toward Cypriot independence.

The decline of nationalism in the first post-1974 years—precisely because Greek Cypriot nationalism was seen as, at least partly, responsible for the catastrophic events of 1974—led the Greek Cypriot leadership to make serious compromises, accepting that there had to be a federal solution to the Cyprus problem and officially renouncing the basic principle of the nationalist–irredentist ideology that had dominated Greek Cypriot politics since the early 1950s—that is, the idea of union with Greece. In an effort to convince not only the Turkish Cypriots but also the international community that it was sincere in its acceptance of a federal solution, the official Greek Cypriot leadership espoused a policy of rapprochement with the Turkish Cypriots, stressing that the Turkish Cypriots were not the enemy and that the two communities could again live together as they had done in the past. In a discourse that fell almost totally silent about the 1960–74 period (when Greek Cypriots saw themselves as the stronger party in the conflict), the Greek Cypriot leadership proclaimed that Turkey and its chauvinistic representatives among the Turkish-Cypriots are the true aggressors, victimizing both Greek and Turkish Cypriots. AKEL went beyond the discourse of the peaceful coexistence of the two communities and even talked about the "brotherly" bonds between Greek and Turkish Cypriots. Even though no other Greek Cypriot political force seemed to be willing to go as far as AKEL in this respect, no doubt rapprochement assumed a dominant role in Greek Cypriot political discourse.

The retreat of nationalism, however, was only temporary, and by the mid-1980s it resurfaced as the dominant Greek Cypriot ideology, albeit in a changed form. What Greek Cypriot nationalists began aspiring to in the 1980s and 1990s was not union with Greece but the reaffirmation of Greek identity in the context of an independent polity that is organically tied to Greek culture and is politically anchored to the Greek state. This new

Greek Cypriot nationalism, however, did not go unopposed. While the ideological clash between Greek nationalism and Cypriotism is by no means a recent phenomenon—being already evident in the early phases of Greek Cypriot nationalism and the opposition it engendered—in the post-1974 years it acquired a greater intensity and still constitutes the major element in the social construction of Greek Cypriot political and cultural identity.

The new Greek Cypriot nationalism's position on the Cyprus problem and its resolution is—more than anything else—expressed as a rejection of the idea of federation. Officially, to repeat, the Republic of Cyprus continues to proclaim its support to a federal solution of the political problem on the island. There is no doubt, however, that, especially since the establishment of a Democratic Rally–Democratic Party coalition government in 1993, the idea of federation has been subjected to considerable criticism, primarily on the grounds that it concedes too much to the other side. The rejectionists stress the undeniably undemocratic character of a bicommunal federation (the 80 percent Greek majority being equated to the 20 percent Turkish minority) and argue that the only "just" settlement of the Cyprus problem would be one that ensures democratic majority rule, providing, of course, for the rights of the Turkish Cypriot minority. The most ardent enemy of federation is the Orthodox Church of Cyprus, which time and again tries to convince its "flock" that a federal settlement "will amount to the complete destruction of Cypriot Hellenism on the island." Although nationalism seemed to be recently in decline, as a result of the accession of Cyprus into the EU (the new European identity is bound to undermine the traditional emphasis on Greek national identity), it is still the dominant Greek Cypriot ideology. The slogan "Cyprus is Greek" dominates political discourse and continues to define the parameters of ideological orthodoxy in Greek Cypriot political culture.

The dispute over the referendum of April 24, 2004, was conducted under the same terms that have been determining Greek Cypriot political discourse on the Cyprus problem for decades. I refer, of course, to the ideological confrontation between Greek Cypriot nationalism and Cypriotism. The resounding "no" of the Greek Cypriots is, above all, a proud victory of Greek nationalism in

Cyprus and, simultaneously, a defeat of Cypriotism and a severe blow to the vision of Cyprus as a common homeland for the Greeks and Turks of the island. As in the past, whenever the international community offered any specific guidelines for a Cyprus settlement, nationalism provided the ideological foundation of Greek Cypriot rejectionism. President Papadopoulos's April 7, 2004, televised appeal to the Greek Cypriots, in which he tearfully requested his compatriots to voice a resounding "no" to the U.N. plan, known as the Annan plan, is a lyric statement of nationalist rhetoric and can leave no doubts concerning the nationalist inspiration in rejecting the Annan plan. The president's speech became a main reference point for those campaigning against the proposed settlement, and many Greek Cypriots kept reiterating Papadopoulos's views or arguments as were heard on the evening of April 7, 2004. "I call on you to reject (the plan). I call on you to say a resounding NO on April 24. I call on you to defend your dignity, your history, and what is right."

The international community was clearly surprised by the enthusiasm with which Greek Cypriots followed Papadopoulos's advice. Here is the bare picture: The Greek Cypriots were offered (for the first time since 1974) a detailed plan for a comprehensive settlement of the Cyprus conflict, along the lines of a bizonal–bicommunal federation with a single international sovereignty (conditions which the Greek Cypriots have officially accepted since 1977). The plan had concrete benefits for the Greek Cypriots—more so, one could claim, than for the Turkish Cypriots, many of whom would have to be relocated if the Annan plan were to be implemented. To be more specific, the Annan plan provided for the return of 100,000 Greek Cypriot refugees under Greek Cypriot administration, the withdrawal of 35,000 Turkish troops, and an end to further emigration from Turkey. And still, the Greek Cypriots voiced a resounding no—mostly on the grounds that the plan offended their "dignity," "their history," and "what is right." President Papadopoulos justified his claim that the plan ought to be rejected by raising a number of objections to (or "disadvantages" of) it. According to Papadopoulos (and these were the views reiterated by many Greek Cypriots), the Annan plan conceded too much to Turkey for it allowed it to perpetuate its military presence on the island and to maintain its guarantor status, granted to Turkey by the London–Zurich agreements. At the same time, Papadopoulos argued, the U.N. plan essentially legitimated the Turkish invasion of 1974, for it allowed most Turkish settlers to remain on the island. Another key objection raised by the Greek Cypriot president was that under the Annan plan, the Republic of Cyprus would be reduced to a constituent state, wholly dependent upon the goodwill of Turkey. The Greek Cypriots, according to Papadopoulos, did not feel they could trust the Turks to actually implement the agreement.

Both U.N. and EU officials who openly favored the Annan plan, along with Greek Cypriot "yes" supporters, considered Papadopoulos's objections rather disingenuous, if not outright insincere. If Papadopoulos honestly supported the idea of a bizonal–bicommunal federation, he could not have possibly rejected the U.N. plan simply on the grounds that it reduced the Republic of Cyprus to a constituent state; isn't this a key ingredient of the Cypriot federation discussed for years—that is, that it will consist of two separate polities without international sovereignty? Almost nobody expected that the settlement would secure the expulsion of all settlers, nor that it would abolish Turkey's institutionalized role in the affairs of the island. After all, it was not the Turks who lost the 1974 war—and why would anyone seriously believe that the Turks would simply give up a right that was theirs since 1960? As far as the issue of trust (or the lack of it) was concerned, one could simply point out to President Papadopoulos that the referendum of April 24, 2004, was precisely about the two sides' willingness to trust each other.

The Greek Cypriots were faced with a plan that could set their relations with the Turkish Cypriots on a fresh and positive basis, and yet they preferred to "defend their history," as defined along nationalist parameters and centered precisely upon the conflict with the Turkish Cypriots. They had a chance to regain the towns of Morphou and Famagusta, along with fifty or so other villages, and they preferred to "defend their dignity." They had the chance to gradually rid themselves of 35,000 Turkish troops, and they preferred to focus on the fact that, under the Annan plan, 650 Turkish soldiers would remain on the island indefinitely. All this came to pass because they felt that they had "to defend what is right." This

type of political rhetoric and political behavior can be little else but nationalism.

As every student of nationalism should know, an ideology's strength does not lie in the rationality of its arguments. Benedict Anderson even referred to the "philosophical poverty" of nationalism, and mentioning this poverty in rational arguments was certainly a trait of President Papadopoulos's April 7, 2004, televised appeal to the Greek Cypriots. Within just a few days of the president's televised rejection of the Annan plan, Alecos Markides, the former attorney general, and George Vassiliou, former president of the Republic of Cyprus, wrote detailed analyses of Papadopoulos's April 7 speech (analyses that were published in various daily newspapers in a small booklet format), criticizing the president's positions and arguments, point by point, and meticulously exposing both the lack of rational power in his positions and his insincerity. If there is one clear conclusion to be drawn from the president's speech, both Markides and Vassiliou cogently argued, it was that Papadopoulos simply did not accept the idea of a bizonal–bicommunal federation, nor that of the political equality of the two Cypriot communities inherent in a federal framework. Still, rationality is not what wins political battles and once again nationalism appealed to popular sentiment—not just any emotions but especially the fears and the national fantasies of the Greek Cypriots. From the moment the Annan plan was submitted in November 2002 (and even during the months before, when the Greek Cypriots were anticipating its submission), many Greek Cypriots argued that the United Nations plan was essentially the product of a foreign conspiracy against Cyprus. The plan serves the interests of Turkey, Britain, and the United States and certainly not those of the Greek Cypriots. Once again, many Greek Cypriots would say, "the powerful of the earth" want to impose upon the Greek Cypriots an unjust solution. The Greek Cypriots, the argument would continue, would not only have to bear the allegedly enormous economic cost of the implementation of the U.N. plan, but they would be left to live with a wide array of other negative consequences (social, military, and even cultural). The U.N. plan, long before the end of the last round of bicommunal negotiations in Burgenstock, Switzerland, was branded "satanic," with Bishop Pavlos of Kyrenia even warning his compatriots that those who planned to vote in favor of the plan would go to hell.

What the results of the April 24, 2004, referendum clearly indicate is that the Greeks and Turks of Cyprus have followed diverse paths since the submission of the U.N. plan in November 2002. Whereas a solid Turkish Cypriot majority managed to essentially marginalize Rauf Denktash, their nationalist and persistently rejectionist leader (who was president of the internationally unrecognized Republic of Northern Cyprus and was for many years justifiably considered the greatest obstacle to a solution of the Cyprus conflict), an even more solid Greek Cypriot majority, including Communist AKEL, rallied around Tassos Papadopoulos, President of the Republic of Cyprus and perhaps the most uncompromising Greek Cypriot politician. Papadopoulos has consistently opposed every international effort for a Cyprus settlement (from the London–Zurich agreements of 1959 to the Annan plan), and he has always justified his position with the same nationalist argument: the proposed solution does not adequately secure the "national interests" of the Greek Cypriots, nor does it secure their Greek identity. Inconsistency is not one of Papadopoulos's weaknesses, and an appeal to national interest and honor was exactly the message he conveyed to the Greek Cypriots concerning the April 24, 2004, referendum. Notwithstanding that they had negotiated the plan (or, to be more precise, five drafts of the plan) put forward by the U.N. for many months, and that they had accepted U.N. mediation, if no agreement could be reached by the parties alone (notwithstanding, that is, that the Greek Cypriot political leadership made clear political commitments that it would support the final result of the negotiating process), the Greek Cypriots were ultimately asked by their president, less than three weeks before the referendum, to voice a resounding "no." And so they did. An overwhelming majority of Greek Cypriots respected their president's wish, showing thus that they preferred the continuation of the status quo, which was created following the Turkish invasion of 1974, and that they preferred to join the European Union, without a solution and thus without the Turkish Cypriots.

To repeat, notwithstanding their official message toward the various international mediators

who have been involved with the Cyprus conflict, most Greek Cypriot politicians do not appear to honestly accept the type of solution Greek Cypriots have officially accepted since 1977. Why then should one rule out the possibility that they are simply not sincere when they claim that they favor a political settlement, which would disrupt the current status quo and reunify the island? The truth is that most Greek Cypriot politicians have used, and continue to use, the Cyprus problem primarily with an eye to internal (inter-, or even intra-party) power struggles in the Greek Cypriot community. Simply stated, understanding the internal logic of Greek Cypriot party politics can throw considerable light on how the Greek Cypriot community and its political leaders view and handle the Cyprus problem.

Since the death in 1977 of Archbishop Makarios, the first President of the Republic of Cyprus, Makarios, Greek Cypriot politics has been characterized by a rather peculiar combination of elements (which I call *neologism clientelistic corporatism*) that, on the one hand, endows politics and politicians with a truly hegemonic role in society and, on the other, perpetuates not only the Cyprus problem but also a wide array of other problems, such as nepotism and corruption, a hypertrophic state, and, more generally, the underdevelopment of Greek Cypriot civil society. Given that every single Greek Cypriot political party claims that its key priority is the solution to the Cyprus problem, one would expect that party alliances would be built around agreements or disagreements concerning the Cyprus problem. However, a careful analysis of Greek Cypriot politics paints an entirely different picture, a picture usually concealed by Greek Cypriot nationalist rhetoric. If their positions on the Cyprus problem were indeed their main priority, the behavior of Greek Cypriot political parties would have been tremendously different in the post-1974 era and there would have been no political alliances between moderate and nationalist forces.[7] However, what has actually guided party politics is simply the determination to build (and to maintain) coalitions to control the presidency of the Republic of Cyprus, irrespective of whether or not those who participate in the coalitions share common views on the Cyprus problem. A logical outcome of the Greek Cypriot party system is the fact that, at least until the referendum of April 24, 2004, or perhaps until the presidential election of 2003, Communist AKEL and Conservative Democratic Rally (DISY), the two largest Greek Cypriot parties, had more or less the same views on the Cyprus problem—both supporting a conciliatory stance on the issue. Yet these two parties have functioned as polar ends of the political spectrum, each displaying the willingness to form coalitions with political parties that adhere to a rejectionist position on the Cyprus problem. Is it unreasonable to assume that what lies beyond the parties' rhetoric (that is, that they truly desire "a just and viable solution" of the Cyprus problem) is the more mundane and less dignified concern to acquire or to maintain power?

How else can one explain why traditionally Cypriotist and moderate AKEL supported Tassos Papadopoulos, a traditionally nationalist and hardline rejectionist politician, in the 2003 presidential election? How else can one explain why AKEL, the only Greek Cypriot party, which had maintained relatively close ties with the Turkish Cypriots, urged its supporters to reject, even if "mildly," the Annan plan on April 24, 2004? The official leadership of AKEL claims that the party voted no in order to cement a future yes, but one would have to be extremely naïve to see the Akelite claim as anything but political hypocrisy. Is it not a more plausible explanation to say that AKEL finally sided with Papadopoulos because, had it gone against him, the party would have had to withdraw from Papadopoulos's government?

TOWARD A RESPONSIBLE POLITICS

The development of a climate of mutual trust between Greek and Turkish Cypriots is a sine qua non for any settlement of the Cyprus problem. It is, to put it differently, a necessary but, of course, insufficient condition for the solution of the Cyprus problem. Bicommunal efforts, supported by the U.N., the United States, and various European countries during the past few decades, have aimed to build trust among Cypriots and to develop a common Cypriot identity. There have been many conflict resolution workshops, usually organized in the buffer zone or abroad, but participation is usually limited to upper-middle-class professionals and intellectuals, who are often accused of being unpatriotic and even treacherous. The fact is that without a climate of mutual trust, the functional coexistence of the two communities in the framework of a bicommunal state and a common homeland is an almost impossible task. In the absence of a minimum level of bicommunal trust, a solution to the Cyprus problem can only be achieved as a result of external pressures (and, as the results of the April 24, 2004, referendum clearly showed, even that may be an unrealistic goal) and will inevitably fail—unless, of course, the foreign powers that engineer the solution are willing to police its enforcement for an indefinite time. With a forced solution, the new Cypriot state is bound to suffer an inescapable legitimization crisis. It will be a polity with no true or loyal citizens who might be able to prevent extremists from either community from sabotaging it. The scenario is all too familiar. The independent Cypriot state that emerged out of the Zurich–London agreements faced the very same legitimization deficit with, of course, grave consequences. A sincere acceptance of a Cypriot polity along with a systematic effort to legitimate it in the minds of all Cypriots constitute rational, as well as moral, imperatives for the political leadership of the island. However, most Greek Cypriot and many Turkish Cypriot politicians continue to operate on the basis of nationalist convictions. The Cyprus problem may simply be an intractable problem—a problem whose very existence serves the entrenched interests of those who control the status quo on the island.

ENDNOTES

1. Paschalis Kitromilides, "The Dialetic of Intolerance: Ideological Dimensions of Ethnic Conflict," *Journal of the Hellenic Diaspora*, vol. 6, no. 4 (1979), 13.
2. Glafcos Clerides, *My Deposition* (Nicosia, Greece: Alithia Publishing, 1990), 367.
3. Michael Attalides, *Cyprus: Nationalism and International Politics* (Edinburgh, Scotland: Q Press, 1979), 104.

4. Ibid., 106.
5. Ibid., 121.
6. Ibid., 117.
7. Caesar Mavratsas, "Approaches to Nationalism: Basic Theoretical Cosiderations in the Study of the Greek-Cyprior Case and a Historical Overview," *Journal of the Hellenic Diaspora*, vol. 22, no. 1 (1996), 77–102.

SUGGESTED READING

There is a vast bibliography on the Cyprus conflict. What follows is a selective list of some works from which this chapter largely draws. For good general accounts of the Cyprus problem and how external and international factors have influenced Cypriot developments, see Attalides 1979, Bahcheli 1990, Bahcheli and Rizopoulos 1997, Calotychos 1998, Crawshaw 1978, Joseph 1997, Kitromilides 1979, Markides 1977. On intercommunal strife and the marginalization of the Turkish Cypriots in the 1960s, see Patrick 1989, Volkan 1979. On the constitutional aspects of the Cyprus problem, see Kyriakides 1968, Polyviou 1980. On Greek Cypriot nationalism, see Kitromilides 1979, 1990, Loizos 1974, 1988, Markides 1974, Mavratsas 1996, 1997, 1998, 2001, 2003.

Attalides, Michael. *Cyprus: Nationalism and International Politics*. Edinburgh: Q Press, 1979.

Bahcheli, Tozun. *Greek-Turkish Relations Since 1955*. Boulder, CO: Westview Press, 1990.

Bahcheli, Tozun, and Nicholas Rizopoulos. "The Cyprus Impasse: What Next?" *World Policy Journal* (Winter 96/97): 27–39.

Calotychos, Vangelis, ed. *Cyprus and Its People: Nation, Identity and Experience in an Unimaginable Community, 1955–1997*. Boulder, CO: Westview Press, 1998.

Clerides, Glafcos. *My Deposition,* vol. 3. Nicosia, Greece: Alithia Publishing, 1990.

Crawshaw, Nancy. *The Cyprus Revolt*. Boston: Allen & Unwin, 1978.

Joseph, Joseph S. *Cyprus: Ethnic Conflict and International Politics: From Independence to the Threshold of the European Union*. London: Macmillan, 1997.

Kitromilides, Paschalis. "The Dialectic of Intolerance: Ideological Dimensions of Ethnic Conflict," *Journal of the Hellenic Diaspora*, vol. 6, no. 4 (1979): 5–30.

_____. "Greek Irredentism in Asia Minor and Cyprus," *Middle Eastern Studies*, vol. 26, no. 1 (1990): 3–15.

Kyriakides, Stanley. *Cyprus: Constitutionalism and Crisis Government*. Philadelphia: University of Pennsylvania Press, 1968.

Loizos, Peter. "The Progress of Greek Nationalism in Cyprus: 1878–1970." *Choice and Change: Essays in Honour of Lucy Mair,* edited by J. Davis, 114–133. London: Athlone, 1974.

_____. "Intercommunal Killing in Cyprus." *Man,* 23 (1988): 639–53.

Markides, Kyriakos. "Social Change and the Rise and Decline of Social Movements," *American Ethnologist*, vol. 1, no. 2 (1974): 309–30.

_____. *The Rise and Fall of the Cyprus Republic*. New Haven, CT: Yale University Press, 1977.

Mavratsas, Caesar. "Approaches to Nationalism: Basic Theoretical Considerations in the Study of the Greek-Cypriot Case and a Historical Overview." *Journal of the Hellenic Diaspora*, vol. 22, no. 1 (1996): 77–102.

_____. "The Ideological Contest Between Greek-Cypriot Nationalism and Cypriotism 1974–1995: Politics, Social Memory and Identity." *Ethnic and Racial Studies*, vol. 20, no. 4 (1997): 717–37.

_____. *1974–1996: Facets of Greek Nationalism in Cyprus 1974-1996: Ideological Contest and the Social Construction of Greek-Cypriot Identity*. Athens: Katarti Press, 1998.

_____. "Greek-Cypriot Identity and Conflicting Interpretations of the Cyprus Problem." In *Greek-Turkish Relations in the Era of Globalization,* edited by D. Keridis and D. Triantaphyllou, 151–79. Dulles, VA: Brassey's, 2001.

_____. *21 National Unity and Political Unanimity. The Underdevelopment of Greek-Cypriot Civil Society at the Beginning of the 21st Century*. Athens: Katarti Press, 2003.

Polyviou, Polyvios. *Cyprus: Conflict and Negotiations, 1960–1980*. New York: Holmes & Meier Publishers, 1980.

Volkan, Vamik. *Cyprus—War and Adaptation: A Psychoanalytic History of Two Ethnic Groups in Conflict*. Charlottesville: University Press of Virginia, 1979.

ABOUT THE AUTHOR

Since 1994, Caesar V. Mavratsas has been teaching sociology at the University of Cyprus, where he is an assistant professor in the Department of Social and Political Science. His main research interests are in the areas of political sociology and the sociology of knowledge, with a focus on nationalism and political culture.

His most recent book, *21 (National Unity and Political Unanimity: The Underdevelopment of Greek-Cypriot Civil Society at the Beginning of the 21st Century)*, was published in 2003 by Katarti Press (Athens, Greece). His previous book, *1974–1996: Facets of Greek Nationalism in Cyprus 1974–1996: Ideological Contest and the Social Construction of Greek-Cypriot Identity*, was also published by Katarti in 1998 and was translated into Turkish in 2000. Mavratsas has published articles in Cypriot, Greek, British, American, Canadian, and French academic journals.

In 1993, he received his Ph.D. in sociology from Boston University where he was also a fellow at the Institute for the Study of Economic Culture. His doctoral dissertation was entitled *Ethnic Entrepreneurialism, Social Mobility and Embourgeoisement: The Formation and Intergenerational Evolution of Greek-American Economic Culture* and was supervised by Peter L. Berger.

Turkish and Greek Cypriots in Conflict

Kenan Atakol

THE ISLAND OF CYPRUS

Cyprus is an island located in the eastern Mediterranean. It is 70 kilometers south of Turkey, 101 kilometers west of Syria, and 824 kilometers east of Greece. The history of the island of Cyprus dates back to the Neolithic Age. Due to its strategic location, Cyprus has been occupied by fifteen different conquerors, the last of which were the Ottoman Turks, who ruled the island from 1571 to 1878.

THE CONFLICT IN CYPRUS

Cyprus is home to Turkish and Greek Cypriots. The Turkish Cypriots came from Turkey and settled in Cyprus following the conquest of the island by the Ottoman Empire in 1571. Ethnically they are Turks. They speak Turkish and religiously are Sunni Moslems. The Greek Cypriots see themselves as Greek descendants. They speak Greek and religiously are Greek Orthodox. As to the time of their settlement in Cyprus and their Greekness, there are conflicting views. Ronald Storrs, writing about the Greeks of Cyprus, offers the following explanation:

The Greek colonists Hellenized Cyprus as early as the fourteenth century B.C.

However, he also notes that some people contend that

the original Islanders had been Asiatic, that there had been Phoenician as well as Greek settlers, that Cyprus had never belonged to any ancient Greek Kingdom, that whatever strain had survived from antiquity had been mingled with Lusignan and Venetian blood, that the language spoken was a corrupt form of Greek: in a word that Cypriots were not Greeks and had no right to call themselves Greeks.[1]

Greek Cypriots see Cyprus as a Hellenic island. Since the early 1820s, Greek Cypriots have been struggling together with Greece to unite Cyprus with Greece. Turkish Cypriots saw and continue to see this as colonization by Greece. For them, colonization remains unacceptable. They have staunchly resisted colonization for several generations. British colonial rule ended in 1960 and was replaced by a binational republic. Greek Cypriots continued their nationalistic aspirations to Hellenize Cyprus. In 1963, fully armed and using their numerical advantage against the Turkish Cypriots, Greek Cypriots attacked Turkish Cypriots. They overtook the binational administration and seized control of the government. This move was strongly opposed by

Turkish Cypriots, who were cofounders and equal partners of the republic. Despite their efforts, Turkish Cypriots were unable to prevent Greek Cypriots from taking over the government. The constitutional order that the events of 1963 destroyed was never restored. Those events turned the binational Republic of Cyprus into a Greek Cypriot state.

In 1974, Greek Cypriots, together with Greece, tried to unite Cyprus with Greece. Turkey intervened, a right it had under the 1960 international Treaty of Guarantee. Turkey's intervention prevented the Greek Cypriots and Greece from uniting Cyprus with Greece. Turkey's intervention precipitated the complete separation of Turkish and Greek Cypriots. After separation, Turkish Cypriots established their own separate state in the northern part of Cyprus. Greek Cypriots, however, dislike this status quo. They continue to strive for reunification so that they can fulfill their national aspirations of Hellenizing Cyprus. The result is a standoff, described by Caesar V. Mavratsas as follows:

> Greek Cypriot nationalists either completely identify the Turkish Cypriots with the Turks (from Turkey) or deny—or at least minimize—their status as a community or a people. They may claim, for instance, that the Turkish Cypriots are actually Islamicized—usually by force—Greek Cypriots, or that the Turkish Cypriots do not really "belong here," but must be seen as "intruders." The simplicity and also the power of the logic of nationalism are remarkable. "Cyprus is Greek" and, thus, the Turkish Cypriots can have no rightful place in it.[2]

To summarize, one can say that the conflict in Cyprus is the result of the struggle between the Greek Cypriots' ambition and the Turkish Cypriots' resistance to it. The conflict has been many years in the making but has not always dominated the Cypriot landscape.

OTTOMAN RULE

During the period of Ottoman rule in Cyprus, the Turkish and Greek Cypriots lived in peace and harmony. For three centuries Greek Cypriots were free to practice their religious, economic and cultural activities.[3]

Prior to Ottoman rule, the Venetians ruled the island from 1489 to 1571. They were Catholic and op-

pressed the Greek Orthodox inhabitants of the island. They limited their religious practices and other activities. For this reason, the Greeks celebrated the conquest of the island by the Ottoman Turks

Following the conquest of Cyprus, the Turkish Sultan, Selim the Second, issued a decree to the governor general of Cyprus, Sinan Pasha, safeguarding the inhabitants' rights and freedoms. Despite its antiquity, the sultan's decree remains a seminal document for parties involved in the conflict. The sultan's decree, issued on September 21, gave the governor the following order:

> The people who are sent to Cyprus for settlement [the Turkish people from Turkey] will obey my commands to the point. Those who do not and instead try to take advantage of the situation and act impetuously will be punished right away.[4]

The treatment by the Ottoman Empire of its subjects was based on tolerance. During the first 200 years of reign, the Greek and Turkish residents of Cyprus displayed tolerance toward one another. The number of mixed villages grew from none to 234.[5]

During the late 1700s, hostility toward the Ottoman Empire began to rise in many European countries. The early 1800s saw the beginnings of Greece's move toward independence from the Ottoman Empire. The 1820s were marked by the beginning of the enosis movement, which aimed to unite Cyprus with what was referred to as motherland Greece. Similar uprisings were occurring in other areas of the Ottoman Empire and were threatening its unity.

Despite Cyprus's attempts to gain independence from the empire, the rules on the island were not tightened. Ottoman officials remained tolerant.

In 1878, the Ottoman Empire turned over the administration of Cyprus to the British, in return for a yearly rent and help in defending the eastern part of Anatolia against the Russians.[6] The agreement did not call for any changes to the island's sovereignty. It remained with the Ottoman Empire.

BRITISH RULE

The tolerance of Ottoman rule is captured in the reflections of Hepworth W. Dixon, a British colonial administrator and author posted in Cyprus:

Where, except in Switzerland and the United States, can governing bodies so republican in origin be discovered as in Cyprus under Ottoman rule? . . . Like a commune in canton Schweiz or canton Zurich, every Cyprian hamlet has a local rule based on the purest form of democracy. The villagers are free and equal . . . their democratic power is good in every way; the peasants, meeting in their free assemblies, have the right to choose not only their rulers but their spiritual leaders The villagers elect the village pope. . . Self-government here is perfect.[7]

Under Ottoman rule the Turkish and Greek Cypriots had control over their own affairs by electing their own representatives to a council. Under British rule, however, the Turkish and Greek Cypriots did not have any elected representatives in the new council. The impact of this change was profound. Dixon's description illustrates how sharp the contrast was.

Formerly the Cypriots had as much control over their own affairs as English people did in their country. Now they are as helpless as a multitude of Russian serfs.[8]

THE ENOSIS CAMPAIGN

After Greece gained its independence from the Ottoman Empire and British rule of Cyprus began, the Greek Cypriots intensified their struggle for enosis. Under British rule, the harmonious relations enjoyed by Greek and Turkish Cypriots declined sharply. The deterioration of relations is reflected in the sharp decline in the mixed villages, charted in the following table. Between the early

Year	Number of mixed villages	Number of Homogeneous Turkish Villages	Total Number of Turkish and mixed Villages
1859	234	118	352
1911	230	85	315
1921	221	89	310
1931	202	88	290
1946	162	110	272
1960	102	130	232
1974	48	105	153
Present	1	–	–

1900s and mid-1970s, mixed villages essentially disappeared.

Events occurring between 1878 and 1974 separated Turkish and Greek Cypriots and created the conflict in Cyprus, which is still unresolved. The enosis campaign that started in the early 1820s and intensified with the beginning of British rule planted the seeds of the conflict.

RISING HOSTILITIES

During the First World War, the Ottoman Empire joined Germany to fight against the British and its allies. The British used this as an excuse to annex the island. After the First World War and Turkey's subsequent War of Independence, which ended with the 1923 Treaty of Lausanne, Turkey accepted the annexation of Cyprus to Britain and Cyprus formally became a British colony. After this, Turkish Cypriots started to feel threatened by the political ambitions of the Greek Cypriots. In 1931, the Greek Cypriots revolted against British rule in Cyprus. They burned the governor's palace and called for enosis again. The British took many measures to punish the people of Cyprus, including Turkish Cypriots who had nothing to do with the revolt. They banned all political parties, prevented the raising of the Turkish and Greek flags and the teaching of Turkish and Greek history classes in schools.[9]

In 1950, the Greek Cypriot Orthodox Church organized a plebiscite on enosis among the Greek Cypriots. Voting was held in the churches of Cyprus. The January 15 plebiscite resulted in a 95.7 percent "yes" vote favoring the union of Cyprus with Greece (enosis). In 1954 Greece asked the United Nations (U.N.) to grant self-determination to the people of Cyprus. The U.N. rejected Greece's request, citing the fact that Turkish Cypriots had an equal right to self-determination.

Determined to unite Cyprus with Greece, Greek Cypriots established an underground terrorist organization called Ethniki Organosis Kiprion Ağoniston (EOKA) to fight for enosis.[10] EOKA was supported and financed by the Greek Cypriot Orthodox Church. On April 1, 1955, EOKA started its terrorist attacks. Terrorists targeted British military personnel, as well as civilian men, women, children, and specific government sites.

The union of Cyprus with Greece, which was the aim of EOKA, would have meant the colonization of the Turkish Cypriots by Greece. This was totally unacceptable to Turkish Cypriots. Trust between the two communities completely dissolved. EOKA's terrorist attacks led Turkish Cypriots to form their own underground organization called Türk Mukavemet Teşkilati (TMT).[11]   Turkish Cypriots first demanded that Cyprus be united with Turkey, its former owner. Later they called for partition.

The Turkish Cypriots' resistance to enosis was marked by EOKA's attacks on everything that was Turkish; and in 1958, fighting erupted between the two communities. For the first time in the history of Cyprus, Turkish and Greek Cypriots were fighting each other. During the EOKA attacks, hundreds of Turkish Cypriots were killed and many more were wounded. EOKA destroyed thirty-three Turkish Cypriot villages. More than 6,000 Turkish Cypriots, equal to 5 percent of the Turkish Cypriot population, became refugees.

THE REPUBLIC OF CYPRUS

While the two communities continued fighting, talks were held in Zurich and London. These negotiations led to the creation in 1960 of the binational Republic of Cyprus. The republic granted shared sovereignty of Cyprus to both Turkish and Greek Cypriots. The 1960 agreements and the Constitution of the Republic of Cyprus accorded political equality to the two peoples. The co-founding partners had equal status and separate rights to self-determination. Under the agreement, each side, which was ethnically, linguistically, and religiously different from the other, separately elected their own representatives to the state institutions. The president, who was Greek, appointed the Greek Cypriot cabinet members while the vice president, who was Turkish, appointed the Turkish Cypriot cabinet members. In the parliament and cabinet, as well as the public service, the ratio was 30 percent Turkish Cypriots and 70 percent Greek Cypriots. The president and the vice president headed the cabinet together, and both had veto power on important legislation and cabinet decisions. Both communities had their own Communal Chamber responsible for educational, marital, cultural, and religious affairs. Each of Cyprus's five major urban centers was given the right to have separate municipalities since Greeks and Turks were living in separate quarters. Turkey, Greece, and Britain were the guarantor powers of the Republic of Cyprus under the Treaty of Guarantee and Treaty of Alliance.

In November 1963, only three years after the establishment of the binational Republic of Cyprus, Makarios, the president of the republic and a Greek Cypriot, proposed thirteen amendments to the constitution.[12]   The Turkish Cypriots believed these changes were designed to take away their rights and refused to accept them. On December 21, 1963, fully armed Greek Cypriots attacked Turkish Cypriots and forced them out of the government and state administration. As a result, 25 percent of the Turkish Cypriots became refugees and the entire Turkish Cypriot population had to live in enclaves and ghettos on 3 percent of the island's land base. Fighting continued.

LESS FREEDOM, MORE FEAR

Three months later, the United Nations sent a peace keeping force to Cyprus, which established a dividing zone between the two peoples in several areas, towns, and villages in order to stop the fighting. Turkish Cypriots had no freedom of movement for five years, until 1968. From December 1963 to May 1968, Turkish Cypriots were confined to fifty-five enclaves spread over the island. They were forbidden by Greek Cypriots to move outside their forcefully enclaved areas. Greek Cypriots erected road bocks. Turkish Cypriots traveling from their enclave to any other area had to cross these roadblocks. This was a deadly affair. Turkish Cypriots, who out of necessity or due to an emergency, had to move out of their enclaves were beaten, humiliated, and returned to their enclave—or taken away and never seen again. The very few Turkish Cypriots who managed to cross the roadblocks had to get permission from the Greek Cypriots through the U.N. or, sometimes, deceived the Greek Cypriot gunmen by speaking to them in fluent Greek. (Many Turkish Cypriots spoke Greek as fluently as the Greek Cypriots.)

During those years, Turkish Cypriots could not exercise their basic human rights. They were hostages in their own country. Once outside designated "safe" areas, there was no guarantee as to what might happen to them. Many Turkish Cypriots were forcefully abducted from their workplaces and homes by the Greek Cypriot gunmen, never to be heard from again. They were not allowed to travel freely or communicate with the outside world. They were deprived of opportunities to cultivate their own land, participate in business and trade, participate in cultural and sports activities, and did not receive their share of the state budget. One hundred and three Turkish Cypriot villages were destroyed. The entire population of several villages was massacred and buried in mass graves.

After the Greek Cypriots forced the Turkish Cypriots out of the state and government institutions, they formed their own administrations. In December 1963, they formed a General Committee comprised of the vice president, three Turkish Cypriot cabinet members, and the president of the communal chamber. During the following eleven years, the Turkish Cypriots further developed their administration. First they formed the Provisional Cyprus Turkish Administration in 1967; in 1971 they formed the Cyprus Turkish Administration.

On July 15, 1974, the Greek Cypriot National Guard staged a coup with the help of the Greek junta based in Greece. They overthrew the president and installed Nicos Sampson as the president of the "Republic of Cyprus." Sampson was seen by many as a "notorious killer" and "Turk-hating fanatic." Sampson had previously been tried and sentenced to death by the British colonial government but was pardoned just before Cyprus's independence. Following the coup, Greek Cypriots, together with Greece, prepared to declare enosis. Aware of this fact, Turkey, using her right accorded by the 1960 Treaty of Guarantee, intervened militarily on July 20, 1974, and prevented enosis. Sampson later went on public record stating, "I was about to proclaim enosis, when I quit."[13]

SEPARATISM

During the 1963–74 period, fifty-four more mixed villages disappeared, leaving just forty-eight. With the Turkish intervention of July 1974 came a population exchange agreement between the two sides. Turkish and Greek Cypriots who wished to move to their own respective areas were allowed to do so. This agreement was provided for in the Vienna III communiqué of August 2, 1975, which was issued by the U.N. Secretary-General as agreed upon by the Turkish and Greek Cypriots. Population exchange provisions included in the communiqué are as follows:

1. *The Turkish Cypriots at present in the south of the Island will be allowed, if they want to do so, to proceed north with their belongings under an organized program and with the assistance of UNFICYP* (United Nations Forces in Cyprus).
2. *The Greek Cypriots at present in the north who, at their own request and without having been subjected to any kind of pressure, wish to move to the south, will be permitted to do so.*

It was under this agreement that the exchange and separation of populations, which currently characterizes Cyprus, took place. All of the Turkish Cypriots moved to the northern part of Cyprus. Greek Cypriots moved to the southern part of Cyprus. As a result of the 1975 agreement, Turks and Greeks became completely separated from each other with the exception of one mixed village, Pile, located in the buffer zone, which is controlled by the U.N. Peace Keeping Force in Cyprus (UNFICYP). Problems between Turks and Greeks are common in Pile. Turkish and Greek Cypriots encounter daily problems concerning the use of telephone, water, electricity, and sporting facilities. These problems are supposed to be addressed by the U.N., Turkish, and Greek Cypriot authorities. The Greek Cypriot administrations' adopted policy is that Greek Cypriots and tourists are not allowed to buy anything, including food, from Turkish-owned shops in Pile. Those who are caught doing so are fined and their goods are confiscated. Turkish Cypriots have not imposed similar restrictions on citizens within their jurisdiction.

COMPETING ADMINISTRATIVE AUTHORITY

Following the Turkish intervention of July 1974, the Turkish Cypriot administration became the Autonomous Cyprus Turkish Administration in 1974, the Turkish Federated State of Cyprus in 1975, and the Turkish Republic of Northern Cyprus (TRNC) in 1983. The events that followed the first attacks on the Turkish Cypriots in 1963 and the measures taken to survive these isolated and lonely years, combined with the need to govern themselves and establish some kind of order, had in the end created a new state within Cyprus's borders. The transformation of the Turkish Cypriot administration from a general committee to a state is the result of the policies of the Greek Cypriots, the failure of the negotiations, and the Turkish Cypriots' need to meet the needs of their people.

From Turkish Cypriots' vantage point, the Greek Cypriot administration, which is recognized by the international community as the representative of the Republic of Cyprus, is an illegitimate and unconstitutional entity. The Republic of Cyprus was established as a partnership republic based on the political equality of the Turkish and Greek Cypriots. When Turkish Cypriots were thrown out of the government and state administration, the Republic of Cyprus lost its legitimacy. The recognition of the Greek Cypriot regime as the representative of the Republic of Cyprus contravenes the principles of the constitution and is illegal. The international community's insistence on recognizing the Greek Cypriot administration as the representative of the Republic of Cyprus is one of the main factors contributing to the persistence of the conflict in Cyprus. Since 1963, international organizations such as the U.N. Security Council (UNSC), U.N. General Assembly, British Commonwealth, Non-Aligned Movement, European Union (EU), and others have adopted numerous resolutions regarding Cyprus. These one-sided pro-Greek resolutions were adopted without allowing the Turkish Cypriots' point of view to be heard. One of the many striking examples of the one-sidedness of these resolutions is the one adopted by the Universal Postal Union at a meeting in 1978 in Rio de Janeiro. The resolution prohibited the sending and receiving of mail, to and from TRNC. The Turkish Cypriots were not allowed to voice their views about this resolution, which deprived them of their basic human right of communication.

EMBARGOES AND THEIR EFFECT

Turkey recognizes the TRNC as an independent state. TRNC, with its constitution and constitutional

institutions, is a full-fledged democratic and secular state. Since 1963, the international community has been subjecting the Turkish Cypriots to discrimination and embargoes. Such one-sided policies that blatantly favor the Greek Cypriots do not help in the finding of a resolution to the Cyprus dispute. Continued nonrecognition of the Turkish Cypriot State and its citizens by the international community has made them look for ways to overcome the difficulties resulting from the aforementioned unjustifiable embargoes. The discriminatory policy of the international community has continued until now and provided the Greek Cypriots with great opportunities at the expense of the Turkish Cypriots. They prospered economically, thus also gaining great political advantage over the Turkish Cypriots. Because the Greek Cypriot regime was recognized as the legitimate representative of the whole of Cyprus, all foreign aid that was given for the whole island was exclusively used for the benefit of the Greek Cypriots. Even the share that the Turkish Cypriots were to receive from the state budget was not given to them after December 21, 1963, and was used for bettering Greek Cypriots' standard of living.

On the other hand, the Turkish Cypriots were forced to survive on aid that came from Turkey. Turkey sent an average of US $18 million to Cyprus each year between 1963 and 1974. This money was barely enough for the minimum subsistence of the Turkish Cypriots.[14] The money from Turkey came in hard currency and was deposited in the Central Bank of Cyprus, which was controlled by the Greek Cypriots. The Central Bank, in turn, gave the money to the Turkish Cypriots in Cyprus currency and used the hard currency for the benefit of the Greek Cypriots.[15]

Because the Turkish Cypriots were not able to produce or import anything, they used almost all of the money that came from Turkey to buy their basic needs in the Greek Cypriot markets. Ninety-nine percent of the service sector was also in the hands of the Greek Cypriots. Therefore, it is not surprising that the Greek Cypriot producers and service providers benefited the most from the money Turkey sent. One can say that the 120,000 Turkish Cypriots lived like "permanent tourists" in their own country, helping the Greek Cypriot economy prosper at their own expense. The U.N. peace keeping force, which was sent to Cyprus after the UN Security Council resolution of March 4, 1964, the presence of which had reached over 7,000 people during the peak of the troubles, also used the Greek Cypriot markets and services for their needs during the many years that they have been in Cyprus. UNFICYP still continues its presence on the island.

Greek Cypriot tourism grew in enormous proportions after 1974 because there was now peace and tranquility on the island. Each year, an estimated 2,500,000 foreign tourists visit south Cyprus. However, only about 300,000 tourists, mostly from Turkey, visit North Cyprus each year.

The international community's discrimination toward the Turkish Cypriots since December 1963 did not in any way help in the resolution of the dispute between the two communities. To the contrary, it reinforced the drifting apart of the two sides from one another.

These embargoes create great hardships that affect every aspect of Turkish Cypriot life. Turkey is the only country helping the Turkish Cypriots overcome these difficulties. Chief among the challenges Turkish Cypriots face are the following:

- Communication with the outside world is impossible unless it goes through Turkey.
- Mail coming in and going out of TRNC can only travel through Turkey.
- Travel documents issued to Turkish Cypriots by the TRNC government are not recognized by the international community. Turkish Cypriot citizens can only travel with passports issued to them by the government of Turkey.
- Foreign countries do not permit direct flights to and from TRNC. Therefore, all passengers and cargo have to go through Turkey.
- Trading directly with other countries is not possible.
- Turkish Cypriots are not allowed to compete or represent TRNC in any field of sports in a foreign country.
- Turkey is the only country that invests in TRNC and gives aid to the Turkish Cypriots.
- The only connection to the outside world that Turkish Cypriots have is through Turkey.

Due to the resulting isolation of the Turkish Cypriots from the outside world for the past forty-four years, they have come closer to and made them more dependent on Turkey.

Of all the damaging embargoes, those emanating from Europe are the most damaging. On December 8, 1972, the EU signed an association agreement with the Greek Cypriots. Article 5 of this agreement states:

> The rules governing trade between the Contracting Parties may not give rise to any discrimination between the Member States, or between nationals or companies of these States, nor nationals or companies of Cyprus.

Despite this article, however, the Turkish Cypriots, their companies, and institutions have been and still are being discriminated against by the EU.

Since the signing of the agreement in 1972, the EU has been helping the Greek Cypriots economically, technically, and politically. From 1977 to 1995, the EU has signed and implemented four financial protocols with the Greek Cypriots and disregarded the existence of the Turkish Cypriots. With these protocols, the EU gave hundreds of millions of dollars to the Greek Cypriots in the form of loans and grants that helped their economy and upgraded their standard of living. On May 22, 1987, the EU signed a customs union agreement with the Greek Cypriots, again without listening to the Turkish Cypriots. In 1990, the Greek Cypriot administration applied for full membership in the EU. The application was accepted without any regard for the Turkish Cypriot objections. It ignored the fact that Cyprus was a divided island with an unresolved problem. The discrimination of the EU against the Turkish Cypriots extended to the Court of Justice of the European Communities, which came out with a judgment on July 5, 1994, forbidding the importation of citrus fruit and potatoes from TRNC to the EU. The reason cited by the court was that phytosanitary certificates for citrus fruit and potatoes imported from TRNC should be issued by authorities in the Republic of Cyprus, namely the Greek Cypriot administration. The Turkish Cypriots believe that the court's decision was political and not based on the rule of law.

For thirty-two years, the EU has done everything necessary to prepare the Greek Cypriots for full membership in the EU, while ignoring the existence of the Turkish Cypriots. Turkish Cypriots believe the EU's policy is one-sided, supporting the Greek Cypriot side and discriminating against the Turkish Cypriots. Turkish Cypriots have received an insignificant amount of foreign aid since 1963. During the difficult years of 1963–74 and afterward, Turkey was the only country that provided aid to the Turkish Cypriots. Greek Cypriots, however, have received foreign aid and foreign investment amounting to billions of dollars over the last forty years. Due to the huge foreign aid and investment that the Greek Cypriots received, their income per capita is more than five times greater than that of Turkish Cypriots. The economic disparity between the two sides has grown enormously. This one-sided pro-Greek policy has become the main obstacle in resolving the Cyprus conflict. Continuing statements made by EU officials that "Cyprus" (Greek side) will join the EU whether or not an agreement is reached, further accelerated the disparity and alienation of the Turkish Cypriots when direct negotiations were continuing.

On December 13, 2002, at the EU summit in Copenhagen, the EU under its enlargement policy decided to admit "Cyprus" as a member effective May 1, 2004. In its decision, the EU stated that "it welcomed the commitment of the Greek Cypriots and the Turkish Cypriots to continue to negotiate with the objective of concluding a comprehensive settlement of the Cyprus problem by 28 February 2003, on the basis of the UN Secretary General's proposals."

The EU further stated that "in case of a settlement, the Council, acting by unanimity on the basis of proposals by the Commission, shall decide upon adaptations of the terms concerning the accession of Cyprus to the EU with regard to the Turkish Cypriot community." The Union also stated that, "The European Council has decided that, in the absence of a settlement, the application of the acquis to the Northern part of the island shall be suspended, until the council decides unanimously otherwise, on the basis of a proposal by the commission."[16]

As of December 2002, there was no new state of affairs in Cyprus. There was no agreement between the Turkish and Greek Cypriot sides, and the Greek Cypriots were one step closer to EU membership. Unless a solution was found in the very near future, the division of the island seemed like a permanent reality.

Following the December 2002 Copenhagen summit of the EU, negotiations between Turkish and Greek Cypriots resumed on January 15, 2003. The two sides were under pressure by the U.N. and the EU to reach an agreement before February 28,

2003. However, it was apparent that the two sides were still far apart on core issues and that it was unlikely they would resolve their differences. Greek Cypriots held presidential elections in February, and a newly elected Greek Cypriot president took office in March 2003.

IDENTITY

Under colonial rule the Turkish Cypriots were identified by the British as Muslims rather than Turkish Cypriots. Their Turkish identity was not allowed to be expressed freely. The British colonial administration changed the only Turkish Cypriot high school's name from "Cyprus Turkish High School" to "Cyprus Islam High School." Turkish Cypriots were not given a chance to acquire a Cypriot identity either. The Republic of Cyprus that was to establish this identity lasted only three years. The president of the Republic of Cyprus, Makarios, who was a Greek Cypriot and the archbishop of the Greek Cypriot Orthodox Church, after signing the agreements in 1960 that established the Republic of Cyprus publicly stated that "the agreements created a state but not a Cypriot nation."

Events following 1963 strengthened the Turkish identity of Turkish Cypriots. Turkey was the only country that provided support and aid to Turkish Cypriots. Their survival depended on Turkey. The dependence of Turkish Cypriots on Turkey was so great that the relations between the two became that of mother and child. Turkey became the motherland. It became impossible for Turkish Cypriots to think of survival without Turkey. This point was proven in 1974 and applies to the present circumstances. Turkish Cypriots only feel safe with the presence of the Turkish army protecting them. Experiences of the past have made them lose faith in the international community. They do not trust the Greek Cypriots. Therefore, they want to have a settlement that will provide a permanent safeguard of their freedom and security.

Cyprus is home to the Turkish Cypriots. They belong to the island, and they are very attached to it. Members of the older generation, now in their mid-fifties or older, who remember the colonial rule and the republic, when the two people lived together, relate to the whole island.

They also experienced and remember the sufferings that the Turkish Cypriots encountered when living together with the Greek Cypriots. A new generation has grown up in North Cyprus and has had nothing to do with the Greek Cypriots. The only common element between this generation in the north and the corresponding generation in the south is that they live on the same island. For members of the younger generation, who have not lived with the Greek Cypriots, Southern Cyprus and Greek Cypriots are as foreign as any other foreign country and its citizens. Even though it has been fifty years since EOKA started its first terrorist attacks (in 1955), stories of what Greek Cypriots did, how Turkish Cypriots fought them, and how they survived are still being told in families and by friends who lived through those times and experiences. A typical story is one told by an architect.

> It was a very hot day in July 1965. I was traveling in a bus from Nicosia to Lefke.[17] When we were passing through Kokkini Trimithia[18] the bus was stopped by the Greek Cypriot gunmen. All fifteen of us, five women and ten men, were taken out of the bus. The women were told to take off their shoes; the men were told to strip down to their underwear. It was 10.00 a.m. and the temperature that day rose to 42°C. We were forced to stay in the sun on the burning asphalt road until 4.00 p.m. before we were allowed to go.

Every Turkish Cypriot family has suffered such humiliation and endured great hardships. Many Turkish Cypriot families became refugees three times in less than twenty years (1955–1974).[19] Many families have lost a close relative. Children have lost their parents. These wounds are still very fresh. The continuation of the conflict and the economic hardships brought about by the embargoes imposed on the Turkish Cypriots have given these wounds no chance to heal. There is no trust between the two communities.

TRAUMAS AND GLORIES

Turkish Cypriots were cofounding partners of the Republic of Cyprus, established in 1960. However, on December 21, 1963, they were attacked and thrown out of the government and state. In one night, the Turkish Cypriots found themselves state-less. Like a highway robbery, the state was stolen from them. The state that was supposed to protect them was using every means at hand to attack, terrorize, and destroy them. They kept their morale up by believing that Turkey would one day come and rescue them. That day was July 20, 1974. Turkey finally came to the rescue of the Turkish Cypriots. The trauma of 1963, ended and the glory of 1974 began. Turkey, which had left Cyprus in 1878, had returned after ninety-six years. The presence of the Turkish army in Cyprus brought peace and tranquility. What the U.N. peace keeping force failed to accomplish in the eleven years after 1963 was achieved with the arrival of the Turkish army in 1974. All the massacres and killings of Turkish Cypriots occurred during the years the U.N. peace keeping force was in Cyprus, from 1963 to 1974. With the exception of a few minor incidents at the borders, not a single person has been killed because of intercommunal strife since the arrival of the Turkish army. The Turkish army remains in Cyprus only to protect the Turkish Cypriots and does not have and has never had any aggressive intentions against the Greek Cypriots.

The continuing physical and political aggression of the Greek Cypriots against Turkish Cypriots, however, is a continuous reminder of past traumas. Examples of Greek Cypriots' aggression include attempts made by organized groups to force their way through the borders and the continuing arming of Greek Cypriots. Greek Cypriots have been purchasing sophisticated arms from Greece, Austria, Brazil, France, and Russia. They went as far as purchasing thirty-six Russian S-300 missiles, capable of hitting the southern part of Turkey from Cyprus. Turkish Cypriots and Turkey have continuously warned Greek Cypriots and the international community against this armament frenzy. Following the purchase of the S-300 missiles, Turkey came out with a strong declaration stating that the missiles would not be allowed into Cyprus. Turkey stated that every action would be taken to prevent this. Turkey's strong and decisive declaration persuaded Greece and the Greek Cypriot administration to divert the missiles to the island of Crete. Turkish Cypriots view embargoes imposed upon them by the international community as a form of political aggression. Any event or action taken by the Greek Cypriots or the international community that has a negative tone is perceived by the Turkish

Cypriots as a threat to their freedom and security. These actions reactivate unpleasant memories and emotions and create doubt as to the true intentions and motives of the Greek Cypriots.

ENEMY PERCEPTIONS

From the very beginning, Greek Cypriots and Greece saw Cyprus as a Greek island. They saw Turkish Cypriots as the main obstacle in their realization of this dream. They tried to rule and colonize Turkish Cypriots without success. They tried to destroy them. In the past forty-four years there has been no visible indication that the Greek Cypriots' ambitions have changed. They continue to see Cyprus as a Greek Island. As long as this belief continues to be manifested in their actions and policies, mistrust will continue and it will be impossible for Turkish Cypriots to think of them as anything other than the enemy. The unjust treatment and economic, social, and political embargoes imposed upon Turkish Cypriots by the international community are another reason for anger toward outside institutions and policy makers.

EFFORTS TO RESOLVE THE CONFLICT

Negotiations to resolve the Cyprus conflict began in 1968 and have been ongoing ever since. The first meeting took place in Beirut. The interlocutors were Rauf Denktash for the Turkish Cypriot side and Glafkos Clerides for the Greek Cypriot side. In the past, there have been times when the two sides came close to an agreement, but the Greek Cypriots' perception of Cyprus as a Greek island has prevented an agreement. It is this wrongful perception that is the main cause of the Cyprus conflict.

The circumstances in which the negotiations have taken place do not give the Greek Cypriots an incentive to negotiate in good faith. The Greek Cypriot side is enjoying the advantages and benefits of recognition, whereas the Turkish Cypriot side lives with embargos and isolation from the whole world. Negotiations have been conducted under the auspices of the U.N. secretary-general on the basis of equal footing. This alone is not enough to yield fruitful negotiations. The international community's preferential treatment of the Greek Cypriots is hin-

dering the negotiation process. That is why thirty-nine years of negotiations have not produced any tangible result. Between 1963 and 1974, the Greek Cypriots saw themselves as the strong party. With all the Turkish Cypriots living in enclaves on 3 percent of the land and out of the government and state administration, Greek Cypriots felt no need to restore constitutional order and allow the Turkish Cypriots back into the government. In 1972, the Turkish Cypriot side made important concessions that were rejected by the Greek Cypriot side. Clerides in his memoirs stated the following:

> In 1972 we could have had a solution of our problem based on a much improved constitution than the Zurich one . . . We rejected it because it did not give us the maximum of our aims i.e. Cyprus, a Greek Cypriot island ruled by the Greek Cypriot majority.[20]

During the negotiation process, from 1974 to present time, the Greek Cypriot side has used international organizations to have pro-Greek resolutions adopted. Instead of concentrating on negotiating a solution, time, energy, and great effort have been spent by the Greek Cypriot side to disparage the Turkish Cypriots and Turkey at international forums.

RECENT NEGOTIATION EFFORTS

The last round of negotiations was initiated by the Turkish Cypriot side on December 4, 2001. These negotiations were direct talks between the two leaders, the Turkish Cypriot leader Rauf Denktash, and the Greek Cypriot leader Glafkos Clerides, held in the presence of the special representative of the U.N. secretary-general. The two leaders negotiated continuously for ten months. The direct talks started with both sides agreeing to the following:

- There will be no preconditions.
- All issues will be on the negotiating table.
- The two sides will continue to negotiate in good faith until a comprehensible settlement is reached.
- Nothing will be agreed until everything is agreed.

To resolve a conflict that has been going on for forty-four years, the starting point must be based on reality. The reality is a violent past and the forced separation of Turkish and Greek Cypriots. The two equal partners of the "Republic of Cyprus," which was destroyed in 1963, are now in two separate states divided by a border. Each has its own political structures, represents its own people, and has no authority or jurisdiction over the other.

Sovereignty, equal status, bizonality, exchange of properties, security, and guarantees are the fundamental issues to be resolved. In the new partnership state, Turkish Cypriots envisage that "the two co-founder Partner States will be sovereign to the extent of their residual powers and the Partnership State will be sovereign to the extent of the functions and competences assigned to it by the co-founder Partner States under a comprehensive settlement." Greek Cypriots, however, seem determined not to relinquish the "Republic of Cyprus," which claims sovereignty over the whole island. From the very beginning the Turkish Cypriot side stated that "each side in Cyprus represents its own people and no one else and neither of the parties can claim authority over the other. Their relationship is, therefore, not one of majority and minority but one of two sovereign States. If there is a new partnership settlement, both peoples will continue to live in the territory of their respective partner State."

The political equality of the Turkish and Greek Cypriots will have to be reflected in the presidency, executive offices, legislature, judiciary, and all the organs of the new partnership state. This will mean a rotating presidency and a decision-making mechanism based on consensus. In his statement of September 12, 2000, the U.N. secretary-general stressed that the object of the talks is to reach a comprehensive settlement enshrining a new partnership in which the equal status of the parties must and should be explicitly recognized. The statement of the U.N. secretary-general also confirmed the fact that each party represents its own side and no one else, as a political equal of the other.

Taking into consideration the forty-four year separation of Turkish and Greek Cypriots and existing realities, a bizonal Cyprus, in which the two peoples will live freely in their respective territories without interference from the other side, is essential to prevent the repetition of the pre-1974 conditions.

The Turkish Cypriot side believes that a global exchange of properties and full compensation provide the only realistic way to settle this issue, again taking into consideration the bizonal nature of the problem. The 1960 Republic of Cyprus was guaranteed under the Treaty of Guarantee and Treaty of Alliance. Turkey, Greece, and Britain were the guarantor powers. The treaties that gave birth to the Republic of Cyprus accorded rights over Cyprus to the two guarantor motherlands, Turkey and Greece, which established a balance between the two. It is understood that the new partnership state will also be guaranteed under the same treaties. Article I, paragraph 2, of the 1959–1960 Treaty of Guarantee states the following:

> It [The Republic of Cyprus] undertakes not to participate, in whole or in part, in any political or economic union with any state whatsoever.

Under this clause, Cyprus cannot join an economic or political union in which guarantors Turkey and Greece are not members. In spite of this treaty requirement, accession to the European Union of "Cyprus" (Greek Cyprus) where Greece is a member and Turkey is not, had already taken place as of May 1, 2004. Accession of Greek Cyprus to the European Union means economic and political union of Cyprus with Greece and the other EU member states. The Greek Cypriot side has aligned itself to the EU. EU officials have continuously stated that "whether or not there is a solution, Cyprus's (Greek Cyprus) accession to the EU will take place." The EU officials kept their word and the accession of Cyprus (only the Greek part of Cyprus) to the EU became a fact. Naturally, these statements left no incentive for the Greek Cypriots to negotiate in good faith for a solution. Accession of the Greek part of Cyprus to the EU with the conflict unresolved is a violation of the 1960 Treaty of Guarantee and the agreements that created the Republic of Cyprus.

In 2002, Denktash and Clerides had nearly sixty meetings. Before the December 12–13 EU summit meeting in Copenhagen, the two leaders met in New York on October 4, under the auspices of U.N. Secretary-General Kofi Annan. After the meeting Annan made the following statement:

> As part of their effort to bridge differences pragmatically, the two leaders have decided to create two ad hoc bilateral technical committees to begin work immediately on important technical issues. The purpose

of these committees is to make recommendations on technical matters, without prejudice to the positions of the two leaders on the core issues concerned. Their work shall be ad referendum, and shall focus on treaties and future "common state" laws. The United Nations will assist the parties in this work.[21]

Before the two sides had an opportunity to form their respective technical committees, the U.N. secretary-general presented, on November 11, 2002, a 145-page document to both sides outlining the "Basis for Agreement on a Comprehensive Settlement of the Cyprus Problem." On December 8, 2002, after reviewing the document, the Turkish and Greek Cypriot sides put their objections forward to the U.N. secretary-general. A revised document was then submitted to the two sides on December 10, 2002. Efforts to have the two sides sign the agreement before the December 12–13, 2002, EU Copenhagen summit failed.

The secretary-general's proposal was submitted in an effort to bridge differences on the issues and facilitate an agreement. Unfortunately, both sides had major objections to many issues outlined in the Basis for Agreement that needed further clarification and negotiation. Issues such as sovereignty, exchange of properties, political equality, bizonality, and guarantees were among the main issues that had not been resolved.

At the Copenhagen summit, the two sides were called upon to negotiate and reach a solution by February 28, 2003. The Copenhagen summit also approved the membership of Cyprus (Greek part of Cyprus), together with the other nine countries. This decision took away all the incentives from the Greek Cypriot side—if there were any left—to reach an agreement to reestablish a partnership republic with the Turkish Cypriots.

After the Copenhagen summit the solution of the Cyprus issue was focused on February 28, 2003. In this context, Kofi Annan sent a letter, a kind of road map, to the two leaders, Denktash and Clerides, outlining the procedure to be followed until February 28. In the meantime, presidential elections took place on the Greek part of Cyprus. Tasos Papadopoulos defeated the incumbent president, Clafcos Clerides, and became the new president of the Greek Cypriot side. Papadopoulos, an EOKA man, is known for his hard-line attitude toward the Turkish Cypriots and his determination to turn Cyprus into a Greek island.

It is a very well-known fact that Papadopoulos has had a much greater role in the division of the island than has Clerides.

The U.N. secretary-general came to Cyprus on February 26, 2003, and had a meeting first with Papadopoulos and then with Denktash. He presented his third revised plan, which met the approval of neither side. On February 27, 2003, Kofi Annan had a second meeting with Denktash and Papadopoulos, at which he called on them to come to The Hague, Netherlands, on March 10, 2003, to give him their answers on his revised plan. At the meeting at The Hague the two sides failed to reach an agreement.

At the EU summit in Athens on April 16, 2003, the Greek part of Cyprus along with the other nine countries signed the agreement of entry into the EU of the "Republic of Cyprus." On April 21, 2003, TRNC Council of Ministers decided to allow crossings, under certain regulations, from the Greek part of Cyprus to TRNC and vice versa. Every day, since April 23, 2003, thousands of Greek Cypriots cross over to the north (TRNC) and thousands of Turkish Cypriots cross over to the south (Greek part) of Cyprus.

For the first time after thirty years, I crossed over to the south in May 2004. I visited the village of Yayla in which I was born and raised. I could hardly recognize my beautiful village. The house that I was born in had been demolished. Our citrus gardens, which extended in front of our house and in which we used to play, were destroyed. The serene river in which I used to play and swim was dried out. In short, my lovely village was mutilated. I wish that I had not gone to see it like this and had kept remembering it as it was in 1974. The same is true for almost every Turkish Cypriot who came from the south. The houses, citrus gardens, vineyards, and business places Turkish Cypriots left in the south had been demolished and destroyed to a great extent. On the contrary, the Greek Cypriot houses and property, which the Greek Cypriots left in the north, have been taken care of by the Turkish Cypriots.

On December 14, 2003 parliamentary elections took place in TRNC, after which a new government was formed on January 11, 2004. On January 24, 2004, Kofi Annan met the Turkish prime minister, Recep Tayyip Erdogan, in Davos, Switzerland. Annan, in his report submitted to the U.N. Security

Council, stated the following regarding his meeting with the Turkish prime minister:

> For its part, the Government of Turkey was putting together the elements of a new policy on Cyprus, which was conveyed to me by Prime Minister Recep Tayyip Erdogan when we met in Davos on 24 January 2004. He told me that Turkey supported a resumption of negotiations. He expressed preferences for dealing with the main issues by 1 May 2004, and a political figure to handle the negotiations, but was open to discussion on these points. He added that, as far as Turkey was concerned, it had no objection to my "filling in the blanks" in the plan should the parties not be able to agree on all issues. He assured me that, henceforth, the Turkish side, including the Turkish Cypriots, would be "one step ahead" in the effort.[22]

Following the elections and the forming of a new government at TRNC and his meeting with Recep Tayyip Erdogan, the U.N. Secretary-General Kofi Annan, on February 4, 2004, invited the two leaders, Denktash and Papadopoulos, to New York for new negotiations. The New York negotiations started on February 10, 2004, and ended on February 13, 2004, without any success. During these negotiations, the Turkish Cypriot side made a very important proposal, which had the support of Turkey. The Turkish Cypriot side proposed a three-stage procedure: if the two sides (the Turkish and the Greek Cypriots) could not reach an agreement on the Annan plan, Turkey and Greece would join the negotiation process. Still, if no agreement were reached, then, Kofi Annan would be entrusted to complete the unfinished parts of the plan ("filling in the blanks"). The Greek Cypriot side also made a proposal asking that the EU become part of the negotiations. On February 13, 2004, the EU announced that it did not want to become a party to the "Cyprus negotiations." At the end of the New York negotiations, the U.N. secretary-general made a statement to the press in which he said the following:

> Following three days of meetings and consultations, I am pleased to announce that the parties have committed to negotiating in good faith on the basis of my plan to achieve a comprehensive settlement of the Cyprus problem through separate and simultaneous referenda before 1 May 2004. To this end, the parties will seek to agree on changes and to complete the plan in all respects by 22 March 2004, within the framework of my mission of good offices, so as to produce a finalized text. In the absence of such agreement, I would convene a meeting of the two sides with the participation of Greece and Turkey in order to lend their collaboration in a concentrated effort to agree on a finalized text by 29 March. As a final resort, in the event of a continuing and persistent deadlock, the parties have invited me to use my discretion to finalize the text to be submitted to referenda on the basis of my plan.[23]

According to the agreement reached in New York, the negotiations reconvened in Cyprus on February 19, 2004, and continued until March 22, 2004, without any positive development. During these negotiations, both sides wanted to make changes to the "Annan Plan," which had already been revised three times. The March 22, 2004, meeting was the last meeting that President Denktash attended during the negotiating process.

As a last effort, Kofi Annan invited the parties to negotiations on March 24, 2004, at Burgenstock, Switzerland, in order to finalize the plan by March 31, 2004. Papadopoulos attended the negotiations at Burgenstock, while Denktash sent his prime minister and foreign minister with full authority to negotiate on behalf of Turkish Cypriots. Turkey and Greece joined the negotiations with their foreign ministers on March 28 and 29, 2004. The EU commissioner for enlargement was present at Burgenstock on March 29, 2004.

By March 30, 2004, it was apparent that agreement was unlikely. So, Kofi Annan "filled in the blanks" on March 31, 2004 and produced his plan entitled "The Comprehensive Settlement of the Cyprus Problem." The plan amounted to over 200 pages with attachments of 131 completed laws, cooperation agreements totaling 9,000 pages, and a list of 1,134 treaties and instruments.[24] Kofi Annan's plan with all the attachments was put to referendum on April 24, 2004, on both sides of the island. Both Denktash and Papadopoulos campaigned against the plan, urging their supports to vote "no." Political parties on both sides were divided between the "yes" and "no" campaigns. The result of the referendum was as follows:

- Turkish Cypriots:
"Yes" 64.91 percent, "No" 35.09 percent, Participation 84.83 percent

• Greek Cypriots:
"Yes" 24.20 percent, "No" 75.80 percent, Participation 96.53 percent

The "Annan Plan," which was originally presented to the two parties on November 11, 2002, and revised four times, was finally put to separate but simultaneous referenda on the Turkish and Greek Cypriot parts of the island. The Turkish Cypriots accepted the plan, but the Greek Cypriots overwhelmingly rejected it.

The referendum itself and its results are a milestone in the history of Cyprus:

• For the first time in the history of Cyprus, the two peoples of Cyprus—that is, the Turkish and Greek Cypriots—voted on their self-determination.
• The Greek Cypriots, who, for the last forty-four years have been deceiving the world that they want an agreement in order to establish a bizonal, bicommunal federation, based on the political equality of the Turkish and Greek Cypriots, rejected the plan. This means that the Greek Cypriots do not want to share anything with the Turkish Cypriots but want to own and rule the island all by themselves. The Greek Cypriots showed the whole world that they are not after a solution to the problem but rather to extend their rule to the Turkish part of the island. This has been their policy from the very beginning.
• The Greek Cypriots who rejected the plan were rewarded with accession to the EU as of May 1, 2004, and the Turkish Cypriots who accepted the plan were left out.

After the rejection of the plan by the Greek Cypriots, the U.N. secretary-general, the EU, the United States, the British government, and the larger international community by and large called for the removal of embargoes imposed upon the Turkish Cypriots to end their isolation. The U.N. secretary-general in his "Cyprus Report" S/2004/437 to the U.N. Security Council made the following appeal:

> The decision of the Turkish Cypriots is to be welcomed. The Turkish Cypriot leadership and Turkey have made clear their respect for the wish of the Turkish Cypriots to reunify in a bi-communal, bizonal federation. The Turkish Cypriot vote has undone any rationale for pressuring and isolating them. I would hope that the members of the Council (the UN Security Council) can give a strong lead to all States to cooperate both bilaterally and in interna-

tional bodies to eliminate unnecessary restrictions and barriers that have the effect of isolating the Turkish Cypriots and impeding their development.

Similar calls were made by EU officials and the United States, British, and other governments.

Regarding his mission of good offices, the U.N. secretary-general made the following assessment in his report:

> As for the future of my mission of good offices, the outcome of the referenda has resulted in a stalemate. Mr. Papadopoulos has stated that he is not prepared to submit the plan to referendum once again unless unspecified changes are made. Others on the Greek Cypriot side speak of a second referendum, and look for unspecified additional guarantees on security and implementation. For their part having approved the plan at referendum, the Turkish Cypriot side is opposed to reopening it for negotiation. Neither of the Cyprus parties has made a proposal to the United Nations or to the other—to my knowledge—to resolve this impasse. I do not see any basis for resuming my good offices as long as this stand-off remains.

The U.N. secretary-general's report, which calls upon the U.N. Security Council to "give a strong lead to all States to cooperate both bilaterally and in international bodies to eliminate unnecessary restrictions and barriers that have the effect of isolating the Turkish Cypriots and impeding their development," could not be adopted by the Security Council due to the veto of Russia and France. As of October 2007, forty-one months later, when this chapter was being written, the U.N. secretary-general's report had still not been adopted by the U.N. Security Council. The report has been shelved and it will never be adopted. The Turkish Cypriots believe that Russia and France vetoed the impartial and realistic report of the U.N. secretary-general because of religious factors.

Prior to the referendum of April 24, 2004, the U.N., the EU, Britain, and the United States were promising the Turkish Cypriots that if they say "yes" to the secretary-general's plan, they will be embraced by the international community, the embargoes will be lifted, and their isolation will end. The Turkish Cypriots overwhelmingly said "yes," but nothing has happened and nothing has changed for them. None of the promises made have been kept. They are still isolated; the embargoes are still there. The EU promised to give $259 million to the Turkish Cypriots for development and allow direct trade between the EU and TRNC. The EU has been talking about these promises since April 2004. Nothing has happened, and with Greece and the Greek part of Cyprus as members of EU, one should not expect anything positive to happen. Now that the Greek part of Cyprus is a member of the EU, Greek Cypriot intransigence is reaching its peak. The last meeting between the Greek Cypriots and the Turkish Cypriots took place in March 2004. Since then, the two sides have not gotten together for any kind of negotiation. The Greek Cypriot side wants to have nothing to do with the "Annan Plan." Calls by the Turkish Cypriot side to meet and talk about differences are left unanswered by the Greek Cypriot side. Instead, the Greek Cypriot president, Tasos Papadopoulos, has come up with a list of twenty-five demands that will destroy the bicommunality and bizonality; abolish the 1960 Treaty of Guarantee; jeopardize the security of the Turkish Cypriots; and leave them at the mercy of Greek Cypriots. Under these conditions and with these unrealistic demands that are totally unacceptable to the Turkish Cypriots, the U.N. sees no reason to take any action using its good offices to start a new process. If the EU, the U.N. Security Council, Britain, and the United States do not change their favoritism for the Greek Cypriots, the separation of the two communities will be further cemented.

CONCLUSION

It has been over four decades since the Turkish and Greek Cypriots were separated from one another. As the referenda of April 24, 2004, demonstrated, the separation of these two peoples is irreversible. The Greek Cypriots do not want to share anything with the Turkish Cypriots; they want all of Cyprus to themselves. Separation arose out of a need to survive the aggression of Greek Cypriots. It has taken a hundred years to complete. Any solution will have to take into account that the sustainability of peace will have to be carefully designed to prevent the repetition of pre-1974 events and the ignition of another bloody conflict. The two sides

will have to live in their respective areas side by side as good neighbors. The overwhelming "no" to the Annan Plan by the Greek Cypriots is a clear indication that they will not accept anything that will not give them sovereignty over the entire island. This means conflict, resumed fighting, and exodus for the Turkish Cypriots. Turkish Cypriots established their state because Greek Cypriots did not want to share power with them. They wanted to rule them. Cyprus has had a violent history. The state, which was supposed to protect its citizens, terrorized them for eleven years. The Turkish Cypriots are not going to relinquish their state. The last four generations have been living with the Cyprus problem. The two peoples have drifted apart from each other. There is great mistrust between the two sides.

Cyprus has changed dramatically during the last forty-four years. Turkish Cypriots are not the party responsible for this change. There are now two separate states in Cyprus, whose citizens are ethnically, linguistically, and religiously different. In an agreement, the two sides must each have their own state and live in their respective areas. Each state will give some of its powers to the common state. Residual powers will stay with the two states. For peace to endure, the two sides will need to have absolute political equality in sharing power in the common state. The political equality of the two sides will have to be reflected in every aspect of the state administration. Decisions will have to be reached by consensus.

As with all the previous decisions made and resolutions adopted on Cyprus by the EU, the decisions made in Copenhagen at the EU Summit on December 13, 2002, did not contribute positively to the resolution of the Cyprus conflict. The overwhelming "no" by the Greek Cypriots in the referenda on April 24, 2004, to Kofi Annan's plan is a sheer indication of this unjust policy that favors the Greek Cypriots. As much as the two sides bear responsibility for resolving this 44-year-old conflict, the unjust and unequal treatment of the Turkish Cypriots by the international community, and particularly the European Union, has been and continues to be the major obstacle in the resolution of the conflict.

The results of the April 24, 2004, referendums have created a new state of affairs. The whole world has seen that it is the Greek Cypriot side that does not want to get together with the Turkish Cypriots but instead wants to rule them and have sovereignty over the whole island. On the other hand, the Turkish Cypriots have categorically stated that they want to live separately in their own part of the island, regardless of the fact that thousands of both Turkish and Greek Cypriots cross the border on a daily basis.

If the state of affairs that has persisted for the past forty-four years continues, the inevitable will happen in the very near future, which is the reality of the permanent division of Cyprus.

ENDNOTES

1. Ronald Storrs. *Orientations.* (London: Ivor Nicholson and Watson Ltd., 1937), 548–49.
2. Caesar V. Mavratsas. "On the Idea of a Reunited Cyprus, *Mind and Human Interaction,* vol. 13, no. 1 (2003): 26–27.
3. Sir Harry Luke, *Cyprus Under Turks: 1715–1878* (London: Clarendon Press, 1921), 15–16.
4. Unofficial translation from the original *Firman* of the Turkish sultan Selim the Second, from the Archives of the Turkish Republic of Northern Cyprus, Girne.
5. Ahmet Sami Topcan. "Report on Turkish Population in Cyprus." (Turkish Republic of Northern Cyprus: Ministry of Interior, 1975).
6. Turkey lies partly in Europe and partly in Asia, and it covers an area of 780,576 square kilometers. A little over 3 percent of this area is in Europe, and the rest is in Asia. Anatolia is the Asian part of Turkey and is called "Anadolu" in Turkish. Anatolia means "sunrise" or the "eastern land." The Bosphorous, the Sea of Marmara, and the Dardanelles Strait separate Anatolia from the European part of Turkey. The European part of Turkey borders Greece and Bulgaria. The Anatolian part borders Iran, Nahicevan (Azerbaijan), Armenia, and Georgia in the east; Iraq and Syria in the southeast; and is bordered by the Black Sea in the north, the Aegean Sea in the west, and the Mediterranean Sea in the south.
7. Hepworth W. Dixon. *British Cyprus* (London Chapman and Hall, 1879), 32, 34–35.
8. *Ibid., 181.*
9. The British closed the New Council (Kavanin Meclisi), which was functioning as a legislative assembly, censored the press, and began to appoint village headmen (Mukhtars) instead of having them elected by the people
10. Ethniki Organosis Kiprion Ağoniston (EOKA) means National Organisation of Cypriot Fighters. EOKA's aim was not an independent Cyprus. The publicly declared aim of EOKA was enosis—that is, the union of Cyprus with Greece.
11. Türk Mukavemet Teşkilati (TMT) means Turkish Resistance Organisation. As the name TMT implies, the aim of the Turkish Cypriot Organization was to fight and resist any kind of Hellenization of Cyprus.
12. Makarios's real name was Michael Christodoulou Mouskos. Later, when he was serving as the bishop of Kition (one of the bishoprics of the Greek Cypriots in Cyprus), he used the name Makarios III. In 1950 he became archbishop of the Greek Cypriot Orthodox Church. In 1960 he was elected president of the Republic of Cyprus. He also continued serving as the archbishop. He was publicly known as "Archbishop Makarios," or simply "Makarios".
13. *Cyprus Mail,* July 17, 1975. 1.
14. In 1973, the last year before the 1974 Turkish intervention, the amount of money sent to the Turkish Cypriots by Turkey was US$22,500,000.00.
15. Turkey kept sending this money, every year, to the Turkish Cypriots. After 1974 the aid from Turkey increased in great proportions. Turkey is still the only country aiding the Turkish Cypriots, whereas the Greek Cypriots continue to receive all kinds of aid from international organizations and individual countries.
16. *Acquis* is a French word that the EU uses in its documents. The word can pertain to legislation, agreements, treaties and relevant rules and regulations of the EU.
17. A Turkish Cypriot town 50 kilometers west of Nicosia.
18. A Greek Cypriot village near the Nicosia airport.
19. The first time was during the 1955–1960 EOKA attacks; the second time was during the 1963–1974 period; and the third time was following the Turkish intervention, when all the Turkish Cypriots moved to the north.
20. Glafkos Clerides. *Cyprus: My Deposition,* vol. 3. (Nicosia: Alithia Publishing, 1990), 367. Clerides had been the main interlocutor of the Greek Cypriot side and was the interlocutor when the negotiations began in 1968; he served two terms (1993–2003) as president of the Greek part of Cyprus. The 1959 agreements that established the Republic of Cyprus were negotiated in Zurich.
21. The two ad hoc bilateral technical committees were formed by both sides and started working in January 2003.
22. S/2004/437 on "His Mission of Good Offices in Cyprus." A report by the UN Secretary General, May 28, 2004.
23. May 1, 2004, was the date on which the Greek part of Cyprus was to become a member of the EU. (A statement to the press by the UN Secretary General).
24. Of the 131 completed laws, "almost all [were] based on Greek Cypriot drafts." From the Cyprus Report of the U.N. Secretary-General, S/2004/437.

ABOUT THE AUTHOR

Dr. Kenan Atakol was born at Yayla, Paphos, Cyprus, in 1937. He received his B.Sc. in civil engineering from the Middle East Technical University, Ankara, in 1961; M.Sc. from the University of New Mexico in 1965; and Ph.D. from the University of Virginia in 1967.

His professional career includes work as a site engineer for the construction of the Dhekhelia Power Plant Extension (Cyprus, 1961–1962); an executive engineer at the Water Development Department, mainly responsible for the investigation and construction of the Argaka–Magunda Dam (Cyprus, 1962–1963); an assistant professor in the civil engineering department of The Pennsylvania State University (1967–1972); and an expert on design and construction of dams and irrigation systems on the comprehensive Morphou–Tylliria Project (Cyprus, 1973–1974). He has published articles in the United States on civil engineering and the "Cyprus Conflict." Atakol's first book—*Turkish and Greek Cypriots: Is Their Separation Permanent*—was published by the Middle East Technical University Press in 2003.

His political career started in October 1974. From October 1974 to December 1998, during the twenty-four years of his political career, he served as Minister of Energy and Natural Resources; Minister of Education, Youth, Sports and Culture; Minister of Interior; Minister of Tourism; and for nearly fourteen years (1978–1994) as Minister of Foreign Affairs and Defense, starting with the Autonomous Turkish Cypriot Administration, then the Turkish Federated State of Cyprus, and finally the Turkish Republic of Northern Cyprus (TRNC).

Dr. Atakol was elected to the Turkish Cypriot parliament for five consecutive terms and served from 1976 to 1998. As a member of parliament he served on the Constitutional Committee, which drafted the 1985 TRNC Constitution and was a member and chairman of the Legal and Political Affairs Committee.

Dr. Atakol is married with two daughters. He lives with his wife in Girne, North Cyprus.

5

Israel/Palestine

The Israeli–Palestinian conflict is thought of as an ethnopolitical conflict that pits Jews and Arabs against each other in a fight for the same territory: the land that lies between the Mediterranean Sea and the Jordan River, comprising Israel, the Gaza Strip, and the West Bank.

Apart from the partition plan dated after World War II, other elements of the conflict can be traced back to the end of the nineteenth century. The Zionist movement started in Europe in the second half of the nineteenth century, holding that Jews should have a state of their own—and not just any state, but a state in their historic homeland, at that time part of the Ottoman Empire and then populated by a large majority of Palestinian Arabs.

Between World War I and World War II, three key pledges were made and became basic sources of the present land dispute. In 1916, the secret Sykes-Picot Agreement was signed by France and Great Britain, with the assent of Russia. This agreement called for the disassembling of the Ottoman Empire and for the division of the region into French- and British-administered areas. That same year, Sir Henry McMahon, the British High Commissioner in Egypt, promised the Arab leaders postwar independence for the former Ottoman Arab provinces. Then in 1917, the British foreign minister, Arthur Balfour, committed to work toward "the establishment in Palestine of a national home for the Jewish people," later known as the Balfour Declaration.

In 1920, parts of the Sykes-Picot Agreement were implemented in the form of mandates legitimated by the League of Nations. France received parts of Turkey, Lebanon, and Syria, while Britain received Iraq and Palestine. In 1923, with the intention of partially fulfilling its commitments with the Arabs, Britain granted limited autonomy to Emir Abdullah I of Jordan and set Transjordan separate from Palestine to the west of the Jordan River.

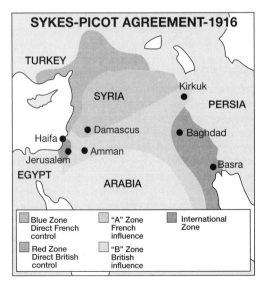

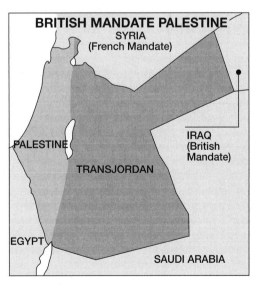

Source: http://news.bbc.co.uk/1/shared/spl/hi/middle_east/03/v3_israel_palestinians/maps/html/british_control.stm

Jewish immigration increased markedly during the 1920s and 1930s. Due to mounting anti-Semitic sentiments in Europe, the British severely limited the exodus of European Jews attempting to enter Palestine and, at the height of the Nazi persecution, declared this immigration illegal. Meanhile, tensions between Arabs and Jews escalated sharply, leading to violent clashes in 1929 and to an Arab revolt by 1936. Britain was having more and more problems maintaining peace and order within its mandate. During and after World War II, despite the mandatory restrictions posed by the British authorities, the Jewish population escaping persecution in Europe increased threefold in Palestine. The Palestinian nationalist movement also started to gain momentum in its struggle against the British mandate and against the Jews who were flocking back to the Holy Land.

In 1947, at the end of World War II, Britain handed over its mandate in Palestine to the United Nations. The General Assembly passed UN Resolution 181, which partitioned Palestine into an Arab state and a Jewish state and made Jerusalem an international city. In 1947, fewer than two million Jews and Arabs lived in Palestine: 67 percent were Arab and 33 percent were Jews. The land was divided, with 56.47 percent assigned to the Jews and 43.53 percent assigned to the native Palestinian Arabs. The partition plan was explicitly rejected by the Palestinian Arabs and, therefore, was never implemented.

In May 1948, two events occurred simultaneously: the British withdrew their troops from Palestine, and the State of Israel was proclaimed. As a result of that declaration, seven surrounding Arab countries declared war on Israel. (This was only the first in a series of wars between Israel and its Arab neighbors.) In 1949, after nine months of combat, Israel, Egypt, Jordan, Lebanon, and Syria signed armistice agreements, which resulted in Palestinian Arabs suffering a significant loss of the territory assigned to them while Israel's jurisdiction increased to 78 percent of the territory. Egypt retained the Gaza Strip, and Transjordan annexed the West Bank, becoming the Hashemite Kingdom of Jordan.

In the following reading, the authors pay significant attention to the wars that occurred once in each decade between the Israeli army and various Arab, Palestinian, and Lebanese resistance groups in 1956, 1967, 1973, 1982, 1991, and 2006. The Six-Day War in June 1967

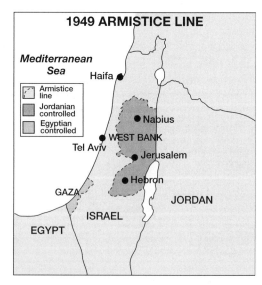

Source: http://news.bbc.co.uk/1/shared/spl/hi/middle_east/03/v3_israel_palestinians/maps/html/israel_founded.stm

AFTER THE 1967 WAR

Mediterranean Sea

SYRIA

Quneitra

GOLAN

WEST BANK

Jerusalem

Gaza City

GAZA

Hebron

Suez Canal

EGYPT

SINAI

ISRAEL

JORDAN

Land occupied by Israel in 1967

Source: http://news.bbc.co.uk/1/shared/spl/hi/
middle_east/03/v3_israel_palestinians/maps/html/
six_day_war.stm

resulted in Israel occupying Arab territories, such as the Sinai Peninsula, the Gaza Strip, East Jerusalem, the West Bank, and the Golan Heights. Israel retained control over Sinai up until the landmark 1979 peace treaty signed between Israel and Egypt—the first Arab state to sign a peace agreement with Israel. The agreement was based on the principle of land for peace: Israel returned all the garnered land and Egypt recognized Israel as a state and established diplomatic relations and a secure border. Above all, this treaty served as the first recognition by an Arab government—in this instance, the most important one—of the existence of a Jewish state.

Because of the restrictive policies implemented by the government of Israel and its military occupation, the Palestinians embarked on major *intifadas* (uprisings) in 1987 and in 2000. During the first *intifada,* protest consisted mostly of nonlethal civil disobedience, general strikes, boycotts of Israeli products, graffiti, and stone throwing aimed at the heavily armed occupation troops.

In 1991, in the aftermath of the Gulf War, a multilateral conference took place in Madrid and opened the way to bilateral negotiations. Meanwhile, following this first *intifada,* the secret Oslo Track II diplomatic negotiations initiated between civil-society Israelis and Palestinians began to take shape and soon involved U.S. President Bill Clinton in framing several agreements. Significant progress was made: the Palestinians recognized Israel's sovereignty in return for the beginning of phased dismantling of Israel's occupations in the West Bank and Gaza. Negotiations included a Declaration of Principles signed by Y. Rabin and Y. Arafat in in 1993 in Washington, D.C., which led to the creation of the Palestinian National Authority in 1994. Also in 1994, Israel resolved disputes with Jordan and signed a peace treaty. In spite of several subsequent agreements, implementation failures on both sides and a last attempt to address all controversial issues at once at the Camp David summit in 2000 resulted in no progress. During the second militarized *intifada,* the Palestinians used firearms and suicide bombings against the occupying Israeli forces, which responded massively with heavy weaponry and the reoccupation of the West Bank and Gaza.

A few months before the Camp David summit in 2000, Israel decided unilaterally to withdraw from southern Lebanon, which it had occupied since 1982. Redeployment without an agreement was also implemented by Prime Minister Sharon in 2005 in the pullout of the Israeli Army and Jewish settlements from the Gaza Strip. Following the kidnapping of one soldier in the Gaza border and two more in the Lebanese frontier in the summer of 2006, however, the Israeli Defense Forces (IDF) launched major aerial and ground military campaigns against Hezbollah ("Party of God"), a pro-Iranian and radical Islamist group. This conflict was perceived to be an indirect battle between the United States and Israel on one side and Iran, Syria, and their clients (Hamas, a major radical Islamist group and political party, and Hezbollah) on the other. During the first years of the twenty-first century, Palestinians witnessed the emergence to political power of Hamas. Early in 2006, Palestinians voted to give Hamas legislators a majority in the Palestinian legislature. After a bloody confrontation in 2007, Hamas took control of the Gaza Strip, leaving the Palestine Liberation Organization (PLO) effectively maintaining power only over the West Bank Palestinans.

The following chapter is cowritten by an Israeli and a Palestinian political scientist who are experts in conflict resolution. It explores jointly the dispute that has expanded from a local confrontation in the middle of the twentieth century to an East–West conflict. The first part examines the centuries-old relations between the Jews and Muslims who have lived side by side and shared common traits of heritage and culture. The chapter continues with an examination of the nationalism that started to take root at the end of the nineteenth century, with both Jews and Palestinians initiating more frequent confrontations. The authors explain in detail the six wars that have occurred between Israel and Palestine, beginning in 1948. The next part of the chapter explores the peace trends that started in 1979 with the Camp David Accords signed by Egypt and Israel. The concluding part examines various peace scenarios aimed at ending this half-century-old conflict and implicating many inside and outside actors.

Understanding Our Israeli–Palestinian Conflict and Searching for Its Resolution

Edward (Edy) Kaufman and Manuel Hassassian

I. INTRODUCTION

Framing a historic period of analysis is a matter of subjective interpretation of history, determined not only by the national ethos of each of us but also by our joint approach. Conventional wisdom has taught us that we should start our analysis from the moment when the two emerging national movements clashed. Indeed, the early Zionist arrival in "the land of the ancestors," *Eretz Israel,* coincided with the Arab awakening to emancipation from the Ottoman yoke. Both processes occurred around the third quarter of the nineteenth century. Jewish nationalism was naturally resisted by the Arab indigenous population as part of an initially wider Arab national movement occurring in the same territory as *Filastin* (Palestine). However, we also could argue that Arab–Jewish relations need to be traced back many more centuries and that we should study relations over a period longer than the last hundred years of bloody confrontations. A colleague of ours has written about the "Common Heritage of Arabs and Jews," and that is how we like to start team teaching the conflict resolution course we have taught for more than ten years at the University of Maryland–College Park.[1] Based on Israeli and Palestinian narratives, watersheds for both nations were the defeat of 1948 and the results of the 1967 conflict leading to the separation of the West Bank from Jordan and Gaza from Egypt. For Israel, peace with Egypt in 1978 was an important landmark. For Palestinians, landmarks were the formation of the Palestine Liberation Organization (PLO) in 1965 and the transition from a call to steadfastness to an active uprising—an intifada (Arabic for "shaking off")—in 1987 that provided a strategy for ending the occupation of the West Bank and Gaza and creating a two-state solution. Again, for both sides, the mutual recognition in the Oslo agreement of 1993 was the first step toward direct negotiations and mutual acceptance.

These preliminary observations led us to develop a fourteen-point approach to teaching and writing about our protracted violent conflict, as is reflected in this chapter.[2] While presentation of an antagonistic black-and-white picture might sharpen readers' grasp of the differences that divide us, it does not highlight the common ground, an understanding of which we hope will move readers not only to understand the Israeli–Palestinian conflict but also to consider alternative solutions. Briefly, our "rules of engagement" in coauthorship are these:

1. *Don't get locked into conventional zero-sum and deterministic interpretations of past conflicts.* Our approach is to take a more imaginative and analytical view of the past, present, and future. We suggest dealing not only with the history that separates us—mostly the ultimate responsibility of our leadership—but also the shared understanding of reality shaped by our academics and intellectuals.

2. *Periodization is a matter of choice.* A significant decision must be made when presenting our common history: Shall it be offered in the context of struggle between two national movements at loggerheads for the same piece of land, Palestine/*Eretz Israel,* or shall we opt for a retrospective on encounters between Arabs and Jews or between Islam and Judaism fourteen centuries ago? If we choose the first option, then conflict epitomizes our relationship. However, if we opt to teach our common heritage and ignore the previous century, one can infer that the interaction throughout the ages in the Middle East and the Iberian Peninsula was a history of coexistence, even in asymmetrical situations in which Jews comprised a minority in the lands of Islam. Surely the Jewish community under Islam enjoyed better privileges and treatment than under Christendom. While courses like ours normally focus only on the era of conflict, we are prompted to salvage the longer historical trajectory to remind ourselves that confrontation is not a permanent feature in our relationship. Since we have had a record of coexistence in the past, a fashionable deterministic prediction that we cannot live in peace in the future is not substantiated when envisioning the long-term perspective. Hence, the main challenge lies in knowing how we can bring it forward without leaving a legacy of violence and denial for future generations.

3. *Historical events are a genuine part of the collective memory of both Arabs and Jews, and we should present both narratives as they are predominantly taught in Israeli and in Palestinian schools.* To understand with empathy the other's subjective perception of realities, it is important to be familiar with both sides of the story. Looking back into our respective nation-building processes, the tendency is to glorify our own role and explain the conflict as an outcome of the adversary's misdeeds or bad conduct. Seeing the other's parallel history can be an important eye-opening experience. We need to respect each other's narratives and, whenever we differ, to include both versions in our analysis. Once we have acknowledged our differences, we have a better hope of affirming our common ground and discovering a shared vision of the future.

4. *In presenting a respective of our own past, we must frame each of the two distinct narratives in their own staged approach.* When introducing the phases of our conflict, we address the prevailing historiography of each side and present it as such, even if the periods and events that marked the Palestinian and Jewish developments at times do not converge. For instance, the periodization of the making of the State of Israel was preceded by the imprint of six distinct migratory waves (*Aliyah,* in the singular), each with different origins, characteristics, and idiosyncrasies. After the "War of Liberation" in 1948, the "wars of Israel" (1948, 1956, 1967, 1982, 1991, and 2006) with established Arab countries (even if triggered or affected by hostile behavior by Palestinians) are often recognized as turning points. From the other perspective, the pre-1948 *Al Nakba* (The Catastrophe) is characterized as the transition of an overall Arab national movement toward a distinct Palestinian patriotism. By and large, from 1948 until the Oslo process, the movement was transformed from a leaderless people through its formative stages of armed strategy to the establishment of the PLO, which was the culminating response to the failures of inter-Arab politics. Even if the causality of events presented in different sequences contradicts each other's official narratives, we contrive to present them with a degree of empathy (rather than antagonism or sympathy) and with a sense of respect for each other's truth.

5. *As with many other parts of our teamwork, we want to respect the references used by both Palestinians and Jews.* One matter over which we have had lengthy deliberations and negotiations is how to name incidents, territories, and wars. In some cases we have made ad hoc decisions to use both sides' formulations. For example, we consider the 1948 war as both Israel's *Milhemet ha-Atzma'ut* (War of Independence) and the Palestinians' *Al Nakba.* And we address a more current controversy as the Palestinians' uncategorical condemnation of the "Apartheid Wall" in the West Bank and Israel's official support of the "Security Barrier." Sometimes we use parallel nomenclature, separated by a dash, as in "Israel–Palestine." In other cases, we have accepted the vocabulary in common usage by most of the world—for example, West Bank of the Jordan River, rather than the Jewish biblical names Judea and Samaria. We have chosen to relate to all these territories as "occupied," using the language of international institutions, rather than the Jewish settlers' reference to "liberated" lands or the official Israeli term "administered" territories. On the other hand, we have related to the Jewish state as "Israel"—its official name as a recognized member of the United Nations (U.N.)—rather than "Occupied Palestine" or the "Zionist entity," terms expressing the reluctance of many in the Arab world to recognize Israel's existence.

6. *We use the tools of social history so that the focus is not only on leadership and elites but also on social and political movements as they developed on the ground.* This is not to say that leaders such as David Ben-Gurion, Hajj Amin al-Husseini, Menachem Begin, or Yasser Arafat

have not played critical roles in determining crucial decisions about our two peoples, but we must recognize that this is a protracted, identity-driven, and ethnopolitical conflict with deep roots. Through the years of prolonged violence and fear, it is not so much a government-versus-government border dispute as a classic protracted communal people-versus-people conflict. It is when focusing on our own communities rather than talking only about governments and leaders that we are able to find, in both camps, individuals and civil society organizations that have reached a high level of agreement about concrete ways of resolving our conflict.

7. *An important challenge in co-teaching and co-authoring is how to stress common stands and avoid adversarial discourse.* Israeli and Palestinian leaders have shown adversarial tendencies, as they often have, have failed to build trust, and have continued to point to the other's failures rather than to look inward and address their own inadequacies. In the pictures that we present, we do not ignore the alternative historic narrative, but we also present the voices of moderation and compromise. Even when those voices represented minority views, their insights are sometimes vindicated, often decades later, when leadership endorses their views. For example, until 1977 Israel's Labor governments stressed the "Jordanian option," which viewed the Hashemite dynasty as partners and ignored the distinctive voices of the Palestinians, even while important Israeli voices called for dialogue with the PLO as the legitimate representative of the Palestinian people, an approach that was duly formalized only with the Oslo Accords in 1993. Likewise, Palestinians advocating a two-state solution were ostracized and often assassinated, only to be vindicated in 1998 when the Palestinian National Council convened in Algiers and adopted such a policy. Likewise, the vociferous opposition of the Likud leadership—led by General Ariel Sharon—included the suggested pullout from Gaza and Jericho (in the east and center of the West Bank) in the Oslo process in 1993. However, this idea became compatible with the 1995 unilateral disengagement plan of Prime Minister Sharon, which included Gaza and four settlements in Samaria (in the north of the West Bank), closer to the city of Jenin.

8. *Understanding the asymmetries between us is an essential element of judgment.* Ugly atrocities, missed opportunities, and leadership mishaps have occurred on both sides, but we must avoid promoting a false parallelism. We must stress the difference in status between the Palestinians (the weaker party, living as an occupied people) and the Israelis (the stronger party, which occupies large parts of Palestinian territory). Although the case is in many ways an example of top-dog Israelis versus underdog Palestinians, we also must be aware of the perceptions of many Jews who see the conflict as little "David" (Israel) facing threatening "Goliath" (the Arab and Muslim worlds).

9. *In sharing our contending stories, the point is not to score debating points, or to argue with selective facts about who came first or who is acting or reacting, or to determine who has more rights.* In reality, we often face a conflict of right versus right. Judging from the stubbornness of both nations to remain on the land in spite of adverse circumstances, it can be agreed that both nations have enough claims and rights. We sense, and rather should emphasize, a common destiny: our nations are "doomed" to live together.

10. In a conflict situation, the natural tendency is to highlight the positive features of each society's history. However, *we do not need to balance the pluses or equally share the blame all through the process, as long as the picture we present recognizes change over time.* For instance, it is clear to us that in the years that preceded Israel's 1948 independence, the Zionist leadership was mostly supportive of moderate options and difficult compromises with the Palestinians, whose leadership was overwhelmingly rejectionist to all plans of reconciliation. At the same time, the peace forces in Jewish society, though insignificant, were more proactive than those well-intentioned individuals within the Arab community. In fact, an opposite trend can be discerned after 1967, when Palestinian institutions increasingly and dramatically changed their policies toward the acceptance of "the other" while fanaticism based on religious and expansionist premises developed intensively within Israeli society and political leadership. As Yeoshafat Harkabi mentioned in his landmark *Fateful Decisions,* in the first fifty years it has been the Zionists who knew to differentiate between

grand design and reality, opting as a small minority in Palestine for incremental and moderate policies. However, when the relative strength of Israel over its Arab neighbors became self-evident, it was the weakening Palestinian side that was giving away its vision of a state from the River Jordan to the Mediterranean Sea. Hence, since historic failure for achieving peace fluctuates over the years, we cannot share responsibility for it equally at all times.

11. *When the contradictory claims to tangible and intangible needs are expressed, the issue of a real conflict of rights calls for innovative ideas of conflict transformation, moving from zero-sum equations to win–win solutions.* We consider this to be not just a slogan but rather a doable approach that leads to alternatives to resolving the core issues (called the final or "permanent status" issues in the Oslo peace process), such as underground water aquifers or Jerusalem or generating new future scenarios.

12. *While the dimensions of the larger Arab–Israeli or "Middle East" conflict have fluctuated over time, we both recognize in our narratives the centrality of the Israeli–Palestinian issue.* Over time, many additional layers have been added to, or subtracted from, the original and continuous strife of the protracted communal conflict of two peoples who consider the same land to be their own. As a result, addressing the core of the issue in depth is an essential way to minimize the added complications created by other state and nonstate actors.

13. *While we recognize the importance of foreign powers in the conflict (nowadays, chiefly the United States), these outside powers have usually been unable to prevent war or impose peace.* The United States was at times able to stop armed struggle and channel such efforts into diplomacy. Yet both in the case of the 1977–1979 Begin–Sadat negotiations (Camp David I) and the 1993 Oslo peace process between Palestinians and Israelis, the main initiative was bilateral, and only later did the White House play a key role.

14. *In short, understanding the historical circumstances that in the past brought about either cooperation or confrontation can be helpful in understanding the future shape that the relations between these two nations may take, but a forward-looking approach is the best* *guarantee for resolution.* Indeed, many aspects of the future can be imagined or predicted by understanding the past. If we can agree and determine that confrontations between Arabs and Jews are a product of historical circumstances rather than a result of inherent contradictions between the two cultural systems, then we know that future relations can, to some degree, be controlled and managed by human decisions. We must seek ways to avoid repeating the historical circumstances that have led to so much confrontation in the recent past, while at the same time we must understand the common cultural dimensions and common heritage that have brought about much cooperation between Arabs and Jews in the more distant past. Yet, using lateral thinking and learning from the costly lessons and best practices for the transformation of other disputes into peaceful coexistence has an inherent value that also needs to be integrated.

II. JEWISH–ARAB RELATIONS THROUGH THE CENTURIES

If we focus on the fifteen hundred years when Arabs and Jews lived together in peace instead of on the last hundred years of conflict, we would observe much commonality between the two groups: Abrahamic religions, Semitic languages, similar archeological sites, historic periods of coexistence, and Arab–Judeo cultures, music, terminology, and body language, as well as food.[3] However, when focusing on the past hundred years, we also can highlight two distinct languages, religions, ethnicities, and preferences toward the East and West. So let us first remind ourselves of the long-term relationship. According to Shukri B. Abed, it is hardly possible to overemphasize the degree of cross-fertilization, mutual influence, and even cooperation that have existed between Arabs and Jews during many periods and in many places as they shared a common history. Although Arab–Jewish contacts have created their share of conflict, oppression, and violence, they have at other times been characterized by tolerance, close cooperation, and cross-fertilization.[4]

Summarizing Abed's important work we concur that since the inception of Islam in the seventh century, Jews living in Muslim lands have played an important part in the intellectual, cultural, economic, and even political life of various Islamic empires. In spite of several unfavorable references in the *Qur'an*, as well as occasional persecution by some rulers, Jews, as one of the *dhimmis* (protected peoples), fared, generally speaking, rather well as a minority in Islamic states.

Under the Abbasid (750–1258), Jews assumed responsible state positions under the caliphate. Within Baghdad, the Abbasid's capital, the Jewish community flourished. By the end of the twelfth century A.D. one finds a similar positive contact between Muslims and Jews in Muslim Spain. When the Muslims conquered Spain in 711 A.D., the Jews of that country welcomed the new rulers, considering them their saviors from the Visigoth Christian kingdom within which they were forced to hide their Jewish identity. Within the new regime, many of the Jews who had previously left Spain to escape religious persecution returned to Spain because they felt protected and saw much better economic prospects.

The economic and social status of Jews further improved under the tolerant rule of the Umayyad. The Jewish community in Spain flourished economically, culturally, and intellectually. Jews occupied high positions in many fields, including medicine, agriculture, commerce, and craft. Jewish scholarship and culture flourished alongside their Arab counterparts and were positively influenced by them. Jewish culture in Spain flourished in many cities to the degree that later Arab geographers referred to certain cities—including Lucena, Granada, and Tarragona—as "Jewish cities." The real cultural prosperity of the Jewish community in Spain, however, began under the rule of Abd Rahman III (912–961). Under him, such people emerged and thrived as the physician and chief negotiator Hisdai ibn Shaprut, the poet Samuel ha-Nagid (who served as vizier and commander of the army of Granada for more than twenty-five years, the astrologer Isaac ibn Albalia (who served as the court astrologer under al-Mu'tamid, who ruled from 1068 to 1091), the scholar Joseph ibn Migash (who was sent on diplomatic missions by al-Mu'tamid), and the great Talmudist Isaac Alfas.

In 1146 another politico-religious Berber dynasty of Morocco, Al-muwahhidun, conquered Muslim

Spain, which was largely under the control of another Arab group. This marked the beginning of uneasy relations between Muslims and Jews as this dynasty persecuted Jews and forced some of them to leave Spain and to seek shelter elsewhere. One of the families that suffered this fate was none other than that of the most famous Jewish thinker Moshe Ben Maymun, known in the West as Maimonides (1135–1204), who is considered to be the most famous Jewish philosopher and physician of the entire Muslim epoch.

The same observations can be made about Jewish–Muslim relations and Jewish–Arab relations during the various successive empires that ruled the Islamic world: the Seljuks, the Fatimites, the Ottoman Empire, and so on. During all these periods, and in almost all cases, one finds that Jews and Arabs continued to maintain relations of peaceful coexistence and cooperation.[5]

Understanding the historical circumstances that brought about either cooperation or confrontation can be helpful in understanding the future shape that relations between these two nations will take. Indeed, many aspects of the future can be predicted by understanding the past, for if we can determine that the confrontations between Arabs and Jews are a product of historical circumstances rather than a result of inherent contradictions between the two civilizations, then we know that future relations can, to some degree, be controlled and managed. We can avoid the historical circumstances that have led to so much confrontation in the recent past while at the same time we can understand our common cultural dimensions and common heritage, which have brought about so much cooperation between Arabs and Jews in the more distant past.

III. THE CYCLE OF WARS IN RETROSPECT: AN OVERVIEW

The first violent episodes between Arabs and Jews occurred under the British Mandate, primarily in 1921, 1929, and 1936. What eventually became a pattern of one major military confrontation in each subsequent decade has lasted until the present. We review key events in the following sections.

1. *The 1948 War of Liberation/Al Nakba:* With the final withdrawal of the British, the decla-

ration of Israel's independence on May 15, 1948, enlarged to *regional* dimensions what had been until then a *local* armed conflict between the Arab and Jewish communities in Palestine. Seven Arab states declared war on Israel, and the actual fight in Israel's southern and eastern front lasted until 1949. Israel and then Transjordan divided between themselves the land of the Palestinian state conceived in the 1947 partition.

2. *The 1956 Sinai Campaign/Suez War:* Israel's concern about the incursion of *fedayin* (armed infiltrations) through its border with Egypt and freedom of navigation in the Red Sea brought about collusion with France and the United Kingdom to reverse Egypt's president Gamal Abdel Nasser's decision to nationalize the Suez Canal. The nature of the conflagration was characteristic as a south/north dispute about sovereignty over national resources, and joint Soviet/United States pressure brought about a territorial withdrawal from Sinai.

3. *The 1967 Six-Day/June War:* This armed conflict brought Israel into confrontation with its three main neighbors, first with a preemptive strike against Egypt, then action against Syria, and then a swift military response after being attacked by Jordan. The fast victory of the Jewish state resulted, respectively, in the occupation of Sinai (including the Gaza Strip), the Golan Heights, and the West Bank. The increased support of Israel by the United States resulted in many Arab countries cutting relations with Washington and the Soviet bloc (except Romania and Cuba), severing ties with Israel, and shaping the Israel–Arab conflict into a typical East–West Cold War case. Eventually a war of attrition followed on both sides of the Suez Canal.

4. *The 1973 Yom Kippur/Ramadan/October War:* In a surprise attack, Egypt crossed the Suez Canal into Sinai and the Syrians regained part of the Golan Heights, but then Israel's troops advanced even deeper into the west side of the Suez Canal and into an enclave within Syrian territory. The Soviet Union considered sending in its own troops, and the initial reaction of the United States was to declare a nuclear alert. This act served to deter further inter-bloc escalation. Subsequent shuttle diplomacy by then U.S. Secretary of State Henry Kissinger brought about a separation of forces between Israel and both Egypt and Syria, but only after months of artillery exchange. The war precipitated an oil crisis, including a sharp price increase and a boycott of Israel's allies by Arab countries. In this we see the global reach of this new round of conflict, including fears of a nuclear war and the economic impact experienced both by oil exporters and importers.

5. *The 1982 Operation of Peace in the Galilee/ Lebanon War:* Collusion between Israel and a short-lived Christian-led government in Beirut brought about an invasion and occupation of a large part of Lebanon, including its capital, Beirut. Aimed presumably only at dismantling the PLO-dominated *Fatahland* (a forty-mile strip of land bordering southern Lebanon), at that time Defense Minister Sharon may have facilitated the displacement of Palestinian refugees through Syria into Jordan, fulfilling a master plan to replace the Hashemite Kingdom with a Palestinian state. The partial occupation lasted for nearly two decades, backed by Israel controlling a strip along its entire northern border in an alliance with a co-opted South Lebanon Army. In this war, no Arab countries came to the rescue of the Palestinians massacred in Lebanon. This reduced the dimensions of the conflict primarily to an Israeli–Palestinian conflict, with Lebanese elites divided mostly across denominational lines and militant Shiite Muslims becoming in favor of the Palestinians and Syrian proxies. With the subsequent exile of the PLO leadership to Tunis and then eruption of the first *intifada* in 1987 the communal conflict focused again on the land under dispute. The militarized response by the Israel Defense Forces, which killed more than a thousand Palestinians, provoked a Palestinian reaction of "limited violence," with fewer than a hundred Israeli casualties. (We present a more in-depth analysis within the "Cycle of Peace" section.)

6. *The 1991 Gulf War/Second Gulf War:* A new war led by the United States in 1991 (considered to be the "Second Gulf War" when the Iran–Iraq War of the 1980s is referred to as the "First Gulf War") successfully caused Saddam Hussein's troops to withdraw from occupied Kuwait and resulted in Iraq's subsequent loss of control over northern and southern Kuwaiti territory. For the first time, Israel was asked by the United States, and agreed, to refrain from reacting militarily to an Arab attack, this time to the long-range missile at-

tacks of the Baghdad regime. Paradoxically, this time the Jewish state was indirectly assisted by a large coalition fighting Saddam Hussein, including both Egypt and Syria.

7. *The Second Intifada:* In September 2000, the second *intifada* began. Compared to the limited violence of the first *intifada*, it was highly militarized and given the eponym *al-Aqsa Intifada* after the mosque on the Temple Mount (also known as the al-Haram al-Sharif) in Jerusalem. This uprising was triggered by the visit to the Temple Mount of Ariel Sharon, the Likud opposition leader. At the very least, this visit further provoked mostly civilian Palestinian and unarmed Israeli victims to suicide bombings and targeted assassinations. What one hundred years earlier was perceived as a conflict motivated by two national movements of liberation had become predominantly a religious one, fueled by fanatic messianic nationalist Jews and extreme political Islamists. This added a dangerous component of fundamentalism to the ongoing struggle. The continuous chain of armed acts and retaliations took place without direct military involvement of any Arab country, although it was encouraged by such Islamist movements as Hezbollah in Lebanon and the Islamist regime in Iran. The unfortunate outcome resulted indirectly in a growing recognition by most on both sides, as well as globally, of the need for a two-state solution.

IIIA. THE ORIGINS OF ARAB–PALESTINIAN AND JEWISH–ZIONIST NATIONALISM (1870s–1948)

In this section, we briefly explain the parallels in the development of both the Arab–Palestinian and Jewish–Zionist movements during the last period of the Ottoman Empire and the British occupation of the Holy Land until the expiration in 1948 of its mandate over Palestine.

The formation of the Jewish national movement was due to three distinct factors: the diffusion of nationalism throughout Europe, the impact of new forms of anti-Semitism, and the keeping of the strong relation between the Jewish religion and the "Promised Land."

The *first factor* reminds us that during the second half of the nineteenth century the sentiment that nations can have a legitimate claim to a state of their own enjoyed wide popularity, and numerous struggles led to the eventual independence of many who had been subjugated for generations. A case in point is Poland. After being split since the seventeenth century under Russia's tsar, the Austro–Hungarian empire, and Germany, Poland once again became independent and united at the end of World War I. The decline of monarchies in Europe raised the issue of people's self-determination. Large segments of Jewish people who were scattered around Europe dreamed that the idea of a nation-state should apply to them.

The *second factor* relates to disillusionment caused by discrimination against Jews in the most advanced and enlightened European states, such as France and eventually Germany. Generation after generation of people had been resigned to the authoritarian Tsarist rule in Russia. Persecutions included pogroms and other raids against innocent Jews, as well as restrictions applied to property, movement, residence, and studies. Much of the movement's origins were attributed to the despotic nature of the regime, so not a few Jews began embracing socialist ideas with the hope that a new ideology based on equality to all would erase ages-old patterns of suffering against a minority whose only crime was to attempt to remain different. France was in many ways an example of an enlightened nation that offered hope and a new relationship to Jews. Beginning with Napoleon, discriminatory laws against Jews and the official banning of the call for formation of a new Sanhedrin (council of judges) to represent World Jewry were defined as examples of discrimination and were no longer tolerated.

Theodore Herzl, an assimilated Viennese journalist, who earlier thought that the solution for avoiding persecution against Jews was conversion to Catholicism, came to Paris as a correspondent and in 1894 encountered the trial of Captain Alfred Dreyfus. Dreyfus, a non-practicing Jew, was charged with and found guilty of spying for the German enemy, while the upper echelons of the army were aware that the real informant was an officer with a noble pedigree. The writer Émile Zola, who with other liberals denounced this new form of anti-Semitism, revealed the conspiracy that pointed to Dreyfus as a scapegoat. Herzl understood that the issue was not only state policies that

discriminated against people but also much deeper societal trends that could not be easily uprooted. For a majority of those Jews who wanted to escape the persecution of the ruthless tsar and Catholic anti-Semites in Europe, the idea of going to another continent was seen as a way of creating a new home, but a minority started to believe that the self-realization of the Jews was not going to take place there either. In 1896 Herzl wrote the famous *Der Judenstaat* (*The Jewish State*). A year later he managed to convene in Basel, Switzerland, a large number of Zionist leaders who formed the World Zionist Organization (WZO). Zionist groups had been active since the 1860s, especially in Russia, but they were united as WZO members in a political movement seeking world legitimacy and power to assert their claim and grant them the possibility of settling in a community and eventually declaring a state in *Eretz Israel*.

This brings us to the *third factor:* the long-standing connection of the Jewish religion with a specific territory, from which Jews were dispersed into exile two thousand years earlier. Since then, Jews have been praying "Next year in Jerusalem." Forgetting Jerusalem was like forgetting one's right arm. Mount Zion was for Jews a symbol and the source of the Old Testament. With this vivid connection, it was obvious for most nationalistic thinkers that the return to Zion was the only option. Even in 1904, sensing the urgency of providing a national home for the Jews escaping persecution, a minority in the World Zionist Organization called for settling in Uganda, but in 1904 the majority of the delegates refused to trade off their deep-rooted link with the Promised Land, as the covenant between Moses and God had established. Some have said that dispersed Jews around the world carried the scrolls of the Bible as their "portable state." By the end of the nineteenth century, the idea of fulfilling their longing for Jerusalem became a reality, a doable proposition. "Nothing can stand against the will of people," it was said. The tragedy was that this was not an "empty land for a landless people." For more than a millennium an established Arab community not only had been settled there but had come to consider the land genuinely theirs by birth and right.

Herzl tried to secure a charter for a Jewish settlement from the Ottoman sultan and from the German Kaiser but did not. After Herzl's death in 1904, the new leader of the WZO, Dr. Chaim

Weizman, continued efforts to secure the support of leading world powers to legitimize and eventually help to realize Zionist claims. Weizman, was a great admirer of the British and preferred to associate the WZO's predicament with the new colonial designs of the British, so he worked together with important Zionist leaders to receive their support. After the outbreak of the World War I, WZO leaders' learned that Mark Sykes, on behalf of Her Majesty's government, and François George-Picot, on behalf of the French Republic, had agreed to a division of Palestine that was supposed to ensure joint dominion. Other potential allies, such as Russia and Italy, were also putting their claims on part of the soon-to-be-defeated Ottoman Empire. Through excellent diplomacy, in 1917 Sykes' Zionist partner, Nahum Sokolov, secured a declaration of sympathy with Zionists' aspirations for a Jewish home in the land of their ancestors from the Director General of the French Quai D'Orsay, Jules Cambon. This statement was used to further lobby the British government to rush into the proclamation of a similar statement, as was issued on behalf of the Cabinet on November 2, 1917, by Lord Arthur Balfour, and known as the Balfour Declaration.

The outcome of World War I was a watershed for the Zionist movement. This unilateral promise was legitimized in the Versailles Peace Conference of 1919 and a year later by formalizing British rule in a mandate on behalf of the League of Nations. The promising new era started with appointment of a pro-Zionist British high commissioner, Lord Herbert Samuel. Over the next decade, the relationship between Zionists and local authorities started to cool as a greater awareness emerged regarding the hostility of the local Arab population to the new *aliyot* (Hebrew for "immigration waves"), the gradual disposition of land, and fears regarding further plans. The change of government in London also precipitated a revision of official policy, which led to commissions of inquiry coming to Palestine and checking the outbreaks of violence. The commissions blamed not only the perpetrators but also Jewish immigration and settlement. Two white papers were issued, both limiting the development of the independent Zionist movement in Palestine.

The obstacles for immigration to Palestine became even more serious after 1933 when Jews started to escape from Nazi Germany and eventually from the vast territories under Hitler's rule. In 1938 an appeal devised at a conference in Évian, France, and addressed to the international community to accept the thousands of escaping Jews was met by only one country, the Dominican Republic, which was willing to accept only four thousand Jews with agricultural experience. Thus, immigration to Palestine became a top objective. Many ships were stopped, and Jews were sent back to their eventual deaths in concentration camps in Europe. Other Jews were sent to a detention camp in Cyprus. The determination of Zionists to continue with illegal immigration through World War II and beyond was confirmed at the WZO conference held in 1942 at the Biltmore Hotel in New York City, during which the WZO openly declared its aim of establishing a Jewish state in *Eretz Israel.*

On the other hand, the Arab people were looking for allies against the oppressive, corrupt, and arbitrary Ottoman rule, and many Arab leaders sealed their loyalties with France (particularly Christians in Greater Syria) and with Great Britain (led by tribal leaders in the Arabian Peninsula). This support came on top of Britain's already strong presence in Egypt. Through an exchange of letters in 1915 between Sir Henry McMahon, the British High Commissioner in Cairo, and Sharif Hussein, the Emir of Hedjaz, the Arabs' expectations of independence were generated by interpretations of the British mentioning specific locations on an unwritten map, which implied the inclusion of most Arab territories.

What led to the misinterpretation of the Balfour Declaration was that Sharif Hussein was not aware that the *villayet* (Turkish for "province") of western Beirut (roughly equivalent to most of Palestine) was not included in the land that was to be given to the Arabs. This news was conveyed to him through correspondence with Sir McMahon. The latter was not in a position to promise Palestine to the Arabs, regardless of the fact that during World War I about 700,000 Muslims were living there, as were 53,000 Christians and 56,000 Jews.

The dual promise meant that the Balfour Declaration's promise—which stated that no acts should be conducted to the detriment of the native Arab population—could not be honored. The clause initially was not followed and later was only partially respected. Most official versions of the history of both sides highlight the armed confrontations or riots that took place in 1921, 1929, and 1936; and often triggered people-to-people clashes. Still, it is important to mention that Palestinian families were known to rescue Jewish neighbors in life-threatening situations in Hebron and Jewish settlers were known to offer friendly gestures toward Arabs when the pressure to leave their lands was mounting in the 1947–1948 war.

Over time, Palestinian nationalism has grown into a distinct submovement within the larger Arab movement. To understand its genesis, we cannot avoid exploring the historical development of Palestinian nationalism in the context of the bigger pan-Arab ideology—that is, Arab nationalism.

Palestine was part of the Ottoman Empire, which ruled western Asia for almost five hundred years. From the seventh century until almost the mid-twentieth century, Palestine was predominantly a Muslim country, although Christian Arabs and Jewish communities also shared this small land. Then the Ottoman Empire encountered many problems: first was the loss of its centralized system of government; second was Turkey's involvement in many wars with Russia, Prussia, and Austria; third was warlords taking action on their own and imposing additional taxes on the poor peasants who comprised various ethnic and national minorities.[6] Moreover, the ideology of the West swept the nation-states in response to the French Revolution. In addition, the ethnic and national minorities always wanted reform, though they never achieved it. The result was more and more frustration for everyone.

Secessionists of many of the minorities grouped themselves into political parties to try to achieve their independence from the Ottoman Empire. Arabs were the ones who really carried the banners of Islam and accepted Ottoman domination of the Islamic Empire. However, when nationalism grew within Turkish society, the imposition of Turkification on all national minorities led to the revocation of this acceptance by national minorities and by the Muslim Arabs who in particular felt that they were treated as second-class citizens. Economic repression and total control of these minorities prompted the feeling that the Turkish sultans were no longer ruling by the principles and tenets of Islam. In response, rebellion against the Ottomans began underground at first and then in the open. One of the most important turning points occurred when, for the first time, the East (meaning the Arab and Muslim world and the Ottoman Empire) was exposed to the West's culture, history, and politics. This crossroad led to the belief among Arabs that Muslim civilization was no longer the leading culture.

This turning point in Arab history started with Napoleon's invasion of Egypt in 1798, at which time the Mamluk governor, Muhammed Ali Pasha, wanted to secede from the Ottoman Empire. However, when Napoleon invaded Egypt he brought all kinds of sophisticated technology with him, such as weapons and a printing press. The Arabs were surprised to learn the extent to which the Ottoman Empire was backward in terms of technology. Consequently, Muhammed Ali sent officers to Paris. When the delegation returned five years later, it opened schools of translation and started to translate into Arabic the literature of the French Revolution and such Western concepts as the nation-state.

Two ideologies emerged at that time. First came the Arab Christian intellectual idea that the Arabic language was the determining factor of Arab identity. Arab Christians in the Ottoman Empire, who felt they were treated as third-class citizens, had ties with the West and spoke more than on language, so they were able to make direct contact with the West. For them, expressing nationalism was best achieved through reviving the Arabic language and not religion, and soon these individuals became leaders. Separation between church and state provided Arab Christians with the same privileges enjoyed by Muslims. Second came the Islamic reformers who did not want to touch Islam but wanted to get rid of certain ideas that distorted Islam, which in the final analysis made all the Ottoman sovereigns abusers of power by their misinterpretation of Islam. Islamic fundamentalists considered Islamic reformism at a later stage to be heresy because they thought that reformists were trying to misinterpret Islam in the context of alien Western ideals. Between Islamic reformism and Arab nationalism, forces were joined against Ottomanism, which represented authoritarianism and repression.

It is important at this point to talk about Palestinian nationalism. The ideas of nationalism and nation-state really found ground in the Fertile Crescent (eastern Mediterranean region) in the latter part of the nineteenth century. However, the development of Arab nationalism was straightforward because the Arabs shared the same language, culture, and history; were rooted in their land; and mostly did not migrate. Several factors led to this sense of shared identity being expressed in a more explicit national form. By 1918 a political movement based in Damascus and Beirut was demanding the independence of Levantine (bordering on the eastern Mediterranean) Arabs from the Turks, after many requests for reform had failed. At that time Palestinians were part of the general Arab national movement that swept the Levantine area. At the San Remo conference in 1920, Britain was given Palestine under its own mandate system. The British Mandate came into existence with its first high commissioner, Herbert Samuel, who was a Zionist and was assigned by the British government to be the commissioner of Palestine. In Arab eyes, Britain acted unfairly. While Britain has been accused of favoring the Arabs on paper, in reality it never curbed Jewish immigration or the buying of land in Palestine by Zionists.

Palestinian nationalism passed through three phases. The *first phase* (1921–1929) is referred to as "peaceful resistance" to the British Mandate. The Palestinians used obstructionist methods, such as civil disobedience (not paying taxes, etc.). In opposing the British, the *second phase* is portrayed as the radicalization process of the Palestinian national movement, which started with the Wailing Wall incident in 1929—the result of a long-running dispute between Muslims and Jews over access to the Western (or "Wailing") Wall—and ended in 1935 with the formation of the Arab Higher Committee and the emergence of Palestinian political parties. The *third phase* was the outright rebellion in 1936, which ended in 1939 with the downfall of traditional leadership in Palestine.

In discussing the social structure of Palestine, it is important to note that the society was traditional, primordial, and tribal, with three social divisions: Bedouins, rurals, and urban centers. Political leaders were from the "notables" (as the ruling elite were called) of the urban centers, and rurals were those who fought and carried swords. The political center was in the cities, and Jerusalem was considered the main location for political activity. When the British came to colonize Palestine, the first thing they did was change the power structure of the notables,

such as the two top political figures: the mayor and the *mufti* of Palestine. The highest religious figure was from the Husseini family; however, two families held most political control: the Husseini and the Nashashibi. Politics of the notables, which were linked to the politics of factionalism that also swept the PLO leadership structure, were considered an important part of Palestinian history.

The Nashashibi family controlled the Islamic *Shariah* courts and controlled considerable amounts of land. According to Islamic *Shariah* law, when the *mufti* dies, an election should take place and *ulamahs* (religious leaders) will determine the elections and decide who will be the next mufti. The British realized that the elected candidate belonged to the opposition, which put the Husseini family in an awkward position. After a riot in Jaffa in 1920 the British ousted the mayor of Jerusalem, Musa Kazen, who was a Husseini, and appointed Rougheb Nashashibi, a leader from this extended family in his place. During the 1920 revolt, a young man named Amin Husseini was considered to be the inciter of the revolt. He fled to Transjordan as a result of the British decision to allow capital punishment. When Sir Herbert Samuel became the first high commissioner to Palestine in 1920, he brought with him as his legal advisor a British Jew by the name of Norman Bentwich, who advised officials to bring back Amin Husseini to create balance.

The encounter between the Zionist and the native Arab population in Palestine was not a success story. Although a few thousand Jews who stayed in the land or came before the 1860s resided in the ancient cities of Jerusalem, Safad, Hebron, Haifa, Tiberias, and Jaffo and were living in friendly relations with their neighbors, the new waves of immigration posed a great threat to the indigenous population. In addition to settling the land and starting new agricultural ventures, at times on land purchased from absentee owners to the detriment of the working peasants, some of the socialist ideas were also perceived to be a threat by the traditional Arab establishment. Members of the new *ishuv* (Jewish settlement, community) brought with them innovative and even revolutionary ideas. Most of their actions between the two world wars were introspective. They tried to build the pillars for a future state in a secluded society but did not prioritize the building of relations with their already difficult Arab neighbors. Some of the more militaristic Zionists—such as Ze'ev Jabotinsky with his Iron Wall concept—did not believe that the Arabs would accept the Jewish state unless convinced that the Jews could not be thrown out or that the socialists were fully merged in building their new society based on new forms of production. Eventually the two trends converged and leaders concurred that the "Arab question" did not need to be fully explored at that time. The fact is that the low priority given in the Zionist agenda to relations with the local Arab population did not allow for anything more than sporadic efforts to reach out. On the other hand, the official leadership of the Arab community was not amenable to such contact with the Zionist "colonizers." Hence, the idea of splitting the land became by default the more realistic option. The British endorsed this idea through the Peel Commission of 1935. It was later endorsed by the UN, through the partition plan offered in 1947 by the United Nations Special Commission on Palestine.

Was the conflict unavoidable? Most likely the collision course was set from the early stages. Yet even after the frustration experienced by the Arabs in relation to the fulfillment of the full territorial promise in the aftermath of World War I, Sharif Hussein's son Feysal agreed in a draft document with the Zionist leader Chaim Weizman to a mutual recognition of their rule, respectively, over Lebanon/Syria and Palestine. Such initiative was not implemented, given that the 1919 Paris Peace Conference granted a mandate to the French and not to the Hashemite to rule over Lebanon and Syria. A second opportunity was the partition plans suggested in 1935 by a British commission of inquiry led by Lord Earl Peel and the UN in 1947. The Palestinian leadership was unwilling to compromise when a disproportionate amount of land was promised to the Jews relative to the population ratio, and that may be an added reason for a more radical rejection of a Jewish state in this Land of Islam.

IIIB. FROM THE WAR OF LIBERATION/*AL NAKBA* IN 1948 TO THE 1967 SIX-DAY/JUNE WAR

From a Jewish perspective, the immediate reaction to Israel's independence on May 15, 1948, was a declaration of war by seven Arab countries, which ended in the Jewish state victory and an enlarging of the territories promised by the 1947 UN partition plan. Israeli officials, in collusion with King Abdullah of Transjordan, conducted a secret negotiation that resulted in splitting between them the West Bank and, after a real military confrontation, a divided Jerusalem. Israel improved its borders and territorial control from 55 percent of Palestine to 78 percent, following the armistice agreements signed with Egypt, Jordan, Lebanon, and Syria in 1949. Between 1949 and 1967 the "armistice lines" became the de facto borders of the State of Israel, recognized as such by the international community and by international law. During these years, no Arab Palestinian state was created in the West Bank, which was occupied and annexed by Jordan in 1950, or in the Gaza Strip, which was under Egyptian military control. The human cost of the war was high (1 percent of the 600,000 Jews in Palestine were killed), and approximately three-fourths of the Arab native population found themselves being removed from their homes and put into refugee camps, mostly in Jordan, Lebanon, and Syria. The figures fluctuate according to contending calculations. Perhaps close to 700,000 Arabs went into exile and 133,000 stayed; others returned by themselves or on a small reunification-of-families plan. The official Israeli version is that most Arabs left of their own volition as a result of the pressure exerted by the Arab governments, which wanted to pave the way for the bombardment and maneuvers of the expectedly victorious Arab armies. On the other hand, the official Arab version is that massacres perpetuated by extremist factions, such as the one committed by Menachem Begin's *Irgun* in Deir Yassin in the outskirts of Jerusalem, as well as deportation acts of mainstream Prime Minister David Ben-Gurion's *Haganah* army, were responsible for their forceful eviction. Books based on currently available official Israeli documents seem to corroborate a mixed picture comprised of fear and panic accompanied by decisions for deportation adopted by local Israeli commanders and official policies to not have Arab populations staying near the frontiers, which all bordered enemy countries.[7]

The leadership and vast majority of the population of Israel were willing to sign a permanent treaty based on the existing borders of the 1949 armistice lines, including a divided Jerusalem.

Under the short tenure of Prime Minister Moshe Sharett, they were even willing to consider the return of a small number of Palestinian refugees. Overall, the consensus was that such an option was not met due to Arab intransigence. Hence, the main effort continued to be introspective. The new "Law of Return" encouraged Jews to come back to their homeland, which multiplied their numbers threefold in eight years. Such an unprecedented historic effort required food rationing for the entire population and the temporary settlement in tents and provisional housing of immigrants—mostly Holocaust survivors arriving in the immediate post–War World II period, and subsequently mostly Jews from Arab countries through the 1950s.

While some indirect and secret contacts with Egypt could have led to some possible agreements, the conventional wisdom of the Israelis was that peace had no chance. Civil societies on both sides were not involved in dialogue. With Jabotinsky's Iron Wall perception of the enemy, it was premature to expect the Arabs to agree to Jewish existence and build a strong Israel. They had no choice but to accept Jews and then negotiate from a position of strength, which has continued to be part of the prevailing ethos.

The 1948 war also strengthened the "Jordanian option," namely that the partner for peace for the Zionists was Sharif Hussein's son, Abdallah. In a secret agreement he agreed that Israel could keep part of the territory promised to the Palestinians in the 1947 UN Partition Plan, while Transjordan would annex the larger part of the West Bank to become the Kingdom of Jordan. Hence, in the view of moderate Israelis the remaining issue needed to obtain peace was a gesture of acceptance of some of the Arab refugees displaced during the war. While waiting for a partner of peace, efforts of civil rights activists within Israel turned domestically to a struggle against discriminatory policies directed at the Arab minority. In the years before 1967, several domestic Arab–Jewish rapprochements occurred within Israel, with projects aimed at fighting against such restrictions as the military authority governing the Arab population of Israel. Most human rights–oriented Israeli forces focused on Arab–Jewish coexistence until 1966, when Arabs came to be regulated a military government.

From an Arab perspective, *Al Nakba* was catastrophic not only in the sense of so many lives and so much property being lost in the war against the Jews, but also in the precarious situation resulting as the majority of Palestinian people became refugees scattered in alien lands. Over the next decades, three main groups became instruments in the hands of others. In Israel, the remaining minority became second-class citizens yet retained full voting rights, mostly represented in the Knesset (Israeli parliament) by the Communist Party. With the incorporation of the West Bank into Transjordan, the West Bankers and the 1948 refugees living there were forcefully co-opted to become Jordanians, the subjects of foreign Hashemite kings, and they joined their displaced brethren who had found refuge in the East Bank. While discriminated against and mistrusted by the ruling elite, at least they were granted documentation that allowed them to travel, and eventually some of them attempted to settle in other countries, such as Kuwait. What was worse was the situation for refugees living in temporary camps in Lebanon, Syria, and the Gaza Strip under Egyptian rule. Added to their daily suffering was the fact that they were denied access to the nationality of their host countries.

Given the subsequent shock and despair, it would have been considered tantamount to an act of treason for any well-intentioned Palestinian leader to come to the Israelis with a message of peace. The only place where cooperation did exist in those early years of the conflict was between the marginalized Marxist groups that found mutual coexistence feasible on a class, rather than an ethnic, level.

Suffering a total loss and weak, manipulated leadership, as well as intra-Arab rivalry, the main belief among most Palestinians then scattered in the Middle East was that only the triumph of pan-Arabism could solve their problem. They were not in control of their destiny until 1964, when Fatah (the Palestinian National Liberation Movement) and the PLO became the Palestinians' representative organizations and triggered some new, now dominant, strategies through their own institutions.[8] At that time, the use of armed struggle was seen by the dispossessed Palestinians as the only way to redress the injustice of the creation of Israel. Ideologically and practically, no legitimacy was given to dialogue with the enemy. The Palestinian National Charter (PNC) of 1964 and the amended National

Charter of 1968, drawn up during drafting of the fourth PNC using the resolutions of the second and third PNCs, emphasized the total liberation of Palestine through armed struggle and self-reliance leading to the creation of sociopolitical and economic institutions that could cater to the needs of a shattered society.

IIIC. ISRAEL IN CONTROL OF THE PALESTINIAN TERRITORIES: FROM 1967 UNTIL THE GULF WAR

The 1967 Six-Day/June War followed a slow escalation of Fatah-sponsored infiltrations and bombs, low-scale Israeli retaliatory acts, artillery exchange, a decision by President Nasser to evict the UN peacekeeping force from Sinai, the closure of the Straits of Tirana in the Gulf of Akaba, the unsuccessful effort of Israeli diplomacy to secure international action for freedom of navigation, massive demonstrations in Cairo and elsewhere calling for the destruction of Israel, signs of preparation for a combined Egyptian attack in the southern and eastern fronts of Israel, and eventually a surprise preemptive strike of Israeli planes that destroyed the air force capability of Egypt. In the subsequent six days, the Israel Defense Forces conquered the entire Sinai. In spite of a message transmitted from Prime Minister Eshkol to King Hussein to keep out, the monarch felt that he could not remain idle and, perhaps misled by false information from Egypt about alleged military victories, he ordered artillery fire on Jewish West Jerusalem and initiated infantry occupation of border posts. Israel then destroyed all convoys coming from the east to the West Bank, conquering the latter and, after heavy fighting, the Old City with its holy places. And within the six days, it also consolidated the take over of the Golan Heights from Syria.

By generalizing, it could be said that the June 1967 War was perceived by Israeli Jews to be a case of an imposed military confrontation that threatened Israel's very survival. The resulting control over the territories was deemed necessary for security reasons, rather than as the result of premeditated annexationist policy. For this reason, Israeli Jews overwhelmingly have not seen the occupation as a colonial one but rather as an unforeseen outcome of an unwanted conflagration because they believe the territories were taken in a just war, one launched by Arab states wishing to destroy Israel.[9] A considerable portion of the Israeli public perceived itself as a nation facing the danger of annihilation.

Israel's occupation of vast territories, bigger than the country itself, produced a polarization within its society between two "camps." On the one hand, the more nationalistic religious and secular wing calling for the annexation of territories grouped themselves in the *Eretz Israel Hashlema* movement (in Hebrew, this literarily means "the complete land of Israel"). Triggered by the new territorial gains, this group "represented the revival of a traditional ideology never renounced by some groups within Israel that had now found new relevance."[10] The Six-Day War was explained in a memorial speech by its victorious military leader Yitzhak Rabin to be a war of self-defense, not one for purposes of conquest. He said that the territories were to be seen as a guarantee for peace. However, soon after the war, the Labor-led government was "pragmatically" experimenting with the crippling annexation by encouraging military/civilian outposts in strategic areas. Labor's reluctance to take a clear stand was recognizable to "doves" and "hawks" within its ranks. By then the settlers' *Gush Emunim* ("Block of Faith") movement had started. Around 1974 settlers started to push for the establishment of their own "illegal" settlements throughout the entirety of the Occupied Territories and announced a return to the "old homes" in Hebron. On the other hand, the "Movement for Peace and Security" could be seen as a countermovement, but it is clear that it would have developed even if the Land of Israel movement had never been formed. For the peace movement, the Six-Day War provided the opportunity to solve the problem of Israel–Arab relations.[11]

The popular terms *right* and *left,* used elsewhere in the world to characterize the forces supporting more capitalist and working-class policies, correlate to a large extent with political groups in Israel, although one could find within the *kibbutz* movement some annexation trends and, among industrialists and large entrepreneurs, a large number supportive of a meaningful compromise with Palestinians. Likewise, within both Labor and Likud, it was possible to find individuals approaching the territorial preferences and policies of the other. Within the two "camps," a silent majority of the Jewish population has been indecisive and willing to follow leadership on such crucial decisions.

Considering the Labor Party's politically pragmatic socialist–democratic platform, which advocated the return of the Occupied Territories for the sake of peace, the Israeli Labor governments in power until 1977 should have enhanced the development of democratic and peaceful tendencies among the West Bank Palestinians. In fact, however, during the first several years of the occupation the Israeli Labor government cultivated alliances with traditional and conservative leaders in the West Bank, who were neither democratic nor socialist. This government was also inclined to trade the West Bank for peace with Jordan but not with the Palestinians, whom Prime Minister Golda Meir, for example, would not consider a nation. Although the Labor government acknowledged for the first time in 1974 the existence of a Palestinian "problem," it continued until its demise in 1977 to seek a Jordanian solution.

From previous European experience, a question that comes to our minds is, To what extent does a colonial situation affect the democratic values of a people in a metropolis? The Occupied Territories are adjacent to the pre-1967 Israel; they are not separate or remote, as were the historical European colonies. Such geographic proximity introduces associations with the type of determinism required to ensure "vital space" (or *lebensraum*)—secure borders and a reservoir for potential Jewish immigration—and the demographic prevalence of a Jewish majority. Furthermore, the consolidation of a Jewish nation-state may still be at a premature stage. Israel's current boundaries are not yet historically well grounded. Israel is a new state, where melting-pot ideas are considered necessary for the formulation of a strong national spirit. The conception of Israel as a Jewish state (rather than as a state for Jews to come to if desired or needed, as well as with equality to all its citizens) does have exclusivist connotations. It puts the remaining 20 percent of non-Jews in a position of unequal access to the same opportunities, a policy rationalized by many of Israel's Jews because of their Arab co-citizens' shared traits with their enemies in the rest of the Middle East.

Israeli governments' expansionist policies came to the fore at a time of postcolonialism, when the processes of self-determination reached an advanced stage all around the globe. The conquest of territories and the expulsion, extermination, or subjugation of populations was a common albeit declining practice until World War II, but only a look into the past can corroborate such policies now that the international protection of human rights has gained a high level of legitimacy.

If the 1967 war gave Israelis a sense of security even when a war of attrition continued along the Suez Canal, the surprise combined attack of Egypt and Syria in the Yom Kippur/Ramadan/October 1973 war was a reality shock and a reminder that the state was not invulnerable. The conception of the impenetrability of the Bar Lev Line (a chain of fortifications built by Israel along the eastern coast of the Suez Canal after it captured the Sinai Peninsula from Egypt during the Six-Day War) became a trap that caused hundreds of Israeli casualties. Some of the *kibbutzim* in the Golan Heights were evacuated when faced with the initial offensive of the Syrian troops. The quick mobilization and excellent military strategy of the Israelis, aided by the United States with a quick refurbishing of military software and hardware, brought a swift recovery over the previously occupied territories of Egypt and Syria, as well as a new incursion into both countries that crossed the Suez Canal and stopped only a few hours away from Cairo and at artillery distance from Damascus. Israel's advance was also stopped by Henry Kissinger with a stalemate, providing for a "no defeat, no victory" policy, whence he became the shuttle diplomat negotiating on both fronts for a separation of forces based on Israeli partial withdrawal. The feeling that the war was a "treacherous attack" on the holiest Jewish day, along with anger against Golda Meir's reluctance to launch a last-minute, though perhaps futile, preemptive strike, further polarized Israelis. A sign that Arabs could not be trusted brought back the concept of a garrison state. This sentiment prevailed and led voters to punish Labor in the 1977 elections and look for the toughest candidate, represented by then Likud leader Menachem Begin. Meanwhile, racist Rabbi Meir Kahane started to speak about the transfer of the "fifth column," the peaceful Arab community that was becoming self-reliant within Israel.

The new facts on the ground for the Palestinians of the West Bank and Gaza were that they were both now formally under the control of one authority: Israel. The possibility of a joint future in an independent entity was regained, as was the understanding that a victorious Israel was a reality, and as such that perhaps the more realistic end would be the now new chance to have a state next to Israel, a sort of new partition. In fact two main factions developed among the Palestinians: those in exile, using the term *Diaspora* as coined in relation to the Jewish people, and those in the Occupied Territories, whose main purpose was their determination to stay in the land—*summud* ("steadfastness" in Arabic)—and not to become refugees, some for a second time. While accepting of being subordinated to the PLO in exile, a process of leadership formation with distinct characteristics was shaped.

Democratic trends and institutions have in fact developed among the Palestinians in the West Bank since 1967 through the formation of many social, professional, and municipal bodies, most of which were elected and operated democratically.[12] They conducted de facto political activities and through a variety of newspapers and journals freely expressed political opinions and views, including severe anti-Israeli expressions. Simultaneously, alongside a prolonged and vigorous struggle against the Israeli occupation, since 1967 significant tendencies have appeared among the West Bank population toward accommodation and coexistence with Israel. The Israeli military authorities, while prohibiting the formation of new political parties, maintained part of the previous quasi-democratic political system in the West Bank. They permitted and often encouraged the functioning of municipalities and village councils in accordance with the 1955 Jordanian law that allowed only men beyond age twenty-one who paid property taxes—primarily members of the wealthy classes—to vote. Indeed, most of the town councilors (and certainly the village *sheikhs*) who operated in the West Bank following the 1967 war and those elected in the 1972 municipal elections belonged to traditional, conservative, rich families. Most advocated the return of the West Bank to Jordan as part of a political agreement with Israel. Yet a few personalities, notably the mayor of Hebron, *Sheikh* Muhammad Ali al Ja'bari, and a small

group of more progressive intellectuals, such as lawyer Aziz Shihada and Dr. al-Taji al-Faruqi, suggested the establishment of a Palestinian entity or state that would peacefully coexist with Israel. Some of these progressive personalities called for the convening of a popular Palestinian congress to discuss these issues and a constituent assembly to elect a new leadership to initiate direct negotiations with Israel.

This new position was articulated and developed by the Palestine National Front (PNF), which was established in 1973 by the outlawed Palestinian Communist Party (PCP), some followers of Fatah, the Democratic Front for the Liberation of Palestine (DFLP), and representatives from labor unions, professional associations, student councils, and other groups. The PCP agenda of a two-state solution to the Palestinian–Israeli dispute, to be achieved by political means, won over significant sections of the Palestinian urban intelligentsia and workers in the West Bank. Unlike the PLO's notion of a secular democratic state, the communist ideas were more pragmatic than those of the PLO. Such pressure was also expressed by a group of mayors elected in the 1976 free elections in the West Bank. Fahd Qawasmah of Hebron, Elias Freij of Bethlehem, and Rashad al-Shawwa of Gaza were among those advocating a peaceful coexistence between the State of Israel and a Palestinian state in the West Bank and Gaza and welcomed U.S. President Jimmy Carter's speech of March 1977 calling for the establishment of a Palestinian homeland in the West Bank and Gaza and initially praised Egyptian President Anwar Sadat's historical visit to Jerusalem in November 1977.

Prime Minister Begin, backed by his hard-line comrades, notably Ariel Sharon, adopted an uncompromising policy regarding the Camp David talks, while prompting Moshe Dayan and Ezer Weizman to resign in 1980 from the Israeli cabinet. With Ariel Sharon as defense minister after 1981, a series of harsh measures were aimed by Israel at eliminating Palestinian representatives and democratically elected institutions and organizations. Several elected mayors were dismissed, the National Guidance Committee (NGC) was outlawed, universities were periodically closed, and newspapers became subject to heavy political censorship. More Arab lands were confiscated while new Jewish settlements were established in the West Bank, and various aggressive and illegal activities of the *Gush Emunim* settlers were tolerated by the Israeli government.

In place of elected officers, the Israeli government endeavored to promote but eventually failed to install an alternative Palestinian leadership, the "Village Leagues." Those individuals were neither elected by nor representative of the West Bank residents but were composed of traditional rural families who collaborated with the Israeli military administration. Moreover, the removal of the representative, partly democratically elected West Bank leaders did not stop the democratization process among the West Bank Palestinians. On the contrary, it enhanced the process. Indeed, partly in reaction to the elimination of the top elected leaders and national institutions, partly as a defense mechanism vis-à-vis Israeli repression, the democratization process further expanded among the grassroots of the Palestinian community through the growing number of and membership in trade unions; professional associations; women, student, and youth movements; and the like. An increasing number of Palestinians regarded their participation in these organizations as a major way to combat Israeli occupation and establish democratic institutions. Thus, for the first time the notion of democracy became, alongside the ideas of national solidarity and struggle against occupation, a major ethos among West Bank Palestinians.

Evidently, the PLO, under Chairman Arafat at the time, vehemently opposed both the return of the West Bank to Jordan and the creation of an independent state in the framework of a political agreement with Israel. This organization was then formally committed to the total destruction of Israel through an armed struggle. Not only did the PLO threaten the lives of Palestinians who supported the establishment of a Palestinian state in the West Bank, but the idea was still premature and heretical among most Palestinians in the West Bank, notably the modern urban intelligentsia and followers of the various radical groups (including multiple guerrilla organizations, the Arab Nationalist movement, the Ba'th Party, and a militant wing of the Communist Party).

Yet this phase was characterized by a marked revision of the PLO objectives, from total liberation to a democratic secular state in which Christians, Muslims, and Jews could live together harmo-

niously. After the October 1973 war, the PLO embarked on a pragmatic course culminating in the declaration of a Palestinian state in the Occupied Territories and the ultimate acceptance of a two-state solution in 1988. This historic decision was not made in a vacuum; it was, rather, a response to such successive important events as the Lebanese Civil War, and the Egypt–Israel peace treaty, the 1982 Israeli invasion of Lebanon, and the *intifada* uprising in the Occupied Territories.

The Lebanon Civil War in 1982

The Israeli official sequence of events starts with the attempted assassination in London of Israeli Ambassador to England Shlomo Argow, which left him incapacitated for life. Retaliation came in the form of heavy air strikes in Beirut, which killed 45 people and wounded 150. This assault was answered by heavy rocket and artillery fire into northern Israel, which drove inhabitants into shelters. Israel's massive reaction was Operation Peace for Galilee. It was perceived initially as a large armed incursion. It started on June 6, 1982, and it is likely that nobody expected it would be twenty years until the unilateral pullout took place under Prime Minister Ehud Barak. The originally declared cleansing of "Fatahland," where the PLO was totally autonomous, was bypassed by the troops already dominating Beirut. Israel declared a ceasefire and insisted that the armed Palestinians (approximately 6,000 in Beirut) leave the country. With the mediation of U.S. envoy Philip Habib, the core of the Palestinian fighters was evacuated in the last week of August. Israeli forces nevertheless moved back around the area of Palestinian refugee camps. Two camps were attacked by Christian militias under the umbrella of vigilant troops of the Israeli Defense Forces (IDF), and hundreds of victims, mostly unarmed civilians, were killed. An Israeli commission of inquiry led by Supreme Court Judge Yitzhak Kahan in February 1983 published a report putting direct responsibility on the Phalange (the Kataeb Party of Lebanon) but concluded that the Israeli authorities carried indirect responsibility and pronounced that Defense Minister Sharon's behavior should bar him from again becoming minister of defense. One of the factors that led to Prime Minister Begin's resignation was his seeing Sharon's betrayal in getting his endorsement only for the original and lesser goals without disclosing from the outset the full range of the operation. Begin's fear was that Sharon had long before developed a grand design to push out the hundreds of thousands of Palestinian refugees from Lebanon via Syria (which would not accept them) and into Jordan and to gather under total control of what was to become the Palestinian state the already large majority of Palestinians living among the Jordanians. Needless to say, such a far-reaching plan failed, but Arafat had to move the PLO headquarters to Tunis, and Palestinians in the Occupied Territories felt the impotence of the Arab world in coming to the rescue of the Palestinians in Lebanon. This aggravated subsequent intrafactional fighting within the PLO. The sense was that *summud* was not conducive to liberation. Palestinians were now on their own and sensed the need to take their destiny in their own hands. This sentiment was one of the main factors leading to the *intifada*.

In September 1983 Israeli troops pulled out from most of Lebanon but maintained, in cooperation with a sponsored South Lebanese Army, control until 2000 of a security zone across Israel's northern border. The Gulf War of 1991 was about the only case in which Israel, when attacked by Iraqi missiles, did not retaliate militarily. The real perception of threat among its citizens was that chemical and biological warheads would be used. In 1980, in an audacious air strike, Israel knocked out an atomic reactor in Baghdad. Even so, the United States insisted that the IDF keep out, which worked, and the Israeli population stoically waited for worse attacks that, fortunately, did not materialize.

IV. THE CYCLE OF PEACE IN RETROSPECT: AN OVERVIEW

The 1948 war ended with a temporary ceasefire and armistice agreements, which were subsequently violated in the cycles of war. It took nearly three decades to reach a formal peace treaty.

1. *Israel and Egypt's 1978 Camp David agreement and subsequent peace treaty* brokered by President Jimmy Carter translated into a full Is-

raeli withdrawal from the territory taken from Egypt in the 1967 war, the institution of normal diplomatic relations between the two countries, the presence of an international force of observers in Sinai, and both sides becoming the recipients of massive economic and security foreign aid from the United States. The border has been quiet ever since, with limited bilateral interaction among the political elites and minimal trade and technical cooperation.

2. *The October 1991 Madrid-based Middle East Regional Peace Conference*, in the aftermath of the Gulf War, was attended by nearly all Arab countries and opened both multilateral tracks of negotiations on issues such as economic cooperation, water, refugees, and the environment and bilateral tracks of negotiations between Israel and a Jordanian/ Palestinian delegation and between Israel and Syria. The initial advance on the multilateral tracks was slowed down when the bilateral negotiations did not advance as expected and was revived again for a short time with the initial advance of the Oslo peace process, discussed in the following section.

3. *The Oslo Track II* unofficial channel of communications between the Palestinians and the Israelis materialized in a number of formal agreements launched at the White House under the auspices of President Bill Clinton in September 1993. Based on an interim period of devolution of power and territory to a Palestinian authority, it was to provide by the year 2000 the formulas for the solutions to the permanent status issues (borders and security, settlements, refugees, Jerusalem). The last-ditch efforts undertaken at Camp David in August 2000 by President Clinton convening Prime Minister Barak and Chairman/President Arafat and subsequent meetings in Taba and Sharm el-Sheikh brought negotiations close to agreement, but it failed to materialize.

4. *The Israel–Jordan peace treaty of 1994* initially produced a "warm peace," which was to include security and economic cooperation, but the outbreak of the second *intifada* (al-Aqsa) after the failure of the Oslo process to be completed in 2000 lowered to a large extent all expectations. Other incipient but promising ties that Israel established with some *Maghreb* (Morocco, Algeria, and Tunisia) and Arab Gulf states were severed.

5. *Israel's unilateral withdrawal from the Gaza Strip and four settlements in the north of the West Bank in the summer of 2005* was an important precedent for the political viability of removal of settlements, although the remaining

limitations to a restricted Palestinian administration in the strip, and the internal weaknesses and fragmentation of the Palestinian National Authority (PNA, or Palestinian Authority) put in question the continuity of such a first step.

IVA. THE SADAT–BEGIN INITIATIVE: A PIONEER EFFORT (1978)

Even in the more limited Israeli–Palestinian focus of our chapter, it is important to put the Sadat–Begin episode into historical perspective. After the Yom Kippur/October War of 1973, Israel and Egypt initiated a peace process, which led to a peace treaty in March 1979. At Camp David in September 1978 Israel, Egypt, and the United States formulated a five-year autonomy plan for Palestinian self-government in the West Bank and Gaza. Yet this formula was not implemented due to lack of political engagement by the Palestinians themselves, as well as lack of serious intent by Israel throughout the 1980s, as evidenced by the continuation of its fait accompli policies of expanding the settlements in the Occupied Territories. Many books and articles have been written about this incredible and often moving story, including the arduous but successful negotiations in Camp David, with President Jimmy Carter as an "honest broker."[13] Not only was Egypt the first Arab country to make peace with Israel—it also was the strongest and most important of the inter-Arab regional system. It also legitimated the principle of "territories for peace." Egypt got "up to the last inch" of Sinai back, mostly in the peace agreement. It got back the remaining few square kilometers in the Taba through a groundbreaking arbitration verdict. Israel got a firm peace with a four-time war opponent. Under the supervision of the Multilateral Force of Observers (MFO), the border became one of the quietest borders in the Middle East. People spoke about a "cold peace" given that the Palestinian issue remained unresolved in the agreement and its aftermath. But the mere existence of a peace with the exchange of embassies; some trade and tourism (particularly with Sinai being one of the preferred locations for Israelis traveling abroad), notwithstanding the negative expressions as reflected in the media, the more recalcitrant left and Nasserite circles; and the Islamists on both sides of the spectrum do not erase the fact that there is peace that has taken away from Israel the existential military threat. In other words, since the peace agreement was struck with Egypt, the subsequent wars with other Arab neighbors or Palestinians did not constitute a threat to Israel's integrity, as the previous 1967 and 1973 wars were perceived to have done. Since then, the wars that Israel has waged have been more a matter of choice than existential self-defense.

The closure of the agreement that cost the life of President Sadat, who was assassinated by extreme Islamists in dramatic circumstances during a military parade, did not encourage an immediate following by other less courageous Arab leaders. However, the main reasons for a delay of more than a decade in moving on with the peace cycle was the debate between incrementalists and maximalists, who resisted any territorial compromise, particularly since the Camp David agreement offered the Palestinians only temporary autonomy and not full independence. On the Israeli side, the additional lesson was that when facing difficult choices in security, the trading of the tangible for the intangible, as provided by more distant borders and peace—an abstract term yet to be proven—the role of leadership can be crucial. Prime Minister Begin could have opted out of the negotiations and gotten the overwhelming support of the majority of voters. Likewise, when opting to accept the formula of "all territories for peace," he took a calculated risk, a decision that eventually made him the most popular prime minister in Israel's history (close to 90 percent support of the agreement). Learning from such a lesson, he also counted on massive support when deciding to annex the Golan Heights to Israel two years later (approximately 80 percent supported that move).

IVB. FROM THE FIRST INTIFADA TO THE END OF THE OSLO PROCESS (1987–2000)

We have been challenged conceptually to decide where to fit the first *intifada* in this dichotomous analysis of war and peace. In respect to past and subsequent levels of violence in the Occupied Territories, the nature of Palestinian rebellion consisted to such a great degree of nonviolen sanctions and civil disobedience that it tilted more toward peace than war. In addition, the political message was one of moderation and acceptance of a small Palestine side by side with Israel.

Palestinian national identity and the process of nation building have become a concrete reality. Between 1982 and 1987 the Palestinians in the Occupied Territories started building an infrastructure that challenged Israeli occupation. In terms of ideology, the *intifada* could not be ignored by the factionalism of Palestinian politics, and it managed to create a national debate among the various political groups within the PLO, between the "interior" and the "exterior," and between the "nationalist" and "religious" camps. This debate reflects the democratic trend within the Palestinian national movement. Differences exist in the national camp over how to pursue the strategy of peace, but detractors are not disruptive and could yet be categorized as "loyal opposition." However, the religious groups spearheaded by the Islamic resistance movement Hamas reject the idea of a Palestinian state side by side with Israel and the convening of an international conference. Hamas espouses the establishment of an Islamic state in the entire area of Palestine and members are willing to fight for it through all forms of violence.

The catalyst for the first *intifada* was a sequence of escalating events, starting with a military track accident in Gaza that left four Palestinians dead. The funerals led to massive stone-throwing demonstrations throughout the Occupied Territories and to subsequent Israeli repression. The level of violence of the 1987 Palestinian uprising in the West Bank and Gaza initially was characterized as an intermediate strategy appropriately placed somewhere between the use of firearms and nonviolence. Proponents, sympathizers, and analysts have called such phenomena "restricted violence," "limited violence," "nonlethal power," "restrained violence," "symbolic violence," "unarmed resistance," "offensive nonviolence," "relatively nonviolent," "predominantly nonviolent," "nonmilitary uprising," "low intensity warfare," "unarmed uprising," "low-level violence," and similar characterizations.[14] Whether downgrading from violence or upgrading from nonviolence to a middle-of-the road form of rebellion, such forms of violence generally have been described as the use of methods primarily intended to intimidate, aggravate, and/or cause minor injuries to the opposing party in the conflict. Acts are not aimed at causing great bodily harm. The main method highlighted has been stone throwing, which has become symbolically important. Prevailing arguments condoning limited violence call for a restricted use of weapons other than firearms. They also often call for a limitation in terms of specific geographic areas (mostly Israel's Occupied Territories); specific noncivilian targets (security forces and settlers); selected occasions (mostly retaliatory to Jewish violence); and a nonlethal or only intimidating or symbolic purpose. Acts may be limited in comparison to previous standards or in terms of available projectiles for resistance (an abundance of stones as compared with scarce quantities of firearms in the Occupied Territories). They may be limited in time, as a conditional and situational stage that may further escalate in the future; limited in the sense of sporadic and spontaneous rather than organized from above; or organized at a level adequate to sustain steadfastness when facing a measurable Israeli reaction of bearable proportions of any type of violence with massive casualties, leading to the forceful ejection of the population. Limited violence was a middle-of-the road compromise between the deep-rooted advocacy and use of violence of major Palestinian organizations and new trends of nonviolence as proposed by some prominent West Bankers.[15] The meaning of *limited* can also be seen in those who stressed that only a minority of acts were of a violent nature and that the overwhelming aspects of the struggle included nonviolent techniques that were not used in previous stages of the Palestinian struggle.[16] It appeared at first as an eclectic and reasonable way of looking for a middle ground, which could provide to such a struggle a significant level of visibility and relevance while at the same time showing a reluctance to inflict large numbers of victims on the opponent. In summing up the issue of the level of violence in the *intifada*, what comes across to Israelis is that "limited violence" is "more violent than limited." "For the children of the Intifada, the STONE is a symbol of protest; for the majority of Israelis, the ROCK that can miss its target or injure can also predictably kill."[17] An Israeli survey showed a more comprehensive list that included explosive devices, assault with a handgun, assault with other types of small arms, throwing hand grenades, knife attacks, throwing Molotov cocktails, and property arson.

To what extent has the moderation of the PLO— moving away drastically in 1988 from the idea of the liberation of all of Palestine toward an acceptance of a two-state solution—been blurred by the only relative move away from terror as a means for goal attainment? Non-violent struggle would arguably be more congruent with what has been perceived as a maximal willingness to compromise on the final objectives. The militarized nature of the current and second *intifada* shows that the Palestinians did not internalize the inherent power of nonviolent action.

The Israeli perception of the uprising had an impact on the acceptance of a two-state solution. De facto, most Israelis felt afraid to step into the West Bank and Gaza—the settlers being the exception to the rule. At the same time, the message became louder and clearer that the Palestinians in the Occupied Territories, even the PLO outside them, were willing to compromise on the 1967 border, the 22 percent of "historic Palestine." Furthermore, an internal debate was generated about the morality of occupation, triggered by the increased level of gross human rights violations. More than a thousand people were killed by the IDF, and tens of thousands were imprisoned. Within civil society, new human rights organizations were set up to focus on protecting the rights of the "other."

These positive trends were undermined by the uncompromising position of Prime Minister Yitzhak Shamir, who opposed splitting the land and was vehemently opposed to negotiations with the PLO, a sentiment that lasted until Shamir lost in the 1992 elections. Yet the outcome of the 1991 Gulf War obliged even Shamir to acknowledge some of the realities of the U.S.-imposed "New World Order" and to agree reluctantly to participate in October 1991 in the Madrid Middle East Regional Peace Conference under explicit pressure from Washington, which threatened to withhold a $10 billion loan guarantee. As the public's determination to leave Gaza and eventually the West Bank increased and settlers became divided over strategies, Likud's internal crisis helped Labor's Rabin—the legendary chief of staff during the Six-Day War—come to power, supported actively by the dovish left-wing Meretz faction and indirectly by the Arab members of the Knesset.

Arafat's initial mediating efforts between Iraq and Kuwait and eventually his declared support of Saddam Hussein not only got the burgeoning Palestinian community expelled from Kuwait but also further isolated him globally and from many Arab states; it was also ruinous for the laborious efforts undertaken in previous years for the PLO to gain recognition by the United States as a legitimate representative. Hence, the Palestinian representatives at the Madrid conference was conditioned on them being concealed within the Jordanian delegation. Israel vetoed participants residing in East Jerusalem (which the Knesset unilaterally declared annexed), as well as declared PLO officials. Many of the points gained with the *intifada* at the international, regional, and Israeli levels were now lost.

The Oslo Peace Process

More than a decade later, retrospective analysis of the Oslo peace process between Palestinians and Israelis highlights more failures than achievements, as we ourselves do in the following pages. We coined the term for the three stages as *WWW: What Went Wrong.* The first "W" relates to problems that occurred during the Oslo agreement. The second "W" represents the failure of leadership when Camp David II negotiations took place in 2000. The third "W" is the current Intifada al-Aqsa, which has brought us back full circle into war.[18]

On the one hand, secret Track II negotiations were conducted in Oslo by two Israeli academics with an entry to then Deputy Foreign Minister Yossi Beilin and through him to Shimon Peres and eventually to Prime Minister Rabin. On the other hand, with Palestinian advisors close to Chairman Arafat, negotiations resulted in a series of agreements beginning with an exchange of letters between Israeli Prime Minister Rabin and PLO Chairman Arafat. Their intense work translated into the official "Declaration of Principles" of September 1993, which was signed on the White House lawn under the auspices of then U.S. President Clinton. The two parties committed themselves to implementing a gradual process of granting political autonomy to the Palestinians, a scheme very similar to the one previously signed at Camp David in 1978, but leading toward full independence, first to manage and ultimately to resolve their conflict exclusively by peaceful means.

According to this framework for peace (more a timetable toward a final treaty), a transitional process of five years would put in place a self-governing Palestinian Authority in the West Bank and Gaza, followed by final status negotiations (no later than three years after the beginning of Palestinian autonomy) about the "core" and most difficult issues, including Jerusalem, Palestinian refugees, Israeli settlements in the Occupied Territories, security and borders, and the underground water issue. Following the Declaration of Principles, a series of interim agreements were signed between Israel and the PLO during the period of 1993–1999: the May 1994 Cairo Agreement on the implementation of autonomy in the Gaza Strip and the Jericho area (of the West Bank); the September 1995 interim agreement dividing the West Bank into areas under direct Palestinian control (area A), civilian Palestinian control (area B), and Israeli control (area C, including settlements and self-defined "security zones"); the January 1997 Hebron Protocol dividing the city between Israelis and Palestinians; the October 1998 Wye Memorandum implementing the interim agreement of 1995; and finally the September 1999 Sharm el-Sheikh memorandum concerning the stipulation and timetable of the final status negotiations on refugees, borders, water, Jerusalem, and settlements. After Israel withdrew political control from less than half of the Occupied Territories and military control from the urban areas, the Palestinian Authority under the elected Arafat government and a legislative council administered all civilian affairs for the cities in the West Bank and Gaza and a large part of the villages.

In its signed agreements, the PLO and the emerging Palestinian Authority promised to stop the violence, arrest terrorists, dismantle the terrorist infrastructures in the territories, collect illegal weapons, and end incitement to violence. Soon mutual recriminations about not fulfilling their parts of the deal and delays of the timetable for implementation poisoned the atmosphere. On the one hand, Israel did not see a contradiction between the continuing expansion of its settlements in the occupied territories and the outcome of the permanent status negotiations that would enable Palestinians to determine their future. On the other hand, the Palestinian Authority, while routinely condemning the use of suicide bombings, did not

act systematically to stop them, and Arafat did not distance himself totally from the perpetuators, who he called *sahyid* ("martyrs," in Arabic). As the peace process continued to unfold, the issue of strong leadership came up once again with the heroe of the Six Days War Prime Minister Rabin's growing openness toward the Palestinians. Then in 1995, toward the end of one of the largest-ever peace rallies in Tel Aviv, Rabin was assassinated by a fanatical Jewish religious student.

IVC. THE CAMP DAVID II, SHARM EL-SHEIKH, AND TABA ISRAEL–PALESTINE–UNITED STATES MEETINGS

After Prime Minister Rabin's assassination, Shimon Peres, an advocate of the Oslo process, was prime minister only briefly until he was displaced, by a small margin, by Likud's Benjamin Netanyahu, who used a negative campaign depicting Labor leaders as terrorist Arafat's buddies. Even if the Hebron agreement and the Wye River understandings were forced upon him, Netanyahu worked to undermine the entire Oslo process, which he opposed. When Ehud Barak's impressive victory brought back renewed hopes for negotiations, his pullout from Lebanon and insistence on moving away from a gradual piecemeal approach to a final agreement sounded promising. He was tempted to move first toward compromising with a moribund Hafez al-Assad, but Syria did not reciprocate and insisted on its demand for five hundred meters to get her to the shore of Lake Tiberiades. Barak then leaned the opposite way and urged to complete an agreement with the Palestinians. The comparison of the two Camp David encounters (the first under the auspices of Jimmy Carter, the second under Bill Clinton) is a fascinating exercise.

The hard issues of the final agreement were put on the agenda. Contending interpretations were provided within and between both sides' participants and analysts. We would like to adopt, with some changes, the shared "third narrative" provided by Arie Kacowicz in his "Rashomon in the Middle East: Clashing Narratives of the Israeli–Palestinian Conflict."[19] Prime Minister Barak showed sincere intentions to compromise, by addressing many of the Palestinians' expectations. He broke the Israeli taboo of negotiating over Jerusalem and accepted the concept of being the capital of the two states, and he offered the return of approximately 91 percent of the West Bank and added to the swap 1 percent more from Israel's land. A settlement range could not be obtained at that time since the "maximum" Israeli offer at Camp David was below the "minimum" Palestinian demands regarding territory. After the publication of the Clinton parameters in late December 2000, the two sides came closer to reaching an agreement at Taba in January 2001, yet these talks collapsed. By January 2001, the two parties had lost their respective legitimacies (especially Barak's minority government), their nerve, and their remaining negligible trust of each other. In addition, the indefatigable mediator and go-between, President Clinton, was on his way out of the White House.

Further more, some of the Israeli negotiating dynamics and procedural aspects of the political interaction contributed to the failure of the talks. By presenting early positions as bottom lines, the Israelis provoked the Palestinians' mistrust. By subsequently shifting their terms in the direction of the Palestinians' political goals, the Israelis whetted the Palestinians' appetite. Moreover, Barak concealed his final proposals, the "endgame," until Arafat had moved. And Yet Arafat would not move until he could see the "endgame"; he came to Camp David reluctantly and insisted that he needed more time for preparation while at the same time he realized that this was a last opportunity for engaging President Clinton in concluding the negotiation process. Also, several Palestinian declarations adversely affected the course of the negotiations. Arafat's doubts about the importance and holiness of the Temple Mount for the Jewish people and the reiteration of an absolute right for every Palestinian refugee to return to Israel derailed any positive dynamic interaction. He remained reactive because he believed that the Americans had not planned enough for Camp David and that the process had not been thought out. In spite of the important fact that the Palestinians agreed to the principle of rectifications along the pre-1967 border on the basis of equivalent territorial swaps, no substantial bargaining or sensible political initiative was offered in Camp David by the Americans, who seemed to convey the Israelis' ideas, which made Palestinians lose confidence in the Americans as honest brokers. In retrospect, the negotiations should be assessed against the different realities in which Israelis and Palestinians found themselves and their inability or unwillingness to understand each other's perspectives. In its aftermath, and even following the outbreak of the Israeli–Palestinian cycle of violence on September 29, negotiations continued for four additional months. The process remains inconclusive, but the "parameters" offered by President Clinton, not at Camp David but albeit too late at Taba, remain the most feasible outline for a shared solution of the Israeli–Palestinian conflict at some point in the future.

V. THE CURRENT CYCLE OF WAR AND PEACE (2000–2007)

The World Zionist Organization was able to manifest its dream of a Jewish State recognized by the international community in a half century (1897–1947). The additional hope that further partitioning and the emergence of a Palestinian state side by side with Israel was shelved during the second half of the twentieth century. The longer cycle of war has emerged again to surpass the shorter cycle of peace. The few years that have elapsed since the collapse of the Camp David talks reveal mixed trends and do not allow us to make any conclusive remarks.

VA. THE INTIFADA AL-AQSA AND ITS AFTERMATH

Since the election of Ariel Sharon as Israel's prime minister followed by his massive stroke and the subsequent succession of Ehud Olmert and the new Kadima Party, no meaningful negotiations have been resumed. After the electoral parliamentary victory of Hamas in 2006, negotiations between the first and the moderate Mahmoud Abbas (Abu Mazen) have been zigzagging back and forth, leaving both sides full of uncertainties. Sharon's policies during his years in office accelerated the ongoing high-intensity conflict that has lasted close to four years and killed more than three thousand Palestinians and a thousand Israelis. In a region where conspiracy theories prevail, where one can always imagine the worst from the enemy and attribute it to post-facto premeditated intentions, the interpretations of the facts that led to the Intifada al-Aqsa are diametrically opposed.[20] The official Israeli version is rather straightforward: this was a terrorist war preplanned and premeditated by Chairman Arafat, as a result of a strategic Palestinian decision to use violence—rather than negotiations—as the primary instrument of advancing the Palestinian political cause. The true roots of the war can be found in the Palestinian rejection at Camp David of the concept of a peacefully negotiated resolution of disputes. Paradoxically, it was the very Oslo peace process and particularly the far-reaching offers at Camp David that caused the Palestinians to respond with violence, following the "precedent" of the unilateral Israeli withdrawal from Lebanon triggered by the successful Hezbollah guerrilla attacks. Therefore, Palestinian terrorists—starting with Arafat himself and including the Palestinian Authority (a "terrorist entity"), Hamas, the even more militant Al Jihad Al Islam (Islamic Jihad), and factions within Fatah—are not opposing the occupation of the territories per se but rather the whole concept of peace through compromise. On the other hand, the Palestinians' prevailing version was that Sharon's forced visit to the al-Haram al-Sharif, protected by a large police contingent, was a premeditated effort to defy Muslim sovereignty over this holy place. It was meant to trigger an Arab popular reaction that would be severely repressed and would escalate into an armed confrontation that Israel would use to crush the PLO and Arafat as the leader of the newly built state institution in the land of the Palestinian Authority.

According to Kacowitz, the second *intifada* was "either a Palestinian war of extermination (the Israeli version) or a Palestinian war of national liberation (the Palestinian version)."[21] A third interpretation suggests the simultaneity of not just two different wars but four. Within each side, one could find two contending goals, as argued by Michael Walzer: (1) a Palestinian war to destroy the State of Israel, as epitomized by the suicide bombing attacks of fundamentalist Islamists and since 2002 of some elements of the more mainstream Fatah faction (such as the al-Aqsa Brigades), directly associated with Arafat and the Palestinian Authority; (2) a Palestinian war to create an independent state alongside Israel, ending the military occupation of the West Bank and Gaza

after 1967, as illustrated by the guerrilla actions against the Israeli army in the occupied territories; (3) a legitimate and just Israeli war of self-defense against Palestinian terrorism, in order to secure Israel within the pre-1967 borders; and (4) an Israeli expansionist war to keep the settlements and hold onto the "liberated" (occupied) biblical territories of "Greater Israel."[22] As throughout the peace process, extremists on both sides kept fighting the illegitimate first and fourth types of war.

If the popular eruption was aimed initially at both the corrupt and malfunctioning Palestinian Authority regime and against Israel, it was rapidly channeled and manipulated by the PLO leadership, first to change the political status quo and improve its bargaining positions in the short term (as indeed happened between Camp David and Taba) and second to focus the resentment and anger from the most marginalized sectors of Palestinian society toward Israel itself. In this sense, Arafat and the Palestinian Authority did not do much to stop the uprising, believing that it might well serve their interests. They preferred to "ride the tiger" rather than to confront terrorism and violence. It seems that the militarized uprising was not Arafat's master plan but rather an exploitation of the violent situation. A "blank check policy" accompanied the often futile post facto "plausible denial," as attempted in the case of the *Karine A,* the ship captured in 2002 in the Red Sea and found to be loaded with weapons.

In the first few weeks following September 29, 2001, the Palestinian uprising was not yet catalogued as a war but rather as a series of confrontations between largely unarmed Palestinians and armed Israeli security forces that immediately resorted to excessive and deadly use of force, fueling a further escalation of the violence. At the same time, it is equally true that members of the Palestinian security forces initiated many of these acts of violence (like the shootings at the Israeli neighborhood of Gilo, in southeast Jerusalem). Moreover, since the collapse of Camp David, Arafat had reneged on the promise to prevent and fight terrorism. By April 2002, even if the Palestinian Authority had wanted to do so, stopping the violence completely might have had no impact on reversing the progressive degradation of internal Palestinian control as a result of Israel's military actions. By adopting the "default option," which increased the number of suicide bombings, the situation on the ground has continued to deteriorate. At the same time, the Israeli government has maneuvered to postpone the reinitiation of political negotiations "under fire." The Israeli military has exacerbated the already precarious humanitarian conditions of the Palestinian civilian population; has turned to extrajudicial killings of alleged terrorists and military incursions into Palestinian cities, towns, and villages; and has violated the rules of war by responding in nonproportional ways, which has led to the death of many innocent victims. The obsession of the official Jewish state to always act from a position of strength brought about an unusual escalation of violence that in itself precluded the negotiations that have been reopened time and again.

Because it stressed the importance of fair and transparent elections in the process of democratization, the election of Mahmoud Abbas as president of the PNA initially provided the first reason for optimism toward the very smooth transfer of government following the death of President Arafat. The task confronting Abbas has been formidable, for he has inherited internal anarchy, polarization, political stagnation, and corruption compounded by the gloomy atmosphere created by five years of a bloody intifada. He intended to break away from Arafat's legacy; specifically, with the help of professionals he hoped to reform Palestinian political, security, and economic systems, and above all to halt the militarization of the intifada. It seems, though, that with Arafat no longer around and with his galvanizing effect gone, the evolving Palestinian leadership is still impotent in dealing with those corrupt officials who could not have survived and thrived that long without their leader Arafat, for whom they always acted as sycophantic and obedient cronies and hangers-on in return for tolerating their leader's indulgences. While the intermediate stage led by Abbas has encountered increasing difficulties, a critical introspection leads to the conclusion that a generational replacement of leadership is necessary.[23] A logical justification for the weakening of the leadership expected to prevent chaos and lawlessness, and possibly a destructive power struggle, can be found within the ranks of the heterogeneous Fatah movement. It is worth mentioning that Fatah's various components had always been kept together by Arafat, often through a combination of financial appeasement and a policy of divide and rule. The movement's institutions

have been controlled by a combination of the old guards of Fatah with more universally appreciated professionals, such as the former World Bank economist and then prime minister Salam Fayyad, thus denying the second and third generations any control of power. The conflict between the "old" and the "young" guards is ongoing, which weakens the movement and strengthens the surging role of Hamas as an opposition enjoying tremendous political importance and relevance. Fatah, on the other hand, cannot transform into a full-fledged political party because of the ideological contradictions within its own ranks, vis à vis Israel, and personal and clannish preferences, and hence it cannot develop a clear political platform.

Fatah's image of corruption compared to Hamas's benevolent work and institutions makes it even worse. One immediate major challenge—albeit weakened by relentless Israeli military efforts that have deprived the faction of several of its charismatic leaders—has been put forth by Hamas's major players with their capabilities and political ambitions. Hence, the tragic mistake of a militarized *intifada*—the leadership should have expected the overwhelming asymmetry to play into the hands of Israel's superiority in this field—has resulted in the victorious and surprising election of a Hamas majority in the Palestinian Legislative Council. A failed effort to create a shared Fatah/Hamas government brokered in Mecca by the Saudi royal family ended in 2007 with the dismembering of the Palestinian National Authority, with Fatah controlling the West Bank and Hamas controlling Gaza. Openly challenged by Hamas's coup d'état in Gaza, Abbas definitely has little time left to wield his power, establish control over the numerous Palestinian security services and factions' militias, and improve the daily living standards of Palestinians before risking any major concession to Israel. Palestinians would want him to lift Israeli travel bans and restrictions, rebuild the shattered economy, root out corruption, and impose law and order. Meanwhile, new but still small political forces have been formed, and much public opinion seems keen to give a chance to a third party other than Hamas and Fatah.

From the outbreak of the Intifada al-Aqsa until the split within Fatah, the emphasis has moved into "how to stop war" rather than "how to make peace." A large number of demarches undertaken by Senator

George Mitchell, CIA Director William Tenet, U.S. envoy General Anthony Zinni, and State Department representative William Burns, as well as other missions, did result in a nominal and conditional adherence to the Quartet's Roadmap to get both sides to cease violence and negotiate.[24] Through creative and extensive "second-track diplomacy," consensus has been reached on nearly all the permanent status agenda items. The components of a possible official accord have been discussed ad nauseam, and the issue is no longer the final status but how to move from the current paralysis into action.[25] The Clinton parameters are considered to be a realistic expression of the consensus found among moderates and pragmatics on both sides.

Peace Prospects

At the end of November 2007, just after we finished writing this chapter, an Israeli–Palestinian meeting was convened by the United States in Annapolis, Maryland, to obtain agreement on a blueprint for a peace accord. Over time, expectations have been lowered to a more general set of principles that can facilitate future negotiations towards an overall peace agreement that needs to be completed over a period of one year. On one hand, the opportunity for a practical agreement has increased because, following the split of Hamas, the government led by Mahmoud Abbas and Salam Fayed is as moderate as the Palestinians can provide and his capacity to deliver "peace dividends" upgraded by the December 2007 Paris conference ending in a commitment to support them with approximately seven billion dollars. On the Israeli side, battered Prime Minister Olmert with charges of corruption being investigated understands that the only way to remain in power—while Qassam rockets continue falling into Israel after the unilateral withdrawal in Gaza and the disastrous Lebanon II war—is to embark on the road to peace. Israeli and Palestinian public opinion has been ready for a long time for "painful concessions"—the vague expression used by Ariel Sharon—if provided by strong leadership. The added asset could be the possible participation of Saudi Arabia, after the ruling dynasty led in 2002 an initiative, ratified by the Beirut Arab League Summit, that calls for "acceptance of Israel as a neighbor living in peace and security in the context of a comprehensive settlement," based on the withdrawal from the Occupied Territories and a just and agreed solution to the Palestinian refugees issue.

However, such an initiative can be derailed easily. On the Palestinian side, violent activities against civilians instigated by Hamas, this time from the West Bank and Israeli retaliations resulting in overkills, can escalate and regain the levels of the Intifada al-Aqsa. On the Israeli side, the components of the Cabinet have expressed different types of reservations and former prime minister and now opposition leader Benjamin Netanyahu is more popular than the leaders of the Kadima and Labor Parties together. U.S. Secretary of State Condoleezza Rice has been investing her energies in an enterprise that at best requires heavy presidential involvement and the ability to gain the confidence of both parties, which clearly is not the case with President George W. Bush. Furthermore, Ehud Olmert and Mahmoud Abbas are transitional types—weak leaders with many internal problems, challenged within their own milieu—and, hence, they may not be able to pull anything together. It may be for another generation of leaders to conclude the deal, after the election of a new president in the United States in November 2008, especially if the Democrats win.

At first glance, we can concur with the premise that "A pessimist is an informed optimist," since many opportunities have been missed by both sides, but when looking forward and backward we can sum up the situation as ambiguous. If we do not focus only on the immediate past and present but speculate in terms of decades, significant progress has been made toward the resolution of our dispute. The legacy of the failed Oslo process has been the consolidation of mutual recognition between the PLO and Israel; the wide bilateral, regional, and global consensus regarding the two-state solution; and the advances made around such thorny issues as refugees and Jerusalem. Even disagreements on specific problems can be overcome when they become part of an overall package that includes other attractive inducements. Furthermore, what was once the agenda of the moderate minorities (two-state solution, sharing Jerusalem, etc.) is now endorsed by most political forces, except the fundamentalists, zealots, and ultranationalists. The impact of such groups as spoilers has been neglected, but the lessons learned could illuminate the searchlight at the end of the tunnel. Since eight thousand Jews were pulled out of Gaza, anxiety seems to be growing in settlers' circles that keeping control over an additional two million Palestinians (in addition to more than a million Arabs in Israel) is widely perceived as a "demographic bomb." The settlers' lobby for "Jordan is Palestine" or for remaining in their homes in the Occupied Territories without citizens' rights is not acceptable to most in the Israeli establishment and public.

Albeit too late, the failure to reach consensus at the Camp David meeting between Prime Minister Barak and President Arafat has been bridged by the Clinton parameters (see the following paragraphs) and by now has become the basis of any pragmatic agreement. What remains is *not what but how* to achieve such increasingly shared goals, and how to move toward reducing violence and provide confidence-building measures that will give to the Palestinians and Israelis a taste of what peace could be if they threw their lot into a treaty. With this in mind, can we look at the future with certainty? In a region where rationality has not seemed to prevail, we conceive of five plausible scenarios for moving toward peace, triggered by different configurations:

1. *A Negotiated Bilateral Agreement.* The disintegration of the Hamas/Fatah government and territorial split in 2007 opened the possibility of direct negotiations that cover both the means to ensure confidence-building measures during the negotiation process, as well as a shared vision about the final peace agreement based on the principle of the two-state solution. At this stage, the commitment to such process is weaker in the Kadima-led government than in the Abbas entourage, a Cabinet composed of independent individual professionals. So far, the release of prisoners and removal of checkpoints is cosmetic rather than meaningful, and the commitment of the Palestinian Authority to curb terror in the areas under its control is still curbed by controversial IDF incursions to crush Hamas and Jihad supporters in the West Bank. Within these limitations, visualizing a promising result to the negotiations is a difficult undertaking.

Many details for how to achieve Palestinian statehood and a long step toward peace in one year are offered by Jerome Segal.[26] In brief, if agreement can be reached along the lines of the Clinton plan, then a comprehensive end-of-conflict/end-

of-claims treaty is signed by Abbas as head of the PLO and brought to a referendum through ratification by the Palestinian people. However, if agreement is not achieved on Jerusalem and refugees but consensus on the permanent boundaries of the Palestinian state is reached, then this limited agreement on permanent boundaries is separated from the other issues and brought to a referendum. Negotiations continue regarding Jerusalem, with a dotted line signifying that the city will be divided but putting off the exact line until the conclusion of this negotiations track. The limited accord provides for the establishment of a Palestinian state and mutual recognition between the two states. However, it is not an end-of-conflict/end-of-claims treaty. Rather it is more than a *Hudna* (long-term ceasefire) but less than end of conflict. The treaty on statehood and permanent borders utilizes the distinction between "de facto" sovereignty (which means that a government actually functions on the ground as a sovereign) and "de jure" sovereignty (which means that a government is recognized as the rightful sovereign over a territory, whether or not it actually controls it).

As soon as the treaty is ratified by a referendum, Israel withdraws from an identified portion of the West Bank. This is a region where the PLO actually exercises a monopoly of political power on the ground, and for the first time exercises de facto sovereignty over part of Palestine and affirms its de jure sovereignty over all of the territory within the agreed permanent boundaries. Israel recognizes it and immediately begins the process of dismantling settlements and withdrawing militarily from all areas where its government is the sole Palestinian entity with weapons. A third party from the international community is established to adjudicate disputes and to assess whether or not the State of Palestine has gained the required monopoly of force.

2. *Palestinian Unilateral Decisions.* Clearly, the option of military struggle has been exhausted. The chances for negotiations between the Hamas breakaway leaders and the PNA are low, but being alone and in case outcomes from the bilateral negotiations fail to materialize, the president comes up with daring ideas. Among them are these:

a. *Unilateral Declaration of Statehood.* In case the Israeli government is unable or unwilling to move along the suggested negotiations into a long-term agreement, the Palestinians have completed their promise to declare a "provisional" state while a large part of the territories remains occupied and has asked the UN to accept Palestine as a sovereign state. (Such a declaration was made by the 19th Palestine National Council meeting in 1988, and now it should ask to be recognized as such by the world community with jurisdiction in the West Bank and Gaza.) The UN Security Council, author of the famous Resolution 242 of November 1967, calling for Israel's withdrawal from occupied territories and the establishment of secure and recognized borders, is now asked to draw a map suggesting what those frontiers should be. Given that both sides are on record as having accepted this resolution, and given the 1947 precedent in which a clearly delimited partition plan was accepted by Israel, it is difficult for the Israeli government to reject a configuration that offers far more than the 1947 plan. Furthermore, room can always be left for border rectification based on mutual agreement. The majority of the Palestinian people favor a sovereign state in the entire West Bank and Gaza with East Jerusalem as its capital: 22 percent of historic Palestine, living side by side in peace with Israel. Time has come to ask that Palestine be given a full seat at the United Nations, and with membership comes the Palestinian undertaking to adhere to all international human rights conventions. In addition, the Chairman of the Palestinian National Authority (in the Oslo accords, it is still "PA" with the "N" omitted) is recognized as the independent country's first president and its representatives abroad as legitimate ambassadors. For the international community, bringing Palestine into the family of nations heals an open wound and atones for the dissonance that resulted from the world's support for the creation of a Jewish state in 1948.

b. *Incorporating Hamas to Fatah's Move Toward the Palestinian State.* Clearly, a second stage is needed to legitimate the daring premises of the previous stage, no less so if declared unilaterally. With respect to the referendum on the treaty with Israel, or the unilateral declaration of statehood, Abu Mazen calls on Hamas to permit the referendum to be held within Gaza and, if approved, to do so also in the West Bank, which will constitute ratification and become binding law that all individuals and organizations must obey. In a "Prisoners' Document," as well as in the Mecca Accord, Hamas accepted that negotiations would be conducted by the PLO and that such treaty would be binding if ratified through a referendum. Because Hamas can urge that the treaty be rejected, it has an indirect way of influencing the terms of the treaty, even though it was not participating in the formal negotiations. If the refer-

endum passes, Mahmoud Abbas will appoint an interim government of the State of Palestine. This government will be in power only until elections can be held for both a president and legislature of the State of Palestine. Participation in the interim government is open to Hamas members provided that they accept the results as binding and to turn over power in Gaza, thereby relinquishing its role as an armed faction.

If, contrary to the preceding scenario, Hamas initially refuses to recognize sovereignty of the State of Palestine, and refuses to relinquish control of Gaza, and refuses to disarm, then the state will expand its sovereign control only in the West Bank. Once Israel has fully withdrawn from West Bank territory, the credibility and well-being of the new State of Palestine will become a popular incentive to a similar outcome in Gaza. Under those circumstances, it may be difficult for Hamas to remain idle and not join its brethren in the independence process.

c. *A Call for a Judicial Decision About the Future Entity by an International Court.* The current building of a fence/wall by Israel, which includes parts of the West Bank and East Jerusalem (different from the fence in the Gaza Strip built along the pre-1967 borders) has been challenged by the UN General Assembly and by the International Court of Justice at The Hague. Rather than asking for an ad hoc decision, once Palestine asks for full membership at the UN, it declares a border dispute with its neighbor Israel and requests a ruling on its final boundaries or requests that the case be determined by arbitration. Under the leadership of former Likud Prime Minister Menachem Begin, Israel accepted the principle of signing a peace treaty with a neighboring country while withdrawing from territories, and outstanding issues, such as ownership of Taba, were determined by arbitration and returned to Egypt.

d. *New Legislative Elections.* Such elections are now scheduled for early 2008., This requires challenging, if necessary and nonviolently, the restrictions posed by the Israeli occupation, including the participation of Hamas's candidates who accept the prior commitment to the Israeli/Palestinian agreements that have led the establishment of the body in which they would like to serve. Furthermore, the candidates will endorse a priori the principles established in the provisional constitution. The political wing of Hamas will meet considerable Arab and international pressure when the electoral option leads to power sharing and, if so, will tell its military wing that no more suicide bombings will be tolerated. It matters little whether Islamist Osama Bin Laden and Al Qaeda's identification with the endgame suffering of the Palestinian people is a ploy to elicit support among the Muslim masses or a cynical stand shared with similar fundamentalist forces who have tried to stop peace and reconciliation efforts between Israelis and Palestinians. The emergence of a third large new party has been discussed, including Wassatieh ("moderation" in Arabic) based on a different interpretation of the Muslim texts, and could ally forces around one shared democracy, social justice, and peace platform.

Past experience has shown that Israeli acts of violence and terror tend to switch the vote toward the more radical groups and individuals. Most likely, Israeli occupation, curfews, building fences on confiscated Palestinian land, increasing military control, collective punishment, and settlers' violence produce radical results among Palestinians. Over time, a long-standing working relationship has been established between civil society organizations of both sides sharing the values of human rights, democracy, justice, and lasting peace. This new party initiative provides a dominant strategy over those forces that emphasize short-term military actions and political schemes that are only reactive to Israeli initiatives.

e. *The Arab Peace Initiative.* Taking into account the inability of the Palestinian leadership to properly organize itself, perhaps the Arab states can upgrade their role as surrogates. The Saudi statement made originally in 2002 and revamped in 2007 as the Arab Peace Initiative offered regional peace to Israel in exchange for a return to the pre-1967 borders.[27] From a practical perspective, we visualize Egypt, Jordan, and other Arab states providing a regional umbrella for Palestinians to conduct staged negotiations in a more attractive framework with Israel. Hopefully, a sustained campaign with professional publicity and the peace and justice camp's active support can bring the conflict to an end, once and for all, and foster acceptance of Israel as a legitimate member of the Middle East region. Such an effort may be enough to motivate many Palestinians, who are sick and tired of security threats and economic deterioration, to go along with it.

3. *Unilateral Israeli Steps.* Unwilling to negotiate with the Palestinian Authority leadership even after Arafat's death, Prime Minister Sharon announced redeployment in the West Bank (the word *withdrawal* has not been considered "politically correct") but left such a legacy to Prime Minister Olmert, who called in the 2006 elections for a "strategy of unilateralism determining the permanent borders of the State of Israel." Instead, following the outcome of the Second Lebanon War, a growing sense of vulnerability is present in Israel today, produced by an enormous shift in how the Israeli public views peace talks with the Palestinians—in particular, how it views withdrawing from the West Bank. While Qassam rockets fired from Gaza have done relatively little damage, future missiles from the West Bank that land on the runways of Ben-Gurion International Airport are an entirely different story. Added to the nightmare of Hezbollah's Katyusha rocket barrages falling into Haifa—Israel's third-largest city—no Israeli leader will withdraw from the West Bank unless he or she is confident of little danger of that sort. Today, the unilateral withdrawal concept is dead. The lesson of Gaza is that it matters a great deal for Israel's security who is in power in Palestine and what kind of relations are had with them. The extent of this shift was exploited by Benjamin Netanyahu when he wrote against negotiating with Mahmoud Abbas on the grounds that turning territory over to a weak government was the functional equivalent of unilateral withdrawal. On the other hand, the PLO demands not less than the 22 percent of what is left of historic Palestine. No single member of the Israeli government is calling for unilateral withdrawal to the 1967 borders, as was the case following the pullout from Lebanon. Hence, the current options of "separation" through redeployment are these:

a. *Replicating Implicitly Another Version of the "Gaza–Jericho" First Step.* Israel agreed with the Oslo agreement to consider pulling out eventually from West Bank areas A and B and annexing the remaining 60 percent. That in itself is not much worse than the continuously deteriorating status quo and the confusing idioms of "allowing for the demographic growth in the settlements," since it will unmask the protracted policy of creeping annexation through settlements. Since the Golan Heights was unilaterally declared annexed by the Knesset without any international legitimacy, governments have been willing to negotiate for that land with Syria. Even if such a move is doubtful and could maintain the current coalition, it may totally isolate Israel.

b. *A Pulling Back Behind the Wall/Fence.* This would imply the de facto annexation of 10 percent to 16 percent of the West Bank while keeping the expanded Jerusalem exclusively as the Jewish capital, thus generating a new de facto situation. It took forty years for the Palestinian leadership in 1988 to recognize Israel's borders within the pre-1967 limits, which neighboring Arab states considered to be only armistice lines. The new Israeli borders, imposed by demographic constraints, are clearly not acceptable now to the Palestinians, but in the eyes of the "Iron Wall" optimists, perhaps forty years from now the Arabs will come to the pragmatic understanding that this imposed solution is permanent and they will live with it.

c. *The Iran Factor.* The early stages of a nuclear race in the Middle East—with Iran's leadership having decided to develop its nuclear capability because of or despite the scrutiny of the international community—challenge that Israel's exclusive holding of such weapons in the region gave them an edge that made negotiations on conventional threats less acute. At this stage, it is hard to predict if this overt challenge, accompanied with statements by Iran's president, Mahmoud Ahmadinejad, calling for the destruction of the Jewish state and the expulsion of Jews to their countries of origin—notwithstanding that the majority are Israeli born—is a scary and worrisome scenario. We need not remind ourselves that an Iranian nuclear device detonated over Israel will kill not only the Arab population but also the Palestinian neighbors. As Manuel Hassassian often says in class, "We are doomed to live together," and now perhaps also to "die together." The idea of a preemptive strike, albeit more difficult than the one successfully conducted in Baghdad in 1981 when Saddam Hussein was building his Osirak reactor, is mentioned without cease. Unchecked balances may result in a self-fulfilling prophecy. However, such a unilateral move may jeopardize at least in the short run the growing chances for normalized relations between Israel and the Arab world. Lately, Iran's increasingly radical role as protagonist in the region has contributed to concerns shared by Israel and the pro-Western Arab regimes. To what extent can Israel use this shared concern, short of speculating about an Israeli military strike? Secret negotiations, within which concessions to the Palestinians would be seen as part of an alliance with the Arab countries could lead to significant results.

d. *The Syrian Option.* It is unclear why negotiations related to abandoning the Golan Heights often address neutralizing the Bath regime in Damascus that is acting as a spoiler and protector of irregular militias fighting Israel. Yet this seems to be a condition for the fulfillment of the Arab peace initiative. The likelihood that the Israeli political leadership could handle withdrawals on two fronts is nil, and opting to prioritize an agreement with Syria at the expense of neglecting a solution to the burning Palestinian problem is ill advised. No pressure has been exerted by the international community, and even less has been wielded by the Bush administration, to resolve what amounts to one of the many latent border disputes in the world. On the contrary, the human rights issues, especially when related not only to individual suffering but also to restricting self-determination, have been highlighted as urgent. The continuous military occupation of the West Bank and the encirclement of Gaza have been the main causes of criticism of Israel, and diverting the attention to Syria, at this stage, is not going to change the threat of terrorist activities.

4. *Imposed Solutions by the International Community.* As mentioned, it has not been possible for the major powers in the international community to act separately or together to force upon Israelis and Palestinians the resolution of this conflict. Yet high-level and persistent involvement has made the difference at crucial moments. The record includes Presidents Carter and Clinton. The latter, still a popular figure with Israelis and not a few Palestinians, may take the challenge again after the November 2008 elections and become the Democrats' special emissary to complete the job that remained unfinished at Camp David. Furthermore, the Quartet's appointment of Tony Blair as special envoy to help the Palestinians rebuild their homeland in concert with Israel may provide added value.

a. *The Idea of a Provisional State.* This option has appeal because an overwhelming majority of member countries are ready to welcome such an initiative. Great Britain has been supportive of a "viable Palestinian State," and Tony Blair may be on his way to joining former U.S. presidents as the appointed. In addition, President George W. Bush has expressed support for the UN's backing of a "State of Palestine" next to Israel. If the Palestinians themselves would endorse it, the international community will easily follow suit.

b. *A Quartet Initiative.* The Quartet, under whose aegis the conference ought to be held, should put forward its own outline, based on UN Security Council Resolutions 242 and 338, the Clinton parameters of 2000, the 2002 Arab Peace Initiative, and the 2003 Roadmap. According to former prominent U.S. foreign policy makers, it should reflect the following:[28]

- Two states, based on the lines of June 4, 1967, with minor, reciprocal, and agreed-upon modifications as expressed in a 1:1 land swap
- Jerusalem as home to two capitals, with Jewish neighborhoods falling under Israeli sovereignty and Arab neighborhoods under Palestinian sovereignty; and special arrangements for the Old

City, providing each side control of its respective holy places and unimpeded access by each community to them

- A solution to the refugee problem that is consistent with the two-state solution, addresses the Palestinian refugees' deep sense of injustice, and provides Palestinians with meaningful financial compensation and resettlement assistance
- Security mechanisms that address Israeli concerns while respecting Palestinian sovereignty

c. *An International Trusteeship over Palestine.* Several ideas have been considered, and the most seriously debated has been granting the United Nations the main role in setting an "International Protectorate."[29] Over time, international interventions have played a key role in various conflict situations around the world, their mandates varying with circumstances and needs. Examples include Namibia (1989), Cambodia (1992), Rwanda (1993), and more recently East Timor (1999) and Kosovo (1999). Within the region, a multinational task force in Sinai and a UN force in the Golan Heights have operated successfully for many years. A transitional international protectorate would provide to each side impartial protection from the violence of the other and generally would create some breathing space. For this to happen, serious muscle is needed, but the aim is not to contain the conflict but to end it. Thus, the security role is not enough. It must be accompanied by a political mandate to assist Palestinians in restoring basic services, reviving civil society, and rebuilding national institutions, with the explicit outcome of the establishment of an independent, democratic Palestinian state after, say, three to five years. Virtually none of these vital tasks could be carried out properly or at all as long as Israel remains the occupying power, both because it would continue to provide a magnet for Palestinian attacks and because it would retain an effective veto over any initiative. The protectorate administration would be divided between the civil and security tasks, with military personnel drawn from countries assented to by both the Palestinians and the Israelis. One proponent, *New York Times* columnist Thomas Friedman, has suggested designating the security task to the North Atlantic Treaty Organization (NATO). Alternatively, it could fall to a "coalition of the willing and acceptable," which may include troops from the United States, United Kingdom, Canada, Australia, and possibly Turkey, Egypt, Jordan or other countries. It is hard to imagine this working without the United States playing a prominent role. Martin Indyk, former U.S. ambassador to Israel, has suggested that the mandate would

initially embrace Oslo areas A and B, comprising some 42 percent of the West Bank, with a possible extension to 52 percent to provide better contiguity.

5. *An Israeli–Palestinian Joint Bottom-Up Initiative.* Some ideas related to this idea come from the laboratory of civil society members, including Track II, think tanks, and individual academics, working together across the divide or separately. The following are a few of those ideas:

a. *A Common Peace Platform:* Over a decade of Israeli–Palestinian civil society cooperation, strong bonds have been established and an epistemic community with shared values of democracy, human rights, and peace has evolved. Many past Track II exercises in different cities and universities around the world, which have produced numerous detailed documents on final status issues (water, Jerusalem, refugees, settlements, borders and security), have shown creative points of convergence that could be used for drafting a common plan of action. In spite of polls showing strong support for the use of extreme retaliatory violence against each other, large majorities of both Palestinians and Israelis approve of a compromise solution based on the side-by-side existence of two states. The problem is that leadership is lagging behind this popular support for a two-state solution, perhaps under the influence of domestic intra- and interparty politics, and the violent extraparliamentary behavior of fundamentalist groups in both societies. Lately, such peace initiatives include, among others, "One Voice."[30] The Ayalon-Nusseibeh Plan ("The Peoples' Choice") has gathered more than 150,000 signatures for a "Civil Pact" (more from the Israeli side).[31] The Geneva Initiative, launched in December 2003 by Beilin-Abed Rabbo, detailed a peace accord covering nearly all points of dispute and incorporating Saudi Prince Abdallah's peace initiative.[32] After being sent to each Israeli household and published as an advertisement in major Palestinian newspapers, the accord has already won support from 47 percent of Israelis and 39 percent of Palestinians.[33] At this stage, we are witnessing a nongovernmental peace accord. If more moderate Palestinian candidates win elections, adherence to a shared peace and justice platform may also occur within Israeli society. Palestinians inside and outside the current factions, as well as independents, have been discussing the formation of a unified force. Different possibilities have been discussed. Clearly, the modes of operation for such processes to take place within the current Palestinian political setting would be very different. The unclear rules of the electoral game will require distinct yet coordinated long-term strategies.

b. A recent initiative of Hebrew University geographer Yehoshua Ben Arieh that was advanced in Track II suggests *a trilateral land swap:* Egypt will give up a bit of territory south of the Gaza Strip (between Rafah and el-Arish), thus making it possible to create "Greater Gaza." The area annexed to the Gaza Strip, which would include a coastal strip at least twenty kilometers in length, would become the site of a new modern city, a resort area, an international airport, and a deepwater port and would triple the size of the Gaza Strip. In return for this territorial concession, Egypt would receive from Israel a slice of land in the area of the Paran Desert and thus would gain an overland route from Sinai to Jordan and neighboring countries.

The Palestinians would concede territory in the West Bank identical in size to the territory that they get from Egypt in Sinai. It is Ben-Aryeh's hope that Egypt will consent to the territorial exchange because of the great economic benefit that would accrue from control of the direct route from the city of Suez to Jordan and because of the prestige that it would enjoy for having brought about a solution to the Israeli–Palestinian conflict.

The other participants in the deal would also get a lot out of it. Israel would be able to hold onto some territory ("settlement blocs") in the West Bank. The Palestinians would receive full territorial compensation in the form of an area with tremendous development potential (in the territory annexed to the Gaza Strip) for the territory it ceded to Israel in the West Bank; they would also receive from Israel at least one (and possibly two) overland passages from the Gaza Strip to the West Bank, as well as access to the overland passage between Egypt and Jordan. This way, the Palestinian state would really have viability.

Of course, ideas are easier than implementation, and the dwindling and aging peace camp is losing ground. Brainstorming is necessary for widening it to include large segments of the vibrant civil society organizations of both sides, active in many walks of life, but alienated for joint or separate peace.

VI. CONCLUSIONS

It seems that none of the five sources of initiatives mentioned in the preceding sections has any chance of materializing on its own and that what is needed is a mixture of the best of the suggested scenarios. The process may begin with secret negotiations parallel to either back channels for Sadat–Begin or Track IIs, as in the Oslo process, and then may be endorsed and mediated by the United States with energetic involvement at the presidential level (as was the case for Presidents Carter and Clinton), accompanied by effective, reciprocal, and unilateral confidence-building measures offered by the Israeli and Palestinian governments. From the Israelis, that would include prisoner release, removal of checkpoints, permits for work in Israel, dismantling of illegal outposts, no government permits, and no new settlements; from the Palestinians, that would include effective curbing of violent threats through cooperative security and a halt to media incitement). The international community could provide endorsement, in terms of both peacekeeping and support of civil-society peace building.

In retrospect, the identity-driven Palestinian–Israeli conflict has become one of the world's quintessential and most intractable ethnopolitical disputes. Several barriers were built over a century, and differentiation was affected by a psychological dimension that resulted from the bloodshed that occurred at least once a decade. Today, we highlight our ethnic, cultural, religious, linguistic, and national differences. Extreme groups in our societies claim control over the entire land of Palestine and Israel and insist on the expulsion of the "Other," but as we reviewed encounters of Arabs and Jews through the centuries, we found strong affinities based on the common ground provided by Semitic languages, Abrahamic religions, shared history of peaceful relations, and joint scientific and cultural contributions to world civilization. Even if conflict resolution is a faraway stage, we should aim for conflict management. Even in these difficult times, conflict should not be perceived as a zero-sum game because taboos have been broken. Israelis and Palestinians have taken steps toward peace in the past. The lack of mutual trust is a major impediment in this process. Acknowledging history is not enough. Rather, we must look toward the future by analyzing what is happening today. Living in a state of trauma exacerbates people's fears and frustrations, which leads to irrational behavior.[34] We need conditions that are conducive to easing tensions and making our lives easier so we can become reengaged in the political process.

Historically speaking, it is hard to deny that the Jewish quest for national independence is one of the success stories of the twentieth century, albeit following the great suffering incurred by their brethren in Europe. Israeli Jews may associate contemporary events with previous traumatic experiences in which survival in the Diaspora was seriously at stake during centuries of persecution, and particularly during the single and most brutal event in human history: the Holocaust. However, for many Palestinians, there is no question about who has been the victim of more recent history or about the necessity for the Israelis to redress the injustices they have inflicted. Depending on different stages of the peace process and political violence, each civil society understandably weighed the situation with its own self-interests in mind.

Hence, suicide bombings prompted Israelis to expect Palestinian society to give up the monopoly of the role of "victim" and share with them a sense of empathy. Palestinians contrasted this with the reference to the "structural" violence of the Israeli government's practices in the Occupied Territories, combined with its seeming disregard for the value of Palestinian life.

In addition to gross human rights violations and the collective punishment of an entire population through restriction of its freedom of movement, the economic situation also must be factored. According to some estimates for 2005, almost 60 percent of Palestinians were unemployed or underemployed; almost 70 percent lived under the poverty level. With no food and high unemployment, and with generalized repression, people become frustrated and turn into walking bombs. We must understand that meeting some basic needs and supporting economic development can also increase peace building.

September 11, 2001, and the defeat of Saddam Hussein undoubtedly constituted a watershed in the world and in regional political trends, with direct and indirect implications for our "narrow" Israeli–Palestinian conflict—albeit that very conflict has been identified by large numbers of people worldwide as a potential cause of a world crisis. A *crisis,* as the Chinese language represents this word, is combined with the characters of both "danger" and "opportunity." Major catastrophes

during the last century have created opportunities for significant new developments that have spilled over into the Jewish–Arab struggle for Israel–Palestine. World War I, the dissolution of the Ottoman Empire, the Balfour Declaration supporting the idea of a Jewish national home, and President Woodrow Wilson's Fourteen Points together paved the way for the British mandate over Palestine. World War II and the post facto revulsion toward Nazi genocide strengthened support for the establishment of a Jewish state. After the 1991 Gulf War, President George H. W. Bush announced a "New World Order" that triggered the Madrid Peace Conference, which was followed by the Oslo breakthrough of mutual Israeli–Palestinian recognition and the call for "No more war."

The Palestinian quest for statehood is an urgent call to give back their dignity to the people of the West Bank and Gaza and to allow them to master their destiny in a manner nonprejudicial to its neighbors, and to Israel in particular. Within this context, our protracted Israeli–Palestinian dispute has shrunk back to its original dimension: two nations fighting for a small piece of land. And now, when most of the people on both sides are willing to settle for a part of the land, the national conflict has been sidetracked by Muslim and Jewish religious zealot minorities, who through their violent and undemocratic acts are determining our destiny, fostering confrontation, and postponing a peaceful resolution.

More and more, our national identities seem to be based only on how we differ from each other, from the enemy. Our identity-driven conflict seems now to be confined to the two major issues being contested: geography and demography. "Separation" is a poor second best to interactive cooperation between two sovereign entities. Failure to move in the direction of the solutions mentioned in the previous section may necessarily lead to the "one-state solution" that would include all the Palestinian territories currently under military control and pre-1967 Israel. An unwilling coalition with "Greater Israel" supporters emerged when some reputable Palestinians suggested warning the Israeli government that the dissolution of the Palestinian Authority will require in the near future that it take full responsibility over the territories and grant full citizens' rights to the natives of Palestine. This dramatic act, in their eyes, should not mean the dismantling of the PLO as the legitimate partner in power sharing.[35] Some academics have been saying for many years that it may already be too late for a two-state solution and point deterministically to the need to address realistically the picture in which Arabs and Jews will live together in one state, in competitive numbers. If this is the case, the challenge would be to make the best of a binational state with an adequate political superstructure, multiculturalism, and equality. But this is unfeasible. What many Israelis see as a demographic threat may also harbor some unfounded expectation on the part of Palestinians who prefer to wait until the time that Jews will be outnumbered. Rather than prolonging the suffering for another generation or more, some other radical options, such as ethnic cleansing or forcing the Palestinians into fragmented "homelands" (as happened to Bantustans in South Africa during the apartheid era), may perpetuate the conflict indefinitely.[36]

A quick assessment of the present political realities show that the present use of violence against each other signals even more the hatred and animosity of the two nations toward each other. Most Palestinians were born after 1967 and identify Israelis only as soldiers and the instruments of their oppression. Jews relate emotionally to the civilian victims, now reaching two-thirds of the total in Israel, who have been harmed through acts of terror and suicide bombings; this sense of a "home front" brings them back to the insecure situation of 1948, since more than 90 percent of the deaths afterward have been of soldiers killed on the borders of Israel. Like leaders such as Gandhi and Arafat's successor Mahmoud Abbas, Arafat could have disowned and totally condemned the violence as illegitimate. As much as suicide bombings had popular support, endorsement of nonviolent methods had even more support, but Arafat preferred to be silent on the alternative, losing the opportunity, after the failure of terror, to tilt the balance in a more peaceful direction.

It has often been said on the Israeli side that facing a common enemy is the glue that keeps a very diverse society together. Israelis are 20 percent Arab, secular and religious, and Jews come from more than ninety countries and are rich and poor. Still, the idea of uniting to face the "Zionist enemy" has been a convenient delaying factor for democratic change in the neighboring Arab countries and for the Palestinians. Achieving peace is not neces-

sarily a factor of disintegration, since in the democratic context, diversity and multiculturalism are inherent features of pluralistic societies in which hyphenated identities exist and flourish. In fact, the political stability in Israel has been decreasing steadily since putting the politicians face to face with the peace option. During the first twenty-nine years following independence, the Labor Party ruled effectively. Paradoxically, it was Begin's Likud that formalized the first peace option (with Egypt) and kept itself in power for fifteen long years. However, in the equivalent amount of time since the 1993 Oslo peace process, seven heads of governments of both parties have been unable, so far, to complete even one full electoral period.

At this stage, the strengthening of civil society linkages seems to be as important as a signed peace of paper. At first glance, the assumption would make sense that people share similar values that could help bridge the divide, and the potential of such interactions would be strong. However, if such is the case, why has cooperation been so difficult to achieve? While it seems logical for people with similar professional backgrounds and attitudes toward each other to work together, what makes such a relationship the domain of only a small fringe of both communities? In addition to technical and financial restrictions, other political and psychological barriers may well exist. In general, we need to realize that this effort to work with the "enemy" is initially more difficult than working for peace or justice separately. This is the case particularly now, when the expectation gap on both sides between the expected benefits and dividends from the peace process and the gloomy reality makes for a sense of frustration and depression. Keeping the Israeli–Palestinian interaction based on a sense of equality and reciprocity, while acknowledging the asymmetries resulting from the forms of dominance in an occupier–occupied relationship, is no doubt a complex enterprise. Such exchanges generate a high level of emotional involvement that could fail or result in a long-term commitment that could help overcome other practical obstacles.

As in other intrastate conflicts, the peace issue is strongly related to the relevance of human rights and clearly must be an essential part of any solution.[37] It is here that the societal involvement in peace building may represent a powerful ingredient in the problem-solving process. A sustained search for common ground and the advancement of "sectorial peace" (through academics, professional groups, artists, target sectors, women, children, etc.) can be the most effective way to change attitudes through frequent encounters. This can lead to the development of epistemic communities that share a common understanding of the issues at stake and the ways to resolve it and generate new discourse and ideas.

With all these complexities, if we look ahead into centuries beyond our lifetime, we all know that these hostilities resulted from political conflicts that can, hopefully, be solved. The cultural ties between Arabs and Jews are too deep and too pro-found to be totally undermined by the current state of political hostility. This is why we believe that a settlement of the political problems is both desired and possible. It is desired because we know that a peaceful coexistence is of mutual benefit for both Arabs and Jews, and it is possible because we are equipped with a rich common heritage that is strong enough to carry us through this difficult enterprise.

Our journey in this presentation needs to come to an end. We thank the editors for this opportunity "to tell our own stories in our own words," and we hope that our joint analysis has made a modest contribution toward understanding and peace.

Appendix

The Clinton Parameters, December 23, 2000

Source: The Web site of the Foundation for Middle East Peace, http://www.fmep.org/resources/peace_ plans/clinton_parameters.html.

Note: After the failure of the Camp David Summit in July, 2000 to achieve a peace agreement between Israeli and Palestinian delegations led, respectively, by Prime Minister Ehud Barak and Palestinian President Yasser Arafat, negotiations continued between the two sides and gaps between the parties on various issues were narrowed, but there was no comprehensive agreement. In a last ditch effort, U.S. President Bill Clinton offered the following "Parameters" on December 23 to Israeli and Palestinian negotiators at a meeting in the White House. President Clinton's "Parameters" were not the terms of a final deal, but guidelines for final accelerated negotiations he hoped could be concluded in the coming weeks. He said his terms would not be binding on his successor when he would leave office in January 2001.

Arafat, after a delay, accepted the Clinton parameters, but with questions and reservations. Barak accepted the parameters, but Israel's position was also equivocal. The parameters laid the foundation for the final negotiations that took place in January 2001 at Taba before the election of Ariel Sharon in February 2001 that effectively ended the peace process. [See "Taba Agreement" below. The text of the Clinton Parameters follows. PCWilcox, 7/7/03])

TERRITORY

Based on what I heard, I believe that the solution should be in the mid-90%'s, between 94–96% of the West Bank territory of the Palestinian State.

The land annexed by Israel should be compensated by a land swap of 1–3% in addition to territorial arrangement such as a permanent safe passage.

The parties should also consider the swap of leased land to meet their respective needs. [There] are creative ways for doing this that should address Palestinian and Israeli needs and concerns.

The Parties should develop a map consistent with the following criteria:

- 80% of the settlers in blocks
- Contiguity
- Minimize annexed areas
- Minimize the number of Palestinians affected

SECURITY

The key to security lies in an international presence that can only be withdrawn by mutual consent. This presence will also monitor the implementation of the agreement between both sides.

My best judgment is that the Israeli withdrawal should be carried out over 36 months while international force is gradually introduced in the area. At the end of this period, a small Israeli presence would remain in fixed locations in the Jordan Valley under the authority of the international force for another 36 months. This period could be reduced in the event of favorable regional developments that diminish the threats to Israel.

On early warning situations, Israel should maintain three facilities in the West Bank with a Palestinian liaison presence. The stations will be subject to review after 10 years with any changes in status to be mutually agreed.

Regarding emergency developments, I understand that you still have to develop a map of relevant areas and routes. But in defining what is an emergency, I propose the following definition:

Imminent and demonstrable threat to Israel's national security of a military nature requires the activation of a national state of emergency.

Of course, the international forces will need to be notified of any such determination.

On airspace, I suggest that the state of Palestine will have sovereignty over its airspace but that the two sides should work out special arrangements for Israeli training and operational needs.

I understand that the Israeli position is that Palestine should be defined as a "demilitarized state" while the Palestinian side proposes "a state with limited arms." As a compromise, I suggest calling it a "non-militarized state."

This will be consistent with the fact that in addition to a strong Palestinian security force, Palestine will have an international force for border security and deterrence purposes.

JERUSALEM AND REFUGEES

I have a sense that the remaining gaps have more to do with formulations than practical realities.

JERUSALEM

The general principle is that Arab areas are Palestinian and Jewish ones are Israeli. This would apply to the Old City as well. I urge the two sides to work on maps to create maximum contiguity for both sides.

Regarding the Haram/Temple Mount, I believe that the gaps are not related to practical administration but to the symbolic issues of sovereignty and to finding a way to accord respect to the religious beliefs of both sides.

I know you have been discussing a number of formulations, and you can agree on any of these. I add to these two additional formulations guaranteeing Palestinian effective control over Haram while respecting the conviction of the Jewish people. Regarding either one of these two formulations will be international monitoring to provide mutual confidence.

1. Palestinian sovereignty over the Haram and Israeli sovereignty over [the Western Wall and the space sacred to Judaism of which it is a part][the Western Wall and the Holy of Holies of which it is a part].

    There will be a firm commitment by both not to excavate beneath the Haram or behind the Wall.
2. Palestinian shared sovereignty over the Haram and Israeli sovereignty over the Western Wall and shared functional sovereignty over the issue of excavation under the Haram and behind the Wall as mutual consent would be requested before any excavation can take place.

REFUGEES

I sense that the differences are more relating to formulations and less to what will happen on a practical level.

I believe that Israel is prepared to acknowledge the moral and material suffering caused to the Palestinian people as a result of the 1948 war and the need to assist the international community in addressing the problem.

An international commission should be established to implement all the aspects that flow from your agreement: compensation, resettlement, rehabilitation, etc.

The U.S. is prepared to lead an international effort to help the refugees.

The fundamental gap is on how to handle the concept of the right of return. I know the history of the issue and how hard it will be for the Palestinian leadership to appear to be abandoning this principle.

The Israeli side could simply not accept any reference to right of return that would imply a right to immigrate to Israel in defiance of Israel's sovereign policies on admission or that would threaten the Jewish character of the state.

Any solution must address both needs.

The solution will have to be consistent with the two-state approach that both sides have accepted as the [end to] the Palestinian–Israeli conflict: the state of Palestine as the homeland of the Palestinian people and the state of Israel as the homeland of the Jewish people.

Under the two-state solution, the guiding principle should be that the Palestinian state will be the focal point for Palestinians who choose to return to the area without ruling out that Israel will accept some of these refugees.

I believe that we need to adopt a formulation on the right of return to Israel itself but that does not negate the aspiration of the Palestinian people to return to the area.

In light of the above, I propose two alternatives:

1. Both sides recognize the right of Palestinian refugees to return to Historic Palestine. Or,
2. Both sides recognize the right of the Palestinian refuges to return to their homeland. The agreement will define the implementation of this general right in a way that is consistent with the two-state solution. It would list five possible final homes for the refugees:
   1. The state of Palestine
   2. Areas in Israel being transferred to Palestine in the land swap
   3. Rehabilitation in a host country
   4. Resettlement in a third country
   5. Admission to Israel

In listing these options, the agreement will make clear that the return to the West Bank, Gaza Strip, and the areas acquired in the land swap would be a right to all Palestinian refugees.

While rehabilitation in host countries, resettlement in third world countries and absorption into Israel will depend upon the policies of those countries.

Israel could indicate in the agreement that it intends to establish a policy so that some of the refugees would be absorbed into Israel consistent with Israel's sovereign decision.

I believe that priority should be given to the refugee population in Lebanon.

The parties would agree that this implements Resolution 194.

I propose that the agreement clearly mark the end of the conflict and its implementation put an end to all its claims. This could be implemented through a UN Security Council Resolution that notes that Resolutions 242 and 338 have been implemented through the release of Palestinian prisoners.

I believe that this is an outline of a fair and lasting agreement.

It gives the Palestinian people the ability to determine the future on their own land, a sovereign and viable state recognized by the international community, Al-Qods as its capital, sovereignty over the Haram, and new lives for the refugees.

It gives the people of Israel a genuine end to the conflict, real security, the preservation of sacred religious ties, the incorporation of 80% of the settlers into Israel, and the largest Jewish Jerusalem in history recognized by all as its capital.

This is the best I can do. Brief your leaders and tell me if they are prepared to come for discussions based on these ideas. If so, I would meet the next week separately. If not, I have taken this as far as I can.

These are my ideas. If they are not accepted, they are not just off the table, they also go with me when I leave the office.

ENDNOTES

1. When we started team teaching in 1992, we called the course "The Israeli–Palestinian Conflict," but with the Oslo process a sense of optimism led us to try to avoid perpetuating calling our relation a "conflict." Initially, we considered highlighting the term *peace*, but cautionary intuition suggested that we replace the original title with "Conflict Resolution: The Israeli–Palestinian Experiment."

2. For a description of previous coauthoring efforts, see "Israeli–Palestinian Co-authoring: A New Development Towards Peace?" *Journal of Palestine Studies* XXII, 88, no. 4 (1993), 32–44.

3. Since the pioneering writings of the late S. D. Goitein (d. 1984) on contact between Arabs and Jews through the ages, no major work has been produced to reexamine the

long history of contact between these two Semitic peoples.

4. Shukri Abed, "The Common Heritage of Arabs and Jews: An Historical Perspective" (unpublished manuscript, 1996). "While the medieval epoch may have been exceptional in terms of Jewish–Arab productive relationships, from antiquity to the present and whenever their destinies met, some Jews and some Arabs found ways to cooperate-mostly within the limits of their time and place, and sometimes transcending these limits." Arabs and Jews are the two surviving representatives of the Semitic people, and their respective languages–Arabic and Hebrew–have preserved the major characteristics of the mother Semitic tongue. As two languages that have many semantic and structural similarities, they reflect a major cultural affinity between the two peoples who use them: Arabs and Jews, respectively. Similarities between Arabs and Jews, indeed an overlapping of world views, are codified in the patterns of these languages. Likewise, notwithstanding the variations in narratives and emphasis, much of the teachings of the *Qur'an,* Islam's holy book, can be traced back to Jewish and Christian origins as reflected in the Bible. Thus, Arabs and Jews share linguistic and religious traditions that were handed over to them by their forefathers and the founders of their respective religions. The linguistic and religious elements they share created the cultural affinity, provided the platform for a historical bond, and led to intellectual and political cooperation between them for many centuries. This cooperation is reflected in the works of many scholars, scientists, philosophers, and artists, of both peoples, who worked together throughout the various Islamic empires and produced one of the most profound and important cultures known in history, the Judeo–Arabic culture.

5. The persecution of Jews that began in medieval Christian Europe was alien to Muslim lands. Religious and ethnic tolerance continued to characterize Muslim societies even when the horrible crimes against Jews in modern history were taking place in Europe. Jews continued to enjoy the protection and the friendship of their Muslim and Arab neighbors until the two respective national movements, Zionism and the Arab National Movement, began to clash on political, not cultural, grounds. The creation in 1948 of Israel as a Jewish state in the heart of the Arab world signaled the beginning of strained relations between the Jews and Muslims/Arabs. The wars, the acts of violence, and the hostility that have erupted as a result of the political developments in the Middle East over the last hundred years are unwelcome phenomena for both peoples.

6. When we talk about national and ethnic minorities, we typically refer to Arabs in general who overwhelmingly were Muslims; the Armenians who were Christians; and the Serbs, Croatians, Greeks, and other minorities who lived within the Ottoman Empire, which engulfed many different communities under a community system of control (the "millet system") for which the head of the church and the head of the community were accountable.

7. Benny Morris, *The Birth of the Palestinian Refugee Problem: 1947-1949* (Cambridge: Cambridge University Press, 1988).

8. Manuel Hassassian, "The Democratization Process in the PLO: Ideology, Structure and Strategy," in *Democracy, Peace and the Israeli-Palestinian Conflict,* ed. E. Kaufman, S. Abed, and R. Rothstein (Boulder, CO: Lynne Rienner, 1993), 257–88.

9. A colonial situation is one in which "one ethnic group rules over another, ethnically different, group within the same territory. The ruling group holds a monopoly of power, as well as a disproportionately large share of the territory's economy resources." Emmanuel Sivan, "The Intifada and Decolonization," *Middle East Review* (Winter 1989/1990), 2–6.

10. Rael Jean Isaac, *Israel Divided: Ideological Politics in the Jewish State* (Baltimore: Johns Hopkins University Press, 1976), 45.

11. Ibid., 73.

12. The following pages have condensed the chapter by Moshe Maoz, "Democratization Among West Bank Palestinians and Palestinian-Israeli Relations," in ed. E. Kaufman, S. Abed, and R. Rothstein, *Democracy, Peace and the Israeli-Palestinian Conflict* (Boulder, CO: Lynne Rienner, 1993), 213–44.

13. Shibley Telhami, *The Path to the Camp David Accords* (New York: Columbia University Press, 1990).

14. The different sources of the terms are given in E. Kaufman, "Israeli Perceptions of the Palestinians' 'Limited Violence' in the *Intifada,*" *Journal of Terrorism and Political Violence, no. 3* (Winter 1992), 1–38.

15. Sari Nusseibah, Faysal el-Husseini, and particularly Mubarak Awad develop this idea in *Nonviolent Resistance as a Strategy for the Occupied Territories* (Santa Cruz, CA: New Society Publishers, 1983).

16. An analysis of the first sixty leaflets of the Unified National Command of the Intifada by Nafez Assaily, Palestinian Center for the Study of Nonviolence, Jerusalem (June 1991), can be obtained by contacting mawad@iyaf.org.

17. Edy Kaufman, "The Intifada's Limited Violence," *Journal of Arab Affairs,* no. 9 (Fall 1990), 120–21.

18. A critical analysis of the "WWW," including articles of both authors, can be found in E. Kaufman, W. Salem, and J. Verhoeven, eds., *Bridging the Divide: Peacebuilding in the Israeli/Palestinian Conflict* (Boulder, CO: Lynne Rienner Publishers, 2006).

19. Arie Kacovicz, "Rashomon in the Middle East: Clashing Narratives of the Israeli-Palestinian Conflict" (unpublished manuscript, Hebrew University, Department of International Relations, 2003).

20. Sari Nusseibeh and Edy Kaufman, "The Al-Aqsa Intifada: Reflections on a Turning Point," *Palestine-Israel Journal,* vol. VII, no. 8 (2000), 32–45.

21. Kacovicz, "Rashomon in the Middle East: Clashing Narratives of the Israeli-Palestinian Conflict."

22. Michael Walzer, "The Four Wars of Israel/Palestine," *Dissent Magazine* (Fall 2002).

23. Khalil Shikaki, "A Palestinian Civil War?" *Foreign Affairs* (January–February 2002), 89–105.

24. This "Roadmap for an Israeli-Palestinian Peace"—developed by the United States and subsequently endorsed by the United Nations, the European Union, and Russia (the Quartet)—was clear in its early stages and then vague in

showing the road toward the establishment of a viable Palestinian state.

25. Among the more elaborate plans, see "Middle East Endgame I: Getting to a Comprehensive Arab-Israeli Peace Settlement," *Middle East Report No. 2* (Amman/Washington/Brussels: International Crisis Group, July 16, 2002).

26. Jerome Segal, "How to Bring a Unified Palestinian State into Existence," published in *Al-Quds* in Arabic, September 27, 2007.

27. Shafeeq Ghabra, "The Arab Peace Initiative: The Necessities of Reviving the Initiative and the Risk of Stagnation," *Common Ground News Service,* November 18, 2003.

28. This statement was coordinated by the International Crisis Group in October 2007 and included as signatories Zbigniew Brzezinski, former national security advisor to President Jimmy Carter; Lee H. Hamilton, former congressman and co-chair of the Iraq Study Group; Carla Hills, former U.S. trade representative under President George H.W. Bush; Nancy Kassebaum-Baker, former senator; Thomas R. Pickering, former undersecretary of state; Brent Scowcroft, former national security advisor to Presidents Gerald Ford and George H. W. Bush; Theodore C. Sorensen, former special counsel and advisor to President John F. Kennedy; and Paul Volcker, former chairman of the board of governors of the U.S. Federal Reserve System.

29. "An International Protectorate for the West Bank and Gaza Strip?" Summarized from a study undertaken by Tony Klug (London: Middle East Policy Initiative Forum, May 2003).

30. The aim of "One Voice" is to achieve consensus at the grassroots level to reach a ten-point agreement based on security, dignity, respect, and the right to build a better future for the next generation of Palestinians and Israelis. For more information, see www.onevoicemovement.org.

31. This short document endorses the two-state solution along the pre-1967 border with mutually agreed modifications: Jerusalem as the capital of the two states, Jews returning only to Israel (no settlements), and Palestinian refugees given compensation and the choice to return to Palestine. See www.mifkad.org.

32. For an analysis of the Saudi peace initiative and the endorsement at the Beirut Arab League Summit in March 2002, see Shafeeq Ghabra, "The Arab Peace Initiative: The Necessities of Reviving the Initiative and the Risks of Stagnation," *Common Ground News Service,* November 17, 2003.

33. For the full peace treaty, covering in detail maps for borders, Jerusalem as a capital for both states, refugees, and settlements (only chapters on water and economic cooperation are missing), see www.heskem.org.il. For the full results of the public opinion poll conducted by the Truman Research Institute for the Advancement of Peace and the Palestinian Center for Policy and Survey Research, see http://truman.huji.ac.il.

34. Vamik Volkan, *Bloodlines: From Ethnic Pride to Ethnic Terrorism* (New York: Farrar, Straus & Giroux, 1977).

35. Gazi Hamad, "To Dissolve or Not to Dissolve," *Palestine Report Newslist,* January 31, 2004.

36. Many publications have compared the South Africa and Israel–Palestine realities, although not predicting as yet the same one-state outcome. See Manuel Hassassian, "NGOs in the Context of National Struggle," in ed. Benjamin Gidron, *Mobilizing for Peace: Conflict Resolution in Northern Ireland, Israel/Palestine, and South Africa* (New York: Oxford University Press, 2002), 130–50. See also E. Kaufman and Mubarak Awad, "Back from South Africa: Lessons for the Israeli-Palestinian Peace," *Tikkun,* vol. 10, no. 5 (September–October, 1995), 63–64, 93–94. Also see Yair Hirschfeld, Avivit Hai, and Gary Susman, *Learning from South Africa: Lessons to the Israeli-Palestinian Case* (Tel Aviv: Tel Aviv Economic Cooperation Foundation and Friedrich Ebert Stiftung, 2003).

37. Edward (Edy) Kaufman and Ibrahim Bisharat, "Introducing Human Rights into Conflict Resolution: The Relevance for the Israeli-Palestinian Peace Process," *Journal of Human Rights,* vol. 1, no. 1 (March 2002), 71–91.

ABOUT THE AUTHORS

Edward (Edy) Kaufman served as Executive Director of the Harry S. Truman Research Institute for the Advancement of Peace at the Hebrew University of Jerusalem from 1983 until 2005. Since 1991 he has also been a Senior Research Associate at CIDCM, having served as the center's director from 1994 to 1996. Prof. Kaufman has dedicated much of his time to applied research, the teaching and training of conflict resolution, and human rights in Israel and worldwide. Through his involvement in human rights and peace organizations, he has endeavored through the years to contribute to the international citizens lobby on both issues. At the global level, he has served for many years as a member of the International Executive Committee of the Nobel Peace Laureate, Amnesty International, and the Committee for Scientific Freedom and Responsibility, and he continues to serve on the advisory board of Human Rights Watch/Middle East. Within Israel, he served as Honorary Secretary of the Council for Jews in Arab Countries and is the Past Chair of the Carter-Merill Human Rights Award–winning organization B'tselem. Prof. Kaufman holds B.A. and M.A. degrees in political science, international relations, and sociology from the Hebrew University of Jerusalem and a doctorate from the University of Paris (Sorbonne). He conducted his postdoctoral studies at the University of Michigan, Ann Arbor. He has authored and coauthored thirteen books and more than sixty academic articles in the area of international relations, with an emphasis on human rights and conflict resolution and a regional specialization on Latin America and the Middle East, having coauthored in the latter area with seven Palestinian colleagues. He has taught in leading U.S. and Israeli universities and has conducted workshops and lectures in over forty countries and fifty North American universities. His current research and advocacy interests are in merging the paradigms of human rights and conflict resolution.

Manuel Hassassian is a professor of international politics and relations. He has served as Executive Vice President of Bethlehem University for fifteen years. His areas of specialization are comparative politics with emphasis on Middle East politics, the Armenian nationalist movement, and political theory. He has published in both areas extensively and his latest books are *Palestine: Factionalism in the National Movement—1919–1939* (English), *The Historical Evolution of the Armenian Question and the Conflict over Nagorno Karabagh* (English), and *Citizenship in the Middle East*. He has published extensively in academic journals domestically, regionally, and internationally on the PLO, the peace process, democracy and elections, refugees, and civil society in Palestine.

Prof. Hassassian is a member of the editorial board of the *Arab Political Science Journal* and the *Palestine–Israel Journal*. In addition, he was editor-in-chief of *Bethlehem University Journal*. Prof. Hassassian is a board member of the Center of Non-Violence in Palestine and a member of the Arab Association for Human Rights. Prof. Hassassian was appointed by the Palestinian Authority to the position of General Secretary of the Bethlehem District Elections Commission in 1996. He also has served by appointment as a consultant to the Palestinian Ministerial Higher Commission on Church Affairs. He has participated in many Track II diplomacy initiatives and has been a visiting scholar to many American universities, lecturing on models and practices of conflict resolution and management.

In September 1996, Dr. Hassassian was awarded an honorary doctorate from the Université de Reims in France for his academic contributions in the field of political science. He also has served as the head of the Jerusalem Task Force in the Negotiations Affairs Department. He was president of the Rectors' Conference at the Palestinian Ministry of Higher Education, and since 2001 he has been president of Palestinian/European Academic Cooperation in Education (PEACE), located in UNESCO's Paris headquarters. In 2005 he was appointed as Palestinian Ambassador to Great Britain.

6

Rwanda

First and foremost, when discussing Rwanda we have to underline the identity-based nature of the country's conflict. The dynamics of the clashes have always been characterized by a few psychological tendencies, such as victimization, dehumanization, stereotyping, and demonization. Before colonialism, this country's history had been compiled in the oral tradition. In relating this history those who had power put the emphasisis on glorious episodes and conquests, while those who were ruled systematically told stories about being poor and oppressed victims; thus, there always have been two sides to the same story.

In addition, 85 percent of Rwanda's population is Hutus, who comprise the second ethnic group to settle in the area (around 2000 B.C.), after the Batwas. The latter were the original inhabitants of the region, and they were mainly hunters. Most of the Hutus were farmers,

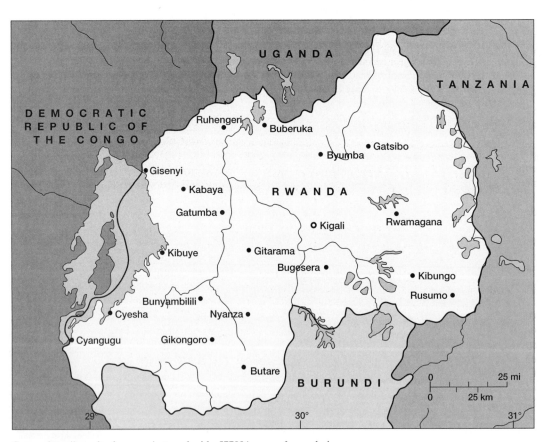

Source: http://travel.yahoo.com/p-travelguide-577884-map_of rwanda-i

and their social structure took the form of lineages and clans ruled by several chiefs. Both groups coexisted peacefully. A few centuries after settling in Rwanda, Hutus were divided into small states ruled by specific clans, which were ruled by a *mwami* who assumed the role of king.

The Tutsis appeared around 900 A.D. Their relation with the Hutus was characterized by agricultural product exchanges. Both groups benefited from heavy rainfalls and fertile lands. However, some Hutu extremists maintain even today that the Tutsis conquered the country by violent means, even though there is no historical evidence confirming their assertions.

Rwanda progressively took the form of a unified country with the merger of the small statelets into one entity.

Then came the colonial period, which exacerbated the feelings of difference between the two main groups. The Germans arrived first, in the 1880s. They pointed out the physical differences they noted between the two ethnic groups. They described Hutus as short, dark, flat-nosed, thick-lipped, and simple-minded negroes, whereas they saw the Tutsis as a group of tall, noble, majestic, and civilized born-rulers.

Furthermore, the Germans created a colonial administration characterized by indirect rule systems. They decided that it was natural for the Tutsis to rule the Hutus even though the country's original institutions were not an exclusive Tutsi creation. Thus, they totally ignored the Hutus' large contribution to this system.

In 1916, the Belgians replaced the Germans. The latter decided to maintain the same indirect style of ruling. They perpetuated the *Tutsification* of Rwanda. For instance, they eliminated the remaining Hutu chiefs. They also offered administration, justice, and access to education exclusively to Tutsi elites.

This process continued until 1955. At that time, crucial changes and a wind of freedom were blowing through the entire African continent. As the Belgians considered their exit strategy, the Tutsis grew determined to preserve their power in a newly independent country and become the local bourgeoisie.

Meanwhile, a group of Hutu intellectuals, led by G. Kabiyanda, produced an important paper the "Hutu Manifesto." The key of their writings was that the Hutu elite had to take control of the country before it gained its independence. They also pointed out the racist monopoly of the Tutsis, which has been fueled by the colonial rhetoric about Tutsi superiority. Hutus expressed their bitterness and anger over the fact that they have endured 900 years of domination by a group that only makes up 14 percent of Rwanda's population.

Moreover, they underlined the double-colonization phenomenon—one by the Hamites, the other by the Europeans—and they finally concluded their essay by rejecting the idea of independence, saying that it would create an even more terrible form of Tutsi-rule over them. Instead, what they really craved was power. They also put the blame entirely on the Tutsis, ignoring the fact that colonialists had used the latter as a tool to serve their global interests.

Those radical ideas led to the creation of a new political party, Parmehutu, which was pro-colonial. Its main goal was not to oust the Belgians but to replace them and put Tutsis in the dominating position. This goal had to do with the psychological phenomenon of *mimetic desire*, which is explained in the following chapter. Another Hutu leader, Joseph Habyarimana, emerged in that period (1957). He was backed by the Belgian administration and the Catholic Church. He gained confidence and became more aggressive in his speeches against the Tutsis, encouraging his people to use violence and kill them. The problem is that the Hutu extremists had a distorted view because, in fact, only 3.3 percent of the Tutsi population was benefiting from the privileges offered by the colonial administration.

In the 1950s, Rwanda experienced a time of political pluralism, and several political parties were founded. In November 1959, rumor had it that two important Hutu leaders had been killed by Tutsis. This sparked a movement called the Hutu Social Revolution. Tutsis were killed, and their houses were burned. This major clash happened over the course of two weeks.

This event marked the beginning of a phase of impunity in which Tutsis became the target of extreme violence. The fact that they were a minority group made them even more vulnerable to Hutu attacks. In 1991 there was a significant decline in the Tutsi population, which went from 14 percent (in the 1950s) down to only 8.5 percent. Some Tutsis fled Rwanda, others switched identities and presented themselves as Hutus. The 1970s were characterized by a growing tension between northern and southern Hutus. The latter were accused of monopolizing the power. To avoid serious clashes among themselves and to divert their aggressiveness, they found a common target and an ideal scapegoat: the Tutsis.

These conflicts led to a coup d'état in which Joseph Habyarimana, then an army major, took power. Thus, in 1975 Rwanda became a single-party state MRND, each Rwandan was systematically made a member, no matter their age or views. Habyarimana built a very strong political monopoly. He was simultaneously head of the state, head of the party, and head of the army.

Even businessmen had to deal with Habyarimana to pursue their ventures, and they often had to give a financial contribution to the party in order to fall into Habyarimana's good graces and ensure their safety. At that time, the term *Akazu* emerged to indicate all the people who were part of the president's network and support system and to exclude all those who were not. This private circle soon became a criminal group, Zero Network, whose mission was to kill anyone who was a threat to the country's totalitarian system.

The 1980s were greatly influenced by foreign assistance that allowed Rwanda to build large infrastructure projects such as roads and extended electric services. During that period, the country was seen as a model of what could be done in Africa with the assistance of international aid. Unfortunately, that money was not fairly distributed and most of the population remained poor. In the late 1980s, the price of coffee suddenly dropped, creating a deep crisis and plunging the country into a huge debt.

The government also created a system of quotas, the Ethnic and Regional Equilibrium, which pretended to offer an equal share of Rwanda's resources to all citizens. In reality, this program was used to block Tutsis' access to employment and education. It also excluded Hutus who were not part of *Akazu*.

In the early 1990s, the government experienced internal and external pressures to return to a multiparty system. Exiled Tutsis organized themselves and created the Rwanda's Patriotic Front (RPF). In October 1990, the RPF went on a mission to attack the country.

In 1991, Habyarimana finally changed the constitution to allow a multiparty system. The Arusha Peace Agreement was negotiated in Tanzania with the RPF and signed in 1993. Its main goal was to ensure the long-term political and military integration of Rwanda's many internal and external components.

On April 6, 1994, Burundi and Rwanda's presidents were both killed when the jet they were traveling in was shot down. In the following days, Prime Minister Agathe Uwillingiyimana and other politcal personalities were killed by Hutu extremists. These events triggered the Hutus who implemented their "Final Solution." Tutsis were accused of killing the president, and Hutu civilians were told by radio and word of mouth that it was their duty to massacre as many Tutsis as possible. This death sentence was also applied to moderate Hutus who were not anti-Tutsi.

The genocide was carried out by Hutus who constituted themselves as a transitional government led by Jean Kambanda, who was condemned in 1998 to life in prison for his crimes. According to Rwanda's authorities, at least 800,000 moderate Hutus and Tutsis were massacred during this genocide.

In July 1994, the Tutsi RPF finally defeated the Hutu regime and stooped the killing. Approximatively two million Hutus fled into neighboring countries, including Burundi, Tanzania, Uganda, and Zaïre. Since then, most of them have returned to Rwanda.

Today, the biggest challenge Rwanda faces is reconciling two groups who have been deeply hurt, wounded, and traumatized and to enable people to forgive each other despite the ugliness, tremendous violence, and hatred they have expressed in the past.

In this chapter on Rwanda's conflict, Richard Batsinduka asserts that the Rwandan conflict is the result of false recollections and distorted views of the country's history. Extremist Hutus have always placed themselves as victims, while Tutsi leaders have described their group's past in terms of conquests and glory. The text also underlines the key role that colonization played in those clashes. Indeed, their racist thesis seriously aggravated an already tense situation, which ultimately led to the infamous 1994 genocide.

The Rwandan Conflict

Richard Batsinduka

Rwanda has a long history of ethnopolitical conflict that has caused much suffering. The most recent, horrific example is the 1994 genocide of Tutsis. The roots of Rwanda's ethnopolitical conflict are deep and complex. In this chapter, I explain the underlying causes and history of identity-based, deep-rooted conflict in Rwanda.

Rwanda's historic heritage contains factors that are identified as classic intensifiers of identity-based conflict. They include reservoirs of recollection, difficult life circumstances, loss of face, victimization, dehumanization and demonization, stereotypes and ideology of difference, real or perceived historic enmity, bystander compliance or encouragement, and narcissistic wounding. People in Rwanda keep experiencing situations in which most of these factors are present in their lives. After discussing the legacy of Rwanda's past, I show how it presents major obstacles to the process of reconciliation.

ISSUES AND INCIDENTS THAT CAUSED THE CONFLICT

The history of Rwanda, at least the precolonial period, was exclusively documented by the oral tradition. The extreme malleability of data compiled only through the oral tradition makes history a very dangerous tool. Stories that are told by Rwandans about the past are either ethno-narratives of glory or ethno-narratives of victimization for those who had less power. Knowingly or unknowingly, the use of these stories has been at the core of ethno-nationalism that exacerbates the ideology of difference, stereotypes of "self" and "other," and scapegoat mechanisms.

Distortion of the Reservoirs of Recollection

The Rwandan Settlement The people of Rwanda are divided into three identity groups: the Hutus who are mainly labeled farmers and make up 85 percent of the population, the Tutsis who are defined as cattle breeders and comprise around 14 percent of the population, and the Batwa or Pygmies who account for almost 1 percent and are mainly hunters and gatherers. The available documentation suggests that the first inhabitants of Rwanda were hunter-gatherers and forest dwellers, the ancestors of the Batwa. The same sources suggest that they inhabited the area from as early as 2000 B.C. Around 1000 A.D. a migration of Bantu or Hutu farmers began, part of the so-called Bantu expansion from the savannahs of present-day Cameroon to the Great Lakes subregion. Their social organization was based on lineages and clans, which were under the leadership of chiefs. Apparently, there was a peaceful coexistence between Hutus and Twas, who bartered skins and meat in exchange for salt and iron products. Around 1400 A.D. Hutus were organized into small states, and each "statelet" was controlled by a dominant clan. Clans were composed of many different lineages and fell under a ruling lineage headed by a *mwami* (king). The mwami was a land chief and a ritual leader. There is evidence that some lineages were already in possession of cattle at that time and that some states had already emerged before the arrival of the Tutsis.

The Tutsi immigration, which began around 900 A.D., occurred gradually and peacefully. Interaction with Hutus was based on the exchange of cattle products for agricultural products. Hutu cultivators and Tutsi pastoralists lived interspersed in most areas of the fertile country that enjoyed regular rainfall, to the satisfaction of both agriculturalists and cattle breeders.

No one would think that the settlement of a country by successive migrants would be an issue, but in the case of Rwanda this part of the country's history is part of the conflict. The way the story is told by Hutu extremists suggests that the Tutsis–Hamites conquered the country of the Hutus–Bantus by violence, even though there is no evidence of violence in the integration of the Tutsis. Nothing is said about the settlement of the Hutu in the land of the Twas. As there is no historical evidence of any fight, the assumption is that everything went smoothly, even though it is obvious that the lifestyle of the hunter-gatherers was likely totally shaken by the arrival of agriculturalist newcomers. One thing is sure: there is no evidence of confrontation either in oral or written history related to the settlement of Rwanda.

The "Unification" of the Country   The amalgamation of the statelets into a united Rwanda was a process spread over several hundred years. Amalgamation began with the Nyiginya kingdom, the core state in eastern Rwanda, which slowly expanded by conquering and giving protection, in return receiving tribute. Not until the second part of the nineteenth century under mwami Kigeri Rwabugiri was Rwanda united as one country. Rwabugiri is perceived to be the one who brought Rwanda to the height of its power. During its expansion, Rwanda attacked neighboring peoples, regardless of whether they were ruled by Tutsis or Hutus and regardless of whether they were organized in lineages or states.

Both Hutus and Tutsis created Rwandan institutions. Even though the power of the ruler derived from control over the military and over the size of his cattle herds, his authority relied largely on rituals strongly rooted in agricultural practices. Mwami Rwabugiri was the source and symbol of all authority in the politically centralized state. He governed the central regions closely through a number of hierarchies of competing leaders who administered men, cattle, pasturage, and agricultural land. He exercised a kind of loser suzerainty over some smaller states that were dominated by powerful lineage groups, some of them Hutus and some of them Tutsis. Some of these entities stayed autonomous until 1910–20. An example was the northern region near Ruhengeri, which was only incorporated into the Rwandese monarchy under German colonial rule. It took several military expeditions led by the German Schutztruppe, assisted by Tutsis, from central Rwanda between 1910 and 1912, to defeat the northern Hutu, also known as Bakiga. The defeat left considerable bitterness toward both the Tutsis and the Southern Hutu, or Banyanduga, who came with them.

In the 1920s, the Belgians made things even worse, when they decided to put these entities under the total control of the central state. This part of Rwandan history is very sensitive as it was subject to distortion by extremists who used it to explain the origin of the "historic enmity" between Hutus and Tutsis. During the sixteenth century, statelets led by Hutu or Tutsi lineages were basically similar, with each king trying to expand his territory either peacefully or by violent means. For instance, the Tutsi king Mutabazi gave his daughter, Nyirantobwa, in marriage to Mashira, son of his rival, the king of Nduga. Gahindiro, son of Mutabazi, married Bwiza, daughter of Mashira. Later, during an armed confrontation, Mutabazi killed the king of Nduga, but Mashira, his son-in-law, managed to escape. Mutabazi reigned Nduga for some years until Mashira returned from exile and reestablished his Babanda clan's power and expanded his territory by annexing the Ndiza, Bwanamukali, and Marangara kingdoms. Mutabazi was forced to flee to Bushi in the Republic of Democratic Congo. Upon his return from exile, Mutabazi managed to kill Mashira and all his male children (his own grandchildren!), thereby establishing his Nyiginya clan's power in the kingdom of Nduga.

In a society governed by lineages and clans, a military victory necessarily ended with the death of the overpowered monarch and the killing of all male members of his lineage. That was the only way of securing and strengthening one's victory. Wars between Hutus and Tutsis were battles between dynasties; royal lineages were in armed conflict. Sometimes there was a conflict opposing royal Hutu lineages or Tutsi lineages; some other times it was a battle between a Hutu royal lineage and a Tutsi royal lineage. The deadliest conflict, known as the Rucunshu war of 1896, involved two opposing Tutsi clans: the Banyiginya and the Bega. Despite their history of conflict, toward the end of the nineteenth century Hutus and Tutsis developed a single and very strong sense of connectedness based on three shared fundamental characteristics: one language, one faith, one culture.

Rwanda was then a major state, and its rulers measured their power by the number of subjects and measured their wealth based on the importance of their cattle, and the two were usually related. Giving or temporarily granting cattle was a way of winning supporters, and a large number of supporters helped to win cattle, especially through conflicts with other members of the elite. The link created between the cattle granter and his follower was called the *ubuhake*. This system was later manipulated and misinterpreted. Ubuhake ended up with a connotation of "feudalism," if not "slavery," which some say was imposed by Tutsis on the Hutus.

The Misinterpretation of the Ubuhake Pastoral Contract

The ubuhake system involved reciprocal bonds of loyalty and exchange of goods and services between two individuals. It first occurred under the reign of Yuhi IV Gahindiro. Mwami Gahindiro used ubuhake to gain more control over the Tutsi aristocracy and reinforce his seizure of their cattle and land nationwide. In the mid-1800s, under the reign of Mutara Rwogera, ubuhake was not frequently practiced and involved only rich cattle breeders seeking the protection of powerful and influential individuals. Pastoralists who had few cattle were not involved in the ubuhake system, nor were agriculturalists.

Toward the end of Rwabugiri's reign, the Rwandan state grew in strength and sophistication. The administration system became larger; the kingdom had developed a complex and highly organized administrative structure comprised of provinces, districts, hills, and neighborhoods. Provinces were administered by high chiefs or army commanders who were Tutsis, while districts were administered by two chiefs appointed by the mwami: one cattle chief (a Tutsi) in charge of cattle taxes and one land chief (a Hutu) responsible for agricultural levies. The districts were divided into hills administered by chiefs responsible for handing over the levies for the two district chiefs. Ubuhake expanded and involved relationships between Tutsis looking for political protection from the newly appointed authorities. One can also note, but more rarely, the creation of ubuhake relationships between influential Tutsis and rich Hutus seeking protection for their cattle.

After World War I, the ubuhake relationship quickly lost its political meaning as the mwami and his entourage had limited power as they were under the control of the colonial administration. The ubuhake relationship became essentially economical and involved more and more people. Those who possessed huge numbers of cattle gave some to Tutsis and Hutus who had few or no cows. In return, recipients had to pay back in loyalty, goods, and services to their granter. In the early 1930s, clients of Hutu origin began to cultivate the land of their patron. These changes were made by the Belgian administration for reasons I will explain later.

Many inaccurate reports have been written about ubuhake. They consisted mainly of claims that this relationship existed for many centuries on the one hand and that ubuhake was an exclusive tool for the exploitation of Hutus by Tutsis on the other hand. Ubuhake relationships did not exist before the second half of the nineteenth century and in the beginning involved only a very limited minority of cattle breeders. One exception worth noting is that a few Hutus were involved in ubuhake relationships in pre-colonial Rwanda. Unfortunately, manipulation and distortion of facts led to a process of "ethnic" amalgamation, particularly among Hutus. The result was an "ethnic" Hutu–Tutsi dichotomy.

The Colonial Changes and the Ideology of Difference

When the Germans arrived in Rwanda in the 1880s, they were amazed by the extent to which the country was organized and also by the people of Rwanda themselves. Richard Kandt, the first German administrator, describes Rwanda and its people, using Adolf Gustav Von Goetzen's observations of 1898:

> He found a country extremely green which from the East to the West rises gradually from 1500 meters to 2500 meters, rich in water and with a wonderful climate; unlike in the other regions of the colony, he didn't find a sparse population but instead, a population amounting up to hundreds of thousands of Bantu Negroes called Wahutu. He found this population in a position of slave subordination towards the Watutsi, a cast of noble strangers of semitic origin, whose forefathers, coming from the Galla countries of Southern Ethiopia, had subjected the entire region of the Great Lakes. He found the country divided into provinces and districts under the administration of the Watutsi, whose impressive height, up to two meters, took him back to the universe of tales and legends, and on top of them, a king who restlessly crossed the country, building his residences here and there.

This description is based on the racial theories developed by Charles Darwin and Joseph Arthur de Gobineau. These theories generated stereotypes that became the foundation of the ideology of difference between Hutus and Tutsis. On one side, we have the Tutsis who are noble, with an impressive height, came from Ethiopia, conquered the Great Lakes, and enslaved the local Negroes. On the other hand, we have the Hutus who, according to Louis de Lacger "have the physical type of the common Negro with an average type of 1.67 metres, very dark in complexion, with prognathism, flat nose and thick lips and who live a simplistic settled way of life." De Lacger goes even further and defines Tutsis as Caucasians who were born rulers. Their unchallenged superiority relyied on three fundamental elements:

- The racial element first: Tutsis' physical superiority. They are tall, noble and have a majestic bearing which gave them a prestigious impact on simpleminded and semi-civilized people.
- The second element is economical: Tutsis are magnates whose wealth comes from their cattle.
- The third element is political: Tutsis are people who are born to rule like the Romans were in the time of Virgil.

The Germans established a colonial administration, ruling the country for the least cost and the most profit. They decided to administer Rwanda by the indirect rule system, making use of Rwanda's impressive indigenous state government system. Believing the Tutsis to be more capable, the Germans found it logical for the Tutsis to rule the Hutus, just as, to them, it was logical and reasonable for Europeans to rule Africans. The Germans were not aware of the Hutus' contribution to the building of Rwanda; they only saw that the ruler of this impressive state and many of his immediate entourage were Tutsis. This led them to assume that the sophisticated institutions had been exclusively Tutsi creations.

Building the Rwandan infrastructure necessitated linking the country to the world economy, and this required a very high proportion of Rwandan goods and labor. The colonial power's demands were dictated to the indigenous Tutsi administration, which turned to the local population to satisfy the master's needs. This situation created very hard life conditions for the local population, especially for Hutus but also for Tutsis of modest means. The colonial exactions included hard labor and various physical and demeaning abuses, which included whipping as a punishment.

Some Tutsis welcomed the European idea of their superiority, which coincided with their mythical beliefs. According to one of the most common myths, Immana (the Creator) created Gahutu, Gatwa, and Gatutsi. He gave a jar full of milk to each of them and asked them to keep the milk and stay awake until his return. Gatwa, who was playful, spilled the milk. Gahutu, who was hungry and not patient enough, drank the milk. Gatutsi waited until the return of Immana. Immana decided that Gatutsi would be the master of both Gahutu and Gatwa.

This is an extremely important turning point as far as the origins of the Rwandan conflict are concerned. In many other African countries, there are numerous tribes. Each tribe speaks its own language or dialect and has its own values, beliefs, traditions, and territory. Actually, going from tribe to tribe is like going from one country to another. Rwanda has only three identity groups. The two groups in conflict—Hutus and Tutsis—are brothers in every aspect of life. There is no basis whatsoever for supposed differences between Hutus and Tutsis. In fact, during the 1994 genocide, Hutu killers manning roadblocks had to ask potential victims for their identity cards, as this document shows the ethnic group to which the cardholder belongs.

Rather, the roots of the conflict stem from the historical relationships between Tutsis and Hutus. As Vern Neufeld Redekop explains:

> Deep-rooted conflict takes place in the context of relationships. Relationships take place within relational systems—a set of factors that brings individuals or groups into significant contact with one another; this is frequently geographical proximity. Within a relational system, there is a Self, the individual from whose vantage point the story is told, and there is an Other, to whom the individual or group relates.[3]

In the case of Rwanda, the relational system is extremely closed and exclusive, because only two groups are involved in that relationship, as the Twas were ostracized by both Hutus and Tutsis. In many other African countries, the multiplicity of tribes and other ethnic groups is very high, so each group has access to many other groups and relationships. In Congo, for instance, if the Bakongo tribe for some reason had a problem with the Bangala tribe, each tribe has still more than two hundred other tribes with whom to get along.

In a closed relational system, such as the one in Rwanda, mimetic dynamics are extremely active. Mimetic theory, developed by René Girard and explained by Redekop, sheds a tremendous amount of light on the Rwandan conflict. One of the dynamics is identified as the *mimetic desire*. As Redekop explains, the word

> "mimetic" comes from the same root as "mime" and "imitate." To have a mimetic desire is to have a desire that imitates the desire of another person. The object of desire may be for a physical object, a relationship, prestige, a skill, recognition, status, life conditions or sex. We become jealous of another person's position or covetous of possessions because we are convinced that the other person really desires or is attached to the position or possessions. We wish more than anything to get what the other desires. The potential for mimetic desire increases as people become closer in class or status. The closer people are the greater the mimetic desire might become.

Hutus and Tutsis are so close, identical in every aspect that the potential for mimetic desire is extremely high. According to Redekop,

if individuals cannot picture themselves in the position of the others their mimetic desire is at a minimum, for example, a janitor might have a very little mimetic desire aroused by the president of a company but might have strong mimetic desire generated by a fellow janitor.

In these dynamics, both Hutus and Tutsis play the roles of Self and Other (the model to imitate), while the Object of desire is nothing else but the prestige coming from the status granted by the colonial administrator. According to Redekop,

> As the Self identifies with the Model, the Self feels that it has a right to have the Object since the Self is as good as the Other. The more intense the perceived desire of the Model, the more intense is the mimetic desire. If the object of desire is a zero-sum commodity—the more one has the less the other has—mimetic desire leads to frustration as the Model becomes the obstacle to acquiring what is desired. Mimetic desire can lead to mimetic rivalry.

During the colonial era, the Tutsi elite were gradually granted a "prestigious" status by Germans, which became even more pronounced under Belgian rule and a source of more frustration among Hutus.

The Belgian Administration and the Tutsification Process

When the Belgians replaced the Germans in 1916, they decided to continue the same indirect style of administration in the country. This kind of administration was supported by Belgian missionaries, who saw it as the best strategy for achieving the county's conversion to Christianity through its natural chiefs. Both the Belgian administrators and the clergy thought that Tutsis could serve their interests. The Belgians decided to set up what was called the "Tutsification of the country." This process was done in two phases.

Phase 1: The first phase involved the elimination of the multiple and diversified hierarchy established by the kings Gahindiro, Rwogera, and Rwabugiri. This happened twice:

- First, the Belgian authorities suppressed the autonomous Hutu entities of the north and northeast who had been integrated into the central state in 1912 but still enjoyed their autonomy. Belgian authorities reorganized these entities into chieftaincies. Hutu traditional chiefs were deposed and immediately replaced by Tutsi chiefs.

- Second, the Belgians eliminated Hutu chiefs throughout the country. Hutu chiefs who were appointed in the triple hierarchy as chiefs of the land from the reign of Gahindiro were replaced in 1926 by Tutsi chiefs appointed by Belgian administrators under what they called the Mortehan Law. The Mortehan Law reinforced the power of the Tutsi chiefs. It also tightened and expanded the pastoral clientelism (ubuhake), and, of course, increased the bitterness of the Hutus.

Phase 2: Belgian administrators and missionaries reserved administration, justice, and access to education only to Tutsi elites. Even while under German rule, in a letter dated April 28, 1911, the Roman Catholic bishop Classe wrote to his superior, *"In my humble opinion, the vital work, the most important in Rwanda, is one of the Batutsi chiefs. The struggle between us and the Protestants is about who will win the confidence of the chiefs. Without the chiefs, we will not have the people."* The Roman Catholic Church became the strongest defender of the Tutsis during the colonial administration, and when in 1927 the Belgian administration wanted to replace some stubborn Tutsi chiefs with educated, more efficient, more obedient Hutus, Bishop Classe reacted very firmly:

> If we are looking for the real interest of this country, we have an incomparable element of progress within the Tutsi youth. Thirsting for learning, anxious to know anything from Europe and willing to imitate the European lifestyle, they understand that their traditional culture has no more reason for being. These young people are the strength for the well being and the economical future of this country. If you ask the Hutus if they would prefer to be ruled by plebeians or by noble people, their answer is clear; their choice goes to Tutsis, and for a genuine reason: Born to rule, they are used to being in command. This is the secret of their settlement in this country and of their seizure of it.

Both the myth of Tutsi superiority and the myth of Tusti conquest are present in Classe's letter. In addition, Bishop Classe adds that Tutsis "are noble" people and that they are "pro Europeans, ready to abandon their traditional culture" to live a European lifestyle. One has to remember that Rwanda is probably the only country in the world in which traditional beliefs were totally wiped out by missionaries. Anything related to Rwandans' traditional faith was labeled as being pagan and forbidden. Thus, one of the three common traits on which Rwandans founded their sense of connectedness was totally destroyed: their traditional faith.

The tutsification process was mainly a political strategy. Only "good Tutsis" were selected for positions of responsibility. Only those Tutsis who had the combination of being traditional authorities and at the same time defending the new colonial order were selected. This process excluded 90 percent of the Tutsis who were not wealthy, as well as those Tutsi aristocrats with anti-colonial attitudes.

King Musinga came to the throne in 1896. He was the incarnation of the monarchic tradition. With the chiefs of his generation, he was very attached to the independence of his country. He posed a problem for colonizers. In 1923, Bishop Classe decided to "attack the foundation of the social organization" of ancient Rwanda by introducing a new land ownership system based on private property. The same year, thirty young Tutsis whose fathers were chiefs completed their education at the European school of Nyanza. Belgians ousted the old traditional chiefs who were anti-Belgian and replaced them with their educated sons. These educated young aristocrats received properties, clients, and cattle from the colonial power. In this manner, the Belgians were able to gradually erode the authority of King Musinga.

A new colonial bureaucracy of young European-style Tutsis replaced the ancient traditional, pro-independence system. The royal entourage was divided into traditionalists on the one side and the new elite on the other side. This new elite welcomed and internalized the racist colonial fables of "the superiority of the Tutsi," their "innate ability to rule," and their "superior intelligence." With the new system, the real power of Rwandan society was henceforth in the hands of the colonizers. The ancient royal power of King Musinga and the ancient Rwandan religion belonged to the past from then on.

In 1931 Bishop Classe (head of the Roman Catholic Church), General Tilkens (Governor General of the Belgian Congo), and Mr. Voisin (Vice-Governor of Rwanda–Urundi) decided to "destroy the ancient monarchy with its political and ideological foundations and replace it with a Christian, pro-colonial monarchy." King Musinga was deposed and deported. The colonial power replaced him with his son, Mutara III Rudahigwa, who was more open to the new colonial order, and the Roman Catholic faith became the new ideology.

The Role of the "Tutsis" in the Colonial Oppression   It is a fact that the traditional Rwandan system was stratified. It is true that the cattle breeders and agriculturalists had to pay tribute to the mwami and his aristocracy, but one can say that strong social contradictions started when land became scarce and pushed rich cattle breeders into conflict with farmers and cattle breeders of modest condition. In addition to that, the colonial system brought an oppression of another nature: capitalism.

The Rwandan people started feeling the burden of fiscal pressure in 1924 when the Belgian administration started to pay a bonus to chiefs who collected peoples' minimum fiscal contribution and tax on cattle. At the same time, forced labor increased tremendously, due to the construction of the road network, national and regional development, forestation, and portage—not to forget the introduction and imposition of new cash crops such as coffee, tobacco, and cotton. All this colonial exploitation was added to traditional charges, passed through the control of the "Tutsi chiefs" who were responsible for the execution of the orders from the colonial administration. This is yet another "good reason" for the "Hutu masses'" hatred toward the "Tutsi race." This bitterness exploded in 1959 following the joint action of the new Hutu middle class and the colonial power, which suddenly decided to take the side of the "Hutu race" in what has since been labeled the "Social Hutu Revolution."

Some people say that the colonial burden was carried by both Hutu and Tutsi masses, the situation being even tougher on chiefs who were not obedient. Tutsis who did not have clients had to cultivate, by themselves, the lot given by the administration to grow cash crops like any Hutu. Remember that in 1936 the Belgian administration introduced Rwandan identity cards that stated the ethnic identity of the holder. As *Hutu* increasingly became a synonym for *poor* and *Tutsi* meant *wealthy*, all those who did not own a certain number of cows were automatically Hutus, and this was mentioned in their new identity card! Chiefs had to inspect crops and see if people were taking good care of them. They would whip those who did not take care of the crops; otherwise, the agriculture inspector would whip the chief.

Another fact worth noting is that both Hutus and Tutsis disliked the colonial presence. In 1904, a Hutu armed attack was made against the missions of Nyundo and Rwaza in the northwest, where the Tutsi presence was low and King Musinga was totally ignored. In 1911–1912, Ndungutse, who claimed to be the son of King Rutalindwa and the rightful successor of Rwabugiri, launched an insurrection aimed at ending the chores imposed under the reign of "the impostor" King Musinga and "kicking the Europeans out of the country." In this revolt, Ndungutse was followed by Hutus, Tutsis, and Twas.

The Genesis of a Genocide
The Colonial Shift   The tutsification process continued until 1955. Then the colonial administration found it crucial to reevaluate its strategy in a world undergoing important political changes. Since the Algerian liberation war and Ghana's declaration of independence in 1957, a wave of freedom had been sweeping through the entire African continent. The Belgian administration was desperately looking for a strategy that would allow it to get through the inevitable, tough process of independence without losing its economical control over Congo and Rwanda–Urundi. Tutsi elites wanted to become national bourgeosie in a totally independent country. They already had traditional authority plus the experience of Western and modern administration as assets and the support of the majority of the population. A tiny number of Belgians supported the idea that once in power the Tutsi bourgeoisie would maintain the good terms they had always enjoyed and continue relying on Belgium. The Cold War and colonial conservatism were good reasons for most Belgian politicians not to trust anybody talking about independence. Those Belgian politicians who wanted to maintain the status quo had an alternate ally: members of the new Hutu bourgeoisie who were willing to seize power and fight for an independent Rwanda. The Hutu bourgeoisie, besides being

educated, had a deadly weapon, one that had ironically been provided to them by the colonial system: the racial card!

For half a century, the Belgian administration promoted the fable of "the superior Tutsi race" and reserved the most important political and administrative role to this "race." Over the years, the Hutu bourgeosie had an opportunity to mobilize and focus all the oppressed Hutu masses' resentment and bitterness toward the "Tutsi oppressor."

Grégoire Kayibanda and Hutu intellectuals began playing that card in 1953 and, in 1957 with valuable assistance from some European priests, produced a very important document, known as the Hutu Manifesto. The key point made in the manifesto was that the Hutu bourgeoisie must take control of Rwanda before it became independent. The authors of the document identified the fundamental problem as being the racist monopoly of the Tutsis, "a caste that hardly makes up to 14% of the population." They talk about a "double colonization, one by Hamites, and another by Europeans," emphasizing that the "first one was the worst." The document talks about the "violent conquest" of Rwanda by the Hamites/Tutsis, which is an invention aimed at justifying the "bitterness of over 900 years of Tutsi domination." Authors of the manifesto declared their fierce opposition to independence, claiming it would open the door to "a worse Hamite colonization on the Hutu."

Obviously, the Hutu bourgeoisie were against the idea of independence: what they needed from Mother Belgium and the King of Belgium was not the end of the colonial system. They needed power, and as some myths declared that the Tutsis were born rulers, the new myth of Hutus as "born democrats" was created, based on the simple fact that they happen to make up the majority of the Rwandan population!

The reality is that Rwanda needed change through a genuine national revolution, a revolution against the colonial system, and a social revolution against Tutsi elites, who were used by Belgium as their executioners. Both oppressed the weak and the poor. There were genuine reasons to fight both against oppression and the few Rwandans who supported the status quo. Instead, the Hutu elite decided to put the blame on the entire Tutsi community, knowing that probably more than 90 percent of Tutsis were living under double oppression, the same as ordinary Hutus were.

A progressive political movement would have put a desire for a genuine and inclusive struggle forward, but the Belgian colonial power and the Roman Catholic Church were allergic to anything that had a Marxist flavor within the Belgian colonies. The Parmehutu (Parti du Mouvement de l'Émancipation Hutu—Party of the Movement of the Hutu Emancipation) was pro-colonial and anti-socialist. Grégoire Kayibanda and his team were not against Belgian colonial rule. What they desperately needed had nothing to do with social change. They needed to replace the pro-European Tutsi elite created in the 1930s. They only wanted the Belgians to change their footmen, thus allowing them to reach the object of their mimetic desire. In other words, instead of relying on the Tutsi "race" to establish their domination, Belgian authorities were being asked to rely on the Hutu "race." The "race" tool was crucial for the Hutu bourgeoisie to achieve their goal, as it was impossible to convince the Hutu "masses" to turn their back on traditional authorities without using the weapon of the anti-Tutsi "racism."

Hutu leaders received support from both Belgian administration and the Roman Catholic Church. When Hutu leaders became more confident about this double support, their rhetoric became vociferous about the fate reserved for Tutsis in the near future. On September 27, 1957, Joseph Gitera Habyarimana, the leader of the Association pour la Promotion Sociale de la Masse—Association for Social Promotion of the Masses (APROSOMA) organized a party to "celebrate the liberation of the Hutus from the Tutsi slavery in Rwanda." In his speech, he mentioned that "the cohabitation of Hutus and Tutsis is like having a wound, a leech on the body, or a cancer in the stomach." Seeds of violent conflict were sown many years ago. The following year, thirty-four years before "The Final Solution," Habyarimana distributed handouts inciting Hutus to kill Tutsis: "Listen carefully: Tutsis used to cut people's throats. They will have their throats cut and this moment is close. They have looked for trouble. Let's get rid of Tutsi slavery. He who wants to eradicate rats doesn't have mercy for the one that is pregnant."

Efforts were not made to provide a more accurate view and counterbalance rising racism. On February 11, 1959, Roman Catholic Bishop Perraudin sent a letter to be read at churches throughout the country, stating, "Differences and inequalities are mostly related to racial differences in a sense that the wealth on the one hand, the political and judiciary power on the other hand are the monopoly of people who belong to the same race." Belgian author Jean-Paul Harroy supported Hutu racist views but noted that "among the 300,000 people labeled as Tutsis in 1956, only 10,000 enjoyed the privileges granted by the feudal system." Only 3.3 percent of "Tutsis" were enjoying the privileges granted by their status, but the Belgian administration, Catholic Church, and Hutu bourgeoisie preferred to include 96.7 percent of innocent Tutsis in their scapegoating campaign. Again, Belgian administrators ignored mentioning that those "privileged Tutsis" benefited far more from the privileges granted by the colonial power rather than from the feudal system.

In contrast, Perraudin's message was clear: in his view, wealth and power were not limited to a tiny minority of Tutsis. They were in the hands of all those who belong to the Tutsi "race." The demonization of Tutsis had begun.

The "Hutu Social Revolution" and the First Republic

Political Pluralism and the First Pogroms Between 1952 and 1962, Rwanda experienced tremendous political effervescency. The ubuhake system was abolished in 1954; the political movement Mouvement Démocratique Progressiste (MDP) was created in 1955 and renamed Rassemblement Démocratique Rwandais (RADER) in 1959; the Mouvement Social Muhutu was founded by Grégoire Kayibanda in June 1957 and became PARMEHUTU in October 1959; the Association pour la Promotion Sociale de la Masse (APROSOMA) was founded by Joseph Habyarimana Gitera; and the Union Nationale Rwandaise (UNAR) was created in September 1959. These are the four most important political parties, but sixteen other small parties were in existence. King Mutara III Rudahigwa died mysteriously in Bujumbura in July 1959 and was succeded by his half brother, Jean-Baptiste Ndahindurwa, who became King Kigeli V.

The Belgian colonial administration and the Roman Catholic Church invested everything at their disposal to support PARMEHUTU and fight UNAR, which was labeled a Tutsi/Monarchist and

Socialist party linked to the Islamic faith. Amazingly, many Hutus belonged to UNAR, including François Rukeba and Michel Rwagasana—the cousin of Grégoire Kayibanda—respectively president and secretary general of the "monarchist party."

On November 1, 1959, rumors began spreading in central and north Rwanda that two prominent Hutu leaders, Dominique Mbonyumutwa and Balthazar Bicamumpaka, had been assassinated by Tutsis. Those rumors triggered what is known as the Hutu Social Revolution. On November 3, Hutus started killing Tutsis and burning their homes in Gitarama and Ruhengeri. The unrest lasted two weeks; some Tutsis fled to neighboring countries, others were internally displaced, seeking refuge mainly at the closest parishes. When the situation returned to normal, Rwanda was placed under military rule by the Belgian administration, which appointed Colonel Guy Logiest as "Résident Militaire." On November 17, Logiest organized a meeting, during which the decision to remove all the Tutsi chiefs and replace them with Hutu chiefs was taken.

In January 1960, 544 subchieftancies were reduced to 229 municipalities administered by burgomasters. Later that year the "Front Commun" or "Joint Front," a joint initiative of PARMEHUTU, APROSOMA, and RADER, officially dissociated itself from the king, and a month later Parmehutu requested the removal of King Kigeri IV. This party declared it was against the monarchy and changed to Mouvement Démocratique Republicain Parmehutu, or MDR–PARMEHUTU. In June, the National Guard was created and election of municipalities councilors was held. They were largely won by PARMEHUTU candidates and boycotted by UNAR. As a result, UNAR was excluded from the Interim Government Council led by Grégoire Kayibanda.

The Scapegoating of the Tutsis and the Reign of Impunity It is worthwhile to note that, before 1959, the majority of the ordinary Hutus were still attached to their traditional institutions and did not have negative attitudes toward the king. As a matter of fact, those who were leading the Hutu mobs in Ruhengeri and Gisenyi had to convince them first that the burning of the Tutsi homes was ordered by the king, who was taken hostage by

UNAR because he wanted the Tutsis to give up their land to Hutus. However, the most efficient means of driving ordinary Hutus to adopt the racist agenda was the impunity guaranteed by the colonial rulers, the missionaries, and the Hutu leaders once they committed any crime against Tutsis. They were free to kill Tutsis, pillage their properties, slaughter their cattle, and rape Tutsi women without being punished. Some priests preached that killing a Tutsi was not a sin. The replacement of Tutsi chiefs by Hutu chiefs and later by Hutu burgomasters facilitated the spread of the racist ideology within the Hutu masses.

The Tutsis have the genuine characteristics of a perfect scapegoat, which is described by Redekop: "Through mimetic desire, there is a build-up of violence within the community, society or tribe. The violence must be dissipated or it will destroy a community through reciprocal violence. One safe way to dispense with the violence is to direct it to a sacrificial victim who becomes a scapegoat." Since 1959, Tutsis have been identified as feudals, conquerors, and members of a minority group. History explains the origins of the two first attributes. The majority/minority issue is based on the premise that there are two races: Hutus, comprising 85 percent of Rwanda's population, and Tutsis, accounting for 14 percent of the population. Race-based conflict was presented as an inevitability. Since then, Rwandan political life has fluctuated between a racial majority and racial minority. When the Hutus are the majority, any crime, any kind of discrimination, any trouble done to the Tutsi is done in the name of "democracy." On October 26, 1960, Parmehutu president Kayibanda said, "It is a victory of democracy over feudality. From the minorities, I am expecting common sense which goes with the respect of the real rights of the majority."

Tutsis are a minority and a very vulnerable group, two characteristics that make them an ideal scapegoat, according to Redekop, who says,

To function in an optimal way, the scapegoat should have the following characteristics:

1. He or she should be powerful enough to evoke some mimetic desire so that the violence should be easily directed against the individual.
2. He or she should be perceived as having done something wrong or somehow be a threat to the

community in order to legitimate being made a scapegoat.
3. The scapegoat must be vulnerable. Either he or she must be weak enough, in the minority, or in a vulnerable position. Otherwise the potential scapegoat could resist, fighting back in such a way that would trigger reciprocal violence.*

The triple label of conquerors, feudal leaders, and minority group gives the Tutsis the unique combination of power and vulnerability. In the past, there have been many good reasons for Hutu extremists to explain their violence against the Tutsis. From 1961 to 1967, Tutsi refugees attacked Rwanda ten times. After each attack, Hutu politicians led reprisal attacks on Tutsis who were still in the country, accusing them of having helped the assailants called "Inyenzi" or "cockroaches." Nkeramugaba, the prefect of Gikongoro, declared after the attack, "We have to defend ourselves. The only way is to neutralize the Tutsis. How? By killing them." After a particular attack in 1963–64, 15,000 Tutsi men, women, and children were massacred by Hutus, using machetes, spears, and clubs. In 1965, as a reward for his actions, Nkeramugaba was elected as a member of parliament by the Hutus of Gikongoro. He promised them that, once elected, he would make sure there was no investigation into the Gikongoro Tutsi massacres. There was an investigation conducted by republic prosecutor Gatwa Tharcisse. In his report, Tharcisse concluded that eighty-nine Hutu officials, including two ministers, were involved in the killings, but President Kayibanda rejected the report and asked for another investigation, which acquitted almost all of the officials. Those who were found guilty were very lightly sentenced. Impunity was guaranteed to whoever committed a crime against a Tutsi, even when they had mounted attack whatsoever.

There was a popular song in Kinyarwanda, "Akanyirangwegwe," which says:

The reason I like my people,
They bend their bow, shoot and kill (the Tutsis).
Who cares if the news reached the White people (the international community),
Who cares if Parmehutu is found responsible,
Since Kayibanda won Rwanda?

In a 1964 speech Kayibanda predicted the 1994 massacre. His message for Tutsi fighters was this:

Tutsis who remained in Rwanda, who are afraid of the popular furor caused by your incursions, are they happy with your behavior? Who is responsible for genocide? Let's talk about your future and about your children. We ask you to think about these innocent human beings who can still be spared from the death to which you are leading your ethnic group. We are particularly addressing Tutsis. You are responsible for your families. If by any chance you manage to capture Kigali, how can you measure the chaos for which you will be the first victims? I do not insist: you can guess. You should not be acting like desperate henchmen! You talk about it among yourselves. It would be the total and hurried end of the Tutsi race. Who is responsible for genocide?*

In 1991, the percentage of Tutsis in the Rwandan population declined sharply. Many had been massacred, so the percentage of Tutsis in the Rwandan population declined sharply. Many had been massacred, others fled the country, some found ways to redefine themselves as Hutus. Said to represent 17.5 percent in 1952, Tutsis were counted as only 8.4 percent. In the late 1960s and early 1970s, others fled the country and some found ways to redefine themselves as Hutus. At the same time, there was a growing split between the Hutus from the south and those from the north. The northerners saw that all rhetoric about solidarity was pure manipulation. In their view, the southerners were monopolizing the benefits of power. As in any other social, political, or economic crisis, in early 1973 Tutsis became the first targets of so-called "public safety committees." Their campaign of intimidation is a good example of scapegoat in action: Hutus targeted Tutsis, the common enemy, as a scapegoat to dissipate the violence that was threatening to plunge the southern and northern Hutus into reciprocal violence. The "disorder" legitimated a coup d'état by the army. Major General Juvenal Habyarimana took power and promised to restore order and national unity. The Second Rwandan Republic was born.

The Second Republic and Habyarimana's Era

The Single-Party State and the "Akazu"
In 1975, two years after the coup, Habyarimana made the country officially a single-party state under the MRND. Every Rwandan, regardless of age, was automatically a member of MRND. Over

twenty years, Habyarimana constructed a cohesive monolith: he was the president of the republic and the president of the party. At each level below him, every relevant government official simultaneously headed the corresponding level within the MRND Party. Habyarimana was the head of the army and had the allegiance of his troops, most of whom came from the north, his home region. He strengthened his power by ensuring that all the heads of para-statal corporations were his own people, as well as from the intellectual elite, including professors at the university and heads of hospitals. Businessmen needed his approval for state concessions that made their business prosperous. In return, they were ready to contribute financially and politically to the president's cause. It was déjà vu of the ubuhake system that had been abolished long ago! Habyarimana had enormous support from the Catholic Church hierarchy. Even though some estimate that 70 percent of the clergy, religious brothers and sisters, were originally Tutsis, seven of the nine bishops at the beginning of the genocide were Hutus. Vincent Nsengiyunva, the archbishop of Kigali, was an unconditional supporter of Habyarimana and served as a member of the Central Committee of the MRND. The president of the Presbyterian Church was a member of the prefectural committee of the same party in Kibuye. Both the Catholic and Protestant clergy served as MRND chains of communication by passing state announcements from the pulpit and by serving on councils. There was a smaller, but by far the strongest, circle within the network of personal connections that supported Habyarimana: the "Akazu" or "Little House."

The original meaning of the term "akazu" is not one of a prestigious connotation. A family that has a leprosy gene is called "akazu" in Kinyarwanda. Rwandan people avoided any kind of contact with such a family. In the case of a political "akazu," though, it was the reverse: its members excluded anybody who didn't belong to the "family." Habyarimana's Akazu was composed of people from his home region, with his wife's relatives playing a major role. Some of them played an openly political role, such as Protais Zigiranyirazo or "Mr. Z," who was prefect of Ruhengeri. Others were heads of powerful enterprises, such as Seraphin Rwabukumba at La Centrale. Yet others operated behind the scenes, such as Colonel Elie Sagatwa, private secretary to the president. Other Akazu members included some military officers: Theoneste Bagosora, the main organizer of the 1994 "apocalypse"; Leonard Nkundiye and Pascal Simbikangwa, who helped secure Habyarimana and Akazu members' undisputed hold on power; and others. This closed circle was at the core of the infamous "Reseau Zero" or "Zero Network," which carried out many criminal activities, including the killing of anybody who opposed total control of the state.

In the 1970s and 1980s, international assistance helped Habyarimana's regime reach a remarkable economic achievement. Rwandans had constructed an impressive infrastructure, including roads, communication network, and electric services, and Rwanda was regarded as a "model" of what could be accomplished with foreign assistance in Africa. Yet prosperity was uncertain and superficial. While Rwandans working directly for the state and those employed by its offshoots were getting rich, the mass of the people stayed poor and expected to get even poorer. The land available to ordinary farmers diminished while the population growth continued steadily. In some parts of the country, some local Hutu officials and members of the Hutu elite bought fields from the poor families for development projects.

In the late 1980s, the price of coffee, the cash crop that accounted for 75 percent of the county's foreign exchange, dropped on the international market. Rwanda became a debtor nation on which the World Bank and the donor community imposed strict fiscal measures. In 1989 a drought in Gikongoro reduced harvests. A large number of peasants were short of food, and the Habyarimana government ignored the gravity of the situation. Meanwhile, there was an obvious increase in discrimination not only against Tutsis but also against Hutus from regions other than the "Holy Land" of the Akazu members, the northwest. Habyarimana established the "Ethnic and Regional Equilibrium" policy, a system of quotas supposed to ensure equitable distribution of resources and opportunities to all Rwandans. In reality, the system was used to refuse Tutsis access to employment and higher education and, gradually, to exclude Hutus from areas other than Gisenyi, Ruhengeri, and Byumba.

Threats to the Akazu: The Internal Opposition and the RPF Attack

Economic decline, increasing corruption, and barefaced favoritism on the part of Habyarimana and his Akazu supporters provoked reactions among intellectuals, politicians, and journalists who demanded reforms. Some pressure also came from the international and donor community, which demanded political reforms and said they were necessary for economic improvement. In July 1990, civil society declared that Rwanda should be returned to a multiparty system. In September 1990, Habyarimana named members of a commission to examine political reforms. In October 1990, the Rwandan Patriotic Front (RPF) attacked Rwanda.

Beginning in 1960, a large Rwandan community lived in precarious conditions in Uganda, Burundi, the former Zaire, and the democratic Republic of Congo (DRC). Among the countries of exile, only Tanzania had encouraged the integration of the refugees into the local population, while Rwandans were allowed extremely limited guarantees and rights everywhere else. In 1982, the then president of Uganda, Milton Obote, expelled thousands of Tutsi refugees to Rwanda, and they were pushed back again across the Uganda–Rwanda border. The will to return to the motherland was increasing in the Tutsi community in exile, who were again told by the Rwandan regime that the country was too overpopulated to accept their return. In 1988, at a meeting in Washington D.C., Rwandans affirmed their right to return to their motherland. Faced with this potential threat, the Rwandan regime created a commission to jointly examine the refugee issue with the Ugandan government, but the RPF decided to go home anyway.

For Habyarimana and the Akazu, the RPF attack presented a risk: internal opposition might widen and look for an alliance with the RPF. It was also an opportunity for Habyarimana to resort to a tool that had proven its efficiency before in similar crises: the Tutsi scapegoat. During the night of October 4, 1990, heavy firing shook the capital, Kigali, all night long, and in the morning the national radio announced that the town had been under attack by RPF infiltrators. After this fake exercise, more than 15,000 Tutsis were arrested and detained for "security reasons"; many were tortured and killed. The fake attack on Kigali helped Habyarimana to secure help from his foreign friends. Belgium, France, and Zaire sent troops to support Kigali. They drove the RPF back toward the Ugandan border, and in the process Rwandan troops accused 1,000 unarmed Bahima civilians, a group identified with Tutsis, of having helped the RPF—and then massacred them.

In 1991, the Habyarimana regime was extremely worried about internal opposition, which was becoming stronger and stronger. Habyarimana was especially concerned about the "Kanyarengwe effect," which he considered to be a major threat to Hutu unity. Colonel Aloys Kanyarengwe fled Rwanda in 1980, after being accused of plotting against Habyarimana. He joined the RPF and was serving as its president. Besides being a Hutu, he was from the north, and his involvement in RPF was an example of the union of Hutus in the opposition and the Rwandan Patriotic Front.

RPF pressure on the regime encouraged the foundation of most of Rwanda's human rights movements that demanded more rapid change. In June 1991, Habyarimana was forced to accept the constitutional amendment that made multiple political parties legal. The MRND was reorganized and fifteen other parties were formed, the most important of which were the Social Democratic Party, the Liberal Party, and the Democratic Christian Party. Now the opposition had parties that could conduct protests against the regime. The parties first demanded a coalition government that would share power among all parties and the MRND. Habyarimana rejected the idea, but after huge demonstrations in early 1992 he was forced to engage in talks with the opposition. In the midst of these talks a group of Hutu hardliners announced the foundation of a new party: the Coalition pour la Défense de la République, or Coalition for the Defense of the Republic (CDR). CDR members claimed the party was born out of frustration. As nobody had been able to defend the interests of Hutus, they decided to take their fate in their own hands, but it was a secret for nobody: CDR was an offshoot of MRND hardliners.

The Creation of the Interahamwe Militia

When Habyarimana agreed to incorporate major opposition parties in a coalition government in April 1992, CDR was not included due to the small number of its adherents. Opposition parties' strength increased steadily, and the more they con-

solidated their positions within the government, the weaker MRND became and the more Hutu hardliners were engaged in terrorists activities against Tutsis and moderate Hutus. The atmosphere became very tense, and parties created youth wings that engaged in violence against rivals. "Inkuba" or "Thunder," the MDR youth wing, harassed MRND members, and "Abakombozi" or "Liberators," the PSD youth wing, assisted Inkuba. MRND decided to transform its youth wing, "Interahamwe" or "Those who aim to the same target," into a militia. From 1992, Interahamwe members received military training from regular forces and were backed by the "Impuzamugambi" or "Those who have the same purpose," the CDR youth wing. In 1993, Interahamwe and other terrorist groups attacks claimed more than 200 lives in different communities.

Impunity and insecurity increased sharply as attacks by unidentified assailants claimed more and more lives. Of course, the Rwandan army blamed the attacks on RPF infiltrators and their Tutsi "accomplices." The political opposition blamed Habyarimana's death squad, Réseau Zéro, for the attacks. Obviously, no matter who was responsible for the violence, the government either was unable or did not want to protect its citizens. National police and soldiers joined thugs rampaging the communities they were supposed to defend.

When the Rwandan forces backed by French and Zairian troops repulsed the RPF in 1990, the armed movement resorted to guerrilla warfare. RPF made several incursions, and the combat was punctuated by a series of cease-fires and negotiations. When the opposition parties joined the government in 1992, they forced Habyarimana to enter into serious negotiations with the RPF, and at the same time the Front launched an important offensive that drove back the Rwandan troops from several communes in the Byumba, along with more than 300,000 Rwandans who became internally displaced and started years of despicable misery. After that attack, the government signed a cease-fire at Arusha (Tanzania) in July 1992. The following month, both parties signed the first of a series of agreements, the Arusha Accords.

The Rwandan army that had grown from 7,000 to 30,000 troops was frustrated by the Byumba defeat. The MRND and CDR spread rumours that the accords might push the government to demobilize thousands of troops. In May and June 1992, soldiers mutinied in Gisenyi and Ruhengeri, killing civilians and looting and destroying properties. Pressure from the Hutu hardliners and the soldiers pushed Habyarimana to disavow the agreements he had signed three months before, calling the Arusha Accords a "scrap of papers."

Defining the Enemy   On September 21, 1992, the army chief of staff, Colonel Deogratias Nsabimana, circulated a top secret memorandum to his commanders, identifying and defining the "enemy." The memorandum divided the "enemy" into two categories: the principal enemy and the partisans of the enemy. The principal enemy was "the Tutsi inside or outside the country, extremist and nostalgic for power, who have never recognized the realities of the 1959 social revolution and who wish to re-conquer power by all means necessary including arms." The partisans of the enemy were defined as *anyone who supported the principal enemy.* The memorandum stated that the enemy and its partisans were mainly recruited among the Tutsi refugees, the Ugandan army, Tutsis inside the country, and the Nilo–Hamitic people of the region.

The same rhetoric, threats, and stereotypes used against the Tutsis during the "Hutu Social Revolution" in 1959 were back again. Radio Télévision Libre des Mille Collines (RTLM) was created. Together with other hatred media, such as the journal *Kangura*, its purpose was to preach hatred against the Tutsis. The regime used well-known artists, such as Simon Bikindi, the bard of genocide, to spread the sinister gospel. In its December 1990 edition, *Kangura* published the infamous **"Ten Commandments of the Hutu:"**

The Ten Commandments of the Hutu

1. All Hutus must know that female Tutsi, wherever they are, work in the interests of their Tutsi ethnicity. Because of this, any Hutu is a traitor who:
Marries a Tutsi woman
Makes a Tutsi woman a concubine
Makes a Tutsi woman his secretary or protégé
2. All Hutus must know that our Hutu women are more dignified and more conscientious in their role as woman, wife and mother of the family. Aren't they beautiful, good secretaries, and more honest!

3. Hutu men, be vigilant and lead your wives, your brothers and your sons toward reason.
4. All Hutus must know that all Tutsis are dishonest in business. They only consider the supremacy of their ethnic group. We speak here in the name of experience. By consequence, a Hutu is a traitor:
who makes alliances with Tutsis in business
who invests his money or state money in a Tutsi enterprise
who borrows or lends money to a Tutsi
who gives Tutsis favors in business (granting import licenses, bank loans, construction parcels, public markets)
5. Strategic political, military and security posts must be confined to Hutus.
6. The education sector (elementary students, secondary students, teaching corps) must be majority Hutu.
7. The Rwandan army forces must be exclusively Hutu. The experience of the October 1990 war teaches us. No military personnel may marry a Tutsi woman.
8. Hutu must cease to have pity on Tutsis.
9. Hutu, wherever they are, must be united, in solidarity and preoccupied with the situation of their Hutu brothers.
The Hutu in the interior and the exterior must seek out constantly friends and allies for their Hutu cause, beginning with their Bantu brothers.
They must constantly thwart Tutsi propaganda.
The Hutu must be firm and vigilant against their common Tutsi enemy.
10. The social revolution of 1959, the referendum of 1961 and the Hutu ideology must be taught to all Hutus and at all levels. All Hutus must disseminate widely the present ideology. Any Hutu is a traitor who would prosecute his brother Hutu for having read, taught and followed this ideology.

Ethno-nationalism was at its climax. Cutting across party lines, a new movement called "Hutu-Power" was born. It embodied the Hutu solidarity that Habyarimana wanted for years. Rupert Emerson defines ethno-nationalism as follows: a nation is "the largest community which, when the chips are down, effectively commands [people's] loyalty, overriding claims both of lesser communities within it, and those which cut across it or potentially enfold it within still a greater society."

Hutu Power used artists like Simon Bikindi to gain the solidarity of Hutus. Bikindi and his group were definitely the champions of ethno-nationalism.

They created a common ancestor named "Sebahinzi" or "The Forefather of the Cultivators." Bikindi called for the solidarity of the "Sons of Sebahinzi," asking them to remember how Tutsis killed their kings without mercy, emphasizing that the same fate was waiting for them if they did not stick together. Bikindi's "masterpiece" "Jyewe Nanga Abahutu," or "Me, I Hate Those Hutus," cites the names of kinglets who were killed by Nyiginya kings during the conflict over the unification of Rwanda and of those who died as rebels fighting the central traditional authority. Some of those mentioned belonged to other identity groups. Examples are Ndungutse, who claimed to be the son of the Tutsi king Rutalindwa, and Batwa like Rukara, son of Bishingwe.

Soldiers and militia, the spearhead of the killing machine, were ready to wipe out the "Tutsi race." They just needed a spark to ignite their hatred and explode. This happened on April 6, 1994, when the plane carrying Habyarimana and Burundi's President Cyprien Ntaryamira was shot down. In less than a hundred days, more than one million Tutsis and nonextremist Hutus were killed. The killers used the most unsophisticated weapons a human being can imagine. Their purpose was not only to kill but to make victims suffer as long as possible before they died. Killing such a large number of people in such a short period of time required a large, organized force, but torturing them and enjoying it took a tremendous amount of hatred and dehumanization.

HOW TUTSI IDENTITY, SENSE OF BELONGINGNESS, AND SECURITY ARE BEING *IMPACTED* OR *THREATENED* BY THE CONFLICT

Being identified as a Hutu or as a Tutsi meant life or death during times of crisis in Rwanda. An identity card in which the word *Tutsi* was highlighted was equivalent to having the yellow Star of David on one's chest under the Third Reich's rule in Germany. Those who were targeting Tutsis in order to exterminate them did not make any distinctions: to them, any and all Tutsis should die. One would expect that being under the same threat would bring Tutsis together, because their fate was the same. The following section discusses the Tutsis' identity and how the conflict impacted their need to be connected as an identity group.

The myth of Tutsi superiority introduced by Germans and reinforced by Belgians through the "Tutsification process," the "Hamitic origin" of Tutsis, and the introduction of the identity card were the first factors that impacted Tutsis' identity. The first two sowed the seeds of Tutsis' "otherness" as an alien conqueror. The last event segregated Tutsi families in two ways. First, it identified those who didn't have the required number of cows to qualify as "Tutsis"; they became officially "Hutus." It was then used to identify victims whenever the government needed a scapegoat to defuse violence.

The Hutu "Social Revolution" impacted the identity of every Rwandan. It marked the beginning of the ethno-nationalism era, when being Hutu or Tutsi was far more important than being a Rwandan. Since then, Tutsis have felt increasingly alienated, as being Tutsi was like being on death row.

When the pogroms started, many Tutsis fled to neighboring countries, where they were treated as aliens. The sense of belongingness of both refugees and those who stayed in the country was deeply affected. As for security, those who stayed in Rwanda were permanent prey for violence, while refugees were victims of local ethnic violence in Burundi, Uganda, and Congo, even though they were under the protection of the U.N. High Commissioner for Refugees (UNHCR).

Some Tutsi refugees spent as much as thirty-five years in exile before returning after the 1994 genocide. This long period of separation impacted relations between Tutsis who had left Rwanda and those who stayed in the country. "Far from the sight is far from the heart." Contact between refugees and those who stayed in the country was extremely limited; no visits were possible. Coming back from exile meant death. Getting a national passport as a Tutsi and being able to visit other countries was close to impossible. Any contact with refugees was considered by the Rwandan government to be collaboration with the enemy, which also meant death. From the Rwandan perspective, countries that had Tutsi refugees were not perceived the same way: Burundi was considered a permanent potential threat, as most of the "Inyenzi" attacks were launched from there. For the Tutsis inside Rwanda, even listening to Radio Burundi could cause serious trouble.

It is worth mentioning that Rwanda and Burundi are like Siamese twins: anything that happens to one country has a big impact on the other. The 1992 massacres of Hutus in Burundi intensified the harassment of Tutsis in Rwanda. When the first Hutu-elected president was killed in Burundi by some Tutsis in 1992, Rwandan Tutsis were harassed as part of the increasing ethno-nationalism that was promoted after the Hutu Revolution. The suffering of the Tutsi refugees in Burundi and Uganda was not necessarily brought to the attention of Tutsis inside Rwanda, who were faced with their own suffering. The two communities were deeply entrenched in their narcissistic wounding. In fact, Tutsis outside Rwanda felt betrayed by those who stayed in the country; they perceived them as being either too greedy or unable to face the hardships of living in refugee camps. For that reason they were seen as being not very different from Hutus and were treated likewise. Between 1959 and 1963, Hutu mobs feasted on cows that belonged to Tutsis who were killed or who had managed to flee. Some Tutsi refugees accused Tutsis who stayed in Rwanda of having joined the Hutu mobs. Basically, whoever decided to stay in Rwanda was defined as a Hutu. Many Hutus and even Batwa fled because they were monarchists or UNAR members.

When the RPF was launched in 1990, Tutsis inside the country paid the price of being seen as accomplices of the invaders. They knew the magnitude of danger they were in, but dared to believe that RPF success on the battlefield and the creation of a coalition government would prevent major massacres. When the genocide started, they understood that stopping it was not the RPF's aim, but it was too late. The RPF's objective was to crush the Rwandan army and take control of the country. The genocide did not change RPF's objective. The genocide stopped because there were no more Tutsi left within the killers' reach, and the presence of the RPF in the liberated zone did not permit the extermination of those who managed to survive.

The Tutsis who survived the genocide felt betrayed by the RPF, which they believe did too little to protect them. Even RPF soldiers who had their families in Rwanda were not allowed to go to protect their beloved ones. Survivors felt they were used as bait to lure Hutu killers and make it easier for the RPF to crush their enemies who were busy carrying out the genocide.

Tutsi survivors' angst intensified when they were questioned by Tutsi returnees. They suffered a secondary victimization when those who were supposed to show more support and understanding preferred to torture them psychologically while the wounds were still open. As a result, Tutsi survivors who could, fled the country. Some Tutsis were accused of being an obstacle to the reconciliation process. Today, Tutsi survivors are being sacrificed in the name of unity and reconciliation while prominent Hutu hardliners who belonged to the former Rwandan army and planned and carried out the genocide elude accountability.

In 2004, as promised, the government released killers who "confessed" their involvement in the 1994 genocide. To show that they did not have any remorse for their horrible crimes, after their release they started killing Tutsi survivors—leaving observers to wonder if the genocide of the Tutsis is over. The security of Tutsis in Rwanda is still at high risk.

PAST GLORIES AND TRAUMAS REACTIVATED BY THE CONFLICT

This section discusses how past glories and traumas have been reactivated by the current situation. Like many other countries that relied on oral traditions to keep data, most of Rwandan history was preserved orally, especially the history of Rwanda's unification and expansion. Rwandans know their heroes through traditional songs and poems, including epic poems. Some heroes left auto-panegyric poems that are real masterpieces in Rwandan literature. The nineteenth century was particularly rich with poetry that celebrated heroic deeds of Tutsi heroes such as Nyiringango, son of Nyagahinga, during the reign of Kigeli IV Rwabugiri. In Rwandan history, Rwabugiri can be compared to Napoleon, Chaka Zulu, or Soundjata. He had a great army and his conquests went as far as Kisangani in northeastern Congo.

The RPF attack in October 1990, its victory in July 1994, crushing the former Rwandan armed forces or ex-Forces Armées Rwandaises (FAR) in Zairian forests, the incredible three-month krieg in

1996 from Kigali to Kinshasa, and the victory over Mobutu and his Zairian armed forces, all reactivated the prestigious glories of the Tutsis throughout their history. On the other hand, those recent successes will naturally become another negative memory and contribute to future deep-rooted conflicts.

The Tutsi pogroms since the Hutu revolution left the Tutsis extremely traumatized. Those who stayed in the country were easy prey whenever Hutu officials needed a scapegoat. Tutsi children born during that time developed survival skills, as they had to learn how to cheat danger on a daily basis. When their parents sent them to fetch water or wood, buy something at the marketplace, or to school or to church, children were constantly aware that any Hutu could harm them on their way, and this happened very often. Political songs such as "Ibigwi by'Aba Parmehutu" or "The Heroic Deeds of Parmehutu's Militants" were broadcast on national radio during the 1960s and 1970s, often on special occasions such as Independence Day and Kamarampaka Day. When Tutsis passed by a group of Hutus while such songs were being played on the radio, anything from sarcastic remarks or racist insults to beating or torture could happen to them.

Tutsis who fled the country during the pogroms were considered aliens, second- or third-rate "inhabitants." They were easy prey for nationals in their country of asylum. In countries such as Uganda or Congo, children were given Ugandan or Congolese names by their parents so they could have access to education. In Burundi, Rwandan adults had to renew their identity cards each year, which was costly given their limited budgets. For those who could not afford renewal fees, the municipal jails became their home!

After the RPF victory, most Tutsi refugees came back home. Interestingly, the number of returnees who decided to resettle in the region of their origin is close to none. Even those who were totally aware of the availability of the property they left behind before the exodus preferred to settle somewhere else, in areas they feel are more secure, such as the provinces of Kigali, Umutara, or Kibungo. Their choices reflect their fear. Who knows what might happen if they returned to their remote villages and lived side by side with "the enemy"?

Who Is the Enemy?

From the Tutsi perspective, the enemy is the Hutu who thinks that "the only good Tutsi is the dead one." Hutus were bombarded with Parmehutu–CDR ideology, teaching that Tutsis are aliens from Ethiopia, extremist feudals, nostalgic for power, who have never recognized the realities of the 1959 social revolution.

Rwandan history was rewritten by Hutu intellectuals to create the foundations of the historic enmity between Hutus and Tutsis. This distorted reality was taught to schoolchildren, both Hutus and Tutsis. Hutu children were taught how their ancestors were enslaved by Tutsis who were then perceived as evil. Tutsi children developed a sense of culpability and could not understand how their ancestors could be that bad. Some felt that they actually deserved to be victimized. Those Hutus who taught hatred to children are the real enemies of the Tutsis.

Most of the killers during the genocide were people who were not even born before the 1959 Hutu Revolution. Some of them never experienced anything negative from Tutsis but absorbed the hatred ideology as gospel. In a deep-rooted conflict, the reasons for victimization do not have to be proven; they are a matter of "faith." Many horrific stories were told to Hutu children about the cruelty of the Tutsis. One example is the story of Kanjogera or Nyirayuhi, mother of King Musinga. It is said that every morning when she woke up, she planted two swords in two young Hutu boys, using the swords as supports to stand up from her bed! Amazingly, not a single Hutu family can claim a loss of a child who had been killed by Kanjogera! It is true that Kanjogera was not a tender person, but her victims were people who were close to her: Tutsis!

The other enemy is the missionaries who ironically chose to teach the gospel of hatred instead of the Christian message of love. One could say that some of them have a pathological hatred of the Tutsis. There are missionaries who try to explain away their hate by claiming they want to be on the side of the weak and the poor. This is an extremely ridiculous mockery of their mission. As had happened in many other places in the world, the first thing the missionaries did when they stepped onto Rwandan soil was to grab huge properties for themselves. They lived a life of luxury in their mansions and were not ashamed by the misery surrounding them. It appears they needed a scapegoat, and the Tutsis were a perfect one!

Some missionaries come from countries where their own ethnic group is dominated by another group, and once in Rwanda they instantly perceive Tutsis through their own frustration. Some Roman Catholic networks are conducting a rear-guard struggle, either to deny that there was a genocide of Tutsis in 1994 or to promote the idea of a double genocide.

From the Hutu extremists' perspective, during the settlement of the country, they arrived after the first inhabitants of the country, the Twas. They carried out all the development work to make the wild country viable. Therefore, they deserve the first-come, first-serve treatment. Tutsis are alien feudal lords who conquered the land of the Hutus, killing Hutu kings and enslaving their ancestors. Tutsis are a tiny and arrogant minority who forced their dominance onto the Hutu majority.

Tutsis imposed the most humiliating exploitation system on the Hutus: ubuhake. Through that system, Hutus were enslaved by Tutsis: they cultivated the fields of their Tutsi lords, carried them and their luggage on hammocks, built and maintained their houses, and gave them half of their own limited crops. Tutsis inflicted humiliating punishment on Hutus by whipping them for no reason. As Tutsis' cattle grew in numbers, they grabbed more and more land from the Hutus. Tutsi lords were warmongers. They conducted wars of expansion against their neighbors. The role reserved for Hutus in those fights was a humiliating one: they carried food for the Tutsi warriors, which repressed the fact that they could be warriors themselves. Tutsis worked hand in hand with the German and the Belgian colonial administrations to exploit and oppress the Hutu people. Hutu children did not have access to education. When brave Hutu leaders stood up and fought peacefully for political changes, the arrogant feudal lords felt that their privileges were threatened and they declared that they had nothing to share with their slaves. They started assaulting peaceful Hutu leaders, and the Hutu masses could not stand the Tutsi arrogance anymore. Hutus stood up and defended their dignity by killing those Tutsis who wanted to keep the Hutu majority in a despicable slavery.

The son of Gahutu conducted a legitimate struggle that put an end to both slavery and colonialism. Between 1961 and 1967, the Tutsi–Inyenzi, who were the enemy of Rwanda and never accepted the reality of the Hutu Revolution, conducted several attacks from neighboring countries and were helped by their brothers inside the country, but the brave Hutus defended themselves and defeated both the internal and the external enemy. From 1967 to 1973, people of Rwanda left peacefully, but Tutsis were becoming more and more arrogant as they held the best positions in every sector of Rwandan life. This led to the 1973 troubles, when Hutus decided again to fight for fairness.

When President Habyarimana came to power, peace and harmony were restored for seventeen years. In 1990, the nostalgic Tutsi–Hamites, backed by the Ugandan army and calling themselves the Rwandan Patriotic Front, invaded Rwanda. For four years, they destabilized the country with terrorist attacks, killing tens of thousands of Hutus, forcing others to abandon their homes and to live a miserable life as internal displaced refugees. When President Habyarimana's plane was shot down, Hutus responded immediately: From the Hutus' point of view, the genocide was a civil war. It was, in fact, a double genocide, because the RPF killed many more Hutus in Rwanda and Congo than the number of Tutsis who were killed by Hutus.

EFFORTS MADE TO RESOLVE THE CONFLICT

The Rwandan social fabric has been deeply affected by the 1994 genocide. The country is slowly recovering from destruction, and in many sectors life is getting back to normal. To survive as a nation, Rwandan people need reconciliation. The following section covers the initiatives undertaken by the Rwandan authorities to launch the process that is necessary to rebuild Rwandan society.

When Tutsi refugees claimed their right to return home, the response they received from the Habyarimana government was that the country was overpopulated and that the refugees should settle permanently in the countries that offered them refuge. The RPF pressured Habyarimana to accept negotiations with the armed rebels, but there was an obvious lack of trust between the two parties. The success of the RPF, the loss of face of the Rwandan army, Hutu hard-liners, and Habyarimana's death resulted in the most horrific genocide of the end of the twentieth century.

Several years have elapsed since the 1994 genocide. Rwandan government officials believe it is time for reconciliation. To coordinate those efforts, the National Commission for Unity and Reconciliation was created. The commission's first task was to find strategies for bringing genocide suspects to justice. Ten years after the genocide, more than 130,000 genocide suspects were in Rwandan prisons. According to some experts, with the judicial means that the country has, it would take 200 years to schedule trails for all suspects. Rwandan authorities are fully aware of the fact that justice is the prerequisite to any kind of reconciliation.

In the attempt to tackle what looks like an impossible task, the government and the National Commission for Unity and Reconciliation resorted to a traditional conflict management tool known as Gacaca or "Smooth Lawn." Gacaca has a metonymical connotation as the process takes the name of the place it was traditionally held: people engaged in the process are seated on a smooth lawn, preferably under the shadow of a tree. As a traditional community-based dispute management tool, Gacaca was used to deal with minor offenses, including property damage, vandalism, domestic abuses, and minor thefts. Gacaca was not used to deal with murder or cattle plundering, as those two particular crimes were punished by death, the offender most likely being lynched as soon as he was caught. In Gacaca, the complainant approached the elders to lodge his or her complaint against the offender. A day was determined when the elders would gather. Both parties were called and asked to tell their stories. After deliberation, the elders would decide what fine the offender should pay the victim or what other punishment should be applied. Gacaca was inadequate to deal with the crime of genocide. To make it work in the post-genocide context, Rwandan authorities made some changes to Gacaca.

"Remodelled Gacaca" courts have replaced elders with people chosen by official authorities, based on their "integrity" within the community. They are called "Inyangamugayo" or "Those who are against degrading deeds." Inyangamugayo are not trained lawyers, yet they have to deal with suspects of crimes against humanity. Reasons the government gave for resorting to Gacaca are as follows:

- Neither victims nor suspects will have to wait for years for justice to be done. This means the process will be speeded up.
- The cost to the taxpayer for the upkeep of prisons will be reduced, enabling the government to concentrate on other urgent needs.
- The participation of every member of the community in revealing the facts of a situation will be the best way to establish the truth.
- Gacaca courts will enable genocide and other crimes against humanity to be dealt with much faster than in the formal justice system. This should end the culture of impunity that currently exists.
- The new courts will put into practice innovative methods in terms of criminal justice in Rwanda, in particular sentencing people to community service to aid the reintegration of criminals into society.
- The application of the law should aid the healing process and national reconciliation in Rwanda, which is seen as the only guarantee of peace, stability, and future development of the country and obliges the Rwandan people to take political responsibility.

The people accused of genocide fall into four categories:

- Category 1: the planners, organizers, and leaders of the genocide, those who acted in a position of authority, well-known murderers, and those guilty of rape and sexual torture
- Category 2: those guilty of voluntary homicide, having participated or been complicit in voluntary homicide or acts against persons resulting in death, having inflicted wounds with intent to kill, or committing other serious violent acts that did not result in death
- Category 3: those who committed violent acts without intent to kill
- Category 4: those who committed crimes against property

The accused in the first category will be judged by the ordinary courts—that is, Courts of First Instance/Magistrates' Courts. For all other cases the government created about 11,000 Gacaca jurisdictions, each made up of nineteen elected judges known for their integrity. Over 200,000 of these civil judges were elected between October 4 and 7,

2001, and received training in 2002 before the courts began to function. There are four levels of jurisdiction for each different category of crime (2, 3, and 4). Only defendants in the first and second categories can appeal judgments on them. Judgments are to be examined by the highest district and provincial levels of the administration.

The trouble with "Remodeled Gacaca" courts and the civil judges overseeing them, Inyangamugayo, is that they have been accused of participating in the same crimes! On Rwandan hills, genocide survivors asking for justice live in constant fear. Not all killers are in jail; they are a real threat to anybody who testifies against them. Relatives of imprisoned suspects are also a threat to witnesses. Besides being an inappropriate process, a mockery to justice for such a horrendous crime, Gacaca puts at risks the victims of the 1994 genocide.

To prove their openness toward reconciliation, the RPF government or "Government of Unity and Reconciliation," as it is called today, incorporated a large number of members of Habyarimana's army, even though some of them are accused of genocide and crimes against humanity. Their presence is again a great source of fear for still-traumatized survivors of the genocide. While Hutus who executed orders to kill Tutsis are incarcerated in overpopulated Rwandan prisons, those who delivered the orders are being recycled in the new army or given first-rate attention in a "five-star resort," the International Criminal Tribunal (ICTR) Prison in Arusha. The international community created the ICTR to bring the organizers of the genocide to trial. Given the huge amounts of money that has been spent since the ICTR's creation and the job done to date, Rwandans wonder what is going on. This is the same international community that turned a blind eye to the extermination of the Tutsis in 1994. In Arusha, the attention given by the international community to those who planned the genocide is immoral, especially when one knows the living conditions of those who survived the genocide. This lack of empathy is confusing for victims who are wondering why the international community that pulled out of Rwanda when the killing started is coming back and awarding criminals with such an enviable lifestyle. From the Rwandans' perspective, it looks like all the "efforts" that are being made or that have been made

fail to address the root of the problem, either by lack of will, or by lack of vision.

WHAT COULD BE DONE

There is no quick fix formula for a post-genocide situation; nonetheless, urgent needs must be addressed prior to any long-term recovery process: survivors of the genocide need assistance, suspect criminals have to be brought to justice, and the reconciliation process cannot be a "placebo."

Addressing Survivors' Basic Needs: Dealing with the Pain

The suffering of those who survived the genocide is beyond understanding and that may be the reason why very few people dare to confront the challenge of offering them help. Compared to those needs, Rwanda's resources are extremely limited and international aid being provided is insufficient. The donor community has to take a very important step: it must recognize that no matter where you are, no matter your skin color, a life is a life.

It is hard for some people to acknowledge that our differences are just skin deep! Memories of international community members pulling out during the genocide are troublesome indeed. It was unbelievable to see people trying to get their pets aboard cars taking them to the airport, while leaving behind endangered Rwandan children, colleagues, and employees. They were concerned about the stress or trauma their dog or cat went through, but to date little has been done for traumatized Rwandans. Is there any worse kind of dehumanization?

The more traumatized and deprived people are of their basic needs, the more they are likely to entrench themselves in narcissistic wounding and the more faint chances of reconciliation grow. Victims of genocide do not demand much: just a pair of ears to listen to them, an open and empathetic heart—a little but significant gesture that shows them that they have not been left alone or singled out.

It is unfortunate that suffering is only acknowledged after it affects us or people close to us. Instead of being compliant or apathetic witnesses of people's suffering, bystanders should learn to assist any endangered human being, not because they know him or her but because he or she is a human being and deserves to be assisted and protected when needed.

Genocide survivors experienced many terrible things: they saw their loved ones being tortured before dying, they lived in constant fear while hiding, some were raped and are dealing with HIV–AIDS, others are maimed for life, children became heads of families, and sometimes, while their suffering is being ignored, they are being accused of not cooperating with unity and reconciliation efforts! These attitudes encourage the entrenchment of narcissistic wounding. Reconciliation is not possible as long as the victim is not strong enough to see the human face of his or her offender and that a remorseful offender is also suffering.

Justice

Bringing genocide suspects to justice is a precondition for the reconciliation process. The international community should consider providing Rwanda with the judiciary means to judge Rwandan criminals where crimes were committed. Money engulfed by the ICTR could have covered much of the need. Reluctance to move the ICTR from Tanzania to Rwanda is unreasonable; those who are opposed to or resist the move probably have something to hide. It is the international community's responsibility to make the right decision. It is important that the suspects receive legal support, as well as fair judicial treatment, but individuals whose only purpose is to milk the international community as long as possible should not hold fairness hostage.

Pretending that suspects cannot get a fair trial is just another arrogant assumption. Some ICTR defense lawyers are said to be bribing suspects to keep their contracts. If the ICTR is employing Rwandan investigators who took part in the 1994 genocide, one should at least expect the ICTR to grant Rwanda the benefit of doubt. If the death penalty is the obstacle to the move, who needs the death penalty? It won't bring back those who lost their lives. Bringing suspects to trial should not be a process for revenge but rather a process aimed at reconciliation.

Reconciliation

Rwandans need reconciliation. There is no way to survive as a nation if Rwandans are not reconciled,

but given the purpose of the process and the magnitude of the task, there is no room for a fake process: it is about the recovery of a nation's humanity, as Rwandans have been dehumanized by the genocide, both victims and offenders. From the Tutsi perspective, there is no way fellow human beings should be treated as they were during the genocide. What kind of human being are you, if you cannot be moved by the voice of a frightened four-year-old girl who promises to sing and dance for you if you spare her life? What kind of human being are you when an eight-month-old baby wakes up and smiles at you because he knows your face, and after having raped and killed the child's mother, you choose to bash the child's head on a concrete wall?

When the survivors are told about reconciliation, the question that comes to their mind is, With whom and why should we reconcile? What have we done to deserve all the atrocities we went through? How can you reconcile a crippled child who is the only survivor of a family with the adult who killed the family and left the child maimed for life?

It is hard to find the right answers to these questions, but again we need reconciliation, and in the Rwandan context it has to be a multidimensional process: it will have to include justice, education, healing, forgiveness, compassion, empathy, and much, much suffering. First of all, though, time is required. One cannot expect compassion and empathy from parties deeply entrenched in their own suffering who refuse to recognize the human face of the other. Narcissistic wounding is not something that people gain control of overnight, and that is why the time factor is critical. Politicians might genuinely want to hasten the process because their time (chronos) means business, but unfortunately the reconciliation process does not work within the limits of that kind of time: for this process to succeed, matters must be left until the right time (kairos). Obviously, the wounds are still open in Rwanda, and ten years are not necessarily enough to overcome the narcissistic wounding. The worst thing officials could do is push people to reconcile or forgive against their will. It is critical to find steps that can launch the process smoothly, taking the interests of all the stakeholders into consideration.

The first step, in our opinion, should be made by the Rwandan state itself. The crime of genocide is basically a state crime. It is the state that planned the genocide, armed the killers, and made the means available to maximize the outcome of the diabolic plan. The Rwandan state turned ordinary Hutu citizens into criminals, dehumanized Tutsi citizens, and denied their right to live. The Rwandan state can set the tone by coming forward and admitting to all citizens its full responsibility for all those crimes. If the Rwandan state asks sincerely and genuinely for forgiveness from its victims, that would be a major step forward, which would set the tone and show the direction in which the process should be heading. One could argue that the current government has nothing to do with crimes committed by the one who organized and carried out the genocide. Governments are not perennial but states are. If the current government is willing to pay the bills left by the government it ousted, including bills for machetes, guns, and bullets used to exterminate the Tutsis, common sense would suggest that the current government should assume responsibility for leading the reconciliation process. Reconciliation requires people who are qualified to be its custodians: those are exceptional individuals with whom Rwandan people from all identity groups can easily identify themselves. In the Rwandan context, this is the squaring of the circle. In South Africa, for example, state and religious leaders Nelson Mandela, F. W. de Klerk, and Archbishop Desmond Tutu were custodians of the Truth and Reconciliation Commission process that followed the end of apartheid.

According to Redekop, "Reconciliation means to stop imitating the entrenched patterns of past violence and imagine, imitate and create life patterns of well-being, meeting the identity needs of Self and Other." There is one particular pattern that is a challenge to the reconciliation process in Rwanda: most of the problems stem from the monopolistic access that an elite within one identity group—the group that holds power—has to resources. Based on ethnicity, regionalism, or any kind of kinship, either real or fabricated, the powerful group ignores both material and identity needs of other groups. As John Burton said, "when non-negotiable, non-material human identity needs are threatened, people will fight."* Explains Redekop, "these needs are universal, but their satisfiers are related to individual cultures. Needs include those for meaning, self actualization, recognition, security, connectedness, and well being." When one looks at Rwanda's history, it is clear that these basic human identity

needs have been and indeed are still threatened: we have seen how Hutus were treated during the colonial era; we have seen how Tutsis have been victimized ever since 1959.

Today, matters have changed: it was a wonderful idea on the part of the current Rwandan government, for example, to stop mentioning people's identity group on their national identity card, but in a society with an oral tradition written records are in some ways irrelevant. Nowadays, in addition to having three "ethnic" groups in Rwanda—Hutus, Tutsis, and Twas—there are new identity references indicating where people came from after the RPF victory in 1994: they are called Ugandans or Abasagya, Abarundi or Burundians, AbaDubai (for those who came from the former Zaire), abaTZ (for those from Tanzania), and abaSopecya for those who were in Rwanda. Access to resources and new social identities are being based on these labels. This pattern is a major potential source of future violence in Rwanda.

Reconciliation is one of the Rwandan government's top priorities. The government is therefore the de facto custodian of the process. The problem is that the government is not perceived as a neutral, "clean" third party by all Rwandans. Hutus who lost their beloved ones in 1990 are still waiting for the government to acknowledge their loss, and they point an accusatory finger at the RPA. Whether accusations are true or false is not the issue; as long as there is insufficient trust, the process will be counterproductive if the government plays the central role.

One would think that church leaders might play a central role. Despite the horrors that took place, especially in Roman Catholic churches throughout the country, and despite the crimes committed by church leaders, churches are still the only places where Rwandans choose to gather voluntarily every Friday, Saturday, or Sunday, depending on the religious faith. There is a tiny little spark of hope there, not because the churches are neutral but because they are the only place where Hutus and Tutsis share a positively centered activity: prayer. Church leaders may be able to play a significant role in the restoration of the lost humanity of the Rwandan people.

The Truth and Reconciliation Commission process in South Africa brought Blacks and Whites together to build mutual forgiveness on mutual suffering. In Rwanda, Tutsis' and Hutus' truths should first be reconciled because history was distorted. That should be achieved through education, not propaganda. There is a lot to do to achieve reconciliation in Rwanda, but most important there must be a political will to achieve reconciliation for the only and genuine purpose and interest of restoring the torn fabric of a nation.

In the end, the reconciliation of Rwandan people will be meaningless if people in the Great Lakes of Africa are not at peace. Once your neighbor's house is on fire, yours is surely next, and if you are accused of being an arsonist, you better be prepared for the backfire, sooner or later. Since 1996, the relationship between Rwanda and the Democratic Republic of Congo (former Zaire) has not been good. Congolese are accusing Rwanda of having caused the death of more than two million Congolese citizens. Again, the die-hard demons are at work: the Tutsi–Hamites are accused of achieving a long-planned genocide of the Bantu people. A conflict like the one that caused the 1996 Rwandan invasion of Congo is at the core of increasing ethno-nationalism in the region. The eastern Congolese are very close to Rwandans and Burundians as they share most aspects of their culture, thus making mimetic phenomena very strong among them. Tutsis are perceived as evil by them. If things are not dealt with properly as soon as possible, one can easily foresee the fate awaiting Tutsis in the future. The massacre of 160 Banyamulenge refugees in the Gatumba refugee camp in August 2004 confirms the threat. The massacre was claimed by a Burundian Hutu rebel movement called PALIPEHUTU–FLN. Banyamulenge are Tutsis from Congo, but in the Great Lakes region of Africa ethno-nationalism still preavails on nationality.

CONCLUSION

It is hard to accurately determine the causes or origins of a deep-rooted conflict. Once examined from a certain distance, causes brought forward by the parties involved sometimes look extremely ridiculous to uninvolved foreign bystanders. Looking at the Rwandan past, one can find many similarities with other countries in the world. For instance, the creation of France did not happen overnight, nor was it achieved peacefully. The same is true for other European countries. Ironically, Rwandan historical facts were not distorted by un-

educated people: they were manipulated by evil, educated extremists.

It is important that Rwandan history be taught with respect for the truth. Nasty things happened in the past. They should be interpreted in relation to the nation's zeitgeist, and as a nation Rwandans should take ownership of their history. Picking out what happened five centuries ago and judging that according to twenty-first-century moral principles makes no sense.

Rwandans share a common historical heritage, which has positive and negative aspects to it: it is time Rwandans learned about the positive things they have achieved together. For example, the bravery of Hutus, Tutsis, and Twas prevented slave traders from scouring Rwanda in search of slaves. The reservoirs of recollection, instead of intensifying the deep-rooted conflict, should be a resource for building a better Rwanda. Colonial powers that colonized Rwanda, especially Belgians, share some responsibility for the Rwandan conflict. They initiated and promoted the ideology of difference, they created and widened the gap between Hutus and Tutsis, and they institutionalized the exclusion of Hutus and the promotion of only the Tutsi elite, thus fueling negative mimetic phenomena between the two groups. Belgian administrators and Roman Catholic missionaries share the blame in dividing and antagonizing Hutus and Tutsis.

It would be unfair to put all the blame on Belgian administrators and missionaries. Rwandans should acknowledge their part in the conflict; if the Belgian administrators and their religious accomplices sowed the seeds of hatred, Hutus and Tutsis were obviously a well-prepared field. Something in Rwandan culture has to change. Giving up part of one's cultural identity to achieve a goal is scary: it is hard to understand why Rwandans accepted that their traditional faith was evil. If traditional cults such as the ancestors are respected everywhere else in the world and coexist with Christianity, why should they be labeled as paganism in Rwanda? Traditional Rwandan values and beliefs included strong and positive interdicts that would have probably prevented genocide. For instance, Hutus and Tutsis who underwent the *kubandwa* initiation together considered themselves to be brothers; they were unable to harm one another under any circumstances. This is just one example to support the idea that traditional Rwandan spirituality should be restored and given the place it deserves in the people's life.

Hutus and Tutsis need to have the same understanding of the 1959 events. Yes, a revolution was necessary and democracy and change were needed, but the systemic ostracism, scapegoat mechanisms, dehumanization, and victimization of the Tutsis since the Hutu Revolution still have no justification. The Hutu Revolution did not bring much change to ordinary Hutus. Those who were poor became poorer. Critical issues such as land redistribution were never addressed. In reality, Tutsi elites were replaced by Hutu elites.

It is the despicable poverty of the masses that is used as a tool by Hutu extremist politicians. Their message is simple: kill your Tutsi neighbor and you can have his land and will not be punished. For people described as "farmers," the message was well received because having land gave them a sense of meaning. As impunity was totally guaranteed to Hutus who victimized Tutsis, killing Tutsis became, in Hutus' minds, a national duty, not a crime. Hutu killers described their actions as *gukora*, meaning "work." They were carrying out a national duty and expected a reward instead of punishment. This is one of the reasons why the vast majority of genocide suspects are remorseless. Actually they may feel betrayed, especially when they learn that those who planned the genocide are enjoying a five-star lifestyle in Arusha or are sharing power with the current government, while perpetrators are rotting in overpopulated prisons.

There is no chance of achieving genuine reconciliation in the current sociopolitical context in Rwanda. There cannot be reconciliation without justice, and the traditional Gacaca courts are not designed to achieve genuine reconciliation. Besides, wounds are still open. Ten years are not enough time for healing, especially when so little has been done to bring killers to justice. Instead, survivors feel victimized by a system that was supposed to help them recover. Those who can afford to are fleeing the country. Hutus are still waiting for signs of recognition from the government: not all the Hutus killed by the RPF were criminals. Hutus believe that their dead deserve equal respect and should officially be regretted and remembered.

The RPF government has changed Rwanda's national flag, coat of arms, and national anthem. All these symbols have been there since the independ-

ence of Rwanda. The official reasons for the changes were that "the old symbols were designed in 1962, at a time when Rwanda was rocked by state sponsored ethnic divisions and killings, human rights violations and bad governance."

Hutus believe that the RPF government is making a clean sweep of Hutu Revolution symbols, and this may wake old demons related to Rwanda resettlement. Not everything designed between 1962 and 1990 was necessarily negative; besides, it is part of Rwandans' common heritage and nobody can change the past. In addition, nothing can guarantee that the new symbols will remain. Change is another potential provocation of Rwanda's identity-based, deep-rooted conflict.

The Akazu system is a die-hard pattern. It replicates constantly; it has been there since Rwanda came into existence. Rwanda is one of the poorest countries in the world; it is landlocked, overpopulated, and has extremely limited resources. In Kinyarwanda, it is said that *"Iyo amazi abaye make aharirwa impfizi"* (When water becomes scarce, it is stored for the bull.). In Rwanda, scarce resources are always stored for those who hold power and power's entourage. During the monarchy, the king and his entourage monopolized resources. During the First Republic, Kayibanda and people from his region of origin did exactly the same thing. During the Second Republic, the term *akazu* was used to describe leaders' exclusive monopoly of wealth and power. Today, akazu is still going strong: having been a refugee in Uganda opens doors to a lot of opportunities, but even as you are accepted as *Uwacu* or "the one that belongs to us" (even if you have not been in Uganda), the same ubuhake pattern is being repeated.

Even if Rwandans believe that the 1959 "revolution" abolished the "ubuhake system," it is still alive in people's mind. The only way to get help and protection from those who have access to resources is to "pay allegiance" to them. It was the case during the monarchy era, it was the case under Kayibanda and Habyarimana, and it is still the case today. The genocide of Tutsis was a result of the presence and alignment of numerous constellations of humanity, each dangerous enough to cause important damages on its own. These constellations are still in place. More violent alignments can occur as long as the people of Rwanda are stuck in the entrenched patterns of their past.

ABOUT THE AUTHOR

Richard Batsinduka was born in Rwanda in 1955 in the southern province of Butare. His parents were Tutsis. He fled Rwanda in May 1973 and completed high school at the Junior Seminary of Bujumbura (Burundi) in July 1975. He received a B.A. degree in Roman philology from the University of Burundi.

Batsinduka taught French at the Rutovu Teachers Training College (1980 to 1982) and the Junior Seminary of Bujumbura (1982 to 1986). In 1987, he signed a contract to teach French for the Ministry of Education of the Kingdom of Swaziland, where he taught until December 1990, when he was granted resettlement opportunities from Immigration Canada. After immigrating to Canada, he obtained a teaching certificate from Laval University. He moved to Ottawa in May 1992, where he taught French at La Cité Collégiale.

In 1994, during the genocide of Tutsis, Batsinduka lost his entire family and all his references and former work colleagues. The following year, he decided to devote the rest of his life to conflict resolution and peace education.

After completing the Canadian Institute for Conflict Resolution's Third Party Neutral training program, he was accepted for a one-year residency program offered by the institute. He drafted a proposal entitled "Community-Based Conflict Resolution in the Rwandan Setting." It was turned into a pilot project proposal, and funding from the Canadian International Development Agency (CIDA) was sought. CIDA funded the eighteenth-month project. Batsinduka coordinated the project from 1998 to 2000. He then joined Initiatives for Change International in the Agenda for Reconciliation Program.

In 2002, Batsinduka began working as a mediator for Canada's Department of National Defence at its base in Borden, Manitoba. He is married to Christine Kayirangwa and has two children, Kevin Nkhosinathi Batsinduka and Jacqueline Nkhosazana Batsinduka.

SUGGESTED READING

1. Bangamwabo, Francois—Favier et alii *Les Relations Interethniques au Rwanda à la Lumièrede l'Agression d'Octobre 1990*. Editions Universitaires du Rwanda (E.U.R), 1991.

2. Canadian Institute for Conflict Resolution. "Understanding Deep-Rooted Conflict," seminar series, 1998 version. Ottawa: Vern Neufeld Redekop.

3. Chrétien, Jean-Pierre, Jean-François Dupaquier, Marcel Kabanda, and Joseph Ngarambe. *Rwanda: Les Média du Génocide*. Paris: Editions Karthala, 1995.

4. D'Hertefelt, and A. Coupez. *La Royauté Sacrée de l'Ancien Rwanda*. Tervuren: Musée Royale de l'Afrique Centrale, 1964.

5. De Lacger, Louis. *Rwanda, Première Partie, le Rwanda Ancien, de Louis de Lacger du clergé d'Albi*. Namur: Les Grands Lacs, 1939.

6. Donat, Murego, *La Révolution Rwandaise 1959–1962*. Louvain-la-Neuve; Institut des Sciences Politiques et Sociales, 1975.

7. Gamaliel, Mbonimana. *L'Instauration d'un Royaume Chrétien au Rwanda, 1900–1931*. Université Catholique de Louvain, thèse de doctorat, 1981.

8. ICPCRIA. *Les Catastrophes Rwandaises: Ses Causes Profondes et les Remèdes*. Nairobi, Kenya: ICPCRIA, 1995.

9. Kayibanda, Grégoire. *Discours, Messages et Instructions du Président Kayibanda, Président du MDR Parmehutu, 1960–1973*. Kigali, Rwanda: ORINFOR, 1993.

10. Lemarchand, René. *Rwanda and Burundi*. New York: Praeger, 1970.

11. Mfizi, Christophe. "Le réseau zéro," Kigali: August 15, 1992.

12. Nahimana. *Rwanda Émergence d'un État*. l'Harmattan, 1987.

13. Prunier, Gérard. *The Rwanda Crisis: History of a Genocide*. New York: Columbia University Press, 1995.

14. Redekop, Vern Neufeld. *From Violence to Blessing*. Ottawa: Novalis, Saint Paul University, 2002.

15. _____. *Scapegoats, the Bible, and Criminal Justice: Interacting with René Girard*. MCC Canada Victim Offender Ministries, 1993.

16. Reyntjens, Filip. *L'Afrique des Grands Lacs en Crise*. Paris: Editions Karthala, 1994.

17. Rutayisire, Paul. *La Christianisation du Rwanda (1900–1945)*. Éd Univ. de Fribourg, Suisse

18. Seruvumba, Emmanuel. *Rwanda—Naissance d'Une Idéologie du Genocide. La responsabilité de l'Église*.

19. Theunis, Guy. " Le Role de l'Eglise Catholique dans les Evénements Récents." In *Les Crises Politiques au Burundi et au Rwanda*, 2nd edition, edited by André Guichaoua. Lille: Université des Sciences et Technologies de Lille, 1995.

7

Sri Lanka

Sri Lanka, formerly called Ceylon, is a small tropical island off the coast of the southern India province of Tamil Nadu, is constituted of an ethnic and religious mosaic composed of two principal ethnic and religious groups: the Sinhala–Buddhist in the southwest and the Tamil–Hindu in the north and the east. For more then twenty years, Sri Lanka has been enmeshed in a devastating civil war between the government and the Liberation Tigers of Tamil Eelam (LTTE). The LTTE wants a distinct state for the Tamil minority, which represents approximately 18 percent of the nineteen million Sri Lankans, whereas the Sri Lankan government wishes to preserve a unitary state. The war has destroyed much of the development potential of the country.

The origins of the disagreements between both communities have been amplified by the religious nationalism of the twentieth century. Although historical studies show that the major groups in Sri Lanka—Tamils and Sinhalese—belong to a similar ethnic blend of migrants from distinct regions of India, the different groups tend to lead highly segregated lives and live within their own communities.

Regardless of which ethnic groups arrived first, both communities have been deeply influenced by the strategy of "divide and rule" promoted during European colonization. As colonial rulers, the British authorities established complete control by 1830 and began to play each group against the other, deepening religious and ethnic antagonism on the island. To counterbalance the Sinhala majority, Tamils resident in the north were integrated into the British education system, while the Sinhalese majority was strictly excluded from forms of employment dominated by British and Tamil professionals. The employment discrimination raised nationalist reactions within the Sinhalese population and caused strong animosities toward the British and Tamils.

After 150 years of British presence, Ceylon finally became independent in 1948, inheriting a secular parliamentary system dominated by the Sinhalese majority. Despite their strong presence on the island, the Buddhist Sinhalese were worried about the proximity of India and the fact that the Tamil community enjoyed a privileged position under British rule. The Sinhalese undertook a series of chauvinistic measures—controlling the police, the justice system, the administration, the army, and the economy—which caused deep animosity within the Tamil community. With the passage of time, the Sinhalese operated "detamoulisation" of the public office, which culminated in 1959 with the signing of the Sinhala Only Act replacing English with Sinhala as the official national language. The government was clearly functioning like a unified nation-state, whereas the social structure of the country was obviously binational.

Facing the banishment of the Tamil language and the feeling of being wrongfully treated by the government, the Tamil population began pointing out the "dictatorship of the minority." Most of the Tamils' fears and insecurities came from the belief that they had lost the advantageous position they enjoyed under British rule in many sectors of public life throughout the country. Decades of tension between Tamils and Sinhala led to intense communal riots from

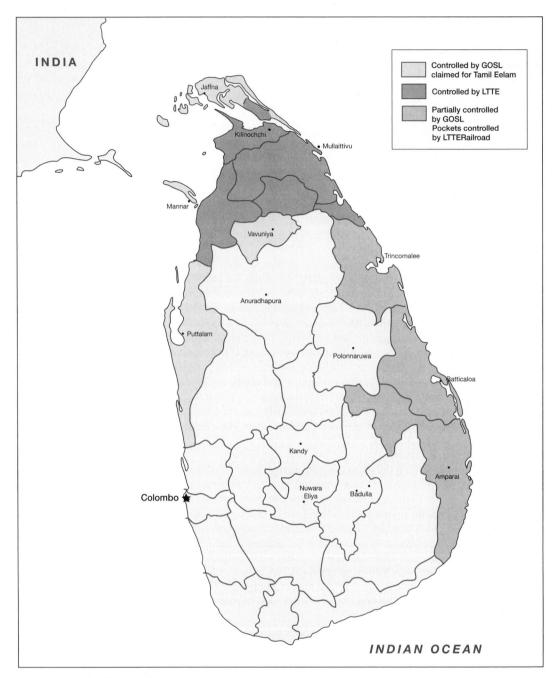

Extent of Territorial Control in Sri Lanka
http://en.wikipedia.org/wiki/Ethnic_conflict_in_Sri_Lanka

the 1950s to the 1970s that targeted Tamil communities and economic interests in many parts of the island. In 1972, an organization known as the Tamilian New Tigers (TNT) appeared, led by a young militant named Velupillai Prabhakaran; in 1983 he became supreme chief of the LTTE. The LTTE adopted a nationalist ideology, with its main goal being the formation of an independent Tamil state in the northeastern section of the island.

In the early 1980s, Tamil efforts to force the creation of a separate Tamil state grew to the point that Tamil militants engaged in guerrilla attacks against the government. The conflict continued through the 1990s with occasional cease-fires, followed by a return to fighting. LTTE bombings continued when the government refused to enter peace talks. In 2000, the Sri Lankan government submitted to the parliament a proposal for a federal constitution that would give an important part of power to Tamils. However, the tensions still remain explosive in Sri Lanka, and the conflict between the two communities is not over.

In the following essay David Ratnavale shows how identity mechanisms transformed community frictions into a civil war. Relying on the old and contemporary history of Sri Lanka, the author reminds us of the principal causes of the emergence of exclusive nationalism and explains the toughening of the Tamil independence movement. Moved by conflicting objectives and strategies, the attitudes and actions taken by each community can be explained by the weight of the identity and a negative perception of the enemy, which lead both communities to distrust and reject one another. Ratnavale underlines the undeniable influence of the media on the behavior of the two communities, whose treatment and censure strongly contributed to the sustained rigid mental representation of the "evil" Tigers. Since 1987, there have been several attempts to initiate a constitutional accommodation between successive Sri Lankan governments and the advocates of Tamil nationalism. These initiatives have often failed to answer prevailing political and military realities, and a definitive solution to the ethnic problem remains elusive.

The author exposes the difficulties encountered in securing a lasting peace between these two populations, and this, in spite of international efforts to support the processes of peace on a national and regional scale. The existing institutional framework hinders the attainment of national consensus on the resolution of Sri Lanka's ethnic conflict. Peace negotiations, headed by Norway, were undertaken in an effort to find a solution to the conflict. The Sri Lankan government is under national and international pressure to carry out a constitutional reform leading to a lasting solution to the conflict. Dialogues have taken place between the Sinhala and Tamil communities and with policy makers on the importance of making reconciliation an integral part of the peace and conflict transformation processes.

Changes in government, as well as the many rounds of negotiation, are shown to be doomed to failure if they are not built on community initiatives. The resolution of conflict is a gradual, uncertain process, prone to hitches in which "achievements gained may be easily lost."

Ethnic Communities and Religions

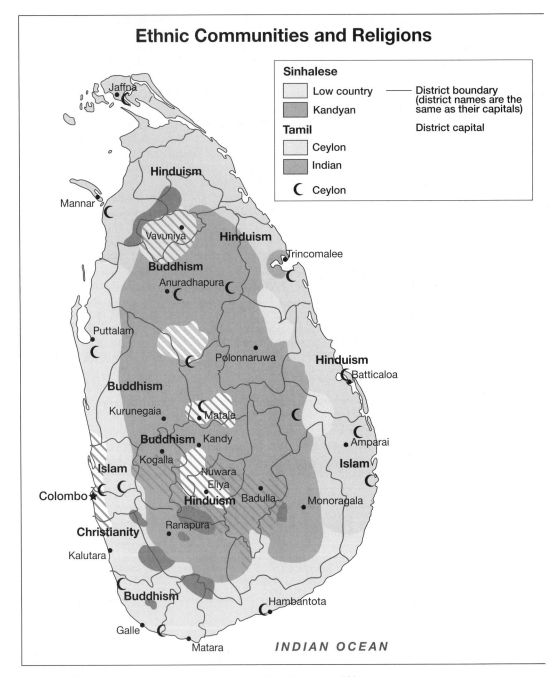

Legend:

Sinhalese
- Low country
- Kandyan

Tamil
- Ceylon
- Indian

(Ceylon

— District boundary (district names are the same as their capitals)

• District capital

Map labels: Jaffna, Mannar, Vavuniya, Hinduism, Hinduism, Trincomalee, Buddhism, Anuradhapura, Puttalam, Polonnaruwa, Hinduism, Batticaloa, Buddhism, Kurunegaia, Matale, Buddhism, Kandy, Amparai, Kogalla, Islam, Nuwara Eliya, Islam, Colombo, Hinduism, Badulla, Monoragala, Christianity, Ranapura, Kalutara, Buddhism, Hambantota, Galle, Matara, INDIAN OCEAN, Islam

Sri Lanka's "Ethnic" Conflict

David Ratnavale

INTRODUCTION

Twenty miles off the southern tip of India shines the tropical island nation of Sri Lanka, once named Serendib by ancient Arab seafarers who serendipitously chanced upon this resplendent isle.

Myths and legend surround how and when the island's original people landed there, who belongs, and who does not. Conflicting versions of the island's 2,000-year history are regularly manipulated to justify the fierce struggle between the Sinhala, a predominantly Buddhist ethnic majority (75 percent) and the mostly Hindu Tamil ethnic minority (13 percent). The population of 18 million includes Muslims (8 percent) and some smaller communities. About 15 percent of the Singhalese and 10 percent of the Tamils are Christian. Many Christians are the descendants of people who converted to Catholicism 400 years ago, when Portuguese influences dominated the island. Others are descendants of people who became Protestants when the Dutch and British were in Sri Lanka.

Independence from Britain's 150-year occupation and another 250 years of Portuguese and Dutch domination before that has made self-rule a difficult undertaking for this island's people. They are still struggling to define their separate but unique identities within a nation-state, freed just fifty-five years ago. Racked by unrelenting violent conflict since 1983, massive infrastructure damage, war-related uprooting of thousands, and a toll of over 60,000 deaths have left Sri Lanka a deeply divided and traumatized society, with its image seriously tarnished.

In late 2001, however, a cease-fire was signed between the Sri Lanka government and the Liberation Tigers of Tamil Eelam (LTTE), a militant organization made up of Tamils, whose initial demands included the establishment of an independent state of Eelam as a Tamil homeland. At an internationally televised ceremony, the nation witnessed the prime minister and a representative of the rarely seen LTTE leader attesting their signatures to a memorandum of understanding, with Norwegian mediators standing by.

The accord held with occasional but not disastrous violations. Yet, given the lengthy period of conflict, deep-seated distrust and multiple regime changes, issues concerned with safeguarding ethnic identity and territorial integrity have kept the nation tense and economically hard pressed.

Neither side may claim innocence. The Tigers remain burdened by their reputation as a deadly terrorist organization that uses suicide bombers and child soldiers in their quest for secession and independence. The Sri Lanka government also stands accused of divisive policies, deception, carpet bombings, and human rights violations. With the nation so wounded, healing the psyche became a daunting task. Providentially, in this island famed for tea, spices, and hospitality that was transformed into a cauldron of fire and hatred, a yearning for peace has been drawing on the country's innate resilience.

With the media unshackled and checkpoints removed, people can move about more freely. Buddhists, Hindus, Muslims, and Christians actually are seen praying together. Thoughts of peace and reconciliation are articulated on both sides of the divide, and as roadways open and former enemies meet face to face, negotiations continue. As conditions of symmetry approached, the perception of the "enemy" started to change, with the divide closing very slowly.

During peace talks held in Thailand, a surprising but welcome development emerged as the LTTE team announced its commitment to seeking a political solution within a framework of regional autonomy. This marked a dramatic change in the "rebels'" strategy and attitude—a willingness to settle for a nonsecessionist solution helped greatly to calm the fears of the Singhalese masses.

Amid doubt and debate over power sharing, signs of a possible settlement began to appear. Encouraging discussions hosted in Oslo, Paris, and Tokyo were directed to exploring several models of federalism, like those in nations such as Switzerland, Canada, and Belgium.

Trust continued to be harshly tested, though, as opposition parties and chauvinist Singhalese challenged the government's political motivations, hurling accusations that it was giving away too much space and power to the Tigers or stalling the peace process only to hold on to power. Alliances were forged and broken in the horse-trading context of retaining parliamentary majority. The LTTE also begun to see similar splits within its fold as renegade elements linked up with government factions and smaller parties aiming to break the tiger's spine.

The Norwegian mediator/monitors stayed committed despite many frustrations and accusations of being partial to the Tamils. The donor community stood by with concern, watching for the psychological moment.

ANALYSIS: HISTORY AND BACKGROUND

With the price of Sri Lanka's war-to-peace transformation costing more lives, more destruction, more suffering, and lasting much longer than anyone can justify, it is useful to explore the dynamics that drive the engines of conflict.

Tracing the evolution of Sri Lanka's ethnic conflict as though it had a definite beginning in time and place, or trying to explain transformations as if they occurred stepwise, is no simple task. Neither does the label *ethnic conflict* adequately encompass other factors that get pulled in to bolster or weaken, respectively, the antagonism and separateness existing between groups. In configuring the "enemy," there is clearly much more to the conflict than Singhalese Buddhists versus Tamil Hindus.

Nor is it a simple matter to gauge the deep aspirations and conflicts of the leaders involved as they struggle to hold on to power. It is even harder to discern the pressures exerted by the inner circles of politics, caste, and clan or know to what extent the intergenerational transmission of enmity keeps peace at bay.

Besides, the evolution of Sri Lanka's war-to-peace transformations cannot be interpreted apart from significant world events, terrorism, September 11, the December 26 (2004) tsunami disaster, and the maneuvered political allegiances that compromise national stability.

Origins

Although both ethnic groups trace their origins to India, there are conflicting versions of the story of Sri Lanka's original people. Ancient dynastic history in the region reflects phases of turmoil in the subcontinent, but they seem to have alternated with lengthy periods of shared cultural harmony. It is, therefore, not wholly accurate to explain the ethnic conflict of today as a manifestation of a phenomenon rooted in the historical experience of the nation.[1]

However, the haunting echoes of tragic mythology, complicated by nearly four hundred years of foreign colonial subjugation, have created a sharp "us" versus "them" divide in Sri Lanka, a split that has generated two strands of nationalism along ethnic lines.

If "History is dynamite," as Michael Roberts has written, "Sri Lanka has too much history" and "history-talk has been a powerful powder serving to ignite or exacerbate the ethnic conflict."[2]

NATIONALISM: A LIBERATING FORCE SHAPING COLLECTIVE IDENTITY

Singhalese nationalism had its beginnings in the nineteenth century, when many Singhalese came to fear that their ancient culture had been and was continuing to be threatened by a series of hostile external forces: Indian expansionism, international trade, Christian missionaries, colonial powers, the corrupting influences of "alien" modernity, and disproportionate Tamil influence in business and government administration.

After Sri Lanka gained independence from the British in 1948, latent animosities linked to these concerns rose to the surface. Singhalese people saw independence as an opportunity to revive a former "golden era" and regain the supreme position they had once held, and then to put the Tamils in their place—figuratively, geographically, and above all psychologically.

The *Mahavamsa,* a sixth-century historical legend, is often cited to explain a unique and powerful Sinhala identity and legitimate Singhalese "manifest destiny" over the island. This endowment was linked with an obligation to protect the Dhammadeepa, "the island of the just word," dedicated by Lord Buddha himself, to be the safe repository of pristine Buddhist culture.

For the Singhalese, increasing Tamil militancy revived fears of past invasions of their gloried civilizations and temples and of intolerable humiliation and shame. Tamil agitation came to be perceived as an obvious threat to the Sinhala peoples' identity, security, and sense of territorial integrity.

Although Sri Lankan Tamils' links with India are predominantly linguistic and religious, the very existence of a large Tamil-speaking population in the southern state of Tamil Nadu loomed as an anxiety-provoking threat for the Sinhalese situated in their one-and-only island homeland. Indeed, when the numbers and regional powers are interpreted against the backdrop of the island's long-term history, the Singhalese rarely view the world with the confidence of a conventional majority. In effect, they have become "a majority with a minority neurosis," a situation described by many scholars.[3]

For the Sinhalese, the presence of the Tamils remains a haunting reminder of alien influence and of the way their inherent rights were compromised by the Tamils' ill-gotten, undeserved advantages manipulated under the divide-and-rule policies of the British. To the majority Sinhala population endowed with such primordial claims, the audacious demand for equal status and a separate state implied yet another ominous threat of boundary violation and traumatic dismemberment. In short, the existence of the Tamils threatened the deeply ingrained collective self-image of the Singhalese as a "chosen people" destined to live on "chosen land."

To bolster Sinhala nationalism Buddhist monks were inspired to claim their hallowed role as both *buddhaputra,* sons of the Buddha, and *bhumiputra,* sons of the soil. This underscored Sinhala Buddhism's exclusivist tendencies that had threatened the status of Hindu Tamils and other minorities. In challenging Hindu Tamil aspirations, the role of the *bhikku* (monk) took on a new shape. No longer were they content to play an ascetic role devoted solely to fulfilling the ritual needs of the lay. Instead, they began to assume an activist role, taking all measures to defend Buddhism and Buddhists.[4] Vehemently rejecting the devolution package that was proposed, some insisted they be given the imprimatur of the state to lead the Sinhala people. Others groups of Buddhist clergy felt no compunction in pressing for war and annihilation of the LTTE.

Explaining a group's behavior in the context of existing crises requires some insight into the history, beliefs, and values that have shaped the group members' collective identity. Burned into the psyche of the Singhalese people is the belief that the island belongs to them, legitimately inherited, and chosen, according to the Buddha's words. The

country is also projected as a mysterious fantasy island, a garden paradise where precious gems lie under the ground, tea and spices above.

If, to any extent, geography determines the history and life of a people, the Tamils' ability to survive the island's northernmost and hottest climatic zone, with its flat, parched, and ungiving soil, bears consideration. The folk from the northern regions seem to have become by nature a modest, cautious, and conservative community, endowed with the characteristics of tenacity and resilience. By contrast, a commonly articulated self-image of the Singhalese people is assumed to mirror the fertile generosity of their southern green landscape and its rambling relaxed hills.

Growing Tamil nationalism was the consequence of a challenge to the legitimacy of the Tamils, who had long regarded themselves and the Singhalese to be founders of the island's culture. Buddhist revivalists strongly repudiated this view, asserting their unique Aryan roots, claiming lighter skin and a Singhalese/Buddhist culture to be superior to the Hindu Tamils of darker Dravidian origin.

The Tamils, who have drawn inspiration from a cultural and linguistic identity originating from a "golden period" of Chola domination over a vast South Asian regional kingdom, resented the Singhalese put-down. The Chola influence of the ninth, tenth, and eleventh centuries is known to have extended beyond Thailand and Cambodia in the east and to Bali in the south. The Tiger emblem of the Chola Empire is what adorns the LTTE flag.

Earlier gestures by the Singhalese to devolve power to the Tamils were perceived to be half hearted, the true rights of the Tamil ignored in order to relegate them to second-class status. In 1956 the Singhalese government enacted a "Sinhala only" language policy. To further dignify themselves, the Singhalese introduced a quota system for entry to universities but did not anticipate resistance, no less retaliation from the Tamils. Seeing their futures to be seriously compromised, the Tamils experienced a not-so-subtle form of job exclusion. Furthermore, Tamil leaders were not accommodated or even consulted when the new constitution was being framed.

Following the pogrom of 1983, Tamil leaders were actually expelled from parliament for refusing to make a declaration of renouncing secession.[5]

The Tamils interpreted the Singhalese-dominated government's tyranny in terms of ethnic cleansing and genocide. Faulting the Singhalese for their of pursuit of a philosophy contrary to the teachings of the Buddha, the Compassionate One, they cried out, "Buddhism betrayed!"

With discrimination and tensions growing, a more aggressive attitude began to ferment among the Tamil people traditionally regarded as conservative and even passive. Frustrated youths took on a militant character aiming to shape a vigorous new collective identity—a victim-to-warrior image change—closely matching that which has occurred among the Israelis.

THE "INCIDENT," 1983

The incident that precipitated all-out war began in 1983 as riots that followed the killing by Tamil Tigers of thirteen soldiers of the Sri Lanka army. As news of the "outrageous" event spread like wildfire, fear and vengeance were triggered within the Singhalese population. The country's president, a Singhalese and Buddhist, remained unresponsive for several days as the bloody riots continued. He finally broke his silence to make harsh pronouncements implicating "those Tamils" to be the wrongdoers. The Singhalese, unified in their rage, wrought devastating anti-Tamil violence, in a burning and killing spree. Analysts now conclude the event was merely the flash point for the release of a preplanned pogrom.

The "83 riots," as they are called, marked a turning point, the conflict gaining the label of an interethnic struggle. Within a short time, Tamil militancy, spearheaded by a guerrilla organization (the LTTE), escalated into a full-scale war, the militants determined to create their very own special and separate state. The Singhalese majority's resolve was, of course, to thwart the Tamil's secessionist aims and preserve their sovereignty over an undivided country, whatever the cost.

Although gestures of appeasements by the Singhalese were forthcoming, these were perceived to be mere sops to manipulate and soften the Tamil political leadership. As tensions mounted, both sides stood firm, and into the fray came the full arsenal of the government's military might and the much smaller but deadly LTTE guerrilla force.

THE QUEST: SHARED GOALS AND CLASHING STRATEGIES

For each side, the quest for recognition of their unique heritage, connectedness, and autonomy became the defining feature for sustaining a secure identity. The raison d'étre for the Singhalese became preserving sovereignty over a singular state; for the Tamils it was separation and independence. In common was their quest for identity and mutual respect.

From a nonpartisan perspective it appears as if both parties to the conflict have labored under similar threats, but the strategies chosen for overcoming them have been certain to clash and be self-defeating in the long run. The repudiation of each other's collective self-image has instead heightened the conflict and widened the divide.

As there can be no self without the other, each side has remained ensnared in the conflict because of the manner in which they defined their identity. Ironically, each side was facing the conundrum of "Who are we?"—and "Who are we if we are not different from them?" "Because we define them, and they define us, we must need each other. But who needs enemies?"

Predator or Prey

The conflict pitted the two sides against each other but, alas, only to become locked in a hateful embrace of war, from which escape is difficult. Pushing and pulling, attacking and defending, they seemed destined to stretch out the drama of who is predator and who is prey.

Consequences of Threat

In the years preceding the cease-fire, the Singhalese-dominated government, faced with the threat of Tiger infiltration, introduced extensive travel restrictions. Heavily armed police and military personnel manned checkpoints at city intersections and highways. Police passes and ID cards showing name, birthplace, and (by implication) ethnic origin elicited new fears and discord. Tamils living in harmony in largely Sinhala communities far from the war zone came to dread the profiling surveillance and harassment at checkpoints, where armed

Sri Lanka military personnel, themselves at risk, nervously judged who was friend and who was foe.

Mounting fear and suspicion led both communities to distrust and reject one another. In ethnically mixed neighborhoods of the major cities, former friends turned cool. Children who played together stayed apart, and in the schools, already divided by a language policy, the atmosphere was ripe for germinating hatefulness.

Every conceivable strategy for outmaneuvering the other side was tried and countered. When, for example, the Sri Lanka government began provoking Muslim–Tamil discord, this was immediately suspected as a clever Singhalese sponsored divide-and-rule strategy. Likewise, Tamil treachery was detected as Tamils sought to exploit the splits within the Singhalese population.

WHO IS FIGHTING WHOM?

The government fighting forces are youthful volunteers, entirely Singhalese from the rural south, their officers usually trained according to conventional western systems of warfare. They enlisted to the rallying strains of "defending the motherland" and for preserving "territorial integrity" (oft used phrases), but for substantial numbers military service was a well-paid government job. A high desertion rate among government forces became a source of much embarrassment and concern but was due primarily to poor selection criteria, frantic recruitment, and inconsistent frontline backup.

Tiger *cadres,* as they are commonly referred to, consisted of Tamil youth, volunteers mostly from Jaffna (the capitol of their northern peninsular homeland), neighboring areas, and the eastern province. Drawn by LTTE propaganda, or some personal or family experience of discrimination, they rallied around a charismatic leader who promised to recover their "inalienable rights."

The Tigers, unlike the government forces, have relied entirely on smuggled armaments and those they captured in battle, their funds derived primarily from the Tamil diaspora, consisting of those who had fled as refugees to Canada, the United Kingdom, Australia, and several European nations following the 1983 debacle. Considered to be a disciplined but harsh dedicated guerilla movement, it lost much of its "liberation movement" image gaining instead, a deadly "terrorist" label due to their fear tactics, recruitment of child soldiers, and training of suicide bombers. All of these developments brought considerable international censure, especially after 9/11, when suspected terrorist groups suffered proscription and their funding resources started to shrink.

DEEPER CONNECTIONS

The contestants possess deeper connections rarely acknowledged. The metaphors used to describe the Sri Lanka conflict are revealing in this respect. In the Singhalese language *singha* means "lion," the symbol of courage, and some Singhalese are known to boast, "We are the lion race." Yet "singha" is a common last syllable in both Singhalese and Tamil surnames. One might therefore encounter a Singhalese named Gunasinghe or a Tamil with the name Gunasingham. The irony lies in the meaning of *guna,* which is healthful in both languages.

Another island state, Singapore, combines *singha* (lion) and *pura* (land), suggesting a wide swathe of cultural links between Asian people connected by a common symbol.

Paradoxically, the conflict has ensnared young people. Buddhist Singhalese youth from the south enlisted in a Sri Lanka (government) army, and Tamil (mostly Hindu) youth from the north, all of them legitimate citizens, siblings, or cousins in their common motherland, constituted a rebel force. Here indeed are two groups closely connected, sharing customs, spiritual attitudes, and similar superstitions, yet yearning to be distinguished as pure and distinct, a phenomenon nicely described by Freud as "the narcissism of small differences."[6]

By the 1990s the Sri Lanka armed forces constituted a modern military machine, comprising more than 100,000 recruits from the Sinhala south, set to wage a largely conventional war with the Tigers, a force of less than one-tenth that size, employing cunning guerilla tactics. The danger of a sudden terrorist attack kept the cities tense. While the government's military recruitment doubled, their combined forces kept pounding the Tiger-controlled areas, and the economy kept declining as the government's defense funding climbed steeply.

As politicians heightened the divisive rhetoric, and the military forces kept shooting back and forth, there was little relief for the nations' internal frustration and rage. Yet, with military debacles occurring on each side, leaders assassinated, villages ransacked, temples, churches and mosques desecrated, one impasse led to another, and yet another, year after year.

When escape seems impossible and wounds intolerable is when an external intermediary is welcomed to mediate, to disentangle or at least lower the tension. In desperation, the government sought foreign military assistance.

First, India was persuaded to send a peacekeeping force that was frequently pulled into vicious combat. The initiative turned out to be a disaster not only for the Tamils in the peninsula—it cost the lives of several thousand peacekeepers. Eventually Sri Lanka's President Chandrika Kumaratunga looked to Norway to mediate the conflict.

These developments provided new justifications for both sides to harden their antagonism toward "the enemy," the situation breeding a chronic conflict and provocative assaults hardening each side's resolve to keep fighting.

In certain phases of the war the Tamils have dared to twist the tail of the Sinhala lion, bearding him in the den of his sacred palaces and temples. This hardened the perception of "those" arrogant Tamils in a tiger's coat with an appetite for a lion's share. The demand for a separate state came to be seen as just the first step toward annexing the whole island. The *Eelam* quest became an *Ellarm* quest for "everything." Any wonder the Singhalese came to feel threatened?

TERRORISM

Held responsible for the assassination of political leaders, bomb attacks on government institution, raids on cities, and damage to holy places, the Tigers gained a label for themselves as a formidable "terrorist" organization. By recruiting and indoctrinating children into their fold, a new breed of combatant was born, and when their campaigns involved suicide bombers, the threats, fears, and surveillance grew harsher. Any parcel was presumed to be a bomb waiting to explode, and any suspicious-looking characters were perceived as potential human dynamite. Suicide bombers magnified the Tigers' terrorist image, bringing swift

censure from the United Nations (U.N.) and child rights organizations worldwide.

However, numerous instances of torture and human rights violations by the ranks of the Sri Lanka army, and the penchant of certain groups to strike terror among Tamil civilians, remained largely hidden as a result of tight media censorship. Consequently, the international community restricted to the government-controlled south tended to focus almost entirely on the Tigers' misdeeds.

Along a circuitous path that included the dissolution of rival Tamil parties, the LTTE aspired to be interpreted not only as a formidable military force but also as the voice of Tamil aspirations. This was achieved despite their hard-to-erase "terrorist" label and splits within the larger Tamil community, many living far from the militarized zone. Military prowess, dogged determination, and an emerging political consciousness ultimately pointed the LTTE to a place at the negotiating table.

PERCEPTIONS OF THE ENEMY

Through the early years of massive civilian displacements, disappearances, reports of torture, and heavy military casualties, the international community appeared helpless to intervene. Because of government propaganda and restrictions on foreigners from entering LTTE-controlled areas, the diplomatic community could view the ground situation only through the telescope of scant nongovernmental organization (NGO) and U.N. presence. Although several diplomatic missions sought to bring reconciliation, most watched only their security and commercial interests.

Despite heavy military casualties the war did not let up, both sides stubbornly refusing to give in, as territory was captured, briefly held, lost, and reclaimed.

Sustaining the image of the enemy as an evil force usually requires the regular reminding of the evil hurts and traumas previously inflicted. Propaganda on both sides of the divide followed this trend, while political entrepreneurs, in echoing age-old *chosen traumas* stirred the instinct for war; linked to these remembered traumas were the *chosen triumphs,* proud periods of glory that had been destroyed.[7] Through this phenomenon of a *time collapse,* all the horrible traumas suffered by one's ancestors at the hands of the enemy could be made to sound and feel as if they had occurred just yesterday.[8]

History can be dredged up as inflammable material or an inspiration for learning, insight, and peace. Misreading outdated history can become uranium in wrong hands.

In a letter to his daughter Indira on how to read history, Jawarhalal Nehru, India's first prime minister wrote, "To understand a person who lived long ago, you must look upon it with sympathy and with understanding. To understand a person who lived long ago you will have to understand his environment, the conditions under which he lived, the ideas that filled his mind. It is absurd for us to judge of the past, people as if they lived now and thought as we do."[9]

ROLE OF THE MEDIA

Press censorship and government propaganda were major contributing factors in sustaining a rigid mental representation of the evil Tiger, thus generating more support for the war, boosting recruitment, and inducing more fear. Photos of grieving mothers receiving the ashes of their sons and families unable to fulfill traditional funeral rites stirred strong emotions. The media portrayed the LTTE as a tiger waiting to pounce, conjuring images of a shadowy anthropomorphized force. With no face to be met, fear mixed with awe kept mounting.

Because local and international radio and television programs were jammed, and ordinary civilians were victims of wild rumor or left to (mis)read between the newspaper lines. Stressed communities succumb easily to rumor, fear, and superstition.

During the early period of the war, far from the combat areas, and in the southern cities, government military operations could be judged only on the basis of news reports in the censored press, but reports of heavy civilian casualties and displacements trickled via the NGOs working in LTTE-controlled areas. Only the civilians under LTTE domination felt the awesome firepower of the government's sophisticated weaponry, its army's skill, the navy's long-range shelling of the coastline, and the air capacity for a carpet blitz.

LTTE propaganda was limited to clandestine "Voice of the Tigers" radio transmissions from within the organization's jungle fortifications. Information originating from the Tamil diaspora could not reach the isolated Tamil population, but in the cities anxious Tamils with Internet connections barely whispered their fears. With a literal press blackout and a permanent power outage for nearly a decade in the Tamil-occupied northern territories, rumor excited fear and drove the will for revenge.

Remembering the Past

Concern with collective memory—its control, manipulation, and preservation—is not a monopoly of certain groups. For many people, safeguarding memory is integral to saving and preserving identity. This is true for individuals, families, and large groups. The urge to preserve identity by preserving memory and preserving identity is heightened among subjugated people *or those fearing extinction*.[10]

It is well known that in refugee camps and in other situations where the survival of uprooted and traumatized groups is precarious, memory in terms of tracing precious history and tradition is kept alive in both word and action. Aiming to preserve their threatened culture, displaced communities are quick to create makeshift schools for their children, to keep memory afresh through song, play, dance, and drama, whenever possible. Themes pointing to past glories and traumas were intertwined in these exercises. Everyday events, victories or losses, fresh graves, killings or rapes—all were *triggers to reflex their recall*.

Why bring up history? writes India's Anita Pratap. "We love harping on our great past, we love harping about our future potential but the stumbling block is our present."[11]

Godfrey Gunatilleke explains, "The historical fixations of a community are analogous to the psychopathological conditions of an individual's life. When the movement to the future is obstructed by inability to adjust and overcome present problems, there is a regression to the past which begins to overpower and hold the present captive to the emotional states and fears of the past."[12]

Perceptions of enemies and their deeds are variously articulated according to the aims of competing political elements. They often differ widely between those of military commanders, combatants in the field, wounded civilians, and people in remote villages. Perceptions easily become distorted when shaped in an environment of fear, rumor, disinformation, censorship, a natural disaster, or even an impending peace.

How impressions are influenced by a generation's experience is illustrated in a study by Michael Roberts who surveyed the perceptions of Sri Lankans alive today as they relate to the experience and vulnerability of five generations. His analysis reveals why Generation A, identified as those who reached the age of majority before 1940 and whose tertiary education was in English, has very different perceptions from Generation C, who reached voting age between 1961 and 1980 and were educated in the vernacular at a time when extreme hostility was shown to the English language, and Generation D, which witnessed a brutal underground civil war, and *a national fear psychosis* involving mass killings.[13]

The enduring perception on both sides of a divide is always that "they," the enemy, are the agents of evil, unlike "us," who remain consistently noble. Sustaining that demonized image of the other calls for interpreting each new hostile encounter to be affirmative. Broadly speaking, the "mirror image" described by Frank explains why these images (of the enemy) are remarkably similar, no matter who are the conflicting parties. Enemy images mirror one another, each side attributing the same kind of virtues to themselves and the same vices to the enemy. "We" are trustworthy, peace loving, honorable, humanitarian; "they" are treacherous, warlike and cruel.[14]

Parallels could be drawn to the 2003 war in Iraq, the United States/British alliance being the good "us" ready to fight against "them," the axis of evil, to protect democracy and Western values. Saddam Hussein countered by distinguishing his kith and kin as the "true believers" unlike "them," the unbelievers. Don Ronen neatly captures this phenomenon in his description of the way people might justify violent action by asserting, "We had to destroy their towns and villages to protect ourselves from 'those people' who have no respect for human life."[15]

CHANGING PERCEPTIONS

Following gestures of reconciliation, such as the signing of an accord, when adversaries come together for a settlement, the upsurge of emotion—in celebration or remonstrance—should surprise no one. At the same time, a peace accord does present a threat to those who profit from war, among them the arms dealers. It also might portend a reckoning, payback time, and liability for war crimes. Some may call for closer scrutiny, while others may regard any show of sympathy for the enemy's plight as outright betrayal.

A dramatic stimulus for a perception change was the wide TV coverage given to the signing of the cease-fire agreement. Closed minds started to open when this was followed by the lifting of censorship, prompt dispatch of food and medicines to the needy on "the other side," removal of barriers and checkpoints, and reopening of roadways and telecommunication links.

With the cessation of hostilities, as Tiger leaders and soldiers emerged from their jungle fortifications, the Singhalese population and the nation as a whole were obliged to confront the "tiger" with a human face, and as more talks opened, former enemies began to be seen communing together.

As the cease-fire continued to hold, perception(s) of the enemy on both sides began to alter even more. Parallel to increasingly open dialogue on the political scene ran important exchanges on the ground. When the military engagements came to a halt, space and time were made for the nation to absorb the media-splashed images of former adversaries standing on common ground. Peace, a notion that people had assumed to be impossible, could at least be pictured.

As checkpoints were removed and boundaries became porous, civilians were free to travel without fear, as never before. Members of the expatriate community started to visit relatives they had not seen for decades and felt inspired to support relief, rehabilitation, and reconciliation efforts. Organizations of mothers of those missing and killed in action on both sides even held meetings of solidarity.

Encouraged by the leaders of the four major religious communities, Buddhist monks, Christian ministers, Hindu priests, and Muslim clergy prayed together, sharing their centers of worship. Through programs emphasizing the theme "One Sri Lanka," the radio and television media contributed hugely to interethnic understanding. These collective community efforts gradually began to bring some calm to the badly fractured society.

A burning curiosity to see the "other side" followed soon after the cease-fire. Busloads of Singhalese headed northward for the Jaffna peninsula without even caring if they would find accommodation. On returning, they regaled their friends with stories of people—real human beings—who received them with warmth and great kindness. These visits bore the same characteristics of the excited "en masse" excursions of Israelis to Egypt after the Egyptian–Israeli peace treaty, as well as Israeli curiosity to come to know Palestinian Arabs in the West Bank after the Six-Day War.[16]

With the reopening of the north–south A9 highway and airline connections, "people exchange" began on an unprecedented level, as they once again assembled in temples and churches, at funerals and weddings. Family and school reunions were up as interschool sporting events were revived. As barriers were lifted, people from both ethnic groups, former good neighbors, could reunite as friends again. Foreign tourists started to pour in.

Although the cease-fire period has helped to recast former prejudices, erasing an encrusted mindset takes more than the passage of time. Indeed, akin to chronic mental states inhered with seemingly immutable mental representations—of self and other—long-standing intergroup conflicts sharpen the dichotomy. Just as distorted and paranoid perceptions rupture individual relationships, nations may also remain opposed in much the same way.

The leader of a demonized enemy must be repeatedly shown to be the devil incarnate, his shape and character unalterable, this image sharpened and reinforced with every new confrontation. By contrast, "our" leader is unshakably good and godlike.

The dichotomy was difficult to sustain when newspaper front pages carried photos of a smiling LTTE leader, dressed in a safari suit and shaking hands with government and international dignitaries. Internalizing an image (object representation) that does not fit that which was rigidly held—a menacing tormentor garbed in military camouflage—required tricky mental jugglery. The wary exclaimed, "A wolf in sheep's clothing!"

For the Tamil civilians also in their cut-off northern towns and villages, and for the LTTE cadres in their isolated bunkers, a similar shock awaited them. All of a sudden, the menacing Singhalese attackers "who burned our homes, killed our families, and destroyed our villages" were proffered as compassionate friends. No longer would they rely entirely on the message of hatred churned out via a clandestine transmitter.

Intervention Efforts

Innumerable efforts to resolve Sri Lanka's violent and deadly conflict were attempted from both sides of the divide, but it was not until 2001, following years of haggling and the horrors of war, that a cease-fire became possible. Getting to that point was accelerated by the change of regime, a chance for a new and safer bargaining climate to unfold with continuing facilitation by the Norwegians, who stayed on the job despite many frustrations.

The government's new approach, as reflected in the Memorandum of Understanding (MOU), revealed a significant change of heart on the issue of the devolution of power. It began to sound reasonable and workable and to resonate more harmoniously with the new attitude of the LTTE negotiators, as well as the overarching ambitions of Norway and other international supporters.

Media Coverage

Because the peace process received wide media coverage and debate, the public at large stood witness to civil debate again, and friendly exchanges replaced the heavy mortar fire of previous years. The longer the cease-fire could hold, peace talks ongoing, paralleled by continuing "familiarity exchanges," the more normalizing influence of everyday human interactions would prevent a relapse, it was reasoned.

Growing Trust

Mutual trust usually evolves from improved information sharing and the opportunity for each side to appreciate empathetically the needs and sufferings on either side. However, the issues raised in debate have for the most part been focused on power sharing, how much to give, or how far to go, with neither side willing to concede that a balance has been reached.

The Tigers' Stripes

Although the Norwegian-backed peace initiative began before September 11, 2001, LTTE leaders saw the need to eradicate the "terrorist" label that haunted them. This was difficult in the face of assassinations assumed to be LTTE backed and a robust Singhalese chauvinism. In addition, international sources of funding for the LTTE cause were drying up.

As splits within the Tamil parties began to narrow, the LTTE laid greater claim to be the unified voice of all the Tamil people, a claim bolstered by their reputation as a formidable military force and a readiness for a negotiated settlement. Yet other Tamil parties vigorously argued this assumption, and most of the Tamils living in predominantly Singhalese areas silently agreed.

Negotiation

Negotiating processes are said to "function best under conditions of equality" and should take place when the parties "have some form of mutual veto over the outcome." Conditions of asymmetry are "generally un-conducive to negotiation." A negotiating space was thus created as the conflict had reached the "mutually hurting stalemate," one that constitutes conditions of "conflict ripeness" a concept that is both a structural condition and a perception.[17]

In keeping with election promises to negotiate a peace with the Tamil separatists, positive gestures in that direction included an offer of a "devolution package" to the Tamils, but opposition elements obstructed these offers, contending that the president was "giving too much." True to Sri Lanka's political traditions, no sooner had the election brought the former opposition to power than they too were accused of giving away even more goodies than promised, thus threatening the issue of balance.

The creation in 1988 of the Presidential Task Force National Program on Human Disaster Management, mandated to address the psychological suffering of the nation as a whole and of its vulnerable populations, was a remarkable strategy that won the applause of the international community. The Norwegians in particular saw the gesture as a small window of opportunity for managing and containing the human-caused disaster, but even this initiative, which contained clear guidelines for a multi-hazard approach to disaster management, got overlooked in the ensuing shuffle.

By far the clearest indication of Sri Lanka's desire to bring peace was President Kumaratunga's initial invitation to Norway to play a mediating role. Nordic acceptance brought immediate relief and hope and has persisted despite accusations of partiality toward the Tamils. The task was often bogged down by government flip-flops due, in part, to conflicting policy decisions. Despite many useful initiatives, including support for NGO's humanitarian services, ambivalence and double-talk crept into policy decisions and raised doubts concerning the government's sincerity.

Admittedly, political efforts for a peaceful outcome were hampered by the slipping margins that successive governments had to preserve. This has been considered a perennial curse. Even though the promise of bringing a final peace was always the foremost election promise, the prospect of losing the majority in parliament meant even more: the threat of losing political power altogether.

Legality

A major legal impediment to establishing legitimacy for negotiations between the parties has centered on the LTTE image and label as a terrorist organization, including contravention of Geneva principles and the forcible recruitment of children. Proscribed by Sri Lanka's government, the LTTE has been regarded as a "rebel" organization banned in several of the countries known to be funding them. Increasing pressure for reform from the United States, U.N., and rights organizations was brought to bear on the LTTE, especially in the aftermath of 9/11. The question of legitimacy (to make a deal) was raised even earlier when the LTTE declared a unilateral cease-fire, a gesture viewed with deep suspicion by Singhalese hawks, who believed it was a sinister move.

For the government, battling an unlawful force was justification enough for prosecution of war to the finish and a reason for not negotiating with terrorists. Fighting an unconventional war left the government forces with ample room for the rules of combat to be stretched.

REGIME CHANGE BRINGS RELIEF AND OPPORTUNITY

November 2001 brought a dramatic change. SLFP, the party to which the executive president belonged, was defeated. The democratically elected United National Party government, echoing what the previous one had done, vowed to bring a lasting settlement. Seizing the political moment, the new government not only reaped the gains achieved by its predecessors but also found it easier to break the deadlock, jump-start the complacent bureaucracy, muffle the saber rattling, and deal more directly with the Tigers.

With the prospect of being extinguished altogether by the ire of global antiterrorist efforts the LTTE accelerated its commitment to image change. These changes progressed to the point where the prime minister (whose party had engineered the cease-fire), in a gesture to exonerate the Tigers, declared at a meeting with Japanese leaders in Tokyo that the LTTE had no links with Al Qaeda.[18]

Another crucial pronouncement of the new administration was its commitment to workable negotiations and its resolve to remove the proscription placed upon the LTTE, even if on a temporary basis, to get the talks on track and deal directly with the Tigers.

Negotiating from Strength and Respect

Prior to the cease-fire, the channels for LTTE to negotiate were seriously limited by the lack of a political/administrative structure comparable with standard government ministries. They depended instead on members of their political wing isolated inside TIGER territory supported by expatriate experts and negotiators living overseas.

Having entered the political arena, the LTTE in collaboration with smaller entities created its own "Peace Secretariat" to match that formed by the government. Symmetry engendered mutual respect. The LTTE secretariat, funded and supported by the Japanese government, helped internationalize the process further and widen the scope of development assistance.

The regime change afforded Sri Lanka an opportunity to overcome the inertia created by the rigid perceptions of the former president's inner circle and the key ministries of defense and foreign affairs. Thus, the new government not only created a practical "We mean business" image but also stealthily stole advantage, typical of Sri Lankan politics, by exaggerating the shortcomings of the former administration.

Using the previous government's "Presidential Action Plan" as a template, the new leadership capitalized by swiftly taking 3R (Relief, Rehabilitation and Reconciliation) to the war-damaged northern and eastern regions.[19] Policies emanating from a newly created ministry for rehabilitation also reflected a much more generous attitude to the dispatch of "food and basic necessities" to civilians living in the nonstate, so called "uncleared" areas. Basically *uncleared* meant areas yet to be wrested from LTTE control.

As the Norwegian facilitation regained credibility, new energy was pumped into easing the sufferings of all civilian victims of the conflict, strengthening human rights commissions, analyzing defense problems more seriously, and inviting more international partners into the peace planning.

INTERNATIONAL COMMUNITY ATTENTION TO EXTERNAL DIMENSIONS: THE ECONOMY

Sri Lanka is not without loyal friends. With the advent of globalization, the country became integrated with international systems. Many nations wanted to be partners in its development as they recognized Sri Lanka's potential. International donor meetings coinciding with ongoing government–LTTE negotiations provided the climate for cooperation. The positive attitude of Western donors reaped unprecedented results. In July 2003 Japan, new to the aid business, with its reputation for knowing where to invest, pledged a generous US$4.5 billion aid package for Sri Lanka.

The Media and Civil Society

With the guns silent and the media freer, the voice of civil society began to influence the peace process, energizing debate and, through workshops, sharing information on systems of governance evolved elsewhere and illustrating how and why societies suffer unique struggles to gain independence. Through their linkages, they fostered community education projects, foreign exposure for young politicians, and later support for building "civilian" links between the two peace secretariats. By extending their reach to district level NGOs, grass-roots societies, and trade unions, the larger society was no longer a voice in the wilderness.

The Peace Process

For a nation battered by two decades of war and mounting military casualties, civilian displacements, economic unrest, and heavy restrictions, the cease-fire agreement brought immense relief and a long-awaited ray of hope.

But one of the lessons from peace processes is that achievements gained may be easily lost. Even painstaking diplomatic and confidence-building work can be wiped away, with the situation regressing almost to square one, severely demoralizing the parties ready to heal their differences, as well as the facilitators, mediators, and donors.

Detractors of a peace process are not necessarily harmful if their purpose is examined in proper context. As every action has an equal and opposite reaction, whenever negotiations are nearing almost a perfect point, fears emerge, as if from nowhere. Change, even for good, can be experienced as a threat.

SIGNS OF GROWTH AND INSIGHT

The experience of conflict can bring insight. Signs suggest that the public has learned from years of experience. They are not as gullible as before and not such easy prey to rhetoric that taps on historical fear. Whereas in the past minor skirmishes were projected as ethnic tension and became flash points for civil unrest, no longer is there a knee-jerk response to violence every time a crisis arises.

Although there is greater insistence on promises being kept, the undercurrent of distrust has remained. Even as their fields were cleared of mines and people returned to their damaged homes, they hesitated to rebuild, still uncertain if development objectives and so-called peace dividends will be properly shared.

As newly emerging and previously unrecognized players strove for attention, the Singhalese in the south reacted to development activity in the north and east, exclaiming, "How about us?" Relief, rehabilitation, and reconciliation, they said, was a two-way street. The pervading question: Was there balance?

The Muslims, a previously marginalized community, refuse to be ignored. Their deep-seated resentments have surfaced with a vengeance. Like the Tamils before them, the Muslims laid claim as a valuable and viable minority with ancient ties to the island. Since independence, the Muslim community has struggled to establish a political identity, no longer willing to serve as convenient coalition partners only for the purpose of gaining a majority. Like the Singhalese and Tamils, the Muslims themselves struggled for identity, dignity, and a place to call their own, with the call getting louder for a Muslim state to be carved out of the island's eastern region.

The Tamils were cautioned to the danger of creating their own victims, the Muslims. As Cherian points out, "If the case of the Jewish state of Israel and its treatment of the Palestinians can be an example, being a victim's victims is the ultimate irony."[20] A fear that the Tamils might do to the Muslims what the Singhalese did to them risked the prospect of spawning a new breed—in this instance, Muslim extremism: liberation fighters demanding their own special homeland.

Another paradoxical gain from the conflict for both the Singhalese and Tamils has been a lessened focus on previously existing rigid distinctions of caste and class. This seems to have evolved from a sense of common suffering or of suffering in common. In facing the horrors of bloody war, skin-deep differences lost their meaning. The desperate efforts to recruit fighters for the Sri Lanka forces created another leavening influence as sons from different regions and social classes became comrades within the military establishment.

Another Regime Change: 2003

In the snap elections called for precipitously by the president in 2003, the JVP, a strange bedfellow was co-opted into a coalition with the UFPA to win by a thin margin. This administrative change helped accelerate the peace-building gains of the previous UNP government, but the JVP link tended to slow the new administration's peace initiatives because they (the JVP) were and remain totally against devolution of power to the Tamils.

The government seemed ready to address its own human rights violations, unlawful arrests, torture, and revelation of mass graves, all this in the light of the LTTE's request for war crimes tribunals. Truth commissions were instituted.

Although reconstructive development on the ground and gestures of reconciliation became high priority for the governments' three-R programs (relief, rehabilitation, and reconstruction), from the Tamil perspective, especially from the diaspora, it was not enough to talk reconciliation, and many started to come and see for themselves.

That the LTTE should lay down its arms as a precondition for peace brought out all the issues that had plagued the peace process in Northern Ireland, and the dilemma of what to do after demobilization and how to manage the huge numbers traumatized by the war came into clearer focus.

Why War

Oftentimes, battles end when war weariness sets in. This author is of the opinion that both militaries had reached symmetry in terms of military capability, each side quietly and discreetly conceding that the price of a military engagement would be self-defeating in the long run. Weary with worry and warring, all want to go home to live.

Societal Trauma

Ethnic conflicts, like any other collective trauma, are best understood as "societal trauma." "Because a society is both more and less than the sum of all individual identities, its response to trauma is a mix of the signs and symptoms of social breakdown, evidence of societal resilience and restitution, as well as the effects of remedial interventions (by local and external resources) towards repair and reconstitution."[21]

Just like individuals, whole societies are prone to trauma—the trauma they bring upon themselves and trauma they visit upon their adversaries—but diagnosing the signs and symptoms of collective trauma is not a clear process. This is because the consequences of collective trauma are variously interpreted and the signs or symptoms are hard to measure. There are no standard remedies, and healing usually occurs in patches. Many societies may conveniently ignore the existence of the smaller (usually poor and disadvantaged) communities lying within. Besides, the underlying psychological processes affecting societies under stress or in transition are invariably intertwined with unstable political, security, social, and economic forces. All these are difficult to measure from within or outside the system, especially during wartime, when

trauma is collectively waged and each side aims to traumatize the other.

Unrecognized and untreated, distressed individuals exert a heavy burden upon the community, which in turn constrain the community's capacity to support and contain its distressed members. Distressed societies will likewise exert a threat and burden upon its neighbors and the region as a whole. Like a cancer, conflicts may feed upon the tissues of a society, straining its immunity and increasing all risk factors and susceptibility to opportunistic infections.

AN UNEASY PEACE

Precipitated by a suicide bombing incident in June 2004 (the first in over two years), a fear psychosis remitted across the land, the instability of the LTTE from renegade elements within its ranks adding to the tension. The government stood accused of widening the split through covert support while the neutrality of Norwegian mediators was questioned again and again.

Talks slowed with increasing calls for a new negotiator—India, the U.N., or others—none wishing to be the new thankless sandwich meat. At least the generals were not pressing for war.

Ironically, even when foreign governments listed Sri Lanka as a risky place to visit, tourist traffic increased dramatically, and by mid-2004 Sri Lanka's economy was emerging as Asia's top gainer, with its market racing forward despite fears of war. As economists analyzed growth factors and measured risks, few could explain why Sri Lanka was described in an edition of a leading travel magazine as "the Island to visit," one that is "evolving from an utterly intractable problem to a workable solution."[22]

Nevertheless, during this increasingly anxious period with Sri Lanka manipulated by a shaky Marxist-backed government, the peace process straggling, and the Tamil rebels warning of war, everyone was anticipating a change.

TIDAL CHANGES: THE TSUNAMI DISASTER

It was on December 26, 2004, when the tsunami that shook the world lashed Sri Lanka with an intensity that killed 38,000 people, rendering 1.5 million coastal residents homeless. The natural disaster showed no favor to friend or foe, cleared or uncleared land in the nation's political scenery. It was a natural disaster superimposed on a manmade conflict.

Suddenly a theoretical illustration became reality: What if a disaster strikes both a government and an un-cleared area (LTTE controlled)? "Such a situation would arise—if a tornado's sweep encompasses both cleared and un-cleared region, disaster management may require the cooperation of parties not ordinarily in partnership and/or through the intervention of mutually acceptable liaison intermediaries.[23]

The unprecedented outflow of international sympathy brought with it massive financial donations and emergency assistance. What disaster research recognizes as the initial honeymoon phase in post–disaster recovery began with an intense period of societal unification and collective group-cohesive strategies as the nation as a whole confronted its common enemy. The tsunami's ravages triggered a coalition of compassion and a proliferation of unifying gestures and initiatives bringing disparate and previously antagonistic groups together as one, everyone anticipating the peace process would accelerate; similar hopes were stirred concerning Indonesia's internal conflict.

But the fantasy of continued unification in the face of a common enemy, the tsunami, was a dream of short duration. The period of cooperation gave way to the disillusionment phase as discrimination surfaced again along ethnic lines, accentuating fault lines in the government/LTTE peace process, political instability, and squabbling over inequitable distribution of emergency assistance.

In the ensuing disillusionment or facing-reality phase, serious flaws in disaster management came to light, bringing sharp criticism upon the government's responsibility for public safety and security. The rage at nature's loss of control and all the grief and guilt it had wrought was laid on the doorstep of "leadership failure" and a demand for change, just as happened after 9/11 and then post-Katrina. Disasters are political events. They begin and end as local events.

As usually occurs, into this climate of discord rushed the political entrepreneurs berating the tsunami relief efforts, the ensuing corruption, un-

necessary outsourcing of rebuilding contracts, and NGO mismanagement, all contributing to a cry for bringing down the government, another election, regime change—the usual merry-go-round.

Increasingly frustrated by the attitudes of her Marxist coalition partners, though, Sri Lanka's president finally kicked them out, convinced their anti-peace moves and unshakable stand against devolution of power was a serious block to the prospects for a lasting peace.

This act of presidential brinkwomanship propelled these saboteurs into an alliance with like-minded, chauvinist, ultra-nationalistic Singhalese–Buddhist parties, threatening mass demonstrations and hunger strikes, pounding the bargaining table as the nation prepared for a crucial presidential election scheduled for November 2005.

The prime minister created yet another split. Seeking to gain votes he sealed a special MOU with the party's former coalition partner (the Marxists) and, by proclaiming the alliance from the steps of the nation's most sacred Temple of the Tooth, once again linked Buddhism to a Singhalese territorial imperative, sans federalism. Once again, the same old issues pushed the nation back to square one, just when peace was nearly at hand.

ANOTHER REGIME CHANGE

The disaster's impact, the way it has been managed, and the presidential election reawakened old fears and "chosen traumas." Once again people saw the frantic coalition horse-trading to win by the thinnest majority. If history were to repeat itself, the risk is of a new administration with the same old policies, a government too weak to endure and easy enough to topple—the insecurities of limited sovereignty. And yet, again, all the party's election slogans echo a determination to break the vicious cycle, stop the merry-go-round, and create a united Sri Lanka and a lasting peace.

Ultimately, it took a natural disaster to expose the nation's basic fault lines to the naked eye—not just as a shallow seafront but a disaster-prone coastline population that was poor and neglected long before the tsunami struck. Although post-tsunami recovery response has amply illustrated the value and potential of humanity acting to ease the distress of fellow humans, the challenge of applying the same human spirit to solving socioeconomic and security problems will be the final test.

Resilience

To bring balance and comfort, the tsunami tragedy has revealed inherent resilience and innovativeness. This is seen in the multitude of grass-roots initiatives sponsored by low-profile, nontraditional, homegrown social organizations focused on self-help and benevolent neighbor-in-need (*shramadana*) traditional activities partnered with hundreds of little-known humanitarian groups worldwide getting down to rebuilding homes and reuniting families—and not waiting for government action. These unifying social strategies are showing results—real enduring building blocks—characteristically in remote affected areas where people are facing the truth together.

If civilian safety and economic development remains in focus, the practical efforts will be mutually enhancing, for in Sri Lanka, as in many other nations torn apart by internal divisions, social and economic inequality remains the common enemy.

Epilogue: Of Lions and Tigers

The prospect of pitting the fabled Lion, King of the Beasts, against another stealthy wildcat, the Tiger, brings our attention to the bonding dimension in this ethnic conflict. A mutual respect is said to exist between these feline species. Though the full-grown adults keep each other at a respectful distance, they are not immune to preying upon the other's cubs, as happens in war.

Respice finem, looking to the end, the reader is urged to winnow the material to sift out sociopolitical analysis and psychological theorizing from acceptable pride in one's birthplace and wishful thinking.

ABOUT THE AUTHOR

Dr. David Ratnavale is a Sri Lanka–born, American- and British-qualified psychiatrist with professional, academic, and administrative experience in the fields of psychiatry, behavioral sciences, disaster management, and humanitarian relief work. He holds a medical degree from the University of Ceylon (now Sri Lanka) and has won awards and recognition for work in widening the scope of mental health services, pioneering research in cross-cultural psychiatry, and for exploring the causes and consequences of disaster-related trauma from both individual and large group (collective) perspectives.

The first Western-trained psychiatrist to be invited to China (1973), he was involved in psychiatric training programs over a twenty-year period. As professor of psychiatry at the Shanghai Medical University, he taught psychotherapy and community mental health. In the United States as professor of psychiatry and behavioral sciences and residency training director at the Eastern Virginia Medical School, he researched war-related trauma and post-traumatic stress syndromes at Veterans and Portsmouth Naval Hospital. As a National Institute of Health's Distinguished Visiting Scientist, he traveled to refugee camps on the Thai-Cambodian border and in Hong Kong, Malaysia, and the Philippines, working to develop innovative rehabilitation programs for displaced persons.

In 1997, Dr. Ratnavale spearheaded a Presidential Task Force on Human Disaster Management, mandated to investigate and address psychological issues emanating from the country's prolonged ethnic conflict. The task force "Action Plan" became an integral part of Sri Lanka's current peace-building strategy. It involved programs for disabled soldiers, former child combatants, families of the MIA and KIA, and trauma management courses with NGOs, the International Committee of the Red Cross, and the international community.

Certified by the American Board of Psychiatry and Neurology, Dr. Ratnavale is a Fellow of the Royal College of Psychiatrists in the United Kingdom, a Distinguished Life Fellow of the American Psychiatric Association, and a Founding Fellow of the Pacific Rim College of Psychiatrists. He has authored several papers and book chapters and has lectured and conducted workshops in Japan, China, Australia, France, Germany, Sweden, Denmark, the USSR, India, The Maldives, Malaysia, The Philippines, Indonesia, Mexico, Colombia, South Africa, Nigeria, Viet Nam, and the former Yugoslavia.

The Asian tsunami disaster brought him to assist in relief programs and offer consultation to the new national disaster management administration.

Presently in private practice in Bethesda, Maryland, Dr. Ratnavale remains active in disaster-related, mental health–related programs and continues as an advisor to Sri Lanka's president on disaster management. He is a senior associate for South and East Asia programs at the Institute of World Affairs.

David Ratnavale is married to Ann-Kristin. They have two sons, John and Marcel.

ENDNOTES

1. Pathmanathan S. Tamil Identity, History and Historiography, a seminar on History, identity and historiography, Marga Institute. Quoted in "Tamil Nationalism. In A History of Ethnic Conflict in Sri Lanka: Recollection, Reinterpretation & Reconciliation." No 5 of 19. Pg. 17.
2. Michael Roberts, "History as Dynamite," *The Island Newspaper*. January, 2000, Perspective.
3. Michael Roberts. "Sinhala-ness and Sinhala Nationalism. A History of Ethnic Conflict in Sri Lanka.", 20.
4. H. L. Seneviratne. The Work of Kings, 131.
5. Devanesan Nesiah. "Tamil Nationalism." In *The History of Ethnic Conflict in Sri Lanka: Recollection, Reinterpretation & Reconciliation.* 17.
6. Sigmund Freud. *Group Psychology.* (1921), 67–143.
7. Vamik Volkan, "The Tree Model: A Comprehensive Psychopolitical Approach to Unofficial Diplomacy and the Reduction of Ethnic Tension," *Mind and Human Interaction*, 10, no. 3: 142–210; reference to *chosen trauma* and *chosen glory* (not *chosen triumph*): 153.
8. Ibid., 179.
9. Jawaharlal Nehru. *Glimpses of World History: Being Further Letters to His Daughter, Written in Prison, and Containing a Rambling Account of History for Young People.* Reissue edition. (Oxford, England: Oxford University Press, 1990).
10. Michael Roberts, "Primordialist Strands in Contemporary Sinhala Nationalism," *Marga Quarterly Journal* (December 2002): 7.
11. Anita Pratap. *Island of Blood: Frontline Reports from Sri Lanka, Afghanistan and Other South Asian Flashpoints.* (New Delhi: Viking, 2001).
12. Godfrey Gunatilaka, personal communication, 1999.
13. Roberts, "Primordialist Strands."
14. J. D. Frank, in Rafael Moses, "A Perception of the Enemy; A Psychological View," *Mind and Human Interaction* 7, no. 1 (1996):40.
15. Don Ronen, "The Cause and Mechanism of Conflict," *Mind and Human Interaction*, 11, no. 1: 47.
16. Rafael Moses, "A Perception of the Enemy: A Psychological View," *Mind and Human Interaction*, 7, no. 1, (1996): 73–43.
17. William Zartman. *Ripe for Resolution: Conflict and Intervention in Africa*, New York and Oxford: Oxford University Press, 2002. (Quoted by J. Uyanoda, "Beyond Negotiation: Towards Transformative Peace in Sri Lanka," *Marga Quarterly Journal* (November 22, 2002): 3.
18. Ranil Wickremesinghe, "LTTE Not Linked to Al Qaeda, PM Tells Japan," *The Island Newspaper*, December 8, 2002.
19. Presidential Task Force Human Disaster Management Action Plan. Sri Lanka Presidential Secretariat Archives, 1999.
20. R. Charian. *The Sixth Genre: Memory, History, and the Tamil Diaspora* (Colombo, Sri Lanka: Marga Institute, 2001).
21. David Ratnavale. "Are We a Traumatized Society?" (unpublished paper).
22. Thomas Wallace, "The Peace Dividend: Sri Lanka the One to Watch," *Conde Nast Traveler*, July 2004.

8

Greece and Turkey

Greece and Turkey share a small common border on land. Both countries also border the Mediterranean Sea and the Aegean Sea. Delineating territory, boundaries, and territorial waters have been the key issues of the Greco–Turkish dispute. Some important peace treaties and agreements have been signed, but the distrust each other has lived on.

As neighboring countries, relations between Greece and Turkey have a long history. In the fourteenth century, the Ottoman Empire expanded and occupied most of Greece and continued to do so until the nineteenth century. During the five-century Ottoman rule, Turks migrated to settle extensively in Thrace, north of the strategic Bosporus strait and a region that has been disputed by both countries. (Parts of Thrace are presently in Greece, Turkey, and Bulgaria, bordering the Aegean Sea, the Marmara Sea, and the Black Sea,)

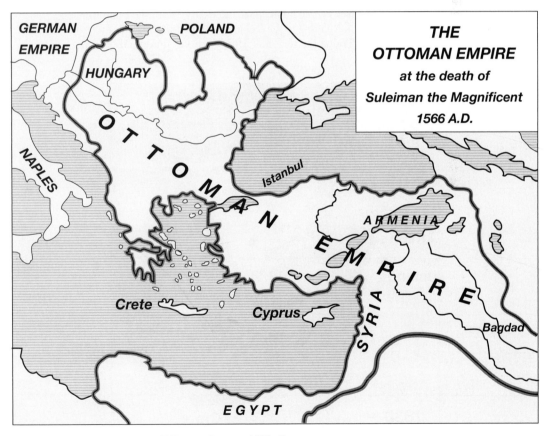

Source: http://en.wikipedia.org/wiki/Image:Ottoman1566.gif

It was not until the nineteenth century that Greece, supported by France, Britain, and Russia, pushed back the Turks and proclaimed independence in 1821 that was later recognized in 1829.

During the nineteenth and early twentieth centuries, in a series of wars with the Ottomans, Greece sought to enlarge its boundaries to include the ethnic Greek population of the Ottoman Empire. It gradually gained more territory and population, reaching the present configuration under the Treaty of Paris in 1947.

After World War I, Greece, which had supported the Allies against the Ottoman Empire, was promised territorial gains in exchange for its support, including western Anatolia, and eastern Thrace. Although the Treaty of Sèvres (1920) that defined these new territories for Greece was signed by the defeated Ottoman Empire, it was never legally ratified and was the prelude to the War of Asia Minor.

The War of Asia Minor (1919–1922), which took place when the Greeks invaded the Thrace region and part of Turkey's mainland (or Anatolia), is an important landmark in Greco–Turk relations. In 1922, Greece demanded support from the Allies for a proposal of armistice with Turkey. The proposal was unacceptable to Mustafa Kemal, a nationalist leader in Turkey. Kemal then led an attack against the Greeks in western Anatolia, leading the Turks to victory and exposing the Greeks to defeat and expulsion. The Treaty of Lausanne was then signed in 1923, between Turkey and the Allies, including Greece. Apart from a population exchange forcing people to return to their ethnic homelands, the treaty established important territorial laws, such as the Convention Relating to the Regime of the Straits and other instruments to delimit boundaries, and it divided the region of Thrace among Turkey, Greece, and

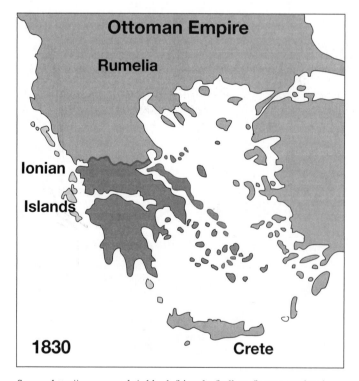

Source: http://www.zum.de/whkmla/histatlas/balkans/haxgreece.html

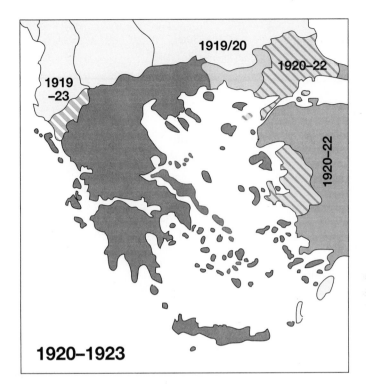

1919/20

1920–22

1919
–23

1920–22

1920–1923

Albania

Yugoslavia

Bulgaria

Turkey

1947

1949

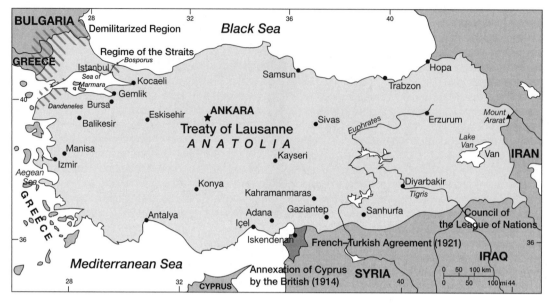

Source: http://upload.wikimedia.org/wikipedia/en/5/58/Turkey-Greece-Bulgaria_on_Treaty_of_Lausanne.png

Bulgaria. The peace treaty also established the territorial waters of both Turkey and Greece at three nautical miles.

Mustafa Kemal, who was later named Atatürk (Father of the Turks), founded modern Turkey in 1923. He then formed a new government and led the country for the next fifteen years. After the Treaty of Lausanne, while Kemal was governing in Turkey, Eleftherios Venizelos governed a number of years in Greece. Both leaders undertook initiatives to normalize and improve relations between the two states. In 1930 Venizelos paid an official visit to Turkey and established a personal friendship with Atatürk. The good relations reached a high point in 1934 with the signature of the Balkan Pact.

During World War II, Turkey signed a peace treaty with Germany and officially remained neutral until near the end of the war, while Greece was invaded first by the Italians, who were defeated, and then by the Germans into 1944. The final World War II settlement with Italy was the Treaty of Paris, signed in 1947, in which Greece recuperated Greek-speaking territories and united the Greek state, a configuration that still holds today. The only region in Greece with a large minority of Turks today is western Thrace.

The period following the war was marked by the beginning of the Cyprus conflict, when different national movements were taking root and dividing the Greek Cypriots from the Turkish Cypriots. Greek Cypriots wanted to unite with their "motherland," Greece, while the Turkish Cypriots rejected that idea. By the end of 1964 the Cypriot Greeks occupied 97 percent of the land and Cypriot Turks were forced to live in various enclaves. The relations between Greece and Turkey deteriorated seriously. The dispute peaked in 1974 when Turkey sent troops to the island using her rights of unilateral intervention provided by the 1960 London and Zurich agreements between Turkey, Greece, and Great Britain. Fighting with the Greeks the Turkish army gained 37 percent of the island which was *de facto* divided into northern Turkish and southern Greek sections. The 1974 crisis was a considerable setback in relations, fueling mistrust. It also marked the beginning of the Aegean dispute.

The Aegean dispute included several points of tension, such as limits on the continental shelf, territorial waters, airspace, demilitarization, and the "gray zone." The Aegean dispute also coincides with the search of oil on its perimeter. The military crisis over the Kardak Rocks–Imia islets in 1995–1996 is a clear occurrence of the disputed gray zone.

Friendly neighbor agreements were signed in 1988 and in 1997. Relations were boosted when two earthquakes hit Greece and Turkey in 1999 and both nations were moved to action. Furthermore, Greece, which had veto power in the European Union (EU) on Turkey's possibile candidacy, approved Turkey's candidacy. Turco–Greek relations have since been improving. Turkey's entrance to the EU will have positive effects on Greco–Turkish relations, setting both countries in a larger European context. However, the future is still not secure: in May 2006 an air collision between Greek and Turkish fighter jets in disputed airspace proved how unsettled border limits remain.

The following readings, "Historical Context, National Narrative, and Prospects of Reconciliation in the Aegean: The View from Athens" and "Turkish–Greek Relations," show different national perspectives on Turkish and Greek relations. While Kostas Ifantis and Onur Öymen identify the same landmark events in modern history, they expose the different views of and consequences on the populations of each country. The authors examine mechanisms to improve relations that have already advanced significantly since the Kardak Rocks–Imia-islets crisis.

Historical Context, National Narrative, and Prospects of Reconciliation in the Aegean: The View from Athens

Kostas Ifantis

Greeks and Turks have been locked in an ethnopolitical conflict for over five centuries. The conflict can be traced back to the fall of Constantinople in the mid-1400s. As international events and borders have changed, the intensity of conflict has flared and waned. In the nineteenth century, however, the conflict escalated and became a source of international concern. In fact, the Greek–Turkish dispute became a major source of instability in the eastern Mediterranean and a worry to the NATO allies of both Greece and Turkey. During the last four decades, the potential for a major clash between the two countries has been salient to the regional security equation, albeit overshadowed by Cold War dynamics. In the summer of 1974, the two NATO allies crossed the threshold of a "hot" confrontation. A generalized war over Cyprus was averted, thanks, in large part, to United States and NATO intervention. Since that time, Greece and Turkey have engaged in a costly and protracted arms race in their matching attempts to establish a favorable balance of power. In 1976, 1983, 1987, 1996, and 1998–99 crises erupted in the Aegean and/or Cyprus that brought the two countries near the brink of war.

There have been short periods of denouement. One example is the well-publicized "Spirit of Davos" between the Greek socialist prime minister, Andreas Papandreou, and his Turkish counterpart, Turgut Özal following a meeting of the World Economic Forum in 1988. Another example is the climate of relaxation and mutual understanding that existed in the early 1990s between Özal and his Greek counterpart, Constantine Mitsotakis. The respite provided by attempts to reduce tension in the 1988–92 period did not evolve toward lasting reconciliation. This was due in part to the acute criticism in both countries, exercised by opposition forces, of what they perceived—each from their own perspective—as asymmetrical accommodation. Following the logic of a zero-sum game, both governments (with the full backing of their publics) were engaged in cycles of tension and détente.

In the post–Cold War era, the Aegean has remained a dangerous flashpoint. This has been a consistent concern in both Europe and the United States. It has been and still is a situation that has the disturbing potential of escalating to a more serious crisis with alarming destabilizing effects at a regional level. In January 1996, in one of the most recent crises, the two countries nearly went to war over the islet of Imia. Only a last-minute, high-level U.S. intervention prevented a military clash between the two nations. Moreover, in the wake of the incident, the air forces of both sides continued to engage in mock dogfights, increasing the risk that an accident or unplanned incident could spiral out of control and lead to armed conflict. The so-called Imia–Kardak episode has been one more case confirming the operation of an intense security dilemma. In late 1999, following two more crises over the S-300 antiballistic missiles and the capture of Abdullah Ocalan, bilateral relations began to warm. In the spring of 1999, the two countries opened a dialogue on nonsensitive issues such as trade, the environment, and tourism. This process was given greater impetus by unfortunate events: the catastrophic earthquake in Turkey in August 1999 and one in Athens in September of the same year triggered an outburst of mutual sympathy in both countries. This was followed by Greece's support for Turkey's EU candidacy at the Helsinki summit in December 1999 and a visit to Ankara by the Greek minister of foreign affairs in January 2000. Since then, Greek–Turkish relations have acquired a new "quality." Although relations have in large part retained their antagonistic and conflictual nature, the EU factor seemed to direct the bilateral dynamics away from military confrontation. One can argue that now the prospects of a more peaceful and cooperative coexistence have increased significantly.

This chapter focuses on how the Greek–Turkish conflict is sustained by Greeks' perceptions and understandings of the interaction between the two regions. Successive sections deal with the way Turkey is embedded in Greeks' historical memory and national identity, their perception of being threatened, what Greek elites and public opinion

call "Turkish revisionism," and the way that is reinforced and legitimized by instances of crisis. In the final section, a brief evaluation of the current phase of détente is attempted and the qualifications for a viable rapprochement are presented. The conclusion is that the key to a lasting reconciliation in the Aegean is Turkey's safe anchoring in the EU.

What, for most, is puzzling is how feelings of mistrust and threat perception have persisted in institutional contexts that should have led to the emergence of shared norms, understandings, and a sense of collective identity paving the way for the peaceful resolution of the two nations' disputes.[1] This failure to comprehend the roots of the Greek–Turkish conflict may be true for NATO, a defense alliance that could not by its nature create an incentive that would lead to the mitigation of the Greek–Turkish conflict.[2]

TURKEY IN GREEK HISTORY AND IDENTITY

In view of Greece's painful and difficult process of integration within the international community of developing nations, it is probably inevitable that Greeks' national identity should have espoused the "defensive" form more commonly associated with societies striving to consolidate their national dignity. Identifying the "other" in such a context becomes almost inevitable. It can be argued that Greece's sense of security forms an organic part of the modern national cultural discourse. An attempt to pin down the historical particularities of Greek national discourse over time, taken by itself, is beyond the scope of this discussion.[3] However, a few words about the shifting (or nonshifting) perceptions and attitudes of Greeks toward Turkey and the extent to which these are embedded in the dominant national cultural patterns can be useful.

Within the ambit of the subjective dimension, the main stumbling block to a genuine rapprochement is arguably the national historical narrative and the resultant national identity, an essential ingredient of which is the need to belittle and demonize "the other." In this context not only the solution, but even the discussion of the existing outstanding disputes, is hampered by the distrust between the two peoples created by their "living history." In both Greece and Turkey, history is not past; the past lives on in the present. Of course, their national historical narratives could hardly have been otherwise. After all, both have shaped their national identities through struggle against and interaction with each other. Most people in Europe and in the United States know that Greeks and Turks have been fighting off and on for several centuries—from well before the fall of Constantinople in 1453 through the Greek war of independence in the nineteenth century to the Turks' recovering of Asia Minor from the Greek troops in 1922. They fought each other in Cyprus in 1974, and they have come to blows over the Aegean on at least three occasions since the mid-1970s.[4] In Greece, the presentation of Turkey as the national enemy was quite an easy and persuasive task since Greece's war of independence was fought against the Turks. Making Turkey into the "historical enemy" played a decisive role in strengthening and solidifying Greek national identity. Through such discursive exhortations, the "historical enemy" and the absolute, even existential, struggle against it appeared as a critical complement to the foundation of the nation's identity in the Hellenic classical heritage. Throughout the history of the modern Greek state, the image of Turkey as the "historical enemy" has transformed cultural and identity discourse into actual policy options and security preferences.

As one of the most prominent contemporary Greek diplomats, Alexander Philon has observed that the relationship between Greeks and Turks is influenced by the fact that the two peoples have for many centuries lived together and apart, in peace and war, in trust and suspicion. Some elements bring them together; others drive them apart. Geography, history, culture, psychology, religion, business and economic activity, education, social, and many other factors provide the elements of the equation.[5] Popular attitudes in both communities are influenced by images from the Byzantine and Ottoman Empires. In the Greek historical memory, the Turk is perceived as the barbarian, the Asian invader who destroyed the Byzantine state and kept Hellenism in bonds for centuries. Greeks see Turks as being responsible for contemporary substandard levels of political, economic, and social development. They allege that in the second part of the twentieth century, Turkey has reemerged as aggressive and expansionist as ever.[6] As a result, the Turks are also perceived to be unethical, sneaky,

dishonest, and so on. Greeks see themselves as being the opposite of all these: almost the perfect race.[7]

In broader political terms, conflict with the Ottoman empire and modern Turkish state has been central to the development of Greek nationalism and the evolution of the modern Greek state. Greece and Turkey became independent states by fighting each other in what could plausibly be portrayed—and in many respect was—a valiant struggle for cultural and physical survival as a nation and state.[8] Greece's very existence as an independent state arose out of war against the Ottoman Turks, while the Turkish republic had its genesis in the Greek–Turkish war of 1919–22. "The war of independence is an act of resurrection of the Greek nation, a transition from darkness to light. The existence of a negative 'other' appears as indispensable both to justify the revolution for 'liberty' and to vindicate the 'slavery.'"[9] The protracted process, lasting over a century, by which Greece achieved its present boundaries mainly involved conflict with the Turks.

The essence of the Greek–Turkish conflict is the clash of historical narratives. It is these very narratives cum resultant collective identities that are irreconcilable as they stand today. As the Greek narrative goes, the national struggle for independence from the Ottoman rule, imposed on her in the fifteenth century, after 1,000-plus years of rule under the Byzantine Empire, became the rallying point of the Greeks around the world. This revolutionary movement was inspired by the nineteenth-century ideas of freedom, equality, and nationalism. Furthermore, once the nucleus of a state was formed in Greece, the effort continued to free the other Greeks who were still under Ottoman rule. At the same time, other people in the Balkans rose up against the collapsing imperial system.

The dominant perception in Greece is that the fact that the Greeks were one of the first who led the charge against the Ottoman Empire and inspired others to revolt against it has never quite been forgotten by the Turks—notwithstanding the admonition of Mustafa Kemal (the founder of modern, post-imperial, secular Turkey in the 1920s) urging them to honor Greek independence. Later the events of Asia Minor in the period 1919–22 and especially the military campaign directed toward the Anatolian heartland and the "catastrophe" that followed the collapse of the Greek effort, have left strong memories on both sides.[10] Paschalis Kitromilides has shown how the symbolic language of "Great Idea" was elaborated on in the nineteenth century.[11] For the Greeks, 1922 and the subsequent 1923 Treaty of Lausanne signified the end of Greek irredentism and the "Great Idea." Of the remaining "unredeemed" territories, Cyprus was officially ceded to Britain and the Dodecanese to Italy. Asia Minor and eastern Thrace were returned to Turkey. The remaining Greek population was evacuated in an agreed compulsory exchange with the Muslims of Macedonia, Epirus, and Crete. The Greeks of Istanbul, Imvros, and Tenedos, as well as the Turks of western Thrace, were exempted from the exchange. Close to 1.5 million Greeks descended upon a country of less than five million while about half a million Turks went in the opposite direction.[12]

The "Asia Minor Catastrophe" was a landmark in the subsequent development of Greek–Turkish relations and the Greek (as well as the Turkish) perception of the "other" in the Aegean, despite the courageous efforts of Eleftherios Venizelos—who came back to power in 1928—and Mustafa Kemal, during the interwar years, to reverse the trend and create a rapprochement between the two nations as an example for future generations.[13] Although rapprochement was achieved, it was only due to considerable concessions on the Greek side. Since then, many of the principles Mustafa Kemal advocated have been violated by his successors.[14] Although lip service has been paid to some of them, in practice the Turks have acted quite differently, adopting a much narrower and more traditional nationalistic view.

If anything, elite perceptions of Turkish revisionism were and still are much more pronounced than their Turkish analogues. The view in Greece, typically, is that Turkey, since the late 1930s, has been acting as an unsatisfied and revanchist state toward its neighbors. Turkey's "flexible and evasive" behavior throughout the years of World War II when Ankara would tilt in the direction of Germany or toward the British and the Americans in accordance with the vacillating tactical and strategic fortunes of the war has always been noted in Greece.[15] Turkish diplomacy, having reneged on previous commitments to the Allies, made parallel contacts with the British and the Americans and the Axis powers in an effort to negotiate Turkey's entry into

the war on the side of the highest bidder. In each instance, as Turkey approached the brink of entering the war on one side or the other, it consistently sought to link its entry to acquisition of Greek territory. The sought-after prize included the Greek islands of the eastern Aegean, as well as the Dodecanese.

"The Threat from the East"

For Greece and Greeks, Turkey has been the focus of the country's security policy and the driving force behind most foreign policy initiatives and responses. The perception of a threat from Turkey has traditionally dominated Greek thinking about the strategic environment, including defense planning.[16] According to Monteagle Stearns, it would not be far from the truth to suggest that since the creation of modern Greece in the 1820s, its foreign policy has taken no major initiative that was not, directly or indirectly, intended to create a more favorable balance of power and to neutralize the "threat from the east."[17] However, the year 1974 was instrumental in further reinforcing contemporary anti-Turkish attitudes. The Cyprus crisis then was regarded as the major turning point in shaping the post–World War II Greek security culture. The Turkish invasion and subsequent occupation of part of the island marked, for Greeks, a point of radical departure from more traditional "Cold-Warish" security thinking. Even before then, Cyprus had been a critical flashpoint. Since the early 1960s, a well-known string of events resulted in the transformation of the Cyprus problem from an isolated political problem concerning the island itself into a key factor in broader Greek–Turkish relations. Any escalation concerning Cyprus had a direct negative impact upon Greek–Turkish relations and was viewed as a proliferation of Turkish claims against Greece.

In the view of the majority of Greeks, the 1974 invasion of Cyprus and the continued occupation of the northern part of the island have been perhaps the strongest indications of Turkish expansionism. They are considered to be part of an undisguised attempt to partition Cyprus by force of arms. For most Greeks, Turkish behavior in Cyprus has reinforced an image of a neighbor that will not hesitate to attempt to revise the territorial status quo by the use of force whenever a low-risk opportunity is presented.

The Greek perceptions of an ever-present Turkish threat were and continue to be reinforced by structural changes in the demographic conditions of the region. A number of Greeks see Turkey as literally suffering from "growing pains." While Greece's population has remained nearly static at around the ten million mark since the 1960s, Turkey has experienced one of the fastest population growth rates in the world. Doubling its size every thirty years, Turkey's population had reached almost seventy million people in 2000. The colossal population gap, close proximity, and territorial asymmetry between the two countries clearly reinforced the perception of threat, increased Greek insecurity, and in some cases invoked geopolitical analyses and scenarios of Greek preemptive action.[18]

Greek policy makers have sought throughout the years to solidify a strategy of adequate deterrence founded on factors of internal as well as external balancing. Despite differences in style, Greek political parties have, almost without exception, shown remarkable continuity in agreeing that Turkey is the country's major security concern.[19] Thus Greece has been spending around 5 to 6 percent of its GDP for defense purposes over a number of years and has constantly sought to maintain sufficiency in land, air, and naval power vis-à-vis Turkey. The vast majority of Greek citizens has unquestionably supported successive governments' decisions to keep defense expenditures at an unbelievably high level, even in times of extremely tight fiscal policies and austerity programs, as during the 1990s when the country was struggling to achieve its membership in the European Monetary Union, the symbol of European integration.[20] Defense spending is considered to be responsible for Greece's budget deficit, as well as for the lower-than-desired quality of social services, but both the elite and the public perception is that "Greece is neither Ireland nor Portugal." The implementation of extensive armament programs is deemed necessary "in order to secure the country's national interests."[21] At the same time, Greek policy has sought to deepen its international ties, especially with the European Union, on the premise that Turkish policy makers would think twice before attacking a country that is highly integrated into the EU.[22] Unquestionably, strategic uncertainty regarding Turkey has absorbed enormous energy and resources on the Greek side.

The list of Greek grievances, in addition to Cyprus, is indeed long, and each grievance has reinforced perceptions of Turkish threat and revisionism, but the two most important include the status quo in the Aegean and the treatment of the Greek Orthodox community of Istanbul. In very recent times, what has added to the Greek perception of threat has been the Imia–Kardak crisis. To the Greek mind, Imia is the most vivid reminder of ever-present Turkish aggression.

Turkish "Revisionism"

In the view of most of Greece's foreign and defense elites, Turkey has been pursuing a calculated revisionist policy in the Aegean, Thrace, and Cyprus. This, above everything else, reflects a grand strategic consensus in Greek domestic and foreign policy in the last three decades. This consensus has come about for many reasons. Turkey's revisionist stance in the Aegean (especially since the 1970s) has been highlighted by partitionist demands with respect to the Aegean continental shelf, air space, and NATO command and control arrangements. Turkish claims are seen as an attempt to, in effect, to create an enclave of most major Greek islands, while Turkish suggestions for shared sovereignty and resource utilization in the Aegean are seen as only the beginning of long-term demands, in light of Turkey's potentially explosive overpopulation problems.[23] The pivotal points are rights to the continental shelf and extension of Greek territorial seas rights to the now almost universal twelve-mile limit. With or without the thorns of ethnic contention, these two issues would present great difficulties since they involve control over (potentially) important resources in a unique setting with unclear legal precedents.

According to the Greek narrative, Turkish "revisionist actions" underlie a determination to change the status quo by challenging existing Greek sovereign rights. For Athens, all boundaries except the continental shelf have been adequately fixed by existing treaties (the 1923 Lausanne Peace Treaty, the 1932 agreement between Turkey and Italy, and the 1947 Treaty of Paris) and established practice. On the continental shelf, Athens proposes recourse to the International Court of Justice (ICJ) in The Hague. As for territorial waters, Greece asserts that the 1982 Law of the Sea (LOS) Convention unequivocally gives it the right to extend maritime boundaries around its Aegean islands to the now standard twelve miles. Greece reserves this right, even though Athens has no current plan to invoke it.[24] A plethora of statements made by Turkey's high-level political and military elites challenging the territorial status quo in the Aegean and complaining about the close proximity of Greece's islands to Turkey's Aegean shores has only served to intensify Greece's perception of threat.

Greeks' perception of threat reflects not fear of an all-out war but rather a well-concerted Turkish strategy of threatening to move aggressively against a number of possible territorial targets, thus creating a series of military fait accomplis.[25] The presence of the Turkish "Army of the Aegean," which is supported by a large fleet of landing craft and special forces units and is located near Izmir, has been fueling Greek concerns. Its "westward" order of battle has meant that the Turks' Aegean army was seen as stalking the area waiting for an opportunity to strike the Greek islands of the eastern Aegean.

THE GREEK ORTHODOX MINORITY OF ISTANBUL

The treatment of the Greek Orthodox minority in Turkey both during World War II and since then is another example of the efforts of the Turkish authorities to upset the balance established by the Treaty of Lausanne in 1923. In June of that year, according to the official Turkish census, 279,788 Greek Orthodox people were living in Istanbul, plus about 26,000 Greek citizens, as established by international agreement. Today, the Greek Orthodox population of Istanbul has been reduced to 3,000 or less. For the Greeks, Turkish policy during World War II was instrumental in the destruction of the Greek minority of Istanbul.

When Greece was fighting off the attack by Mussolini and resisting the Nazi occupation forces in 1942 (while Turkey remained neutral), the Ankara government took the opportunity to impose a special confiscatory tax (purportedly directed against war profiteers). The *Varlik Vergisi* was used to bring about the financial and economic ruin of the minorities and to deport to eastern Anatolia the heads of families who could not pay it.

Other measures were also introduced that forbade members of minorities from exercising their traditional professions, conscripting them unfairly, and so on. All these contribute to the remembrance of past wrongs, real or imagined, suffered by the Greeks at the hands of the Turkish state.[26]

After the war, government-inspired riots in September 1955 inflicted death, rape, and destruction on the Greek minority. In 1964–65 Greek citizens, established by international agreement in Turkey, and their families were the victims of mass expulsions. Pressure was put on the Greek Orthodox population, which constituted the majority on the islands of Imvros and Tenedos, to abandon their ancestral homes through expropriation of their land, the use of Turkish convicts to terrorize them, the closure of the Greek schools, and similar activities.

Furthermore, all institutions of learning and charitable foundations of the Greek Orthodox minority had to face a systematic effort by the Turkish authorities to close them. The theological seminary in Halki and the printing press of the patriarchate were among the victims of this policy. Other examples of this vigorously discriminatory policy include the imposition of illegal taxation, the dismissal without replacement of school boards and teachers, and the refusal to register properly constituted legal documents showing the patriarchate or other religious and charitable foundations as the beneficiary. All this took place in addition to the constant bureaucratic delays, harassment, and deliberate official obstructionism.

In Greek history, and in the context of relations with Turkey, Turkey's treatment of the Greek minority of Istanbul constitutes a dark page that runs deep in Greeks' collective memory.

THE IMIA CRISIS

In the Greek mind, the Imia crisis could not but be understood as a clear demonstration of Turkish revisionism—a revisionism that was reinforced by changes in the function of the Turkish state caused by an alarming neoauthoritarianism and a nationalist hatred brought about by the Kurdish problem. As Alkis Kourkoulas, one of the most respected Greek correspondents in Istanbul, has indicated in a best-selling monograph, the military campaign in southeastern Turkey resulted in a situation in which the use of force or the threat to use force has become totally accepted as a legitimate foreign policy behavior by large parts of Turkish society. The dominant position of the military in Turkish political life reinforces these tendencies.[27]

The dominant understanding in Greece has been that Ankara saw in Imia an opportunity "to fabricate a case so as to put forward the idea of 'gray areas' and push Greece to the negotiation table" in order to revise the status quo in the Aegean.[28] The Turkish position during the crisis "became a much wider challenge to Greek sovereignty over small islets along the maritime border, as well as to the border itself."[29] The issue of "gray areas" in the Aegean had never been raised by Ankara before the Imia crisis. This incident should be viewed in the context of Turkey's fear of the extension of Greek territorial waters from six to twelve miles. The Turkish argument was that Turkey would lose out with regard to its Aegean high-sea rights. The importance of this issue for Turkey was evident in its threat to Greece that any extension would be a cause of war.

Knowing well the weakness of its case, Turkey was reluctant to take the matter to The Hague. In such a case, it seemed that the foreign policy and defense establishments in Ankara invented the notion of "gray areas"—choosing thus to stoke tension in the Aegean—in order to put more pressure on Greece. As Ekavi Athanassopoulou has noted, for Turkey it was a chance to try and "push its borders westwards and thus strengthen its position regarding such questions as the delimitation of the continental shelf, the extent of national air-space and territorial waters."[30] In the months that followed Imia, Ankara pursued the concept with rigor.

In an article published on June 13, 1996, the Turkish daily *Milliyet* listed the inhabited islets of Farmakonisi and Agathonisi as "gray areas." Along with disputing Greek sovereignty over islets close to its coast, in June 1996 Turkey also disputed Greece's sovereignty over the island of Gavdos, which lies southwest of Crete and is inhabited by some 300 Greek fishermen. During the planning of the NATO exercise Dynamic Mix, the representative of the Turkish general staff submitted a statement according to which Turkey opposed the inclusion of the Greek island of Gavdos in the exercise "due to the disputed situation regarding

sovereignty." It should be noted that the regime of the islet of Gavdos had nothing to do with the Treaty of Lausanne, since it is under Greek sovereignty in accordance with the arrangements of the 1913 Treaty of London.[31] Indeed, this Imia aftermath steeled Greek public opinion enormously.

THE RAPPROCHEMENT POST-HELSINKI 1999: PROSPECTS AND IDEAS

A view widely held in both Greece and Turkey is that it was the earthquakes of August and September 1999 that brought about the recent, considerable change in relations. If this popular view is an accurate depiction of reality, then we are faced with the phenomenon of public opinion swaying reluctant governments. According to Alexis Heraclides, there are

> four possible explanations of the uncharacteristic attitude of the Greek public: the salience of human suffering and disaster; the sense of common fate before insurmountable natural forces; the vivid image of the concrete "other" which contrasted sharply with what is expected of him/her as a representative of a merciless foe; and in the Greek case at least, the exceptional levels reached by the nationalist rhetoric, of a presumed unending confrontation along deterministic and existential lines à la Carl Schmitt ("Friend-Foe") with no conceivable way out of the quagmire save perhaps in a final showdown. This latter view may have convinced several more optimistic segments of the Greek public, perhaps even the silent majority, to be more receptive and ready for any sign of breakthrough from the impasse.[32]

However, in the explosive Greece–Turkey realm, where vital national interests are at stake, what are the prospects for a real and lasting consolidation of the ongoing rapprochement? Can we identify a set of ideas that can form a mutually accepted path toward a historic "Aegean" settlement? My conviction is that cooperation and security in the Aegean can be achieved, if the two countries—governments and people—succeed in redefining their interests so as to allow a security-regime type of relationship to develop. At a more analytical level, redefinition of interests can be the result of the two actors' power location and capabilities, as well as the domestic interplay on both sides of the Aegean. In the post-Helsinki (December 1999) era, the domestic interplay in both countries has been more favorable than ever before. Greece's success joining the European Monetary Union—contrary to most predictions—contributed to the establishment of a favorable bilateral balance-of-power arrangement vis-à-vis Ankara that made Athens more confident in undertaking its Turkish policy initiatives.

Greece's long-standing policy of "conditional sanctions" vis-à-vis Turkey (through the employment of vetos and other qualifying mechanisms within the EU's institutional nexus) was abandoned at the December 1999 council meeting in Helsinki in favor of a policy of "conditional rewards." The rationale behind this approach has been to create appropriate conditions for a political and diplomatic "peace dividend" by pursuing a strategy of engagement with Turkey. It is a strategy that seeks to maintain and enhance relations with Turkey as much as possible in the various policy realms. It refers to a policy of increasing contact and producing a widening network of relationships.

The logic behind this drastic reversal was simple, yet compelling. The damages of a putative Greek–Turkish clash, apart from the obvious human costs, would be strategically damaging to many other groups. War would certainly undermine stability on a transregional scale. It would be fatal for the fragile settlement processes in the Balkans. It would derail all chances for a successful NATO and EU enlargement strategy. At a minimum, Greek–Turkish brinkmanship, apart from the permanent foreign and security damage to both countries, would make it almost impossible for NATO to adapt to the post–Cold War challenges and would kill the prospects of EU's Common Foreign and Security Policy (CFSP) and European Security and Defence Policy (ESDP). With the potential for destructiveness and escalation far greater today than in the past, a clash would have profound implications for Turkey and the West. It would also have operational consequences for the United States. In strategic terms, a conflict could lead to a permanent estrangement of Turkey and extremely high economic and security costs for Greece.

The rapprochement has, therefore, a sound strategic rationale on all sides. Athens calculated that it would be much better off with a next-door neighbor meeting all the Copenhagen (1993) and Helsinki (1999) criteria for EU membership. The current détente has been the "jewel on the crown" of the new proactive and confident Greek policy, and the future of this relationship will have important implications for the success of Greek foreign policy as a whole. The changes in the Greek approach toward Turkey are strategic, even "grand strategic" in nature, and not simply tactical. Although there is still potential for deterioration in relations with Ankara, the risk of conflict is now reduced. For this reason, Athens and Ankara have a shared stake in ensuring that Turkey's EU candidacy moves forward steadily. Both countries have a longer-term strategic interest in seeing Turkey's EU aspirations succeed. Such a success has the potential of changing Greece's perception of threat and fostering political and economic reform in a Turkey reassured of its place in Europe. The stakes involved in bringing to fruition this strategy of reciprocal accommodation are extremely high. The added advantage, from a Greek perspective, is that conditional rewards (carrots rather than sticks) will continue to be offered by an all-EU policy that no longer isolates Greece as the intransigent partner or odd man out.

Greece's Helsinki policy shift did not escape serious criticism at home. Critics were quick to point out that a policy of "unilateral accommodation" would be interpreted in Turkey, and elsewhere, as a sign of weakness and would encourage Turkey to escalate its demands. To support their point, critics argued that following the lifting of Greece's veto on Turkey's candidacy in the European Union, there was no gesture, not even a symbolic one, indicating Turkey's willingness to reciprocate. For their part, supporters of Greece's policy shift agree that the probability of a Turkish strategy of matching goodwill gestures is quite low. However, the expectation is that if the "Turkish bet" is eventually won, the benefits of cooperation and peace in the relations of the erstwhile antagonists will be immense.

THE REALM OF THE GREEK STRATEGY: ENGAGING TURKEY

The engagement policy of Athens has three elements. With respect to economics and trade, engagement means seeking an expansion of relations and growth of exchanges. Politically, engagement means seeking to maximize bilateral contacts at various levels, while placing traditional disputes in the diplomatic freezer. Under this approach, Athens—during the 1999 Helsinki European Council—agreed to the Turkish candidacy for EU membership, a major political risk for the Greek government. Militarily, Greece has agreed to a policy of enhancement of military-to-military contacts in the framework of NATO-regulated CBMS, with the specific aim of increasing mutual confidence and reaching agreement on "rules of the game."

The engagement strategy of Athens rests on the hope that growing economic, political, and military contacts and cooperation will either help transform Turkey into a more democratic (with the functional impetus of the EU) and cooperative state or, at a minimum, bring about some kind of convergence of interests. In Greek calculations, integrating Turkey into the European system will help socialize Turkish elites in the European norms of behavior and will increase their stake in reforming their course. The more Turkey is integrated into the European system, the less likely it will be to employ force. Rather, it will act as a prudent and satisfied member of the international system, once it becomes accustomed to the "rules of the game" and understands the benefits that it can safeguard as well as bestow.

For many in Athens, this is seen as quite an innovative strategic approach. The stakes are extremely high, but in the post-Helsinki era such a policy is not only desirable but also possible. It is possible because of what could prove to be the catalytic insertion of the EU into Greek–Turkish relations. At the same time, under such a strategy Greece may be wise to enhance economic, political, military-to-military relations and cultural ties at all levels.[33] This may help curb any tendencies toward military adventurism that might crop up on either side from time to time. One should never forget that there is always the potential for conflict over issues such as Cyprus and the Aegean or the extent to which Greeks perceive Turkey as an actor seeking regional hegemony. It should be stated that this strategy remains undecided on some of the key judgments about Turkey's future. For example, it is unknown whether Turkey's enmeshment in the European integration system will modify its long-term objectives and behavior, enhance the process

of democratization, or, alternatively, lead it to pursue an aggressive policy and challenge the status quo as is feared by many Greeks. The "bet" now is for a lasting and comprehensive solution to the problems dividing Greece and Turkey based on a gradual but dynamic process in which the two "adversaries" are truly engaged in assessing and redefining their interests so as to allow a cooperative security regime to emerge and take roots. Of course, there are—at least in the short and medium run—significant qualifications, which should still be taken into account.

THE POLITICAL AND STRATEGIC QUALIFICATIONS

Greece and Turkey share common land and sea borders and both have extensive coastlines along the Aegean Sea. The geographic imperatives of both countries can moderate as well as exacerbate actions. These imperatives are long term and can transcend governments and ruling elites. They are also interconnected, so that if one imperative is altered, it will probably affect others. Within this framework, five practical principles have remained constant over time.[34]

First, progress in Greek–Turkish relations should be possible even when Athens and Ankara have politically weak governments. It is true that modern governments in postindustrial countries are prompted to adopt cooperative relations. Nevertheless, some limited but important steps can be taken even when governments are weak. Regardless of the relative strength of each government, the militaries of Greece and Turkey will continue to conduct exercises in the Aegean, pursue their national objectives, and protect their interests. This factor normally leads to a regular cycle of increased tensions and serious incidents, some of which involve loss of life and military equipment. Yet even weak governments want to keep friction to a minimum. Within this framework, it is important that each government remain sensitive toward the concerns and opinions of the public of the other side. Further, even weak governments want to eliminate or limit the impact of domestic factors that could contribute to the continuation of the conflict, such as serious domestic political, economic, and social problems. However, weak governments are sometimes more likely to be tempted to resort to a "foreign policy adventure" to deflect attention away from domestic problems. Clearly, therefore, the exercise of strong leadership in both countries is highly desirable, if not sine qua non.

Second, it is better to move slowly on Aegean disputes. Perceptions need to be changed gradually, trust must be built, and bureaucracies and populations must be prepared for change. Avoiding high expectations reduces the chance of great disappointment and disillusionment. There is a deep-rooted conviction that it is almost impossible to return to the status quo if a country "loses out" on an Aegean issue. These are not the types of issues for interested parties to experiment with, and it is counterproductive to pressure either country into taking too many risks without having a good expectation of an acceptable outcome. In that respect, a low-key, low-publicity approach on both sides, backed by a continuing dialogue that keeps holding the notion of common interests as the basic premise, can be extremely helpful.

Third, one should not underestimate the importance of geography. The 1996 Imia crisis brought both countries to the brink of war. Turkey's current "gray areas" (or zones) policy, which raises sovereignty questions concerning selected Aegean islands and islets, could lead to a serious confrontation if it is not pursued in a cooperative and mutually agreed manner with the Greek government. In this regard, the Greek view of referring legitimate disagreements about sovereignty to the International Court of Justice is still worth implementing.

Fourth, specific Greek–Turkish disputes should not be viewed in isolation without, however, being formally linked to "package deals." There is a delicate interconnection among the issues. For example, Greece's claim to a national airspace of ten nautical miles may appear to have nothing in common with Turkey's pursuit of a "'fair" share of the Aegean seabed, yet no Greek government would consider changing its policy until there was a mutually agreed settlement on the delimitation of the seabed. To do otherwise would be viewed as a sign of weakness and could thus adversely affect Greece's negotiating position on this or any other bilateral issue.

Fifth, the active and balanced involvement of international actors (mainly the United States, NATO,

and the EU) in the confidence-building process is clearly vital and, for that matter, instrumental. Of course, the ingredients of a lasting settlement, given the current international setting, can only be based on the assumption that Turkey and Greece, will cement their integration into the larger European community.

CONCLUSION

What makes the Greek–Turkish conflict appear intractable is above all its subjective dimension, namely the awesome psychological barrier resulting from years of antagonism and enmity. Like most ethnopolitical conflicts, the Greek–Turkish conflict is characterized by a total lack of mutual confidence, suspicion bordering on paranoia, and demonization of the "other." In the final analysis, the state of relations between Greece and Turkey is a product of the attitudes and perceptions of ruling elites and the general public operating within global and regional settings. However, developments of the past five to six years show that historic patterns can change. Consider the following proposition: country dyads with advanced and interdependent economies and consolidated democracies (sustained by civil societies) can avoid conflict and choose cooperation as an optimal foreign policy goal. If Turkey's goal of meeting the criteria of EU membership is achieved, future generations may be talking about Turkey and Greece in a fashion similar to the manner in which German–French reconciliation was described after World War II.

Differences between Turkey and Greece are not new. As long as they remain unresolved, some unforeseen incident could touch off open conflict and large-scale warfare. Continuing disputes over Cyprus, the Aegean, relations with the EU, relations with NATO, and issues related to bilateral and multilateral relations with other regional and extraregional actors all have the potential of threatening Turkish–Greek and regional peace, security, and stability. The history of the two countries' bilateral relations shows that such a situation might repeat itself more easily than many think. Regardless of the merits and demerits of the case of each of the disputants, the central question is whether Greece and Turkey will be better off in a condition of protracted conflict, as compared to entering into a new phase of mutual and active engagement and even cooperation. Unequivocally, the answer is that both countries would be much better off if they were to reach a final reconciliation, a new historic compromise. Moreover, the Greek–Turkish discord, though difficult, is hardly a zero-sum game as a whole or in its various parts.[35] The impact of a clash on political, social, and economic progress would be devastating. A war is unthinkable because it would isolate both belligerents from their Western institutional affiliations. The ingredients of a lasting settlement, given the current international setting, can be based only on the assumption that Turkey and Greece will become peaceable members of the the European community.

Rapprochement is intimately linked to the positive development of the relationship between Ankara and Brussels. The start of accession negotiations could be instrumental. Stagnation or deterioration of the EU–Turkey relationship would almost definitely complicate and perhaps threaten the Greek–Turkish rapprochement. With Ankara's candidacy confirmed, Turkey's relations with the EU have become less uncertain. At the same time, though, they have moved into a more highly structured and legalistic pattern, with fixed criteria and fewer opportunities for arguments on strategic grounds. Joining the EU increasingly emerges as

Turkey's best strategic option. In both the security and modernization—political, economic, social—realms, the EU's influence is great, as has been demonstrated in other southern, eastern, and central European states. Athens appears committed to Turkish EU vocation and to a step-by-step engagement. It believes that this strategy will produce many benefits by moderating Turkish behavior, increasing opportunities for trade and investment, and improving the situation in Turkey itself as its modernizers struggle to respond to European integration challenges.

At the end of the day, for many Greeks Europe is the only actor powerful enough to transform Turkey into a modern democratic state. This is more so since, as the foregoing discussion has argued, Greeks believe that their country has always been motivated by benevolent intentions while the other—Turkey—has not. Perceptions and historic grievances have been powerful determinants of policies, especially when they refer to structural arrangements, external and domestic, as is the case in the Aegean. Stereotypes, prejudices, perceptions, ideological bias, and historical memory have played a decisive role in producing "knowledge" and "evaluation" in the sociology of the Greek–Turkish relations. History and cultural differences are major explanatory variables.

ENDNOTES

1. Bahar Rumelili, "Liminality and Perpetuation of Conflicts: Turkish-Greek Relations in the Context of Community-Building by the EU," *European Journal of International Relations*, vol. 9, no. 2 (June 2003), 214.
2. See Ronald Krebs, "Perverse Institutionalism: NATO and the Greco-Turkish Conflict," *International Organization*, vol. 53, no. 2 (1999), 343–377.
3. An excellent account of the Greek national identity discourse can be found in Constantine Tsoukalas, "Greek National Identity in an Integrated Europe and a Changing World Order," in *Greece, the New Europe, and the Changing International Order*, eds. Harry J. Psomiades and Stavros B. Thomadakis (New York: Pella, 1993).
4. M. James Wilkinson, "The United States, Turkey, and Greece—Three's a Crowd,", in *Turkey's Transformation and American Policy*, ed. Morton Abramowitz (New York: The Century Foundation Press, 2000), 188.
5. Alexander Philon, "Greek-Turkish Relations since 1974," in *United States Foreign Policy Regarding Greece, Turkey & Cyprus: The Rule of Law and American Interests*, American Hellenic Institute Conference Proceedings, April 29–30, 1988 (Washington, DC: AHI, 1989), 1.
6. Byron Theodoropoulos, *The Turks and Us* (Athens: Fytrakis, 1988, in Greek), 16.
7. Hercules Millas, "National Perception of the 'Other' and the Persistence of Some Images," in *Turkish-Greek Relations: Escaping the Security Dilemma in the Aegean*, eds. Mustafa Aydin and Kostas Ifantis (New York: Routledge, 2004), 153–156.
8. Alexis Heraclides, "The Greek-Turkish Conflict: Towards Resolution and Reconciliation," in Aydin and Ifantis, *Turkish-Greek Relations*.
9. Millas, "National Perception of the 'Other.'"
10. During the negotiations in the 1919 Paris Conference, the Greek delegation with Prime Minister Eleftherios Venizelos argued before the Supreme Council of the Allies the Greek claims for the annexation of northern Epirus, Thrace, the Dodecanese and the internationalization of Constantinople. Venizelos also demanded most of the vilayet of Aydin, including Smyrna, to safeguard the security of the Greeks of Asia Minor. Of these claims, northern Epirus was denied to Greece through Italian pressure, while the return of the Dodecanese would not be realized until after the Second World War. The other claims were

conceded to Greece by the Treaty of Sevres (August 1920). Following Lloyd George's proposition—which was endorsed by President Wilson—Greek troops were dispatched to Smyrna to protect the Christian population. At the end of 1920 Venizelos was voted down by a war-weary electorate and King Constantine was restored to his throne. The return of the royalist party to power triggered a change in French policy. France's discontent with the Treaty of Sevres, which had created an enlarged ally—Greece—for Britain and, therefore, a potential threat to French interests in the Levant, became manifest. At a London conference in 1921 the representatives of Kemal, who was fighting against the concessions of the captive Istanbul government, negotiated with the French and the Italians. In June the Italians left the region, and in October France started arming the Kemal's forces. Kemal had in the meantime signed a treaty of friendship with the Soviet Union in March 1921. In August 1921 the Greek army, having stretched its line of communication with the coast to a breaking point, was stopped by stiff Turkish resistance outside Ankara. A year later, the Turkish offensive split Greek defenses, captured Smyrna, and led to the mass exodus of the Greeks of Asia Minor that was completed with the 1923 population exchange. On this, see M. L. Smith, *The Ionian Vision: Greece in Asia Minor, 1919–1922* (London: Allen Lane, 1973).

11. Paschalis M. Kitromilides, "'Imagined Communities' and the Origins of the National Question in the Balkans," in *Modern Greece: Nationalism & Nationality*, eds. Martin Blinkhorn and Thanos Veremis (London: Sage-ELIAMEP, 1990), 59.

12. Thanos Veremis, *Greek Security Considerations* (Athens: Papazisis, 1980), p. 27.

13. A series of agreements was signed between the two countries, the most important being the 1930 Greek–Turkish Friendship Accord and the 1933 treaty for the diplomatic guarantee of the "common border". On a more multilateral front, the two countries were instrumental in the conclusion of the 1934 Balkan Accord.

14. Richard Clogg, "Greek-Turkish Relations in the Post-1974 Period," in *The Greek-Turkish Conflict in the 1990s: Domestic and External Influences*, ed. Dimitri Constas (Basingstoke, England: Macmillan, 1991), 13.

15. Theodore A. Couloumbis, *The United States, Greece, and Turkey* (New York: Praeger, 1983), 128–29. One of the most "popular" and most footnoted books in Greece has been Frank G. Weber's *The Evasive Neutral: Germany, Britain and the Quest for a Turkish Alliance in the Second World War* (Columbia: University of Missouri Press, 1979).

16. Ian O. Lesser, F. Stephen Larrabee, Michele Zanini, and Katia Vlachos-Dengler, *Greece's New Geopolitics* (Santa Monica: RAND, 2001), 20.

17. Monteagle Stearns, "Greek Foreign Policy in the 1990s: Old Signposts, New Roads," in *Greece Prepares for the 21st Century*, eds. Dimitri Constas and Nikolaos A. Stavrou (Baltimore: John Hopkins University Press, 1995), 60.

18. The best example of this reasoning is found in Panajotis Kondylis, *Theory of War* (Athens: Themelio, 1997, in Greek), 381–411. What the late Kondylis proposed for reversal of the gradual shrinkage of Hellenism was a "massive first-strike" against Turkey. His "proposal" is based on the false assumption that a Greek–Turkish war is inevitable due to the growing demographic gap and the great development deficit of Turkey. Such a war would result in Greece's destruction. But even in the case of peace, Greece would sooner or later end up becoming Turkey's satellite. Greece might end up having no other choice but to preempt on a massive scale now that the balance of power is more or less symmetrical. The best critique of this line of reasoning comes from Alexis Heraklides, "Geopolitics, Machtpolitik and a Greek-Turkish War: A Critical Approach," in *Current Issues*, no. 66 (January–March 1998, in Greek).

19. Panayotis Tsakonas & Antonis Tournikiotis, "Greece's Elusive Quest for Security Providers: The "Expectations-Reality Gap,'" *Security Dialogue*, vol. 34, no. 3 (September 2003), 303.

20. Following the 1996 crisis over the Imia Kardak islets, a decision was made for a further intensification of defense effort with an increase of the resources devoted to defense. In 1996, an armaments program worth almost €15–17 billion was agreed upon and implemented in the following five years. In 2000, a second five-year (2001–2005) program was agreed upon, which if implemented in full will amount to more than €20 billion. Throughout this period, Greek military procurement has put exclusive emphasis on the acquisition of modern weaponry and the development of high-quality defense capabilities (C4, force multipliers, etc.).

21. This phrase used by Prime Minister Kostas Simitis in a speech in 2000. Quoted in Tsakonas & Tournikiotis, "Greece's Elusive Quest for Security Providers," 303, fn. 4.

22. Theodore A. Couloumbis, "Strategic Consensus in Greek Domestic and Foreign Policy Since 1974," in *Greece and the New Balkans: Challenges and Opportunities*, eds. Van Coufoudakis, Harry J. Psomiades, and Andre Gerolymatos (New York: Pella, 1999), 419.

23. Van Coufoudakis, "Greek Political Party Attitudes Towards Turkey: 1974–89," in *The Greek-Turkish Conflict in the 1990s: Domestic and External Influences*, ed. Dimitri Constas (Basingstoke, England: Macmillan, 1991), 42.

24. Wilkinson, "The United States, Turkey, and Greece," 194.

25. See Constantine Arvanitopoulos, "Greek Defence Policy and the Doctrine of Extended Deterrence," in *Security and Cooperation in the Eastern Mediterranean*, eds. Andreas Theophanous and Van Coufoudakis (Nicosia, Cyprus: InterCollege Press, 1997), 154.

26. On the *Varlik Vergisi*, see Faik Okte, *The Tragedy of the Turkish Capital Tax* (London: Croom Helm, 1987); Thanos Veremis, *History of the Greek-Turkish Relations, 1453–1998* (Athens: Sideris, 1998, in Greek), 107–110; Alexis Alexandris, "The Historical Context of Greek-Turkish Relations 1923–1954," in *Greek-Turkish Relations, 1923–1987*, eds. Thanos Veremis et al. (Athens: Gnosi, 1988, in Greek), 105–108; and Alexis Alexandris, *The Greek Minority of Istanbul and Greek-Turkish Relations 1918–1974* (Athens: Centre for Asia Minor Studies, 1983).

27. Alkis Kourkoulas, *Imia: A Critical Approach of the Turkish Factor* (Athens: I. Sideris, 1997, in Greek), 26.

28. Ekavi Athanassopoulou, "Blessing in Disguise? The Imia Crisis and Turkish-Greek Relations," *Mediterranean Politics*, vol. 2, no. 3 (Winter 1997), 86.

29. Wilkinson, "The United States, Turkey, and Greece," 200.
30. Athanassopoulou, "Blessing in Disguise?" 86.
31. Thanos Veremis, "The Protracted Crisis," in *Greek-Turkish Relations in the Era of Globalization*, eds. Dimitris Keridis and Dimitrios Triantaphyllou (Herndon, Virginia: Brassey's, 2001), 44–45.
32. Heraclides, "The Greek-Turkish Conflict."
33. In terms of trade and business transactions, by 2000 the exports–imports between the two countries had more than doubled to over US$900 million; investment had gone up by 775 percent from US$2.4 million in 1999 to US$14.7 million in 2000, and apparently it is far greater. The joint ventures in both countries and elsewhere abroad are also apparently impressive though it is difficult to access their magnitude. As to developments at the state-to-state level, by 2002 no fewer than nine bilateral agreements were signed (all by now ratified): (1) coopera-

tion on customs administration, (2) economic cooperation, (3) promotion and protection of investments, (4) cooperation on environmental protection, (5) cooperation on tourism, (6) maritime transport, (7) science and technology, (8) cultural cooperation, and (9) combating crime, especially terrorism, organized crime, illicit drug trafficking, and illegal immigration. The two countries now have a fairly adequate and more up-to-date institutional–legal framework on matters of low politics. In addition, the two governments have signed a protocol on the reentry of illegal refugees; they also have decided to draft an agreement on sea and air transportation and to address the outstanding question of double taxation, which hampers economic transactions.
34. S. Ross Norton, "Geography Never Changes," *The Strategic Regional Report*, vol. 3, no. 4 (June/July, 1998).
35. Heraclides, "The Greek-Turkish Conflict."

ABOUT THE AUTHOR

Kostas Ifantis is an associate professor of international relations in the Department of Political Science at the University of Athens. He studied law at Aristotle University of Thessaloniki and international relations at the University of Bradford, United Kingdom, where he received his Ph.D. He worked as a lecturer in international and European politics at the universities of Bradford and Portsmouth, United Kingdom, in the early 1990s. In 1998, he was a research fellow at the Center for Political Studies at the University of Michigan. In 2002, he was a Fulbright Scholar at the John F. Kennedy School of Government at Harvard University. His papers have appeared in edited books and in periodicals such as *Democratization, Review of International Affairs,* and *Turkish Studies.* His books include *NATO in the New European Order* (London: Macmillan, 1996); *Theory and Reform in the European Union* (Manchester, England: Manchester University Press, 2002); and *NATO and the New Security Paradigm* (London: Frank Cass, 2002). With Mustafa Aydin he recently edited *Turkish-Greek Relations: The Security Dilemma in the Aegean* (New York: Routledge, 2004).

Turkish–Greek Relations

Onur Öymen

Turkey and Greece have a long seesawing history of cooperation and conflict. The past century bore witness to alternating waves of tension and acrimony interspersed with conciliatory gestures and initiatives. This chapter highlights the ups and downs of recent and historic Turkish–Greek relations. It also details the disputes at issue. To conclude, suggestions on how relations might be improved are proposed.

The geographic area of today's Greece was an Ottoman territory for more than three centuries. Greece gained her independence from the Ottoman Empire in 1821. During the first years of independ-

ence, the population of Greece was around one million and her territory less than 50,000 square kilometers. Over the decades that followed Greece expanded her territory to the detriment of the Ottoman Empire. Greece's expansion took place with the support and assistance of the Western powers. The enlargement of Greece toward the north forced a great number of Turks, who had settled in that territory and lived there since the fifteenth century, to leave their homes and properties and move to Turkey.

An important episode of Turkish–Greek relations was the Greek invasion of parts of western

Anatolia between 1919 and 1922, again with the encouragement and support of the Western powers. The Greek invasion of Anatolia had a devastating effect on the civilian population of Turkey. As Ismet Inönü, then the head of the Turkish delegation at the Lausanne Peace Conference in 1923, declared, a total of 98,000 houses in twenty-seven cities and 1,400 villages were destroyed during the Greek invasion. The cost of that invasion for the Turks of western Anatolia was calculated at the time to be four billion golden franks. The Greek forces were defeated in 1922 by the Turkish troops under the command of Mustafa Kemal Atatürk.

According to Professor Justin McCarthy, five million Muslims, most of them Turkish, were killed and 5,381,000 refugees were forced to migrate from the beginning of the Greek upheaval for independence until the end of the Greek invasion of Anatolia.[1] This was a tragic result. Despite these bitter memories, the new leaders of Turkey decided to start a new page in Turkish–Greek relations, based on mutual trust, friendship, and cooperation after regaining Turkish territories.

At the Lausanne Conference, the border issues between Turkey and Greece, as well as the situation in western Thrace, were discussed. The Turkish side presented concrete data about the then current population of western Thrace: 129,118 Turks, 33,904 Greeks, and 26,266 Bulgarians. Turks possessed 84 percent of the land.

Another important issue was the status of the Greek Orthodox Patriarchate of Istanbul. The Turkish side proposed that the patriarchate be moved outside Turkey since it had been involved in the past in a number of political activities against Turkish interests. In the end, the following compromise was reached: the patriarchate would remain in Istanbul but would never again be involved in any political activity. The Turkish side agreed to keep the patriarchate in Turkey with the understanding that it would not hold and use an ecumenical title. It would merely be the church of Turkish Orthodox people.

The Lausanne Treaty, signed on July 24, 1923, was not only a landmark in the history of Turkey but also formed the cornerstone of the relations between Turkey and Greece. This treaty, while establishing the new borders of Turkey, created a careful balance between Turkey and Greece. During the conference at Laussane, then Greek Prime Minister Elefteros Venizelos complained to Ismet

Inönü that the Western powers, which had urged with him to dispatch Greek troops to Izmir and invade Anatolia, had left him alone at the conference table.

After the Lausanne Conference, Atatürk and Venizelos were able to turn a new page and create a new spirit of cooperation between Turkey and Greece. The two countries signed a number of agreements, particularly on the exchange of population and the rights and privileges of Greeks in Istanbul and Turks in western Thrace. Prime Minister Venizelos paid an official visit to Turkey in 1930, during which he established a personal friendship with Atatürk. He shared his impressions with Richard N. Coudenhove-Kalergi, the author of the book *Crusade for Pan-Europe*, who wrote:

> Venizelos convinced me that Turkey, under the rule of Kemal Atatürk, had become an integral part of Western civilization and that whatever the future of pan-Europe, Turkey must be made part of it. He assured me that Greece could only cooperate with our movement if Turkey also were included. He spoke with admiration of Mustafa Kemal Atatürk.[2]

Venizelos had expressed these views not only to Coudenhove-Kalergi. He also sent a letter to the president of the Nobel Peace Committee on January 12, 1934, in which he wrote:

> In 1922, after Mustafa Kemal's struggle was victorious and the Turkish Republic was proclaimed, the previously prevailing instability and intolerance [were] brought to an end. In fact, the realization of such radical transformations in a society in such a short lapse of time is very rare. From the ashes of a theocratic empire in decline, where religion and legal affairs were intermixed, a modern, healthy and dynamic nation was created. The Great Reformer Mustafa Kemal Pasha abolished the absolute regime of the sultans and introduced a strict secular character to the state. With the aspiration to reach the level of civilized nations, the whole society is undergoing rapid transformations. Peace was consolidated concurrently with the realization of the internal reforms that shape present-day Turkey. . . . Thus, as a country totally satisfied with its ethnic and political borders emanating from treaties, Turkey has become the pillar of peace in the Near East.[3]

We Greeks, who have been in a constant state of disagreement and war with Turkey, have been the first ones to feel the effects of the profound changes in the successor of the defunct Ottoman

Empire. In the aftermath of the tragedy of Asia Minor, we obtained the possibility of reaching an understanding with Turkey, which had emerged from the war as a newly established nation state, and extended our hand of friendship, which Turkey took with sincerity.

The rapprochement, which came about when these two states sincerely initiated efforts to make peace, became an example for conflicting peoples, and it not only served the Hellenic and Turkish nations, but proved useful for peace in the whole of the Near East as well.

The person to whom we are indebted for this valuable contribution to peace, is Mustafa Kemal Pasha, President of the Turkish Republic.

As the Head of the Hellenic Government in the Year 1930, when a new era on the way to peace was opened in the Near East with the signing of the Greco-Turkish Pact, I have the Honor to nominate Mustafa Kemal Pasha for the Nobel Peace Prize.[3]

Few documents better describe the level of Turkish–Greek relations of the period.

Mustafa Kemal Atatürk's feelings for the Greek people and for Turkish–Greek friendship were also very warm. Atatürk sent a letter to the Greek Minister Yorgi Pezmazog lu who was on a bilateral visit to Turkey, in which he wrote:

The Hellenic and Turkish nations, which are nations harboring positive sentiments for one another, have brotherly feelings and have transformed obscurity into lucidity, have gathered here tonight. I am sure that the ever growing Hellenic-Turkish fraternity, will in the near future, dawn upon humanity, a bright and dazzling horizon. . .

The noble views expressed by Venizelos and Atatürk were reflections of the true feelings of Turkish and Greek nations. Thanks to the farsightedness of their leaders, Turkey and Greece had not only developed friendly relations but also jointly played a positive role in the field of regional cooperation. The two countries signed a friendship pact in September 1933. They further concluded in Athens on February 9, 1934, a Balkan Pact, together with Yugoslavia and Romania.

The successor of Atatürk and second president of Turkey Ismet Inönü also maintained friendly relations with Greece. During the Second World War, when Greece was invaded by Nazi German troops, some nongovernmental organizations established

in Turkey helped a number of Greeks to escape. The late George Papandreou, a former prime minister of Greece, was among them.

During and after the Second World War, Greece lived though some difficult periods. A great number of Greek citizens perished as a result of a civil war that lasted until 1949. The Greek economy was in ruins. Turkey was among the few countries that sent Greece food and humanitarian assistance. Both Turkey and Greece profited from the Marshall Plan after the war. The two countries joined NATO together on February 18, 1952, and became allies. Turkey's Prime Minister Adnan Menderes, who came to power in 1950, maintained friendly relations with Greece. A visit to Greece in 1952 by the new president of the Turkish Republic, Celal Bayar, was a landmark. He was warmly received in Athens by the Greek government and people. His name was given to a Turkish college in western Thrace. Bayar described Turkish–Greek relations as being "The best example of how two countries who mistakenly mistrusted each other for centuries have agreed upon a close and loyal collaboration as a result of recognition of the realities of life."[4]

On February 28, 1953, a second Balkan Pact was signed in Ankara by Turkey, Greece, and Yugoslavia. The following year another agreement was concluded between the same countries in Bled, which stipulated that the parties would regard an attack against any of them as an attack against all of them and would take all appropriate measures, including the use of force, to defeat this attack. Unfortunately, the Balkan Pact lasted only seven years and ended in 1960.

After thirty years of friendship, Turkish–Greek relations began to deteriorate. The most serious event, which damaged Turkish–Greek relations, was Greece's attempt to annex Cyprus. Armed attacks perpetrated by the National Organization of Cypriot Fighters (EOKA), a Greek Cypriot terrorist organization, began on the April 1, 1955. The climate of friendship among the people of both countries disappeared rapidly.

A coup d'état in Cyprus organized in July 1974 by the Greek junta aiming to annex Cyprus to Greece was met with a swift response from Turkey. When the diplomatic efforts failed, Turkey, using her rights of unilateral intervention provided by the London and Zurich agreements of 1960, sent troops to the Island to protect the Turkish Cypriots and to prevent enosis, the annexation of Cyprus to Greece. The Turkish intervention saved not only the Turkish Cypriots but also many Greek Cypriots from the oppression and violence of the former terrorists, who took over the Greek Cypriot leadership after the departure of Archibishop Makarios.

After these events, a number of old and new problems emerged that further aggravated the situation. These problems still dominate the agenda of Turkish–Greek relations and are summarized in the following section.

Continental Shelf Issue

The continental shelf dispute between Turkey and Greece is of particular importance because the settlement of a number of other issues is somehow dependent on the solution of the continental shelf question. Turkey argues that this issue should be solved through diplomatic negotiations between the two countries, whereas Greece wants to refer the matter to international adjudication. Greece applied unilaterally to the International Court of Justice on August 10, 1976, but failed to get a result. The court, in its decision of December 19, 1978, refrained from ruling in favor of Greece and took a decision of "non-jurisdiction."

Greece claims that all her islands, including those that are close to the Turkish mainland, should have the same rights over the continental shelf as the land mass of Turkey. This position is neither justified by international law nor accepted by Turkey. The international arbitration bodies, dealing with similar problems, usually give priority to the determination of the continental shelf areas between the mainlands before starting to study whether islands in the area should be granted some rights. The arbitration decision of 1977 on the French–English continental shelf dispute is a case in point.

The Law of the Sea Convention of 1982 stipulates that small islands that are not inhabitable cannot have a continental shelf. A number of treaties state that the islands closer to the mainland of a different state should be content with territorial waters only. The treaty signed between Australia and Papua New Guinea on December 18, 1978, is an example of this understanding.

Since the first diplomatic note sent by Turkey to Greece on February 27, 1974, Turkey has defended the idea that the continental shelf in the Aegean

should be delimited with an agreement to be concluded between Turkey and Greece. Turkey contends that the principle of natural extension should be the main reference to delimit the continental shelf. An important part of the Aegean continental shelf is the prolongation of the Anatolian peninsula. It is unthinkable that the existence of Greek islands in the Aegean prevents Turkey from having her fair share. A ruling of the International Court of Justice on the North Sea continental shelf, taken in 1969, confirms the rightfulness of the Turkish position.

Turkey also argues that the delimitation of the Aegean continental shelf should be done in accordance with the principle of equity. While delimiting the continental shelf, the special characteristics of the Aegean—such as the semi-closed nature of the sea, its natural resources, and the security requirements of Turkey and Greece—should be taken duly into consideration. In a diplomatic note delivered on February 27, 1974, Turkey rejected the principle of equidistance suggested by Greece. The decisions of the International Court of Justice on the North Sea in 1969, the Tunisia–Libya dispute in 1982, the United States–Canada dispute in 1974, and a Britain–France dispute in 1977 sustain Turkey's position.

Territorial Waters

When the Lausanne Treaty was signed in 1923, the territorial waters of both Turkey and Greece were three nautical miles. In 1936, Greece unilaterally enlarged her territorial waters to six miles. Later, when Turkey also extended her territorial waters to six miles, a new situation emerged. Since Greece possesses about three thousand islands in the Aegean, the extension of territorial waters to six miles altered the balance established by the Lausanne Treaty in favor of Greece. Today, the territorial waters of Greece represent 43.68 percent of the Aegean Sea, whereas Turkey's portion represents only 7.47 percent. The remaining 48.85 percent are international waters.

On several occasions, Greek governments claimed that they have the right to further extend Greece's territorial waters up to twelve miles. Greek politicians argue that the U.N. Law of the Sea Convention allows such an extension. Turkey, which is not a party to that convention, contends that Greece's intention of extending the territorial waters beyond the six-mile limit contravenes the principle set forth by Article 300 of the convention, which prohibits the abuse of rights. Turkey raised its objection during the Third Law of Sea Conference in Caracas, arguing that there is no general rule identifying the breadth of territorial waters that can be implemented in every sea in the world. Should the territorial waters be extended to twelve miles, the Aegean would practically become a Greek lake. It would then be practically impossible for Turkish vessels to reach the Mediterranean from Turkish harbors through international waters. It would not be possible for the Turkish air force to conduct exercises over the international waters. The result would be a total collapse of the Lausanne balance and would lead to the establishment of a Greek hegemony over the international waters and airspace of the Aegean. Furthermore, the extension of territorial waters in the Aegean would further complicate the continental shelf problem.

Finally, it should be noted that an extension of territorial waters would be valid only if other interested nations did not oppose the extension. This rule has been cited in the decision announced by the International Court of Justice regarding the fishing rights problem between Britain and Norway in 1951 and between Britain and Iceland in 1974.

For all these reasons, a unilateral extension of the territorial waters in the Aegean is unacceptable to Turkey and may cause irreparable damage to relations between the two countries.

Demilitarization of the Islands

According to the Treaty of Lausanne, as well as the Treaty of Paris of 1947, Greece is not allowed to station her armed forces and conduct military activities in Lemnos, Samothrace, the eastern Aegean islands, and the islands of the Dodecanesee. Greece, claiming that the Montreux Convention of 1936 abrogated the demilitarized status of the Greek islands imposed by the Treaty of Lausanne, started to deploy troops and conduct military activities on these islands, and even tried to include the island of Lemnos in NATO plans and exercises.

Article 12 of the Treaty of Lausanne clearly stipulates that the islands of Lemnos, Samothrace, Mytilene, Chios, Samos, and Nicaria were given to

Greece provided that they remained demilitarized. The content of this article was based on a decision made in 1914 by superpowers at the end of the Balkan Wars, with the consent of all parties involved. In addition to that, a convention annexed to the Treaty of Lausanne regulating the status of the Turkish Straits, stipulated that the islands of Lemnos and Samothrace would be subject to comprehensive demilitarization measures.

The Montreux Convention signed in 1936 permitted Turkey to militarize the Turkish Straits but not to change the demilitarized status of the Greek islands. In fact, the preamble of the Montreux Convention refers to Turkey's security interests only. No reference is made in the minutes of the Montreux Convention that this convention would replace relevant provisions stipulated in the Treaty of Lausanne. Therefore, the militarization of Greek islands cannot be legally justified.

There is no political justification for militarizing the islands either. A goodwill statement of the then Turkish foreign minister in 1936, often used by Greece to attempt to prove the validity of its position, cannot be regarded as a document replacing a formal agreement duly signed and ratified. Responding to a note sent by Turkey in 1969 referring to the illegally militarized Greek islands, Greece stated that no fortification had been built on the islands against the treaties and made particular reference to Lemnos.

The Greek initiative to include Lemnos in NATO plans was not accepted by the Alliance and created new disagreements between Turkey and Greece, which damaged NATO's interests as well. A number of NATO exercises in the Aegean have been cancelled as a result of these disputes.

Turkish–Greek problems began to be an issue in NATO, particularly during the reintegration of Greece into NATO's military structure. Greece had left NATO's military alliance in 1974 after the Turkish intervention in Cyprus. Turkey and other Allies, accepting a compromise solution proposed by NATO's supreme commander for Europe, General Bernard B. Rogers, approved the reintegration of Greece into NATO's military system on October 16, 1980. After joining the military structure, however, Greece claimed that the full implementation of the Rogers Plan was not possible. Greece's attitude created further tensions and additional problems. A number of NATO projects have been postponed or canceled. In short, Greece's insistence on militarizing the demilitarized islands created serious problems going beyond the Aegean and Turkish–Greek relations. It is still one of the unresolved issues.

THE QUESTION OF KARDAK ROCKS
AND THE "GRAY ZONE"

An unexpected problem was added to Turkish–Greek conflicts over the Aegean at the end of 1995. A ship named *Figen Akad* ran aground on the Kardak Rocks, situated less than four miles off Turkish shores and more than five miles from the closest Greek island. A sovereignty dispute over the uninhabited Kardak's twin rocks became an international problem. High-level diplomatic talks and an exchange of notes between the Turkish foreign ministry and Greek embassy in Ankara did not produce any results. Turkey suggested starting negotiations between the two countries to clarify the status of the rocks and, in the meantime, argued that the status quo ante be maintained. Greece did not accept this proposal. When the incident was reported to the public by the Greek press, both Turkish and Greek citizens reacted strongly and emotionally. Some inhabitants of a neighboring Greek island raised the Greek flag over the rocks. Turkish journalists reacted immediately and replaced it with a Turkish flag. Finally, the Greek government stationed soldiers on one of the rocks and again raised a Greek flag. The Turkish government, realizing that the Greeks would not withdraw their troops despite diplomatic pressures, sent Turkish SAS[5] commandos to the second rock, not yet occupied by the Greek forces in the early hours of January 31, 1996. Throughout that night intensive diplomatic contacts took place between Turkey, Greece and the United States. Then U.S. Assistant Secretary of State Richard Holbrook played an important role in negotiating a settlement. Greece finally agreed to withdraw its troops early in the morning and the status quo ante was restored. Turkey withdrew her troops also. Both countries promised not to send civilians or military personnel to the rocks until the problem was resolved.

Greece used the Kardak incident as a pretext to block EU financial assistance to Turkey, which was promised as compensation for the economic burden sustained by Turkey by entering into a customs union with the EU. The Greek government started a sizable diplomatic attack in all possible international fora, claiming that Turkey had invaded a Greek rock.

The reality was that Kardak Rocks, named Imia by the Greeks, had never been a Greek territory. No article of the Treaty of Lausanne established the sovereignty rights of the islands and the islets of the region or mentioned or defined Kardak Rocks. No article of the Paris Peace Treaty of 1947 referred to Kardak either. The arrangements made to transfer sovereignty rights to Italy in 1932 over Meis (Castellorizo) Island and adjacent islets do not cover Kardak either. It is true that some talks were conducted between Turkey and Italy at a technical level and some notes were exchanged between January 4, 1933, and January 8, 1937, but no formal agreement whatsoever was signed or ratified by the two countries and registered by the League of Nations, whereas an agreement on Meis in a similar case was duly signed, ratified, and registered with the League of Nations as required by international law.

Sovereignty rights over the Aegean Islands are referred to in the Articles 6, 12, 15, and 16 of the Treaty of Lausanne. Article 16 stipulates that "Turkey hereby renounces all rights and titles whatsoever over or respecting . . . the islands other than those over which her sovereignty is recognized by the said Treaty, the future of these territories and islands being or to be settled by the parties concerned." The reference in the Article 16 of the Treaty of Lausanne to "to be settled" indicates that all sovereignty problems have not been settled and some issues have to be discussed in the future, among the parties concerned. One should also note that in Article 16, Turkey agreed to cede sovereignty rights. In this article there is reference to "islands" only. In other related articles of the treaty, "islets" are mentioned as well. Therefore the absence of a reference to "islets" in Article 16 should be carefully noted.

According to international law, the secession of a particular territory to another country cannot be done unless the political will for that secession has been explicitly stated in an agreement. No bilateral agreement has been concluded between Turkey and Greece for the transfer of sovereignty rights over islets or the rocks in the area of Kardak.

In summary, since the maritime borders between Turkey and Greece are undefined, the Kardak problem, as well as issues related to other islands, islets, and rocks, collectively called the "gray zone" remain unresolved. The status of the islands, islets, and rocks that have not been clearly defined and regulated by international treaties should be negotiated between Turkey and Greece. As a matter of fact, Greece sent several verbal notes to the Turkish foreign ministry between 1955 and 1963 inviting Turkey to start talks regarding maritime borders between mainland Turkey and the eastern Aegean Islands. Greece has made diplomatic overtures aimed at finalizing inconclusive negotiations started between Turkey and Italy in 1932 about the delimitation of sea borders in the Dodecanese region, covering the Kardak Rocks area as well. This fact alone shows that the Greek side was aware that no maritime borders between Turkey and Greece were legally drawn in that region.

AIRSPACE

A Greek royal decree published in 1931 unilaterally extended Greece's airspace to ten miles, far beyond territorial waters. The existence of such a decree was first mentioned in a Greek aeronautical information publication issued in 1975. International law and the Chicago Convention of 1944 require that the breadth of national airspace correspond to the breadth of territorial sea. Besides violating international law, the Greek royal decree risked upsetting the balance created by the Treaty of Lausanne in Aegean airspace. Turkey has not accepted this fait accompli. Greece's claims over ten miles of airspace are among the causes of the decades-long disputes between Turkey and Greece. Since Turkey has not recognized the Greek ten-mile airspace in the Aegean, Turkish military aircraft continue to fly over the international waters up to the six-mile limit of the territorial waters of Greece. The Greek government continues to protest all Turkish flights within ten miles. Greek aircraft often engage in dogfights with the Turkish aircraft, which, on some occasions, result in fatal air crashes.

Besides the disputes over the airspace, another conflicting issue emerged as a result of unfair distribution of responsibility areas for air control services in the Aegean. In the early 1950s the International Civil Aviation Organisation (ICAO) gave Greece a much larger zone of responsibility than Turkey. Greece wanted to use this factual and technical situation to gain political advantages. Greek governments attempted to use the limits of the Flight Information Region (FIR) as a borderline of Greek sovereignty. This has created further tensions between the two countries.

Greece maintains that all issues related to the Aegean are internal matters over which Greece alone has authority, with the exception of the continental shelf. Other issues do not have an international aspect, which needs to be discussed with Turkey. Greece holds that the only way to solve the continental shelf issue is to bring the matter to the International Court of Justice. In reality, extensive talks on the continental shelf were held in the late 1970s between the undersecretaries of the ministries of foreign affairs of both sides. Several proposals have been discussed, but no agreement has been reached. Recently, the undersecretaries of the two countries have started to discuss this matter again, but so far no concrete result has been obtained.

THE TURKISH MINORITY IN WESTERN THRACE

Ethnic Turks have resided in western Thrace since at least the fifteenth century. The Treaty of Lausanne regulates the rights and privileges of the Turkish minority in Greece and the Greek minority in Turkey in the fields of religious, civil, and cultural rights and recognizes their equality before the law. Although in the early 1950s the Greek government accepted the use of the words *Turk* or *Turkish* to describe the minority rather than *Muslim*, the Greek position changed afterward, and subsequent Greek governments began to persecute and ban organizations and individuals that called themselves "Turkish." A Helsinki Watch report describes the situation in western Thrace as follows:

> The very existence of a Turkish Minority is officially denied in Greece. Indeed any allusion to it is punishable by law. The post office refuses to accept written communications that contain any reference to the

Turkish identity of the minority. Government leaders, even the Parliament, turn down petitions on behalf of the minority when addressed in the name of the "Turkish" Minority.

Greek courts also have outlawed the use of the term "Turkish Minority." In 1988, the Greek High Court upheld a 1986 decision by the Court of Appeals of Thrace shutting down the Turkish Teachers Union of Western Thrace. The Court held that the use of the word "Turkish" to describe Greek Moslems endangered public order. As a result of the High Court's decision, most Turkish associations have remained closed.[6]

In 1923, at the time of the Lausanne Conference, the number of Turkish people in western Thrace was 129,120, representing 68 percent of the total population of the area. The Turks possessed 84 percent of the land. Today, the Turkish population of the region is about 150,000 and represents only 35 percent of the region's total population. By the early 1990s, the Turkish minority held much less than 40 percent of western Thrace's land due mainly to the expropriation of land throughout many decades of public works.

Greece has pursued a policy of reducing the population of the Turkish minority. To achieve this end, the law of Greek citizenship, adopted in 1955, contained discriminatory measures against the Turkish minority. Article 19 of this law reads as follows:

If a person of non-Greek origin is to depart from Greece with the intention of not returning, it can be judged that the said person has lost Greek citizenship. This provision is also applicable to persons of non-Greek origin, born and residing abroad. It can be declared that those who live abroad, who are under age and whose parents alive have lost his/her/their Greek citizenship, have also lost their Greek citizenship. Based on the resolution adopted by the Citizenship Council, the Interior Ministry judges on this subject.[7]

This article differentiates Greek citizens according to their ethnic origins. Such an approach is a clear violation of the Universal Declaration of Human Rights and of U.N. and Council of Europe instruments related to human rights. The Greek parliament finally abrogated Article 19 on June 11, 1998, But from 1955 to 1998 approximately 60,000 Turks lost their citizenship as a result of the enforcement of the above article. Practically none of

them has been allowed to regain Greek citizenship after the abrogation of the article. Because of this and other discriminatory measures, the Turkish minority of Greece has not increased in the way it should have naturally increased. Given an annual 2 percent growth rate, the Turkish minority, using 1951 census figures as a base, would have been expected to number close to 300,000 today. The actual figure is about half of that.

A large part of western Trace, bordering Bulgaria, where tens of thousands of Turks are living, was declared a "forbidden military zone" for many decades. Entry to and exit from this zone was subjected to strict formalities and for many years no foreigners, including diplomats and journalist, were allowed to enter this zone. Former Greek Minister of National Defense Gerasimos Arsenis announced that this restriction ended in 1995.

Furthermore, since western Thrace was declared a border region in a decree dated 1938, selling or purchasing immovable property in this area requires special permission of the authorities. This has created further hardships for the Turkish minority.

By the mid-1980s, these discriminatory practices sparked a civil rights movement by members of the Turkish minority, led by the late Dr. Sadik Ahmet, a former parliamentarian and communal leader. In January 1990, Dr. Ahmet was found guilty of disrupting public peace under Article 192 of the Greek Penal Code. In October 1989, while campaigning for parliament, he had distributed leaflets that spoke about the "Turks," "Turkish Muslims," and the "Turkish Muslim minority of Western Thrace." Dr. Ahmet was imprisoned from January to March 1990. On February 15, 1991, the Court of Cassation rejected the appeal of Dr. Ahmet and ruled that "there was no Turkish minority in Western Thrace." The European Commission of Human Rights declared in April 1995 that Greece had violated Dr. Ahmet's right of free expression under Article 10 of the European Convention on Human Rights.

In the field of education, as well, Turks continue to face serious restrictions. There are 230 minority primary schools with 8,500 students; two minority junior high schools with 200 students; two minority senior high schools with approximately 400 students; and two Muslim religious schools (*Medrese*) with 200 students. The Greek authorities have not properly implemented the cultural agreements signed with Turkey in 1951 and 1968. There are more than a thousand children graduating every year from the primary minority schools of Xanthi (Iskeçe) and Komotini (Gümülcine). Of these, only 150 in Komotini and 100 in Xanti are allowed to attend minority high schools. Very few go to Greek high schools. Most other students stop their education. The nine years of mandatory education all children in Greece are required to attend is not practically available to Turkish children.

The Greek authorities limit to sixteen the number of Turkish teachers trained in Turkey, whereas this number was thirty-five in 1955. Schools are overcrowded and most of the other teachers do not have proper Turkish language training. Textbooks are decades out of date.

The Treaty of Athens of 1913, which became part of the Greek legal system, permitted Turks to elect their religious leaders (mufti). However, Greece later abrogated this act. The Treaty of Lausanne granted the Turkish minority the right to organize and conduct religious affairs free from government interference. For many decades, however, Greece has directly appointed muftis—against the wishes of the overwhelming majority of ethnic Turks. Law No. 1920 legalized this policy in December 1990. Also in 1990, the Turkish community held unofficial elections for muftis and elected Mehmet Emin Aga in Xanthi and Ibrahim Serif in Komotini. Both were tried by Greek Courts and condemned on several occasions on the grounds that they tried to perform their religious duties "illegally."

Even efforts of the Turks' religious charity organization, Vakiflar, have been thwarted. Violation of the independent Vakiflar first began in 1967, after the colonels seized power in Athens. Even after the return to civilian rule, the situation did not change. Law No. 1091 of November 12, 1980, further restricts the activities of Vakiflar and the Turkish minority's right to administer them. A presidential decree of January 3, 1991, allows the state to appoint members of Vakiflar's managing boards.

Comprehensive reports published by Helsinki Watch after 1990 describe extensively the hardships suffered by the Turkish minority and criticize the Greek government.

Thus, despite the rights and privileges granted by the Treaty of Lausanne, Greek citizens of Turkish origin have suffered a number of difficulties in maintaining their citizenship, property rights, and access to education for their children.

TURKISH–GREEK RELATIONS WITHIN THE FRAMEWORK OF THE EUROPEAN UNION

Turkey and Greece simultaneously signed association agreements with the European Economic Community in 1963. The European Union treated both countries fairly and equally in the following years. In the mid-1970s, when Greece applied for full membership, the Union tried to maintain a fair position with Turkey. On January 29, 1976, in its report about Greece's eligibility for full membership, the EU Commission stated the following:

> The membership perspective of Greece will highlight the problems between this country and Turkey. Turkey is also an associated member to the Union and the declared goal of this association is Turkey's full membership. The Union is not a party to the conflicts between Turkey and Greece and should not be party to them. Until today the balance in the relations of the Union with Turkey and Greece was determined by the association status that both countries posses on equal footing and each of these countries have, as the ultimate goal, the possibility to become a full member albeit with different calendars. The membership perspective of Greece brings unavoidably a new element to this balance. . .The Commission believes that the examination of the Greek membership application should not affect the relations between Turkey and the Union and that special measures should be taken to concretize its decision that the rights granted to Turkey by the Association Agreement should not be modified.[8]

However, in practice the full EU membership granted to Greece in 1980 had negative effects on Turkey–EU relations. One of the first actions of Greece in the early 1980s was to block the implementation of the Fourth Financial Assistance Protocol of the EU to Turkey. As a consequence, the EU has failed to pay to Turkey the €600 million promised by this protocol. In the beginning of 1996, Greece used the Kardak crisis as a pretext to block EU assistance to Turkey aimed at compensating Turkey for the losses it would face as a result of the customs union. Turkey was deprived, for several years, of any meaningful assistance from the EU due to this negative attitude of Greece.

When the European Council met in Helsinki in December 1999, attending heads of state and governments made a formal decision about Turkey's candidacy for full membership. In paragraph 4 of their decision the following indirect reference to Turkish–Greek relations was made:

> In this respect the European Council stresses the principle of peaceful settlement of disputes in accordance with the United Nations Charter and urges candidate states to make every effort to resolve any outstanding border disputes and other related issues. Failing this, they should within a reasonable time bring the dispute to the International Court of Justice. The European Council will review the situation relating to any outstanding disputes, in particular concerning the repercussions on the accession process in order to promote their settlement through the International Court of Justice, at the latest by the end of 2004.[9]

Before the end of the meeting, the Finnish prime minister and EU term president, Paavo Lipponen, sent a letter dated December 10, 1999 to Turkish Prime Minister Bülent Ecevit explaining the meaning of this reference, as follows:

> Today, the European Union has set out on a new course in its relations with the Republic of Turkey. I am very pleased to inform you officially on our unanimous decision to confer Turkey the status of Candidate State, on the same footing as any other candidate.
> When, in the European Council, we discussed the draft conclusions annexed to this letter, I said, without being challenged, that in Para. 12 of the conclusions there was no new criteria added to those of Copenhagen and that the reference to Para. 4 and 9 (a) was not in relation with the criteria for accession but only to the political dialogue. The accession partnership will be drawn up on the basis of today's Council decisions.
> In Para. 4 the date of 2004 is not a deadline for the settlement of disputes through the ICJ but the date at which the European Council will review the situation relating to any outstanding disputes.
> Regarding Cyprus, a political settlement remains the aim of the EU. Concerning the accession of Cyprus, all relevant factors will be taken into account when the Council takes the decision."

Finally, Greece used its EU membership rights to make Turkey's full membership conditional to the prior membership of Cyprus. The Greek prime minister stated that the membership of Turkey would pass from the Green Line in Cyprus, which is the border dividing Turkish and Greek areas, and that Greece would veto the membership application process of all candidate countries if the EU does not accept Greek Cypriot membership, even if no solution has been reached in the Cyprus conflict.

RECENT DEVELOPMENTS

Problems spanning the last four decades of the twentieth century damaged Turkish–Greek relations. Some of these problems could have been solved through diplomatic negotiations. Instead, Greece chose to use confrontation instead of reconciliation. In addition, it used a massive propaganda campaign to blame Turkey for Turkish–Greek disputes in virtually all international organizations and media.

According to Greek defense doctrine devised during the Cold War years, the threat to Greece no longer comes from the north but from Turkey. This perception has not changed, despite the new climate of rapprochement between the two sides following the end of the Cold War.

During this period, several politicians and high-ranking officials both in Turkey and Greece thought that the absence of dialogue would further deteriorate relations between the two countries. Turkey made some gestures to normalize relations. The late president of Turkey, Turgut Özal, met with then Greek prime minister Andreas Papandreou on a number of occasions at international conferences and tried to establish a new relationship through personal contact. Although no concrete results emerged from these talks, at least the need to normalize relations was recognized.

In 1996, the then deputy foreign minister, Georges Papandreou, suggested informal talks with his Turkish counterpart, the author of this paper and then undersecretary of the Turkish Foreign Ministry. We met several times in different European capitals and tried to create a new avenue, which might lead to a better understanding between the two countries. As a result of these talks,

Papandreou and I agreed, on an ad hoc basis, to establish a group of Turkish–Greek "wise men" who would be in charge of studying existing problems and making unbinding proposals to their respective governments. Turkey and Greece later elected two eminent experts each. Hans van Mierlo, foreign minister of the Netherlands and the EU term president, invited a group of wise men to an opening meeting in The Hague. The Greek side did not accept this proposal and suggested that the experts should exchange written opinions instead of meeting. Some letters were exchanged, but no meetings took place. This was a lost opportunity.

Another factor that deteriorated Turkish–Greek relations toward the end of the 1990s was the support that Kurdish terrorist leader Abdullah Öcalan received from some circles in Greece. News that Öcalan hid in the Greek Embassy in Nairobi before being arrested created strong reactions in Turkey and resulted in the resignation of some ministers and high-ranking government officials in Athens. During his trial, Öcalan accused Greece of being involved in helping the Kurdistan Workers Party (PKK) in its terrorist activities waged against Turkey, which infuriated the Turkish public.

Turkish Foreign Minister Ismail Cem, in a letter he sent to Greek Foreign Minister Georges Papandreou on May 24, 1999, referred to the links between some groups in Greece and a terrorist organization attacking Turkey. He proposed signing an agreement of cooperation between the two countries against terrorism. In a letter dated June 25, 1999, Papandreou accepted this proposal and suggested initiating talks between Turkey and Greece regarding tourism, environment, culture, trade, and regional cooperation. The two ministers met in New York on June 30, 1999, and six mixed groups were established.

The severe earthquake that caused the death of about 20,000 people in August 1999 in Turkey and the subsequent earthquake in Athens created sympathy and a sense of rapprochement between Turkish and Greek people. This new and positive climate permitted the two governments to further deepen their contacts. The two ministers decided to start talks, bilaterally and within the framework of NATO, to adopt confidence-building measures. Both sides decided to organize a ministerial meeting each year, exploratory talks between the undersecretaries of the foreign ministries, regular political consultations between political directors, and working group meetings. Since then, twenty-five agreements have been signed on several areas of potential cooperation, but no tangible results have been achieved so far on the major issues. On confidence building, no concrete achievement has been reached besides the confirmation of what has been agreed between the two countries in 1988. No measure has yet been adopted to prevent tensions or dogfights between Turkish and Greek airmen over the Aegean. At the same time, Greece has denied overflight rights to Turkish aircraft assigned to the NATO mission in Kosovo and did not allow Turkish troops to use Thessalonika harbor on their way to Kosovo.

In 2004, formal and informal visits of prime ministers and several exchanges of nice words and good intentions occurred, but no concrete results have been obtained. In the meantime, Greece has secured the full membership of Greek Cypriots to the European Union without any political cost. The balance of power between the two countries was thus further tilted in favor of the Greek side.

CONCLUSION

The way to find concrete and lasting solutions to the existing Turkish–Greek problems is to intensify already existing mechanisms of dialogue covering not only secondary issues but also the real problems, taking into account the national interests of both countries and the balance established by the Treaty of Lausanne. Furthermore, it should be understood that no international pressure or propaganda using foreign governments or lobbies abroad will lead to viable solutions. Early membership of Turkey to the EU may facilitate the solution of a number of problems. Until then, the two sides should refrain from any action, statement, or fait accompli that might make the resolution of existing problems even more difficult. The Turkish and Greek press have an important role to play in this regard. Emotional approaches, provoking the feelings of the people against each other, may result in irreparable damage.

The Turkish minority in Greece and the Greek minority in Istanbul should be treated according to international commitments and standards. Religious leaders should refrain from any action or statement that could damage friendly relations between the two countries. The Greek government should reconsider its basic strategic concepts and stop considering Turkey as a threat. Both governments should revise schoolbooks and eliminate any unfriendly references about each other. Both Turkish and Greek diasporas should stop operating as instruments of destruction for the interests of the other side. Cooperation, mutual understanding, and friendship should replace confrontation. A culture of reconciliation should be developed together. Each segment of Turkish and Greek society has an important role to play in the establishment of a new climate of trust and cooperation.

ENDNOTES

1. Justin McCarthy, *Death and Exile: The Ethnic Cleansing of Ottoman Muslims 1821–1922,* Darwin Press, 1996, pp. 339.
2. Richard N. Coudenhove-Kalergi, *Crusade for Pan-Europa. Autobiography of a Man and a Movement,* Putnam Press, New York, 1943, Chapter 12, pp. 126–127.
3. The Daily *Milliyet,* 28 October 1998.
4. Tözün Bahçeli, *Greek-Turkish Relations since 1955,* Boulder: Western Press, 1990, p. 16
5. SAS commandos stand for "Underwater Defence" in Turkish.
6. A Helsinki Watch Report, *Destroying Ethnic Identity: The Turks of Greece.* August 1990, pp. 18–20.
7. Helsinki Watch Report, *Greece: The Turks of Western Thrace,* January 1999, Vol. 11, No. 1
8. Presidency Conclusions, Helsinki European Council, 10 and 11 December 1999, Available on http://www.consilium.europa.eu/uedocs/cmsUpload/Helsinki%20European%20Council-Presidency%20conclusions.pdf
9. Presidency Conclusions, Helsinki European Council, 10 and 11 December 1999, Available on http://www.consilium.europa.eu/uedocs/cmsUpload/Helsinki%20European%20Council-Presidency%20conclusions.pdf

ABOUT THE AUTHOR

Onur Öymen is a retired diplomat from Turkey. Born in Istanbul, Öymen graduated from Galatasaray Lycee and the Political Sciences Faculty of Ankara University, where he also completed his Ph.D. He speaks English, French, German, and Spanish. Öymen began his career with Turkey's Ministry of Foreign Affairs. Following his military service, he worked with NATO and the Council of Europe during the 1960s. During the 1970s, he was head of policy planning, a counselor for the Turkish Embassy in Nicosia, and a special advisor to the minister for foreign affairs. Öymen was a counselor in the Turkish Embassy in Prague and, later, Madrid. He served as Turkey's ambassador to Denmark in 1988 and ambassador to Germany in 1990. He was undersecretary of the Ministry of Foreign Affairs and permanent representative to NATO.

During his career, Öymen has received many awards. In 1995 he was chosen Civil Servant of the Year by *Nokta* magazine. The Turkish Industrialists' and Businessmen's Foundation named him Diplomat of the Year in 1995, 1996, and 1997. In 1997, he won the Abdi Ipekçi Peace Award, an honor bestowed by the Turkish daily *Milliyet.*

After retiring in 2002, Öymen entered politics and was elected a member of Parliament and was chosen vice president of CHP in 2003.

His publications include "Türkiye'nin Gücü" or "Turkish Challenge" (1998), which has been translated into English and German, and "Gelecegi Yakalamak: Küresellesme ve Devlet Reformu" (2000) and "Silahsiz Savas: Bir Mücadele Sanati Olarak Diplomasi" (2002).

Öymen is married and has two children.

9

Northern Ireland

The conflict in Northern Ireland is one of Europe's most violent conflicts since World War II. Ireland, the third-largest island in Europe, is composed of the Republic of Ireland, which covers five-sixths of the island (south, east, west, and northwest), and Northen Ireland which covers the northeastern sixth of the island that still belongs to the United Kingdom. Northern Ireland has been characterized by systematic social segregation between the "Nationalists" or "Republicans," the Catholic minority (44 percent), who defend the formation of an independent country, and the "Unionists" or "Loyalists," the Protestant majority (53 percent), who want to remain part of the United Kingdom.

The conflict is rooted in the seventeenth century, when the British promoted Protestant settlements in the northeastern corner of the predominantly Catholic country. In the nineteenth century, the Irish independence movement intensified and hardened, fueled by the Irish nationalism of the Catholic community. The island was finally partitioned in 1921, dividing the Protestant and Catholic communities into two camps with two parliaments: all the provinces of Ireland, except the six provinces of the north, were united in a state subject to the British crown in exchange for the independence of the remainder of Ireland.

This partition was rejected by the Catholic minority in the north and the majority of the Irish population in the south. For Irish Catholics, this was cause for a nationalist fight for self-determination, as they referred back to what they regarded as the historical integrity of the island. However, Protestants perceived the conflict in terms of security. They were interested in preserving unity with Great Britain and resisting the perceived threat of a united Ireland. In 1949, Catholics in the south of Ireland unilaterally proclaimed independence and took the official name of Republic of Ireland, whereas Northern Ireland, mainly Protestant, continued to be attached to Great Britain.

Nevertheless, the tensions could not be controlled. The Irish Republican Army (IRA), the military branch of the Sinn Fein political party, turned its activities against the British army. A paramilitary group was formed to defend the interests of the Protestant population. The Catholics, who felt treated like second-class citizens, fought to have their rights respected and tried to reverse the political order. Armed hostilities between Catholics and Protestants—named "the troubles"—intensified during the late 1960s between Irish Nationalists and the British Unionists. Their claims culminated at the end of 1960. In 1968, a campaign calling for respect of the civil laws was also launched by the Catholic community.

In 1998, after decades of violence and unsuccessful reconciliation attempts, a peace settlement was reached. It was known as the Good Friday Agreement and was signed by Northern Ireland and the British and Irish governments and is now being implemented. The Good Friday agreement gave the province political autonomy under an elected assembly with proportional representation for the Catholic minority and Protestant majority. The assembly will guarantee power sharing between the communities.

In his essay "The Politics of Peace and War in Northern Ireland," Sean Byrne tries to capture the brittleness of the process of peace signed in Northern Ireland in 1998. He explains initially the multiple causes at the origin of the conflict by exploring the historical, religious, demographic, psychocultural, economic, and political context of that time. He centers on the phenomenon of identity allegiances of the Protestants and the Catholics, fueled with the fear

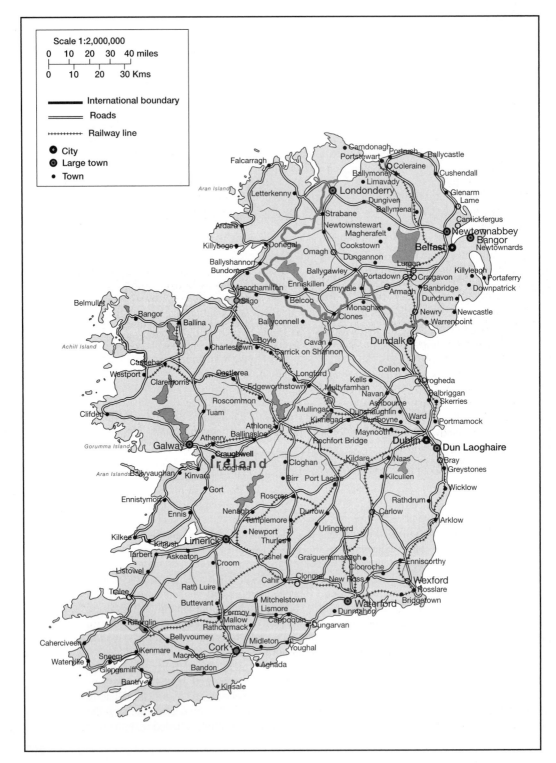

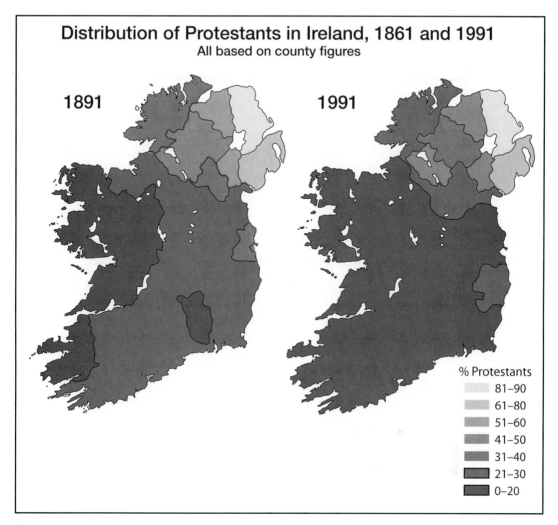

Distribution of Protestants in Ireland, 1861 and 1991
All based on county figures

1891

1991

% Protestants
- 81–90
- 61–80
- 51–60
- 41–50
- 31–40
- 21–30
- 0–20

Source: http://www.wesleyjohnston.com/users/ireland/maps/island_protestants_1861_1991.gif

of seeing their political power, economic interests, and religious freedom threatened by the opposing community. Byrne also studies the impact of past traumas, often marked by a skewed perception of the "other," which maintains mistrust between the various actors of the two communities: "Identity-based group conflict is at the very heart of the Northern Ireland conflict." Then the author examines the mitigated results of a series of political initiatives launched by the United States and the European Union and the British and Irish governments to solve the conflict and to support social reconciliation, before coming to an analysis of the agreements signed for disarmament by the IRA in 1998, which claimed to guarantee the pacification of the situation in Northern Ireland. The author evaluates different prospects of pacification and mentions the challenges of sociopolicies, when attempting to address the question fully.

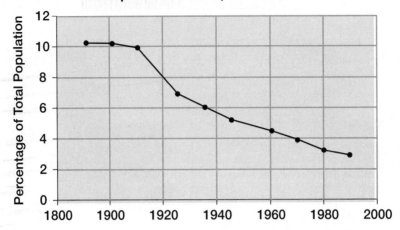

The Declining Protestant Population in the Republic of Ireland, 1891 to 1991

Note: For the period before 1921, these figures are for the twenty-six counties that later constituted the Republic of Ireland.

Source: http://www.wesleyjohnston.com/users/ireland/charts/declining_prot_1891_1991.gif

Percentages

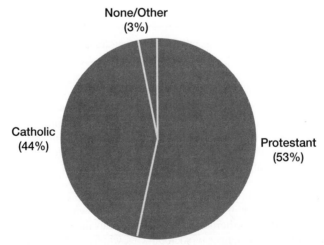

None/Other (3%)

Catholic (44%)

Protestant (53%)

Source: http://www.statistics.gov.uk/cci/nugget.asp?id=980

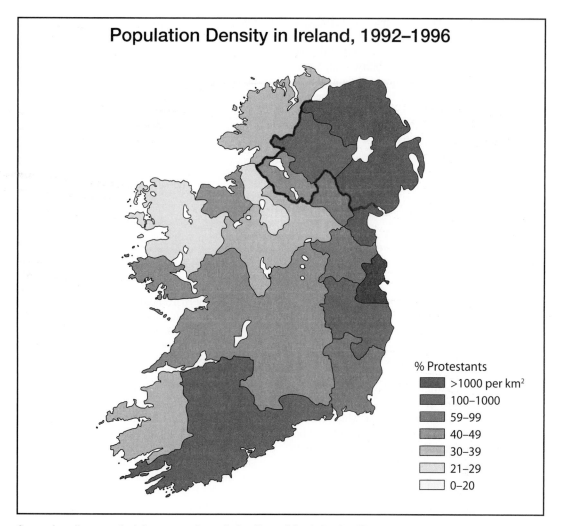

Population Density in Ireland, 1992–1996

% Protestants

■ >1000 per km²
■ 100–1000
■ 59–99
■ 40–49
■ 30–39
■ 21–29
□ 0–20

Source: http://www.wesleyjohnston.com/users/ireland/maps/island_density.gif

"The Role of Constructive, Transcultural Storytelling in Ethnopolitical Transformation in Northern Ireland" by Jessica Senehi explores the essential role of storytelling on identity formation and constructive and destructive narrations, while it is based on the sociocultural experiment of Northern Ireland. The essay also explains how the story-based approaches to peacemaking and peace-building may get at some of the key dilemmas in post-conflict peacemaking and peace-building by developing shared identities and mutual understanding. This essay explains initially the concept of storytelling and examines the diversity of the forms that it takes. Senehi analyzes the conditions supporting the positive or negative transformation of ethnic conflicts and highlights the differences of perceptions characterizing the historical memories of the two communities.

The author also evaluates the effectiveness of this means of promotion on mutual cultural understanding, the construction of communities, the evolution of intercommunal life on the construction of a social peace: "In constructive storytelling, facilitators and participants establish an environment of safety, respect, openness, and inclusion." The resolution of conflict by the use of storytelling within the context of the end of the conflict underlines the importance of ensuring storytelling's accessibility to all levels of society in order to allow the development of knowledge in both camps, while paying heed to the ignored voices and reducing social inequalities. The author also notices the intellectual and material accessibility of this practice, which encourages mutual comprehension and development of shared knowledge. The author stresses the importance of "learning lessons" for the future so that this process brings results in the reconciliation of the communities.

The Politics of Peace and War in Northern Ireland

Sean Byrne

INTRODUCTION

Much has been written about the Northern Ireland conflict, which embodies two distinct ethnic communities locked in a historic fatal embrace. For thirty years over three thousand people have perished in the political violence that has torn apart the fabric of the community there.[1] The protracted conflict in Northern Ireland was shaped by the 1601 Protestant Plantation of Ulster, which created a bipolar society in which loyal Protestants felt besieged by an indigenous disloyal Catholic community who since 1178 had fought a continuous guerrilla war with the British monarchy.[2] With the 1920 Partition of Ireland, a devolved Protestant state took on a sectarian nature, discriminating against its Catholic minority in employment, housing, and positions of economic and political power.[3]

Catholics became reenergized politically in the late 1960s, modeling their civil rights association on that of Dr. Martin Luther King in the United States. Civil strife erupted when Loyalists attacked civil rights marchers, pogromed Catholics from mixed neighborhoods, and created a state of anarchy in Northern Ireland.[4] Violence and counterviolence brought direct rule and direct British involvement in the conflict and ignited the long war with the Provisional Irish Republican Army (PIRA).[5]

The failure of a number of efforts to prod the political elites to collaborate on a power-sharing arrangement promulgated efforts by the British and Irish governments in the early 1990s to culti-

vate the middle ground to develop a pluralist third pillar in Northern Ireland's society.[6] This strategy combined with international pressure, especially the primary mediation role of the United States, resulted in the 1998 Good Friday Agreement (GFA) that broke the political deadlock, brought the Republican and Loyalist paramilitaries in from the cold, and created the prospects for long-term accommodation between both communities.[7] However, a fragile frosty peace has taken root over the past five years as key political issues need to be resolved to build a lasting peace in Northern Ireland.

This chapter provides a historical background of the conflict and outlines perceived threats to each group's identity and way of life. Second, past glories and traumas are discussed within the context of the current peace process and of each community's perceptions of the causes of the conflict. Third, efforts to resolve the conflict are highlighted. Fourth, the actions and policies of both governments and other external third parties, such as the United States and the European Union (EU), to resolve the conflict are addressed. Finally, some brief tentative conclusions are drawn about the future of the conflict.

HISTORICAL BACKGROUND

The underlying cause of the conflict between Unionist Protestants and Nationalist Catholics is whether Northern Ireland is part of Britain or part of the Republic of Ireland, as well as how this important political issue is tied to ethnonational identities.[8] In 1920, Ireland was partitioned by the Government of Ireland Act to end the war with Britain, leaving a large minority of Nationalist Catholics within Northern Ireland. The legitimacy of the state of Northern Ireland encouraged some populist Unionist Protestant politicians to discriminate against the minority Nationalist Catholic community in housing, education, employment, and voting so that the Northern Ireland state took on a sectarian nature.[9] Deliberate discrimination against Nationalist Catholics by Unionist Protestants, who wished to keep Northern Ireland British, acted as a catalyst during the late 1960s for the Northern Ireland Civil Rights Association (NICRA).[10]

NICRA protests for civil rights were met with resistance from the Northern Ireland state, Loyalist Protestant pogroms, and PIRA violence.[11] The British army was sent onto the streets of Belfast and Derry to keep law and order but ended up in a thirty-year war with the PIRA.[12] However, the Northern Ireland conflict is not only about political and economic issues; it is also about psychocultural issues, history, religion, and demographics.[13] Sectarianism and voluntary segregation have created two socially distanced communities.

In Northern Ireland, a small middle ground made up of the Alliance Party and the Women's Coalition provides the balance between Protestants and Catholics. The principal Unionist Protestant constitutional parties, the Official Unionist Party (OUP), and the Democratic Unionist Party (DUP) represent mainstream and working class political opinion. Unionist Protestants give their allegiance to the maintenance of the union between Northern Ireland and the United Kingdom. Some working-class Loyalist Protestants in the Ulster Volunteer Force (UVF) and the Ulster Defense Association (UDA) believe that they have a right to use political violence to keep Northern Ireland part of Britain.[14] Loyalists are loyal to the Queen of England (the Queen) but not to the Queen's government. The Progressive Unionist Party (PUP) and the now defunct Ulster Democratic Party (UDP) represent this shade of political opinion.

Within the Catholic Nationalist community, middle-class and working-class voters tend to vote for either the Social Democratic and Labour Party (SDLP) or Sinn Fein (SF), which represents the political interests of the PIRA. Nationalists wish to eradicate the border between Northern Ireland and the Irish Republic. The Nationalist SDLP's goals are centered on Irish unity based on the consent of a majority of the people of Northern Ireland. Republican SF, the political wing of the PIRA, wants to end the British presence in Ireland and create a united thirty-two county socialist Republic.[15]

Paul Bew and Henry Patterson have argued that from 1972 to 1985 British policy toward Northern Ireland was one of bungles, mistakes, and miscalculations.[16] The British government continually reacted to the situation in a mode of crisis management rather than creating a political process that represented the context of the conflict.[17] The Irish diaspora in the United States, as well as Libya, channeled arms and monies to Republicans in Northern Ireland to continue the armed struggle to end British rule.[18] At the same time, the South African Defense Force (SADF), defending apartheid South Africa, funded various Loyalist paramilitary organizations fighting to keep Northern Ireland British, thus preventing any political examples of radical groups overthrowing government for the African National Congress (ANC).[19] In addition, the ANC and the PIRA had strong political links during this period.[20]

In Northern Ireland, Britain is the representative of the majority of Unionist Protestant interests, while the Irish government guarantees the political interests of the Nationalist Catholics. From the 1985 Anglo Irish Agreement (AIA) onward, both external ethno-guarantors—the British and Irish governments—have successfully worked together to impose a "coercive consociational" power-sharing government on their internal co-nationals—Unionist Protestants and Nationalist Catholics—so that both communities have to work together to find a resolution.[21] Unionist Protestants now distrust their external ethno-guarantor, the British government, which is working closely with the Irish government to impose a political solution. They fear being pushed into a united Ireland and are, therefore, a community under siege.[22] In general, Nationalist Catholics trust their external ethno-guarantor, the Irish government, and feel that the 1998 GFA has promised them political parity with Unionist Protestants and a strong voice for the future prospects of Irish unity.[23] Cooperation between both governments that resulted in the GFA brought about a cold peace because key issues in the dispute, such as decommissioning of weapons, were not resolved until the historic July 28, 2005, PIRA declaration to dump its arms.[24] Political pressure is now on Loyalists to follow suit.

PERCEIVED THREATS TO WAY OF LIFE

Part of what has driven and continues to drive the conflict in Northern Ireland is the threats that both the Catholic and Protestant communities each perceive. These threats concern identity, political power, religious freedom, fear of genocide, access to economic resources, majority/minority dichotomy, and way of life as part of an interconnection of social forces that shape and drive the conflict.[25]

The Protestant Community

Protestants of Ulster believe that two distinct peoples inhabit Northern Ireland: the Protestants and the Catholics. The core of the problem is the refusal of the Catholics to recognize that Protestants have the right to remain loyal British subjects. Protestants remain loyal to the Queen, even when the British government is an unreliable ally who is willing to sell out their birthright and force them into a Catholic-dominated, united Ireland.[26] They believe the British government gives in to the Catholics and their allies, the PIRA, and the government of the Republic of Ireland. Protestants see themselves as being different from the Catholics in the Republic of Ireland and do not want to be forced into a Rome-dominated united Ireland in which they will be a minority dominated by priests. Protestants are under siege from the Ulster Catholic fifth column, which works hand in hand with the PIRA, the Catholic hierarchy, and the Irish government.[27] The Protestants' position is that they will not "give an inch," hence the political slogan "No Surrender!"

Protestants feel that Northern Ireland is far better off as part of the United Kingdom than it would be as part of a united Ireland. The "Celtic Tiger" in the south is perceived as having a weak economy that is kept from collapsing by a high emigration rate of young people to Britain and other countries. Protestants feel they have excellent British social services, housing, education, and regional economic support, while the Irish government has a huge economic debt around its neck.[28] Protestants do not want to be forced to join a bankrupt united Ireland, with inequality in income and regressive social mobility. Proud Protestants of Ulster are psychologically bound to Britain with bonds of blood, history, and loyalty that cannot be bartered away by any British government.[29] They have an allegiance to the Queen, whom they fought and died for in World Wars I and II. Protestants see themselves as loyal British subjects who deserve to keep their British nationality and travel on British passports. The Protestants of Northern Ireland will not give in to PIRA campaigns of terrorism intended to force them against their will to give up their British citizenship.[30]

Protestants feel that the Catholic Church in the Republic of Ireland is authoritarian and coercive because it is in control of education, the constitution, divorce, and the Irish way of life. If a Protestant marries a Catholic, he or she has to bring the children up Catholic, not Protestant. In the past, the Irish Constitution was full of Catholic moral values, traditions, and social teachings. Conservative Protestants such as the Reverend Dr. Ian Paisley believe that Irish politicians from the south are controlled by the Vatican. Protestants are suspicious of the power and intentions of the Catholic hierarchy because they perceive that Catholic priests control the minds and attitudes of Catholic people.[31] Protestants do not want their children to have to learn the Irish language and religion in Catholic schools.[32] These are not a part of Protestants' British culture. They are afraid of how they might be treated in a united Ireland.

Protestants argue that Catholics exaggerate when they say that Protestants discriminated against them in the past. Protestants did gerrymander some local-government electoral boundaries so that only Protestants could be elected.[33] They sometimes discriminated against Catholics in housing, education, industrial location, and employment, but it was the Catholics' own fault because they reserved their loyalty for a foreign government—the government of the Irish Republic. Protestants feel they have to be on their guard against treasonous collaborators. They believe the Irish government has provided a safe haven for PIRA terrorists who attacked innocent Protestants. They contend that it is the British government's responsibility to protect Protestants and to keep Northern Ireland British because Protestants are a distinct community.[34] Protestants are strongly committed in their allegiance to Britain.

The Catholic Community

Catholics perceive that the people of Ireland form one nation, and the fault for keeping Ireland divided lies with the British government. They believe that Protestants are a minority on the island of Ireland, and their opposition to a united Ireland is worked up by the British who prevent a peaceful settlement to the "Troubles" by exploiting differences they created and fostered among the Irish people.[35] The British government partitioned Ireland in 1921 so that the Conservative party could stay in office. In addition, Catholics believe that condescending attitudes and racial stereotyping warped the attitudes of British Conservative politicians in their dealings with Ireland. They maintain that Northern Ireland was viable only because the British government paid vast subsidies to the Northern Ireland government between 1921 and 1972, before it imposed Direct Rule from London.[36] Catholic Republicans also feel that the Protestants of Northern Ireland would not have been intransigent toward them or to a united Ireland if they had not been able to count on British economic and military support. Catholics feel that if British influence and financial interests were withdrawn, the natural interdependence of the two parts of the country would allow Protestants to rejoin a unified Ireland.[37]

Islands are seen by the international community as integral political natural boundaries; and, as the majority nation on the island, Catholics feel that they should not be prevented by a Protestant minority from being united with Catholics in the Republic of Ireland.[38] It was the British policy of "divide and rule" that brought Protestant settlers to Ireland in the seventeenth century and enforced the partition of Ireland in 1921 against the wishes of the majority of its citizens.[39] Now the Protestants of Northern Ireland do not want to be part of a united Ireland because the British government has stirred up animosities between both groups.

In general, Catholics feel that their ethnonational and political identity ties are with fellow Catholics in the Republic of Ireland. At the last all-Ireland elections in 1918, the Nationalist Catholic majority voted overwhelmingly for a united Ireland and viewed the 1921 partition of the island as illegitimate under international law.[40] Generally, Catholics look to their historical roots and cultural traditions, which are tied to the whole island. Catholics are a homogenous political bloc and realize that Northern Ireland took on a sectarian nature so that the Protestant political and economic elites could maintain their power by keeping the working classes divided.[41] In the past the Catholic Church influenced the political policy-making process in the Republic of Ireland and intervened as a third-party mediator in the 1980 hunger strikes between Republican prisoners and the British government. However, recent public scandals highlighted clergy physical and sexual abuse of young children, severely limiting the political influence of the church in politics north and south of the Irish border.[42] In contrast to Protestants, the British monarch is regarded by Catholics as a symbol of the British presence in Northern Ireland.[43]

Catholics feel that the British have egged on the Protestants into taking up more extreme positions than they otherwise would have done. Between 1921 and 1972, Catholics were discriminated against in housing and employment; they were harassed and abused by the B-Specials and Royal Ulster Constabulary (RUC) and were forced to leave Northern Ireland to try to make a decent living elsewhere.[44] When the Civil Rights Association marched in 1969 for equal rights for Catholics in housing, jobs, and voting, extremist Protestants attacked the marchers and burned Catholics out of their homes. The British government sent in the troops to protect Catholics, but they broke into their homes and put their young men in jail for no reason. British paratroopers shot dead fourteen innocent unarmed Catholic civil rights demonstrators during Bloody Sunday in 1972 in Derry.[45] Catholics know that the Protestants are afraid of change, but Catholics have suffered a lot of injustice and feel alienated. They have not been allowed to display their cultural identity—the Irish flag—

play the Irish national anthem, or speak the Irish language. In general, Catholics want political rule from Dublin, not from London.

It is obvious to Catholics that the British presence has not brought peace to Ireland. From their perspective, it is the British military and political presence that distorts the political situation in Northern Ireland and keeps both communities apart. British policy has propped up sectarianism, damaged the economies of both parts of Ireland, given insufficient recognition to the Irish identity of Catholics, allowed continuing differences in levels of unemployment and deprivation between Catholics and Protestants, and allowed security policies such as shoot-to-kill that made the situation worse.[46] Catholics believe that British misrule in Northern Ireland has perpetuated the conflict and kept Protestants and Catholics divided. The partition of Ireland in 1921 was never legitimate from a democratic point of view. Catholics are deeply committed to eventual Irish unity.

PAST GLORIES AND TRAUMAS REACTIVATED BY CURRENT PROBLEMS IN THE PEACE PROCESS

Vamik Volkan writes that a traumatic event experienced by an ethnic group is passed down orally through the generations and becomes the basis for future retaliation by that group against the other.[47] Rituals are needed so that the group can express its emotional state and thus heal from the trauma or the seeds that are being sown for future violence.[48] Within the Northern Ireland context, chosen traumas of victimhood make it difficult for the Protestant and Catholic communities to understand each others' fears, to take responsibility for their role in the conflict, and to reconcile differences. Both groups feel persecuted and present themselves as victims of the other side. For Protestants, Republican terrorist attacks and assassination of Protestant members of the police and security forces indicate Catholics' intentions to annihilate the Protestant people. Catholics argue that foreigners invaded and then occupied the land and dispossessed them. Both groups see themselves not as an illegitimate invader but as an indigenous group with exclusive rights to the territory. Different perceptions of the causes of the conflict and the true intentions

of the other side lead to threat and insecurity with any concession seen as a loss. Two examples of past traumas that exacerbated the conflict and continue to thwart peace efforts in Northern Ireland are described in the following sections.

Bloody Sunday

On January 30, 1972, fourteen unarmed Catholic civilians were shot dead by British paratroops in Derry while they protested nonviolently as part of a civil rights march.[49] These deaths signaled the beginning of an offensive by the PIRA whose ranks burgeoned as a result of this tragedy. The subsequent Widgery Inquiry set up by the British government to investigate the event exonerated the actions of the British troops who claimed that they were fired on by a PIRA sniper. The events of Bloody Sunday demonstrated to the Catholic community that if they protested against socioeconomic and political injustices the power of the state would come crashing down around them. Bloody Sunday ensured that a majority of young Catholics turned to the traditional force tradition of armed insurrection against the state and to the PIRA to defend the Catholic community.[50]

In 2002, British Prime Minister Tony Blair's government established the Bloody Sunday Inquiry to reopen the case and examine old wounds. The evidence thus far points to the fact that the paratroops had orders from the British government to teach the demonstrators a hard lesson. The new tribunal gave all the people of the city of Derry the opportunity to reconcile and repair their strained relationships. The inquiry will go a long way in assisting the Catholic community to heal from the trauma of Bloody Sunday.

Marching Season

Protestants march every July 12 to celebrate the 1690 victory of William of Orange over the Catholic King James at the Battle of the Boyne and on August 12 to celebrate the Apprentice Boys' defense of the city in the Siege of Derry. For Protestants the marching season is a cultural event whereby Protestants march to celebrate their culture and to demonstrate their loyalty to the Queen.[51] Catholics insist that the marching season is an expression of triumphalism and not of culture. The government has put the Northern Ireland police service on the front line to prevent most of these marches from entering Catholic areas such as Garvaghy Road in Portadown and lower Ormeau Road in Belfast. Police efforts to prevent Orange marches have drawn the wrath of the Loyalist community and the support of the Catholic community. The celebration of historical victories or massacres illustrates how both communities are trapped in a historical time warp in which the past and present merge so that it is easy for extremist leaders to pass these traumatic events down to other generations.

PERCEPTION OF THE "OTHER" AND THE "ENEMY'S" VIEW OF THE NORTHERN IRELAND CONFLICT

Northern Ireland's "Troubles" are being played out by an array of groups whose members generally coalesce around differing political ideologies. Leading ideological groups include Nationalists, Republicans within the Catholic community, and Unionists and Loyalists within the Protestant community. Historically, the British government has represented the interests of Protestants while the Irish government has represented those of Catholics. In many cases, group members' ideology is linked to their history and identity. As a consequence, group members' positions are inclined to be immutable. Moreover, members of one group tend to see members of other groups as enemies, with different, irreconcilable views and aims. Understanding the origins and aims of Northern Ireland's many groups is essential to understanding the complexity and intractability of the conflict.[52]

John Whyte argues that there is an intensity of attachment to identity that is at the heart of any understanding of the Northern Ireland conflict.[53] This clash of identities ensures that Protestants act as a besieged minority in a religiously segregated society. Unionist Protestants are unsure of their ethnonational identity, while Catholic Nationalists report that they are Irish. The only identity that is secure for Unionists is evangelical Protestantism as it binds together classes, moderates and extremists, and the various denominations in a public band to resist political threats to their constitutional position within the United Kingdom.[54] Identity-based

group conflict is at the very heart of the Northern Ireland conflict.

Unionists

The majority of Protestants in Northern Ireland are Unionists. About 80 percent of Unionists give their allegiance to the ideology of Unionism—the maintenance of the union between Northern Ireland and the United Kingdom. The national argument asserts that Unionists feel themselves to be of British nationality. Invariably, though not necessarily, Unionists are Protestants. The economic argument against Irish unity is that Northern Ireland is far better off as part of the United Kingdom than it would be as part of a united Ireland. The Republic of Ireland is seen by Unionists as having a weak economy, kept from collapse by high emigration. Unionists believe it would be a disaster to join Ireland because of its economic hopelessness and huge economic debt.[55] Unionists feel that they are psychologically bound to Britain with bonds of blood, history, and common ancestry and culture, which cannot be bartered away. Religious objections to Irish unity have been partly in reaction to specific items of law, which enshrine Catholic values, such as the church's control of education.[56] Many Protestant leaders are deeply suspicious of the power and intentions of the Catholic hierarchy.

The OUP, also known as the Ulster Unionist Party (UUP), is located in Belfast, Northern Ireland. The OUP is no longer the largest Unionist political party in the province, securing about 40 percent of the Protestant vote. The OUP traces its origins to the Ulster Unionist Party, which was founded in 1892 and remained the sole voice of the Protestant population of Northern Ireland until the late 1960s, and the governing party from 1920 to 1972.[57] The OUP government collapsed during divisions that ensued over civil rights, the fall of Stormont (devolved the parliament in Northern Ireland), and power sharing with Catholics.[58] The OUP is split between integrationists—those who want full integration with Great Britain—and devolutionists—those who want a return to devolved government in Northern Ireland. Devolutionists oppose the 1985 Anglo Irish Agreement (AIA) and 1995 Framework for Peace that gave the Irish government a say in the government of Northern Ireland. The leader of the OUP, David Trimble, received the Nobel Peace Prize for his efforts during the 1998 Good Friday peace process. He supports a power-sharing government with Northern Ireland's moderate Nationalists. However, he insisted that the PIRA had to hand in its guns if Sinn Fein was to take its seats in the new Stormont government in Belfast.[59]

Founded in 1971, the Democratic Unionist Party (DUP) regards itself as being right wing in terms of being strong on the constitution but leaning to the left on social policies. Currently, the DUP attracts about 60 percent of Unionist votes representing hard-line Unionism and political Protestantism. It opposes power sharing and an Irish Dimension. It strongly opposes the AIA of 1985, the 1995 Framework for Peace, and the 1998 GFA that gave the Irish government a say in the government of Northern Ireland. Its leader is the Reverend Dr. Ian Paisley, founder of the Free Presbyterian Church. Paisley believes that the Catholic Church is the anti-Christ and that Protestants cannot share power with people who are dominated by the "church of Rome."[60] He is highly suspicious of the government of the Irish Republic, which he perceives to be in league with the Catholic hierarchy in the Vatican.[61] Paisley does not want Unionists to form a power-sharing government with Northern Irish Republican Catholics.

Loyalists

Loyalism is a more extreme form of Unionism. Loyalists come predominantly from the Protestant working class, and they believe that they have a right to fight to keep Northern Ireland part of Britain.[62] They represent only about 30 percent of the Protestant population, but they have military training and weapons. Loyalists, ironically, are likely to place more emphasis on not becoming part of an all-Ireland state than maintaining the link with the United Kingdom. Loyalists believe that they have signed their loyalty to the Queen with the blood they shed "for Queen and country" in World Wars I and II. Loyalists give their allegiance to the Queen on condition that she fulfills her duties to them, the most important of which is protection.[63] The union with Britain is seen as a safeguard against absorption into the Irish Republic. Loyalists believe that they entered simultaneously into a political contract and a religious covenant with the British monarch when Ulster

was being planted with loyal Protestants during the seventeenth century.[64] The concept of the contract becomes politically significant when Protestants perceive the British government as not fulfilling its side of the bargain. Loyalists do not believe it is disloyal to the Queen to refuse loyalty to ministers of government who fail in their duty to give loyal subjects the blessing of the Queen's peace.[65] The irony of their ideology is that they believe that Protestants have to behave in a disloyal manner to demonstrate their loyalty to the Queen.

The Combined Loyalist Military Command (CLMC) represents all of the powerful Protestant paramilitary groups in Northern Ireland. The CLMC, comprising the now defunct Ulster Democratic Party (UDP) and its military wing, the Ulster Defense Association (UDA), and the Progressive Unionist Party (PUP) and its military wing, the Ulster Volunteer Force (UVF), called a reciprocal cease-fire on October 13, 1994, ending their campaign of sectarian attacks against the Catholic community.[66] The CLMC cease-fire was on-again, off-again in the wake of the collapse of the 1998 power-sharing government and the PIRA's reluctance to hand over its weapons to the British authorities.

The now defunct UDP was the political wing of the UDA. It favored maintaining the link with Britain under its former leader Gary McMichael. The UDP was founded in September 1971 as a co-coordinating body for the great variety of Loyalist vigilante groups. The UDA is Northern Ireland's largest paramilitary organization. It is legal although its nom de guerre, the Ulster Freedom Fighters (UFF), is proscribed. The UDA advocates independence for Northern Ireland and publishes the magazine *Ulster*.

The PUP supports keeping Northern Ireland British. The organization is the political wing of the UVF. Gusty Spence is the president of the PUP. An illegal Protestant paramilitary force, the UVF is sometimes described as the "secret Protestant army."[67] In 1966, it revived the title of the Unionist UVF established in 1912 to fight Irish Home Rule.

Irish Nationalists

The majority of Catholics follow the ideology of nationalism and are looking for the creation of a united Ireland through peaceful consent. Nationalists give their allegiance to the percepts of Irish nationalism, namely the abolition of the border between the north and the south of Ireland and the unification of Ireland.[68] Invariably, though not necessarily, nationalists are Catholic. Nationalists support constitutional politics and want a united Ireland obtained with the consent of a majority of the people of Northern Ireland. Constitutional Nationalists seek a united Ireland, but only by peaceful democratic means. The majority of Nationalists accept that the greatest obstacle to Irish unity lies within the Ulster Protestant community. Nationalists recognize Northern Ireland's Protestants' strong expression of political allegiance to Britain and understand that it cannot be ignored if both communities are ever to work together toward eventual Irish unification.[69]

The Social Democratic and Labour Party (SDLP), located in Belfast, Northern Ireland, speaks for a majority of moderate Catholics in Northern Ireland. It attracts about 40 percent of the Catholic vote, mainly from middle-class and trade-union voters. Founded in 1970 by a group of ex–civil rights activists, it is an umbrella party. It brought together the remnants of the old Nationalist Party, which stood for unity with the rest of Ireland and little else, the National Democratic Party, and the Republican Labour Party. Its long-term goals are to promote the creation of a socialist state in the European social democratic tradition and Irish unity based on the consent of a majority of the people of Northern Ireland.[70] The SDLP is generally split between those who hew to a strictly nationalist line—"the Greens"—and those who do not. Past party leader John Hume received the Nobel Peace Prize for his efforts to promote the current Northern Ireland peace process.

Irish Republicans

Catholics who want to get the British government out of Northern Ireland support the Republican ideology, a more extreme form of nationalism. Currently, Republicans represent about 60 percent of Catholics. Republicans support the formation of a socialist Republic of Ireland consisting of thirty-two counties. The term *republican* has become synonymous with support for Sinn Fein, with its socialist orientation, and the PIRA's military

campaign, although not all Republicans would necessarily support either.[71] Republicans call for British withdrawal or a declaration of intent to withdraw as the first step toward bringing about a united Ireland. For Republicans, the root of the conflict is the British presence in Ireland. They argue that Ireland has a right to self-determination and that the British presence prevents the Irish people from exercising that right. Unionists do not have the same right to self-determination because they are a national minority—a significant minority but a minority nevertheless.[72] Republicans also argue that the British presence has not brought peace to Ireland; it has propped up sectarianism, damaged the economies of both parts of the island, and stunted the development of class politics.[73]

The Provisional Irish Republican Army, also called "the Provies" or "the Provos," and its political wing, Provisional Sinn Fein (or just SF), came into being in January 1970 after the IRA Army Council voted to give token recognition to the parliaments in Dublin, London, and Belfast, which effectively meant the end of abstentionism, or the refusal to take their seats in the Irish Dail and the British Parliament.[74] SF candidates now run for seats in each of these parliaments.[75] However, in the past, if elected, candidates did not serve since they regarded these institutions as being either illegal or foreign. Those who disagreed with the Army Council's ruling walked out, effectively splitting the Republican movement into the Provisional IRA and Provisional SF, founded by those who walked out, and the Official IRA and Official SF.[76] Provisional SF usually gets around 80 percent of the working-class Catholic vote. The Official IRA abandoned its military activities in 1972 and disbanded sometime afterward. PIRA, however, sustained a twenty-eight-year military campaign to end what it terms the "British occupation" of Ireland.[77] SF advances its views in its publication *An Phoblacht/Republican News*. The PIRA would not surrender its arms to the British government, even though SF had seats in the new Stormont Assembly and the power-sharing government.[78] Two fringe groups—the Rea IRA and the Continuity IRA—reject the peace process and have splintered from the PIRA as a result of its refusal to carry on the war against the British government.

EFFORTS TO RESOLVE THE NORTHERN IRELAND CONFLICT: SUCCESS OR FAILURE?

In recent years, various members of the international community have endeavored to broker peace in Northern Ireland. Their efforts have met with mixed results.

The United States and the European Union

In the mid-1990s, the United States put political pressure on Britain to get all of the political parties in Northern Ireland to the table and to provide economic aid through the International Fund for Ireland (IFI).[79] President Bill Clinton's visits to Northern Ireland, and his appointment of Senator George Mitchell as mediator, enabled an outcome to be negotiated in the form of the 1998 GFA. Confidence-building mechanisms—the decommissioning of paramilitary weapons, reform of policing, prisoner release, and withdrawal of emergency legislation and the British military—are all embodied in the GFA.[80] The European Union (EU) also provided economic resources to build the peace dividend through the 1994 EU Special Support Program for Peace and Reconciliation. It has met with mixed reviews.[81] The EU has also become a political forum for the Irish and British governments to collaborate with each other on an internal political solution to the conflict.

The British Government

The Northern Ireland conflict has been an ongoing problem for the British government, which has annual summit meetings to discuss the evolution of the Northern Ireland conflict with the Irish government. The political interests of Northern Ireland's Protestant community are represented by it. Going back in recent history, to March 1972, the British government suspended indefinitely the Northern Ireland Parliament after Brian Faulkner, the province's prime minister, balked at handing over all security power to Westminster.[82] The British government took full control of Northern Ireland by appointing a Secretary of State for Northern Ireland to implement Direct Rule and a Northern Ireland Office to administer it economically, legally, and politically. The British presence in Northern Ireland has helped to reduce the risk of civil war between Protestants and Catholics. If the British government were to withdraw, outright conflict would result. The British presence prevents the conflict from becoming worse, at a cost of approximately £400 million a month to the British government.[83]

British governments have specifically acknowledged, since the 1985 AIA, Northern Ireland's right to secede from the United Kingdom if the majority of the population votes to do so. In the past, the British government has favored a power-sharing arrangement between Protestants and Catholics within Northern Ireland and an Irish Dimension that includes involvement of the Irish government and political process. The 1995 Framework for Peace Document and 1998 GFA recommended joint authority, suggesting that Northern Ireland be governed equally by both the British and Irish governments.[84] This new proposal highlighted a possible British readiness to detach itself from the Northern Ireland problem. Protestants looked upon this new proposal as a staging post or an attempt to trundle Northern Ireland into an all-Ireland Republic. The British government has no wish to impede the realization of Irish unity, if it is to come about by genuine and freely given mutual agreement and on conditions acceptable to both Protestant and Catholic communities.[85] If, in the future, the majority of Protestants and Catholics of Northern Ireland should indicate a wish to become a part of a united Ireland, the British government would support that wish. Prime Minister Tony Blair's British government has worked hard with the Irish government to put together the April 1998 GFA with all of Northern Ireland's political parties. The GFA peace agreement set up a new, devolved power-sharing government and parliament in Belfast. The power-sharing government is temporarily suspended because the PIRA refused to decommission its arms. The peace process has often seemed in danger of unraveling.

The Irish Government

The Irish government represents the political interests of the Northern Ireland Catholic community in its annual summit meetings with the British government. The current Irish prime minister is Bertie Ahern. The *Irish Dimension* is a term that came into popular usage in 1973 with the Irish government acknowledging the desire of the majority of the Catholic community in Northern Ireland for an eventually united Ireland, with assistance in this process by the Irish government.[86] It is a counterbalance to the British Dimension, the term used to express the Unionist attachment to Britain. It was given institutional expression by the British government in the plan for a Council of Ireland in the 1973 Sunningdale Agreement, the AIA of 1985 in the form of the intergovernmental body. Today it has institutional expression under the 1995 Framework for Peace and 1998 GFA that proposed a north–south institutional body to formulate policies on an all-Ireland basis on a scale between consultation on any aspect of designated matters to executive action in consultation with the British and Irish governments.[87] The Irish government declared its intention in the Framework for Peace document to amend its constitutional claim to the territory to Northern Ireland. The aspiration toward Irish unification retains majority support in the Republic of Ireland, but a much smaller proportion of the Irish population is prepared to suffer any serious inconveniences to help that to happen.[88] The Irish government will introduce and support parliamentary legislation to give effect to the establishment of a United Ireland if, in the future, a majority of the people of Northern Ireland clearly wishes unification. The Irish government drafted the April 1998 GFA with the British government and Northern Ireland's political parties. The GFA established a parliament and a new devolved power-sharing government at the Stormont Assembly building in Belfast. However, the Northern Ireland government was suspended and the peace process jeopardized by the paramilitary arms issue.

ACTIONS AND POLICIES TO RESOLVE THE NORTHERN IRELAND CONFLICT

In April 1998, the GFA was signed by all parties to the conflict. On July 28, 2005, the PIRA agreed to decommission its arms, which led to a breakdown of the new power-sharing government. The murder of Billy Wright, outlawed leader of the Loyalist Volunteer Force (LVF), in the Maze prison by members of the Irish National Liberation Army

(INLA) on November 15, 1997, and the Real Irish Republican Army's (RIRA) bombing of the town of Omagh that killed more than twenty-five civilians nearly restarted the political violence that had shaken the province over the preceding thirty years.[89] The death of Billy Wright and the stalled Mitchell–de Chailiand negotiations also led to the breakdown of the CLMC's cease-fire. In addition, the UDA/UFF ended its three-year, two-month cease-fire and resumed its violent campaign against perceived Republicans. The commencement of paramilitary activities killed twelve Catholics and four Protestants. However, with a lot of goodwill, Senator Mitchell was able to keep the negotiations on track. The PIRA split into the Continuity Irish Republican Army (CIRA) and the RIRA, whose members perceived that Gerry Adams and Martin McGuinness had sold out to the British and Irish governments. Members of the PIRA were disillusioned over the lack of movement and progress in the formation of a second power-sharing government in Belfast between Protestants and Catholics.[90] Both governments feared that the PIRA and the CLMC would break their cease-fires and resume their violent campaigns. There was a general fear of a resurgence of political violence.

The peace process in Northern Ireland appeared to have stalled for a number of reasons. First, former U.S. President Clinton's visit to both parts of Ireland toward the end of November 1995 failed to set the tone of the peace talks between the British and Irish governments, Unionists, Nationalists, and paramilitaries. U.S. President George W. Bush focused on the wars in Afghanistan and Iraq so that U.S. foreign policy shifted away from the Northern Ireland conflict, though he was dismayed by the ongoing violence and wanted the peace process to continue.

Second, the "Twin-Track" approach to progress on the Northern Ireland problem of former U.S. Senator George Mitchell and Canadian General de Chailiand reached an impasse on the decommissioning of paramilitary arms and munitions.[91] There was a danger that the CLMC might end its cease-fire in the wake of the PIRA's refusal to give up its arms.

Third, Tony Blair, then the British prime minister, and Bertie Ahern, the Irish prime minister, were unable to break the logjam in negotiations about getting guns out of Irish politics. The PIRA and the CLMC's initial refusal to decommission all their weapons clearly demonstrated that both organizations were not permanently renouncing violence. President Bush pressed Prime Minister Blair to find a peaceful consensual solution to the Northern Ireland conflict. President Bush needed to appease the Irish-American lobby in Congress when he was running for a second term as U.S. president. Prime Minister Blair's government was in a relatively strong position in the British parliament. He did not need the votes of the Unionist MPs to stay in power.

Fourth, Bertie Ahern, the Irish Taoiseach (Prime Minister), tried eagerly to influence the peace process because of pressing political and economic needs in the Republic of Ireland. Economic pressures emanating from national and international investors link possible economic investments to the Celtic Tiger with the development and enactment of a permanent peace agreement among all the key stakeholders involved in the conflict.[92] Looking to future prospects for the tourist industry, economic investors, and other industries, Bertie Ahern sought a framework for peace to bring economic prosperity to the whole island. He wants SF, the PIRA, and the Loyalists to renounce violence and decommission their weapons. However, looking at past history, he knows the monumental problems that any agreement will have to surmount.

Fifth, the Unionist political parties are uneasy sitting at the table with representatives of the UDA and PUP—representing the interests of the UVF—because these political parties threaten the traditional Unionist position of just saying "no." However, the OUP now realizes that if there is ever to be a lasting peace in Northern Ireland, Protestant Unionists have to share power with the Catholic Nationalist minority within Northern Ireland.[93] The OUP and the DUP strongly rejected pressure from the PIRA and refused to sit at the table with SF because the PIRA did not surrender its arms. Both political parties are now waiting to see if the CLMC (UVF and UDA) and LVF will end their violence in the wake of the PIRA's stated claim to decommission its weapons.

Sixth, the LVF and the INLA—extremist Loyalist and Republican fringe paramilitary organizations—initially refused to call cease-fires or decommission their arms. The LVF assumed a hard-line position because of its members' loyalty to the Queen and fear of being pushed into a Catholic-dominated United Ireland in which Protestants would be a minority. The LVF does not fully trust Tony Blair's British Labour government and is suspicious of any involvement of the Irish government in any political discussions over the future of Northern Ireland's position within United Kingdom.[94] The LVF has used violence in the past against Catholics and would use violence again any time in the future to keep Northern Ireland British, especially as the PIRA has not decommissioned its arms.

Finally, Gerry Adams, the political leader of SF, the SDLP, and the government of the Republic of Ireland were all caught off guard by the breakdown in the power-sharing government and fear that the peace process could end. Gerry Adams and Martin McGuinness were in danger of assassination by RIRA members, who believed that they were traitors. SF is a small but well-trained organization that politically represents the interests of the PIRA. SF wants the British government to leave Northern Ireland so that the United Irish nation can form. The PIRA was concerned that the RIRA would take center stage and it would become marginalized. The British and Irish governments persuaded SF to convince the PIRA to decommission its arms.[95]

The moderate Nationalist SDLP party waged a highly successful strategy by moving the cause for Irish nationalism forward in the United States and getting former President Clinton and the U.S. Congress to fully support the peace process. The SDLP wants a United Ireland that would be integrated into the EU and would respect the rights of the Protestant community to be different and have equal treatment within a united Ireland. The SDLP wants to include SF and the Loyalists as an integral part of this political peace process—provided they renounce the use of violence to resolve the conflict. All key stakeholders must be part of any movement to sustain a just peace for all in Northern Ireland.

A comprehensive peace process must address structural macro factors, as well as micro agency factors, in transforming relationships and structures, and working to forge a shared identity.[96] A multi-track approach that involves politicians, religious leaders, journalists, conflict resolvers, and businesspersons, as well as grassroots groups, is necessary to build the peace process in Northern Ireland.[97] A process that engages every sector of society at multiple levels of intervention is crucial to build a sustainable peace in the long term.[98]

THE FUTURE OF THE NORTHERN IRELAND CONFLICT

Within Northern Ireland, a bad-tempered peace now exists between both communities even though there has been little violence over the past five years other than the punishment beatings meted out by Loyalist and Republican paramilitaries to maintain their power base within the Protestant and Catholic working class communities.[99] The institutions of devolved governance are in place in Belfast as Protestant and Catholic politicians sat in a general assembly and worked together to develop a second power-sharing government.

While the political elites from both sides attempt to govern, local grassroots organizations are attempting to build bridges of contact across the intercommunal divide so that people can work together to forge new relationships and build a civic culture.[100] For example, parents and children in the integrated schools are sharing their cultural stories with each other, negotiating their identities, and in the process, developing a shared identity.[101]

The future looks bright that a lasting peace can bring about the end of the conflict in Northern Ireland. However, it is critical that Loyalist guns are now taken out of Irish politics forever if the Troubles in Northern Ireland are to end. South Africa provides a good example upon which the people of Northern Ireland can model their peace process: Nelson Mandela and F. W. de Klerk were able to negotiate the end of the apartheid state and preserve the face of the white minority community while ending the intergroup violence that had plagued that country.[102] Only time will tell if the people of Northern Ireland have the will to make the GFA work.

CONCLUSION

This chapter has outlined the conflict in Northern Ireland as it presently manifests itself. Today, the relative absence of political violence favors the prospects for a lasting, peaceful solution. However, Republican and Loyalist paramilitary intimidation and punishment beatings, coupled with church burnings, Loyalist marches through Catholic neighborhoods, and the decommissioning of Loyalist arms, could block any constructive, devolved, governmental power-sharing initiative from moving forward.

Former Prime Minister Tony Blair did not want to hold new elections for the Northern Ireland Assembly because he was not convinced that paramilitary arms were decommissioned and that the violence and the PIRA's long war were over. Prime Minister Blair's political position following the Iraq war was dominant but not hegemonic. While OUP leader David Trimble was well regarded by the British prime minister, he will need all his political skill to pull together a Unionist Protestant community disenchanted with the peace process as it now stands.

Trimble is willing to share political power with both Nationalist and Republican Catholics provided that guns are permanently taken out of Northern Ireland politics. Meanwhile, Republicans take the position that political progress is impossible in Northern Ireland owing to the monolithic tensions within Orangeism. The current state of the Northern Ireland peace process suggests that if elections are not held and a new power-sharing government put into place, joint authority by both the British and Irish governments will likely result.

This chapter has argued that the weight of history bears down heavily on both communities, whose identity fears are extremely potent. In the past, solutions have failed because the political center was weak and the paramilitaries were not included in the political process. Nevertheless the 1998 GFA ushered in a new era in Northern Ireland politics and with it the promise of an enduring peace. The majority of the people of Northern Ireland desire peace. The challenge for political leaders from both communities is not to let the opportunity slip away. A constructive peace can be built and relationships restored in a process that engages all sectors of society.[103] People want to share their stories and heal from the past.[104] Peace and justice in Northern Ireland depend on pluralist thinking that engages all of the people in Northern Ireland in a new, shared destiny.

ENDNOTES

1. S. Byrne, "Consociational and Civic Society Approaches to Peacebuilding in Northern Ireland, *Journal of Peace Research,* vol. 38, no. 3 (2001), 327–52.

2. N. Carter and S. Byrne, "The Dynamics of Social Cubism: A View from Northern Ireland and Quebec, in *Reconcilable Differences: Turning Points in Ethnopolitical Conflict,* eds. S. Byrne and C. Irvin (West Hartford, CT: Kumarian, 2000), 41–65.

3. J. McGarry and B. O'Leary, *Explaining Northern Ireland: Broken Images* (Cambridge, MA: Blackwell, 1995).

4. B. O'Leary and J. McGarry, *The Politics of Antagonism: Understanding Northern Ireland* (Atlantic Highlands, NJ: Athlone, 1993).

5. P. Bew and H. Patterson, *The British State and the Ulster Crisis: From Wilson to Thatcher* (London: Verso, 1985).

6. Byrne, "Consociational and Civic Society Approaches to Peacebuilding."

7. S. Byrne, "Transformational Conflict Resolution and the Northern Ireland Conflict," *International Journal on World Peace,* vol. 28, no. 2 (2001), 3–21; and A. Guelke, "International Dimensions of the Belfast Agreement," in *Aspects of the Belfast Agreement,* ed. R. Wilford (Oxford, England: Oxford University Press, 2000), 245–63.

8. S. Byrne, "Conflict Regulation or Conflict Resolution: Third Party Intervention in the Northern Ireland Conflict: Prospects for Peace," *Terrorism and Political Violence,* vol. 7, no. 2 (1995), 1–24.

9. P. Bew, P. Gibbon, and H. Patterson, *The State in Northern Ireland, 1921–72: Political Forces and Social Classes* (Manchester, England: Manchester University Press, 1979); and P. Bew, P. Gibbon, and H. Patterson, *Northern Ireland, 1921–94: Political Forces and Social Classes* (London: Serif, 1995).

10. J. Ruane and J. Todd, *The Dynamics of Conflict in Northern Ireland: Power, Conflict and Emancipation* (Cambridge, England: Cambridge University Press, 1996).

11. P. Arthur and K. Jeffrey, *Northern Ireland Since 1968* (New York: Basil Blackwell, 1998).

12. C. Irvin, *Militant Nationalism: Between Movement and Party in Northern Ireland and the Basque Country* (Duluth, MN: University of Minnesota Press, 1999); and O'Leary and McGarry, *The Politics of Antagonism.*

13. S. Byrne and N. Carter, "Social Cubism: Six Social Forces of Ethnoterritorial Politics in Northern Ireland and Quebec, *Peace and Conflict Studies,* vol. 3, no. 2 (1996), 52–72; and Carter and Byrne, "The Dynamics of Social Cubism."

14. S. Bruce, *God Save Ulster! The Religion and Politics of Paisleyism* (Oxford, England: Clarendon, 1986).

15. P. Dixon, *Northern Ireland: The Politics of War and Peace* (London: Macmillan, 2002).

16. Bew and Patterson, *The British State and the Ulster Crisis.*

17. P. Dixon, "Consociationalism and the Northern Ireland Peace Process: The Glass Half Full or Half Empty," *Nationalism & Ethnic Politics,* vol. 3, no. 3 (1997), 20–36; "Paths to Peace in Northern Ireland (I): Civil Society and Consociational Approaches," *Democratization,* vol. 4, no. 2, 1–27; and "Paths to Peace in Northern Ireland (II): The

Peace Processes 1973–74 and 1994–96," *Democratization,* vol. 4, no. 3 (1997), 1–25.

18. A. Guelke, *Northern Ireland: The International Perspective* (Dublin: Gill & Macmillan, 1988)

19. A. Guelke, *The Age of Terrorism and the International Political System* (London: I. B. Tauris, 1995).

20. Guelke, "International Dimensions of the Belfast Agreement."

21. O'Leary and McGarry, *The Politics of Antagonism.*

22. A. Aughey, "The 1998 Agreement: Unionist Responses," in *A Farewell to Arms? From "Long War" to Long Peace in Northern Ireland,* eds. M. Cox, A. Guelke, and F. Stephens (Manchester, England: Manchester University Press, 2001), 62–77.

23. O'Leary, B, "Academic Viewpoint: The Nature of the Agreement," *Fordham International Law Journal,* vol. 22, no. 1 (1999), 628–43.

24. S. Byrne, S. "Toward Tractability: The 1993 South African Record of Understanding and the 1998 Northern Ireland Good Friday Agreement," *Irish Studies in International Affairs,* vol. 13, no. 1 (2002), 135–49.

25. S. Byrne, N. Carter, and J. Senehi, "Social Cubism and Social Conflict: Analysis and Resolution," *Journal of International and Comparative Law,* vol. 8, no. 2 (2002), 725–40.

26. D. Miller, *Queen's Rebels: Ulster Loyalism in Historical Perspective* (Dublin: Gill & Macmillan, 1978).

27. Bruce, *God Save Ulster!*

28. S. Byrne and C. Irvin, "A Shared Common Sense: Perceptions of the Material Effects and Impacts of Economic Growth in Northern Ireland," *Civil Wars,* vol. 5, no. 1 (2002), 55–86.

29. Byrne, "Transformational Conflict Resolution and the Northern Ireland Conflict."

30. D. Bloomfield, *Peacemaking Strategies in Northern Ireland: Building Complementarity in Conflict Management Theory* (Basingstoke, England: Macmillan, 1996).

31. M. Fitzduff, *Beyond Violence: Conflict Resolution Processes in Northern Ireland* (Tokyo: United Nations University, 1996).

32. S. Byrne, *Growing Up in a Divided Society: The Influence of Conflict on Belfast Schoolchildren* (Cranbury, NJ: Associated University Presses, 1997).

33. S. Byrne and N. Carter, "Social Cubism."

34. S. Byrne and A. Delman, "Group Identity Formation and Intra-Group Conflict," *Journal of Intergroup Relations,* vol. 25, no. 4 (1999), 35–57.

35. J. Darby and R. McGinty, *The Management of Peace Processes: Ethnic and Intercommunity Conflict* (New York: St. Martin's Press, 2002).

36. M. Hechter, *Internal Colonialism: The Celtic Fringe in British National Development, 1536–1966* (London: Routledge & Kegan Paul, 1975).

37. Irvin, *Militant Nationalism;* and F. Wright, *Northern Ireland: A Comparative Analysis* (Dublin: Gill & Macmillan, 1987).

38. Guelke, *Northern Ireland.*

39. J. Whyte, *Interpreting Northern Ireland* (Oxford, England: Clarendon, 1990).

40. Guelke, *Northern Ireland*

41. Bew et al., *The State in Northern Ireland* and *Northern Ireland, 1921–94.*
42. B. McSweeney, "Security, Identity and the Peace Process in Northern Ireland," *Security Dialogue*, vol. 27, no. 2 (1996), 167–78.
43. Byrne, *Growing Up in a Divided Society.*
44. S. Byrne and M. Ayulo, "External Economic Aid in Ethno-Political Conflict: A View from Northern Ireland," *Security Dialogue*, vol. 29, no. 4 (1998), 219–33.
45. McGarry and O'Leary, *Explaining Northern Ireland.*
46. Byrne, "Conflict Regulation or Conflict Resolution,"
47. V. Volkan, *Blood Lines: From Ethnic Pride to Ethnic Terrorism* (Boulder, CO: Westview, 1998).
48. D. Sandole, "Virulent Ethnocentrism: A Major Challenge for Transformational Conflict Resolution and Peacebuilding in the Post-Cold War Era," *The Global Review of Ethnopolitics*, vol. 1, no. 4 (2002), 4–27; J. P. Lederach, *Preparing for Peace: Conflict Transformation Across Cultures* (Syracuse, NY: Syracuse University Press, 1995); and J. P. Lederach, *Building Peace: Sustainable Reconciliation in Divided Societies* (Washington, DC: United States Institute of Peace, 1997).
49. S. Byrne, "Northern Ireland, Israel, and South Africa at a Crossroads: Understanding Intergroup Conflict, Peace-Building, and Conflict Resolution," *International Journal of Group Tensions*, vol. 28, no. 3/4 (1999), 231–53.
50. Irvin, *Militant Nationalism.*
51. S. Byrne, "Power Politics as Usual in Cyprus and Northern Ireland: Divided Islands and the Roles of External Ethno-Guarantors," *Nationalism and Ethnic Politics*, vol. 6, no. 1 (2002), 1–24.
52. D. Horowitz, *Ethnic Groups in Conflict* (Berkeley, CA: University of California Press, 1985).
53. Whyte, *Interpreting Northern Ireland.*
54. Bruce, *God Save Ulster!;* Miller, *Queen's Rebels.*
55. S. Byrne and C. Irvin, "External Economic Aid and Policy-making: Building the Peace Divided in Northern Ireland," *Policy and Politics*, vol. 29, no. 4 (2001), 414–29; and Byrne and Irvin, "A Shared Common Sense."
56. T. Northrup, "Dynamics of Identity in Personal and Social Conflict," in *Intractable Conflicts and Their Transformation*, eds. L. Kriesberg, T. Northrup, & S. Thorson (Syracuse, NY: Syracuse University Press, 1989), 55–82.
57. Bew et al., *The State in Northern Ireland;* and Bew et al., *Northern Ireland, 1921–94.*
58. M. T. Love, *Peace Building Through Reconciliation in Northern Ireland* (Aldershot, England: Avebury, 1995).
59. Byrne, "Toward Tractability."
60. Bruce, *God Save Ulster!*
61. Dixon, *Northern Ireland.*
62. McGarry and O'Leary, *Explaining Northern Ireland.*
63. Miller, *Queen's Rebels.*
64. Ibid.
65. Ibid.
66. Byrne, "Conflict Regulation or Conflict Resolution."
67. Bruce, *God Save Ulster!*
68. Byrne, "Consociational and Consociational and Civic Society Approaches to Peacebuilding."
69. J. Agnew, "Beyond Reason: Spatial and Temporal Sources of Ethnic Conflicts," in *Intractable Conflicts and Their*

Transformation, eds. L. Kriesberg, T. A. Northrup, and S. J. Thorson (Syracuse, NY: Syracuse University Press, 1989), 42–52.
70. J. Hume, *A New Ireland: Politics, Peace and Reconciliation* (Boulder, CO: Roberts Rinehart, 1996).
71. S. Byrne and L. Keashly, "Working with Ethno-Political Conflict: A Multi-Modal and Multi-Level Approach to Conflict Intervention, *International Peacekeeping*, vol. 7, no. 1 (2000), 97–120.
72. Guelke, *Northern Ireland.*
73. Irvin, *Militant Nationalism.*
74. O'Leary and McGarry, *The Politics of Antagonism.*
75. Whyte, *Interpreting Northern Ireland.*
76. Irvin, *Militant Nationalism.*
77. Byrne, "Conflict Regulation or Conflict Resolution."
78. Byrne, "Toward Tractability."
79. Ibid.
80. Aughey, "The 1998 Agreement."
81. Byrne and Irvin, "External Economic Aid and Policy-making"; and Byrne and Irvin, "A Shared Common Sense."
82. Bew and Patterson, *The British State and the Ulster Crisis.*
83. Dixon, *Northern Ireland.*
84. O'Leary and McGarry, *The Politics of Antagonism.*
85. McGarry and O'Leary, *Explaining Northern Ireland.*
86. O'Leary, "Academic Viewpoint."
87. McGarry and O'Leary, *Explaining Northern Ireland.*
88. Byrne, "Consociational and Civic Society Approaches to Peacebuilding."
89. M. Cox, "The War that Came in from the Cold: Clinton and the Irish Question," *World Policy*, vol. 16, no. 1 (1999), 60–78.
90. Byrne, "Toward Tractability."
91. Ibid.
92. C. Irvin and S. Byrne, "The Perception of Economic Aid in Northern Ireland and Its Role in the Peace Process," in *Peace at Last? The Impact of the Good Friday Agreement on Northern Ireland*, eds. J. Neuheiser & S. Wolff (Oxford, England: Berghahn, 2002), 167–91.
93. Byrne, "Consociational and Civic Society Approaches to Peacebuilding."
94. Dixon, *Northern Ireland.*
95. Byrne, "Toward Tractability."
96. J. Galtung, *Peace by Peaceful Means: Peace and Conflict Development and Civilization* (London: Sage, 1996); and J. Rothman, *Resolving Identity Based Conflicts* (San Francisco, CA: Jossey-Bass, 1997).
97. L. Diamond and J. McDonald, *Multi-Track Diplomacy: A Systems Approach to Peace* (West Hartford, CT: Kumarian, 1996); and R. J. Fisher, *Interactive Conflict Resolution: Pioneers, Potential, and Prospects* (Syracuse, NY: Syracuse University Press, 1996).
98. L. Keashly and R. J. Fisher, "A Contingency Perspective on Conflict Interventions: Theoretical and Practical Considerations, in *Resolving International Conflicts: The Theory and Practice of Mediation*, ed. J. Bercovitch (Boulder, CO: Lynne Rienner Publishers, 1996), 235–63; and S. Woolpert, C. D. Slaton, and E. Schwrin, (Eds.), *Transformational Politics: Theory, Study and Practice* (Albany, NY: SUNY Press, 1998).

226   Sean Byrne

99. Byrne, "Toward Tractability."
100. Byrne, "Consociational and Civic Society Approaches to Peacebuilding" and "Transformational Conflict Resolution."
101. Byrne, *Growing Up in a Divided Society*.
102. Byrne, "Toward Tractibility."
103. L. Kriesberg, *Constructive Conflict: From Escalation to Resolution* (Lanham, MD: Rowman & Littlefield, 1998); and Lederach, *Building Peace*.
104. J. Senehi, "Language, Culture and Conflict: Storytelling as a Matter of Life and Death," *Mind and Human Interaction*, vol. 7, no. 3 (1996), 150–64; J. Senehi, "Constructive Storytelling in Inter-Communal Conflicts: Building Community, Building Peace," in *Reconcilable Differences: Turning Points in Ethnopolitical Conflict*, eds. S. Byrne and C. Irvin (West Hartford, CT: Kumarian, 2000), 96–115; and J. Senehi, "Constructive Storytelling: A Peace Process," *Peace and Conflict Studies*, vol. 9, no. 2 (2002), 41–63.

SUGGESTED STUDY QUESTIONS

1. The globalization and fragmentation in world affairs today might seem to oppose rather than complement each other. Why is this information useful to the student of the Northern Ireland conflict?
2. In dealing with identity conflicts, to what extent are we prisoners of history and to what extent can we successfully innovate?
3. How does history shape people's view of the political conflict in Northern Ireland? How do psycho-cultural and structural factors interact with economic factors and with the international milieu?
4. What effect did the existence of a state of emergency have on community relations in the Northern Ireland conflict?
5. How do economic conditions influence relations between Protestants and Catholics?
6. Does EU integration make Irish unity inevitable?
7. What factors encouraged President Clinton to become engaged in the Northern Ireland peacebuilding process?

WEB SITES RELATED TO THE NORTHERN IRELAND CONFLICT

CAIN Web Service (Conflict Archive on the INternet) http://cain.ulst.ac.uk
CAIN Web Service (Conflict Archive on the INternet)
Guide to Web Sites Containing Information on the Conflict and Politics in Northern Ireland http://cain.ulst.ac.uk/bibdbs/newlinks.html
School of Politics, International Relations, and Philosophy, Keele University, Northern Ireland Government and Politics on the Internet http://www.keele.ac.uk/depts/por/ni.htm
International Conflict Research, University of Ulster http://www.incore.ulst.ac.uk

ABOUT THE AUTHOR

Sean Byrne is a native of Ireland. He is Professor and Director of the Arthur V. Mauro Centre for Peace and Justice at St. Paul's College, University of Manitoba, Canada. Previously, he was Director of the Doctoral Program in the Department of Conflict Analysis and Resolution at Nova Southeastern University, Ft. Lauderdale. Byrne has written many publications in the areas of third-party intervention, ethnic conflict analysis and resolution, and children and conflict. His books include *Growing Up in a Divided Society: The Influence of Conflict on Belfast Schoolchildren* (Cranbury, NJ: Associated University Press, 1997), and he has edited with Cynthia Irvin *Reconcilable Differences: Turning Points in Ethnopolitical Conflicts* (West Hartford, CT: Kumarian Press, 2000). With Cynthia Irvin, he has received research grants from the USIP and SSHRC to explore the role of economic assistance in building the peace dividend in Northern Ireland.

The Role of Constructive, Transcultural Storytelling in Ethnopolitical Conflict Transformation in Northern Ireland

Jessica Senehi

Northern Ireland encompasses six counties in the northern region of the island of Ireland and is part of the United Kingdom. The conflict between the Catholic and Protestant communities there—like other ethnopolitical conflicts—is driven by a complexity of interconnected factors, including psycho-cultural, linguistic, historical, political, economic, and geographic dimensions.[1] Of course, the identity of these communities are not monolithic. Within each community, there are differences among how people view the conflict and the degree of their commitment, if any, to violent struggle. Further, the degree of community mobilization around intergroup conflict varies at different historical moments and in different situations.

The Northern Ireland conflict has historical roots going back centuries, which are memorialized in word, song, art, and ritual passed from one generation to the next.[2] Images of the conflict and the "other" encoded in these expressive traditions fuel an us-versus-them mentality and justifies violence against the other group. Meanwhile, structural issues—such as access to the economic and governance systems—have fueled a sense of frustration on the part of Catholics and moderate Protestants who mobilized for civil rights beginning in the late 1960s, which led to violent escalation of the conflict. This marked the beginning of the recent period of conflict, characterized in popular parlance as the "Troubles." For the Protestant community, despite their slight majority in Northern Ireland, their minority status within an all-island context and in Great Britain fuels political insecurity. More than 3,200 people have died in intercommunal violence during the "Troubles."

Currently, the conflict is in a "post-conflict" or "post-accord" phase, characterized by a "negative peace" or a "cold peace"—that is, while direct violence has for the most part ceased and processes of conflict deescalation have more momentum than their opposite, contention remains over political and economic issues, as well as lack of familiarity and mistrust between communities. The transformation of the intercommunal relationship to one characterized by mutual recognition, power sharing, mutual trust, and a shared understanding of history and vision for the future is an incomplete project.

This essay is based on the understanding that this peace-building and community relations work needs to be undertaken by people in all levels of society and along multiple tracks.[3] Approaches along different tracks and at different levels of society will have different characteristics and meet different types of needs. The focus of this essay is on the potential role of storytelling in peace-building in ethnopolitical conflicts, specifically Northern Ireland, now in a post-accord peace-building stage. Storytelling is not seen as a panacea, but rather as one among many significant types of peacemaking and peace-building approaches.

Ethnopolitical conflicts involve the collision of two stories, two cultural narratives. These narratives underpin cultural identity, knowledge, and history in ways that actually encode the conflict into the identity of one group by excluding the knowledge system of the other community and defining that community as an enemy. This creates one means through which the conflict is sustained, remains resistant to resolution and transformation, and is transmitted (along with the trauma associated with it) transgenerationally. Conflict transformation requires that both parties become aware of the constructed nature of narratives without discounting their legitimacy, learn to understand the narrative of the other community while recognizing its legitimacy, and are able to craft a shared narrative and identity without losing hold of each community's distinct experience and need for healing and social justice. Drawing on the case of Northern Ireland, it is argued that constructive storytelling approaches to conflict resolution and peace-building are one significant way to get at these issues.

Using the case of Northern Ireland as an example, the thesis of this chapter is that story-based approaches to peacemaking and peace-building may get at some of the key dilemmas in post-conflict peacemaking and peace-building. After more than a decade of experience with the post–Cold War era, characterized by intense—often genocidal—ethnopolitical conflicts, some key insights and concerns have emerged among conflict intervenors on the front lines and researchers. First, ethnopolitical conflicts are complex, requiring multiple interventions by multiple actors at multiple levels of society. Second, conflict is not erased with the swish of a pen on a treaty, accord, or pact crafted by political elites, but rather lasting peace requires building relationships between communities. Third, it is critical to draw on the material and intellectual resources on the ground at the conflict zone in designing and implementing conflict resolution interventions and development projects. Fourth, rebuilding an inclusive society requires the development of a shared identity without erasing the identities of the different communities within that society. Fifth, communities need to heal and move on while at the same time honoring their past; this requires both advocacy and connection, both social justice and reconciliation.

CONSTRUCTIVE STORYTELLING

Storytelling, as used here, refers most of the time to the art of telling a story, includes both oral (and signed) narrative, involves a teller and at least one listener, and, thus, is a social interaction.[4] Some forms of written storytelling are also mentioned in the following examples. Storytelling may involve relating of fictional tales or personal experience and group history, but all narratives are never pure fact or fiction. A fantastic tale may be used as a parable to express something that the teller sees as true. Meanwhile, narratives of personal or group experience are constructed and interpretive. Historical accounts are selected, framed, and used—often to make a point about the present in order to affect the future.[5]

While the relationship between narrative and truth is complex, not all narratives are equal. They may be evaluated and some deemed better than others.[6] Different people may respond to a narrative differently, by embracing the story, by taking an oppositional stance to it, or reframing the story in some way.[7] Within communities, meaning is negotiated through narratives, and certain versions will not have currency with the group and will not be circulated.[8]

It is critical to recognize the interrelationship of story and social structures. Even though group history and personal narratives may be formulated in the interests of the narrator, the fact that a particular event occurred may be undeniable. Just because cultural knowledge is socially constructed does not mean that conflict is all in one's head. One cannot conclude that there are no structural bases of conflict (e.g., structural and social inequalities) nor that socially constructed ideas (e.g., gender or race) do not have material consequences. Rather, the production of meaning is an important process in social life that in intractable conflicts can have high stakes. It is the role of storytelling in the production of meaning and access to that process that is the focus here.

Again, this is not to suggest that storytelling is necessarily good or peaceful. Discursive practices—here, storytelling—may intensify social cleavages when they privilege some cultures while silencing others, generate or reproduce prejudicial and enemy images of other groups, mask inequalities and justice, inflame negative emotions, or misrepresent society. On the other hand, discursive practices may enhance peaceful relations when they involve a dialogue characterized by shared power, engender mutual recognition, promote consciousness-raising, serve to resist domination, or teach conflict resolution strategies.

Constructive storytelling refers to storytelling that is characterized by shared power—or "power with"—and is alternative to coercive power—or "power over." It is a highly inclusive and collaborative process through which persons can participate in the social construction of meaning and establish bonds of community. Storytelling is *not* constructive if it is characterized by a power imbalance and only one person or one group in power is doing most of the talking or controlling the production of knowledge. Even silence can be used as a power play by superordinate individuals or groups to prevent commentary or dialogue that challenges the status quo. Constructive storytelling is characterized by everyone having access to and inclusion in the storytelling process. It allows for a diversity of stories to be told and presents an opportunity for the de-silencing of experience. In these ways, the storytelling process is congruent with the concepts of mutual recognition (inclusion), empowerment (power sharing), and critical consciousness (honesty and awareness-of-self-in-context) that are fundamental to positive peace.

Stories have been used in all societies throughout time in many ways and for many reasons, including for purposes of mediation, diplomacy, cross-cultural relationship building, social activism, and social change.[9] Meanwhile, many people in Northern Ireland, Western Europe, the United States, Canada, and the rest of the world have described themselves as storytellers and have used storytelling and story-based projects in intentional ways in diverse social and professional contexts, including building community, resolving conflicts, and building peace.[10]

Often, these contemporary storytellers tell stories within cross-cultural or culturally heterogeneous contexts. I call this *transcultural storytelling*.[11] While, it is well recognized that storytelling is a means of sharing knowledge and building culture within community, less consideration has been given to how storytellers might represent their culture to others. This may be a critical means through which minority communities may negotiate their identity within the wider society or within multicultural societies. Such transcultural storytelling, however, is not something resulting from modernity. Storytelling has always been used not only to build culture but also to negotiate cross-cultural boundaries.

Many of the key events in the history of the Northern Ireland conflict have been memorialized in word, song, murals, and rituals passed from one generation to the next. These expressive forms are produced within the subcultures of the Protestant and Catholic communities.[12] They are a means through which each community articulates its identity—including understandings of the past, current values, and visions of the future—and speaks out to the other community and the world. Even though these communities may recognize or be audiences (perhaps unavoidably) of each other's popular expressive culture, these are parallel—not interactive—processes. Both Protestants and Catholics see each other's murals, understand their symbolism, and read these symbols as messages about who is safe in a particular geographic location. Both Protes-

tants and Catholics memorialize historic battles with yearly parades. These parades are read differently in different communities and at different times. During times of relative peace before the "Troubles," the parades celebrating the historical interpretation of one side might be seen as a recreational day out for both communities. However, in tenser times, the parades can be an expression of triumphalism or interpreted that way by the other community. There can be mutual understanding without mutual recognition; that is, both sides can understand what the other is saying but be unable to walk in the other's shoes and get the other's viewpoint at an empathetic level and with regard to the other's legitimacy. In these ways, the communities do not make sense of collective experience collectively.

In Northern Ireland, the Protestant and Catholic communities are very segregated in terms of residential patterns, schooling, religion, and culture. While there is an integrated school movement, it accounts for less than 10 percent of schoolchildren. The cultural geography reflects the ethnopolitical divide. In Belfast, eighteen-foot-high walls form a "Peace Line" that separates Protestant and Catholic neighborhoods. Other markers, including murals and painted curbs (painted either the colors of the British or the Irish flag) indicate whether a particular block's residents are Protestant or Catholic. Even sports are quite segregated, with Gaelic football and hurling being mostly Catholic sports and cricket and rugby generally Protestant sports.

Storytelling may provide a means to contribute to breaking down stereotypic images of the conflict and the other community. Story-based approaches to peacemaking and peace-building might provide a means for parallel tracks of cultural meaning making to meet, cross, or converge. In an assessment of storytelling activity in both Northern Ireland and the Republic of Ireland, conducted for the Verbal Arts Centre in Londonderry, including a survey of sixty-seven people involved in storytelling projects, Pat Ryan found that 97 percent of respondents felt that "storytelling was a powerful vehicle for better understanding between individuals from different backgrounds," and 55 percent of those agreed that "there are specific roles for storytelling in increasing mutual understanding, especially as defined by the Northern Ireland curriculum."[13] The report describes storytellers, storytelling clubs, storytelling festivals, and storytelling projects on the island. Clearly, this is a significant cultural and local resource that might play a role in future projects aimed at conflict transformation.

RECOGNIZING CONFLICT COMPLEXITY

Ethnopolitical conflicts are complex, which contributes to their intractability, but complexity can also be a resource as it suggests multiple modes of intervention. Protracted ethnopolitical conflicts play themselves out in multiple planes of social life. The cultural dimension is one of these. In Northern Ireland, as discussed, conflict is articulated and explained in story, poetry, song, and art. Ethnopolitical conflict transformation will require some new stories, metaphors, symbols, and paradigms. Movement toward conflict transformation can occur in different social arenas and along different tracks, suggesting many roles and types of intervention that foster conflict transformation and social change. This includes storytellers, other artists, and the media—all of whom are involved in reproducing and producing culture.

Conflict transformation requires not only participation from different sectors of society but also participation at all levels of society—grassroots, middle-tier, and elite levels.[14] Storytelling is an effective way to promote the expression of grassroots knowledge, which can perhaps trickle up and shape a revised and more nuanced master narrative. Whether conflict transformation occurs at the grassroots, middle-tier, or elite level, this process can only happen person to person. It is a one-on-one process. Transformation can only occur one person at a time, one heart at a time, one mind at a time. Conflict transformation almost always involves storytelling.

Conflict resolution involves addressing both structural and psychocultural causes. Addressing psychocultural issues is critical for creating the relationship and trust necessary for parties' constructive collaborative problem solving.[15] A focus on storytelling gets at some of these more intangible factors. For example, storytelling is a means of creating and articulating identities; storytelling is critical to the processes of children's cultural and political socialization; and storytelling expresses emotions that can promote healing and empathy.

The analysis and resolution of conflicts is also complicated by the fact that conflicts vary in terms of their stage of development and intensity. Intervention approaches are contingent on these factors.[16] Storytelling is more appropriate and applicable in later peace-building stages of conflict. However, these stages are not completely distinct. Social change does not happen in a lockstep manner. Within each community, people will take different positions on the conflict, with some people doing relationship building across the divide that provides the groundwork for a future peace process. However, storytelling can be relevant for conflict mitigation at all stages, sometimes inviting a paradigm shift. In Northern Ireland, during a break in negotiations between elites, sharing stories and musical talents created a relaxing and unthreatening setting for interpersonal relationship building that was critical for motivating parties in the next go-round of negotiations and taking them to the next step.[17]

TRANSFORMING INTERCOMMUNAL RELATIONSHIPS

Storytellers consistently emphasize that storytelling builds community. This process occurs on many levels. First, storytelling creates and gives expression to personal and group identity. Narration fosters empathy as listeners identify with the person telling the story or the characters in a story, even across conflict divides. Storytellers of one culture telling to listeners of another culture report being motivated to represent their culture positively in order to counteract stereotypes and prejudice and create goodwill for their group. Stories also engender emotions that may invite compassion, understanding, and a change of heart. Storytelling in a cross-cultural setting may create a shared identity encompassing both groups even momentarily as individuals identify with the storytelling. Dan Bar-On and others have brought together people from different sides of protracted social conflicts, including in Northern Ireland, in seminars called "To Trust and Reflect."[18] During these seminars, participants share their personal experiences and listen to those of others. Evaluations of some of the first seminars, involving Palestinians and Israelis, emphasize the value of storytelling: "Hearing the stories of the 'other' and learning more about their pain and suffering was something that left an impact on me. Storytelling and the care, support, safety, and protection of the TRT group made it easy to open up and trust."[19] A significant aspect of storytelling is that even though individuals can develop their storytelling skills as a performance art, storytelling is something that everyone can participate in without any training at all, including youths and even very young children. For eighteen years, Reverend Doug Baker has developed and led programs for children in Corrymeela, a residential ecumenical center at the northern tip of Northern Ireland. He reflects, "Only after they find what they have in common, through storytelling and sharing of experiences such as family habits or outside interests, and establish some identification with each other, can we move on to questions on which the kids will likely disagree. If they can develop some degree of relationship, the course will be different from that point forward. They can agree to disagree and begin to understand each other's points of view."[20]

Storytelling is critical to this process. As Baker puts it, "There is a particular value in storytelling as a contribution to communication between opposing groups and to building peace. You cannot reconcile anyone; they must do that themselves. But you can enable people to hear each other's stories, which in itself often leads to awareness and bonds which facilitate reconciliation."[21] Storytelling is a way of knowing that combines both the sharing of knowledge with the sharing of feelings, resulting in a profound exchange that creates new social bonds.

While every culture has stories, each culture has its own stories and cultural norms may differ in regard to storytelling style and what stories are appropriate to tell, when, and by whom. While Northern Ireland's culture is known for the wit and everyday storytelling skills of its members, the Northern Irish are also known for being extremely reserved when it comes to speaking publicly about the conflict or revealing themselves through direct personal stories. Such cultural communication norms will affect storytelling projects. For example, the United States Institute of Peace wanted to promote dialogue and interpersonal storytelling among Catholic and Protestant youths in Northern Ireland. However, in keeping with their cultures, the youth were reserved in their interactions. Yet when given the opportunity to travel to Bosnia, where they met Muslim and Christian youths who were also dealing with a violent ethnopolitical conflict and who were engaged in dialogue and peacemaking, real dialogue could begin. The change in context, the example of others in dialogue, and the realization that Northern Ireland was not the only region dealing with conflict were factors in the youths' recognition of their shared experience of violence across the divide.[22] Such relationship building across a sectarian divide and a huge geographic divide is by definition empowering. Storytelling creates bonds, and in this case storytelling is creating an international network of young adults who have experience in peace-building in the aftermath of violence. This helped the youths engage in community building.

Storyteller Liz Weir, a professional storyteller in Northern Ireland, established a yarn spinner's group (or storytelling guild) in Belfast to build community across the sectarian divide. Weir stated:

> Storytelling has an extremely important part to play in the modern world. This bringing together of people on a personal level. It creates personal connection. In storytelling, you don't ask a person who they are when they come to a storytelling group, but you know. One person would tell a story about going to Mass. Somebody else would tell a story about going to an Orange Lodge dinner. So you know one's a Catholic and one's a Protestant.[23]

The storytelling guild provides a context within which people can build relationships on a personal level simply by telling folktales or relating stories about their lives. Because storytelling is a flexible process and because the storytellers are in control, they are able to reveal only as much as they are comfortable revealing. However, even one's choice of story indicates one's values and interests. As storytellers often say, "You are known by the stories you tell." Ireland is a culture known for its storytelling. However, in this situation, in a community often characterized by sectarian separation and conflict, Weir is using the Celtic storytelling tradition in a new, transcultural context. Through this process, a broader, shared identity is developed.

Because storytelling can be pleasurable and fascinating, it motivates people to be involved, to participate, and to collaborate in storytelling programs or story-based projects. This increases participants' willingness to resolve their differences. For example, Northern Ireland's Pat Ryan reports the following incident:

> A storyteller recounted how he was visiting various schools around Castlederg. Two schools in the area shared the same bus route. Although the children from the two schools rode the bus together every day, the groups never spoke to one another. Each viewed the children from the different school as being of the "other" side.
>
> Around the end of the storyteller's residency, the principal of the school informed him that a "miracle" had occurred. Overhearing one of the children from the "other" school talking about a "surprise" visit from the storyteller who was to come that day, the eavesdropper and his friends began to regale their opposites, proclaiming that the storyteller was "brilliant." They even proceeded to reveal the teller's entire repertoire, performing all his stories, riddles, and songs. By the end of the bus journey no one could have stopped the two groups chattering to each other even if they wanted to![24]

Shared pleasurable activity and happiness build genuine bonds among people.

In constructive storytelling, facilitators and participants establish an environment of safety, respect, openness, and inclusion. Storytellers reveal their values with the stories they tell. In constructive storytelling, listeners are interested in the stories of others. Storytelling promotes mutual understanding as people get to know each other beyond the surface level. Tellers and listeners share the pleasurable experience of storytelling together. They laugh and cry together. Such interpersonal interaction creates bonds of community that are felt and sensed. Through storytelling, people can name their problems and experiences and engage in a collective process of developing shared meaning.

INCLUDING LOCAL STAKEHOLDERS AND THEIR KNOWLEDGE

Conflict resolution and peace-building approaches must not be guided solely by intervenors who come from outside the conflict zone.[25] It is increasingly recognized that conflict resolution interventions—even when facilitated by insiders—are best when they are elicitive, include the perspectives of all stakeholders, and respect the knowledge that those

in the setting already have. For example, a program to bring peace education to a school should not exclude or marginalize local schoolteachers from the process. In many conflict interventions, there is often a desire to meet one's objectives as soon as possible; eliciting knowledge and collaboration from others is time-consuming. But this can be seen as the long-short way: it is more time-consuming in the short run but leads to easier implementation and greater success and stability in the long term. Local knowledge is encoded in stories of personal experience and folklore.

Storytelling—if focused on promoting voice rather than didactic storytelling—by its nature is elicitive and empowering. Storytelling fosters inclusion because it is so inclusive. Storytelling requires little or no equipment, money, or personnel; storytelling is low-tech. Culture is always being created and produced through the stories people tell about themselves. Thus, the accessibility of storytelling is significant for increasing people's participation in defining their culture, their community, and themselves regardless of financial circumstances and even under dire conditions in conflict zones. Storytelling is intellectually accessible; everybody "gets it." Everybody can understand stories and participate regardless of age, culture, or background. Storytelling does not require costly or time-consuming training, so all groups can participate in cultural production with little gatekeeping.

In fact, this is why colonization and oppression rarely fully wipe out culture; as James Scott put it in his study of slave folklore: "Short of killing its bearer, the human voice is irrepressible."[26] Storytellers include people by reminding them that "everyone is a storyteller" as we tell stories frequently in our daily lives. Storytelling happens in person; the storyteller is accessible and accountable to the listener in person. Listeners are close to the sources of cultural production. Post-story discussion allows for a shared process of knowledge development. Thus storytelling is an appropriate methodology for meeting the need to include the knowledge of all stakeholders in a particular intervention.

An example of how storytelling can be used to promote peace-building can be found in the work of Ian White, director of the Glencree Centre for Reconciliation. In 1998, the center established a program of victim–combatant dialogue in Northern Ireland called "Let's Involve the Victim's

Experience (LIVE). The goal of this dialogue program was to promote personal and collective healing and relationship building. It also sought to de-silence and include those who had been affected by the conflict as victims or perpetrators or both.[27]

The Arts Council of Northern Ireland Fund supports a not-for-profit initiative aimed at raising the status of children's writing and artwork by validating children's own creative skills and providing them with a rich arts experience. This program also includes an effort to promote "unheard voices" to reduce social inequalities. Less privileged groups in Northern Ireland, as in most conflicts, typically experience the more direct ill effects of violence. Therefore, part of this program involves a focus on "Young L'Derry Voices," which is a cross-community collaboration designed to provide a space for youth to collaboratively explore their experience of violence and interpret and express those experiences through art.

ACHIEVING DIVERSITY WITHIN UNITY

Ethnopolitical conflict transformation requires a paradoxical need to both honor the distinct identities of different communities and simultaneously promote the co-creation of a shared identity and set of common understandings that allow for unity. This is complicated by the fact that in the context of conflict the identity of belonging to one community has been bound up with *not* belonging to the other community. However, as storytelling can account for complexity, paradox, and stories within stories, it is possible for shared narratives to exist. Simply recognizing the legitimacy of another's perspective, even if one disagrees with it, is a move toward mutual recognition and respect.

In 1998, some schools in rural South Tyrone, near the southern border of Northern Ireland, established a program called "Pathways to Peace and Reconciliation," based on the belief that the arts can unite people from two different cultures by focusing on interests that are common to both. The program brings together children from different religious and class backgrounds to explore cultural diversity, as well as their common heritage, in order to (a) empower the children by improving their self-confidence and self-efficacy, (b) reduce social exclusion and marginalization, and (c) promote

understanding and respect for cultural differences. Children are instructed to collect stories from grandparents, other relatives, and neighbors and to use these as the basis for their own story construction and other artwork.

Unity in diversity is the goal of an integrated education program in Northern Ireland called "Education for Mutual Understanding," which includes many storytelling activities. Storytelling is part of many programs in schools and is one of the many activities of National Integration Education Week. Storytelling embodied in folklore is recognized as a means through which children can locate themselves culturally in the world and also can recognize that others have traditions and worldviews.[28]

NEGOTIATING THE NEEDS FOR REMEMBRANCE AND MOVING ON

The transformation of ethnopolitical conflicts needs to satisfy the paradoxical needs of moving on (forgetting) and honoring (remembering) the past.[29] Honoring the past may be associated with loyalty to one's community and be an obstacle to reconciliation. However, storytelling offers a means by which these two seemingly polar goals can be achieved. It is possible that a collective history embraced by previously conflicting communities might no longer exclude or misrepresent whole groups of people. If collective trauma is acknowledged and healed, it may be possible for it also to be honored in the collective memory in written record, cultural production, ritual, and interpretive sites.

Truth and reconciliation commissions are a collective process of public storytelling. They have been one means through which this forgetting–remembering paradox has been negotiated although such commissions' work is not simple and can be controversial in many ways.[30] In 1998, people from Victim Support Northern Ireland and the Northern Ireland Association for the Care and Resettlement of Offenders consulted with Dr. Alex Boraine, then Deputy Chair of the South African Truth and Reconciliation Commission and others, about developing a healing process in Northern Ireland. As a result of these efforts, in 1998 the Healing Through Remembering Project was established with funding from the Community Relations Council. In June 2002, the project issued a ninety-eight-page report with recommendations. The report emphasizes storytelling, especially testimony:

> Stories and narratives will be collected from all who wish to tell of their experiences of the conflict in and about Northern Ireland. These stories—collected by those already undertaking this type of work and by community groups through a flexible but standard method—would form part of an archive housing the stories of past and serving as a vehicle to learn lessons for the future.[31]

Such storytelling is both straightforward and incredibly complex as it requires numerous choices ranging from how such projects are crafted to considerations regarding managing emotions and achieving a respectful and dignified process.

RECOMMENDATIONS

This chapter describes the nature of interventions that use a storytelling approach but does not evaluate them. There is little empirical evidence regarding how such approaches might actually impact conflict and lead to structural change. However, Saunders argues that sustained dialogue and relationship building over a twenty-year period between Palestinians and Israelis was critical to the Middle East peace process and its progress.[32] The significance of cultural aspects in sustaining ethnopolitical conflicts is well recognized, so it is likely that interventions involving constructive cultural production and relationship building must move in the right direction. It is important for future research to strive to evaluate these approaches.

For those considering using a story-based intervention, the following questions can serve as a guideline.

1. *What are the objectives?* Storytelling is a medium not a model. Again, one of the key attributes of a story-based practice is that a particular project can be highly tailored to the particular needs and resources of a situation. A constructive storytelling process may take shape in innumerable ways. Be reflective, detailed, and open-minded in considering your objectives and how you can appropriately achieve them. Objectives should be broad. Designing a project to get people to think a certain way would be overly prescriptive and objectify participants. Didadicticism contravenes the spirit of constructive storytelling, which emphasizes the process of co-creation among the teller and listeners.

2. *Who will be included?* In the design of your project, ensure a balance of power as constructive storytelling provides for power inequality. Such storytelling must provide people with space to speak.

3. *What possible form might a project take?* Because storytelling is so inexpensive and doable, small inexpensive projects tailored to the specific needs of parties or communities are possible. Storytelling approaches to reconciliation may involve working with personal narratives or creating new forms. Consider artistic or other story-based projects that allow for multiple perspectives and experiences to coexist. For example, the stories of diverse persons in one community can be collected and woven together in one dramatic form. Storytelling can be combined with other artistic forms, such as dance, music, and art.

4. *Is there room for the unexpected?* Empowering people by giving them a forum in which to tell their story and engage in a truly creative endeavor always creates an element of unpredictability, which can make people uncomfortable. It is important to have a safe place to examine all perspectives respectfully.

5. *Will there be guidelines?* While the goal of storytelling is to encourage people to express themselves as freely as possible, it may be helpful to set up some guidelines to ensure participants' interactions are respectful. It is best if the participants in the project have a role in establishing those guidelines.

6. *A word about content:* Constructive storytelling is about empowering storytellers and sharing stories, rather than using stories dogmatically or didactically to promote a particular point of view. However, storytelling can be a means of providing models for positive conflict resolution. For example, it is critically important to tell the stories of success involving persons and groups who have been successful in transforming conflicts and achieving reconciliation. The international nongovernmental organization Search for Common Ground has developed an Arts and Culture Program that develops and promotes films that show how individuals on opposite sides of social divides have found common ground and friendship. The goal is for the films to be followed by a facilitated discussion among the members of the audience. A relatively structured, formal, or planned storytelling session becomes the precursor and catalyst of additional storytelling immediately following. In many traditional and contemporary contexts, this spontaneous storytelling is an important part of the overall event.

7. *Have fun!* The fact that storytelling can be pleasurable adds to its power as a potential peacemaking and peace-building methodology.

Community decision makers and opinion leaders must take seriously the power of storytelling:

1. *Be conscious of stories.* Listen to the stories of all the communities in the conflict. At which point do disputing parties' versions of the story come into conflict? Such differences may seem zero sum in the sense that they cannot be reconciled. Consider whether or not there is a way to expand the narrative pie and tell the story in such a way that different experiences coexist. How can a larger diversity of stories enter the public transcript? Listen to the cultural voices and include them in the process. At a storytelling workshop at the University of Colorado in April 2003, Northern Irish storyteller Liz Weir reported that members of the Northern Ireland Assembly met with singer and songwriter Tommy Sands the previous December. Sands told a story about two buses coming from opposite directions in each other's way on a narrow street. The drivers—like the government—needed to back up before they could go forward again.

2. *Value arts education.* Art for art's sake is wonderful because it allows people to be themselves rather than focusing on meeting some prescribed standard as is usually the case in school, on the job, and in so many arenas of life. This is arguably more true of the folk arts (rather than so-called "high" arts), such as storytelling, because the art forms are more flexible. Through storytelling and other arts, students learn skills of creativity that are necessary for problem solving and envisioning alternatives to conflict and strife. Equally important, they learn communication skills that are critical for participating empathically and persuasively in social life.

3. *Listen for new, changing, and alternative stories.* While cultural identity, collective history, and shared knowledge have a storied character, no one story can capture the complexity and fluidity of forces. Cultural understandings of self, past, and future goals are not a coherent whole or fixed. Rather culture contains contradictions. Its boundaries are porous, allowing for cultural connections and multicultural identities. Its history is complex, encompassing a diversity of experiences and social forces. Future goals may be uncertain and contested. This does not necessarily create disorder or chaos but rather a complex social conversation and negotiation, which is a community resource that generates a body of knowledge born of dialogue and which holds the possibility for new meaning to be synergistically generated in the face of new challenges.

4. *Value cultural participation.* Research has suggested that storytelling not only gave people the space to voice their perspectives; it also gave them a space to expand their philosophies. Peace requires building relationships and participating in building society. This is deep democracy. Thus, the ability to express one's experience and perspective, to listen, to share in pleasurable celebrations, and to negotiate meaning within community are critical for citizenship in a democratic society. Storytelling can be one way to promote these processes. Paradoxically, storytelling is accessible and flexible at the same time that it is also complex and operates on multiple modalities—emotional, intellectual, even spiritual— at the same time that it is an interpersonal interaction. Communities need to be grounded in one-to-one personal contact and relationships. Storytelling and folk arts provide a way for people to come together in a context of pleasure to—as storyteller Francis Parks put it—"share political notions, economic notions, and notions of justice."[*]

Endnotes

1. Sean Byrne and Neal Carter, "Social Cubism: Six Social Forces of Ethno-territorial Conflict in Northern Ireland and Quebec," *Journal of Peace and Conflict Studies*, vol. 3, no. 2 (1996): 52–71.

2. The Northern Ireland conflict has a long history of grievances, claims to sovereignty, and violence that has shaped the sectarian behavior of the Protestant and Catholic communities. For example, the historical narrative from the Catholic perspective would emphasize the conflict as beginning with the Norman invasion and conquest of the island in 1171, after which point Ireland became a colony of England. For the Protestants, the conflict began with the 1603 Ulster Plantation, when King James I of England granted land in the province of Ulster to Scottish Calvinist settlers, resulting in the displacement of Catholics from their land. Because of religious differences and views about the other side, these communities rarely intermarried and remained largely distinct communities over the centuries.

   From 1692 to 1760, Penal Laws were instituted by England. This legislation barred Catholics from practicing their religion, owning land, speaking the Gaelic language, running for governmental offices, and voting. There were also statutes regarding other religious groups, such as Jews and Quakers. From 1884 to 1888, the Potato Famine decimated the population of Ireland as many people died of

[*]*Many thanks to Sean Byrne, Judy Carter, and Ariann Kara Kehler for their comments on this paper. However, the responsibility for the contents and any inaccuracies are the author's own. The research and writing of this paper were supported by a University Research Project Grant from the University of Manitoba for the study of "The Role of Storytelling and Popular Expressive Traditions in Peacebuilding."*

starvation or emigrated to the United States, Australia, or Canada, reducing the island's population by half. In the 1870s, a struggle arose between landlords and tenant farmers. In the context of severe poverty and scarce resources, there as was struggle between Catholic and Protestant tenant farmers. The idea of "Land for the Farmers" became defined by Catholics as "Ireland for the Irish." Meanwhile, in the industrialized northeast of Ulster, wealthy industrialists wanted to keep the union with Britain, which was the market for their manufactured products, and "Unionism" became the unifying ideology of Protestants. Nationalism (Home Rule for the island, with a devolved parliament in Dublin) became the unifying ideology for Catholics. The salient identity for the people was a nationalist–religious identity rather than a class identity, arguably dividing the poorer classes and benefiting the wealthy in Northern Ireland and Britain.

Beginning in 1905, Catholic Nationalism became a call for independent statehood for the island, which resulted in the 1916 Rising in Dublin by the Irish Republican Army and the 1919 War of Independence. The latter resulted in the Anglo—Irish Treaty that was ratified in Dublin and gave independence to twenty-six of the thirty-two counties in Ireland, while the other six counties in the northeast of Ulster remained part of Britain. Anti-treaty IRA forces rejected the treaty, leading to a year of violent civil war followed by a truce.

In 1926, the former IRA forces became the Sinn Fein opposition government in the Irish Free State. Within Northern Ireland, an alienated Catholic population opted out of politics. The Ulster Unionist party, in effect, became a one-party government that discriminated against its Catholic minority in housing, employment, and voting. In the 1960s, young Northern Irish Catholics attended Queen's University in greater numbers due to British government funding. Many of these youths formed the Northern Ireland Civil Rights Association with moderate Protestants to agitate and protest nonviolently for civil rights for all of Northern Ireland's citizens. In 1968, extremist Protestants in the Royal Ulster Constabulary and the B-Specials (an auxiliary police force) attacked the marchers. Law and order began to break down, and the British army sent to Northern Ireland to protect Catholics from sectarian violence was attacked by a resurgent Provisional IRA.

Since that time, a number of political initiatives by the British government to create a power-sharing government in Northern Ireland failed because of Unionist opposition. The 1985 Anglo–Irish agreement ended the Unionist veto and changed the political milieu in Northern Ireland. A civil society approach combined with a political process facilitated by the British and Irish governments and mediated by U.S. Senator George Mitchell resulted in the 1998 Good Friday Agreement (GFA), ratified by elections in Northern Ireland and the Republic of Ireland. The GFA created a devolved power-sharing government in Belfast, brought the paramilitaries from both sides into the peace process, reformed the police force, and set in place a decommissioning of weapons. Currently, a "cold peace" exists in Northern Ireland as the political parties try to create a formula for government, and the decommissioning of weapons has yet to be resolved.

3. John Paul Lederach emphasizes the needs for conflict transformation to include the elite, middle-tier, and grassroots levels of society in *Preparing for Peace: Conflict Transformation Across Cultures* (Syracuse, NY: Syracuse University Press, 1996); and Louise Diamond and John MacDonald delineate nine tracks for diplomacy involving government, conflict resolution professionals, business, private citizens, academics, activism, religion, funding, and media in *Multi-Track Diplomacy: A Systems Approach to Peace,* 3rd ed. (West Hartford, CT: Kumarian, 1996).

4. Pat Ryan, *Storytelling in Ireland: A Re-awakening* (Londonderry, England: The Verbal Arts Centre, 1995).

5. Donald Consentino, *Defiant Maids and Stubborn Farmers: Tradition and Innovation in Mende Story Performance* (Cambridge, England: Cambridge University Press, 1982); Harold Scheub, *The Tongue Is Fire: South African Storytellers and Apartheid* (Madison: University of Wisconsin Press, 1996); and Elizabeth Tonkin, *Narrating Our Pasts: The Social Construction of Oral History* (Cambridge, England: Cambridge University Press, 1992).

6. Donna Haraway, *Primate Visions* (New York: Routledge, 1989).

7. Jacqueline Bobo, *Black Women as Cultural Readers* (New York: Columbia University Press, 1996).

8. Barbara Myerhoff, *Remembered Lives: The Work of Ritual, Storytelling and Growing Older* (Athens: University of Georgia Press, 1992); and Greg Urban, *Metaphysical Community* (Austin: University of Texas Press, 1996).

9. Julie Cruikshank, *The Social Life of Stories: Narrative and Knowledge in the Yukon Territory* (Lincoln: University of Nebraska Press, 1998) ; Scheub, *The Tongue Is Fire*; and Thomas A. Hale, *Griots and Griottes: Masters of Words and Music* (Bloomington: Indiana University Press, 1998)

10. Ryan, *Storytelling in Ireland;* Marian Liebmann, *Arts Approaches to Conflict* (London: Jessica Kingsley, 1996); Margaret Read MacDonald, *Traditional Storytelling Today: An International Sourcebook* (Chicago: Fitzroy Dearborn, 1999); Jessica Senehi, "Constructive Storytelling: A Peace Process," *Peace and Conflict Studies,* vol. 9, no. 2(2002), 41–63; and Allison M. Cox and David H. Albert, eds., *The Healing Heart—Communities: Storytelling to Build Strong and Healthy Communities* (Gabriola Island, BC: New Society, 2003).

11. Senehi, "Constructive Storytelling."

12. It is critical to emphasize that culture is not monolithic or clearly bounded. References to the Protestant and Catholic communities are meant to be construed as a very generalized category.

13. Ryan, *Storytelling in Ireland,* 68.

14. John Paul Lederach, *Building Peace: Sustainable Reconciliation in Divided Societies* (Washington, DC: United States Institute of Peace, 1997).

15. Vamik D. Volkan, Demetrios A. Julius, and Joseph V. Montville, eds. *The Psychodynamics of International Relationships,* vols. 1 and 2. (Lexington, MA: Lexington Books, 1990, 1991) ; Jay Rothman, *From Confrontation to Cooperation: Resolving Ethnic and Regional Conflict* (Newbury Park, CA: Sage, 1992); Marc Howard Ross, *The Management of Conflict: Interpretations and Interests in*

Comparative Perspective (New Haven, CT: Yale University Press, 1993).

16. Loraleigh Keashly and Ron Fisher, "A Contingency Perspective on Conflict Interventions: Theoretical and Practical Considerations," in *Resolving International Conflicts: The Theory and Practice of Mediation,* ed. J. Bercovitch (Boulder, CO: Lynne Rienner, 1996); and Sean Byrne and Loraleigh Keashly, "Working with Ethno-Political Conflict: A Mutli-Modal and Multi-Level Approach to Conflict Intervention," *International Peacekeeping,* vol. 7 (2000), 97–120.

17. George Mitchell, personal communication, April 18, 2000.

18. Dan Bar-On, ed, *Bridging the Gap: Storytelling as a Way to Work Through Political and Collective Hostilities* (Hamburg, Germany: Körber-Stiftung, 2000); and Joseph H. Albeck, Sami Adwan, and Dan Bar-On, "Dialogue Groups: TRT's Guidelines for Working through Intractable Conflicts by Personal Storytelling," *Peace and Conflict: Journal of Peace Psychology,* vol. 8, no. 4 (2002), 301–02.

19. Ifat Maoz, "Expectations, Results and Perspectives: The Evaluation Report," in *Bridging the Gap: Storytelling as a Way to Work Through Political and Collective Hostilities,* ed. Dan Bar-On (Hamburg, Germany: Körber-Stiftung, 2000).

20. Miriam Saul, "The Real Peacemakers," *Presbyterians Today* (April 2002), 10–13.

21. Doug Baker, "Bringing Peace to the City of Belfast," *Northern Friends Peace Board Newsletter,* December 1998.

22. Neil McMaster, "Peacemakers or Troublemakers? Young People and the Transition to Peace," presentation made at the Conference on Peacebuilding after Peace Accords, Joan B. Kroc Institute for International Peace Studies, Notre Dame University, September 13, 2003.

23. Liz Weir, personal communication, May 7, 1995.

24. Ryan, *Storytelling in Ireland.*

25. Lederach, *Building Peace.*

26. James C. Scott, *Seeing Like a State: How Certain Schemes to Improve the Human Condition Have Failed* (New Haven, CT: Yale University Press, 1998).

27. Ian White, "Victim-Combatant Dialogue in Northern Ireland," in *Reconciliation After Violent Conflict: A Handbook,* eds. David Bloomfield, Teresa Barnes, and Luc Hyse (Stockholm: International Institute for Democracy and Electoral Resistance, 2003).

28. Sean Byrne, *Growing Up in a Divided Society: The Influence of Conflict on Belfast Schoolchildren* (Cranbury, N.J: Associated University Presses, 1997).

29. Lederach, *Preparing for Peace* and *Building Peace.*

30. Martha Minow, *Between Vengeance and Forgiveness: Facing History After Genocide and Mass Violence* (Boston: Beacon, 1998).

31. Healing Through Remembering.

32. Harold Saunders, A Public Peace Process: Sustained Dialogue to Transform Racial and Ethnic Conflicts (New York: St. Martin's Press, 1999).

ABOUT THE AUTHOR

Dr. Jessica Senehi has been engaged in teaching, research, and practice in the area of conflict analysis and resolution since 1997. Her area of focus is on the role of storytelling in conflict and peace-building in intercommunal conflicts. From 2000 to 2003, she taught in the master's and doctoral programs in conflict analysis and resolution at Nova Southeastern University in Florida. Since 2003, she has been associate director of the Arthur V. Mauro Centre for Peace and Justice at St. Paul's College within the University of Manitoba in Canada. She holds an interdisciplinary Ph.D. in social science from Syracuse University.

10

Serbia/Croatia

Many wars have taken place in the Balkans over the last hundred years. The many nationalities present in the Balkans have been forced to share a small geographical region, which politically and structurally has been changed many times. From the nineteenth century, when the Ottoman Empire controlled the southern part of the Balkans and the Austro–Hungarian Empire controlled the northern part, to the end of the twentieth century, Yugoslavia went through a process of unification and dismemberment.

At the end of World War I, the Treaty of Versailles (1918) established a new state in southern Europe: the Kingdom of Serbs, Croats, and Slovenes. The name was changed in 1929 under King Alexander I to Yugoslavia, the land of the Southern Slavs. During that period the Serbs dominated the government, exercising authoritarian rule and provoking anti-Serb sentiments in the rest of the Yugoslavian state. Croatia was particularly resentful and would have preferred independence to being a mere republic in Serb-dominated Yugoslavia. In 1934, a Croatian radical group fighting against the Serbian-dominated regime assassinated King Alexander while he was in Marseilles, France.

During World War II, German Nazi troops invaded Croatia and allowed a fascist movement, already growing in popularity, to gain power. Croatia followed in the footsteps of the Nazis and established concentration camps to exterminate especially Serb and Jewish minorities. By 1945, Soviet-supported partisans expelled the Nazis and Croatia became part of Yugoslavia under the leadership of Marshall Josep Broz Tito. Tito ruled until his death in 1980, after keeping together for thirty-five years the six part republics (Serbia, Croatia, Slovenia, Montenegro, Bosnia–Herzegovina, and Kosovo) that formed modern Yugoslavia. In 1974 a new constitution was adopted, extending basic rights and decentralizing power.

The decade following Tito's death was marked by a lack of leadership that weakened ties among the republics, and the country started to crumble. In 1986, Slobodan Milosevic, a charismatic Serbian leader, appeared on the political scene. Milosevic became famous during a speech he gave publicly defending the Serbian population in Yugoslavia. His main political instrument was populism and stirring nationalist sentiments in the Serbian population. In 1988, Milosevic was elected president of Serbia, where he ruled for the next thirteen years. While gaining support from the Serbs, other ethnic groups, including the Croats, disliked his politics, deepening already tense ethnic relations in Yugoslavia. Foreseeing the dissolution of Yugoslavia in 1990, he adopted a new constitution for the republic in Serbia.

The Milosevic regime began to weaken, which was noticed by the entire European political establishment. The European Union (EU) favored multiparty elections, especially in Croatia and Slovenia. Nationalist tendencies were replacing a discredited form of socialism as the dominant force in the region. Thus, Croatia went ahead and held multiparty elections in May 1990. The leader of the Democratic Union Party whose intention was to gain more independence for Croatia, responded to the demands of the population and was elected. When he took power, he proposed many economic, political, and social changes in the new constitution; one proposal was that Serbs would retain the status of minority equal to the other minorities in Croatia. The Serb Croat political party rejected the constitution. Unsurprisingly, the already divergent views of the Serb Croats and Croats deteriorated further and aggravated tensions. In response to the constitution, the Serbs in the mountainous Krajina area of Croatia declared their own Autonomous Region of the Serb Krajina. The Republic of Serbian Krajina was never recognized by Croatia, and when police tried to intervene they were blocked by the Yugoslav National Army, mainly composed of Serbs present in the region.

Following Croatia's declaration of independence, the Serbs who had already self-proclaimed the autonomous region in Krajina, looked for support from Belgrade. In December 1991, the Serbian separatists had acquired one-third of Croatia's territory. The Serbian government provided weapons and supplies to the Croatian Serb rebellion movement.

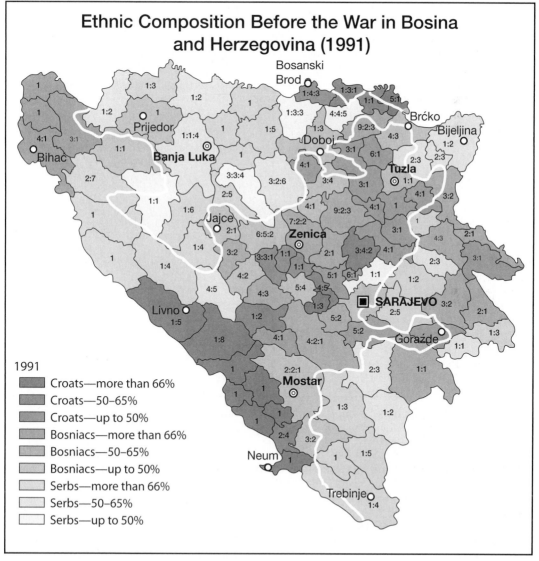

Source: http://en.wikipedia.org/wiki/Image:Ethnic_Composition_of_BiH_in_1991.gif

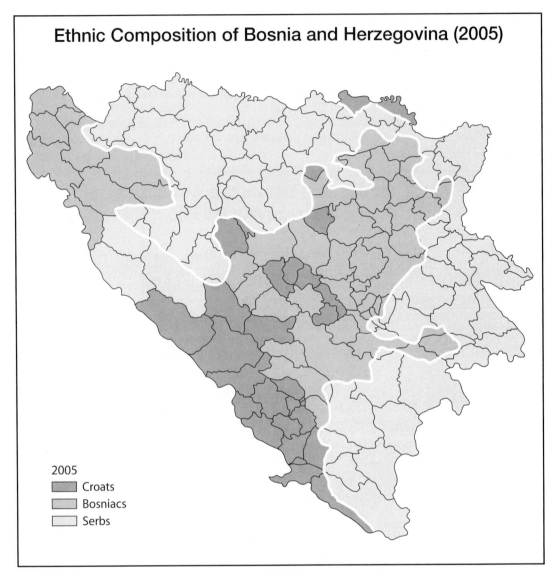

Ethnic Composition of Bosnia and Herzegovina (2005)

2005
- Croats
- Bosniacs
- Serbs

Source: http://en.wikipedia.org/wiki/Image:Ethnic_Composition_of_BiH_in_2005.GIF

Belgrade's support of the Serb minority and neighboring territories grew stronger. In 1992, Serbia led various military operations in an effort to unite all the ethnic Serbs and consolidate "Greater Serbia." At the height of the conflict Serbia extended its territory to include 20 percent of Croatia and 75 percent of Bosnia. The conflict continued until 1995 when the Dayton Accords were signed.

In the same way, Bosnia and Herzegovina suffered tremendous losses during the dissolution of the former Yugoslavia. As in the case of Croatia, in 1990 Bosnia and Herzegovina held a multiparty election in which a tripartite coalition intending to oust the Communist party was elected. The coalition, partly composed of the Serb political party, soon split due to divergent views on the future of Bosnia: whether it would stay part of Yugoslavia or would claim

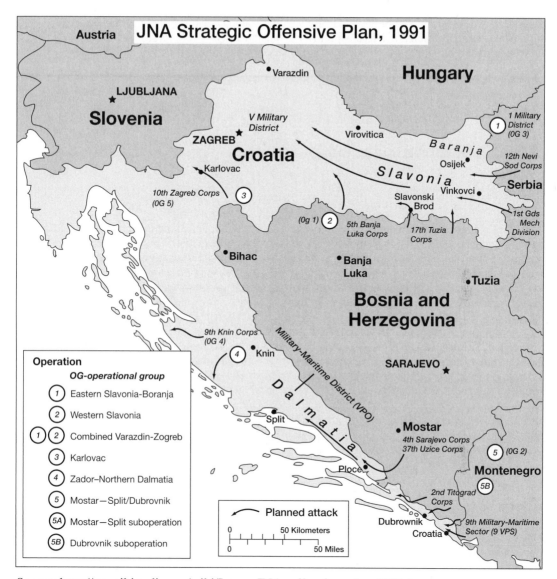

JNA Strategic Offensive Plan, 1991

Operation

OG-operational group

1. Eastern Slavonia-Boranja
2. Western Slavonia
1. 2. Combined Varazdin-Zogreb
3. Karlovac
4. Zador–Northern Dalmatia
5. Mostar—Split/Dubrovnik
5A. Mostar—Split suboperation
5B. Dubrovnik suboperation

Source: http://en.wikipedia.org/wiki/Image:JNA_offensive_plan_1991.jpg

independence like neighboring Croatia and Slovenia. Although in October 1991 Bosnia declared its sovereignty, only in March 1992 did it get international recognition after holding a referendum on independence. The referendum in Bosnia was boycotted by the Bosnian Serbs; the proposal was accepted by 98 percent of the voters. Again, the Bosnian Serb minority was strongly supported by Belgrade and Milosevic fully supported the Yugoslav National Army against the Bosnians. War broke out in April 1992. It lasted three years and caused more than 100,000 deaths and two million internally displaced refugees.

This chapter by Sonja Biserko examines the roots of Serbian nationalism and Serbia's relationship with the other republics of the former Yugoslavia. Following international intervention and the setting up of the International Criminal Tribunal for the former Yugoslavia to prosecute Milosevic and other Serbian leaders, violence stopped but the region had to deal with the crisis and its traumatic effects on the Serbian community.

In his chapter, Eduard Klain takes a psychodynamic approach to analyze the conflict. He focuses his analysis on different groups of individuals and nationalities to establish the effect of the war in the former Yugoslavia during the pre- and post-conflict periods.

Serbia: Between Archaism and Modernity

Sonja Biserko

This chapter aims to throw light not only on causes and consequences of the former Yugoslavia's dissolution but also on Serbia's perpetual clash with modern times. What I discuss here, therefore, are long-standing policies and ideological patterns that triggered the collapse of a federation, their leading actors and factors, and the bloody outcomes of the so-called national program Serbia has not yet abandoned. I explain why, in my view, Serbia is unable to come to grips with both its recent past and its reality, as well as what chances it has of coping with its current needs and constraints. I show that Serbia today is more prone to fragmentation than ever before—because it is still seesawing between archaism and modernity, unready to give up delusions about itself and the contemporary world.

DEFINING THE PROBLEM IN HISTORICAL PERSPECTIVE

Development of the Serb people and their state during the past two centuries has been marked by a conflict between patriarchy and modernity that has slowed and made the cultural integration of Serbs and creation of a "complete state" more difficult.[1] As a result, there is currently an acute lack of institutions, border issues are still unresolved, and other problems persist in Serbia. The clash between patriarchy and modernity marked the end of the twentieth century, largely because emancipation was always perceived as a loss of identity. The foregoing resulted in a revival of a "greater Serbia" concept, which drew its strength from the patriarchal, collectivist model of state and society and ethnic-religious understanding of *nation*. That concept

drew additional strength from the reliance on tradition of the medieval Serb empire.

The ethno-national greater-state ideologies lay at the very foundatons of the breakup of Yugoslavia and the war. In the judgment of Serb nationalists, the historical climax presented the greater-Serbian state idea and its advocates with a singular opportunity to capitalize on the breakup of Yugoslavia and redraw the borders according to a national program nearly two centuries old.[2] The Serb elite based its ambitions on several very important premises: the international environment or vacuum that emerged as a result of the collapse of communism, Serbian supremacy over the Yugoslav People's Army, and the Kosovo myth, which mobilized Serbs, and perceptions of Russia as Serbia's natural ally.[3]

The Serb national program was not unique in the Balkans. Balkan nations that have lived on the periphery of two large empires for centuries were also nourishing national aspirations—and had nation-states as their goals. The nineteenth and the beginning of the twentieth centuries saw their wars of liberation and their efforts to build modern states of their own. The creation of Yugoslavia in 1918 laid the foundation for the realization of the Serb national program, but at the same time the new Yugoslav state embodied objectively disparate national interests and common southern Slav aspirations. Even as the new state was being built, the proponents of unitarianism and federalism clashed. Their conflict inevitably raised questions about the survival of the Yugoslav state. The Serbs, who wanted to become the leading nation in Yugoslavia and the Balkans, had always been strong. They believed that they ought to be given a vanguard role in the Balkan Entente, the collective defense agreement designed to discourage the constant territorial claims of various European countries.

The adoption of the 1974 Yugoslavian Constitution was preceded by extensive public debate throughout the country. At the time, dissatisfaction was already felt in Serbia about the direction in which the changes were drifting. Serbian elites looked upon the confederation of Yugoslavia as a plot to completely break up the Serb people and argued that Serbia's boundaries at the time were "neither national nor historical borders" and that, for that matter, the "boundaries between all republics were administrative, rather than political."

The Serbs' largely traumatic and frustrating experience with the 1974 constitution exerted considerable influence on their later behavior during the disintegration of Yugoslavia. Most Serbs believe that the constitution destroyed the unity of Serbia, brought about scores of problems for it, and led to the breakup of Yugoslavia. Most Serbs are deeply convinced that the constitutional transformation of the republics into states rendered a satisfactory solution to the Serb national question even more remote. Having decided that the 1974 constitution marked the beginning of the end of Yugoslavia as they saw it (i.e., as an extended Serbia), Serbian community and opinion leaders set about reviving the Kosovo myth. This myth served to rally and cohere Serbs politically, just as it did at the beginning of the nineteenth century.

SERBS MOBILIZED OVER THE NATIONAL PROGRAM

The Albanian demonstrations in Kosovo in 1981 were used as a pretext for raising the Serb national question and fomenting Serb nationalist sentiments. The Yugoslav People's Army (YPA) pushed its way onto the political stage and virtually occupied Kosovo.

The struggle for Josip Broz Tito's inheritance in 1980 started amid a deep crisis, for which the political and intellectual elite and establishments had no answers.[4] The country's general unpreparedness for change was largely exacerbated by Yugoslavia's sui generis position during the preceding fifty years, a position based on its geostrategic location and the bipolar division of the world during the Soviet Union–United States Cold War. This position

gave Yugoslavia special treatment and a special role on the international political stage that was far greater than its real importance. The Serbs, whose unwillingness to address the open issues and their resistance to change resulted in national homogenization: any attempt to refashion Yugoslavia under new circumstances was perceived as a scheme to deprive them of a state of their own. Serbs' ethnic identity and the leaders of the time used the slogan "Firstly, the state—secondly, democracy" to block democratization and prevent the necessary pluralization of interests. The Serb elite, led by Slobodan Milosevic, reverted to its national program, which had been in preparation at an informal level since the early 1970s and was articulated with the publication in 1986 of the Academy for Science and Art (SANU) Memorandum.

In trying to influence the outcome of the Yugoslav crisis through the memorandum, the academy was anxious that it should reach those whose purview was the solution of current problems. The memorandum was at once pro-Yugoslavia and anti-Yugoslavia in that it suggested a transformation of the country through its recentralization. The authors of the memorandum argued that the Serb people could not look to the future serenely amid so much uncertainty. For this reason, the memorandum's authors stated that all the nations in Yugoslavia needed an opportunity to state their aspirations and intentions. Restated, this meant *Serbia could make its own choice and define its national interest.*[5] In essence, the memorandum merely copied the parameters of the Serb national program from the end of the nineteenth century and the beginning of the twentieth calling for "the liberation and unification of the entire Serb people and the establishment of a Serb national and state community on the whole Serb territory."

The impotence of the federal leaders to confront Milosevic, who proceeded to destroy everything that crossed his path—institutionally and extra-institutionally—with gathering speed, was due, above all, to the fact that the Yugoslav model of socialism has been worn out, while they themselves were unprepared for any radical change. Besides, afraid of Serb nationalism, they adhered to opportunism, which soon destroyed the already fragile balance in the federation.

The mass support Milosevic won turned quickly into a national movement in Serbia. Drawing on the energy of that movement, Milosevic established his authoritarian rule, which enabled him to raise the Serb question in Croatia and Bosnia–Herzegovina and present it as a state question that could only be solved by establishing a Serb state in these republics precisely in keeping with the position promoted by Dobrica Cosic, Serbia's most popular writer, and his circle.[6] Key concerns were the imperilment of the Serb people, the exhaustion of the Yugoslav framework, the need to amend the 1974 constitution, and the resulting unequal position of Serbia vis-à-vis the other republics.

THE PROPAGANDA WAR

Revival of Serbian nationalism in the 1970s, in response to the trend of decentralization of Yugoslavia, was based on the idea that Serbs were "the backbone of Yugoslavia and the Balkans." Such a conviction stemmed from fabricated myths, which held that Serbs had liberated all other Yugoslav peoples, hence their right to primacy, and that Serbs possess state qualities far superior to those characterizing other peoples. The Serbian Orthodox Church, Serbian Academy of Arts and Sciences, Association of Writers of Serbia, and Belgrade University contributed to an awakening of national energy. Simplified truths about centuries-long sacrifices made by the Serb people mobilized the entire Serb populous in Yugoslavia. The media's contribution to the ensuing course of events was also substantive. The media became the principal war-generating and peoples-harassment mechanism in Yugoslavia in the prewar period. By recalling the World War II genocide of Serbs in Croatia and the suffering of Serbs under Turks and hyping the terroristlike characteristics of the Albanian people, the elite and media plunged Serbians into a state of frenzy, in which no rational reasoning was possible.

The Serb national question was raised using the following arguments: confederalization of Yugoslavia was an attempt to destroy the Serb nation, while the borders of Serbia were "neither national nor historical borders." It was a signal to the Serbs to fight for their "severely jeopardi[z]ed national identity, and make that aim the main prerequisite of their future survival." The revival of the Kosovo myth served to mobilize Serbs and eventually help bring about anti-bureaucratic revolution, which was in fact a crusade against Yugoslavia.

The well-thought-out portrayal of the "enemy," (i.e., one's neighbors of yesterday) as inhuman laid the groundwork for their destruction. The Croats were referred to exclusively as Ustashi and the Muslims were derogatorily referred to as *balije* (Serbs converted to Islam). Greater Serbian advocates pointed out that "Muslims are genetically defective people who converted to Islam, so now, of course, that gene is simply condensing from generation to generation. They are getting worse and worse, express themselves in simple terms, and dictate such a way of thinking and behaving. This is already implanted in their genes."[7] Prominent leaders and intellectuals propagated war and ethnic cleansing in all their public utterances as a legitimate means of achieving justifiable objectives. Biljana Plavsic is remembered for the following statement: "I'd rather we completely cleansed east Bosnia of Muslims. Speaking of cleansing, I wouldn't like anybody to take this literally as meaning ethnic cleansing. However, they have imputed to us this quite natural phenomenon as ethnic cleansing and termed it a war crime."[8] Plavsic counted on the great numerical preponderance of Serbs and was convinced that the Bosnian war must be won by them because "there are twelve million of us, so even if six million are killed, the remaining six million will live decently." Cosic put forward a similar thesis back in 1990 when he said, "Eighty thousand Serb casualties would be an acceptable price to pay for the realization of the national objectives."

To mobilize Serbs throughout Yugoslavia, every method was used, including the recollection of Second World War crimes against Serbs, the revival of myths created at the time of Turkish occupation, and lies. The Serbs' supremacy, "statehood," and the ability to organize their state were continually pointed out.

Mindful of the changes in the international environment, especially the collapse of Communism, Serbian propagandists made much of the fact that Serbia had always been anti-Communist. They cited the "collapse of the Communist regime and Communism" in support of their new thesis that the "AVNOJ boundaries have lost all foundation in history and possess no regularity under international law."[9] They argued that the collapse of the social order created by the Communist Party meant the "collapse of its historical–political determinant—that is, the AVNOJ boundaries." As one of the main architects of the Serbian program, Cosic also argued that the "Serb people cannot accept a confederation of the present republics because their boundaries are illegitimate both in a historical sense and under international law, for they were drawn to conform to the political objectives and criteria of the Communist Party and according to the Brioni Constitution."[10]

THE MILOSEVIC ADVENT

The idea of recentralizing Yugoslavia gained increasing support in Serbia in the political vacuum left after Tito's death. Milosevic strengthened his standing with dogmatic members of the party by accusing reformers of "washing their hands of Socialism." His advice to them was to "get out of the League of Communists and its forums."

Milosevic's visit to Kosovo in April 1987 made him aware of the potency of nationalism and marked a turning point in the treatment of the Kosovo problem. Having won by his defense of Titoism the support of the military leadership, which strove to preserve the state intact, Milosevic proceeded to reshuffle all editorial staffs, especially those of the daily *Politika* and the weekly *NIN* (Serbia's two principal newspaper houses) and state-run television, sacking seventy-two editors. The new editorial teams became part of Milosevic's inner political team. They played a key role in starting the war and enlisting the support of the popular masses. Milosevic could not have grown into the national leader he was if the people, dissatisfied and eager to change the petrified leadership personified by Ivan Stambolic, president of Serbia from 1986–87, had not been in the right mood. The people were obviously ready for a new leader and saw Milosevic, on the strength of his utterances in and about Kosovo, as the man fit to rule.

Milosevic based his policy on populism. His meteoric rise to power had not been lost on the intellectuals, so they went over to his side in the second half of 1988. The national program of Cosic and his group finally came into the open once a political leader had at long last been found to espouse it. Power was in the hands of Milosevic, but the future

of Serbia was charted in the home of Cosic, who was hailed by Serbs as the architect of the program. In spite of their moral and political differences, the two worked in harness: Cosic pursued his nationalist goals, and Milosevic—the pragmatic leader—pursued his political interests. It was this commonness of purpose that held them together.[11]

COLLAPSE OF YUGOSLAVIA

The period preceding the outbreak of fighting was characterized by three phases: attempts to preserve the old system, the crystallization of two concepts for resolving the crisis, and war. In the first phase, shortly after Tito's death, members of the political and intellectual establishment strove to preserve their positions without making much effort to resolve the crisis by systemic reform, for any bold move threatened to alter the correlation of forces and upset the balance established in Tito's day. The second phase was marked by the 1986–87 rise of Milosevic, the first politician to step forward with a proposal for overcoming the Yugoslav crisis by reinforcing federal institutions and central government with Serbia playing a dominant role. This was diametrically opposite to the view that had meanwhile evolved in Slovenia, which saw Yugoslavia's future only through substantial decentralization and greater roles for the republics. At that time, Croatia did not declare itself, but during 1989 it joined Slovenia in its demands. The appointment of Ante Markovic as federal prime minister was the last attempt to find a solution to the Yugoslavian problem. His program advocated economic reform in hopes of initiating political change, an expectation that had already been proven illusory during the 1970s.

The Eighth Session of the Serbian Central Committee (September 1987) marked the turning point in efforts to resolve the Yugoslav crisis and brought about a rift within Serbia's political establishment. The installation of Milosevic and the political execution of Stambolic gave victory to the nationalist political orientation leading to the breakup of Yugoslavia. Following the Eighth Session party coup, Milosevic engineered the largest purge of the party (much more sweeping than the ones following the Cominform resolution in 1948 or the removal of the liberals in 1972) with the object of consolidating Serbians' power. The purge was not merely about intraparty conflict; it was important for the disposition of forces for the upcoming showdown in Yugoslavia. The Eighth Session was the key event in the dissolution of Yugoslavia. The so-called antibureacratic revolution managed to homogenize both the then Serbian Communist Party and the nation. It brought down institutions and initiated deregulation with the full support of the army. During July 1988, Milosevic toppled the Vojvodina leadership in the so-called "yoghurt revolution" and proceeded to centralize Serbia under the slogan "One people, one state, one court of law."[12]

The annexation of Montenegro followed in January 1989 after the fall of the republic's leadership. Under the pretext of a "replenishment of cadres," Milosevic's cronies and errand boys were installed in federal posts. The purging of the representatives of Vojvodina, Kosovo, and Montenegro gave Serbia a controlling majority in the federal leadership. With his unification of Serbia, Milosevic simultaneously prepared a campaign against Slovenia and Croatia.

The scenario for unmaking Yugoslavia was worked out in detail in advance. Because events followed each other with great speed, other republics were unable to react. Following the isolation of Slovenia, the Belgrade scenario focused increasingly on Croatia, which for the most part failed to react to Belgrade's provocations. It was only after a long period of vacillation that Croatia decided to resist, so a confrontation between Serbia and Croatia started. A wave of Serb nationalism erupted, which Belgrade manipulated and skillfully doled out through the media, and the Serb population was used to organize rallies in Croatia.

After the dissolution of the League of Communists of Yugoslavia at its XIII Congress in January 1990, Milosevic announced to his collaborators that "Serbia has to prepare itself to live without Yugoslavia." The adoption of the new Constitution of the Republic of Serbia in September 1990 marked the end of the first phase of preparations to destroy Yugoslavia. This constitution usurped two paramount federal functions: national defense and foreign relations (Articles 72/1 and 72/3). It deprived autonomous provinces of their constitutional functions (Articles 108–112) and excluded Serbia from

the legal system of the Socialist Federal Republic of Yugoslavia (FRY) (Article 135). It was the first secessionist document, especially as it is quoted in Article 135, which states that Serbia will enforce federal legislation only if it is not "contrary to its interests." In fact, this article practically nullified all Serbian obligations toward the rest of the country. On the other hand, Serbia continued to claim all the rights allotted to it by the federal legislation and federal constitution, the most important of which was preserving its representatives (three, including provinces) in the Socialist Federal Republic of Yugoslavia (SFRY) presidency. Even Milosevic in one of his speeches on Radio Television of Serbia (March 15, 1991) declared, "Yugoslavia does not exist any more." This constitution helped Milosevic to stay safe in Serbia, "which was not in war" and had nothing to do with the evolving "tragedy."

Having failed to export his "anti-bureaucratic revolution" to other republics, or to occupy Yugoslavia in one fell swoop, Milosevic went ahead with implementing his plan with the help of his supporters, namely other parties who had previously set out Serbia's war aims in their programs, in which the frontiers of the future state coincided with those of Moljevic's "Homogeneous Serbia." These parties were the Serbian Renewal Movement (SPO) led by Vuk Draskovic, the Serbian Radical Party (SRS) of Vojislav Seselj, and the Serb National Renewal (SNO) party of Mirko Jovic.[13] All these parties effectively promoted the Chetnik movement and drew on its traditions.[14]

PLANNING AND PREPARATIONS OF WAR

Preparations for war took a long time and were carried out at several levels, including the media, institutions, schools, universities, churches, the army and informal discussion groups gathered in coffee bars and homes. From the inception and formulation of the project to its implementation, various people were assigned various tasks. The role of chief warmonger was entrusted to Vojislav Seselj, one of the most diligent operatives and Milosevic's alter ego for the preceding ten years. He was the one to apply violence to the extent his master deemed necessary at any given moment. At the same time, his gross manner and thuggery made Milosevic seem decent and acceptable in comparison.

Disintegration of Yugoslavia cannot be understood without previous knowledge of the important role of the (YPA) Yugoslavia People's Army. The YPA grew more powerful and influential in Yugoslav society in the 1980s, which clearly indicated that its key role in future developments was inevitable. In view of the continuing militarization in Yugoslav society, it was only logical for the army to consider a coup d'état. The army and Serbian leaders were in full agreement that Serbs were an integrating factor in Yugoslavia because they were most populous and also most widely dispersed throughout the country; furthermore, they contributed to both Yugoslavias. The then prime movers also suggested that Serbian national awareness ought to be acknowledged as a counterbalance to other nationalisms not based on statehood, but that position was viewed with great mistrust by other republics.

The Hegemonic centralism of Serb policy coincided with the centralist position of the army. That position was a source of inspiration for all future YPA-taken actions. It was also the cause of the YPA's downfall, because in the process the YPA relinquished its founding principles. Actions that ultimately brought about the historical and moral downfall of the YPA were the boycott of the federal parliament, subjugation and decommissioning of the Territorial Defen[c]e Units, siding with the Serb government during wars in Slovenia, Croatia and Bosnia–Herzegovina, and mobilization of volunteers to replenish the swiftly diminishing army rank and file. In 1990, when the YPA de facto became the Serb army, General Veljko Kadijevic described the war objectives in the following fashion: "The YPA shall defend the Serbs and define borders of future Yugoslavia."

The Serbian Orthodox Church (SOC) had a special role in promoting the Serb national program. After five decades of the communist era, the SOC became public with Milosevic coming into power. His aim in opening public space for it was to obtain the support of the church in mobilizing Serbs for the national program. The church played the role it had been assigned. It strongly encouraged the rise of an ethno-nationalistic spirit combined with aspirations for the "Greater Serbia" project on all levels of society: religious and na-

tional feelings were manipulated for overtly political purposes. At the same time, the church openly backed the regime of Slobodan Milosevic. However, its comeback failed to reach an institutional form, due to an ambiguous attitude of the Milosevic regime toward the Communist ideological heritage.

The most important role of the church in its political comeback was the one symbolizing the idea of pan-Serbian unity. Thanks to its great influence on the people, the church obtained much logistical support from the state and the army. Army support to the church was even more open after the changes that took place in October 2000 because the church became the only institution, after military and political defeat, that continued to inspire the Serbs spiritually, culturally, and politically the teritory that had failed to be united in a single state.

The SOC never recognized the borders of Serbia within Yugoslavia after World War II. At the beginning of 1992, at a time when the war for reshaping these borders was already underway, the Congregation of the SOC issued a declaration saying it acknowledeged not the borders set up by the AVNOJ, while Bishop Atanasije Jevtic qualified their revision as a question vital for Serbian people, which in itself justified the Church's interference into politics. In the summer of 1995, the SOC Patriarch declared that in Dayton Milosevic was entitled to negotiate the borders in the name of Bosnian Serbs. However, after the Dayton Accords were signed, the Congregation of the SOC, dissatsfied with the solution reached, declared the Patriarch's signature invalid.

Due to this position, which in fact justified war crimes and ethnic cleansing, the SOC never dissociated itself from the war crimes committed in Croatia, Bosnia and Herzegovina, and Kosovo. Although the SOC claimed that one should dissociate oneself from all crimes, it also stated that among "all the war crimes committed in the Balkans in the 20th century, where the Serbian people suffered the most, only the 'Serbian' crimes are singled out," which was then turned into "an ideology of de-nazification, sentencing the Serbian nation to a deprivation of its right to have a historical voice." The SOC believed that "the ideology of Serbian crimes" was being used for a civilizational and value excommunication of the Serbian people as immaturate for the global family. The SOC believed that "a geopolitical interest of breaking down a great and important historical nation on the South-East of Europe is in the question.[15]

INTERNATIONAL RESPONSE TO THE YUGOSLAV CRISIS

With the YPA on its side, Serbia became superior to other Yugoslav nations and was able to quickly achieve its military goals in Croatia and Bosnia. Because of Yugoslavia's military superiority, the international community became involved in the Yugoslav crisis. From the beginning, international intervenors tried to mediate a peaceful resolution to the war. In 1991, the international community's response to the Yugoslav wars was to convene The Hague Conference, which was mediated by the European Community. The aim was to discuss the future of Yugoslavia. The conference was the last attempt to preserve the Yugoslav framework and find a solution that would satisfy two fundamentally opposed concepts of the future arrangement of Yugoslavia—namely, a confederation and a federal system featuring a loose federation and a strong central government, respectively.

On September 3, the conference passed a declaration on Yugoslavia that laid down the principles that were to "ensure the satisfaction of the opposing aspirations of the Yugoslav peoples in a peaceful way." The underlying principles were that there would be no alteration of boundaries with the use of force, that the rights of all in Yugoslavia would be protected, and that all legitimate interests and legitimate aspirations would be fully respected.

At the first meeting of The Hague Conference, Milosevic employed the well-known strategy of the Serb nationalists, the implementation of which was already in progress on the ground: he requested equal respect for the right to self-determination of all Yugoslav peoples and guarantees that they could all exercise that will to self-determination. He supported this position by arguing that Yugoslavia was a community of equal Yugoslav peoples, not republics. He also argued that any right to secede would lead to the eventual delimitation of new international frontiers of Yugoslavia because the internal administrative boundaries did not have the character of international frontiers. At the

same time, he raised the problem of the partition of assets, human rights, and such Serbia experienced The Hague Conference as an ultimatum to itself, the "abolition of a state by dint of some sort of freakish political engineering coupled with a flagrant violation of international law." After rejecting the offer from The Hague conference, primarily because of the military supremacy, Milosevic continued to create new problems by occupying Croatia (20 percent of its territory) and Bosnia (75 percent of its territory) while the international community struggled to contain the resulting humanitarian disaster.

Only Srebrenica's tragedy was able to push the West into making decisive moves. Srebrenica had been targeted by General Ratko Mladic since 1992. In the Serbs' opinion, Srebrenica, together with Gorazde and Zepa, lay in an Islamic corridor linking Sarajevo with Turkey through Sandzak, Albania, and Kosovo. For this reason, Mladic expelled (July 1995) 14,000 people, of whom 8,000 went missing, from these defenseless enclaves. The Dutch battalion in Srebrenica requested no assistance from the United Nations Protection Force (UNPROFOR) and let the Serbs expel the helpless Muslim population and shoot males of all ages. Though the reaction of the international community came too late for the population of Srebrenica, it saved Gorazde from a similar fate.

From a moral point of view, Srebrenica was both a turning point in the Bosnian War and a symbol of the impotence and indifference of Western foreign policy. The Srebrenica massacre provoked some serious moral soul-searching throughout the world about the international community's duty to intervene in Serbia. The ensuing NATO strikes and the Croat–Muslim offensive threatening to "liberate" Banjaluka reduced Serb territorial possessions to 46 percent. The Croat-Muslim push was halted outside Banjaluka because the West, having witnessed the Serb exodus from Krajina, feared a new refugee crisis. It was then that Milosevic realized for the first time that negotiations alone could save the tottering Serbs from an utter rout.

The use of force had created a new reality on the ground and made possible the peace agreement known as the Dayton Accords. The accords were initialed in Dayton and then ratified in Paris on December 14, 1995. The Serbs were given half of Bosnia. The international community did not modify the 51:49 percent territorial apportionment. The Muslims, the most populous nation in Bosnia, saw themselves as being on the losing side, while Slobodan Milosevic regarded Dayton as a victory.

The Dayton Accords were viewed by many as a de facto partition, though parts of it could have, had they been implemented, reversed some aspects of the Bosnian tragedy. Having brought peace to Bosnia, the accords achieved the best possible results under the circumstances. The fundamental worth of the agreement was that it established peace in Bosnia and secured it militarily. It committed all three parties to an integral Bosnia within internationally recognized borders, reaffirmed Bosnia's international status, and established the right of refugees and displaced persons to return. It also laid the foundations for military stabilization of the region through confidence-building measures and arms control aimed at achieving a military balance based on reduced armament.

The Serbian opposition criticized the Dayton Accords in the strongest terms. It perceived Milosevic as a Western collaborator for handing over Serb territory for which fierce battles had been fought. Over time, Serb nationalists realized that the Dayton Accords were the best deal they could have clinched at the time. For Dayton's output, Republika Srpska was not only sealed as a territorial gain but also seen as an almost ethnically pure state. By developing a strategy of preventing the return of non-Serb refugees, nationalists practically managed to preserve the effect of the bloodshed, while looking forward to opening the door to Republika Srpska's unification with Serbia.

THE HAGUE TRIBUNAL

The Yugoslav crisis provided an opportunity to establish a new International Criminal Court for the Former Yugoslavia. The main objective of the tribunal was to deter the warring sides from committing war crimes. The court was challenged in Serbia from the very beginning because of its perceived anti-Serb bias and failure to realize that "in fact, the Serbs are the victims, the Muslims and the Croats the perpetrators." However, by the time of the outbreak of the Kosovo crisis, the tribunal had been ineffective in this regard. Several major indictments had been raised, such as those against

Radovan Karadzic, Ratko Mladic, and the "Vukovar troika," but no principal suspect had been handed over by the Serb side.

The indictment against Milosevic was made public during the Kosovo intervention. Milosevic claimed that he "always considered the Hague tribunal to be an immoral and illegal institution, invented as a form of retaliation against disobedient representatives and disobedient peoples, just as once there were concentration camps for superfluous races and superfluous people. This tribunal exists first and foremost for the Serbs. It is the same form of intimidation that the Nazis used first against the Jews and later against all the Slav peoples."[16]

The Albanian rebellion in southern Serbia united both governments, republican and federal, in their determination to crush it. Cooperation with the international community, in this case NATO, was of key importance in the suppression of the rebellion and the adoption of solutions for southern Serbia. Apparently, over time, as events in Croatia and Bosnia have shown, an international presence has proven to be of crucial importance for Serbia, which no longer enjoys the advantage it enjoyed over its neighbors in the early 1990s. Thus, as explained by Nebojsa Covic, Serbia's interest "lies in co-operation with KFOR and UNMIK and in making sure that resolution 1244 is respected, that it should remain in force as long as possible while a long-term solution for Kosovo and Metohija is being prepared." Serbia still has hidden agendas but less and less potential to implement them. Judging by Serb nationalists, they would like to see a rearrangement of the Balkans and the drawing of new boundaries as had been done at the Berlin Congress in 1878.

THE PRESENT SITUATION IN SERBIA

The international presence in the region and the dynamics in Serbia itself (the October 2000 removal of Milosevic, the March 2003 assassination of Prime Minister Zoran Djindjic, and the massive victory of the radicals in the December 2003 early parliamentary election) clearly indicate that Serbia is only now coming to grips with its own reality. Milosevic's legacy is difficult to deal with, including acknowledging its recent criminal past, which makes Serbia a sui generis case in the post-Communist world.

The current situation in Serbia may serve as a new key for understanding the disintegration of Yugoslavia. The early 1990s dominant thesis about "the civil war" and "accountability of secession-minded republics" now requires a fresh look or reappraisal. The lack of ability of the Serb elite to define and mainstream modern Serbia and place it in a contemporary international context were key reasons for the disintegration of the Yugoslav federation.[17] It is further illustrated by the potential to finalize that disintegration with the breakup of Serbia and Montenegro. On the domestic scene, this is best reflected in the prevailing stand on minorities as exemplified by the numerous anti-minorities incidents that occurred in the wake of the December 2003 elections. Total misunderstanding of contemporary processes and trends jeopardizes Serbia proper and makes it prone to further fragmentation.

Regressive trends—namely attempts to revive, or rather continue, the national program and forcibly create a national state with much help and support from traditional institutions, notably the Orthodox Church, and the painfully slow latching on to European processes—are embodied in the ideas and stands of the incumbent Prime Minister Vojislav Kostunica. Lack of readiness of the Serb elite to comply with its international commitments, notably The Hague Tribunal, has set Serbia on the path of isolation, thus making room for the reassertion of the far-Right political groups. It is an established fact that the stand on The Hague tribunal reflects the position on the recent past and the near future alike. Furthermore, stands on reforms and the assassination of Djindjic mirror both.

Even after Milosevic, the vacuum of authority caused by disputes over basic constitutional structures remains a continuing source of instability in Serbia, as well as the region as a whole. With the basic situation still unresolved in each of the entities or states in the region, little progress can be made in addressing the broader institutional problems in the region. An additional problem for Serbia's democratization agenda is the unresolved status of Kosovo and Montenegro, which lack both a political agenda and the energy necessary for transition. Such a precarious situation nourishes

the hopes of nationalists that they may get away with a recomposition of the Balkans. That is why the preservation of Macedonia and Bosnia–Herzegovina is essential. The very existence of these two states stands in the way of hegemonic aspirations in the Balkans, for Greater Serbia, Greater Croatia, and Greater Albania ambitions all imply partition of Bosnia and Macedonia. The role of Bosnia and Macedonia is, therefore, in many respects similar to that of Switzerland or Belgium: an alternative border scheme can only be accomplished through prolonged war and instability. For the same reason it is necessary to prevent any attempt to partition Kosovo. As long as the border issue is pending in the region, democratization agendas will be obstructed both by political agendas and corruption.

ACKNOWLEDGING AND RECONCILING THE PAST

Acknowledging the past is the biggest and most painful problem in Serbian society. Srebian elites did not renounce the Serbian national program and its aspirations of territorial expansion, though recent messages from the international community indicate that such illusions have no prospects. However, Serbian leaders keep nourishing these illusions as they make it possible for them to mold Serbia's responsibility for the recent past to relativism. With such goals Vojislav Kostunica hastened to set up his Commission of Truth and Reconciliation, which is tasked with "organising investigative activities aimed at disclosing documentation on social, ethnic and political conflicts which led to the war and consequently casting light on the chain of events and causes."

Reconciliation is an indispensable process that gives society new life and new hope. Reconciliation presupposes that the two parties to the conflict can find a basis on which they can live together. However, reconciliation construed as a debate about the past is not reconciliation at all. Reconciliation must ascertain the truth and take a stand on the historical injustices at issue. The bigger the mistake and the bloodier its consequences, the harder for people to own up, says historian Carlo Sforza. The war that Serbia waged not only against the peoples of the former Yugoslavia, but also against Europe and the United States, has led to internal decay, the extent of which is not publicly known because no defeat or guilt has been acknowledged.

In the last ten years, Serbia has made no effort to enter into dialogue with any of the parties to the conflict with the object of achieving reconciliation. For one thing, there can be no reconciliation with Croatia while a number of questions remain unsolved. These questions involve, among other issues, the Serb's silence about the fate of 1,500 missing Croats. As regards relations between Belgrade and Bosnia, the state of affairs is even more uncertain and complex. To begin, the Dayton Accords essentially cement the defeat of the victim, namely the Muslims. Dayton was framed according to the situation on the ground, not according to the principles of justice. In other words, the accords themselves have not created any preconditions for a process of reconciliation. Republika Srpska is a creation founded on crime and, therefore, intrinsically condemned to ruin. Nine years after Dayton, only a small number of refugees have returned to Republika Srpska, and Mladic and Karadzic, the symbols of ethnic cleansing and mass murder, are still at large. Furthermore, while paying lip service to an integral Bosnian state, the Bosnian Serbs are busy hacking away at its very foundations with a view to a union with Serbia. This project is being promoted as the "rounding off of Serb cultural and spiritual space." The Republika Srpska has already been incorporated in the economic, educational, military, and media structure of the Former Republic of Yugoslavia. While pretending to be willing to be part of a multiethnic Bosnia has paid off in terms of Western donations, no one has any intention of facing up to the past. This is the more so since the army of the Republika Srpska has been amply financed by official Belgrade.

As far as Bosnia is concerned, an initial error was made. The first Truth Commission failed in its task because each of the three parties had its own version of the truth that it consistently propagated, which was totally contrary to the spirit of the Dayton Accords and contrary to the spirit of a just peace. A new commission under U.N. auspices was set up only recently, but unless the truth is established and the character of the war qualified, the new commission is not likely to make any progress.

A similar situation is evident in Serbia, following Milosevic's fall from power and intensifying since his transfer to The Hague. After ten years of frustration with Milosevic, the West has settled for a "normalization of Serb nationalism"—blaming all crimes committed by Belgrade on Milosevic the Communist. No attempt has been made to fathom the deeper roots of Serb nationalism, which throughout the twentieth century threatened the survival of the former Yugoslavia and finally was the principal cause of her breakup. Indeed such efforts have been discouraged by Western diplomats, who are eager to have normal relations with Belgrade and willing to give new leaders the benefit of the doubt. Instead of making a clean break with the remnants of Milosevic's regime, new leaders perpetuate the same policy by other means. They are awaiting different international circumstances and even a redrawing of the Balkan map. According to Cosic, that would create a war for ethnic states. Citizens have nothing to lament, for history has created an ethnic state. Admittedly, Cosic has not defined its boundaries yet.

Serbia has not come to terms with recent changes in the world and the end of the Communist illusion, which opened up the space for disillusionment and new manipulations. Serbian resistance to new challenges resulted in lengthy and thorough preparation for new egalitarian ideology through Communist party dogma urging unity, church preaching about the superiority of Orthodoxy and of the East over West, a military doctrine extolling Serb warriors, and literature and historiography. Serbs' worldview, their very outlook, stems from the totalitarian character of the political and cultural model upon which it rests. Without an alternative and with no possibility of retreat, the inculcation could not but lead to the use of force. This cultural pattern wreaked unprecedented destruction: the razing of towns, the obliteration of centuries-old monuments, and the murder of citizens. As one prominent Serb architect remarked, "This lunacy is also permeated by the avenger's hatred of urbanism and urban civilization."

Evolution of a new cultural pattern will require both time and the engagement of the small marginalized segment of Serbian elites who consistently oppose Serb nationalism, as well as the international community. Thus far, parties' preferences have been for simple solutions ensuring peace rather than investing in efforts to fundamentally change the cultural pattern essential for reconciliation.

The ad hoc Hague Tribunal established in 1993 for former Yugoslavian leaders represents a key mechanism for the individualization of crimes and the satisfaction of justice, but it is not sufficient in itself to bring about reconciliation. The Hague Tribunal is in the interest of nations because it holds individuals responsible for crimes. It proves the crime and prevents a nation from deluding itself and building a new myth in which it figures as the victim. Another important feature of the Hague tribunal is that it compels states to accept limited sovereignty with regard to humanitarian law and human rights violations.

On the other hand, The Hague Tribunal has its limitations: for example, it has no built-in moral dimension, which can therefore result in responsibilities being glossed over. For example, Milosevic's transfer, under outside pressure, was presented to the Serbian domestic public as a concession opening the door to Western financial support. Such an approach devalues the moral component of the responsibilities of Milosevic and The Hague. In other words, The Hague Tribunal is potentially problematic in that it may leave a state with the impression that it has fulfilled its moral obligation. Furthermore, the tribunal deals with individual culpability without condemning, as the Nuremberg trials did, the policy that caused the crime.

A truth commission can correct these shortcomings. However, a truth commission cannot by definition be a valid state truth commission if the state in question does not acknowledge its responsibility for the crimes. The Kostunica state commission was composed for the most part of people whose books furnished the arguments in favor of starting the war. Its credibility and prospects were doomed from the start.

The task of a truth commission or anything similar to it is, among other things, to diagnose the political context in which a criminal policy could have been embraced and implemented. Unless this is done, a society cannot examine its responsibility for these policies. We are dealing here not with collective guilt but rather with the historical responsibility of a society that agreed to such a policy and elected leaders who prompted it or merely kept silent regarding crimes such as the siege of Sarajevo, the massive killings of civilians in Srebrenica, and ethnic cleansing. Facing such truths is the hardest task for a society attempting to come face to face with itself.

It is obvious that, at this point, Serbia is not prepared to come to grips with both its past and its reality and that a process as such cannot be launched, let alone proceed, unless fully backed by the state, its programs, its institutions, and its media, above all TV and radio. The state must adopt a set of values to guide the commission and must build them into its system of values and its institutions such as education, media, and such.

If we consider Serbia, for example, we may say that she has made small steps in the desired direction. The reality of Serbia today is fragmented, as are the activities of the international community. Everything is taking place at several different levels at the same time, so there is no succession of events that could launch a process of reconciliation. At one level, Serbia is being saved from implosion; on another, the state union is being artificially maintained; on a third, the decentralization of Serbia is being blocked by new Belgrade politicians; on a fourth, an idea to partition Bosnia and Kosovo is being circulated with the expectation that the international community will come around to this sensible realistic idea.

Looking ahead, current events bode poorly. Turning a blind eye to crimes, glorifying criminals like Mladic and Karadzic, and overrating an army deep in crime are also policies of the new government. Unless exposed, this link could set the stage for a new war. As the well-known German historian Holm Zundhausen put it, "No society can avoid confrontation with the dark pages of its past. Every democratic community must sort itself out. Silence is destructive."

Confrontation with the dark pages of Serbia's recent past presupposes a clear-cut break with the Greater Serbia policy. Unless this policy is delegitimized, the crime cannot be condemned. Only once the Greater Serbia project is defeated can the region restore its balance and start its painful process of reconciliation.

SUMMARY

Serbia is a wasteland. The prime minister who was a strong alternative to Serb conservatism and nationalism was killed. Fully aware of the depth of

Serbia's problems, Zoran Djindjic invested enormous energy in Serbia's U-turn, but failed. By his assassination Serbia suffered yet another defeat. Orchestrated campaigns against close allies of Djindjic, nongovernmental organizations, and individuals who understand the broader implications of Djindjic's assassination are tantamount to an essential revival of Milosevic's concept and ideology. Boris Tadic, who was elected president of Serbia on June 28, 2004 (and was far more acceptable than his competitor, Tomislav Nikolic, the candidate of the Radical Party), in his first public statements, expressed the same attitude as Vojislav Kostunica relating to the recent past. Despite denial of Serbia's accountability, Kostunica's government will obviously be obliged to hand over indicted generals charged for war crimes in Kosovo. It is only when the pressure comes from the outside that today's Serbia "faces its recent past," but the manner in which it faces it lacks the moral dimension it should owe to itself.

Despite continuing attempts of the nationalistic block to deny the existence of a pro-European alternative, the problem of modernity continues to impose itself as a key issue in Serbia. Modernity at this moment of time has no inner strength. It could fully emerge as a strong alternative only if the international community makes efforts to that end. The future of Serbia and its relationship with Europe primarily depends on its potential to give voice to a modern alternative and on the international community's ability to understand the gist of the problem. The international community, primarily the European Union and the United States, would have to play a key role in that process, because their engagement in the past decade has turned them into main protagonists of all developments in the Balkans. Attempts to resolve problems only at the political level, without essential insight into the society proper and recognition of the genuine alternative, which can survive only if international backing is rendered, will not be sufficient.

ENDNOTES

1. The term *complete state* was coined by Zoran Djinjdjic. Emblematic of that idea is his study "Yugoslavia as an Unfinished State," and Nenad Dimitrijevic's essay "Serbia as an Unfinished State."
2. A new Serbian state, removed to the southwest, while leaving a part of Kosovo behind, makes the sum and substance of the so-called national program. The following quote probably best illustrates the idea: "This is the time of territorial-ethnical reshuffle of the entire Balkan region, the time of forced adjustment we shall have to accept as a fact of life. Epochal changes make it necessary for the Serbian people to congregate in the territory [where] it can live, it can cover by its civilization and wherefrom it will be enemy to no one. Even this disaster brings forth something useful—ethnical appeasement of the region. The Serbian people unifies and homogenizes; it rounds up its living space that gets ethnic borders. A change as such implies establisment of a new nation state in the territory only aggressors may call into question. In other words, we are forced to create a state suited to us and to our power." (Dobrica Cosic, "Chasing the Wind.")
3. The Battle of Kosovo took place in 1389 and marked the beginning of five centuries of Ottoman supremacy. However, Serbs have been gloriyfing this heavy defeat ever since. The defeat has been turned into martyrdom, while Kosovo proclaimed itself "the soul of the Serbian nation." Accordingly, without Kosovo, Serbs will be wiped out as a nation. This is why "the Kosovo myth" implies continuity with the medieval Serbian state.
4. Tito was the Yugoslavian statesman who led the resistance to Nazi occupation during World War II, established independence from the Soviet Union (1948), and as president (1953–1980) pursued the policy of "socialism with a human face" while stressing nonalignment in foreign affairs. By the strength of his personal authority and political insight, he managed to adjust differing interests of ex-Yugoslav republics and maintain the federation. After his death, differencies increasingly came to light.
5. Kosta Mihajlovic and Vasilije Krestic, *Memorandum SANU (The SANU Memorandum): Odgovori i Kritike (Replies and Criticism)* (Belgrade: SANU, 1995.)
6. Though a self-proclaimed dissident, Dobrica Cosic has always been under the wing of people in power—from Josip Broz Tito and Milosevic to present-day "democratic" leaders. He is both the actual and intellectual architect of Serbian nationalism but keeps changing its clothes. His popularity and influence are mostly based on the thesis threading all his writings: "Serbs are winners in wartime, but losers in peacetime."
7. Biljana Plavsic (one of three main Bosnian leaders indicted for war crimes), *Svet,* Septembar 6, 1993.
8. Ibid.
9. AVNOJ is the acronym for the Anti-fascist Committee for Yugoslavia's National Liberation. At its historic session in the town of Jajce (Bosnia–Herzegovina) in 1943 the AVNOJ decided that the future Yugoslavia would be a federation and outlined the borders between Yugoslav republics.
10. Cosic Interview in *Politika.*
11 Slavoljub Djukic, *Izmedju slave i anateme* (Between the Glory and the Anathema).
12. The Vojvodina leaders who tried to address the rally were pelted with yogurt cartons.

13. The SPO program looked upon the Serb entity as independent of the other republics, which implied that Yugoslavia was entirely Serbia's creation, and declared that "neither the territories which, on 1 December 1918, the day Yugoslavia was created, were part of the Kingdom of Serbia, nor the parts in which Serbs were in the majority before the Ustasha genocide, may secede from present-day Yugoslavia or be confederated at the expense of the Serb people—these territories are the inalienable historical and ethnic property of the Serb people." As to Croatia, the program was explicit: "Croatia within its present borders cannot be confederated before an autonomous province of Serb Krajina is established in Baranja, parts of Slavonia, Kordun, Lika, Banija, and northern Dalmatia, and before autonomy is guaranteed to Istria and Dubrovnik." Should Croatia nevertheless secede from Yugoslavia, "the autonomous province of Serb Krajina would be incorporated into the Serb state."

The Programmatic Declaration places special emphasis on Kosovo, urging the "suppression of the Albanian separatist rebellion by all means" and the taking of such essential measures as preventing any form of Kosovo—Metohija politico-territorial autonomy, expelling allegedly 360,000 Albanian immigrants, preventing extension of state grants to national minorities, declaring a state of war and imposing military rule, dissolving the local organs of civil government financed from the state budget, closing down or conserving all local factories and production facilities, abolishing all welfare payments to Albanians, especially those conducive to excessive birth rate, and a host of others.

14. When World War II broke out, Chetniks initially stood for "the Yugoslav Royal Army in homeland," led by General Draza Mihajlovic. However, rather than fighting against the German army (they more often than not collaborated with it), Chetniks turned into a strong nationalistic movement aspiring to create a "Greater Serbia."

15. *Pravoslavlje*, February 15, 2004.

16. *La Stampa*, February 3, 2001.

17. According to Slobodan Vucetic, the President of the Constitutional Court of Serbia, "after December 2003 elections Serbia cannot be a regional state, for it lacks the experience of regionalism."

ABOUT THE AUTHOR

Sonja Biserko is head of the Helsinki Human Rights Committee in Serbia, a Belgrade-based post she has held since 1991, and a member of the executive board of the International Helsinki Federation, based in Vienna. From 1974 to 1991, Biserko was a career foreign service officer with the federal Ministry of Foreign Affairs in Belgrade. She served as a special adviser on European affairs in London and Geneva. In 2001, she was a senior fellow at the United States Institute of Peace.

Biserko has planned and organized nongovernmental organization (NGO) activities in the field of human rights promotion. She has initiated national and international NGO projects in cooperation with various international human rights bodies, including Helsinki Watch, the Lawyers Committee for Human Rights, the U.N. Center for Human Rights, the International Helsinki Federation, and the International Tribunal for War Crimes in the Former Yugoslavia. She has organized national and international activities aimed at protecting refugees and displaced persons and returning them to the places of their origin. She has worked with regional and international human rights and political bodies to protect human rights in the Federal Republic of Yugoslavia (FRY), and, in particular, in Kosovo. In addition, she has organized regional and international activities related to war crimes in the former Yugoslavia, collected and documented crimes committed in the region, and initiated confidence-building activities among different groups in the FRY and former Yugoslavia.

Biserko helped found the Center for Anti-War Action; the Belgrade Forum for International Relations; the European Movement in Yugoslavia; and the Serbia Helsinki Human Rights Committee. She has organized, lectured, and participated in many international conferences in the United States, including foreign relation conferences, a Senate Foreign Relation Council hearing, and several international meetings on the situation in Serbia during and after the NATO campaign. She has organized meetings and courses related to human rights and humanitarian law. She has been involved in projects related to the return of the refugees to Croatia, Serbo–Albanian relations, a Serbo–Croatian roundtable, self-determination in Kosovo, international tribunals, and war crimes.

Biserko has edited and published several books, including *Yugoslavia: War, Collapse, Crime, The Shattering of the Soul, In the Name of Humanity, Self-Determination: Between Autonomy and Separation*, and *Radicalization of the Serbian Society*. In 1996, she founded and began editing a monthly bulletin *Helsinki Charter*, which focuses on the problems of refugees and war crimes. In addition to regular columns in *Helsinki Charter*, she writes articles and does interviews in major regional and international media, including the *New York Times, Le Monde, La Stampa, Frankfurter Allgemeine Zeitung, Frankfurter Rundschau, Security Dialogue, Koha Ditore, IWPR*, and others. In 1994, she was awarded a prize for human rights work by the Lawyers Committee for Human Rights in New York.

SUGGESTED READING

Books, Articles, and Published documents

Akhavan, Payam, ed. *Yugoslavia the Former and Future: Reflections by Scholars from the Region*. Geneva: UNRISD, 1995.

Anderson, Benedict. *Imagined Communities: Reflections on the Origin and Spread of Nationalism*. London and New York: Verso Press, 1991.

Arsić, Mirko, and Dragan R. Marković. *68—studentski bunt i društvo*. Belgrade, Serbia: Istraživačko izdavački centar SSO Srbije, 1988 (treće izdanje).

Bakić, Radovan. "Kretanje stanovnika po nacionalnom sastavu u SAP Kosovo u periodu od 1961 do 1971 godine." *Glasnik Srpskog geografskog društva*, no. 51 (1971): 97.

Baletić, Milovan, ed. *Ljudi iz 1971: prekinuta šutnja* Zagreb, Croatia: Dopunski izdavački program Vjesnik, 1990.

Banac, Ivo. "Bosnian Muslims: From Religious Community to Socialist Nationhood" and "The Dissolution of Yugoslav Historiography." *Beyond Yugoslavia: Politics, Economics, and Culture in a Shattered Community*, prepared by Sabrina Petra

Ramet and Ivo Banac

——.*The National Question in Yugoslavia: Origins, History, Politics*. Ithaca: Cornell University Press, 1984.

——.*With Stalin Against Tito: Cominformist Splits in Yugoslav Communism*. Ithaca and London: Cornell University Press, 1988.

——."Political Change and National Diversity." *Daedalus*, no. 119 (1990): 141–61.

——."Post-Communism as Post-Yugoslavism: The Yugoslav Non-Revolutions of 1989-1990." In *Eastern Europe in Revolution*, edited by Ivo Banac, 168–87. Ithaca: Cornell University Press, 1992.

Banac, Ivo. *Raspad Jugoslavije*. Zagreb, Croatia: Durieux, 2001.

Biberaj, Elez. *Yugoslavia: A Continuing Crisis*. London: Research Institute for the Study of Conflict, 1989.

Bilandžić, Dušan. *Historija Socijalističke Federativne Republike Jugoslavije: Glavni procesi, 1918–1985*. Zagreb, Croatia: Školska knjiga, 1985.

Bilić, Jure. *'71: koja je to godina*. Zagreb, Croatia: Centar za informacije i publicitet, 1990.

Biserko, Sonja i Slavija Stanojlovic. *Radikalizacija drustva u Srbiji* (zbornik radova). Belgrade, Helsinski: Odbor za ljudska prava u Srbiji, 1997.

Blagojević, Marina. "Iseljavanje Srba sa Kosova: trauma i/ili katarza." *Republika*, no. 7 (Novembar 1-15, 1995): I–xx.

Bogdanović, Bogdan. *Grad i smrt*. Belgrade, Serbia: Beogradski krug, 1994.

——.*Mrtvouzice: Mentalne zamke staljinizma*. Zagreb, Croatia: August Cesarec, 1988.

Bogosavljević, Srđan. "Drugi svjetski rat—žrtve u Jugoslaviji." *Republika*, no. 7 (June 1-15, 1995): xi–xvi.

Bojić, Nada. *Ko ste Vi Vojislave Šešelju?* Belgrade, Serbia: Dereta, 1992.

Božić, Ivan, Sima Ćirković, Milorad Ekmečić, and Vladimir Dedijer. *Istorija Jugoslavije*. Belgrade, Serbia: Prosveta, 1972.

Budding, Audrey Helfant. "Yugoslavs into Serbs: Serbian National Identity 1961-1971," *Nationalities Papers*, no. 25 (September 1997): 407–26.

Bugarski, Ranko. *Jezik od mira do rata*. Belgrade, Serbia: Beogradski krug, 1994.

Cavoški, Kosta. *Slobodan protiv slobode*. Belgrade, Serbia: Dosije, 1991.

——.*Zatiranje srpstva*. Belgrade, Serbia: Hriscanska misao, 1996.

Ćimić, Esad. *Politika kao sudbina*. Zagreb, Croatia: Stvarnost, 1989.

Cohen, J. Philip. *Tajni rat Srbije*. Zagreb, Croatia: CERES, 1997.

Čolović, Ivan. "Fudbal, huligani i rat." *Republika*, no. 7 (June 1-15 1995): i–x.

Ćosić, Dobrica. "Za jugoslovenstvo nacionalnih kultura," *Naprijed,* no. 9 (November 28, 1952): 49.

——.*Stvarno i moguće: člunci i ogledi*. Ljubljana i Zagreb, Croatia: Cankarjeva založba, 1988.

———.*Srpsko pitanje—demokratsko pitanje*. Belgrade, Serbia: Politika, 1992.

———.*Piscevi zapisi 1951–1968*. Belgrade, Serbia: Filip Višnjić, 2000.

———.*Piscevi zapisi 1969–1980*. Belgrade, Serbia: Filip Višnjić, 2001.

———.*Piscevi zapisi 1981–1991*. Belgrade, Serbia: Filip Višnjić, 2002.

———.*Srpsko pitanje I*. Belgrade, Serbia: Filip Višnjić, 2002.

Čubrilović, Vasa. *Istorija političke misli u Srbiji XIX veka*. Belgrade, Serbia: Narodna knjiga, 1982.

"Da li je nacionalizam naša sudbina," *Delo*, no. 17 (1971): 1–35.

Danilović, Rajko. *Upotreba neprijatelja: politička suđenja 1945–1991 u Jugoslaviji*. Valjevo: Anecija Valjevac, 1993.

Denitch, Bogdan. *Ethnic Nationalism: The Tragic Death of Yugoslavia*. Minneapolis: University of Minnesota Press, 1994.

Dimitrijević, Vojin. "Međunarodna zajednica i jugoslovenka kriza," *Republika*, no. 8 (February 1–29, 1996): i–xii.

———."Sukobi oko Ustava iz 1974." In *Srpska strana rata: trauma i katarza u istorijskom pamćenju*, edited by Nebojša Popov, 447–71. Belgrade, Serbia: Republika, 1996.

Dizdarevic, Raif, *Od smrti Tita do smrti Jugoslavije*. Sarajevo: Atudio OKO, 1999.

Djilas, Milovan. *Članci 1941–1946*. Belgrade, Serbia: Kultura, 1947.

———.*Druženje s Titom*. Harrow: Aleksa Đilas, 1980.

Druga Srbija. Belgrade, Serbia: Beogradski krug, 1992.

Đekić, Mirko. *Upotreba Srbije: optužbe i priznanja Draže Markoviča*. Belgrade, Serbia: Beseda, 1990.

Đorđević, Mirko. "Književnost populističkog talasa." In *Srpska strana rata*, edited by Nebojša Popov, 394–418. Belgrade, Serbia: Republika, 1996.

Đukić, Slavoljub. *Lovljenje vetra*. Belgrade, Serbia: Samizdat FREE92, 2001.

———.*Čovek u svom vremenu: razgovori sa Dobricom Ćosičem*. Belgrade, Serbia: Filip Višnjić, 1989.

———.*Kako se dogodio vođa*. Belgrade, Serbia: Filip Višnjić, 1992.

———.*Između slave i anateme: politička biografija Slobodana Miloševiča*. Belgrade, Serbia: Filip Višnjić, 1994.

———.*Kraj srpske bajke*. Beograd, Samizdat FREE92, 1999.

Ekmečić, Milorad. "Odgovor na neke kritike 'Istorije Jugoslavije'." *Jugoslovenski istorijski časopis*, no. 13, br. 1/2 (1974): 217–80.

Garde, Paul. *Vie et mort de la Yugoslavie*. Paris: Fayard, 1992.

Gellner, Ernest. "Nationalidm in the Vacuum." In *Thinking Theretically About Soviet Nationalities,* edited by Alexander Otyl, 243–54. New York: Columbia University Press, 1992.

Goati, Vladimir. "The Disintegration of Yugoslavia: The Role of Political Elites." *Nationalities Papers*, no. 25 (September, 1997).

———.*Jugoslavija na prekretnici: od monizma do građanskog rata*. Belgrade, Serbia: Jugoslovenski institut za novinarstvo, 1991.

Gojković, Drinka. "Trauma bez katarze. Udruženjen književnika Srbije: rađanje nacionalizma iz duha demokratije." *Republika*, br. 118 (June 16–30, 1995): i–xvi.

Gow, James. *Legitimacy and the Military: The Yugoslav Crisis*. New York: St. Martin's Press, 1992.

Halberstam, David. *War in a Time of Peace*. New York: Scribner's, 2001.

Kovacevic, Slobodanka and Dajic Putnik. *Hronologija jugoslovenske krize*. Belgrade, Serbia: IES, 1994.

Inić, Slobodan. "Potraga za državom: Republika Srbija u DF/FNR/SFR Jugoslaviji." *Republika*, vol. 7 (December 16–31, 1995): i–viii.

———.*Portreti,* Beograd: Helsinski odbor za ljudska prava u Srbiji, 2001.

Intelektualci i rat. Belgrade, Serbia: Beogradski krug, 1993.

Isti, ed. *Srpska strana rata. Trauma i katarza u istorijskom pamćenju*. Belgrade, Serbia: Republika, 1996.

Jakovljev, N. Aleksandar. *U vrtlogu secanja I i II*. Belgrade, Serbia: Forum pisaca, 2002.

Jovanović, Slobodan. "Jugoslovenska misao u prošlosti i budućnosti." *Srpski književni glasnik*, vol. 59 (1940): 29–38.

Jović, Borislav. *Poslednji dani SFRJ: izvodi iz dnevnika*. Belgrade, Serbia: Politika, 1995.

Jovičić, Miodrag. "Ustavnopravni položaj srpskog naroda u jugoslovenskoj federaciji." In *Srpsko pitanje*, edited by Aleksa Đilas, 117–30. Belgrade, Serbia: Politika, 1991.

———."*Jako srpstvo—jaka Jugoslavija*"—izbor članaka iz "Srpskog glasa" organa Srpskog kulturnog kluba *1939–1940*. Belgrade, Serbia: Naučna knjiga, 1991.

Judah, Tim. *The Serbs: History, Myth and the Destruction of Yugoslavia*. New Haven and London: Yale University Press, 1997.

———."The Serbs: The Sweet and Rotten Smell of History." *Daedalus*, vol. 126 (ljeto 1997): 23–26.

Kadijevic, B. Veljko. *Geopoliticka stvarnost Srba (zbornik radova)*. Belgrade, Serbia: Institut za geopoliticke studije, 1997.

Kočović, Bogoljub. *Žrtve drugog svetskog rata u Jugoslaviji*. London: Veritas Foundation Press, 1985.

Konstantinović, Radomir. *Filozofija palanke*. Belgrade, Serbia: Prosveta, 1971.

Koštunica, Vojislav, and Kosta Čavoški. *Party Pluralism or Monism: Social Movements and Political System in Yugoslavia, 1944–1949*. Boulder, CO: East European Monographs, 1985.

Knezevic, Milos. *Kosovo i Metohija, izazovi i odgovori (zbornik radova)*. Belgrade, Serbia: Institut za geopoliticke studije, 1997.

———.*Balkanska pometnja*. Belgrade, Serbia: Djuro Salaj, 1996.

Kostunica, Vojislav. *Izmedju slave i prava*. Belgrade, Serbia: Hriscanska misao, 2000.

Krestić, Vasilije. "Suštinska sporna pitanja Srba i Hrvata tokom istorije." *Glas Srpske akademije nauka i umetnosti CCCLXXII, Odeljenje istorijskih nauka, knj. 8* (1993).

Krstic, Branislav. *Kosovo izmedju istorijskog i etnickog prava*. Belgrade, Serbia: Kuca Vid, 1994.

———.*Kosovo pred sudom istorije*. Belgrade, Serbia: Izdanje autora, 2000.

Madžar, Ljubomir. "Ko koga eksploatiše." *Republika*, vol. 7 (September 1–15, 1995): i–xvi.

Magaš, Branka. *The Destruction of Yugoslavia: Tracing the Break–up 1980–92*. London: Verso, 1993.

Magas, Branka and Ivo Zanic. *Rat u Hrvatskoj i Bosni i Hercegovini 1991–1995*. Zagreb, Sarajevo: Naklada Jesenski i Turk, 1999.

Malcolm, Noel. *Bosnia: A Short History*. New York: NYU Press, 1996.

Maliqi Shkëlzen. "Kosovo kao katalizator jugoslovenske krize." In *Kosovo—Srbija—Jugoslavija*, edited by Slavko Gaber and Tonči Kuzmanić, 69–76. Ljubljana, Slovenia: Knjižnica revolucionarne teorije, 1989.

Mamula, Branko. *Slucaj Jugoslavija*. Podgorica, Montenegro: CID, 2000.

Mesic, Stipe. *Kako je srusena Jugoslavija*. Zagreb, Croatia: Time of Truth, 1994.

Mihailović, Kosta, and Vasilije Krestić. eds. *"Memorandum SANU": odgovori na kritike*. Belgrade, Serbia: SANU, 1995.

Mihailović, Srećko et al. *Od izbornih rituala do slobodnih izbora*. Belgrade, Serbia: Institut društvenih nauka, 1991.

Milivojevic, Marko. *Yugoslavia's Security Dilemmas: Armed Forces, National Defense, and Foreign Policy*. New York: St. Martin's Press, 1988.

———.*Yugoslav People's Army: The Political Dimension*. West Yorkshire: University of Bradford, 1988.

Milosavljević, Olivera. "Jugoslavija kao zabluda." *Republika*, vol. 8 (March 1–31, 1996): i–vxi.

———."Upotreba autoriteta nauke." *Republika*, vol. 7 (July 1–31, 1995): i–xxx.

Milošević, Slobodan. *Godine raspleta*. Belgrade, Serbia: BIGZ, 1989.

———.*Od Gazimestana do Sevenginena*. Belgrade, Serbia: Harprom, 2001.

Mirić, Jovan. *Sistem i kriza: Prilog kritičkoj analizi ustavnog i političkog sistema Jugoslavije*. Zagreb, Croatia: Centar za kulturnu djelatnost, 1984.

Nenadović, Aleksandar. "Politika u nacionalističkoj oluji." *Republika*, vol. 7 (April 15–30, 1995): i–vxi.

———.*Razgovori s Kočom*. Zagreb, Crotia: Globus, 1989.

Nove stranke Srbije: dokumenti novih političkih stranaka i grupa u Srbiji. Zbornici Dokumenata. Belgrade, Serbia: Institut za političke studije, 1990.

"O predlozima za izmenu nekih odredaba Ustava SFRJ i tezama za izborni sistem." *Anali pravnog fakulteta u Beogradu*, vol. 16, no. 4 (1968): 487–526.

Nisic, Stanko. *Strategija Srba*. Belgrade, Serbia: Nikola Pasic, 1995.

Pašić, Najdan. *Nacionalno pitanje u savremenoj epohi*. Belgrade, Serbia: Radnička štampa, 1973.

Perović, Latinka. *Zatvaranje kruga: ishod političkog rascepa u SKJ 1971/1972*. Sarajevo: Svjetlost, 1991.

———.*Beg od modernizacije, Srpska strana rata*. Belgrade, Serbia: Republika, 1996.

Pešić, Vesna. "Rat za nacionalne države." In *Srpska strana rata. Trauma i katarza u istorijskom pamćenju*, edited by Nebojša Popov, 3–59. Belgrade, Serbia: Republika, 1996.

———.*Serbian Nationalism and the Origins of the Yugoslav Crisis*. Washington, DC: United States Institute of Peace, 1996.

Pfaff, William. "Invitation to War." *Foreign Affairs*, vol. 72 (ljeto 1993): 97–109.

"Plava knjiga." In *Upotreba Srbije: optužbe i priznanja Draže Markovića*, edited by Mirko Đekić, 123–74. Belgrade, Serbia: Beseda, 1990.

Popov, Nebojsa. "Srpski populizam: od marginalne do dominantne pojave." *Vreme*, br. 135 (May 24, 1993): specijalni dodatak, 1–33.

Popović, Danko. *Knjiga o Milutinu*. Belgrade, Serbia: Književne novine, 1986.

Popović, Srđa, Dejan Janča and Tanja Petovar. *Kosovski čvor: drešiti ili seći*. Belgrade, Serbia: Hronos, 1990.

Popović, Nikola. *Srpski nacionalni program, dokumenti i misljenja*. Belgrade, Serbia: DMP, 2000.

Protic, St. Milan. *Mi i Oni*. Belgrade, Serbia: Hriscanska misao, 1996.

Radakovic, Ilija. *Besmislena YU ratovanja*. Belgrade, Serbia: Drustvo za istinu o antifasistickoj Narodnooslobodilackoj borbi u Jugoslaviji (1941–1945), 1997.

Radić, Radmila. "Crkva i 'srpsko pitanje.'" *Republika*, vol. 7 (August 1–31, 1995): i–xxiv.

Rak, Pavle. *Nacionalisticka internacionala*. Belgrade, Serbia: Forum pisaca, 2002.

Ramet, Sabrina Petra. *Balkan Babel: The Disintegration of Yugoslavia from the Death of Tito to Ethnic War*. Boulder, CO: Westview Press, 1996.

———.*Nationalism and Federalism in Yugoslavia, 1962–1991*, 2nd revised edition. Bloomington and Indianapolis: Indiana University Press, 1992.

Rančić, Dragoslav. *Dobrica Ćosić ili predsednik bez vlasti*. Belgrade, Serbia: Crno na belo, 1994.

Raskovic, Jovan. *Luda zemlja*. Belgrade, Serbia: Akvarijus, 1990.

Šešelj, Vojislav. "Esej o socijalizmu i intelektualcima," *Savremenik*, vol. 30 (March–April 1984): 269–84.

———.*Hajka na jeretika*. Belgrade, Serbia: KRRZ, 1986.

Šijaković-Blagojević, Marina. "Etnički aspekt migracija u Jugoslaviji." *Marksistička Misao* (1986): 202–14.

———."Iseljavanje Srba sa Kosova: trauma i/ili katarza," *Republika*. vol. 7, no. 127 (November 1–15, 1995), i–xx.

Silber, Laura, and Allan Little. *Yugoslavia: Death of a Nation*. New York: TV Books, Inc., 1997.

Simic, Predrag. *Put u Rambuje: kosovska kriza 1995–2000*. Belgrade, Serbia: NEA, 2000.

Stambolic, Ivan. *Put u bespuce*. Belgrade, Serbia: Radio B 92, 1995.

———.*Koren Zla*. Belgrade, Serbia: Helsinki odbor za ljudska prava u Srbiji, 2001.

Stojanović, Dubravka. "Traumatični krug srpske opozicije." *Republika*, vol. 7 (October 1–31, 1995): i–xvi.

Stranke u Jugoslaviji. Belgrade, Serbia: TANJUG, 1990.

Šuvar, Stipe. *Nacije i međunacionalni odnosi u socijalističkoj Jugoslaviji*. Zagreb, Croatia: Naše teme, 1970.

———.*Nacionalno: nacionalističko: eseji i polemički prilozi*. Split, Dalmatia: Marksistički centar, 1974.

———. "Savremeni trenutak međunacionalnih odnosa." *Marksistička misao*, br. 6 (1977): 72–88.

Tasic, Predrag. *Kako sam branio Antu Markovica*. Skopje, Macedonia: NIP Mugri 21, 1993.

Tito, Josip Broz. *Govori i članci*. vols. 1–21. Zagreb, Croatia: Naprijed, 1959–72.

Todorovic, Dragoje. *Ujedinjeno srpstvo: Dr. Stevan Moljevic*. Belgrade, Serbia: Kalekom, 2000.

Vilic, Dusan, and Bosko Todorovic. *Razbijanje Jugoslavije 1990–1992*. Belgrade, Serbia: DIK Knjizevne novine, 1995.

Vujović, Sreten. "Stereotipi o gradu, nacionalizam i rat." *Republika*, vol. 7 (April 1–15, 1995): i–xii.

Vuković, Zdravko. *Od deformacija SDB do maspoka i liberalizma*. Belgrade, Serbia: Narodna knjiga, 1989.

Woodward, Susan L. *Balkan Tragedy: Chaos and Dissolution After the Cold War*. Washington, DC: The Brookings Institution, 1995.

Žerjavić, Vladimir. *Gubici stanovništva Jugoslavije u drugom svjetskom ratu*. Zagreb, Croatia: 1992.

Zimmermann, Warren. *Origins of Catastrophe: Yugoslavia and Its Destroyers—America's Last Ambassador Tells What Happened and Why*. New York: Times Books, 1996.

Zirojević, Olga. "Kosovo u istorijskom pamćenju." *Republika*, vol. 7 (March 1–15, 1995): 9–24.

Zuljic, Stanko. *Srpski etnos i velikosrpstvo*. Zagreb, Croatia: AGM, 1997.

Magazines

Borba (Belgrade)
Danas (Belgrade)
Erasmus: casopis za kulturu i demokraciju (Zagreb, 1990–1994)
Geopoliticka raskrsca (Belgrade)
Glasnik Srpske književne zadruge (Belgrade)
Godišnjak SANU (Belgrade)
Intervju (Belgrade)
Književne novine (Belgrade)
Nasa Borba (Belgrade)
Naše teme (Zagreb)
NIN (Belgrade)
Oslobođenje (Sarajevo)
Politika (Belgrade)
Republika (Belgrade)
Srpska politicka misao (Belgrade)
Srpska reč (Belgrade)
Vjesnik (Zagreb)
Vojska, Beograd
Vreme (Belgrade)

Croatia: The Participant in Large-Group Conflict

Eduard Klain

This chapter explores the collapse of the former Yugoslavia, reasons for wars among various national or religious groups, and the establishment of new states. It investigates psychodynamic processes involved in political conflicts in the former Yugoslavia, with a focus on Croatian perspectives, and analyzes the history of nations in conflict in order to understand current events.

THE HISTORICAL SEARCH FOR A HOMELAND

Ivan Rendić-Miočevic, a professor of history at the Faculty of Philosophy in Zadar, Croatia, who had studied the distant history of the peoples of Il-lyricum, connects the remote past of the peoples who lived in these regions with present-day events. One of his fundamental theses is that the patriarchal society developed in these regions has not changed throughout their history. Rendić-Miočevic writes, "If we can say that this society, usually called patriarchal, has not changed for centuries, or has changed very little, then we must conclude that, in fact, it has no history."[1] Vladimir Dvorniković explained this problem long ago:

> Yugoslavs, like other Slavs, were non-historical people of space a long time, and on entering the history—when they came to the present-day south—historical fate and nature of their new habitation made them turn back into non-historical people of the space. We could even say the life destiny of Yugoslavs as a whole consisted in permanent struggle for that transformation from people of space into people of time. And this struggle is still going on. The Yugoslavs are still struggling with the space, the geographic dominant of their lives. They have not surmounted this dominant, although they have reached the crucial point towards political synthesis and against geographical special forces, which have not favored this synthesis.[2]

Miočević's view includes within Yugoslav's traditional patriarchal territory Montenegro, the mountain regions of Serbia and Bosnia, Herzegovina, the Dalmatian hinterland, Lika, and Macedonia. This is very important, since Serbs, mostly Bosnian and Croatian Serbs, Croats, and, in smaller part, Muslims live in these regions. Dvorniković calls tribes that lead patriarchal lives Dinaric. As Dvorniković explains, a patriarchal man hates work, for work is the death of heroism. This viewpoint is evident in former Serbian President Slobodan Milošević's statement, at the beginning of the present-day Serbian aggression: "We don't know how to work, but we know how to fight."[3] Dvorniković also emphasizes the morality and sanctity of revenge: "A patriarchal man can not

forgive because he equates forgiveness with self-defeat. In this ethical dilemma, he always remains a fighter, a Balkan, and not a Christian soul. The ethos of fighting and solidarity of a patriarchal person has two poles: On one side, undoubted virtues developed through ages of family life, but on the other side, brutality and robbery in their worst forms."[4]

Yugoslavia has been unlucky since its beginnings. It was created by foreign factors—that is, great European countries—rather than as the need of people and nations who populated it. Yugoslavia has always been a group of very heterogeneous peoples pushed to live together.

Let me just remind you how difficult it is to form a small group, even when its members share a common aim. Think of the knowledge and skill that are necessary to overcome the resistances and hostilities among the members of the small group and to train the group for communication, interaction, and participation. I am afraid that the only way to make highly, heterogeneous people live together as a large group in a state is to use authoritarian repression accompanied by an idealized or demonized figure serving as a supreme leader relying on a smaller group. This was the formula by which a large group of twenty million people, called Yugoslavians, functioned.

From 1918 to 1941, the supreme authority was the Serbian king who relied on the Serbian majority and repressed the other two large groups, Croats and Bosnians (Muslims), through the utilization of police. The Croats and Bosnians, as well as ethnic or national minorities, in the state played a subordinate role. While repression of all who were not Serbians established a false cohesion, the three main groups—Serbians, Croats, and Bosnian Muslims—continued to nurture destructive aggression and project their unwanted aspects onto others. The two repressed large groups, as well as the unrecognized nations and ethnic minorities, felt excommunicated and looked for others outside the state with whom to identify.

The Yugoslavia just described disintegrated in 1941 in only one week after the disappearance of its authority—the king and everything around him. The Second World War was an ideal opportunity to unleash all the destructive aggressions suppressed in Yugoslavia since the country's formation. The paranoid projections became dominant, supported by foreign groups: the warring European countries. Lives were destroyed and families were broken. Wilfred Bion's descriptions of the destructive power of antagonistic groups were unleashed.[5] What is important to realize is that through transgenerational transmissions all affected groups continued to "remember" awful scenes of separation, such as the killing of their parents in front of their eyes or a child being dragged away from its mother when she was taken to a concentration camp. The transmitted "memories" were acted out by insulting people in other groups and blaming them as the cause of aggression. This is of utmost importance for anyone wanting to understand present-day ethnic conflicts and other confrontations in Yugoslavia. The best chance of success for dealing with this complicated situation was to offer Communism, which favored poor and degraded people and offered equal positions for everyone.

The end of the Second World War led to the creation of the Communist resistance movement for several reasons. The Communists offered prosperity to the poor and the marginalized, promised equality, and suppressed the sentiments of groups (nations) that had destroyed each other during the war and were afraid of revenge at the hand of denied nations and ethnic minorities. The Communists came out of the war as winners on the side of the Allies and had a charismatic leader, Josip Broz Tito, who inspired a false feeling of security by transposing his own grandiose self onto large groups of Yugoslav citizens. However, Communism discredited religious and monarchic authorities, group leadership, and humanistic ideals and resulted in increasing paranoia within Yugoslavia.

The old "memories" were not forgotten, and the repetition of old grievances reappeared in the Federal Peoples' Republic of Yugoslavia. The group dynamic that occurred in the first Yugoslavia (1918–1941) were repeated in the second Yugoslavia (1945–1991). The repressive authority of the tyrannical leader relied on the police and the army. It also relied directly on members of the leading and only party, accounting for less than 10 percent of the population. It depended on Serbs through an organization that called itself the federal administration (1 to 1.5 percent of the population). The number of confronted groups increased in the new state because new nations and ethnic minori-

ties were accepted in the Communist system as equals, thus further reducing overall group cohesion and increasing tensions. The number of "enemy groups" who became suitable targets for the negative and destructive tendencies of the other groups within Yugoslavia increased. Control of the confronted groups could only be achieved with cooperation from repressive forces: by the police and the army. These two forces were actually unified and conducted from one and the same center.

DIFFERENCES IN THE GROUPS CONSTITUTING YUGOSLAVIA

The charismatic leader felt intuitively that heterogeneous groups could only be kept together if they and their leaders were given important positions in the country. By strengthening leaders' narcissism and nurturing narcissistic group selves, he gave all groups an illusion of power. He increased his authority by saving all national, ethnic, and religious groups within Yugoslavia and their leaders from Joseph Stalin's occupation of Yugoslavia. Three protective agents within the regime—the police, army, and federal administration—succeeded in keeping group tensions suppressed. Each attempt by any smaller group to oppose the authority of the larger group or ruler was quelled, especially if the leaders' names were heard and emphasized again and again. Thus, the names of the leaders could be read on the billboards or shouted by large group members at public meetings. The narcissism of the supreme ruler could not stand any name but his own. Tito and his closest allies offered a quasi-democratic group approach.

GROUP DYNAMIC OF THE DISINTEGRATION OF COMMUNIST YUGOSLAVIA

In the 1970s, a dynamic balance existed among the various groups in Yugoslavia. Foreign credit provided economic stability, welfare and almost total employment. Keeping in mind Bion's description of group dynamics, a "dependency" was created to put the population together.[6] There was a leader who took care of everything and, most importantly, procured financial means. Members of the population in general felt as if they took part in governmental affairs, which means that they had some power through self-managing bodies. Though their power situation was completely false, it satisfied many people's narcissistic needs. While most members of these large groups were not aware of economic and political realities, they were protected by idealization of the leader and projection of unwanted elements on "others." This "adaptation" was disrupted in 1980 by Tito's death. For a while, however, Tito remained a cult figure, even though he was dead, through numerous rituals, beginning with a great show at his funeral, followed by pilgrimages to his tomb and the creation of his museum. A large number of people needed this long mourning process. However, the space for idealization narrowed with time. Idealized illusions began to collapse. Economic difficulties appeared, and splits began to occur within the Yugoslav population. The weakest link, the Communist Party of Yugoslavia, was the first to collapse. Its breakdown was fueled, in part, by the dissolution of the Soviet Union. The rigid rules of the Communist party hierarchical organization deteriorated, the group lost its clear boundaries, subgroups formed, and confronted one another. As the splits occurred within the Communist party, splits among the Yugoslav population also became clear along national lines.

THE WAR IN SLOVENIA: JUNE 27–JULY 2, 1991

The four-day war in Slovenia between the federal army and the Slovene people certainly had many political, economic, military and other causes. From a group-dynamic processes perspective, the external reason for this unusual war was the Republic of Slovenia's proclamation of independence and the Slovene government's move to take control of Yugoslavian border crossings. The federal government was said to have ordered the army to secure the frontier, but some people believe the army itself made that decision.

It seems logical that the federal army reacted with force to Slovenia's attempt to become independent. This act represented a threat to the officers and aroused in them fear of destruction because of the breakdown of Communism (which had already happened but they could not accept) and the federal state being a complete disaster.

Tanks moved in the direction of border crossings, and the Slovenes defended themselves in an organized and disciplined manner. At the same time, they waged a well-organized mass-media war, using the most powerful medium, television. The federal army war operations were mostly performed without direct human confrontation (tanks and war planes). Soldiers, however, appeared ambivalent, not sure whether they should shoot at their own people or not. The army split—many soldiers surrendered or deserted to the Slovene territorial defense; some officers did the same. After four days of the war, the federal army collapsed.

THE WAR IN CROATIA: AUGUST 1990–AUGUST 1995

In the multinational, multiconfessional, and socioculturally diversified state of Yugoslavia, there are many groups with hardly any links but many things that separate them. Yugoslavia has witnessed constant dynamic change in relations among the groups. Smaller groups united into larger alliances, coalitions formed and fell apart, and points of confrontation between the groups changed. Nevertheless, the most important relationship was a dynamic one between the two most populous nations: the Serbs and Croats. Serbs were, as mentioned, brought up in a military tradition based on myths about heroism, believing the best and strongest people should lead Yugoslavia. They identified, sometimes consciously, sometimes unconsciously, with Serbia. They regarded it an honor to be a member of a military or police group. A uniform and arms were symbols of maleness for them. On the other hand, Croats as a group cultivated feelings of subordination and underestimation. Since 1918, they have felt exploited by the Serbs in Yugoslavia. The Second World War and the Communist era contributed to the development of these feelings and the accompanying psychodynamics of these two groups.

It is interesting to note that during the Second World War, extreme groups of Serbs and Croats formed. The so-called Chetniks and Ustashas physically exterminated members of "opposing" groups without any rational motive. Malignant destructiveness, which is always accompanied by irrationality, motivated the actions of extremists on both sides. Extremists treated members of opposing groups as some primitive tribe, and on that basis used destructive projections of paranoia to justify their actions. They believed they had to defend themselves, for otherwise they would be tortured, destroyed, or unconsciously cannibalistically massacred. These irrational fears, together with paranoid projections, spread with great strength and rapidity and led to mass reactions, illustrating Bion's fight–flight response in group dynamics. Unfortunately, both sides had many casualties.

One harmful consequence of these group dynamics was the subsequent interpretation of these events. After the second World War both Serbs and Croats satisfied their self-esteem with repeated stories about the war. This had an enormous impact on education and the emotional development of postwar generations. After the war, Communist propaganda succeeded in presenting the situation as if the Ustashas (extreme Croats) killed innocent Serbian people in large numbers while having a different, much more lenient attitude toward the Chetniks (extreme Serbs). The number of Serbian victims was inflated ten- to a hundredfold. In fact, all those opposing the official politics of the time were systematically exterminated—not only Serbs but also representatives of all other nations, including Muslims, Croats, and others. The two extremist groups perpetrated the same destruction, but Croats have been ashamed of what happened, while Serbs have been somewhat proud. Throughout the postwar period, any investigations of the causes and severity of the crimes in which both Croats and Serbs were involved as were the Ustashas, Chetniks, and Communists were systematically prevented. Thus, incomplete investigations and stories have contributed to the preservation of memories of crimes and, released by the new democratic processes, have burst out with full strength. For better understanding of the group psychology of these two peoples, it should be mentioned that after the Second World War the Serbs in Croatia, where they make 12 percent of the population, held the leading positions in the government and business, as well as in the Communist Party. The president of the Communist Party of Croatia was almost always a Serb. On the other side, the Croats in Voivodina, which is part of Serbia, have never held any leading position.

By his authoritarian behavior, Tito controlled resistances in national groups. When they acted out, he provided some small concessions that temporarily reduced tensions and resistances. When Communist rule broke down, Yugoslavia disintegrated. In the process of disintegration, which is still in progress, Serbs and Croats acted in two different ways. In Serbia, the Communist regime is still in power, albeit somewhat modified, and the Communist Party wins the majority in the parliamentary elections. Serbian election results are difficult to explain psychodynamically, but group processes exerted influence during the late 1980s. One charismatic leader (Josip Broz Tito) was substituted for with another (Slobodan Milošević) who offered narcissistic omnipotence (they are the most capable, their historical heroes are the greatest, their God is the best, etc.) and complete protection from all enemy groups (Croats, Albanians, Bulgarians, Muslims, etc.) in a totally regressive–paternalistic way—for example, through declarations such as "Nobody should beat this people," "We will arrest the enemies," and so on. Such promises resonated with Serbs. Fear of other groups in Yugoslavia, imposed by the great leader, as well as fear of any change or new, unknown situations, were also cohesive factors that attracted Serbs to Communism.

In Croatia, the group process was different but still exhibited some similarities. Communism was defeated in elections. The party that won elections united its numerous members around the idea of nation building. It chose to advance the concept of sovereign Croatia, free to choose the countries with which it will form alliances, and under what conditions, or whether it will proceed toward full independence. Official statements and documents issued by the party guaranteed civil and political rights to all Serbs and other minorities in Croatia, thereby inviting them into parliamentary negotiations.

The advancement of this concept revealed variations in the approach. The basic standpoints were explained both moderately and radically. More extreme statements were used by official Serbian politicians, who were supported by some representatives of the Serbian people in Croatia, to turn Serbs in Croatia away from parliamentary struggle and toward armed fighting. We should not forget that the leaders of the group that won the elections (the Croatian Democratic Union) were mostly former Communist leaders brought up in that regime, which expelled and sentenced them when they rebelled against it. Imprisonment fostered a drive to fight against Communism in groups, but they were not able to confront the invisible Communist in themselves. And, here is the great similarity with the leading Serbian group. Authoritarian behavior in the leading Croatian group was moderate in comparison with Serbian behavior because it was attenuated by a freer, louder opposition and media, which wrested control from the government. Nevertheless, parliamentary elections in Croatia did succeed in achieving considerable democratic freedom. Another very important similarity between the leading Serbian and Croatian groups is their charismatic leaders. The authoritative personality, military education, and origin of Josip Broz Tito were similar to those of Dr. Franjo Tudjman, the Croatian leader. Supporters were entirely dependent on the leader, having little chance to grow up independently. If electoral victory brought a shared feeling of carelessness and satisfaction to the supporters, it did not last long because revelers were soon faced with enemy groups from their environment. As if awakened from a dream, they reacted aggressively and regressively. By not allowing anyone to oppose them, they enlarged resistance and hostility in other groups, especially among Serbs in Croatia, who actually had for years been persistently indoctrinated through cunning propaganda directed from Belgrade. These forces, coupled with group dynamics, created a complex war. Initially, the war was between Serbs and Croats and Communism and advancing democracy. It was between Serbia as a state and Serbs in Croatia. It put the federal army on one side, and the Croatian government and people on the other. An irrational and deeply regressive war has been waged between several groups led by hate, fear, and paranoid projections.

THE WAR IN BOSNIA AND HERZEGOVINA: MARCH 1992–NOVEMBER 1995

The war in Bosnia and Herzegovina was a logical continuation of the war in Croatia. It followed the same pattern: the Serbs proclaimed themselves endangered and attacked the other two national peoples: the Croats and Muslims (Bosnians). The Serbs aimed to occupy a large part of Bosnia and Herzegovina's territory, "clean" it ethnically, and incorporate the territory into a greater Serbia. By massacring civilians, the Serbs put fear in native peoples and forced them to leave the region.

From the beginning, organized and armed resistance to Serbian aggression was waged by Croatian groups in Bosnia because they had experienced the war in Croatia and identified with their own country (Croatia). During the Communist regime, Croatians in Bosnia were suppressed by Serbs and persecuted, especially in Herzegovina. The Croats, as an endangered group, homogenized and formed a cohesive resistance even before the war.

The Muslims, who comprise a large portion of the Bosnian population, did not prepare for war because they had lived with the illusion that Croats and Serbs would fight one another and leave them alone. They were not aware of Serbia's real territorial ambitions and often used negation or denial as a defense. Knowing the historical precedents did not help them either. During World War II, Bosnian Muslims were slaughtered by Chetniks (Serb extremists), a situation that has since been repeated. The Bosnians did not form cohesive resistance groups, nor did they develop an overall object of identification in their own country (like the Croats did in declaring Croatia a sovereign state). Moreover, Bosnians did not have close contacts and alliances with other Islamic countries. Even though their tradition is partly Islamic, it is also partly Slavic, as are their origins.

The religious framework within which Muslims live has much fatalism built into it, which appears to be one of the reasons they withdrew rather than actively resisting Serbian aggression from the start. That is, the group's collective fatalism was, at least initially, expressed in terms of "flight" rather than "fight." As a result, an enormous number of Muslim refugees sought shelter in Croatia and other European countries. The number continues to increase as the Serbian program of "ethnic cleansing" continues. Bosnia's Muslims favor maintaining a large heterogeneous group, living alongside Serbs and Croats in Bosnia and Herzegovina. Serbs and Croats would rather integrate their peoples from that territory, in one way or another, into a separate Serbia or Croatia. These aspirations are an example of a homogeneous group identity that seeks to contain the same people with the same tradition in the same nation.

CROATIAN–BOSNIAN WAR: JUNE 20, 1992– FEBRUARY 23, 1994

The most absurd war in the former Yugoslavia was the war between Croats and the Bosnian Muslims. Croats from Herzegovina were armed by Croatian authorities, and in 1993–94 they started a war against the Bosnians that had characteristics similar to the war that Serbia started against Croatia and Bosnia–Herzegovina. The Croats were ethnically cleansing the territory and forming camps for Bosnian Muslims. To make the situation even more absurd, at the same time the Croats were waging war against Bosnians, more than a million Muslim refugees from Bosnia and Herzegovina were in Croatia. Later in that war, the Croatian army from southern Bosnia and Herzegovina was involved. Toward the end of the war, the Bosnian and Croatian army started fighting together against the Serbs. A typical example of the Croatian–Bosnian war is the division of Mostar, a city with a long history and multicultural center. Serbs were expelled, and Croats and Bosnians were separated, with Croats in the west and Bosnians in the east part of the city. The western part remains preserved; the eastern was demolished. Those most responsible for this war were leaders in Serbia and Croatia who wanted to divide Bosnia and Herzegovina along Croatian and Serbian lines and leave Bosnians one small enclave.

CHOSEN TRAUMA

The role of chosen trauma plays a large role in the conflicts that have been waged in the Yugoslavian region. Vamik Volkan uses the term *chosen trauma* to describe "the collective memory of a calamity that once befell a group's ancestors. It is, of course, more than a simple recollection; it is a shared mental representation of the event, which includes realistic information, fantasized expectations, intense feelings, and defenses against unacceptable thoughts. In time collapse, the interpretations, fantasies, and feelings about a past shared trauma commingle with those pertaining to a current situation. Under the influence of a time collapse, people may intellectually separate the past event from the present one, but emotionally the two events are merged."[7]

An old Serbian chosen trauma, if understood, sheds a lot of light on the wars that have ravaged the territories in and around the former Yugoslavia. History confirms that the Muslim Turks defeated the Serbs in 1389 in the Battle of Kosovo. There is a saying (not a historical fact) that after their victory over Serbs, the Turks killed all male children and raped all young Serbian women so that they would give birth to Turks. Eastern religions proscribe that the father determines the child's religious identity. He is the seed, while the mother represents only the earth into which the seed is planted. This myth about Turkish behavior after the Battle of Kosovo has remained vivid in Serbians' collective memory to the present day. In current wars, it has generated revenge against the Muslims because of the events that happened more than six hundred years ago. During the last ten years, Serbs have been celebrating the Battle of Kosovo as if it were their victory, not a defeat.

Serbs sought revenge for their chosen trauma on a sexual level. They raped Muslim women and left them in camps while they were months pregnant so that they would give birth to Serbs, reversing the myth that if a Turk raped a Serbian woman her child would be a Turk. Men were also raped. Muslim fighters who were caught were mutilated by Serbian women, who cut off their penises and testicles.

Bosnians feel that their chosen trauma occurred when Bosnian Muslim royalty stood up against the Turkish government in 830 A.D. In the first battle, they won over the Turks. Then a Turkish sultan retaliated. He sent a large, stronger army to fight the rebels, and the army killed all the gentry. (It is interesting that this event took place on Kosovo Field.) However, during the events in the former Yugoslavia, Bosnians primarily reactivated their "memories" of how Chetniks had slaughtered them during World War II.

It is not easy to define the chosen trauma of the Croats. I believe that Croats' need to have their own country originates from having to serve someone constantly. Croatia was part of the Austro–Hungarian monarchy. The government of Austria was on one side and Hungarians, resisting the central government, were on the other side. When the Austro–Hungarian monarchy disintegrated, Croatia became subordinated again in Yugoslavia under Serbian authority, which replicated in a certain way what had happened after the Second World War.

OBSTACLES TO SOLVING THE CONFLICT

In various parts of the former Yugoslavia, especially those stricken by the war, including Croatia, Bosnia, and Herzegovina, many victims are still full of hatred and wish for revenge. Hatred exists on all sides. It has stimulated the war, and when people had to surrender territory, under the Dayton agreements, that hatred was even more obvious. Once again, the Serbs seem to have lost at the negotiating table what they had won on the battlefield. Experiences during the events that occurred as the former Yugoslavia was collapsing have left a permanent impression on survivors. Particularly vulnerable are families of missing people, many of whom were taken away by force. Exacerbating the psychological torture, the Serbs refuse to provide any information about them. Hatred in families whose loved ones were killed prevails, as well as wishes to avenge those deaths. The victims of war, notably the disabled, released prisoners of war, refugees, and displaced persons, also suffer serious scars and wish for revenge. It appears that war victims are growing less aggressive and vengeful, due perhaps to the conciliatory attitude of the Catholic Church, which lectures on forgiveness. Still, there are rather frequent and dangerous inducements of children by their parents, primarily mothers, to avenge their killed or missing parents.

The hurts and losses caused by years of suffering and bloodshed in the former Yugoslavia are deeply rooted in the collective psyche of people living in the region. Past experiences can affect current events and future choices in many ways, as outlined here.

1. **Transgenerational Transmission of Trauma**
   Transgenerational transmission occurs when an older person unconsciously projects his traumatized self into a developing child's personality. A child then becomes a reservoir for the unwanted, troublesome parts of an older generation.[8] When elders influence a child, the child absorbs their wishes and expectations and is driven to act on them. It becomes the child's task to mourn, to reverse the humiliation and feelings of helplessness pertaining to the trauma of his forebears. The transmissions of traumatized self-images occur almost as if psychological DNA were planted in the personality of the younger generation through its relationships with the previous one.

2. **Generalized Projection Onto Other Nations**
   The collective psychosis that seized the people in the former Yugoslavia was in fact a generalization of paranoid projections onto another nation and religion within the former Yugoslavia, with no space for critical judgment and rational consideration of the facts. Destructive slogans, such as "Only a dead Chetnik is a good Chetnik" and "Only a dead Ustasha is a good Ustasha" illustrate this pattern. Collective paranoia transcended social strata. As a result, each member of the "enemy" nation was a suspect with whom it became dangerous to associate or work.

3. **Distrust and Prejudice**   Distrust is a minor form of a paranoid reaction and is perpetual to interethnical conflicts. It is accompanied with prejudices against "others." In Croatia distrust was aimed largely at Serbs, especially those who stayed in Croatia. Those fighting against Croatia were out of reach. Serbs fighting in the Croatian army were trusted a little. During the Croat–Bosnian war, Bosnian refugees in Croatia, mainly women, children, and the old were considered enemies and experienced immense distrust.

4. **Retraumatization**   Retraumatization reopens narcissistic wounds. The larger community attitude toward veterans grows worse each day. One can often hear people asking them "Who made you fight? Who made you volunteer for the war?" In the beginning, state authorities did not recognize posttraumatic stress syndrome (PTSD) as a valid condition at all. Now it is seen to be as important as physical injuries sustained in the war. Whenever veterans feel like talking about their sufferings and about what happened in the war, people decline to listen, saying they are bored.

The repatriation of refugees is an ongoing problem. Nobody wants them. The authorities do not want them because they are still trying to maintain the fantasy of having a more-or-less ethnically "clean" country. Neighboring nations do not want refugees to come back. Refugees themselves do not want to return, especially those who escaped to Western countries. Generally, the ones who are returning are elderly and those who did not fare well in Croatia, Serbia, western Europe, or America. Hypocritical politicians talk positively about homecoming in public but actually want ethnically "clean" countries and incite contempt against homecomers. Politicians intend to give as little money as they can to homecomers and do not want to open work positions to refugees. As a result, refugees do not have resources for living. In one case in Bosnia, returnees were killed.

An example of the long-term effects of conflict can be found in the town of Vukovar. It is the most destroyed town in Croatia, and a symbol of Croatian people's suffering. Before the war, Vukovar was a nice small town on the coast of the Danube River. Half the residents were Croats; half were Serbs. They lived together without any conflict for many generations. From August until November 1991, the town was systematically destroyed by the Yugoslav national army, Serbian paramilitary, and Serbs from Vukovar. It is not clear how citizens of Vukovar managed to hold out against such destructive forces for those three months. When Vukovar finally fell wounded, hospital patients and other civilians were taken out and shot, many people ran away through mine fields, and some were returned after being held in captivity by Serbians. Refugees from Vukovar dispersed all over Croatia and other countries. Their problem is not solved even now. Vukovar was peacefully reintegrated into the Republic of Croatia and Croats and Serbs started returning.

Serbs and Croats have very different memories of the day Vukovar fell. During the war, Serbs celebrated it as a great victory. After the war they saw it as the day Vukovar fell, and initially they took wreaths to the cemetery to commemorate the day. More recently, though, Serbs declined to place wreaths, explaining they feared doing so would irritate the Croats. Those few examples illustrate the complexity of interethnic relationships and all the obstacles to surmounting them.

HOW TO OVERCOME THE CONFLICT

Though the victims of the war and destruction are many and little time has passed, steps can be taken to promote cooperation and reconciliation.

Who can help? First, the media can, especially television if it is not politically controlled. Nongovernmental organizations can do a lot to promote reconciliation among the opposing parties. Mental health officers, in the widest meaning of the term, are also important in many areas of life. They have great influence and often serve as objects of identification. Teachers of all types are important because of their influence on children, both for the present and the future. Teachers can help the children who have become links in intergenerational transmission of hatred and other negative emotions. Religious leaders can help in reconciliation. Finally, all people of goodwill can do something positive and useful.

What channels can be used? In the beginning, trading is adequate because traders have the least prejudice and are the most willing to forget hatred if they have a financial interest. If used cautiously, sports can be very useful for reconciliation. Care must be taken to ensure that sporting events, especially football matches, do not wake up a lot of aggressive emotions that players and fans can act out. When teams win sport competitions, the victory celebration can be affirmative, provided no destruction occurs. Entertainers easily cross the line of interethnic conflicts and gladly perform in other nations. Care must be taken of course, as was learned when a group was performing Serbian songs and Croats dropped in and started a fight. Cultural and artistic events such as theater guest performances, such as Croatian theater in Belgrade and theatre from Montenegro in Zagreb, are good ways to help to overcome interethnic tensions. Professional meetings of scientists, doctors, and others are certainly good venues in which people can talk and repair narcissistic and ethnical injuries. Communication between family members of different nationalities are very welcome, though some situations can be more destructive then constructive.

How can people help themselves? One way is to ask for forgiveness. Throughout history, it has been very hard to ask for forgiveness on the state level. When successful, this process has beneficial effects. Unfortunately, that usually happens many years after the trauma has been inflicted by one nation on another. Recently, many legal charges have been pressed against war criminals in international and other courts, but I am not convinced that court judgments satisfy people's psychological need for justice. Revenge rarely produces considerable or meaningful benefits. Far more beneficial, in my experience, are reconciliation groups.

My experience with one such group is described in the following section.

RECONCILIATION GROUPS

For three years (1999–2003), I participated in a reconciliation process involving Croatian, Serbian, Bosnian (Muslim), and Slovenian mental health professionals.[9] One may wonder why mental health professionals were elected to participate in reconciliation groups. One reason is that they are usually influential in their communities and can pass on their ideas and experience in reconciliation groups to their large groups. Optimistically, one could expect them to influence decision makers in their communities to support reconciliation efforts.

Initially, members of the group stated that although they came from different ethnic backgrounds, ethnicity had never been an issue—until conflict erupted. Over time, however, memories and emotions surfaced and participants admitted that they found it difficult to sort out their feelings and work together. Participants shared their memories, stories of loss (some had lost family members), and fears. In some cases, one participant's memories sparked another's memories. Participants discussed the confusion they felt when, during the conflict, interethnic friends had become enemies. They admitted it was difficult to restore trust and rekindle those relationships.

One participant explained, "I fought against Serbs and they were my enemies. I cannot exclude anybody. I had some friends in Serbia, but during the war they shot at me and were my enemies. Today, they are no longer my enemies, but I like things being left as they are."

In one conversation, participants remembered how disappointed they had been to learn that the Yugoslav army had not protected innocent people in Croatia. One participant remembered watching refugees fleeing and atrocities being committed. Such memories elicited memories of atrocities committed during World War II, which in turn led to a discussion about who was worse, Ustashas or Chetniks. When one participant commented that someone should pay for damages inflicted on Sarajevo, Mostar, and Srebrenica, another quickly retorted that someone should pay for Vukovar, Dubrovnik, Šibenik, Zadar, Osijek, Vinkovci, and other Croatian cities demolished in the war.

In post-conflict societies, who has suffered the most and which side is worse off often become contentious topics. In fact, members of both sides have suffered and both end up paying directly and indirectly for destroyed cities and a host of other costs.

The deep-rooted nature of Croatian–Serbian conflict is illustrated in the following comments one participant made: "Serbian hatred toward Muslims goes back for centuries. It was much easier in the war between Croats and Muslims. With Serbs, it was worse. I feel that Serbs do not think of Muslims as humans; they think of them as if they are dirt. Bombs fell on Sarajevo for three-and-a-half years. They tried to destroy people and erase them."

In conflicted and post-conflict societies, symbols and language carry weight that outsiders sometimes fail to perceive or understand. For example, swine are an important symbol of religion and power. In Sarajevo, at one point, it was impossible to buy pork legally; it was only possible to buy it on the black market. In Bosnia, swine are not even included in school textbooks as a domesticated animal. Many Yugoslavians speak more than one language, yet members of the group recalled how the use of a single word belonging to the "other side" could arouse suspicions and cold treatment from others. Some of the persons I worked with recalled switching to languages other than their mother tongue or those they had learned in school because doing so made them feel "much safer." Because language is linked to one's nationality and regional background, it is an ethnic marker. Language is linked to identity. The party that can compel the other to hide his or her identity exerts great power.

On the topic of responsibility for reconciliation, one of the mental health professionals who came together for understanding one another stated that "it would be best if everyone could look for perpetrators in their own nation and apologize for the atrocities done by one's nation." Unfortunately, it is not always easy to identify individual perpetrators and victims. In additional, it is not always easy to determine who is responsible for certain specific atrocities. These mental health workers discussed how their trust in the army had been shattered. Some admitted and condemned atrocities committed by soldiers from their side but stated that more heinous atrocities had been committed by the other side, which was blamed for starting the war in the first place. One participant said soldiers "used to invade Croatian villages, rob houses, and even kill little babies in their cradles." Others reported that some soldiers "murdered people of their own nation." Participants discussed soldiers' motivations. Some questioned whether soldiers should be held responsible for acts committed "for the sake of justice, truth, and future coexistence."

The point at which these mental health professionals began talking about atrocities committed by members of each nation marked a turning point in the reconciliation process. It is surprising that participants said they felt manipulated and used to advance the agenda of the "'new Yugoslavia' or the United States or some other world power." Some individuals indicated they thought that the international community, NATO forces, and medical and other nongovernmental organizations were trying to influence the reconciliation processes and "reconcile the people in the former Yugoslavia by force."

Experience, both on the world stage and in the former Yugoslavia, has revealed how hard, long-lasting, and often unsuccessful reconciliation work can be. For citizens, reconciliation "experiments" can be painful and add to existing traumas. The following two events illustrate how detrimental reconciliation efforts can be.

When international authorities in Bosnia and Herzegovina ordered the cornerstone to be laid for the new mosque in Banja Luka, Serbs organized a huge demonstration, which halted the ceremony. The cornerstone was laid some weeks later, but the police and military had to use tear gas and water cannons to hold back protestors. In Mostar, Croats who returned to their homes were killed. Ironically, they survived the whole war, only to be killed while returning home after the war. Examples like these make citizens wonder about reconciliation and the benefit of the international community's efforts. Such incidents only serve to perpetuate patterns of intergenerational trauma. Resulting sentiments will hardly contribute to reconciliation and a cessation of age-old hostilities.

ENDNOTES

1. Ivan Rendić-Miočević, *The Evil of the Great Spleen: History and Non-History of Croats, Montenegrins, Muslims, and Serbs* (1996).
2. Vladimir Dvorniković, *Karakterologija Jugoslavena* (*The Caracterology of Yugoslavs*) (Beograd: Gecakon, 1939), 85–91.
3. Speech given at the meeting of the Serbian Assembly in 1990.
4. Dvorniković.
5. Wilfred Bion, Experiences in groups New York: Basic Books.
6. Ibid.
7. Vamik Volkan, *Bloodlines: From Ethnic Pride to Ethnic Terrorism* (New York: Farrar, Straus & Giroux, 1997), 33, 43, 44, 48, 133, 226; and Vamik Volkan, "Transgenerational Transmissions and Chosen Traumas: An Aspect of Large-Group Identity." *Group Analysis* 34 (2001): 79–99.
8. Vamik Volkan, "Intergenerational Transmission and Chosen Traumas: A Link Between the Psychology of the Individual and that of the Ethnic Group," in *Psychoanalysis at the Political Border*, ed. L. Rangell and R. Moses-Hruskovski (Madison, CT: International Universities Press 1996), 251, 270.
9. Eduard Klain, "Yugoslavia as a Group," in *Group Process and Political Dynamics*, ed. M. F. Ettin, J. W. Fidler, and B. D. Cohen (Madison, CT: International University Press, 1995); Eduard Klain and L. Pavic, "Countertransference and Empathic Problems in Therapists/Helpers Working with Psychotraumatized Persons," Croatian Medical Journal 40, 4 (1999): 446–72; Eduard Klain, "Intergenerational Aspects of the Conflict in the Former Yugoslavia," in International Handbook of Multigenerational Legacies of Trauma, ed. Yael Danieli (New York: Plenum Press, 1998); Eduard Klain and L. Pavic, "Psychotrauma and Reconciliation," Croatian Medical Journal 43, 2 (2002): 161–64; and Eduard Klain, "Yugoslovia as a Group," Croatian Medical Journal 33 (1992): 1–2.

ABOUT THE AUTHOR

Eduard Klain, M.D., D.Sc., CGP, is a psychiatrist and retired professor of psychological medicine at the Medical School at the University of Zagreb. He is also the retired head of the Department of Psychiatry and Psychological Medicine at the Medical School at the University of Zagreb.

Dr. Klain is a member of the Academy of Medical Sciences of Croatia and a former president of the Collegium for Psychological Medicine. A psychoanalyst, Dr. Klain is a direct member of International Pychoanalytic Association (IPA) and Director of the Institute for Group Analysis at Zagreb. He is also a training and supervising group analyst, as well as a certified group therapist with the American Group Psychotherapy Association.

11

Nigeria

The Federal Republic of Nigeria is located in western Africa and is the continent's most populous country. A former British colony, Nigeria has experienced several ethnic and religious conflicts during its history, and some of these clashes turned violent and deadly. Composed of more than 250 ethnic groups, the leading ethnic groups are the Hausa (29 percent, mainly located in the north), the Igbos (18 percent, dominating the east), and the Yoruba (21 percent, predominant in the south, the sixth-largest oil-producing area in the world), each group having its own language. Islam (50 percent) and Christianity (40 percent) are the main religions. The Hausa conquered the north in the ninth century, and the Yoruba invaded the south. Nigeria is also a member of the Organization of the Petroleum-Exporting Countries (OPEC), which has caused divisions in community interests in the country.

In the nineteenth century, after the abolition of slavery, trade in cocoa and palm oil started to flower in western Africa. Interested in getting control of the region's natural resources, the British instituted a protectorate in southern Nigeria in 1885. The British influence extended gradually to the northern part of the country, and in 1914 the British joined together two protectorates—South Nigeria and North Nigeria—to form the Nigeria of today. Great Britain adopted a system of indirect administration, "indirect rule," rendered through traditional chiefs whose power remained intact. To avoid religious strife, the British discouraged Christian missionaries from converting the Muslim population living in the north. As a result, schools were built in the South, where the indigenous population grew rich and westernized.

In 1939, the country was divided into three parts, each one dominated by an ethnic group: Hausa in the north, Yorubas in the southwest, and Ibos in the southeast. After the Second World War, the political life of Nigeria was shaken by the rise of the nationalist movement, but even after Nigeria gained its independence in 1960 the intense rivalries between ethnic groups continued, and the civil government was then overthrown by a military coup d'état in 1966. The leaders of this new coup increased the power of the federal government and changed the subdivision of the country, which now consists of twelve states. Anger erupted in northern Nigeria when Muslim Hausas fearing Christian Igbo domination of local markets killed hundreds of Igbos.

In 1967, the Christian Igbo minority declared the secession of Biafra, an area of southeast Nigeria rich in oil resources, a situation that degenerated into violent racial tensions between the two communities. A bloody war, as well as a famine that moved international opinion, tore the country apart. In 1970 Nigeria was reunified at the end of the hostilities. Except for a short period between 1979 and 1983, the Nigerian regime was authoritarian and oppressive. The population was dissatisfied with the civil government, and another coup d'état took place in 1983 and a new military government set up. Following the elections of 1993, chief Moshood Abiola was elected as the head of the government, but General Ibrahim Babangida, in power since 1985, canceled the result of the elections.

Since then, Nigeria has always been under military rule despite attempts at reestablishing civilian government. The economic downturn resulting from the fall of the price of oil, accentuated the pressure in favor of democratic reforms. These attempts at reforms were faced by

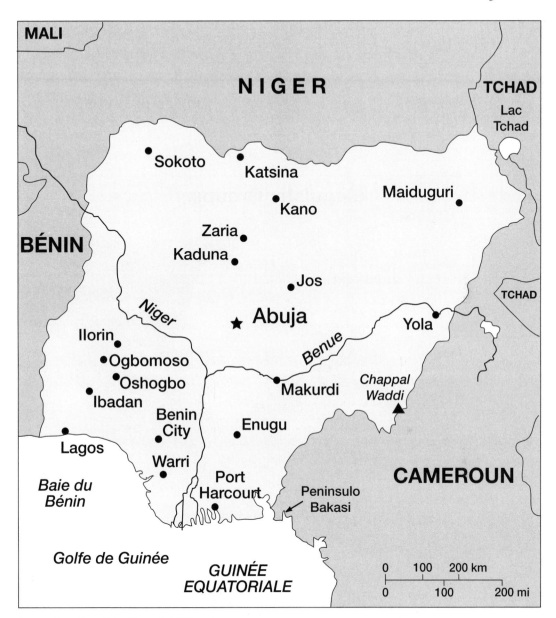

MALI

N I G E R

TCHAD

Lac
Tchad

Sokoto

Katsina

Maiduguri

Kano

Zaria

BÉNIN

Kaduna

Jos

TCHAD

Niger

★ Abuja

Yola

Ilorin

Benue

Ogbomoso

Oshogbo

Makurdi

Chappal
Waddi

Ibadan

Benin
City

Enugu

CAMEROUN

Lagos

Warri

Baie du
Bénin

Port
Harcourt

Peninsulo
Bakasi

Golfe de Guinée

**GUINÉE
EQUATORIALE**

| 0 | 100 | 200 km |
| 0 | 100 | 200 mi |

Source: http://en.wikipedia.org/wiki/Nigeria

stiff opposition from the military. The Nigerian army's attitude and repressive methods were condemned by the international community, before pluralist elections were finally held in the 1990s. Between 1996 and 1999, the country was ruled by dictators who gained power in a series of coups and countercoups. After sixteen years of corrupt and brutal military dictatorship, Nigeria managed to regain democracy in 1999.

The essay by Conerly Casey explores the causes of these conflicts by analyzing the various tensions that took place in Kano, a northern Nigeria city that has experienced many religious and political crises. These clashes opposed different types of groups: Muslims versus Muslims, Muslims versus Christians, and Christians versus Christians. The riots resulted in the deaths of thousands of people, not to mention the thousands of casualties and properties destroyed.

The author explains that the roots of these conflicts are very complex, and several factors have contributed to the current situation. Among them, we can cite the colonial legacy, which

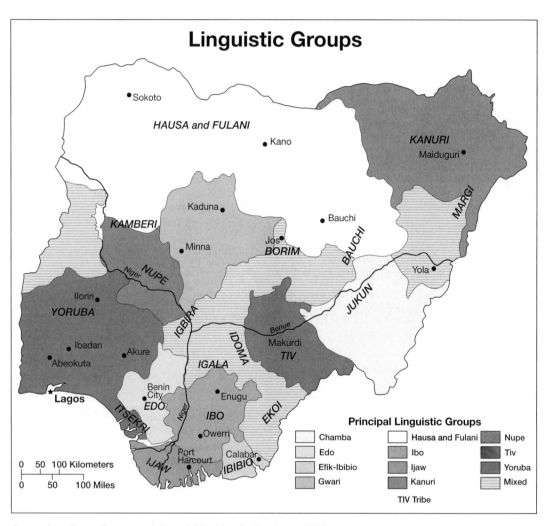

Source: http://www.lib.utexas.edu/maps/africa/nigeria_linguistic_1979.jpg

traced artificial boundaries with no effort to respect the cultural and historical distinctions of the country. Instead, the British chose to mix various kingdoms into one entity and named it Nigeria. Thus, colonialism has played a large part in the religious intolerance and hatred we observe today among ethnic groups. These conflicts reached their climax in the period between 1979 and 1983, and they abruptly reemerged after May 1999, when democracy was finally restored. No less than forty violent ethnoreligious clashes have been recorded during the three years following Olusegun Obasanjo's election in 1999.

Besides colonialism, it would be proper to cite the Nigerian elites as a factor that has fueled these conflicts. This group has shamelessly used religion as a tool to serve its personal interests. Elites have manipulated the various religious groups, creating hostility and tension among them and encouraging them to use violence to gain resources and power from the state and favors from the government.

Poverty also plays a key role in these conflicts because most of the protesters are jobless, uneducated, and rural people. This group constitutes a sort of "reserve army" that can be mobilized anytime to kill people and destroy properties in exchange of a small fee. In this case, religion serves as a cover, hiding a bigger problem, which is the critical state of Nigeria's economy and the misery in which most of its citizens live. The sectarian factor also contributes to the country's tensions. For example, the Muslim community is divided into different competing groups. Since 1906, these sectarian groups have experienced many clashes. Those communities tend to protest either against the government or against people who give a different interpration of the Qur'an. Traditional sects, such as the Quadririyya and the Tijjaniyya, are usually fighting with one another, but they sometimes create a united front against the Izala, another religious group.

In his essay, Dr. Salisu A. Abdullahi shows a different point of view. The author asserts that a new type of "war" has emerged. The concepts of ethnicity, religion, and nation have been crystallized and merged into a larger notion named *cultural identity.*

The essay also underlines the key role the media play in people's identifications. They tend to exaggerate the similarities and differences among various groups, who also tend to transmit chosen traumas from one generation to another. Among these events we can cite Biafra's attempted secession and the civil war that resulted from it. Those chapters of Nigerian history will remain deep-seated in the nation's collective memory.

The author also points out that ethnic and religious nationalisms have resurfaced in the country as a base of citizenship. Conflicts between Christian Igbos and Muslim Hausa have, for example, resurfaced in the north. These tensions prove that the different ethnoreligious groups still carry a lot of anger and grief from the past. In a word, they will not forgive and they will not forget.

After having closely examined the many causes of the Nigerian ethnoreligious conflict, it should be asked why they remain unresolved and what we can do to change the situation. Nigeria first needs to benefit from an honest and real leadership, at every level of the government. The elites have to stop being greedy and have to pursue the national interest instead of their own self-interest. There is also a need to talk to religious leaders and to ask them to stop promoting violence among the youngest and poorest citizens. Because of the misery the poor and young experience every day, they are the most vulnerable group and can be easily manipulated. Instead of brainwashing them with religious or ethnic ideologies, politicians and key opinion leaders need to be more responsible. They should broadcast messages of peace, tolerance, and harmony instead of hatred.

Source: http://en.wikipedia.org/wiki/Nigeria

Mediated Hostility, Generation, and Victimhood in Northern Nigeria

Conerly Casey

Within the last two decades, political antagonisms in northern Nigeria have intensified with political and economic instability, ethnic and religious struggles for political power, and intra- and interreli-gious conflicts—regional, national, and global—all of which are highly mediated.[1] Falola describes the impact of these political changes upon Nigerian social relations as a shift from the "decade of clashes" in the 1980s to the "age of warfare" in the 1990s.[2] Media play an important role in the political identifications that Nigerians make with others, exaggerating similarities and differences among peoples who have become consumers of violence. Network societies, based upon ethnic, religious, or national identification, may use media to channel remembrances of violence, and the emotion it evokes, by filling in what Volkan calls the "cracks" of identification, with mythico–historical ethnic, religious, or nationalist ideologies.[3] Faced with warfare relations and uncertainties about the jurisdictions of and the protections offered by the Nigerian nation-state, states, and municipalities—along with mediated global insecurities, affective and visceral—Muslim youths reposition themselves in politicized social relations and are looked upon by others as perpetrators and victims of violence.

In this chapter, I consider recent political violence in the city of Kano in northern Nigeria and the potent nexus of (1) Volkan's "chosen traumas"—losses, defeats, or humiliations that have been difficult to mourn, (2) transgenerational transmissions of trauma, and (3) subtle, and less than subtle, media transmissions of victimhood and reflections of communal thought, both open and unsurfaced.[4] In northern Nigeria, traumatic memories of colonization by the British and Biafra's attempted secession, resulting in the Nigerian civil war, continue to provide an undercurrent of un-mourned histories and memories.[5] Nigeria's chosen traumas are revisited and surfaced as Nigerians view media accounts of political struggles around the world, particularly those in the Middle East, and as those struggles are echoed within the politics of ethnicity, religion, and region in Nigeria. During the past two decades, northern Nigerians have been dealing with increasingly complex religious identifications brought on by the confluence of Nigerian animism, an influx of reformist Sunnis and Shias from the Middle East, vocal Christian evangelists, and secular and religious concepts of jurisdiction, social justice, and citizenship, transmitted primarily through the media.

I suggest that in the city of Kano the large-scale violence of 1991 and 1995 reverberated with nineteenth-century jihadist and colonial violence and with the violence of the Nigerian civil war, conflating morality, civility and criminality, and historical perceptions of others that reflect and constitute

Muslim and Christian relations through acts of violence. In 1999, resentments among Muslim Hausa about the election and political administration of President Olusegun Obasanjo, a Yoruba born-again Christian, interlocked with the implementation of Shariah law in twelve states of northern Nigeria. During the 1999 crisis, Kano Muslim Hausa *'yan daba* (urban neighborhood gang members) and *almajirai* (Qur'anic students) attacked Muslim Yoruba, claiming revenge for the killings of Muslim Hausa living in Sagamu, a town in the southern state of Ogun. These Muslim Hausa youths, drawing on betrayals from the colonial period, focused on "marginal Muslims," particularly Muslim Yoruba, as saboteurs who collaborated with colonial Christians and would similarly disallow the reenchantment of Muslim orthodoxy, and the potential establishment of Shariah law as Nigerian state law.

On May 11, 2004, Muslim Hausa *'yan daba* and *almajirai* brutally murdered their neighbors and fellow Kano residents, calling them *arna* (unbelievers), *Kiristoci* (Christians), and *baki* (strangers). The crisis followed several months of communal violence in Plateau State that Muslim residents of Kano felt had been condoned through the inaction of the Christian governor of Plateau State, Joshua Dariye, and the Christian head of the Nigerian state, General Olusegun Obasanjo. Local media such as the radio and newspapers detailed horrifying experiences of Muslim Hausa victims who had returned to Kano, along with the bodies of their dead relatives. There were passionate and vivid international components—protests over the killing of Palestinian leaders by the Israeli army and the brutal treatment of prisoners in Iraq by the U.S. army—that culminated in a public burning of the effigies of Ariel Sharon and George W. Bush. The language of Muslims and Christians, "indigenes" and "strangers," used to describe the identities of victims and killers, the spiritual and material power associated with them, and the spatial patterning of the violence, led once again to a conflation of identity, morality, and security, with Nigerian Christians held responsible for the actions of Plateau residents and the Nigerian, U.S. and Israeli presidents.

These salient memories, and memories of the senses, enacted through violence and repressed, exiled, and erased by violence, underscore the betrayals that emerged through what Mamdani refers to as the "decentralized despotism" of colonialism and the mosaics of ethnic, religious, and regional politics, exacerbated by Nigeria's "petro-Capitalism" and "spoils politics," that have emerged since Nigeria's independence in 1960.[6] The 1999 election and political leadership of President Olusegun Obasanjo, whom reformist Sunni and Shia Muslim Hausa refer to as "the U.S.'s boy," deepened regional antagonisms, conflating identity, morality, and security with Nigerian national and world insecurities. Affective rememberings and forgettings of violence, and the insecurities that violence may solve or generate, find new means of political expression through the reformist, anticolonial, antiimperial, Islamic movements such as *'yan Izala, 'yan Shia,* and *'yan Tajdid,* reviving identification with nineteenth-century jihadists to reform and to unify Nigeria's Muslims both to establish Shariah law in Nigeria and to protest the violence of the United States.[7] *'Yan Izala, 'yan Shia,* and *'yan Tajdid* gain momentum through extensive uses of, and responses to, media and telecommunications, embedded in the profiling stratifications of state violence, violence sanctioned by the governments of the United States, the Nigerian nation-state, and Kano's Shariah state, and state, legal, and media legitimizations of violence toward "enemies of the state" under "wars" and "states of emergency."

While there is growing documentation of the contributions of Islamic reform movements in northern Nigeria and in Niger, particularly of *'yan Izala,* to open debate over reigning political and moral orthodoxies and the legacies of colonialism, such movements, as they seize on the signs, objects, and practices they seek to reform, create a "precarious oscillation of democracy and despotism."[8] Over the past two decades, *'yan Izala, 'yan Shia,* and *'yan Tajdid* advocated the "democratic" implementation of Shariah law, set limits on government accountability, and opened new domains for public sentiment and debate that cut across long-standing community barriers, yet they also stratified citizenship among Muslims, "marginalizing" nonreformist Muslims and non-Muslims.[9] They offered new opportunities for Islamic identification and participation, yet through self- and community censorship, these reform movements increased anxiety about salvation, about belonging to the "true" form of Islam, and about the potential for evil, via relations with Christians and non-Hausa Muslims, to enter

oneself and one's community through a lack of ethnic, religious commitment.

Based on eight years of ethnographic research in Kano with religious leaders and healers; reformist Sunni and Shia, Sufi, and Bori (a fusion of animism and Islam); *'yan farauta* (hunters), *'yan tauri* (people who concoct and use herbal medicines against piercing from weapons), *'yan daba* (members of neighborhood youth gangs), and *'yan Hisbah* (Shariah law enforcers), my research findings contradict a primordialist thesis that buried or semiconscious ethnic animosities are responsible for Kano violence. Portrayals of ethnic clashes are often tied to a primordialist argument—an idea that people's sense of group identity draws upon the attachments of kinship or shared claims to blood, soil, or language. The affective force used to bind people of a particular ethnic background is usually cited as the reason for their destructive or violent tendencies against others. Tied to this argument is the idea that present conflicts in Africa have resulted from the imprecise drawing of boundaries inherited during the colonial period.[10]

There are a number of problems with primordialist suppositions. First, as Mbembe suggests, "little effort has been made to understand the imaginaries and autochthonous practices of space—which are, themselves, extremely varied."[11] In Nigeria, allegiances and jurisdictions fluctuate frequently with changing forms of territoriality, so that an interlacing of social ties is never reducible simply to family relationships, ethnicity, or religion. Ethnic or religious conflicts, when they do occur, rarely cross national borders but are closely tied to reclassifications of localities within Nigeria, a process based on colonial associations of family ties, ethnicity, and religious proximity. As Mbembe notes, "This bureaucratic work is preceded (or accompanied) by the invention of imaginary family ties . . . the ethnoracial principle serving increasingly as the basis for citizenship and as the condition of access to land, resources, and elective positions of responsibility."[12]

Scholarship also tends to attribute antagonisms and violence among Nigerian citizens to deteriorating conditions in Nigeria, such as pervasive political corruption, economic disparities, internal political machinations, authoritarian and stratification tendencies as opposed to "democratic" ones, inequitable resource allocations, and religious proselytizing, all of which have international dimensions and pressures.[13] Yet, as Feldman points out, there is a crucial difference between the "conditions of political antagonism" and the "relational practices of antagonism" that "generate different ideological and practical settings and are subject to diachronic frictions."[14]

Among northern Nigerians, the relations of political antagonism—forged during the nineteenth-century Islamic jihad, colonization, the Nigerian civil war, and subsequent violence—intersect with media portrayals of violence against Muslims within and outside Nigeria's national borders. Such antagonisms are rooted in, reproduce, and transform the ideologies and feelings of "affective citizenship," fusions of ethnic, religious citizenship, based on territorialized ethnic customary law and de-territorialized religious law, and on the historical perceptions of enclosure and exclusion that underpin memories of belonging, backed by law, but a law that has, historically, been arbitrary and violent in its application. Ethnic citizenship, with juridical ties to land and resources, and the language of "originality" and "indigeneship," conjoined with substantive, borderless religious citizenship, and similar notions of "originality," "authenticity," and "purity," are volatile forms of citizenship. In northern Nigeria, "affective citizens" join the state, typically dominated by ethnic, religious majorities, to "carve out autonomous material spheres of effect and affect that diverge from formal political rationalities."[15]

> Political enactment becomes sedimented with its own local histories that are mapped out on the template of the body. Formal political rationalities no longer sustain a singular or determining relation to performance dynamics. Rather instrumental rationality has been increasingly redirected to perpetuating the efficacy of symbolic action. Political action and institutionalized ideology form two discontinuous, signification systems. It is within the interstices that oral history emerges as a representational artifact of violence and the body.[16]

Affectively channeled and repeated by media, institutionalized political ideologies and enactments of violence fracture and instantiate the appearance of continuity among political centers, whether they be Mecca, Washington, or Kano, and the *talakawa* (commoners, poor), a majority of whom are Muslim youths seeking belonging, citizenship, and social justice.

Rather than assume the affective power of primordialist identifications or of deteriorating conditions in Nigeria to evoke violence, it is important to ask how, when, and why victimhood and certain categories of victim identity become prioritized, so easily inspiring loyalty. Who has a right to victimhood, to protection from violence, and by whom? When Muslim Hausa youths are recruited into violence, what problems does it solve for them? Is violence and its resulting "reenactments of violence," "mass regression," or "therapeutic terror," methods by which Nigerian youths attempt to distill "truth," to remember collectively, and thus to enact citizenship, jurisdiction, and social justice through violence?[17]

KANO: AN EMERGING ISLAMIC STATE

In July 2000, I returned to Kano, an ancient city of northern Nigeria, with a population of about three to four million. Kano is the commercial capital of northern Nigeria and, as a state capital, is a center for political and religious decision making. Though the people of Kano have been predominantly Muslim Hausa for the past five centuries, Kano includes large communities of Yoruba who are about half Muslim and half Christian, Igbos who are predominantly Christian, and many other minority ethnoreligious groups, including Tiv, Nupe, Kanuri, Fulani, and Jukun. Kano includes large well-established communities of Muslim Lebanese and smaller communities of people from Europe, Asia, and other parts of the Middle East and Africa.

There is continuing tension between the laws and conventions of Muslims living in northern Nigeria and those put forth by the federal government. In 1999 and 2000, this tension reached crisis proportions as twelve states in northern Nigeria, one of them being Kano, declared Shariah law as the state law for all Muslims, redefining morality and criminality. Impassioned discussions ensued about the effects of Shariah upon Muslims and non-Muslims and about human rights, the constitutionality of Shariah, and its impact upon Nigeria as a nation-state. Violence between Christians and Muslims—"indigenes" and "strangers"—broke out all over northern Nigeria, in which several thousand people were killed (and continue to be killed) in face-to-face, hand-to-hand combat made more horrific because of the sheer intimacy of neighbors turned killers. The May 11, 2004, violence in Kano followed a series of conflicts within the past decade, during which memories of colonization and of the Nigerian civil war, particularly of Biafra's attempted secession, along with Israeli violence against Palestinians and, more recently, the U.S.–Bush administration's "War in Iraq" and "War on Terrorism," reactivated past traumas and betrayals, hardened ethnoreligious communal boundaries, and fueled xenophobia, contact avoidance, and conflicts among political communities.

MEMORY AND A POLITICS OF VIOLENCE

In Kano just before Christmas 1994, Gideon Akaluka, a Christian Igbo, was arrested and charged with using the Qur'an as toilet paper. Evaluations of his sanity, morality, and religion were sprinkled through the talk in Kano. A few days later, three Muslim Hausas who claimed to be part of a faction of the Muslim Brotherhood broke into his prison cell, decapitated him, and displayed his head to a crowd gathered in front of the central mosque. Their message was clear: they maintained that "Muslims" were asking for Gideon to be executed, and they intended to apply what they believed was a just sentence whether or not the judge cooperated. The author of a June 1995 article in *At-Tajdid,* a right-wing Muslim newspaper, described Igbos and northern Christians as contemptuous of local values, their hostility fueled by Muslim leaders who "collaborate" with Christians.[18]

On May 30, 1995, an argument between two men, one Muslim Hausa and one Christian Igbo, erupted into violence that swept the city and left several hundred people dead and thousands injured. Initial reports described the conflict as an argument about who was to receive payment for safeguarding an automobile while its owner patronized a bank. Some reports indicated that the automobile had been stolen and the Muslim Hausa owner had angrily pushed the Christian Igbo guard into a nearby refuse fire.[19] Following a police investigation, *The Democrat,* a newspaper published in nearby Kaduna, reported that the theft of a briefcase in Sabon Gari, or the new city, led to hostilities,

fueled by accusations that Igbo traders were complicitous in the theft.[20] Days later many local people described long-standing conflicts between Hausa and Igbo traders over the allocation of stalls in the nearby *Sabon Gari* market as more potent sources of hostility and violence. *A.M. News,* a Lagos-based newspaper, reported the clash as "a climax of hostility between the two ethnic groups since December 26 when an Igbo trader, Mr. Gideon Akaluka, was beheaded in a barbaric act in the precincts of Kano prisons by Muslim fanatics."[21]

Muslim Hausa and Christian Igbos claimed that during the crisis, police teargassed and killed members of both ethnicities. Escaping the teargas myself, I observed hundreds of youths running with handmade weapons, long sticks, nails pointing outward, knives, and machetes. Many of them screamed to me to turn back. As I drove away, I saw two men wearing Western-style shirts and trousers pulled from their motorcycles and beaten to death. Friends and acquaintances of all ethnicities reported witnessing similar atrocities, as well as people pulled from vehicles and beaten, busloads of people shot, people burning in gasoline-soaked tires.

Government-run and secular newspapers attempted to downplay the levels of violence, reporting between five and thirty dead, pointing to "miscreants" as the cause of the violence.[22] The editor of a June 1995 editorial in *The Democrat,* a pro-government newspaper, reported dismay at the violence and exemplified a Muslim Hausa perspective in his description of Kano:

> Cultural beauty has been peacefully consuming several subcultures to the delight of the forces of integration and the glory of its people. Because of this, the Hausa Kano is more, or less, a man of various ethnic combinations effectively and peacefully integrated into the Hausa mainstream culture. In short, Kano is a good example of cultural integration, where even foreigners, particularly from the Middle East, have effectively become Hausanized and consequently Nigerianized. Of Nigerian tribes, the Yorubas, Nupes, Kanuris and Jukuns have without discrimination, been equally Hausanized.[23]

Igbos are not included among those "integrated." Of the ethnic groups that Abutu lists, all have northern populations that include large numbers of Muslims.[24] The idea, though not explicit, is that these groups have assimilated because they share Islamic values, including political ones. In fact, many Igbos feel marginalized at a regional level and that their institutionalized marginalization stems from an historical political exclusion at a national level. In an interview for the Lagos-based newspaper *Third Eye* (1995), Dr. Arthur Nwankwo stated:

> It is true that the military has irretrievably damaged the elements of true federalism in Nigeria. . . . While the Northern and Western peoples of Nigeria appear as subjects in history in that process, the whole of Eastern Nigeria appears as object, the latent engine of history that must be impacted on at will.[25]

Dr. Nwankwo refers to the objectification of easterners, predominantly Igbos, in relation to Biafra's attempted secession, and the politics of exclusive cultural identification that intensified throughout and after the Nigerian civil war.

THE ATTEMPTED SECESSION OF BIAFRA: FOUNDATIONS OF BETRAYAL IN THE 1960s

The night of January 15, 1966, coup leaders who were Igbo and Yoruba, murdered the federal prime minister, the northern and western premiers, the federal finance minister, and some senior commanding officers, all of whom were Hausa and Yoruba. The coup leaders were arrested but never tried, and General Aguiyi-Ironsi, an Igbo, was made president. In May 1966, General Aguiyi-Ironsi announced plans to unify the country by abolishing existing regions, thus making it possible for anyone to get a job, to go to school, or to obtain land for a home or business anywhere in the country, an "opening" of the north to southerners that many Muslims considered "defiling." Anger and rioting erupted in northern Nigeria where Muslim Hausas fearing Christian "contamination" and Igbo domination of local markets killed hundreds of Igbos, razing their properties to the ground. In July, coup members killed General Aguiyi-Ironsi and forty-seven Igbo officers. In September and October, radio reports of Hausas being killed in the eastern, predominantly Igbo region sparked riots and the massacre of at least seven thousand Igbos living in northern Nigeria. In 1967 Igbos began talking of the secession of the entire eastern region, Biafra, to create a safe haven for refugee

Igbos who would necessarily include areas where non-Igbo minorities lived and worked.

Lacking geographical areas that produced food or crude oil, Igbo Biafrans needed the support of people living in the Yoruba-dominated western and the pluralist midwestern regions, as well as that of minorities within Biafra, many of whom felt coerced through violence.[26] According to Last, "the failure of the Yoruba to go along with secession added betrayal to the idioms of a political and economic rivalry which still bedevils reconciliation."[27] The ethnic divisions promoted by the civil war remain on the surface or just below the surface of communal memory. After the war,

> The government's policy of reconciliation focused on Biafra's attempted secession and the ensuing civil war, whereas for many Biafrans the crucial issue was the earlier massacre of civilians in northern towns and the exodus that the riots provoked. For them, secession was forced upon Biafra—it was not their choice.[28]

FROM ETHNIC CONFLICT TO RELIGIOUS WAR

In a June 1995 a headline article, Ibrahim stated that the federal minister of Information and Culture, Dr. Walter Ofanagoro, a southerner, had come to Kano to gather information firsthand about the crisis. According to Dr. Ofanagoro, "Kano state had been a center for commercial activities from time immemorial and as such had been promoting cross fertilization of ideas in view of the accommodative nature of the people."[29] He reported that "disgruntled elements" were responsible for the "disturbances." Shortly thereafter, the Emir of Kano, a Muslim Hausa, called for the Nigerian government to crack down on "immigrants" from outside Nigeria whom he held responsible for increased unrest.[30] When tribal markings or traditional clothes were not apparent, immigration officials, police, and military asked people to pull up their shirts so that could observe the presence or absence of local medical practices or other markings. Political leaders assigned responsibility for the violence to disgruntled youths who were "outside" the body politic: "immigrants" and "disgruntled elements."

As the crisis continued, styles of dress and tribal markings, while initially providing individuals with signs of a shared group, however overdetermined, and a personal history shaped by this group became bodily displays dangerously signifying inclusion or exclusion. Polarization around ethnoreligious identity increased as people associated highly visible tribal markings with the atrocities they had witnessed. Newspapers ran headline articles like "The Unforgettable Riots in Kano," showing pictures of Muslim Hausa murdered.[31] *At-Tajdid* ran a headline article, "Christians Are the Aggressors," and showed a slain body captioned as "Dan Fulani, the First Victim."[32] People also focused on the numbers of churches and mosques that had been destroyed during the crisis.

THE IDENTIFICATION OF ENEMIES

As reports of people being killed came in and bodies were carried back into various neighborhoods, language about the crisis changed. People suggesting that the crisis was caused by "poverty," "a lack of education," or the "influence of corrupt religious and political leaders" typically maintained their perspective. However, people who had initially identified the crisis as an "ethnic clash" began speaking about it as a religious conflict, and later as a "religious war." In June 1995, a group of Muslims protested the handling of the crisis investigation by burning two police stations in the old city. Around the same time, Shu'aib's article in the right-wing *At-Tajdid* reported the violence as a "religious crisis":

> The number of Mosques burnt or destroyed reaches up to nineteen. The words "up Jesus" were even scrawled on the remains of one Mosque on Burma Road. This glaring fact proves that it had not been solely because of an accidental ethnic clash that more than one hundred Muslims lost their lives in a most heinous manner at the hands of the Igbo at Sabon Gari quarters and an inestimable amount of their wealth and properties were squandered or destroyed. The incident was rather a well-planned and properly organised plot, skillfully executed and deliberately orchestrated out of an uncontrollable and fanatical religious zeal and fervour. The way the plot was executed in a very short time, and with the use of modern weapons such as guns by the Igbos all go to show the state of their readiness for the event.[33]

In July 1995, southerners living in Sabon Gari found postings on their houses that reportedly read, "Leave immediately and return home, or the Islamic army will force you out." No one knew to whom the "Islamic Army" referred, though people reported varied explanations ranging from complete dismissal of the event as a "prank" to a plot by Igbos to provoke Hausas, to signs that "Muslims were mobilizing for war." Moreover, Hausa news reporters attempted to assure residents that Igbos were not "preparing for war."[34] Memories of the Nigerian civil war, of Biafra, and of past ethnic conflicts resurfaced for residents of Kano, colored now with militant religious overtones. Metaphors used to describe people of different ethnicities and religions became increasingly those used for "animals" and "witches": "savage," "inhuman," without "morals" or "ideology." This increased focus on religion as a source of conflict coincided with significant changes in Kano Muslim communities—the immigration of large numbers of reformist Muslims in 1995, along with the building of reformist Islamic schools, increased "orthodox" spirit exorcisms, during which spirits, as well as humans, were converted to Sunni orthodoxy, and conversions were made from Sufism to reformist Sunni and Shia sects.[35]

"MARGINAL MUSLIMS" AND THE RISE OF ISLAMIC REFORMISM

While conflicts between Muslims and between Muslims and Christians have been present since the colonial period, in the late 1970s, tensions between and among Kano Muslims and Christians reached boiling points with hundreds of youths fighting bloody street battles, burning mosques and churches, homes, and businesses.[36] Among Muslims, persistent conflicts about whether to sanction religious history and mystical traditions that predate the nineteenth century Islamic jihad, led by reformist Shaihu Usman dan Fodio, have become the norm, with both Qadiriyya and reformist Sunnis claiming him as a member of their sects.[37] Complicating Usman dan Fodio's revolutionary aspirations for northern Nigeria were several anti-caliphate, anti-jihad states, including Argungu (Kebbi), Gobir (Tsibiri), Maradi, Damagaram, Gumel, Borno, Ningi, Abuja, and Daura (Baure).[38]

Factional fighting found momentum during the late 1970s and 1980s under the influence of the well-known scholar Sheikh Abubakar Gumi,

Grand Khadi (Chief Islamic judge) of northern Nigeria. Gumi took inspiration from Muhammad ibn. Abd al-Wahhab, an eighteenth-century scholar who eschewed all *bidi'a* (innovation) and called for a return to the pure teachings of the Prophet while encouraging a more liberal use of *ijtihad* (independent reasoning).[39] Gumi fought most explicitly against Sufism. According to Gumi, Sufi orders did not exist at the time of Muhammad the Prophet, and the Prophet did not conceal any part of the revelation during his lifetime to be delivered to those who came after him. He condemned the worship of saints and spirits, the use of charms or amulets, and the use of drums in mosques, all of which are considered *shirk* (associating partners such as the *jinn* with Allah by the use of magic) or *bidi'a*.

In 1978, Gumi formed a powerful orthodox movement, *Jama'atu Izalat Al-Bidah Wa Iqamat Al-Sunnah* (The Society for the Eradication of Innovation and the Establishment of the Sunna). Popularly known as *Izala*, this movement's stated purpose was *tajdid* (reform and rejuvenation), inspired by Usman dan Fodio's nineteenth-century achievements and Saudi Wahhabism, yet realized through the day-to-day struggle against the *bidi'a* of Bori and the Darika brotherhoods.[40] The intellectualism of the Izala leadership, along with vast funding from Wahhabis in Saudi Arabia and Kuwait, contributed to a rapid explosion of Izala publications, radio and television programs, and cassettes, which cojoined a burgeoning media industry in Nigeria and competed with media from other parts of Nigeria and the world.

'Yan Izala began to denounce in the media and in face-to-face situations the *bidi'a* of other Muslims, literally calling them *kafiri* (unbelievers), and fighting between *'yan Izala*, Sufis, Shias, Muslim Brothers, and *'yan Bori* intensified. One of Gumi's students, Aminudeen Abubakar, led one wing of *'yan Izala*, *Da'awa*, which continued to propagate Wahhabism, stressing the fight against *bidi'a*. A second group, *Umma*, composed mainly of intellectuals, also focused on the propagation of Wahhabism, while the Muslim Brothers took a firm position on the need to implement Shariah and to establish an Islamic state.[41]

Also during the late 1970s and 1980s, a man whom Nigerians nicknamed *Maitatsine* (the one who curses) came to Kano from Cameroon.

Maitatsine claimed that Kano Muslims had no *kibla* (direction), and he repeatedly shouted at them, "May Allah separate you from all of His blessings!"[42] Maitatsine considered himself a prophet, while his followers, *'yan Maitatsine*, were "original" Muslims, uncorrupted by the *bidi'a* and *shirk* of Kano Muslims. *'Yan Maitatsine* refused to accept watches, bikes, or other material goods emblematic of modernization and urbanization.[43] They took over the Kano goat market, lived in cavelike dwellings and trenches, and kidnapped and shared young women, while killing their enemies. Maitatsine and his followers were *'yan Tauri* who made and used ritual herbal medicine against piercing from weapons. Unable to stop *'yan Maitatsine* from their criminal and recruitment activities, the local police enlisted the aid of other *'yan tauri* and the Nigerian military who eventually captured and killed Maitatsine. During this time, checkpoints around Kano, manned by armed young men, looking for the stomach tattoos of *'yan Maitatsine*, contributed to an emerging fear of Kano youths and "strangers."[44] People feared youths who had joined Maitatsine's movement, and those who, alongside the state, had armed themselves to fight against *'yan Maitatsine*.

During 1995, large numbers of Wahhabis from Saudi Arabia came to northern Nigeria to develop Islamic schools and social services. Well-funded at a time when the Nigerian national government was in a state of crisis and unable or unwilling to provide such services, Wahhabis became rapidly absorbed with the needs of Muslims, converting hundreds of Sufis to Wahhabi orthodoxy, fueled by an explicit critique of colonization and neocolonial politics.

In a *New Nigerian* article entitled "The Need for an Imam," Umar described a widespread view about the impact of colonialism on Islamic leadership and a new role for youths within a fragmented Islam:

> With colonialism a new system was introduced. Power was wrestled from the hands of the righteous who were either slayed or subjugated. Thereafter, the remaining religious men refused to have anything to do with the white man's system. His system of education and orientation was totally rejected. The custodians of the Qur'an woke up to become complete strangers in running the affairs of their communities. Those who are ignorant of the Qur'an and those who

are hostile to it were trained by the colonialists who handed over the reins of power to them . . . some religious men with wisdom started to realise that the only way to give back Islam its deserved authority over both the spiritual and temporal spheres is by sending their children to comprehend and master the new system while holding Islam at the core of their hearts.[45]

Umar also wrote that "the future of the Muslim world lies in the hands of these "determined, guided young generation" whom he terms "Islamic revolutionaries" as opposed to their often-used media label, "Islamic fundamentalists.""[46]

That the 1995 Kano crisis was not initiated but was carried out by alienated youths responding to corrupt Islamic and Christian leaders is only part of what many residents describe as a "cause" of the crisis. Others portray a revolutionary role for youths. While Kano youths were implicated in reactionary violence and looting during the Kano crises of 1991 and 1995, and associated with the "gang" activities of *'yan daba,* who were employed by religious and state politicians to strong-arm public opinion, youths are increasingly described as religious martyrs who are able to "purify" Islamic life.[47]

THE QUEST FOR AUTHENTIC IDENTITY

Pressure to conform to secular national and Islamic ideals have led many young people to experience high levels of self-consciousness about their religious identities and practices. After reading *The Divided Self,* a book about psychosis by R. D. Laing, a young man named Musa wrote in his personal diary:

> Even to remain a "religious" person, you need your autonomy and original self, otherwise, soon you will begin to be influenced by others. Soon you find yourself doing something you are not supposed to be doing. I soon realized that I was in another stage of false self. The picture I have created for myself of being a very religious man is actually false in the inner self.[48]

Musa's attention to "authenticity" and his need to identify the workings of a "false self" or "false consciousness" exemplify the complexity of ethnic,

religious identifications in Kano. At the same time, these concerns reflect schematic oppositions between Musa's desire for agency through a present, stable "self" and his "object" value for secular and religious communities. These theoretical oppositions—between subjective, authentic agency and objective, "false" passivity—gained popular attention with the emergences of existentialism and Marxism, both of which informed the writing of *The Divided Self.* These oppositions also mark a religious politics of inclusion and exclusion that measure the compatibility of people, like Musa, with a religionized politics that places political issues and struggles within sacred contexts. Nigerians like Musa seem highly concerned about the dangers of "misnaming" or "misrepresenting" the sacred and the secular, and struggle to "purify" culturally hybrid identities by moving out of unstable spaces, or by "cleansing" them of enemies within. As Bhabha suggests, "Blasphemy is not merely a misrepresentation of the sacred by the secular; it is a moment when the subject-matter or the content of a cultural tradition is being overwhelmed, or alienated, in the act of translation."[49]

Musa produced a splitting image of his identity contoured for idealized others, whom in a later diary entry he specifies as Muslims and Westerners whose social and civil virtues are culturally distinct. He interpreted his alienation, isolation, and desire to migrate as emanating from a "false" image of his "self," which would ultimately be unmasked and discovered. Tethered to false images and historical social relations, Musa finds a path of flight, "to go elsewhere." His attempts to maintain an alliance with one part, his "divided self," lead Musa to vacillate between "anxious identifications" with groups who symbolize and practice his ideals of Islamic and Western virtues and a mistrust of his own perceptions and judgments, leading to withdrawal, depression, and migration.[50]

Conflicts between Sufis, such as Musa, and reformist Sunni Muslims, such as *'yan Izala* and *'yan Dawa,* reformist Shia Muslims, such as *'yan Umma, 'yan Shia,* and *'yan Tajdid,* and *'yan Bori* have emerged in response to the sensory structures associated with Sufi and Bori ritual uses of music, dance, perfumes, and amulets, visiting the tombs of Sufi saints, and excessive feasting and celebrations, practices that draw spirits to humans. Reformist Sunnis considered all of these practices to be forms of *shirk* (polytheism, or the forbidden association of partners such as the *jinn* or witches with Allah), *bidi'a,* and *sab'o* (blasphemy), and to be economically excessive, with reformist Shia concurring that many of these practices were emblematic of, or infused with, animism and Western capitalism.[51] Yet, what constituted *shirk, bidi'a,* or *sab'o,* or the conspicuous consumption of Western capitalism, was always a matter of interpretation and debate. For instance, in times of political conflict, most notably the 1999 violence in Kaduna over the implementation of Shariah law, many reformist Sunnis and Shias relied on the use of "traditional" ritual forms of medicinal protection, heightening enmity between reformist Sunnis, Shias, and Sufis. Umar, a Sufi *'dan tauri,* said:

> Now, *mafarauta* (hunters), *'yan Izala,* and a businessman will all seek to find *tauri* medicine. Before *'yan Izala* condemned these practices, but now it is a lie. During the Kaduna crisis, there was one *'dan Izala* who really fought. He sent a car asking for *tauri* medicine, but nobody sent it to them. They used to condemn the practices of wearing amulets and drinking *rubutu.* They said these are all blasphemy. But, Allah says stand up and I will help you.[52]

The 1999 to 2000 struggle to implement Shariah law in Kano drew together Hausa reformist Sunnis and Shias, and Sufis, against protesting Christians, yet exacerbated conflicts over historical perceptions of Nigerian Islamic identity and belonging. Sufi critics of *'yan Hisbah* complained that the insults, intimidations, and violence of *'yan Hisbah* were outside of Shariah law, insisting that most of the "troublemakers" were not Nigerians, but Nigerienne or Chadian, perhaps *'yan Tatsine.*[53] Addressing the charges of Hisbah abuses of power, Yusuf, a *'dan Hisbah,* told me the following:

> The government said some *'yan Hisbah* are not Nigerian, some are not Muslim, and some are not from Kano. The Governor thought some *'yan daba* had found their way into Hisbah.[54]

National, ethnic, and regional dimensions of religious ideology and practice became central discourses in a shift from the policing of "unIslamic practices" among Muslim Hausa, to the profiling of "un-Islamic people," an ethnicization of Islam that conflated Hausa ethnicity with Islamic "authentic-

ity," differentiating Muslims who supported the implementation of Shariah law across Nigeria, from those who sabotaged it. *'Yan Hisbah* focused on non-Hausa Muslims, particularly Muslim Yoruba, the second-largest ethnic group of Nigerian Muslims, as a powerful stumbling block to Islamic unity and reform.

THE KADUNA AND SAGAMU CRISES

When I returned to Kano in July 2000, conflicts between Muslim Hausa and Christian Igbo had given way to conflicts between Muslim Hausa and Muslim and Christian Yoruba. Residents of Kano were quick to tell me about the horrors of the Kaduna crisis, a city two hours to the south of Kano, engulfed by violent conflicts between Muslims and Christians over the possible implementation of Shariah law in Kaduna State. Residents of Kano related the Kaduna crisis to remembrances of an incident in 1999 in which Yoruba residents of Sagamu, a town in the southwestern part of Nigeria, killed their Hausa friends and neighbors, many of whom were from Kano.

On August 6, 1999, the editor of the Muslim-backed *Weekly Trust* reported:

> The battle-ground was the Sabo area of Sagamu where the Hausas live. Scores of houses and the mosque in this area were razed to the ground. The Hausa community, in this Yoruba town, was besieged by Yoruba warriors for days, with machetes and dane guns, with results not difficult to imagine.[55]

Residents in Kano asked me if I had heard that Muslim Hausa *'yan daba* carried out reprisal attacks in Kano, killing their Yoruba friends and neighbors.

Media reports of the Yoruba–Hausa conflict in Sagamu preceded the arrival of a truck carrying the bodies of victims back to their families in Kano. The emotional recollections of what happened failed to tally with southern news reports, which *'yan daba* felt were deliberate misinterpretations of the conflict meant to pin the blame on Muslim Hausa. One *'yan daba* told me, "We wouldn't have felt as much if it had been just the news, but when we saw the bodies, our emotions were high" (personal communication, January 15, 2001). Factional fighting among Muslims results from, and serves as, communal memory, reactivating past glories associated with the revolution of Usman dan Fodio and humiliating defeats by the British and anti-caliphate states, and contributing to public debate about Yoruba betrayals of Hausa during the Nigerian civil war and identifications of Muslim Yoruba as "marginal Muslims" who would sabotage the implementation of Shariah law in northern Nigeria.

HYBRID IDENTITIES: THE *'YAN DABA*

The complexity of ethnic, religious identifications in northern Nigeria is evident among Kano's *'yan daba*, most often the perpetrators and victims of violence. While predominantly Muslim Hausa, *'yan daba* have incorporated youths of other ethnic and religious backgrounds. They often take non-Hausa words, like *scorpion* or *pusher*, or words combining Hausa with references to people elsewhere, such as *kayaman* (reggae man) or *Takur Sahab* (person who has a leader in India) as street names. *'Yan daba* have adopted a style of dress they associate with "West-side niggers" (Los Angeles-based rappers). In their sunglasses, chains, and baggy jeans, *'yan daba* show a broad interest in youth cultures from around the world, questioning me, through whirls of Indian hemp, about the impact of rappers such as Tupac Shakur and the revolutionary politics of his Black Panther mother. Unlike Musa, *'yan daba* seem capable of holding contradictory identities, such as Muslim–rapper.

'Yan daba self-identify with neighborhoods, hanging out in particular joints, but they shift among modes of violent opposition to other neighborhoods, tolerant separation, and eclecticism. They identify with *'yan farauta*, expert hunters, and with *tauri* ritualists and fighters. Nonetheless, these relationships are tenuous and, in some cases, a potent source of *'yan daba* marginalization. For instance, a *mafarauci* (hunter) described *daba* in a personal communication to me on October 26, 2000 as:

> An acquired habit, not a profession or tradition. Stealing, drinking, smoking hemp, and general anti-social behavior is not the culture or subculture of hunters. What is paining us is that these groups of *'yan tauri* and *'yan daba*, even in the eyes of the law and the Emir, they see them as hunters, which is not so. To us, *'yan daba* are hooligans.

'Yan daba, whose ranks have swollen from between fourteen per neighborhood in 1991 to between fifty and two-hundred today, are often the main caretakers of younger male siblings and *almajirai*.[56] Like younger siblings, *almajirai* serve as errand boys while playing along the perimeters of local joints. Through *'yan daba* do the caretaking, *almajirai* form the main pool of youths from which *'yan daba* recruit. *Almajirai* moral aesthetics develop through ambiguous attachments to social rituals and daily life at the mosque and to those of *'yan daba* and the *daba* neighborhood street economy, a classic Mbembe "imaginary family" social grouping.

'Yan daba recruits speak about getting even with people who have "downgraded" or "underrated" them. Insults and injuries are taken as reenactments of earlier acts, variably related to personal experience and to ethnic, religious, or political mytho-histories, which nonetheless excuse violence. Forceful acts of domination are accompanied by outbursts of ribaldry and derision that seem to mock and mimic officialdom, while creating new forms of officialdom altogether.[57] A *'dan daba*, dressed lavishly in Muslim-style *riga* (dress), smoking a joint reminiscent of Cheech and Chong, slaps an *almajiri* to the ground for forgetting to say his prayers. Once again, the crowd cheers and laughs. Through the arbitrary application of pain, *'yan daba* produce fear that "reinforces certain moral values within society," replacing values of the colonial regime with Islamic ones.[58] *'Yan daba* use such "therapeutic terror" to galvanize and to channel the affective memories of their members.[59]

'Yan daba speak of attractions to power, physical and metaphysical, and the fear they will generate through their associations with *daba*. Recruits say they are impressed with *'yan daba* fighting, a form that uses two sticks that enable someone to beat opponents who are larger or stronger. *Daba* recruits fear *'yan daba* who use *tauri* medicines and who perform the ritual acts and prohibitions that make them invulnerable to their enemies. They enjoy frightening married women into staying home. The felt and expressed qualities of fear and respect emerge as an entanglement with what Mbembe refers to as the "banality of power," part of which is a "distinctive style of political improvisation, by a tendency to excess and lack of proportion, as well as by distinctive ways identities are multiplied, transformed, and put into circulation."[60]

'Yan daba serve as the vanguard for local political and religious leaders, earning the major part of their incomes from politically motivated thuggery. Ironically, in 1999 'yan daba agitated for the implementation of Shariah law, breaking streetlights and destroying public property to persuade the Rabiyu Kwankwaso, the governor, to sign it into law. With the implementation of Shariah law and the increased crackdown on prostitution, drugs, alcohol, and black market petrol sales, 'yan daba have suffered increased poverty, finding it difficult to obtain money for food and clothing, dating, or marriage. Petty theft is down, but the rates of rape and violent crimes have increased and are more often attributed to 'yan daba "rampages," even though there is no evidence tying 'yan daba to these increases.[61]

MEDIA TRANSMISSIONS OF VIOLENCE

In Nigeria, youth groups such as 'yan daba are central to the shaping of the political, religious climate at national and local levels and have developed into what the media variably refers to as "vigilantes," "ethnic militias," or "tribal armies." Youth groups all over Nigeria have entered into the realm of "policing," left open by a crippled police force and the recent demilitarization of Nigeria. Many journalists consider the militant wing of the O'odu'a People's Congress (OPC) in the predominantly Yoruba west, the Bakassi Boys in the Igbo-dominated east, and 'yan daba to be mercenaries navigating a fragmented political space. However, these groups are tied to larger political and cultural associations. For instance, a lead story in the Muslim-funded *Weekly Trust* described 'yan daba as a future Islamic Army:

> The 'Yan daba, a reserve army of unemployed youths, have acted in ways that suggest that they can metamorphose into a tribal army some day. In 1999, when Hausa residents of Sagamu town in Ogun State had a clash with their Yoruba hosts, it was the 'Yan daba group that organized a reprisal attack against Yoruba residents in Kano.[62]

Media stories like this one progressively denuded local incidents and disputes about the particulars of their context, aggregating them by narrowing their detail. This process, which Tambiah refers to as "focalization," is a kind of cascading that may channel remembrances.[63]

The processes of remembering and forgetting are further complicated by affective ethnic or religious exclusions, ideas about a collective predestiny and whether violence under today's circumstances is an appropriate form of *jihad*. A 'dan daba described the complexities of religious affiliation as 'yan daba mobilize for violence (personal communication, October 15, 2000):

> If there's a fight between Muslim Brothers and Tijaniyya, or between Tijaniyya and Kadiriyya, it's the 'yan daba within these groups that will fight. But, if there's a fight between Muslims and non-Muslims, all 'yan daba will get involved in the fight, to help their Muslim brothers, in the name of Muslim brotherhood, to fight in the name of Islam.

Self-consciously, 'yan daba articulate ethnic and religious unity, but not all or even most of Kano's 'yan daba participated in the reprisal killings of Yoruba. As with other large-scale conflicts, 'yan daba who lived in the most ethnically and religiously mixed neighborhoods of Kano were responsible for killing Yoruba. Indeed, most of the violence witnessed in northern Nigeria during the early 2000s occurred in the most mixed areas, in the cities of Kaduna and Jos, which have large minority animist–Islamic and Christian populations, and in newer, mixed neighborhoods of Kano, particularly those along major roads to the south, east, and west.

In northern Nigeria, Hausa ethnicity and the Muslim religion are conflated because of the predominance of Muslim Hausa. By contrast, about half of all Yoruba are Muslim, so that the categories of ethnicity and religion function more readily as independent sources of identification. In a *Weekly Trust* article about Muslim Yoruba killing Muslim Hausa in Lagos, the secretary-general of the Supreme Council for Islamic Affairs was quoted as saying, "We have too many nominal Muslims in the south who are ignorant of their religion . . . they can be used by some other people who think that Shariah is a monster which they must attack."[64]

Similarly, Ado-Kurawa has described the denigration of southern Muslims as a ploy by Christian Yoruba to separate the north and south: "For several years the fanatical Christian Yoruba tribalists have led a propaganda campaign against northern Muslims. The idea being to isolate and demonize northern Muslims, thereby making them ready targets for extermination by all other Nigerians."[65]

Also according to Ado-Kurawa, Christian Yoruba–controlled media, backed by Christian imperialists, are the main force behind the anti-Shariah propaganda:

All the tools acquired from the "psychological job" done on Africans by the imperialists have now been deployed against this adversary (Islam). The use of the tools perfected by their European Christian patrons has been very easy for the Yoruba Christian dominated Nigerian media. They portray the Shari'a as barbaric and uncivilized.[66]

Over the past six years, anti-American media reports have become increasingly common; the authors of these reports argue the need for Shariah as a way for Muslims to separate—physically, psychically, spiritually, economically—from "infidels," especially Nigerian Christians and imperialists. Muslim journalists highlight the arrogance and brutality of the U.S. bombings in Iraq, holding Americans responsible for untold deaths and destruction. They recount the plight of Palestinians and the need for Muslims to fight against social injustice. Osama bin Laden stickers began to adorn Kano buses, while hundreds of youths joined the *Hisbah,* Shariah enforcers, and wider networks of separatist Muslims.

STATES OF EMERGENCY

In March 2001, the deputy governor of Kano State, Dr. Umar Abdullahi Ganduje, announced an Islamic "state of emergency" referring to the inability of Shariah law, as it was being practiced in the state, to stop "prostitution" and the sale and consumption of alcohol. He led Hisbah on a series of raids to local hotels, restaurants, and "cool spots," where the Hisbah abused patrons and destroyed thousands of dollars' worth of alcohol. Because Igbo and Yoruba Christians owned most of these businesses, these raids bankrupted some and scared others into a mass exodus of Christians and Muslims who feared increased violence, a scene not

unlike the mass exodus preceding the Nigerian civil war. Establishments stayed indefinitely closed or operated at odd hours or with armed guards patrolling the gates. Jokes about "dying for a drink" became a permanent fixture as humor rose to meet increased levels of anxiety. Rumors about the arming of Muslims and Christians became more frequent. In response, the Nigerian head of state, Olusegun Obasanjo, called Dr. Ganduje to Abuja, stating in public that the deputy governor had endangered Nigerian state security, thus reframing Kano's "state of emergency" as a national "state of emergency."

The deputy governor's state of emergency spawned other forms of Islamic state-preserving "states of emergency." When asked about an incident of Hisbah burning down a Christian-owned hotel that had been in operation on a daily basis for several years, a Hisbah said:

They (Hisbah) made a mistake. Any human can make a mistake. . . . But, this Hisbah militant group is here to stay. We have to confront the evildoers. The Hisbah exist and have 100 percent support from God. Most of the vices committed by poor people . . . are because of the poor leadership in America, England, and Switzerland. Why did they allow our leaders to go and take our money there? (personal communication, August 8, 2001)

MEDIATED HOSTILITY AND VIOLENCE

In the weeks before the crisis on May 11, 2004, when *'yan daba* and *almajirai* brutally murdered *arna* (unbelievers), *Kiristoci* (Christians), and *baki* (strangers), Muslim Hausa residents were paying close attention to reports of terrorism in Nigeria and to violence in Plateau State, in the Palestinian territories, and in Iraq. Muslims quickly dismissed reports of the U.S. State Department's alleged concern with an Afghani-associated Taliban in Yobe and Bornu States, of the existence of al-Qaeda in Plateau State, and of the Salafist group in Kano State as ploys by the United States to keep a firm grip on the political affairs of Nigeria. As part of a cover story of the Muslim-backed *Weekly Trust*, Sheikh Ibrahim El-Zakzaky, leader of the Islamic Movement in Nigeria, argued that "the 'propaganda' about the existence of terrorist cells in the North (Nigeria) may be part of a general plan by the United States to prepare the ground for coming into the country," a popularly held concern that the Bush administration plans a war on Nigeria to "steal" the petroleum.[67]

The polarization of Western Christian and Eastern Islamic political identities by world leaders such as George Bush and Ariel Sharon has hardened political identifications in Nigeria, not just among Muslims but also among a range of political actors concerned with global justice and security. Muslim youths in northern Nigeria take Osama bin Laden and Saddam Hussein as heroes, adorning their motorcycles and busses with stickers of their images, because they identify not with the religious politics of these men but with Islam, in general, and with the militant masculinity and willingness of bin Laden and Hussein to "stand up" to George Bush and Ariel Sharon, personalities they associate with anti-Islam, elitism, corruption, and violence. Yet, unlike the massacres of Christians and non-Hausa Muslims that took place in Kano during the years 1991, 1995, and 1999, there is evidence that the killings on May 11 were, to some extent, intentional and planned, indicative of genocidal massacre.[68]

CONCLUSION

Among northern Nigerians, the relations of political antagonism—forged during the nineteenth-century Islamic jihad, British colonization, the Nigerian civil war, and subsequent violence—intersect with media portrayals of violence against Muslims inside and outside Nigeria's national borders. Such antagonisms are rooted in, reproduce, and transform the ideologies and feelings of "affective citizenship," fusions of ethnic, religious, regional citizenship, based on territorialized ethnic customary law and deterritorialized religious law, and on the historical perceptions of enclosure and exclusion that underpin memories of belonging, backed by law, but a law that, historically, has been arbitrary and violent in its application. The Kano violence of 1991, 1995, 1999, 2000, and 2004 was an escalation of antagonisms and heightened polarizations of self and other; conflations of identity, morality, and security, that sediment the opposing colonial identities of native and settler; the religious identities of animism, Nigerian Sufism, and Sunni and Shia reformism, in which some Muslims

are "marginal," even contaminating; the Muslim Hausa and Christian Igbo identities that mark the opponents of Nigeria's civil war; and, most recently, the global political identities of George Bush's "You're either with us or with the terrorists." In media-saturated places such as northern Nigeria, youths' ambivalent experiences of adult leadership and of local ethnic and religious media, alongside global media, are best understood in relation to the historical ruptures of identity, memory, emotion, and agency, processes that become embodied within the self and acted out. While not the only means of legitimation and authority, the media have particular relevance for Kano Muslim youths who want to belong, but for whom the social histories and felt qualities of violence make trust difficult if not impossible. With no moral authority, political or religious, media easily suppress historicity, channeling and repeating affective references to the historical ruptures of the nineteenth-century Islamic jihad, colonization, the Nigerian civil war, and, most recently, the U.S.–Bush administration's "War on Terrorism" and "War on Iraq," along with the massacre of Muslim Hausa in Plateau State, shaping the "truths" of violence and of victimhood, ideologically and viscerally, legitimating and authorizing violence, even genocidal massacres, as affective forms of citizenship.

In recent years, the Pan-African contexts of decolonization and democratization have stimulated many forms of historical revision, collective memory, and "truth telling," including South Africa's Truth and Reconciliation Commission and Nigeria's Oputa Panel. These methods of attaining social justice, based on Christian beliefs in confession and forgiveness are not utilized by most Muslim Hausa, who instead focus on punishment as a deterrent, future discretion, and lessening the visibility of immoral or criminal acts. It is important to comprehend what stands as the evidence, or the "truth" of violence, within the contexts of Western academic empiricism; Christian, Shia, and Sunni reformism; Sufism; or from within the perspectives of youths socialized by institutions that authorize competing "truths." How do youths know when someone is "being for real," "being authentic," or "being truthful" under extreme conditions of poverty, scarcity, and boredom, or from within larger politicized conflicts? How are groups such as *'yan daba* and *'yan Hisbah* able to be "for real" while projecting visible and invisible forms of terror? How are "states of emergency" used to regulate the politically seeable and the politically unseeable, whether innocent Iraqis or the poor *'yan daba* and other marginalized groups of Kano? How and why do Nigeria's chosen traumas—colonization by the British, amalgamation of the Muslim north and Christian south, and Biafra's attempted secession, resulting in the Nigerian civil war—continue to underscore unmourned histories, memories, and traumas?

Psychically and spiritually, young Muslim Hausa appear under ethnic, religious pressure from two paradoxical notions of "being for real" or being "authentic." First is the experience of seeing ethnic and religious identity as more and more open to choice, whereas lived experience is increasingly one of ethnic, religious nationalism marked by the search for Muslim Hausa "authenticity" and "originality." Young people experience high levels of anxiety and self-consciousness about intersubjective religious identity, alongside a striving for independence in thinking and behavior. Second, youths express a concern about *boko* (Western education) and viewing media and their tendencies to dwell in imagination and fantasy, all of which conflict with an idealized Islamic self-identity and the ability to be "for real" spiritually. These paradoxes take on additional significance in relation to local Sufi and reformist Sunni and Shia teachings about how one attains religious knowledge—whether, for instance, "authentic" knowledge is embodied or scriptural, and whether global forms of related knowledge and self-expression are sources of knowledge or paths to hell. Faced with the complexities of Islamic identity and with severe political economic hardships, instabilities, and insecurities, young people are vulnerable to the emotional channeling of the media and the persuasive oratory of their political/religious leaders. A growing concern is the mushrooming population of *almajirai,* some as young as five years, who are recruited into violence by *'yan daba* and *'yan Hisbah,* and who, by their late teens, have typically participated in several major crises, their shared experiences of violence serving as collective memory and as identification with, and belonging to, older Muslims.

Following the implementation of Shariah law as Kano State Law, there were efforts to "see" and to address the needs of disputing parties. Governor Ibrahim Shekarau, elected May 29, 2003, developed a government think tank of Muslims whom he assigned to meet with Christian leaders and groups to assure them that Shariah law would not be applied to non-Muslims. Local government chairmen within the old city organized meetings of disputing Muslims. Most notably, the Gwale local government chairman invited *'yan daba* to express their needs to government officials and some *'yan daba* received money for school fees. Across northern Nigeria, a series of conferences were held at major universities to discuss Shariah law and its impact on Muslims and non-Muslims, and majority and minority ethnic, religious politics. While dialogue has improved relations between Muslims and Christians and among Muslims, many Kano residents continued to feel marginalized and feared ongoing communal violence, fears made real by the May 11 crisis.

All disputing parties have a stake in evaluating these stresses on young people since youths are the most likely to be the perpetrators *and* victims of communal violence. Young people need care and guidance from peers and elders who have, themselves, found declassifying, tolerant rather than dehumanizing, nonviolent means through which to confront the brutal contradictions of living in a global world.

Any recasting of the past in fundamentally moral terms requires attention to chosen traumas and their impact on citizenship, social justice, and equity, not simply as concepts but as ways to actively alleviate conflict and violence, including the everyday violence of stereotyping others, of poverty, and of inequitable access to schools, jobs, and resources. This can be dealt with, in part, by international, national, and state government institutions, religious and nongovernmental organizations, and private businesses, but "unofficial" enactments of human recognition, generosity, and compassion are equally important. The epistemological divergences of secular, ethnic customary, and religious law, as well as the moral imperatives and obligations of each, whether at the United Nations or local governments, require significant understandings of historical grievances and communication about reparation and security. While critiques of ethnocentrism and the violence directed at world Muslims and Christians, and at Muslim and Christian Nigerians, have brought attention to identity and equality, to the kinds of mutual recognitions and attunements that are necessary for coexistence, the relations of individuality and individual human rights, communal and historical grievances and desires, and majority interests have yet to garner the balance necessary for peace. All Nigerians benefit from strong public debate and civil initiatives that cut across ethnicity, religion, regionality, and political party to address the needs of the most marginalized Nigerians: ethnic, religious minorities and youths.

ACKNOWLEDGMENTS

I would like to thank all of my friends and colleagues in Kano who have helped to shape my understanding of identity and difference among Nigerians. Though for reasons of confidentiality I am unable to name them, I am particularly grateful to 'yan daba and to 'yan Hisbah who allowed me into their lives under the difficult circumstances surrounding the implementation of Shariah law. I would like to thank Aminu Inuwa, Salisu Abdullahi, Abdulkarim 'Dan Asabe, and Phillip Shea for assistance with this research and for comments on an early draft of this paper, and also Margaret Ostermann and Judy Carter for comments on an early draft of the paper. I am intellectually indebted to Allen Feldman, Uli Linke, Valentine Daniels, and Vamik Volkan. The research for this paper would have been impossible without the generous support of the Harry Frank Guggenheim Foundation and the Fulbright Institute of International Education. Finally, I thank Vamik Volkan, George Irani, and Judy Carter for inviting me to write this chapter.

ENDNOTES

1. J. Hunwick, "Sub-Saharan Africa and the wider world of Islam: Historical and Contemporary Perspectives," in *African Islam and Islam in Africa: Encounters between Sufis and Islamists* (pp. 28–54), eds. D. Westerlund and E. Rosander (Athens, OH, USA: Ohio University Press, 1997); Falola 1998; Larkin 1998; R. Loimeier, "Islamic Reform and Political Change: The Examples of Abubakar Gumi and the 'Yan Izala Movement' in Northern Nigeria," in *African Islam and Islam in Africa: Encounters Between Sufis and Islamists,* eds. D. Westerlund and E. Rosander (Athens, OH: Ohio University Press, 1997), 286–307; Lovejoy and Williams 1997; M. S. Umar, "Changing Islamic Identity in Nigeria from the 1960s to the 1980s: From Sufism to Anti-Sufism," in *Muslim Identity and Social Change in Sub-Saharan Africa,* ed. L. Brenner (Bloomington and Indianapolis, IN: Indiana University Press, 1993), 154–178; Watts 1996; D. Westerlund, "Reaction and action: Accounting for the rise of Islamism," in *African Islam and Islam in Africa: Encounters Between Sufis and Islamists,* eds. D. Westerlund and E. Rosander (Athens, OH: Ohio University Press, 1997), 308–334.
2. Falola 1998.
3. V. Volkan, *Bloodlines: From Ethnic Pride to Ethnic Terrorism* (New York: Farrar, Straus, & Giroux, 1997).
4. Ibid.; also see L. Malkki, *Purity and Exile: Violence, Memory, and National Cosmology Among Hutu Refugees in Tanzania* (Chicago: University of Chicago Press, 1995) 54, where the author defines mythico–history as "not only a description of the past, nor even merely and evaluation of the past, but a subversive recasting and reinterpretation of it in fundamentally moral terms." Some Nigerians, particularly southerners, consider amalgamation of the northern and southern territories of Nigeria a trauma. While Nigerians refer to the "amalgamation of 1914" as a single collective trauma, the processes of amalgamation occurred over a period of several years.
5. Nigerian media includes traditional protest media, such as poetry, praise singing, preaching, music, and storytelling, as well as print media.
6. Mamdani 1996. Watts 2001
7. *'Yan Izala* are Sunni Muslims, while *'yan Shia* and *'yan Tajdid* are Shia. In the late 1990s, members of these groups joined together, referring to themselves as "Nigerian Orthodox Muslims," in preparation for the political struggle to implement Shariah law across northern Nigeria. Twelve states in northern Nigeria presently have implemented Shariah law as state law.
8. Loimeier, "Islamic Reform and Political Change"; A. Masquelier, "Narratives of Power, Images of Wealth: The Ritual Economy of Bori in the Market," in *Modernity and Its Malcontents: Ritual and Power in Postcolonial Africa,* eds. J. Comaroff and J. Comaroff (Chicago: The University of Chicago Press, 1993) 3–33; Umar, "Changing Islamic Identity in Nigeria"; "Westerlund, Reaction and Action"; and J. Comaroff and J. Comaroff, *Ethnography and the Historical Imagination* (Boulder, CO: Westview, 1992), 29.
9. In many parts of Africa, the violence of European "civilizing missions" and, more recently, ideologically charged "development" industries that link technological "development" to changes in peoples' cultures and psychologies have an enormous impact on the use, and deployment, of terms such as *morality, civility,* and *democracy* in arousing public debate.
10. A. Mbembe, "At the Edge of the World: Boundaries, Territoriality, and Sovereignty in Africa," in *Globalization,* ed. A. Appadurai (Durham, NC: Duke University Press, 2001), 25.

Also, only recently have scholars focused on social imagination and fantasy as critical to understanding the formation of identities tied to spatial practices and histories of origin. See B. Anderson, *Imagined Communities: Reflections on the Origin and Spread of Nationalism* (New York: Verso, 1991); A. Appadurai, "Disjuncture and Difference in the Global Cultural Economy," in *Colonial Discourse and Post-Colonial Theory: A Reader,* eds. P. Williams and L. Chrisman (New York: Columbia University Press, 1994), 324–39; Appaduari 1996; H. Bhabha, *The Location of Culture* (London: Routledge, 1994); Comaroff and Comaroff, *Ethnography and the Historical Imagination;* A. Feldman, *Formations of Violence: The Narrative of the Body and Political Terror in Northern Ireland* (Chicago: University of Chicago Press, 1991); and Malkki, *Purity and Exile.*

11. Mbembe, "At the Edge of the World," 26.
12. Ibid., 31–32.
13. Falola 1998.
14. Feldman, *Formations of Violence,* 4.
15. Ibid.
16. Ibid.
17. Feldman, *Formations of Violence;* Volkan, *Bloodlines;* and V. Daniels, *Charred Lullabies: Chapters in an Anthropology of Violence* (Princeton, NJ: Princeton University Press, 1996), respectively.
18. M. A. Shu'aib, "Christians Are the Aggressors" [special issue], *At-Tajdid: Movement for Islamic Revival,* June 3, 1995, 8.
19. H. Abdullahi, "The Unforgettable Riots in Kano," *The Triumph,* July 9, 1995, 3; and B. Abutu, "Kano Under Curfew: Five Killed in Sectarian Violence" [editorial], *The Democrat,* May 31, 1995, 1.
20. M. Oboh and K. Funtua, "Kano Violence: 49 Charged to Court," *The Democrat,* June 14, 1995. 1.
21. B. Otitoju and L. Adeniji, "Mayhem in Kano—26 Die in Ethnic Riot—Curfew imposed," *A.M. News,* June 1, 1995, 1.
22. Abutu, "Kano Under Curfew"; also, Oboh and Funtua, "Kano Violence."
23. Abutu, "Kano Under Curfew."
24. Ibid.
25. A. Nwankwo, "Nigeria: A Dream Turned Nightmare," *Third Eye,* August 28, 1995, 12.
26. Ken Saro-Wiwa, *Genocide in Nigeria: The Ogoni Tragedy* (London: Harcourt-Brace, 1992).
27. M. Last, "Reconciliation and Memory in Nigeria," in *Violence and Subjectivity,* eds. V. Das, A. Kleinman, M. Ramphele, and P. Reynolds (Berkeley, CA: University of California Press, 2000), 318.
28. Ibid., 317.
29. S. Ibrahim, "FG'll Curb Sectarian Conflicts," *The Triumph,* June 1, 1995, 1.
30. S. Ibrahim, "Kano Emir Demands Checking of Illegal Aliens," *The Triumph,* June 20, 1991, 1.
31. Abdullahi, "The Unforgettable Riots in Kano," op cit.
32. Shu'aib, "Christians Are the Aggressors," op cit.
33. Ibid.
34. S. Ibrahim, "Igbos Are Not Preparing for War, *The Triumph,* June 8, 1995, 1, 12.
35. C. Casey, *Medicines for Madness: Suffering, Disability and the Identification of Enemies in Northern Nigeria.* Disser-

tation, University of California. (Ann Arbor, MI: UMI Publishers, 1997).
36. Casey 1998, 2001, 2005.
37. During the transition to independence, the Sardauna of Sokoto, Ahmadu Bello, revived the works of Usman dan Fodio to unify northern Muslims, regardless of brotherhood or legal school (Padeu, 1986).
38. Personal communication with Professor Phillip Shea, Department of History, Bayero University, Kano, Nigeria, July 19, 2004.
39. Hunwick, "Sub-Saharn Africa and the Wider World of Islam," 33.
40. Westerlund, "Reaction and Action," 310.
41. Hunwick, "Sub-Saharan Africa and the Wider World of Islam"; Ibrahim, "Kano Emir Demands Checking of Illegal Aliens"; Loimeier, "Islamic Reform and Political Change"; and Umar, "Changing Islamic Identity in Nigeria."
42. Personal communication with Professor Phillip Shea, Department of History, Bayero University, Kano, Nigeria, July 19, 2004.
43. Watts 1996.
44. Personal communication with Professor Phillip Shea, Department of History, Bayero University, Kano, Nigeria, July 19, 2004.
45. I. Umar, "The need for an imam," *New Nigerian,* July 9, 1995, 13.
46. Ibid. Also see L. Brenner, ed., *Muslim Identity and Social Change in Sub-Saharan Africa* (Bloomington and Indianapolis: Indiana University Press, 1993); Loimeier, "Islamic Reform and Political Change"; and Umar, "Changing Islamic Identity in Nigeria from the 1960s to the 1980s."
47. The 1991 Kano crisis, sparked by the vocal preaching of German evangelist Reinhard Bonnke, in predominantly Muslim Hausa areas of Kano, led to the deaths of several hundred Christians and Muslims. In addition, 'yan daba claimed to receive money and support from political and religious leaders, while religious leaders adamantly denied their support of 'yan daba. See A. 'Dan Asabe, "'Yan Daba: The "Terrorists" of Kano Metropolitan?" *Kano Studies* [special issue: Youth and Health in Kano Today] (1991), 85–101; and Otitoju and L. Adeniji, "Mayhem in Kano."
48. R. D. Laing, *The Divided Self* (New York: Pantheon Books, 1969). Musa is a pseudonym for a Muslim Hausa in his late twenties who grew up in a village to the east of Kano, then moved to Kano, where he encountered pressure to affiliate with Muslim student groups at Bayero University. This quote is from an introduction he wrote to his diary in 1995 before giving it to me for my research.
49. H. Bhabha, *Anxiety in the Midst of Difference,* Distinguished Lecture presented at the American Anthropological Association, Chicago, December, 1996, 225–26.
50. Ibid.
51. *'Yan Shia* and *'yan Izala* consider secular human legislation one of the most egregious forms of *shirk* because it places humans on par with Allah, according to Westerlund, "Reaction and Action," 309.

52. Umar. *Rubutu* is a Muslim Hausa treatment for *rashin lafiya* (imbalance in all areas of life—psychical, spiritual, social, and physical). To take *rubutu*, the afflicted person writes Qur'anic verses on a board or bowl, washes it with water, and drinks the solution, to, literally, internalize the medicinal verses.
53. The sentiment that violence in Kano is a manifestation of aggressive intrusions from the "outside" is widespread and cuts across historical perceptions of violence from colonization to the most recent massacres of Christians in 2004. See Casey 1998; 2006.
54. This is taken from a January 15, 2001, interview with a *'dan Hisbah* who was part of the Independent Shari'a Implementation Committee and the Kano State Shari'a Implementation Committee.
55. "Hausas Massacred in Sagamu," *Weekly Trust,* August 6, 1999, 1–2.
56. 'Dan Asabe, "'Yan Daba."
57. Mbembe, "At the Edge of the World," 102.
58. 'Dan Asabe, "'Yan Daba," 99.
59. Daniels, *Charred Lullabies.*
60. Mbembe, "At the Edge of the World," 102.
61. Some *'yan daba* participate in *'daukar amarya,* the kidnapping and raping of women they feel have "slighted"

or disrespected them. *'Yan daba* admit kidnapping groups of "prostitutes" from hotels and brutally raping them in uninhabited areas of Kano. However, these rapes are rarely reported. According to a magistrate judge in Gyadi Gyadi, cases of reported rape increased six-fold between the implementation of Shariah Law in November 2000 and January 2001. The judge attributed this rise to a decrease in the number of "prostitutes" available for older men, who had instead begun "turning to young girls" (personal communication, January 12, 2001).
62. "Hausas Massacred in Sagamu," 1–2.
63. S. Tambiah, *Magic, Science, Religion and the Scope of Rationality* (Cambridge, England: Cambridge University Press, 1990).
64. *Weekly Trust,* 2000, 3.
65. I. Ado-Kurawa, *Shari'ah and the Press in Nigeria: Islam Versus Western Christian Civilization* (Kano, Nigeria: Kurawa Holdings, 2000), 273.
66. Ibid., 324.
67. "Who Are Nigeria's Terrorists?" *Weekly Trust,* May 1–7, 2004.
68. Casey, 2006.

ABOUT THE AUTHOR

Conerly Casey is an assistant professor at the American University of Kuwait. She maintains close working relations with faculty in the Departments of Sociology and Psychiatry at Bayero University in Kano, Nigeria. Casey holds a master's degree in counseling psychology from the University of Southern California and a doctoral degree in anthropology from the University of California, Los Angeles (UCLA). Funded by the Harry Frank Guggenheim Foundation and by the Fulbright Institute of International Education (IIE) Conerly studies conflict, violence, and peace among youths in northern Nigeria.

Having worked with victims of violence at the University of Vermont Medical Center, Boston City Hospital, and the South Shore Mental Health Center, Dr. Casey developed research and teaching interests in the intersections of culture, violence, and medicine. She has taught numerous classes about conflict, violence, and trauma at UCLA, the University of Chicago, and the Central European University and has delivered lectures about these topics in countries as diverse as Indonesia, England, Chile, Nigeria, and the United States.

Dr. Casey has received numerous awards to support her dissertation research, *Medicines for Madness: Suffering and the Identification of Enemies in Northern Nigeria* (1997), among them a Fulbright IIE Dissertation Award and several research awards from the Department of Anthropology, the Psychocultural Studies Program, and the Division of Social Medicine, all at UCLA. In 1997, the first chapter of Dr. Casey's dissertation, "Suffering and the Identification of Enemies in Northern Nigeria," received the Association for Political and Legal Student Essay Prize and was published in the *Political and Legal Anthropology Review* (1998).

The Harry Frank Guggenheim Foundation funded her latest project, *Youthful Martyrdom and Heroic Criminality: The Formation of Youth Groups in Northern Nigeria (2000–2002),* which because of its timing included a study of the conflicts and violence among Nigerians during the implementation of Shariah law as Kano State law. In the spring of 2002, Dr. Casey was a fellow with the Humanities Institute at Dartmouth College, where she was able to embark on the analysis and writing of the results of this project.

Dr. Casey, along with Dr. Robert B. Edgerton, has edited a volume entitled *A Companion to Psychological Anthropology: Modernity and Psychocultural Change,* which includes several chapters about violence and its aftermath (in press, Blackwell Publishers, Inc.). She is co-editing, along with Dr. Salisu Adamu Abdullahi and Dr. Mohammed Ismail Zango, a volume entitled *Cultural Sociology: An Introduction to Sociology and Anthropology in Nigeria,* which includes several chapters about changing relations that contribute to conflicts, violence, and peace. While in Nigeria, Dr. Casey is revising her dissertation and writing the manuscript for a book based on her research, *Youthful Martyrdom and Heroic Criminality: The Formation of Youth Groups in Northern Nigeria.*

Ethnicity and Ethnic Relations in Nigeria: The Case of Religious Conflict in Kano

Salisu A. Abdullahi

CONCEPTUAL UNDERPINNING

In discussing the issue of ethnicity and ethnic relations in Nigeria, it is pertinent first of all to underline some conceptual issues central to the title of this chapter.

Ethnic is a concept used to classify a person according to his or her group based on culture, race, tribe, and religion. *Ethnic groups* are characterized by common history and shared tradition, among other particulars. These distinctive cultural patterns are what set apart one ethnic group from the other. *Ethnocentricism* is an attribute of all ethnic groups. Leon-Gurerrero explains ethnocentrism as the belief that the values and behaviors of one's own ethnic group are right and better than those of other ethnic groups.[1]

Ethnicity is a claim to belong to a particular group on the basis of the characteristics mentioned. What is said so far permits us to call the following African societies ethnic societies: South Africa, Sudan, Rwanda, and Nigeria. It is worth noting that each of these societies is internally divided on the basis of language, religion, physique, body texture, and so on. Furthermore, in developing democracies such as Nigeria's, sharp and usually hostile divisions exist on the basis of ideological orientation and political belief

BACKGROUND

What is known as Nigeria today once consisted of different societies that existed as centralized states with clearly defined political structures. For example, the Habe (Hausa) and later (mainly) the Fulani Kingdoms occupied most parts of the north, while the Yoruba and Benin Kingdoms resided in the south and uncentralized societies of mainly Igbos also lived in the south. In addition to these kingdoms, several small independent societies resided in both the north and the south. The two main parts of Nigeria have different histories of contact with the outside world. Arab traders came

to the north in the ninth century with the religion of Islam and their system of education. The new way of life was largely accepted peacefully, even though force was used much later. In the fifteenth century European traders came to the south with Christianity and the Western system of education.

By 1914 the southern and northern parts (protectorates) were amalgamated as a British colony. In 1960 these different societies with different religion, culture, history, tribes, and level of development became a single independent nation called Nigeria—a country with three culturally distinct regions: northern Hausa and Fulani people, western Yoruba, and eastern Igbo people. In addition to these main tribes, over 240 tribes are found principally in the middle belt and south-central Nigeria. From 1967 to date efforts were made by different administrations to create more states to ensure national integration that would do away with regional identity. The current political disposition is a zoning system, a dangerous divisive move created by elites to ensure that (as they said) "no section of the country is dominated by the other." The country is divided into six geopolitical zones: Northeast, northwest, north-central, southeast, southwest, and south-south. This division is seen as conforming to the old British regional system.

Islam and Christianity are the main religions, and several traditional religions are practiced. These religions have followers all over Nigeria within the various regions and linguistic groups. Liphart argued that a country is grouped as homogeneous if 80 percent or more of its population belong to the same religion or speak the same language.[2] In reality, Islam had a strong following in the northern region (northwest, northeast, and north-central) and the western region (present southwest) for an appreciable period before the advent of colonialism. In the eastern region (southeast), as stated by Balogun, even though contact with Islam had been made before the nineteenth century many did not accept Islam until the 1960s when it started to develop.[3] Up to now the region has a comparatively smaller number of Muslims. Christianity has more of a following in the south, with the southeast having more Christians among its population than anywhere else in the south. Christianity has many followers among the middle belt population (north-central) and a large following among the northeast population. Given this argument, Nigeria is not only a multiethnic country but also is made up of different religions and a variety of protest movements operating as sects within each religion.

In Nigeria churches started breaking as protest in 1891, and since then several separated churches have been in existence in the country. This separation found in Christianity is equally present in Islam. Consequently, until recently two dominant brotherhoods existed in Nigeria: *Qadiriyya* and *Tijjaniyya*. More recently, a third group, the *Izalatul bidi'a wa ikamatus Sunna* (usually shortened to *Izala*) with an equally large following (particularly among youths) emerged. This seemed to change the nature of the conflict. For example, from 1906 to the early 1970s conflicts were mainly between *Qadiriyya* and *Tijjaniyya*. In the mid-1970s the pattern changed to conflicts between the traditional rival sects (*Qadiriyya* and *Tijjaniyya*) on one side and the *Izala* on the other. Thus, religious conflicts in Nigeria usually take any of the following forms: Muslim–Christian, Muslim–Muslim or Christian–Christian conflict. With the change of government from military to civilian, more cases of ethnoreligious conflicts have been recorded. According to the Kano State Government Position Paper on Violent Crime and Illegal Weapons:

> In the last two decades, hardly would any year come and pass without one or more incidence of ethno-religious and political violence. Since the inception of the Fourth Republic the problem has exploded in an alarming rate. Some of the spectacular incidences of ethno-religious crises include Kafanchan crises (1987 and 2000), Tafawa Balewa crises (1992), Kaduna crisis (2000 and 2002), Jos crisis (2000), Tiv–Jukun (mid 1980s to date), Nassarawa crisis (2001) Ife–Modakeke (from the 1990s) Lagos/Shagamu (2000), Ijawa–Itsekiri (intermittent), Ijaws and Ilaris (intermittent) Umuleri and Uguleri (intermittent) OPC attack. . . . In Kano State the incidences include those of 1991, 1995, 2000 and more recently, 2004.[4]

This chapter attempts to explain the incidences of religious conflicts in Nigeria drawing some cases from Kano.[5]

THE ETHNIC CHARACTERISTICS OF KANO

As indicated by Paden, by 1954–1955 the Sabon Garin Kano had sixteenth ethnic groups out of which ten are Nigerians.[6] The remaining six are from other African countries and other parts of the world. The ethnic groups that do not seem to be reflected in the classification are the ones from the Jema'a Federation (now Southern Kaduna), Plateau State, and what used to be called North-Eastern State (the present Bauchi, Borno, Adamawa, Taraba, and Yobe States). Such ethnic groups were likely to be found in other early immigrant settlements, such as Tudun Wada and Brigade, where the majority of the World War II veterans and Bompai industrial workers settled. The first Yoruba man to settle in Kano came in 1819. Igbos are likely to have settled around 1910 but outnumbered the Yoruba after 1945. It will not be incorrect to say that the present Kano population is made up of all Nigerian ethnic and religious groups.

SOME CASES OF RELIGIOUS CONFLICT IN KANO

Most works on religious and political conflicts in Nigeria and Kano, e.g. Paden, Abdullahi, Balogun, Albasu, and so on seem to agree that from the 1950s to date the entire crisis that took place in Kano had two main undertones: religious and or political.[7] According to Balogun:

> Ethnic and religious differences partly explain the division between the North is sometimes violently torn apart by the *tariqas*—the *Qadiriyya* and the *Tijjaniyya* and their opponent *Izala*. For a long time differences between *Qadiriyya* and *Tijjaniyya* Muslim adherents have created problems at various levels of confrontation including violent physical clashes which left some of the confronting Muslims dead.[8]

Balogun's position seems to be more relevant to Kano than any other part of Nigeria as evident in the following cases.

1. During the first republic attempts were made by both the ruling party (the Northern Peoples' Congress, NPC) and the opposition party (the Northern Element Progressive Union, NEPU) to manipulate sectarian differences. For example, to win the minds of ignorant voters as the 1964 elec-

tion was drawing close, the Sardauna of Sokoto of the NPC allegedly circulated a genealogical tree *(Salsalatu Shajaratu)* tracing his descent to Prophet Muhammad. To counter that move, the NEPU organized a lecture in Kaduna to explain the implication of Sardauna's claimed origin and, that since Prophet Muhammad (his said root) was not a Nigerian, then Sardauna was an alien. The differences and hostility between *Qadiriyya* and *Tijjaniyya* are far from being resolved in Kano and all over Nigeria. The emergence of *Izala* greatly lessens the tension between these two traditional groups. *Izala* is against anything outside the Qur'an and *Sunnah*. This movement effectively started in Jos; from the late 1970s to date Kano seems to have more *Izala* followers than elsewhere in Nigeria. Several interpretations and disagreements (in both print and electronic media) have taken place between either *Qadiriyya* and *Tijjaniyya* or both and *Izala*.

2. In 1953 a riot occurred to cleanse Kano from the non-Muslim tribes. This riot resulted in thirty-six deaths, 241 wounded, and destruction of properties.

3. In April 1980, clashes between Muslim preachers and their audiences left two dead. In May of the same year, *Tariqa* (a name being used for either *Qadiriyya* or *Tijjaniyya*) and *Izala* disagreements resulted in the death of a follower.

4. In December 1980, Maitatsine, a Muslim scholar, wanted to purify Islam. In particular, he was against materialism and a worldly life style. With over 4,000 followers, he led an uprising aimed at bringing about Islam and his thought. Over 4,177 people died, 8,712 were wounded, and properties were destroyed.

5. In October 1982 Muslim students in Kano demonstrated over the building of a church in a mosque area. The riot resulted in death and destruction of properties.

6. In March 1987 a religious riot resulted in response to a preaching by a reverend at the College of Education Kafanchan in Kaduna State. The riot spilled over to Kano.

7. In October 1991 a riot erupted when a magazine used disrespectful language regarding Prophet Muhammad. The conflict started in Katsina State and spread to other parts of northern Nigeria.

8. In October 1991, Muslims demonstrated against the visit of Reverend Bonnke, a German preacher. Initially planned to be peaceful, the demonstration resulted in the most violent demonstration of its kind, with both sides armed with iron rods, swords, knives, and some sophisticated firearms. Eight people were killed and thirty-four wounded. Hotels, cinemas, residential houses, churches, and a mosque were destroyed, and shops were burned and looted.

9. In May 1992 riots occurred when people saw the dead and injured brought to Kano from the Zangon Kataf conflict.

10. In December 1994, a Shi'a group carried out a "sentence" of decapitation passed on Mr. Gideon Akaluka for allegedly arguing that the Bible is superior to the Qur'an and that the Qur'an is nothing more than toilet paper. People present when Mr. Akaluta made the statement wanted to kill him, but he was rescued by the police and taken to Goron Dutse Prison. A Shi'a group abducted him from the prison and carried out the sentence.

11. In March 1996, intra-Shi'ate groups clashed during a lecture at a mosque at Bayero University in Kano. The leader, who was the guest lecturer, was attacked by a faction of his group (*Tadjid al-Islamiyya*), which withdrew from the movement over certain interpretational disagreements. He was rescued and taken to a safe place in the vicinity of the mosque by the university's security force, as police were not invited. The faction was persuaded to leave as time for *Zuhr* (noon) prayer was fast approaching.

12. In June 1996, a Christian service in Theatre One, Bayero University, was attacked on Id-el-Kabir as a result of loud music coming from the service during prayer. Immediately after the prayer, youths (not university students) attacked and injured six people and destroyed the musical instruments. The situation was controlled (mainly) by the university's security force.

13. In August 1996, a clash between Shi'ates and *Tariqa* in Adakawa/Gwammaja during the *Maulud* celebration resulted in three persons being killed, fourteen injured, and property destroyed.

14. Retaliatory religious conflicts resulted in loss of lives and property in July 1999, October 2001, and October 2002 as responses to clashes between Muslims and Christians elsewhere in Nigeria—Plateau, Kaduna, and Shagamu. The most serious and destructive religious conflict in Kano history was the May 2004 two-day conflict that was a response to the attack on Muslims at Yelwan Shandam. Revenge was carried out. The sight of five hundred casualties brought from Yelwan Shandam and the Friday sermon by some of the Imams that very week most likely induced this. As opposed to previous violence, the May retaliation took place in almost all parts of Kano. Many people were killed, several were injured, houses were set on fire, motor vehicles were destroyed, and shops were looted and destroyed.

At this point there is the need to ask what the explanations of these conflicts and clashes are. It is that easy to explain religious conflict in Kano and Nigeria in general using a single factor. This chapter attempts to explain the factors responsible for religious conflict in Kano and to a larger extent in most Nigerian cities

EXPLANATIONS OF RELIGIOUS CONFLICTS

The Colonial Past

For their own convenience, the British merged different kingdoms and societies into one country and called it Nigeria. No effort was made to consider the distinct cultural and historical differences of the societies. This "deliberate" mistake was confirmed in a statement by the Parliamentary Private Secretary of State, British Colonial Office (1952–1959):

> During the debate for independence of Nigeria, the view of the Secretary of State at that time, with which I agreed was that in Nigeria we should attempt to put together a large and powerful state with ample materials resources which will play a leading part in the affairs of the continent and the world. This was attractive but it involved forcing several different ethnic and cultural groups into a single structure. . . . It should now be clear for all but the willfully blind to see that it is extremely dangerous to force diverse racial and social entities into a single rigid political structure.[9]

Thus, colonialism as Kukah observed has greatly contributed to fueled religious intolerance in Nigeria, promoting religious bigotry, suspicion, and hatred among various groups of the citizenry.[10] Consequent to the above, ethnoreligious conflict in post-independent Nigeria had been evident since the early 1950s but reached its peak in the period from 1979 to 1983. It resurfaced intensively after May 29, 1999, when power was handed over to civilians. Jega indicated that no less than forty violent ethnoreligious and communal clashes were recorded in the first three years of the Obasanjo administration.[11] Since then, many more have taken place. These have challenged the idea of a unified Nigeria while pointing to the fact that several contradictions central to national integration and development

that are rooted to the colonial past needed to be resolved. As Umar argued:

> Some of these contradictions were quite fundamental, e.g. the disparity in the economies of the regions, the seeds of neocolonial economy already planted by colonialism. There was also the contradiction of a secular polity in a predominantly religious society, as well as the contradiction of religious pluralism and sectarianism. This last contradiction, sectarianism, was particularly pronounced within the Muslim community.[12]

THE ROLE OF THE ELITES

Kuper and Smith developed an ethnic pluralism model sometimes referred to as ethnic conflict model to account for endemic conflict that sometimes manifest itself into serious violence in racially homogeneous but ethnically plural African societies.[13] They argued that African societies are made of several distinct ethnic groups of varying sizes, influence, and characteristics. These groups live side by side but separately, and they share certain values derived from common culture and race, as well as historical and contemporary experiences. They live and interact together. But because of different interests and the desire to maximize influence in a competitive situation, groups tend to use resources available to assert themselves in relation to other groups. The elite cadres of various groups engage in the struggle for control. This creates a situation of conflict among the ethnic groups.

In Nigeria any explanation of religious conflict will not be complete without mentioning the role the elites are playing in fueling the conflict. Elites are the normative reference group in the society. Accordingly, they are responsible for setting standards relevant to national development and greatness. Instead, they have resorted to manipulating religion for their personal rather than national interest. Elites compete over the nations' valued goods (appointment into office, contracts, influence, and other favors), which are usually scarce. So any move by one group is seen in terms of personal advantage over the other. Creating hostility, tension, and conflict between religious groups often pursues these jostling to get something out of the state resources. When there is conflict, the elites are those invited to solve the problem, and this brings them closer to the government and the attendant benefits. The elites encourage people to use violence so that they can gain greater favor from the government. More than this, the violence is a way of diverting the attention of the masses from the real issue, which is that the masses are suffering because of the elites' greed. As Jega has argued:

> . . . groups are mobilized, identities rigidly re-inforced, often infused with excessive religiosity, violent youth gangs and militia are formed and armed, and ethnic tension and conflict thereby facilitated.[14]

From the first republic to date, politicians—particularly those from the northern part of Nigeria—resorted to using religion to gain followers instead of using convincingly beneficial party programs. To date, politicians are fighting not over locating developmental projects or programs in their constituencies but over who gets what position in the local, state, and federal government boards and agencies. Nigeria is perhaps the only country where politicians start to campaign for another office/term on the day after being sworn into a political office (*Tazarce* syndrome). This explains the persistence of intra- and interparty conflicts throughout the federation. Each section is trying to get the sympathy of the masses, not by using a tangible socioeconomic development agenda but by using verses from the Qur'an and the Bible. This is what one reads and hears daily in all Nigerian print and electronic media.

ELITES AND THE POVERTY TRAP

Discussing the basis of conflict and consensus in Nigeria, Barongo made two propositions: (1) Ethnic and elite conflicts are reflections of the competing economic interests in the society and these interests are class based; (2) Ethnic and elite conflicts will tend to be intensed in a capitalist environment and less so in a society dominated by socialist values.[15]

The selfish interest-promoting activities of elites are made possible by unemployment and the abject poverty in which the majority of Nigerians are trapped since the introduction of the Structural Adjustment Programme (SAP) in the 1980s.[16] To most Nigerians today the attitude is that whatever will keep them alive is welcome. Consequently, people accept and comply with any idea that will give them food to eat that very day. Accordingly,

N100–N200 per person (less than $1.00–$1.50) is sufficient compensation for enlisting, in particular, jobless youth to commit arson, acts of vandalism, and violence, often with looting.

This author has seen people eating what they looted right at the scene and taking remaining goods away. Several poverty alleviation/eradication programs have failed to liberate the majority of the citizenry from the mess created by the SAP. As a result, in most urban and semiurban areas of Nigeria a large population of reserved "armies" is always willing to be mobilized to harass and intimidate people and destroy lives and properties for a small fee. To most of them the given reason for the violence and conflict is religious, which in reality is a cover for a more deep-seated economic hardship. Perhaps this explains why during each of these demonstrations and waves of violence anybody who looks economically okay regardless of tribal or religious background is at risk of being attacked. Even Muslims have been known to have been assaulted in so-called Muslim assaults on Christians. This forces one to really look at the genuineness of religious differences as the cause of these conflicts.

It is worth noting that most of those mobilized are the jobless youth (*'yan daba, 'yantauri, 'yan cuwa—cuwa, Almajirai,* and so on), mostly of rural origin, who are either not fully knowledgeable or are ignorant or unwilling to listen to religious teachings. Indeed, some operate under the influence of marijuana or drugs that can stimulate them and make them hyperactive, fearless, and merciless. The Kano Disturbances Tribunal of Inquiry observed:

> The *Almajiri* system, whereby an Islamic teacher collects young boys from their parents to take them elsewhere other than their home villages for the purpose of teaching them Islam, was in our opinion a major remote cause of the disturbance in Kano, when the tribunal visited . . . prisons where the captured fanatics were kept, we saw a number of children whose ages ranged from 10–14.[17]

Ten years later, a witness told a panel of investigations:

> It was obvious to me on arrival to Kano in the 1970s that unless the problem of juvenile beggars was addressed the late 80s and 90s will bring in the problem of "Adult beggars" and since idle hands are easy tolls to the devil, idle adults can easily be manipulated for

mischief making by those who do not wish Kano well. True to my suspicions these idle juveniles and adults became ready tolls for Maitatsine when he struck in the 80s and *'Yan Daba* when they became a huge threat at the end of the 80s and even now. When I discussed this matter with some highly placed indigenes I was told to leave the matter alone as it would anger some religious leaders if pressed further.[18]

SECTARIAN FACTOR

Scholars such as Alkali, Abdullahi, and Balogun have reported that Muslim communities experience violent protests that were sometimes expressed in religious confrontations between sectarian groups from 1906 to the 1980s.[19] To the present day, most of these protests were either against authorities or due to differences in the interpretation of certain verses in the Qur'an or in response to certain prescriptions or proscriptions in the *Sunnah*. What is consistently clear is that sectarian differences are political. Umar opined:

> The differences among sects cannot be correctly understood without taking the consideration of their concrete political underpinnings and that is why any attempt at resolving such differences will have little chances of succeeding if it fails to pay adequate attention to these political underpinnings. It was precisely this failure, which prevented a lasting solution to the sectarian conflicts within the Muslim community.[20]

As Last argued, sects have given the youth in northern Nigeria a new social grouping and heightened religious experience.[21] He cited the Jihad of 1804 and that those who fought the Jihad in places like Kano were all youths who protested against the dominant order—the sects—first *Qadiriyya* and *Tijjaniyya* in the 1920s, then *Izala* in the 1970s and 1980s. Unlike the first two sects, the followers of *Izala* see themselves as waging holy war against ignorance and mixing of religious values with Hausa traditional values. It is because of this that members of *Izala* are in conflict not only with the "traditional sects" (*Qadiriyya* and *Tijjaniyya*) but also with the authorities (traditional and modern). The Kano Disturbances Tribunal of Inquiry stated:

> In order to place in proper focus the remote causes of the Kano crises, it is necessary to refer to briefly the existence of different Islamic *Tariqa* groups in Northern

parts of Nigeria generally and Kano in particular. The coming of *Qadiriyya Tijjaniyya* . . . to Nigeria brought some slight differences in the method of worship hitherto practiced by the Muslims. The followers of each of these groups eventually saw their leaders as the only link with Allah! This certainly did bring differences between the groups resulting in serious clashes.[22]

RESPONSE TO THE PROBLEM

Panels or tribunals of inquiry are set up by either the federal or a state government following most religious conflicts in Nigeria. Their consistent terms of reference are finding out the root cause of the conflict and suggesting ways of future prevention. These individual bodies of inquiry usually work at uncovering the root causes and proposing remedies. The government usually does nothing, which is why many people believe that these bodies are set up just to cool tensions and not necessarily to address the problem. The reports submitted by such bodies are usually kept under lock and key while the problems keep resurfacing. But why does this do-nothing approach persist? The possible reasons are several.

First, most of these conflicts are precipitated by the elites. And after each incident, elites and their colleagues, with whom they share network and subculture, are made members of the investigative bodies. Thus, the decisions of these bodies are often suspected of being influenced by one group or another in the conflict. Consequently, one finds that complaints of unfair treatment from one or the other party in the conflict often trails the reports of most of these bodies of inquiry

Second, as noted previously, since the mid-1980s Nigerians have been experiencing serious economic hardship as manifested by unemployment and underemployment, inflation, and poor performance of the agricultural sector. Most bodies established to investigate the conflicts implicate the economic hardship that the citizenry is experiencing. Of course, several laudable government programs could no doubt address the problems, but they flounder in the process of their implementation. This explains the evidently rising number of the jobless and underemployed, not only in Kano but also in other Nigerian cities. This group of those negatively affected by economic hardship constitutes the usual pool from which the elites recruit for their egoistic, divisive, ideological propaganda and manipulation to carry out looting and killings, all in the name of "religion." This has implications not only for Nigerians but also for regional and global security.

Other problem-solving measures include the exchange of ideas among leaders of different religious groups. Not long ago the Kano State government conducted a seminar involving Christian and Muslim leaders. The establishment of Unity Colleges is another way of bringing children of different religions and tribes together, in this case for a period of six years. The idea is that through interaction, the students will learn to appreciate each other's way of life. In fact, this author is a product of one of such three schools established by the Government of the Northern Region However, it is not clear whether these measures are having a sufficient impact.

SUMMARY

This chapter addresses the issue of ethnicity and ethnic relations in Nigeria using cases of religious conflict in Kano as a reference point. While religious conflict takes place in most Nigerian cities, the choice of Kano is appropriate because Kano is among those with the highest incidence of religious conflict. Generally the foundation for ethnoreligious crisis was laid in the colonial past, but factors such as the deliberately divisive role the elites are playing and sectarian problems are all relevant in the explanation of religious conflicts, not only in Kano but throughout the Nigerian nation. Specifically for Kano, first, most religious conflicts from the early 1950s to date were direct responses to events in other parts of Nigeria and elsewhere in the world, particularly the Middle East—for example, when the United States attacked Libya, the Russians occupied Afghanistan. During the first Gulf War, the tension was so high that (speculatively) a popular department store in Kano changed its name from Fahad to Sahad Stores for fear of being attacked by people during the demonstration that was likely because the late King Fahd of Saudi Arabia teamed up with the United States against Saddam Hussein. Second, most of the rioters actively stealing, killing, and destroying are either ignorant of the teaching of Islam regarding

coexistence or are not ready to practice the religion according to the teachings of the Qur'an and the *Sunnah*. The majority of these rioters are underemployed or unemployed and mainly of rural origin. Third, the attacks in most cases tend to be indiscriminate, mostly targeting people who "do not look Hausa or Fulani" or that cannot speak Hausa or do not dress in modern ways. This category of people could be attacked even if they are Muslim. Fourth, traders, particularly the Igbos, are consistently targets because they have something to be looted. Fifth, attacks during a religious crisis cannot be adequately explained independently of economic, political, and tribal factors, but judging by the behavior of the rioters, the economic factor appears to weigh more heavily.

CONCLUSION

Even though made up of different cultures and religions, Nigeria has the necessary resources to prosper. For these resources to be meaningfully utilized for development and the betterment of all, sincere and effective leadership is needed at all levels of the polity (local, state, and federal), which this crop of self-centered elites is hardly capable of providing. Instead of working for peace and development of Nigerian society, the elites, particularly the politicians, are busy fighting each other to ensure their continued stay in elected offices. This is because in Nigeria today political office is one of the main sources of acquiring money and other opportunities (quickly) for politicians and their associates. This elucidates why a majority of the people no longer seems confident about the ability of the elites to truly liberate Nigeria from economic hardship, political instability, insecurity regarding life and property, and social injustice. As a result, people are turning to political parties that have the implementation of Shariah in their agenda The argument is that Shariah is a divine law and through it justice and accountability will prevail in all levels of the polity. With Shariah their problems can be solved. This explains why many in the northwest zones (particularly Kano and Zamfara States) voted for governments that have the implementation of Shariah on their agenda. To date, many in the states where Muslims are the majority are calling for the implementation of Shariah, apparently because of the elites' failure to deliver under the secular government. This call is likely to continue, particularly if the Shariah governments of Kano and Zamfara States are able liberate their people from the aforementioned problems.

RECOMMENDATIONS

The following recommendations are offered:

1. Having noted that most participants in urban conflicts are of rural origin, government needs to strengthen policies and programs of agricultural development and rural industrialization. This will stem rural exodus. On the other hand, the urban manufacturing industries that have either closed down or are functioning below capacity should be resuscitated through the creation of an enabling environment by government at both the federal and state levels

Strategy of Implementation
Integrated agricultural development to foster people in rural areas to actively participate in both rainy and dry seasons farming and to further encourage the formation of cooperative societies, which can be funded through short-term loans with soft interest. Construction of road networks to link villages with local government headquarters and headquarters with state capitals. Provision of water and electricity to rural and semiurban areas, and improvement in the supply of water and electricity in urban areas. Establishing capital-intensive industries in urban areas and reviving the closed and partly functioning ones.

2. Schools at all levels of education should be made to review their curricula with a view to incorporating training in citizenship.

Strategy of Implementation
Civics to be taught at all levels of Nigerian education. Secondary school students' visits from one part of Nigeria to the other during long vacations. Experiences acquired from the visits to be documented and utilized by teachers, students, and policy makers.

3. The schools should include equally in their curricula a qualitative environment-oriented functional education that can guarantee a means of producing an independent living in a multiethnic nation.

Strategy of Implementation
Restructuring the curricula at primary and secondary school levels to include not only academic subjects but also vocational training. Emphasis should be placed on technology that is appropriate to the Nigerian environment so that the knowledge acquired can provide the graduates of the schools with a means of earning an independent living rather than relying on the government for white-collar jobs.

4. Government should ensure the provision of religious education that is rooted in nation building

Strategy of Implementation
Compulsory courses on religion and peaceful coexistence to be taught at all levels of Nigerian education. Emphasis placed on peace, tolerance, and consensus as significant elements for the development and survival of one unified Nigeria.

5. Government should embark on reorientation of all categories of elites against greed and self-centeredness.

Strategy of Implementation
Government at all levels to embark on mass enlightenment through seminars, workshops, jingles, and radio and TV drama. Nongovernmental organizations and community-based organizations to be involved in this enlightenment exercise. The exercise should denounce placing personal interest over national interest, in particular the seemingly institutionalized tradition of using money acquired (regardless of the manner) as a yardstick of measuring success and achievement in the society.

6. Government at all levels should resocialize religious leaders and scholars on proper interpretation of religious injunctions to promote harmony, tolerance, and transparency in the society.

Strategy of Implementation
Religious leaders to be educated on the significance of unity, peace, and harmony for the development of the Nigerian nation. This is to be achieved through seminars and workshops with participants from different religions and groups within a religion. The seminar should address the importance of understanding one another and the necessity of accommodating each other in a multiethnic nation for peace and progress.

ENDNOTES

1. A. Leon-Guerrero, *Social Problems* (Thousand Oaks, CA: Pine Forge Press, 2005).
2. Cited in S. P. I. Agi, *Political History of Religious Violence in Nigeria* (Calabar, Nigeria: Pigasiannn and Grace International Publishers, 1998).
3. I. S. A. Balogun, "Islam in Nigeria: Its Historical Development," in *Nigeria Since Independence: The First 25 Years*, vol. ix: *Religious*, eds. J. A. Atanda, et al. (Ibadan, Nigeria: Heinemann Educational Book Limited, 1989).
4. *Report of the Committee for the Presentation of a Position Paper of the Kano State Government to the Presidential Committee on the Control Violent Crimes and Illegal Weapons*, July 2004, 2.
5. Kano is located in the northern part of Nigeria. It has been a commercial center since the trans-Saharan trade of the ninth century. It has been a political and administrative capital since colonial time. Currently, it is one of the most populous industrial cities in Nigeria, second only to Lagos.
6. J. N. Paden, *Religion and Political Culture in Kano* (Berkeley and Los Angeles: University of California Press, 1973).
7. See Paden, *Religion and Political Culture in Kano*; J. N. Paden, *Ahmadu Bello Sardauna of Sokoto: Values and Leadership in Nigeria* (Zaria, Nigeria: Hudahuda Publishing Company, 1986); S. U. Abdullahi, "On the Phenomenon of Religious Disturbances in Nigeria" (presented at the Nigeria Institute of Policy and Strategic Studies, Kuru, Jos, Nigeria, 1984); Balogun, "Islam in Nigeria"; and B. Albasu, "Recurring Eruption of Violence in Kano" (presented at the Kano Peace Forum, 2004).
8. Balogun, "Islam in Nigeria," 62.
9. P. B. Tanko, "Ethnicity, Religion and the Survival of Democracy in Nigeria," in *Ethno–Religious Conflict and Democracy in Nigeria: Challenges*, eds. E. E. O Alemika, and F. Okoye (Kaduna, Nigeria: Human Rights Monitors, 2002).
10. Kukah, 1989.
11. A. M. Jega, "Ethnic Tension in Nigeria: The Way Out" (paper presented at a Conference on The Ethnic Question, organized by the Nigerian Institute of Advanced Legal Studies, Abuja, Nigeria, 2002).
12. M. S. Umar, "Islam in Nigeria: Its Concept and Manifestations and Role in Nation Building," in eds. J. A. Atanda, et al., *Nigeria Since Independence: The First 25 Years*, vol. ix: *Religious* (Ibadan, Nigeria: Heinemann Educational Book Limited, 1989).
13. L. Kuper and M. G. Smith, eds., *Pluralism in Africa* (Berkeley and Los Angeles: University of California Press, 1969).
14. Jega, "Ethnic Tension in Nigeria," 3.
15. Y. R. Barongo, "Ethnic Pluralism and Democratic Stability in Nigeria: The Basis of Conflict and Consensus" (occasional paper, Department of Political Science, Bayero University, Kano, 1981).
16. The economies of developing countries in Africa, Asia, and Latin America are characterized by structural rigidities in the production and consumption sectors, which are said to be the basic impediments to the growth and development process of these countries. The Structural Adjustment Programme is a measure that originated from the international development agencies (notably the World Bank and the International Monetary Fund) to address the problem of these structural rigidities.
17. *Report of the Kano Disturbances Tribunal of Inquiry*, April 1981, 94.
18. *Report of the Panel of Investigation on Kano Disturbances*, October 1991, 18–19.
19. A. H. Alkali, "The Mahdi of Toranke," *Kano Studies*, vol.1, no. 4, (1968): 92–95. Abdullahi, "On the Phenomenon of Religious Disturbances"; and Balogu, "Islam in Nigeria."
20. Umar, "Islam in Nigeria," 79.
21. M. D. Last, "Religion of the Young in Northern Nigeria" (paper for discussion at Satterthwaite, n.d.).
22. *Report of the Kano Disturbances Tribunal*, 89.

ABOUT THE AUTHOR

Dr. Salisu A. Abdullahi is a reader, former head of University Security and former head of the Department of Sociology, Bayero University, Kano, Nigeria. He was a visiting research fellow at the School of African Studies, University of London (1994) and visiting scholar at the Cleveland State University (2005). His areas of teaching and research interests are criminology, social policy, and social problems. He was Special Adviser (Social Policy) to the Chief of General Staff and Vice-Chairman Provisional Ruling Military Council (Vice President) Federal Republic of Nigeria from 1998 to 1999. Dr. Abdullahi has served on various national and international committees and boards. He is a patron and member of different professional, occupational, and social organizations inside and outside Nigeria.

Lessons to Ponder: Insights and Advice from the Front Lines

Judy Carter

Ethnopolitical conflict, as this book's chapters attest, is complex. It is one of this century's gravest threats. Yet, ethnopolitical conflict remains difficult to understand, prevent, and mitigate. This text endeavors to shed light on ethnopolitical conflict and the deadly violence it produces. By sharing their perspectives from the front lines, this book's contributors have given voice to the realities and complexities of ethnopolitical conflict around the globe. They have explained its intransigence, and some have offered actionable recommendations on how to mitigate and prevent deadly ethnopolitical violence. Especially noteworthy is the chapter jointly authored by Edy Kaufman, an Israeli, and Manual Hassassian, a Palestinian. By example, they show that dialogue, respect, and mutual learning deepen understanding and promote peace.

The need for such understanding and new approaches is pressing. Ethnopolitical conflict poses a threat to global security. That broader, deeper understandings and alternative foreign policies and intervention approaches are required is underscored not only by the intransigence and tragic deadliness of ethnopolitical conflict but also by the malevolence aimed at developed Western nations and their citizens. When this anthology was conceived, the world was reverberating from the aftershocks of the September 11, 2001, terrorist attacks on the United States. As the book went to press, the United States' so-called War on Terror was continuing unabated. So, sadly, were many of the ethnopolitical conflicts about which contributors wrote. The Israel–Palestine, India–Pakistan, Nigerian, and Rwandan conflicts were continuing to cost lives. Disputes between people in Turkey and Greece, Croatia and Serbia, Macedonia and Albania, and Cyprus had become simmering stalemates punctuated by isolated but deadly and demoralizing incidents of protest. In Northern Ireland and Sri Lanka, war-weary residents were attempting to preserve fragile peace agreements. In other countries, such as Sudan, Liberia, Sierra Leone, and the Democratic Republic of Congo, however, ethnopolitical violence appeared to be escalating.

Bombings, fatalities, and fears of escalating violence continue to dominate daily headlines. Interest-based negotiation, conceived and promulgated primarily by U.S. academics and widely regarded as the best way to manage and resolve interpersonal conflicts and some inter- and intragroup disputes, has failed to mitigate and eradicate complex intergroup ethnopolitical conflicts afflicting developing nations. Even unofficial Track II diplomacy and other interest-based offshoots have proven incapable of defusing complex, deep-rooted, interstate and intrastate conflicts that have erupted or escalated since the end of the U.S.–Soviet Union Cold War. In previous eras, developed nations may have been able to disregard or dismiss overseas ethnopolitical conflicts. Today, they ignore developing nations' struggles at risk to their own security.

Reflecting on the ubiquity and persistence of ethnopolitical conflict, some questions beg answers. Why do old ethnopolitical conflicts keep recurring and new ones keep erupting? What forces and factors cause and exacerbate ethnopolitical conflict? What role should outsiders, be they individual peacemakers or international organizations, presume to play? What lessons can be learned by studying ethnopolitical conflicts? How can ethnopolitical conflicts be prevented or at least the violence and tragedy associated with them reduced? What steps must the world take to advance and achieve sustained peace?

The aim of this concluding chapter is to summarize and synthesize the lessons that can be drawn from the stories that contributors bravely shared from the front lines of conflict zones around the world. Collectively, contributors' chapters offer illuminating insights into the origins and dynamics of ethnopolitical conflicts, plus advice on preventing, mitigating, and recovering from such conflicts. Contributors' explanations and stories answer many questions. They also make points regarding international actors' intervention practices, ethics, and responsibilities.

This chapter discusses common causes and predictable patterns that characterize most ethnopolitical conflicts. Using contributors' accounts from the front lines, I first describe ethnopolitical conflicts' etiology and devolutionary dynamics. Next, I use contributors' reports to extract insights regarding the forces and factors that exacerbate tensions and incite violence. The role that identity and politics—internal and external or international—play in the origination and exacerbation of interstate and intrastate conflicts are explored. Finally, I summarize the recommendations contributors offer on how to manage and prevent interstate and intrastate war and ethnopolitical violence most effectively and respectfully. Special attention is given to contributors' suggestions that developed nations have an ethical responsibility and vested interest in thinking about and acting differently toward developing nations plagued by ethnopolitical conflict.

While *Perspectives from the Front Lines* is about violent conflict, it is equally about peace. Better understanding of ethnopolitical conflict, I hope, will motivate readers. My sincerest aspiration is that contributors' stories, explanations, and recommendations will deepen and broaden the insights of students, policymakers, decision makers, corporate and religious leaders, the media, and others. I hope these pages will inspire all to act in ways that promote sustainable peace.

CAUSES OF CONFLICT

Defining and understanding ethnopolitical conflict is, of course, a prerequisite to preventing or at least containing it and helping war-torn nations rebuild. Pinpointing the origins of some conflicts can be difficult. In the conflicts discussed in this anthology, land (and access to other natural resources, notably oil and water), power, history, identity, sovereignty, self-determination, politics, economics, race, language, religion, ancestry, ethnicity, and values appear capable of causing and exacerbating conflict. Poverty, injustice, oppression, foreign invasion and intervention, lack of education, corruption, loss of face, victimization, dehumanization, demonization, ideological differences, vengeance, and bystander compliance or encouragement can cloud and intensify ethnopolitical conflict. In reality, most ethnopolitical conflicts are complex and multifactored.

Of the many forces and factors that can cause or exacerbate ethnopolitical conflicts, two that stand out in this collection are identity and politics. Politics seems to precipitate the most volatile conflicts, while threatened large-group identity and conflicting values appear to precipitate the most intractable conflicts. Reasons for ethnopolitical conflicts being so resistant to resolution are that (1) neither identity nor values are negotiable and (2) politics are endlessly vulnerable to internal and external power struggles, manipulation, co-optation, and foreign interference.

Ethnopolitical conflict, this anthology's contributors suggest, is often fueled by ethnonationalism. Ethnonationalism and identity can be difficult to define. They may derive from those sentiments that "when the chips are down, effectively command people's loyalty," (Batsinduka), or they may be "what remains when one has forgotten everything else."[1] Identity is made doubly difficult to define by the speed with which people now revolve around the planet in today's global society. People who relocate frequently sometimes feel they belong to no particular place or group. Yet, the need to belong remains a compulsive drive.[2] Ironically, globalization—arguably only a euphemism for colonization—and modernity are intensifying disputing parties' need to safeguard and assert their identity. Fear of modernity and globalization are especially evident and incendiary in traditional, patriarchal, and Muslim societies such as Nigeria, Sri Lanka, the former Yugoslavian republics, and many others.[3]

The ability of students, policymakers, and power brokers in developed countries to truly understand the devastation that ethnopolitical conflict wreaks on developing regions of the world is pivotal. Few Westerners, insulated and isolated from the realities of ethnopolitical conflict as they are, can truly comprehend ethnopolitical conflict's horrific consequences. For them, the number of people who are dead, missing, or displaced is incomprehensible.

Statistics and stories in contributors' chapters paint a grisly picture, one that is hard for most Westerners to comprehend. An estimated five million Turkish Muslims were killed and another five million refugees were forced to flee when Greece invaded Turkey (Oymen). During its history, Cyprus has been occupied by fifteen different conquerors, which caused considerable hardship (Atakol). People have lost close relatives and been forcefully placed, sometimes several times in quick succession (Atakol; Mavratsas). Yugoslavia endured two waves of ethnopolitical violence, from 1918 to 1941 and 1945 to 1991 (Klain). In 1995 in Srebrenica, 14,000 people were expelled and 8,000 went missing; the fates of 1,500 Croats remain unknown (Biserko). Macedonians endured "unspeakable terror" (Petroska-Beska and Kenig). The Israeli–Palestinian conflict has brought about "bloodshed at least once a decade" (Kaufman and Hassassian) and sent hundreds of thousands of citizens into exile.

Pakistani officials estimate that 60,000 Kashmiris have been killed since 1989. Thousands more languish in jails where they are tortured. Human rights organizations regularly report extrajudicial killings, disappearances, arbitrary detentions, individual and gang rapes, torture, and other large-scale human rights violations, as well as the deliberate destruction of entire villages (Hussain). During two decades of ethnic conflict, an estimated 60,000 Sri Lankans died and many more were injured and displaced (Ratnavale). The outbreak of violence in Rwanda in 1990 caused the internal displacement of 300,000 Rwandans. Other Rwandans who fled earlier spent thirty-five years in exile. One of the most shocking ethnopolitical conflicts included in this text is the 1994 massacre of over one million Rwandan Tutsis and nonextremist Hutus (Batsinduka). Many Rwandan genocide survivors watched their loved ones being hacked to death with machetes. Batsinduka lost his entire family.

Many survivors of ethnopolitical conflict are haunted by nightmare-making scenes of violence. Casey reports fleeing from rioting Nigerian youths who were brandishing guns, machetes, and handmade weapons. While escaping, she saw two men being pulled off their motorcycles and beaten to death. Others who witnessed the riot report seeing busloads of people being shot and others being burned in gasoline-soaked tires. Some Croatians remember soldiers invading villages, robbing houses, and "killing babies in their cradles" (Klain). Others remember heart-wrenching scenes of children being pulled from parents who were destined for concentration camps. Ratnavale recalls Sri Lanka children being turned first into soldiers and second into "cannon fodder." Many victims are plagued by memories of relatives who simply "disappeared."

In addition to memories of atrocities, survivors are dealing with the aftermath of ethnopolitical violence. Many are maimed for life. Some victims are debilitated by post-traumatic stress syndrome (Klain). Others were raped and are dealing with HIV-AIDS; children are being orphaned (Batsinduka).

The horror and barbarity of ethnopolitical conflict's consequences underscore the imperativeness of learning how to effectively prevent and defuse it. As tragic as ethnopolitical conflict's predictability is, that same predictability offers hope. By understanding the down-spiraling pattern that characterizes most conflicts, students and others will be able to see, first, how important prevention and early intervention are and, second, that peace-promoting overtures can be initiated at any time.[4]

PATTERNS OF CONFLICT

When it comes to understanding ethnopolitical conflicts and extracting useful, peace-promoting lessons, understanding their etiology and evolution is a useful first step. As contributors' chapters confirm, nearly all ethnopolitical conflicts devolve following the same sad storyline.[5]

Many ethnopolitical conflicts can be traced back to a specific event or a slow but growing threat. In Sri Lanka, the incident that precipitated the 1983 riots and ensuing all-out war was the killing of thirteen Sri Lanka Army soldiers by Tamil Tigers (Ratnavale). The arrival of Jewish settlers, with their political and economic ideas and ways of living, posed a "great threat" to the indigenous Palestinian population. Each new *aliyah* (wave of immigration) intensified their fears (Kaufman and Hassassian). In many cases, the origins of one ethnopolitical conflict arch back to another ethnopolitical conflict. The conflict between Greece and Turkey, for example, goes back to the Byzantine and Ottoman empires. Rwanda's genocide can be traced back to the country's colonization.

Events and threats that spark ethnopolitical conflict can be classified into five broad, often-interrelated categories: (1) large-scale immigration, foreign aggression, invasion, occupation, or intervention, (2) abuses of power, oppression, unjust control, and corruption, (3) lack of autonomy, threats to democracy or self-rule, and challenges to sovereignty, (4) extreme poverty, fascist authoritarianism, extreme violence, terrorism, and human rights abuses, and (5) threats to identity or way of life. On the topic of threats, it is important to note that they can be real or perceived. Intangible threats to cultural traditions, ethnic customs, language, beliefs and values, religious freedom, and national identity can be as potent as threats to economic resources and political power.

Misunderstanding, miscommunication, misperception, and misinformation exacerbate conflict and fuel mistrust. So do deception, trickery, manipulation, and broken promises (Batsinduka; Hussain; Kaufman and Hassassian; Oymen). India and Pakistan's conflict over Kashmir hinges on Kashmiris' contention that the Instrument of Accession, assigning their principality to India, is invalid if not fraudulent. They resent India's forceful occupation of Kashmir and think India's promise to withdraw is a lie (Hussain). In Turkey's view, Greece's decision to deploy troops and conduct military activities on Aegean islands was a breach of trust that violated the 1932 Treaty of Lausanne and the 1947 Treaty of Paris (Oymen). Turkish Cypriots think Greek Cypriots have deceived the world for forty years with their claims of wanting to establish a bizonal, bicommunal federation (Atakol).

Typically, the persistence of conflict and the violation of trust cause positions to harden and animosities to escalate. Palestinian–Israeli relations, initially characterized by *sammud* or steadfastness against Israeli occupation, degenerated into violence and active uprising. When the first nonviolent *intifada* failed to produce results, the second, more violent al-Aqsa Intifada emerged (Kaufman and Hassassian). Frustration over failed peace processes, the Israeli Defense Forces' brutality in the West Bank and Gaza Strip, and Palestinian president Yassir Arafat's failed leadership led Palestinians to take matters into their own hands.

Mistreatment and breaches of trust leave deep scars, as events in Cyprus illustrate. Although Turkish Cypriots' political equality was enshrined in Cyprus's constitution when the republic was formed in 1960, they became stateless hostages in 1963. Not only did Greek Cypriots steal Turkish Cypriots' state from them, but the former allegedly then "used every means at hand to attack, terrorize, and destroy" the latter (Atakol). Greek Cypriots effectively imprisoned and ghettoized Turkish Cypriots. They denied Turkish Cypriots access to telephone, water, electricity, and government services. Turkish Cypriots could not cultivate their land, conduct business and trade, or participate in sports or cultural activities. They could not communicate or travel freely; mail was restricted, and travelers vanished or were killed (Atakol).

Such systematic discrimination and impoverishment breed resentment, explain Petroska-Beska and Kenig. Gradually, peaceful resistance gives way to radicalization and rebellion. Issues multiply. Bitter feelings over being treated like second-class citizens fester and grow (Kaufman and Hassassian; Ratnavale). So do fear and blaming. When group members become fearful, they magnify threats and seek support from other members of their identity group. To coalesce, groups need something or someone specific on which to focus. They typically attribute the cause of the conflict to the other side or out-group. Each side blames the other for being unreasonable, exacerbating the conflict, and thwarting efforts to peacefully resolve differences. In Northern Ireland, for example, Catholics blamed the British government. They accused political and economic elites of seeking to maintain their power by keeping working-class citizens impoverished and divided. They also accused Britain of encouraging Protestants to "take up more extreme positions" (Byrne). Protestants, on the other hand, claimed the "Troubles" were the Catholics' fault, because they were in league with the Vatican. Protestants believed they must guard against "treasonous collaborators" (Byrne), who were disloyal to the Queen and were willing to sell their birthright and let foreign (Roman) powers influence their affairs.

Once enemy targets have been identified, stereotypes emerge and ostracization follows. Most stereotypes are mythical fabrications used to justify condescending attitudes and "us versus them" behavior (Byrne). Stereotypes can range from mild to extreme. Greeks, for example, consider Turks to be barbarian Asian invaders who destroyed the Byzantine Empire and constrained Hellenism's greatness. They blame Turks for Greece's economic, political, and social underdevelopment. In their view, Turks are dishonorable and unethical, while Greeks are "almost perfect" (Ifantis). From Hutus' perspective, Tutsis are "alien feudal lords who stole their land, killed their kings, and enslaved their ancestors" (Batsinduka). They see Tutsis as an arrogant minority, who imposed *ubuhake,* a feudal system of land tenancy, on the Hutu majority and humiliated and exploited them. They are land grabbers and warmongers. Similarly, Macedonians see Albanians as uncivilized, uneducated, duplicitous, disloyal, and dangerous. They are "naive, ignorant, illiterate peasants who can be turned into terrorists overnight" (Petroska-Beska and Kenig). Albanians' blind obedience to fanatical religious leaders, culturally inculcated worship of weapons, and willingness to die as martyrs allegedly make them capable of, if not predisposed to, unspeakable brutality. Added to this perception are the Albanians' warlike nature, insatiable greed, ability to manipulate the international community, and desire to "take everything that belongs to Macedonians" (Petroska-Beska and Kenig), including their cultural heritage.

As conflicts degenerate, stereotypes are used to justify violence against others who have been labeled as "enemies." As enmity increases, each group tells its members "what merciless, unscrupulous perpetrators *they* are" and "what innocent victims *we* are" (Petroska-Beska and Kenig). "We are trustworthy, peace loving, honorable, humanitarian; they are treacherous, warlike and cruel" (Ratnavale) is a common chorus. At the same time, disputing parties denigrate each other; they often invent stories that aggrandize their own reputation. Serbs, for example, claim to be "the backbone of the Balkans" (Biserko). Their supposed superiority stems from the myth that they liberated all other Yugoslav people and are therefore entitled to their own nation.

The wider the rifts grow, the less contact the disputing parties have with each other. Lack of contact forces members of disputing parties to accept stereotypes. In-group–out-group thinking paves the way for prejudice, racism, and discrimination. An example of such prejudice occurred following the 1920 partition of Northern Ireland. The Protestant-supported majority government discriminated against Catholics, restricting their access to housing, education, employment, and positions of economic and political power. Protestants gerrymandered electoral boundaries. Constabularies harassed Catholics and jailed young men "for no reason" (Byrne). British troops sent to protect Catholics broke into and burned their homes. Another example of discrimination comes from Greece, which outlawed any reference to "Turkishness" because the word "Turkish" "endangered public order" (Oymen). For a time, Greece also stripped people of "non-Greek origin" who left Greece of their Greek citizenship. Greece forbade foreigners, diplomats, or journalists from entering a forbidden military zone, limited Turks' property rights, denied their right to elect religious leaders, provided substandard schooling, limited access to secondary education, and limited their economic opportunities (Oymen). Albanians living in Macedonia experienced similar discrimination. They could not speak their language freely, gain access to education, influence political decisions, or obtain government jobs. They were persecuted, kidnapped, mistreated, interrogated, beaten, and killed or vanished. Police and army officials violated their human rights (Musa). In Rwanda, Tutsis were forced to carry an identity card, which was like "having the yellow Star of David on one's chest under the Third Reich's rule in Germany" (Batsinduka). Anti-Semitism, discrimination, occupation, and mistreatment have played a pivotal role in the Israeli–Palestinian conflict (Kaufman and Hassassian).

Over time, prejudice paves the way for demonization and dehumanization. Name calling begins. Enemies describe each other as animals, aliens, or witches. Yesterday's neighbors become untrustworthy dogs, genetically defective simpletons whose inferiority is implanted in their genes" or uncivilized savages without morals or ideology (Biserko; Casey; Petroska-Beska and Kenig). Gradually, enemies cease to be human; they become a scourge that needs to be expelled or "cleaned" away (Klain).

Denigrating, demonizing, and dehumanizing others make it easier to justify attacking or exterminating them (Casey). Demonization and dehumanization lead to human rights violations and ethnic cleansing, as occurred in Yugoslavia and Rwanda. Popular slogans such as "The only good Chetnik (Serb), Ustasha (Croat), or Tutsi is a dead one" foreshadow violence. At a certain point, violence, torture, and murder become justifiable. They stop being wrong. They become self-defense tactics (Kaufman and Hassassian). Palestinians' *intifada* and the 1967 Six-Day War are cases in point. So was Protestants' assertion that in Northern Ireland political violence was a right (Byrne). When conflict reaches this point, political and opinion leaders often advance the notion that war and ethnic cleansing are "legitimate means of achieving justifiable objectives" (Biserko). Killing becomes, as it did in Hutus' minds, a patriotic duty, not a crime. In Rwanda, explains Batsinduka, killing Tutsis was *gukora* (work), for which people expected rewards, not rebukes.

As violence escalates, disputing groups may commit acts intended to shock or provoke their enemies. For example, the beheading of a Nigerian prisoner was judged to be a well-planned, deliberately orchestrated plot skillfully executed by fanatical religious zealots (Casey). India and Pakistan's decisions to test nuclear weapons served as reciprocal saber rattling that increased tensions in both nations and abroad. In Rwanda, Tutsi parents became reluctant to send their children to school, church, or the marketplace, or to fetch water or wood, for fear they would be insulted, beaten, tortured, or killed, recalls Batsinduka.

As atrocities escalate, disputing groups feel compelled to separate themselves from each other. In Nigeria, Muslims used Shari'a law to separate themselves physically, socially, economically, and spiritually from "infidels" (Casey). Cypriot Turks and Greeks keep to their own. In the absence of contact, there is typically little or no hope of dialogue, much less a reduction in violence. Even conciliatory gestures are interpreted as disingenuous offerings or even threats, in part because they trigger memories and mistrust (Atakol).

Typically, parties become increasingly intransigent; their conflict becomes increasingly intractable. Each incident further justifies intensifying attacks against "the enemy," hardening positions, and calling on group members to redouble their resolve, as happened in Sri Lanka (Ratnavale). Extremism emerges and is condoned. Once violence, torture, and murder become justifiable, terrorist organizations and guerilla groups either emerge or grow in visibility. Often, the emergence of one extremist organization will spark the formation of an opposing organization. Greek Cypriots' formation of the National Organization of Cypriot Fighters (EOKA), a militant reunification organization, goaded Turkish Cypriots into starting their own underground organization. Likewise, increasing Israeli aggression prompted Palestinian Liberation Organization (PLO) members to employ more violent tactics.

Violence begets counterviolence and, in some cases, ignites war.

When violence reaches a certain level, citizens who have purposely remained on the sidelines feel pressured to choose sides. Fear draws them into the fray. When Albanian extremists began attacking civilian targets, ambushing and murdering security forces, and kidnapping innocent people, Macedonians felt compelled to support and seek protection from terrorists, or risked being used as human shields (Petroska-Beska and Kenig). When an entire community is consumed by conflict, no one is left to lobby for peace.

One particularly peculiar phenomenon associated with protracted conflict is implosion, which typically expresses itself as infighting or mutiny. Intrastate ethnopolitical conflict is an example of such infighting. In Yugoslavia, following the end of the U.S.–U.S.S.R. Cold War, long-suppressed animosities and political aspirations were unleashed. Identity groups comprising the federation each strove to assert their agenda and resurrect Greater Serbia, Greater Albania, and the like, using violent means if necessary (Klain; Petroska-Beska and Kenig). Disputing parties' power struggle sped the federation's collapse.

An offshoot of implosion is scapegoating. If intragroup dissension is suppressed, it must be dissipated or the group will self-destruct. A safe way of dissipating intragroup differences and power struggles is to choose a sacrificial victim or scapegoat. Rwandan Tutsis, former Communist leaders, and various Balkan minorities have served this purpose (Batsinduka; Klain).

At some point, disputing groups pass a point of no return. They become locked into an all-out, do-or-die battle. Warring factions become obsessed with annihilating their enemies. They stop caring about costs or their own survival. In the "red heat" of war, combatants with little or nothing to lose adopt the view that "If I'm going down in flames, I'll take you with me." At this point, called entrapment—disputing parties become ensnared in their conflict. They are unable to extricate themselves. They cannot back down, for fear of losing face, political power, or in some cases their lives.

Finally, disputing groups reach an impasse, as is the case in Israel and Palestine, India and Pakistan, Turkey and Greece, and Cyprus. Theoretically, when disputants reach a "mutually hurting stalemate," their conflict is ripe for intervention and peacemaking efforts. When war weariness saps soldiers' zeal, government and private funders have exhausted their resources, and parties are "sick and tired" of fighting, they are supposedly ready to explore diplomatic, legal, and political alternatives. Sri Lanka and Northern Ireland appear to have turned this corner, but most of the other conflicts reviewed in this book have not—a point that calls into question the appropriateness and effectiveness of the Western conflict management theories and approaches employed by international intervenors.

In addition to the financial, political, and social costs, violent and protracted ethnopolitical conflict sets in motion one final, especially insidious pattern that virtually ensures conflict will keep recurring—the transgenerational transmissions of conflict.[6] Transgenerational transmission occurs when adults project their feelings of enmity, anger, vengeance, and trauma onto children (Klain). Children inherit the conflict as if it were transmitted via "psychological DNA" (Klain). Because they model themselves after their elders and want to please them, children absorb and adopt adults' attitudes and motivations. Conflict is transmitted transgenerationally through stories of what the enemy did and how one's predecessors fought back (Atakol; Senehi). Even though children may have no contact with their supposed enemies, they are socialized to despise them. Palestinian and Israelis youths, despite being born after early clashes and having little contact, hate members of the other side (Kaufman and Hassassian). Youths' hatred is inherited. It breeds vengeance. Not only do members of the next generation mourn the past, they also often undertake to avenge the losses and humiliation their forebears suffered. In the former Yugoslavia many citizens are full of hatred and want to avenge the suffering and deaths of loved ones, as well as soldiers and civilians who were killed, maimed, or tortured, reports Klain.

Owing to transgenerational transmission, ethnopolitical conflict becomes ingrained in disputing parties' respective identities. Members of each group define themselves in relation to "the enemy." Eventually, enmity and conflict become the glue that binds the group together and the defining characteristic of its raison d'être (Hussain; Kaufman and Hassassian; Senehi). In such a case, "There can be no self without the other" (Senehi). Disputing parties become ensnared in the conflict because of the manner in which they define their identity. Enmity, hatred, and violence become embedded in disputing groups' collective psyche or culture (Kaufman and Hassassian; Ratnavale). In such societies, children grow up believing fighting is honorable and aggression and violence are justifiable (Klain). Living in a state of chronic conflict—something few Westerners can imagine—makes people fearful and frustrated; it leads to desperate, irrational behavior such as that of suicide bombers.

The insidiousness of transgenerational transfer is exemplified in cases in which the tables turn and the group that was oppressed gains power. Groups that have been oppressed often severely oppress those over whom they have power. Because hatred and vengeance are so deeply ingrained, oppressed groups gaining power know of no other way to rule but to mete out matching malevolence against their former rulers. Victims become victimizers, as occurred in Rwanda. In other cases, oppressed groups find a different group, often a minority, to victimize. In Sri Lanka, minority Muslims are struggling to assert their independent political, religious, and cultural identity and have a place to call their own (Ratnavale). In Nigeria, Yoruba and Muslims are using tools and techniques that "European Christian imperialists" used to suppress indigenous African groups against each other (Casey). In cases in which enmity is central to a group's identity, even if the "enemy" disappears, the group will find a new enemy.[7] At the end of the Cold War, when the Soviet Union no longer posed a threat, propagandists made Turkey the preeminent enemy, claims Oymen. The United States found new threats on which to focus.

The bitterness and vengeance resulting from protracted ethnopolitical conflict and transgenerational transmission can be intensified by poverty and political manipulation. Youths are especially easy to goad into action. In Kashmir, youths have become "desperate and radicalized by decades of political manipulation, misgovernance and corruption, denial of social justice and economic opportunities, and systematic abuse of personal liberties and human rights" (Hussain). In Nigeria, disenfranchised youths want not only to right the wrongs of the past but also to recoup Islam's past glory, authority, and autonomy. Muslim leaders are encouraging them to see themselves as heroic "Islamic revolutionaries" (Casey).

The insidiousness of ethnopolitical conflict is perhaps worst when children grow up in refugee camps or equally impoverished, futureless surroundings. When youths know nothing but war and hopelessness, they see few other options besides more war and violence, stress Kaufman and Hassassian. In some cases, the impetus to act is made all the more urgent by demographic time bombs ticking in conflicted, underdeveloped regions around the world

(Kaufman and Hassassian; Musa). Israelis, Macedonians, and Turkish Cypriots may soon be outnumbered by their opponents. High birthrates, driven in part by political and religious leaders' encouragement, are a threat. Similarly, Turkey's overpopulation problems are driving its demands for more air space and ocean access (Ifantis). People with no hope of gainful employment can easily be co-opted by fundamentalists, extremists, and terrorists.

That ethnopolitical conflicts devolve in a similar manner is clear. The constancy and predictability of the pattern suggests that there should be steps that others can take to prevent ethnopolitical conflict or at least prevent it from becoming violent and deadly. In fact, every turn in conflict's devolutionary down-spiral offers an opportunity to halt hostilities. Intervenors can act at any time. To maximize their effectiveness, though, intervenors first need to familiarize themselves with a range of forces and factors that typically ignite and inflame ethnopolitical conflicts.

FORCES AND FACTORS

Many forces and factors exacerbate ethnopolitical tensions and incite violence. Students and others attempting to deepen their understanding of ethnopolitical conflict should begin, contributors advise, by studying history. Understanding the history of overseas conflicts is an essential prerequisite to understanding their complexity and intractability—and the challenges confronting disputing parties and would-be intervenors (Byrne). Students and others must be able to move beyond their ethnocentric or Americentric perspectives in order to understand the ideological and moral values and political aspirations motivating ethnopolitical adversaries. To understand and judge disputing parties fairly, students and others must understand their history and environment, the conditions under which they lived, the ideas that filled their minds, the values and ideals that undergirded their choices, and the goals that motivated their actions (Ratnavale). Anything less is absurd and potentially irresponsible. Only by understanding history can outside observers hope to respond appropriately to ethnopolitical conflicts (Kaufman and Hassassian).

Because North America is so young, it is sometimes difficult to fathom how deep-rooted some ethnopolitical conflicts are. Conflicts ravaging the Balkans originated during the Middle Ages. The 1389 Battle of Kosovo and the subsequent fall of Constantinople marked the beginning of six centuries of Ottoman domination and ensuing Greek–Turkish discord (Ifantis). Northern Ireland's troubles began in 1178, when Catholics started fighting a guerrilla war with Britain's monarchy (Byrne). The 1601 Protestant Plantation of Ulster and the 1690 Battle of the Boyne further polarized Protestants and Catholics. Rwanda's troubles originate, according to ancient animist myth, when Immana (the Creator) created Gahutu, Gatwa, and Gatutsi, tested each, and decided that Gatutsi (Tutsis) would rule both Gahutu (Hutus) and Gatwa.

In addition to historical events, current forces and factors exert considerable influence on the devolution of ethnopolitical conflicts. Contemporary forces and factors that influence ethnopolitical conflicts' inception and exacerbation fall into two broad categories: internal and external. Interestingly, identity and politics feature prominently in both categories.

Internal Forces and Factors

In surveying internal forces and factors that influence ethnopolitical conflicts, land appears to be closely connected to identity and politics. As Kaufman and Hassassian explain, identity first and foremost requires a homeland. Jews are deeply bonded to the land around Mount Zion; they consider it to be their "promised land"—even though Arabs have occupied the land for more than a millennium. As Kaufman and Hassassian explain, Israelis and Palestinians share a common destiny: they are "doomed to live together."

Related to land and identity are sovereignty and self-determination. People want to influence decisions about their homeland and its politics. Place and space are more important than many North Americans realize. The conflict between Israel and Palestine is about "two nations fighting for a small piece of land," explain Kaufman and Hassassian. Israelis have been seeking a homeland for more than a century. Muslims have been fighting for freedom from foreign rule and influence, first from the Ottoman Empire, then the French and British, and now the United States. In the Israeli–Palestinian conflict, each side believes it is the "chosen people" entitled to the "chosen land" or at least a homeland. Sri Lankans exhibit a similar sense of entitlement and desire for autonomy (Ratnavale).

Israelis' and Palestinians' desire for their own homeland and Sri Lankan Tamils' efforts to secede illustrate the lengths to which disputing parties will go in fighting for an independent homeland. Macedonians have fought for generations to gain freedom from oppression and occupation. For ethnic Macedonians, threats to their homeland and control over it elicit deep-seated fears and strong reactions (Petroska-Beska and Kenig). After centuries of "slavery" and subjugation, their desire to resurrect, express, and nourish their ethnocultural identity is high—and worth defending. The Cypriot conflict also illustrates the potency of homeland attachment. Greek Cypriots see Cyprus as a Hellenic island and want to be reunited with Greece (Atakol). They see Turkish Cypriots as "Islamicized intruders" (Mavratsas) who do not belong on the island.

Beyond place and space, identity hinges on ethnicity, ancestry, race, religion, language, culture, and customs. Northern Ireland's protestants feel "psychologically bound" to Britain and the Queen, with bonds of blood, history, common ancestry, culture, and loyalty that cannot be bartered away (Byrne). Threats to these identificatory markers typically elicit fear and self-protection, as well as intransigence and retaliation. Sri Lankans saw Tamil agitation as a threat to Sinhalese "identity, security and territorial integrity" (Ratnavale). Croats interpreted Serbs' relentless bombing of Sarajevo as an attempt to "destroy and erase them" (Klain). Macedonians saw Albanians as "incomers" threatening their new-found independence and ethnocultural autonomy (Musa). The international community's acceptance of Albanians' rhetoric led Macedonians to fear being wiped off the world ethnic map (Petroska-Beska and Kenig). Turks interpreted Greece's ban against groups and individuals calling themselves "Turkish" as a denial of their identity (Oymen).

Fears of cultural, linguistic, or actual annihilation elicit defensive reactions and can thwart peace plans, as the United Nations discovered in 2004 when Greek Cypriots rejected Kofi Annan's peace plan because it would not adequately "protect their Greek identity" (Mavratsas). Threats to a group's identity can have a long-lasting impact, as is illustrated by the Greek–Turkish conflict. After 1,000 years of Byzantine rule and nearly five hundred years of Ottoman domination, avoiding foreign influence became a defining trait of Greeks' national identity. Greeks' fight for independence ultimately led to the Ottoman Empire's downfall, which Turks still resent. Greeks' thinking and choices, from foreign policy to defense planning, continue to be led by their mistrust of and contempt for the threat from the east. Turkey, on the other hand, remains devoted to preserving as much control in the region as it can. Political choices in and between Greece and Turkey are vestiges of ancient animosities (Ifantis; Klain).

Of course, aggression and violence exacerbate ethnopolitical conflict. But so too do memories of it. In Northern Ireland, marching season may commemorate historical victories for Protestants, but it also reinflicts painful memories for Catholics (Byrne). Likewise, ongoing political power struggles in Israel, Cyprus, and Kashmir serve as continuous reminders of past traumas (Atakol). Past memories are connected to present political events through a historical time warp called "time collapse." In protracted ethnopolitical conflicts, disputing groups each select memories of *chosen glories,* battles they won, and *chosen traumas,* battles they lost.[8] In some conflicts, disputing sides' stories of historic events differ substantively. Serbs and Croats have radically different interpretations of battles they fought. Memories of glories and traumas are kept alive through storytelling, as well as poetry, songs, celebrations, festivals, and other sometimes unconscious psycho-social forces.

Not only are memories of these incidents kept alive, but so are the emotions that accompanied them (Klain).[9] When new struggles or incidents of violence occur, memories and emotions of the past fuse with and often magnify reactions to present events. Thus, contemporary twenty-first-century incidents such as military and guerrilla attacks, bus and marketplace bombings, and mob riots commingle with memories of ancient wars and battles, assassinations, the murder, rape, and torture of innocent civilians, the destruction of sacred or historically significant buildings and monuments, and campaigns that threatened ethnocultural, linguistic, or spiritual annihilation. Even the unearthing of mass graves, trials for war crimes, current political power struggles, or manipulation by the international community can elicit old memories, fears, and hatred. Old emotions trigger reflex reactions. Owing to time collapse, disputing parties react as if they have just relived their chosen traumas and glories. New incidents seem as real as historic battles with the "auld enemy" (Senehi).

How past glories and traumas perpetuate ethnopolitical conflict is illustrated by events in Nigeria. Nigeria's chosen traumas—colonization by the British, amalgamation of the north and south, Biafra's attempted secession, and the resulting civil war—are generating an undercurrent of antagonism (Casey). Arguments about ethnicity, religion, and politics are intense. Ethnoreligious tensions between Muslim Hausas and Christian Igbos have re-arisen. Critics and dissenters, unwilling to accept Shari'a law and grant political power to Muslim clerics, are being ostracized and attacked. Violence is mounting. A similar pattern is evident in Rwanda. Rwanda's 1994 genocide was committed by people who for the most part had never experienced Tutsi *ubuhake,* domination, or discrimination, because they were too young. Rather, they had absorbed ancient enmities and desires for vengeance from others (Batsinduka).

In conflicted societies, stories, songs, poems, and celebrations keep alive memories and emotions associated with them. They memorialize past glories and traumas. They help define and reinforce disputing groups' identity, often in terms of opposition to the "other." Stories and other histocultural transmitters are used to socialize children, transmit ancient enmities to subsequent generations, and keep animosities alive. In Northern Ireland, Catholics commemorate Bloody Sunday, the day that Protestants attacked civil rights activists marching for equal rights and British paratroopers shot and killed fourteen innocent, unarmed Catholic civilians protesting against British occupation. Protestant Unionists gather in local pubs to tell stories the evening before annual Orange Order parades held throughout Northern Ireland to commemorate the victory of William of Orange at the Battle of the Boyne. Local landmarks such as shops, schools, churches, and homes are described with reference to stories about the violence that occurred at them (Byrne; Senehi). In refugee camps, stories, plays, games, and songs play a vital role in the preservation of memories, history, identity, culture, and tradition (Ratnavale). Stories are sometimes used to politicize events, encourage political mobilization, and promote violence. In Rwanda, traditional stories, songs, and panegyric poems honor battle heroes. Modern songs pay tribute to "the heroic deeds of militants" (Batsinduka).

The distortion of old stories and the fabrication of new myths can intensify ongoing ethnopolitical conflicts. German colonialists, missionaries and Belgian colonialists, for example, used the myth of Tutsi superiority to their own advantage. During the Hutu Revolution, Hutus introduced a new narrative aimed at reversing the "Tutsification process." Storytelling played a prominent role. Hutus rewrote Rwandan history books, purposely infusing them with horrific but false stories of Tutsis enslaving and mistreating Hutus. These stories were then taught to schoolchildren. These stories fueled Hutus' sense of victimization and desire for vengeance, which escalated animosities and violence (Batsinduka).

Like stories, some symbols "have great power" and can intensify ethnopolitical animosities. In the Israeli–Palestinian conflict, the 1973 Yom Kippur/October War stands out as a key date. Enemy forces mounted a "treacherous attack" on one of Jews' holiest days (Kaufman and Hassassian). Ethnic languages, old buildings and monuments, and flags are especially potent symbols. Because language and ethnic markers are so closely linked to a group's identity, being forced to hide or give them up is often interpreted as an insult or a threat (Klain). Being compelled to hide their mother tongue for fear of being discriminated against angered Croats. Turkish and Greek Cyriots lamented being forbidden to fly their flags or teach Turkish or Greek history in school (Atakol). In Northern Ireland, Catholics resented being unable to fly the Irish flag, play the Irish national anthem, or speak the Irish language (Byrne). Conversely, Macedonians were incensed that ethnic Albanians insisted on flying the Albanian flag and singing their own anthem. They saw these actions as an affront to Macedonia's sovereignty. The desecration and destruction of centuries-old churches and monasteries by Albanians were regarded as an attack against "the holy core of Macedonian identity," explain Petroska-Beska and Kenig. Albanians were equally incensed that Macedonia's new constitution was adopted without input from their community, that they could not fly their flag or express their cultural heritage, and that their human rights were being violated (Musa).

Beyond identity, stories, and cultural markers, one of the most potent forces affecting the devolution of ethnopolitical conflict is opposing sides' leaders.[10] Chapters in this text illustrate how corrupt, self-serving leaders can seize power and incited hatred, violence, and war. Dictators often exacerbate ethnopolitical conflicts, sometimes intentionally, for their own political and economic benefit. Former Rwandan president Juvenal Habyarimana created an *akuzu (*inner circle) of supporters and henchmen and the "Zero Network," which violently suppressed opposition to his "corruption, barefaced favoritism, and criminal activities" (Batsinduka). Habyarimana reportedly faked an attack on Kigali to justify arresting fifteen thousand Tutsis, many of whom were tortured and killed. In some cases, leaders' apathy proved to be as deadly as malice. Sri Lanka's 1983 riots are thought to have been part of a preplanned pogrom about which senior leaders did nothing (Ratnavale).

Corruption and self-serving opportunism on the part of senior leaders and other power brokers characterize many conflict-ridden regimes. Kashmir, for example, has a long history of manipulation, fraud, and election rigging. Each side's improprieties justify the other side's retaliatory misbehavior. The result is flawed, violent elections, mistrust, misrule, and an "alienated, despairing population" willing to "resort to radical solutions" (Hussain) In many cases, political corruption precludes peacemaking. Greek Cypriots' rejection of Kofi Annan's peace plan is seen by some as little more than a thinly veiled attempt on the part of self-serving local politicians to preserve their power and the "corrupt, nepotistic status quo" (Mavratsas).

In addition to corruption, self-interest, and inaction, malice—sometimes against citizens—is disturbingly common. Israeli prime minister Ariel Sharon is accused of causing three thousand Israeli citizens' deaths (Kaufman and Hassassian). Former Yugoslavian president Slobodan Milošević stands accused of crimes against humanity. Former Cypriot leader Nicos Sampson was considered to be a "notorious killer" and "Turk-hating fanatic" (Atakol).

Ethnopolitical conflicts are often exacerbated and prolonged by the hard-line positions leaders take and stubbornly refuse to budge from. Kaufman and Hassassian blame the inflexible stances taken by Ariel Sharon and Yassir Arafat for compounding the intractability and ongoing violence of the Israeli–Palestinian conflict.

In addition to official leaders, other internal leaders and dissenters, from fundamentalist clerics to terrorists, can manipulate citizens, thwart peace efforts, and topple accords (Mavratsas).[11] In many ethnopolitical conflicts, "religious zealots, warlords, and opportunists" (Batsinduka) are to blame for aggression and escalating violence. Colonial authorities, elites, and warlords fabricate and manipulate ethnonationalistic sentiments to achieve their goals, as evidenced in Rwanda, Nigeria, and the former Yugoslavian republics. According to Kaufman and Hassassian, the Israeli–Palestinian conflict was co-opted by dangerous fundamentalist fanatics.

Whether official or unofficial, despotic leaders seem especially adept at filling political power vacuums. Consider Milošević's "power grab" following the death of Tito, Yugoslavia's long-time president and peacekeeper. The collapse of Communism presented a "singular opportunity" for Serbs to pursue their ancient "Greater Serbia" aspirations. Milošević was quick to capitalize on Serbs' secessionist sentiments. Under the pretext of revitalizing Yuogslavia's underdeveloped economy, Milošević mounted his antibureaucratic revolution. With the army's support, he purged the federal government and installed loyal supporters, as well as "cronies and errand boys" (Biserko). Other federation leaders were powerless to stop him. Milošević preyed on opposing sides' ancient animosities, ethnonationalistic aspirations, and fears that whoever failed to take the offensive would be tortured, destroyed, or massacred (Klain).

Leaders often use co-optation and politicization as means to advance their agendas and fan ethnoconflict's fires. In Cyprus, for example, Greek Cypriots' *enosis* (reunification with Greece efforts) acquired a "messianic character" and became a quasi-religious movement (Mavratsas). Religious fundamentalism is frequently used to attract disenfranchised groups and persuade them that violent aggression is justified, if not necessary, to achieve desired political ends. Nigeria's *'yan daba* recruited youths to join vigilante gangs, ethnic militias, and tribal armies that filled the void left by police ineffectiveness and military inactivity. *'Yan daba* earn most of their income from "politically motivated thuggery," paid for by local political and religious leaders. Opportunistic leaders can and will co-opt youths (Casey). In Rwanda, political parties created youth wings, which initially harassed members of opposing parties. As tensions rose, youth-wing members were given military training and then sent to work with regular forces and terrorist groups (Batsinduka).

As destructive as despotic leaders can be, the absence of a leader and leadership capacity can prove equally dangerous and deadly. Lack of self-governance experience and expertise are particularly problematic in newly created states. The risk is that power will be seized by loyalists bent on re-creating some romanticized "golden era" of the past or recapturing some mythical supremacy, as happened in Serbia and Sri Lanka. Latent animosities may flare up anew, and archenemies may simply resume their battle, as Yugoslavia's Chetniks and Ustashas did. In new nations with no experience governing their affairs democratically and no clear communally held vision of the future, terrorist groups and religious extremists can readily seize power (Casey; Mavratsas). Lack of leadership and self-governance capacity can undermine peace efforts and cause ongoing instability, as is the case in the former Yugoslavia (Biserko). Groups that cannot determine how best to make peace and self-rule often end up mired in more conflict.

In contemplating contributors' front-line stories, we see that, of the internal forces and factors that cause and exacerbate ethnopolitical conflict, history, land, identity, stories, leadership, and politics are especially potent agents. Contributors' descriptions and explanations illuminate reasons why old ethnopolitical conflicts keep recurring and new ones keep erupting.

As virulent as internal forces and factors may be, external forces and factors can play equally, if not, more powerful and detrimental roles.

External Forces and Factors

External forces and factors that influence ethnopolitical conflict's etiology and devolution relate largely to politics and power. Outsiders' ambitions, actions, foreign policies, and intervention efforts are frequently motivated by economic aspirations (greed) and/or a desire to secure more power. Two additional, comparatively new forces and factors, which contributors claim significantly impact ethnopolitical conflict, are the media and modernity.

External forces and factors that cause and exacerbate ethnopolitical conflict can be clustered into three interrelated categories: (1) invasion, colonization, and globalization, (2) mistaken nation making and intervention, and (3) exploitation, usury, and manipulation.

Foreign invaders, colonial powers, and other opportunists have a long history of starting and inflaming ethnopolitical conflict. From the Greek, Roman, and Ottoman Empires, to the British and European competition to colonize new lands, to the globalizing efforts of the United States and multinational corporations, expanding empires have left countless dead and numerous intractable ethnopolitical conflicts in their wake. Foreign invaders, colonizers, and entrepreneurs have left a trail of human carnage and political, economic, environmental, and social wreckage.

Contributors' accounts illustrate how outsiders' ambitions, actions, and political and economic policies have large, long-lasting, and far-reaching effects on developing nations and their citizens. Foreign powers, acting first as exploitive colonizers and then as supposed peacemakers, have adversely impacted every ethnopolitical conflict discussed in this book. Outsiders not only aggravate interstate and intrastate conflict, they often create an enduring culture of conflict. Even when foreign invaders leave, their legacy lives on. As Ratnavale explains, 150 years of British occupation and another 250 years of Portuguese and Dutch domination in Sri Lanka created a sharp "us versus them" split. After 400 years of foreign colonial subjugation, Sri Lankan society is solidly divided and conflict has become embedded in the country's culture.

History and contributors' stories reveal a pattern. Invaders, colonizers, and megacorporations install themselves in foreign countries and exploit their resources and their people. They disrupt and sometimes destroy traditional ways of living. They also impose their economic system and erode inhabitants' self-sufficiency. Compounding the effect of land and resource grabs, they seize political power. Rightful leaders are "slayed or subjugated" (Casey), and citizens wake up to find "complete strangers running their affairs" (Casey). Citizens end up as "powerless as Russian serfs" (Atakol). Outsiders' political domination breeds dependency and despondency, while their oppression and tyranny erode inhabitants' ability to solve their problems and govern themselves. Over time, invaders' modus operandi permeates the societies they conquer. It sows the seeds of ongoing aggression, oppression, and tyranny. Even when outsiders leave, these behavior patterns remain.

Bluntly stated, ethnopolitical conflict begets ethnopolitical conflict.

Rwanda's history illustrates the insidious manner in which foreign invaders and colonial powers' choices can impact ethnopolitical conflicts and the resulting responsibility that rests on their shoulders. In fact, it can be argued that colonization created the animosities that led to the 1994 genocide. When Germans labeled Tutsis as "noble, majestic" people "born to rule" and described Hutus as enslaved, "simple-minded, semi-civilized" people (Batsinduka), they created "us versus them" animosities and skewed each group's identity. Mythical, colonialist-created stereotypes, compounded by the colonialists' decision to hire Tutsis to rule Hutus, pitted Tutsis against Hutus. Belgians' subsequent "Tutsification" program drove Tutsis and Hutus—who had previously shared a common language, religion, and culture—further apart. Colonialists forced both Tutsis and Hutus to work on large infrastructure projects. They also forced Tutsis to whip lazy Hutus. Colonialism brought capitalism and taxation to Rwanda and disrupted its socioeconomic fabric. Formerly self-sufficient farmers were persuaded to switch to cash crops such as coffee, tobacco, and cotton. All these changes eroded Rwanda's political, social, and economic foundations.

Missionaries and their hypocrisy added to ethnopolitical animosities. Religious leaders initially supported colonial governments and Tutsi elites. They claimed Rwandan land and lived well. During the Hutu Social Revolution, however, missionaries did an about-face and gave their support to Hutus and the "new myth" that Hutus are "born democrats." Missionaries' push to outlaw Rwandans' traditional "pagan" beliefs and practices destroyed one of the three identity attributes that linked Rwandans. Finally, missionaries' decision to back Hutu revolutionaries may have contributed, albeit unintentionally, to the 1994 genocide.

In Batsinduka's view, invading colonial powers are responsible for Rwanda's ethnopolitical conflict and ensuring genocide: "They initiated and promoted the ideology of difference, they created and widened the gap between Hutus and Tutsis, they institutionalized the exclusion of Hutus and promotion of Tutsi elites. They fueled negative mimetic phenomena between the two groups. Belgian administrators and Roman Catholic missionaries share the blame in dividing and antagonizing Hutus and Tutsis."

The devastating consequences of foreign invasion, colonization, decolonization, and globalization are evident in ethnopolitical conflicts from Sri Lanka to Nigeria to Northern Ireland. Foreign invasion and intervention carry with them ethical responsibilities much larger and longer lasting than intruders realize. Even suppressing ethnopolitical conflict can cause unexpected, deadly consequences, as evidenced by the rise in intrastate conflicts following the end of the Cold War and the crumbling of Communism. History underscores intervenors' duty to act responsibly and with exceptional foresight.

As devastating as invasion can be to a well-defined ethnonational group, foreign ignorance and the fabrication of false nation-states or accidental cleaving of coherent groups have proven to be equally disastrous. Many of the nations currently plagued by ethnopolitical conflict are artificial. Created by foreign superpowers, they are vestiges of colonialism and post-war nation making. Their citizens share no cohering sense of identity, history, or solidarity (Banerjee; Hussain). Many African and Asian conflicts stand as embarrassing reminders of foreign intervenors' legacy. Kashmir's conflict is the direct consequence of British intervention. Yugoslavia's remains illustrate the consequences of superpowers' cartographic improprieties. Yugoslavia was supposed to be a federation of equal partners: Serbia, Croatia, Slovenia, Bosnia and Herzegovina, and Montenegro (Petroska-Beška and Kenig). Member states, however, came from different identity groups with different sociocultural, religious, and political backgrounds. They held divergent values and national ambitions. Rather than engendering empathy, their shared history of serial occupation and oppression fueled intense aspirations of autonomy.

As Klain makes plain, nation-states should not be fabricated by foreigners, be they European colonizers, international organizations, or peacemakers. Heterogeneous groups of people forced to live together end up fighting to go their separate ways, as happened in the former Yugoslavia. Likewise, forcing separate, well-defined groups to join a new, foreign-imposed nation can cause disastrous results, as happened in Kashmir when Britain forced it and 562 other independent kingdoms to join either India or Pakistan (Banerjee; Hussain). Groups that are forced to live together turn against those forcing them to do so—if they can, which is rare. More often, they turn inward, against each other, hence the ubiquity of intrastate ethnopolitical conflict.

Equally important, foreigners should take care not to accidentally separate identity groups, which is what happened when world superpowers ratified the Treaty of Bucharest and partitioned Macedonia (Petroska-Beška and Kenig). Outsiders' nation-making efforts, concludes Mavratsas, create "legitimization crises" with "grave consequences." False borders create polities "with no true or loyal citizens," leaving opportunists and extremists to run amok. Because identity is so central to nationalism, nations must be born out of the needs and aspirations of the people who populate them (Hussain). They must be supported by the will of the people; otherwise they will crumble.

Worse than false borders are foreign usury and manipulation. Many countries in chronic conflict have been used for economic gain or to achieve international political aims. India and Northern Ireland were used for economic and political gain, respectively.

In reviewing the ethnopolitical conflicts included in this text, two patterns emerge. In some cases, international intruders manipulate countries in conflict. In other cases, countries in conflict use the international community.

In some ethnopolitical conflicts, disputing parties have been treated like pawns by international superpowers. Cyprus is a case in point, having been a pawn in Greek–Turkish relations. Greek and Turkish Cypriots concur that their mutual enmity was initially institutionalized by British manipulation of local politics (Ifantis; Mavratsas). The international community's "insistence" that the Greek Cypriot administration, which seized power, be recognized as the republic's official government exacerbated animosities. Turkish Cypriots considered Cyprus's administration (and others' recognition of it) to be unconstitutional, illegal, and immoral (Atakol; Mavratsas). The decision of the European Union (EU) to admit Cyprus only added insult to injury. Foreign meddling and unfair treatment by the international community, particularly the EU have been and continue to be one of the main factors contributing to the persistence of the conflict in Cyprus and the major obstacle in the resolution of the conflict (Atakol).

Foreign efforts to force disputing nations to de-escalate their conflict and sincerely pursue peace sometimes backfire, and intervenors attempting to be neutral and diplomatic can find themselves being used. Turkey and Greece applied for associate membership in the European Economic Community at the same time. Greece subsequently applied for and was granted full membership. Greece promptly blocked an EU assistance protocol, which deprived Turkey of EU financial assistance. Greece then held the EU hostage by insisting that Turkey not be granted full EU membership until Cyprus was granted conditional membership. Greece threatened to veto all EU membership applications unless its demands were met (Oymen). In Cyprus, Turkish Cypriots saw foreign superpowers' imposition of embargoes as an unjust form of economic discrimination and political aggression. Embargoes intensified Turkish Cypriots' resentment and mistrust of the international community (Atakol). Even Greek Cypriots rebelled. They voted against letting international intervenors "impose an unjust solution," claiming the U.N.'s proposed peace plan was a "foreign conspiracy" designed to "serve the interests" of Britain, the United States, and Turkey (Mavratsas).

Relations between India and Pakistan reveal a different but still manipulative pattern. India has refused to seriously discuss Kashmir's claims and desire for autonomy—unless motivated by "some military crisis," "tactical advantage," or pressure from the international community's "big powers" (Hussain). India has feigned a willingness to negotiate, but its promises have evaporated as soon as tensions have subsided or international attention has shifted elsewhere (Hussain).

Turkey and Greece have taken a different tack; they have taken their debate to the international stage. Each side postures and plays its cards for the sake of regional and international effect and showmanship. Each side uses the threat of regional instability to dramatize its demands (Ifantis).

In such games of showmanship, shifts in international attention can result in unexpected reversals of power or popularity, with sometimes surprising consequences. For half a century, owing to the Cold War, Yugoslavia enjoyed a central position on the international political stage. It was accorded "special treatment" that exceeded the country's "real importance" because of its geostrategic location and U.S.–U.S.S.R. interests in preserving the region's precarious balance of power (Biserko). At the end of the Cold War, Yugoslavia lost its favored-nation status. Compounding matters, the collapse of Communism destabilized Yugoslavia and it disintegrated. International superpowers are blamed for Yugoslavia's collapse, the ensuing bloodshed, and their tardy, ill-informed efforts to restore peace. Macedonians, for example, hold the international community, especially the United States, responsible for Albanians' insurrection. Macedonians blame the international community for allowing arms, soldiers, and violence to spread and for preventing Macedonia's security forces from decisively quashing

Albanian terrorists' attacks. They claim the international community's intervention gave Albanians the impression they had "the world's most powerful allies on their side" (Petroska-Beska and Kenig). Insisting on a peaceful settlement to the conflict, in the Macedonians' view, was tantamount to condoning violence and terrorism.

Outsiders can exert considerable influence on ethnopolitical conflicts. Influence comes from distant and surprising sources. Decisions made by the United States and other nations can, for example, alter the dynamics of ethnopolitical conflicts and aggravate, enlarge, and prolong them. When the United States gives financial, political, military, or moral support to countries with oil, water, or other strategic interests, groups worried about U.S. influence and hegemony act to support one another. The Israeli–Palestinian conflict, for example, is part of a larger pan-Arab movement (Kaufman and Hassassian). Neighboring Arab nations and their conflicts impact and are impacted by Israeli–Palestinian relations. Diaspora communities and neighboring nations can affect ethnopolitical conflicts. The United States, Libya, and South Africa contributed arms, money, and support to Northern Ireland's conflict (Byrne). Up to 70 percent of the terrorists in Kashmir come from elsewhere, and many are acting under the direction of Pakistan (Banerjee).

Foreign support sometimes causes unintended consequences. The India–Pakistan conflict has been fueled, to a certain degree, by the availability of weapons, soldiers, and financial support from West Asian neighbors (Banerjee). U.S. support for Afghanistan's war with the Soviet Union left the region awash in weapons and fighters. A large proportion of these resources went to al-Qaeda and the Taliban. Afghanistan's surplus weapons and overzealous militants, says Hussain, then flowed over the border into Kashmir—and around the world. Surplus weapons and fighters, combined with religious extremism, says Banerjee, turned an "indigenous political dispute that would normally have been expressed through peaceful political protest" into a violent ethnopolitical conflict being waged by insurgents trained and using arms supplied by neighboring nations (Banerjee).

In addition to politics, power, and economic motivators, the media and modernity appear to be having a growing effect on ethnopolitical conflict. Not only does modern communications technology transmit breaking news stories and graphic images of ethnopolitical conflicts around the world, around the clock, but it can be and is being manipulated in ways that influence the conflicts per se.[12] Governments, politicians, clerics, and celebrities use both national and international media to spread their views, incite hatred, and suppress dissent. Owing to media manipulation, information reaching the rest of the world is sometimes restricted or distorted.

The potency of media muzzling, manipulation, and usury is illustrated in contributors' chapters. In Yugoslavia, the media became "the principal war-generating and people-harassment mechanism," reports Biserko. "By recalling the World War II genocide of Serbs in Croatia and the suffering of Serbs under the Turks and hyping the terroristlike characteristics of Albanian people," the church, academics, intellectuals, and the media conspired to spark old animosities, which inflamed the Serb populous and eventually plunged Yugoslavia into war. When Milošević came to power, he dismissed print and TV editors and reporters and replaced them with his political supporters. These propagandists "played a key role in starting the war and enlisting the support of the popular masses," says Biserko.

In Sir Lanka, state-controlled media spread "government propaganda," while local and international radio and television programs were censored and jammed, reports Ratnavale. In Nigeria, state-run newspapers downplayed the levels of violence, claiming ethnic clashes were isolated incidents perpetrated by "miscreants" and lying about the number of casualties. Some media adopted ethnic or religious angles and blamed blacks, Muslims, or *'yan daba* youth gangs for incidents of unrest and violence (Casey). In Rwanda, the media vilified Tutsis. The journal *Kangura* published the "Ten Commandments of the Hutu," which told Hutus to avoid Tutsis. Artists such as Simon Bikindi, "the bard of genocide," wrote songs about how Tutsis killed Hutu kings and Hutu heroes died in battle, which were broadcast on national radio, especially on special occasions like Independence Day (Batsinduka). In Macedonia, senior officials and the media portrayed Albanians as "terrorists" who should be "eliminated" (Musa). Journalists who tried to present balanced coverage were considered "betrayers of the Macedonian nation" Not only did the media decline to publicize Albanians' point of view; it distorted and fabricated stories to make Albanians look guilty.

In addition to inciting hatred and violence, the media have the power to define, distort, and threaten identity. As with storytelling, the media can exaggerate differences, create stereotypes, and embellish or revise groups' histories. They can demonize enemies and fabricate identities based on mythico–historical ethnic, religious, or nationalist ideologies.[13] They can sensationalize news events or downplay disputes. They can publicize current news events in ways that resurrect memories of chosen glories and traumas and emotions related to them. In Nigeria, reports Casey, the media's reports reactivated traumas experienced during colonization and the Nigerian civil war and caused a time collapse.

Even news reports about ethnopolitical conflicts being waged elsewhere in the world can trigger strong reactions. Explains Casey: "Nigeria's chosen traumas are revisited and surfaced as Nigerians view media accounts of political struggles around the world, particularly those in the Middle East" Likewise, reports and documentaries about genocide, ethnic cleansing, displacement, forced migration, minority rights, and victimization provoke old memories and sentiments (Casey).

An overlooked aspect of the media's power is its ubiquity and ability, intended or not, to proselytize democracy, capitalism, and Western moral values. The international media is, in part, provoking developing countries' backlash against modernity and globalization. Developed countries' television, movie, and Internet offerings paint a picture of a permissive, valueless, violent society. Anti-modernity sentiments are in part linked to the clash between sacred and secular values and ways of life.[14] Anti-modernity is sparked by perceived threats to identity and fears of change (Biserko) and a strong desire to avoid the "corrupting influences of alien modernity" (Ratnavale). The clash between tradition and modernity can be seen in Serbia, Macedonia, Sri Lanka, and Nigeria.

Resistance to and contempt for modernity make sense once one understands that eschewing education, urban civilization, and modernity are ways of blocking alien out-group influences; fortifying in-group cohesion, conformity, and loyalty; and preventing social integration and change. Yugoslavians' patriarchal culture, traditional religious values, long history of dependency on the state for decision making, many years under collectivist rule, and individual republics' desire to recapture their former grandeur and independence contribute to citizens' resistance to modernity (Biskerko; Klain; Petroska-Beska and Kenig). Because citizens were unable to express their identity in the past, they are reluctant to accept a new, modern identity (Biserko). In Nigeria, anti-modernity is linked to religious teachings of Mohammed and scholars, who counseled followers to shun *bidi'a* (innovation) and consumer goods representing modernization and to honor Islam's original teachings. Modernity is spurned by many Muslims because they fear it will contaminate their spiritual purity and destroy social and family structures (Casey).

Closely related to anti-modernity are anti-superpower resentment and anti-Americanism.[15] Anti-modernity is in part a reaction against globalization and the U.S.'s hegemonic position in the world and its habit of intervening in others' disputes to protect its political and economic interests.[16] Traditionalists and developing nations see globalization as a thinly veiled attempt to secure control over developing countries' resources and cheap labor. They see it as another wave of colonialism.[17] They fear that globalization will decimate their language, culture, and traditional values. Culture is the U.S.'s biggest export. Traditionalists and developing nations fear developed nations will spread their violent, amoral, materialistic consumer culture.[18]

In some ethnopolitical conflicts, outside intervenors have become a common enemy. In Cyprus, fears that foreigners would dictate their destiny united adversaries (Mavratsas). Ethnic Macedonians hold ambivalent views of superpowers. In their eyes, Western superpowers are unjust, decadent, conspiring, and selfish. They are promoting democracy and peace to achieve their own goals. During Macedonia's conflict with Albanians, U.S. and EU intervention triggered fears that Macedonians' homeland would be torn apart and their rights ignored. In Macedonians' view, U.S. and EU intervention in Macedonia's sovereignty was hypocritical: they were attacking democracy, the same principles the West was promoting. Nevertheless, Macedonia still wants to join the international community (Petroska-Beska and Kenig).

Foreign intervenors' record of success when it comes to preventing and mitigating violent ethnopolitical conflicts is inconsistent at best and escalatory at worst. Many international intervention efforts are ineffective and actually exacerbate tensions. Yet, superpowers continue to foist their values onto developing countries in ways reminiscent of invasion, colonialism, and forced ideological conversion. They continue to misunderstand or distort disputing countries' claims. They negotiate agreements that offend citizens, who ignore or violate them.

Examples of inappropriateness and failure abound. Foreign powers have been "unable to prevent war or impose peace" in Israel, note Kaufman and Hassassian. The international community failed to avert Sri Lanka's ethnopolitical carnage, despite early reports of massive civilian displacement, torture, disappearances, and heavy military casualties, laments Ratnavale.

International efforts to find a peaceful solution to Yugoslavia's conflict failed. The Srebrenica massacre is a symbol of Western impotence and indifference, says Biserko. The U.S.-facilitated 1995 Dayton Accords, seen as a success by Western powers, were an affront to Muslims. Outsiders looked only at the current situation; they did not look at history or principles of justice. When Serbs were forced to relinquish territory, they lost at the negotiating table what they had won on the battlefield. From Serbs' viewpoint, the Dayton Accords were a loss that "cemented the defeat of the victim" (Biserko).

The 2001 Ohrid Framework Agreement and its enforcement by the international community humiliated, degraded, and betrayed Macedonians. The United States and the EU forced Macedonia to negotiate with terrorists. By taking sides, the international community turned Albanians into winners and Macedonians into losers. By overlooking Albanians' violent tactics and mandating preferential treatment for them, the international community sanctioned extremism and sowed the seeds for a "whole new cycle of the ethnic conflict," explain Petroska-Beska and Kenig.

In Northern Ireland, the U.N. is blamed for a litany of "bungles, mistakes, and miscalculations" (Byrne). Cypriots are equally disenchanted. They see the international community's actions as ineffective, unfair, and immoral. "All the massacres and killings of Turkish Cypriots occurred during the years the U.N. Peace Keeping Force was in Cyprus," reports Atakol. As soon as the Turkish army arrived, intercommunal killing stopped. The army accomplished overnight what U.N. Peace Keeping Forces had been unable to do during their eleven-year mission. The U.N. not only failed to resolve Cyprus's conflict; it actually supported punitive trade embargoes. After nearly four decades of failure and abuse, Cypriots have "lost faith in the international community" (Atakol) and have no incentive to negotiate in good faith.

Pakistanis, Indians, and Kashmiris hold the international community equally culpable for the conflict in Kashmir. Foreign powers created the conflict and have failed to remediate it. Appeals to the U.N. have been met with resolutions that are "irrelevant and incapable of implementation" (Banerjee). Efforts to negotiate an end to the conflict, hold a plebiscite, or even get parties to the negotiating table have failed. In Hussain's view, the conflict in Kashmir illustrates the ethical responsibilities facing the international community.

The international community's role—and ethical questions about its responsibilities—are perhaps most poignantly underscored by events in Rwanda. Because Rwanda lacked valued resources or strategic importance, the international community ignored evidence indicating genocide was imminent. When mass killing began, members of the international community fled, abandoning Tutsis and Hutus. The international community's initial lack of concern, rapid retreat, and ongoing disregard "devalued and dehumanized" Rwandans (Batsinduka). These actions also call into question the international community's duty to protect.[19]

At the crux of the conundrum are two questions: should the international community intervene in other countries' ethnopolitical conflicts, and if so, under what circumstances?

Although international superpowers have a long, embarrassing history of invading and colonizing other countries and bungling peacemaking efforts, the consensus is that there remains a superordinate duty to protect innocent civilians.[20] As well as a moral obligation, affluent developed countries have a vested interest in advancing global human security and a culture of peace. Even those who have lived through violent ethnopolitical conflict and failed superpower intervention initiatives, including this text's contributors, still believe the international community has a vital role to play in mitigating ethnopolitical conflicts. Ifantis, for example, believes that "Europe is the only actor powerful enough to transform Turkey into a modern democratic state." According to Byrne, the "British presence in Northern Ireland has helped reduce the risk of civil war between Protestants and Catholics. If the British government were to withdraw, outright conflict would result." Albanians credit the international community with stopping ethnopolitical violence in Macedonia and saving many lives. They also want the international community to assist with economic development and other initiatives (Musa).

The need for international involvement and cooperation is driven by three intertwined global imperatives: economic, ecological, and social.[21] Failure to reconcile and rebalance these triple-bottom-line exigencies puts the planet and its inhabitants in peril. Conflict is, in many cases, rooted in economic, environmental, and sociopolitical imbalances. When the environment in which people live cannot fulfill their basic daily needs or they are unable to earn a living, when people's basic human rights are being violated or their values and dignity are being disrespected, when the social fabric of their community and their identity risk being torn apart, and when the political or government system on which they rely to protect them fails to do so, conflict typically erupts. Because the earth is a closed system, excesses in one region can create shortages and dissent or conflict in other regions. As 9/11 and other acts of terrorism in London have shown, conflict, like air and water pollution, can move rapidly around the globe.

Ethnopolitical conflicts waging halfway around the world are superpowers' business. In many cases they caused or contributed to them, and their choices are exacerbating them. Superpowers face a serious risk. Terrorism's impacts can be symbolic, economic, social and political. The growing threat of international terrorism underscores the need to care about and attend to distant countries' ethnopolitical conflicts. The benefits of global security highlight the importance of international engagement and commitment.

While conventional approaches to peacemaking and conflict resolution have helped to curtail violence and end some conflicts, they have proven to be incapable of addressing deep-rooted, protracted ethnopolitical conflict. Repeated attempts to broker peace between Israel and Palestine have all failed (Kaufman and Hassassian). Most international intervenors take an interest-based view of and approach to ethnopolitical conflict. Interests and positions, however, do not adequately explain or account for the violence associated with ethnopolitical conflict. Nor are interests and positions able to end such conflicts. To make a difference, international intervenors must look much deeper. They must look at identity and values.[22]

Not all nations, especially those in the Muslim world, want to embrace Western values. Given the media reports and programs they see, it is understandable that political, religious, and community leaders and citizens in developing countries are disinterested in, or even repulsed by, capitalism, consumerism, secularism, and even democracy. Modernity and its social consequences must look positively unenticing, if not frightful.

While agreement seems to be growing that the international community has a responsibility to care about "have not" countries in conflict, there is less concurrence about what kind of assistance to offer and how to provide it. Previous presumptuous, prescriptive intervention efforts have failed and sometimes backfired. Moreover, it is elitist and egocentric for developed nations to think that developing nations would want to emulate them and adopt their values. The challenge facing international intervenors is how to help in ways that respect others' values. Such approaches should take into account other nations' history, accept their beliefs and political choices, preserve their culture and dignity, and safeguard their identity.

RECOMMENDATIONS

This anthology's contributors offer many insightful lessons worth pondering. Of particular note is the advice they offer on how to effectively manage and end violent ethnopolitical conflict. What makes contributors' recommendations so valuable is that they stem from their first-hand knowledge of what it is like to endure years or generations of ethnopolitical conflict—and lose family and friends to violence and war. Their stories suggest that the process of managing, preventing, mitigating, and recovering from ethnopolitical conflict is firstly about human compassion and mutual understanding. It is secondly about internal and global governance and policy choices. It is interesting that contributors emphasize the former, while outside intervenors typically dwell more on the latter.

Recommendations offered by this anthology's contributors can be succinctly summarized as follows: (1) ask, listen, and learn, (2) act responsibly and respectfully, (3) support reconciliation and rebuilding, (4) share power and empower, (5) take a holistic approach, and (6) address systemic issues and effect structural change.

Broadly speaking, ameliorating ethnopolitical conflict revolves around reversing the forces and factors that caused and/or exacerbated it. Respect, dialogue, understanding, tolerance, and mutual learning are required to undo the effects of old, intractable ethnopolitical animosities.[23] Misunderstanding, miscommunication, misperception, misinformation, and mistrust need to be replaced by their opposites. Disputing parties and international intervenors alike need to understand how history has influenced and continues to shape people's identities and aspirations. Threats to identity need to be alleviated (Ratnavale). Stereotyping, discrimination, and the transgenerational transfer of enmity need to end. Former enemies need to be undemonized and rehumanized. Strong, peace-promoting leaders and leadership are required. Those advocating extremism or guilty of co-optation, corruption, and manipulation must be stopped. Attention must be paid to disputing parties' political aspirations.

Justice and fairness loom large as common goals in states plagued by ethnopolitical conflict.[24] Demands for a homeland, political autonomy, self-determination, and sovereignty must be addressed (Atakol).[25] As this volume's contributors emphasize, all parties want respect and recognition. They want understanding and decent treatment from each other, intervenors, and others (Atakol; Byrne; Mavratsas; Musa; Ratnavale). In some cases, an end to oppression and the use of dialogue and mutual learning are promising solutions. In other cases, though, structural change, sometimes of global proportion, is required.

One especially striking feature of contributors' chapters is the importance they ascribe to dialogue, reconciliation, mutual learning, and peace-building. Standing in equally striking contrast to the weight given to rights and interests in conventional conflict intervention models and processes is the importance contributors accord to responsibility. In their view, adversaries need to honestly admit the past and take responsibility for their actions—and make amends. They need thorough, purposeful reconciliation and peace-building processes. At the same time, international superpowers and developed nations' citizens need to shoulder responsibility for ways in which they have contributed or are contributing to ethnopolitical violence. Developed nations' ignorance, denial, and usury must stop. The effects of globalization and modernity must be weighed, internalized, and in some cases curtailed.

Despite the atrocities they have seen and experienced from their front-line vantage point, contributors are unanimous in their commitment to and calls for peace. Their advice on how to mitigate and prevent current and future interstate and intrastate wars and ethnopolitical violence is practical, implementable, and adaptable. Their recommendations, summarized in the following pages, call on individuals and groups at all levels and in all sectors of society to think and act differently. Collectively, contributors underscore the need to put people before politics.

To reduce ethnopolitical tensions, reverse the impacts of ethnopolitical conflict, and begin restoring relations, political will and international support are required. An even more important precedent is face-to-face contact between adversaries (Ratnavale). Contact undemonizes and rehumanizes members of the opposing group. It puts a face on the other side. Frequent encounters change attitudes (Kaufman and Hassassian). Contact dissipates fabricated images and stereotypes. Merciless foes turn out to be both human and victim (Ifantis). Increased contact can be officially orchestrated or accidentally triggered. In Sri Lanka, roadways were opened to encourage increased "people exchange." When former enemies met face to face, they discovered "actual human beings, who received them with care and great kindness" (Ratnavale). Natural disasters brought Greeks and Turks together. Catastrophic earthquakes triggered "an outburst of mutual sympathy" in both countries, which significantly improved relations (Ifantis; Oymen). Acknowledgement of shared suffering can be cathartic.[26] In ethnopolitical conflicts, both sides have suffered. Loved ones are dead, displaced, and missing (Mavratsas). Victims need apologies; perpetrators need forgiveness (Klain). All parties need "a pair of ears to listen to them, and an open, empathetic heart," says Batsinduka. Acknowledging each other's suffering and losses creates common ground and empathy. So does grieving together.[27]

Following South Africa's example, truth and reconciliation commissions (TRCs) are being used to acknowledge harms done, demonstrate compassion, and restore relations. For TRCs to work well, certain criteria must be met. Contributors offer three recommendations regarding TRCs. First, TRCs must be authentic and effective. Poorly designed processes frustrate and further victimize victims (Batsinduka). TRCs founder if their aims, process managers, and approaches are poorly chosen. Serbia's Kostunica commission, for example, was managed by the same people who had "furnished the arguments in favor of starting the war." As a result, the commission's "credibility and prospects were doomed from the start" (Biserko). Its integrity declined further as parties continued to propagate their own interpretation of the truth and political agendas (Biserko). In Rwanda, commissioners appointed to manage the National Commission for Unity and Reconciliation had planned the genocide. They chose to use *Gacaca*, a traditional community-based conflict management process meant for minor offences, to deal with 130,000 genocide suspects imprisoned in Rwandan jail cells. Such inappropriate, ineffective approaches trivialize horrendous crimes, make a mockery of justice, and retraumatize victims, veterans, and citizens (Batsinduka; Klain).

Second, TRCs must protect victims from further victimization and trauma. In Rwanda, Tutsi survivors and returnees are suffering a second round of victimization. Not only did they have to relive their nightmares, but political insiders, Hutu hard-liners, and soldiers accused of genocide and crimes against humanity also eluded accountability and continued to kill Tutsis. "Tutsi survivors were sacrificed for the sake of national unity and reconciliation" (Batsinduka).

Finally, TRCs must have teeth. They must encourage reconciliation and rebuilding. The Dayton Accords did not contain any preconditions for a process of reconciliation. As a result, the agreement was flawed and failed (Biserko).

In all reconciliation processes, the state must accept responsibility for ways in which it caused or contributed to ethnopolitical violence, advises Biserko. Governments' duty is to protect its citizens. As Batsinduka explains,

> The crime of genocide is basically a state crime. [In Rwanda, it was] the state that planned the geno-cide, armed the killers, and made the means available to maximize the outcome of the diabolic plan. The Rwandan State turned ordinary Hutu citizens into criminals, dehumanized Tutsi citizens, and denied their right to live. (Batsinduka)

In Biserko's view, a truth commission is invalid if the state does not admit its culpability. The state's willingness to admit responsibility for its role in ethnopolitical conflict sets the tone for TRCs' proceedings and witnesses' testimony. Both victims and offenders have been dehu-manized. Reconciliation efforts should focus on recovering "a nation's humanity," says Batsin-duka. By admitting responsibility, apologizing to citizens and victims, and asking forgiveness, the state can lay the foundation for authentic reconciliation and systemic societywide change.

Like the state, citizens must be willing to accept responsibility for their choices and actions (Batsinduka). In protracted ethnopolitical conflicts, both sides are usually guilty. In Sri Lanka, for example, Tamil Tigers used deadly terrorist tactics, suicide bombers, and child sol-diers. The government used divisive policies, deception, extensive bombings, and human rights violations (Ratnavale). Each side must admit its atrocities—"No society can avoid con-frontation with the dark pages of its past. Every democratic community must sort itself out. Silence is destructive."—(Zundhausen in Biserko). Acknowledging the past and coming face to face with its history, hatreds, and barbarity is the hardest, most painful task a society at-tempting to recover from ethnopolitical conflict must confront (Biserko). "The bigger the mistake and the bloodier its consequences, the harder it is for people to own up" (Sforza in Biserko). Ideally, "everyone should look for perpetrators in their own nation and apologize for the atrocities done by one's nation" advises Klain.

Governments and citizens should look hard at the systemic forces and factors embedded in their culture that cause and exacerbate conflict. They should analyze and publicly discuss the political context in which deadly violence emerged, was accepted, and then was encour-aged. Citizens on both sides must examine and internalize responsibility for choosing and fol-lowing their leaders, supporting or at least tolerating their policies, and condoning or ignoring the use of violence. Government officials and citizens must internalize responsibility for standing silently on the sidelines when violence was being planned and perpetrated. Commu-nities must take responsibility for any vestiges of the past that could reactivate conflict. Turn-ing a blind eye to crimes, glorifying criminals, and overlooking an army involved in crime could set the stage for a new war (Biserko). Critical self-reflection and honest admission of culpability are vital to reconciliation, reconstruction, and efforts to prevent the recurrence of conflict. Enduring peace requires that each side "stop imitating the entrenched patterns of past violence" and create new ways of interacting and collaborating (Batsinduka).[28]

For reconciliation to work and peace to endure, sincere remorse, accountability, and jus-tice are required. "There is no room for fake processes," emphasizes Batsinduka. In post-conflict societies, which group has perpetrated the worst offenses and which group has suffered the most can become contentious topics (Mavratsas). In many ethnopolitical conflicts, both sides have paid and suffered dearly (Kaufman and Hassassian; Klain). Yet resentments and misgivings about who got how much can persist and cause conflict to recur. Score keeping and score settling can compromise reconciliation efforts. In Sri Lanka and Macedonia, Tamils and Albanians, respectively, are despised for their ill-gotten, undeserved gains or the prefer-ential treatment they receive.

The question of whether soldiers can or should be held responsible for acts they commit-ted can become contentious and difficult to resolve (Klain). In Ratnavale's opinion, all crimes, torture, killing, unlawful arrests, and human rights violations should be surfaced and addressed, whether they were committed by government representatives, military officers, or guerillas. In addition, those profiting from war, from arms dealers to government insiders, need to be held accountable, stop what they are doing, and make amends when possible.

Justice is a prerequisite for reconciliation and enduring peace, emphasizes Batsinduka. Without justice, peace-building's gains rarely endure. Consider Rwanda. Its history of impunity contributed to its culture of conflict. Because colonial rulers, missionaries, and Tutsi leaders did as they wished, Hutus felt free to "kill Tutsis, pillage their properties, slaughter their cattle, and rape Tutsi women without fear of reprisal" (Batsinduka). Reconciliation must ascertain the truth and take a stand on the historical injustices at issue (Biserko). Authentic, well-designed, and well-managed reconciliation and peace-building efforts offer disputing parties a fresh start. They offer "new life and new hope" (Biserko).

In societies experiencing or recovering from ethnopolitical conflict, the kind of assistance outsiders can offer falls into the categories of relief, rehabilitation, and reconciliation ("the three R's") and demobilization, disarmament, and reinsertion (DDR). In particular, contributors suggest that members of the international community assist with confidence building and capacity building measures (Ifantis; Kaufman and Hassassian; Ratnavale). Demining, weapons decommissioning, repatriation, reconstruction, and other initiatives aimed at "hard," tangible challenges help. Equally important are efforts aimed at "soft" challenges, such as civil society rebuilding. Refugees and soldiers can present and experience difficult problems, as "nobody wants them" (Klain). Politicians may talk about homecoming and reinsertion but provide few or no resources or fail to protect homecomers from discrimination. As a result, returnees have trouble making a living. To make repatriation and return to civilian society attractive, employment opportunities are required (Ratnavale). Otherwise, with no food and high unemployment, people become "walking bombs" (Kaufman and Hassassian).

The international community can play a role here, provided it acts with caution and respect. Displaced persons and soldiers will lay down their arms when they have alternatives to which they can turn. When soldiers are afraid to turn over their weapons for fear that violence might recur, foreign intervenors can help by securing peace militarily, as was done in Bosnia, or by using U.N. peacekeepers (Byrne). International superpowers can help promote peace by recognizing disputing nations' fears, issues, and borders, confirming their standing in the international community, and supporting the right of refugees and displaced persons to return home (Biserko). They can promote national and regional stability by addressing underlying systemic economic, political, and power issues (Biserko; Byrne).

As vital as reconstruction assistance is, consultation and commitment are even more essential. International intervenors must take care not to impose their agendas or values. They must weigh carefully the ethics of aid programs that benefit voters and taxpayers back home. They must ascertain what kind of assistance is desired. They must also keep their promises (Ratnavale).

Vital though international assistance may be, it is important not to overlook grassroots, bottom-up peace-building efforts (Kaufman and Hassassian).[29] Grassroots actors and their peacemaking efforts have tremendous, untapped potential power to effect change. Regrettably, conventional conflict resolution efforts typically involve only senior government representatives, academics, and a few elite others (Mavratsas).[30] A significant number of ethnopolitical conflicts are characterized by a disconnect between what is happening at senior political and grassroots levels.[31] Politicians and government representatives negotiate agreements but cannot "deliver their constituents," enforce agreements they sign, or preserve peace. The inability to maintain credibility and power is blamed for the collapse of Israeli–Palestinian peace talks early this century (Kaufman and Hassassian). Often, officials have failed to adequately consult with grassroots actors, address their concerns, and win their support. Representatives' priorities and vision do not match those that citizens hold.

Because their concerns are not being addressed, grassroots groups pursue their own goals, often using violent means.

Occasionally, though, the roles reverse and grassroots groups ignore senior officials' power-based negotiations and work independently toward peace. In Northern Ireland, Protestants and Catholics jointly pursued peace. While politicians and extremists battled away, local grassroots organizations built "bridges of contact across the intercommunal divide" (Byrne). Small, middle-ground groups such as the Alliance Party, Women's Coalition, and Northern Irish Peace People came together. Protestants and Catholics began "telling their stories, negotiating their identities, and developing a new shared identity," reports Byrne. Citizens forged new relationships and created a new culture.

The Kashmir Study Group developed a proposal recommending that Kashmir be reconstituted as a new sovereign entity with access to and from both India and Pakistan, which would jointly guarantee its sovereignty (Hussain). Some Cypriots are advancing a two-state solution. In Israel and Palestine, a number of individuals and civil society organizations have reached a high level of agreement about concrete ways of resolving the conflict. Many Arabs and Jews favor creating a Palestinian state that would exist alongside Israel (Kaufman and Hassassian). In Nigeria, a think tank comprising Muslims and Christians met to ensure Shari'a law would not be imposed on non-Muslims; conferences were organized to improve understanding. Local government leaders undertook to mediate disputes and, in one case, invited 'yan daba to advise government officials (Casey). Author Onur Oymen and his Greek counterpart attempted to create a group of Turkish and Greek "wise men" to study existing problems and propose possible solutions to them. These examples illustrate grassroots actors' ability to help themselves and effect systemic change.

To be effective and enduring, peace-building efforts should be inclusive. Conflict transformation requires the engagement of "all sectors and all levels of society"—grassroots, middle-tier, and senior levels.[32] Intervention efforts should not focus just on official government representatives, business leaders, and other elites; they should focus as much, if not more, on civil society groups (Kaufman and Hassassian).[33] Peace-building and conflict transformation can sometimes best be advanced using unofficial, grassroots channels (Senehi).[34] Multitrack processes that engage every sector of society increase the odds of achieving sustainable peace.[35]

Conflict resolution and peace-building efforts should not be shaped exclusively by outside intervenors. Ideally, they should be initiated and managed by disputing parties.[36] Increased contact and outsiders' confidence-building support may thaw relations, but peace-building requires engagement, empowerment, and capacity building. Unless disputing parties take ownership of peacemaking and peace-building initiatives, they are unlikely to be implemented or endure.[37] Taking ownership and control of peace-building programs increases social capital, confidence, and internal capacity.[38] First, self-selected and jointly managed initiatives prove to parties that they can work together. Second, they teach valuable lessons about problem solving and conflict management that stay resident within the community after international intervenors have left. Interactive conflict resolution and multilevel dialogue surmount the superficiality that plagues conventional top-down international intervention efforts.[39]

Contact, dialogue, and joint problem solving have remarkable restorative powers. Disputing parties and civilians need to express their views, listen to one another's perspectives, build new relationships, negotiate new understandings and agreements, and co-construct new narratives and shared visions for the future (Byrne; Kaufman and Hassassian; Senehi). Former rivals need to develop new paradigms and plans. They need to create new ways of interacting. Kaufman and Hassassian demonstrate how people from opposite sides can work together. In writing their chapter, they focused on the similarities, including their shared Semitic languages, the Abrahamic roots of their respective religions, their Arab–Judeo cultures, their music, food, dress, and customs, their history, their scientific and cultural contributions to world civilization, their shared significant archeological sites, and their shared history of peaceful relations. They found common ground, and they discussed how to deal with differences. By avoiding prevailing "either/or" thinking in favor of integrative "both/and" framings, Kaufman and Hassassian found ways to respect each other's history, identity, values, narratives, and sensitivities. With that foundation, they were able to model their shared vision of the future.

Joint projects and mutual learning have the ability to repair relations, build understanding and capacity, and help prevent future conflicts from erupting or, if they do, escalating out of control. When people work together, they learn about each other, find common ground, develop new, shared understandings, and discover that they can work together. Through joint projects, they can address and change structural challenges and benefit the entire community.[40] Joint projects and mutual learning are especially important for youths, says Musa. They inspire hope and counteract the transgenerational transmission of ethnopolitical conflict.

Dialogue and storytelling hold similar promise. They can be used to facilitate conflict resolution, post-trauma healing, intercommunal reconciliation, peace-building, and conflict transformation efforts. In post-conflict societies, people initially need to "share their stories and heal from the past" (Byrne). Dialogue and storytelling are simple, widely accessible ways of getting started. Storytelling is a safe way to express the pain and loss suffered. It is a nonconfrontational way for former enemies to hear and internalize how they hurt each other. Storytelling encourages inclusion, honesty, shared responsibility, and critical self-awareness, all of which contribute to peace-building. It can foster understanding, empathy, and compassion, and engender changes of heart. Storytelling can undemonize enemies, reduce prejudices, end stereotyping, reduce animosities, and create goodwill.

Storytelling also sheds light on the "intangible dimensions" of ethnopolitical conflict. It is a way for groups to explain their identity, history, and aspirations. Through stories and dialogue, groups can share "who they are, where they have come from, and where they are going" (Senehi). Such conversations provide a forum for disputing parties to describe their experience, develop shared understandings, and build trusting relationships across historical ethnopolitical divides. Storytelling satisfies the paradoxical needs of moving on (forgetting) and honoring (remembering) the past (Senehi). Publicly acknowledging traumas helps with healing. Ceremonies, rituals, written records, cultural productions, and interpretive sites can facilitate "healing through remembering" (Byrne; Senehi).[41] Such outlets for expression make healing easier and reduce the risk of future violence (Byrne).

Storytelling has cohering power. It gives voice to elites, intellectuals, ordinary people, and previously voiceless stakeholders. Listening to stories together builds bonds and closes chasms of conflict. It builds community. Storytelling can raise disputants' consciousness, increase their willingness to resolve conflicts, and inspire them to initiate or participate in collaborative reconciliation and reconstruction projects. Storytelling can be educational, for both disputing parties and international intervenors. It can impart important lessons about resisting domination, sharing "power with," as opposed to having "power over," and making meaning jointly (Senehi). Storytelling affords disputing parties an opportunity to craft new stories and plans for a peaceful future. It provides a forum for new voices and alternative ideas to emerge and grow. Storytelling is an effective way to tap into grassroots knowledge and encourage its expression so that indigenous knowledge and traditional conflict management and reconciliation techniques can "trickle up" and inform senior officials and their peace-building and conflict transformation strategies.

In addition to learning from and with their former enemies, disputing groups can learn much from others who have endured the ravages of ethnopolitical conflict. Conflicted states may have as much, or more, to learn from one another than from Western "experts." For example, Northern Ireland modeled its peace-building efforts on the approach South Africa used (Byrne). Key lessons that can be gleaned from others' peace-building efforts include

> The importance of appreciating how complex ethnopolitical conflicts are, the need to transform intercommunal relationships, the importance of including local knowledge and local stakeholders in the process, the need to maintain diversity within unity in addressing cultural difference, and the need for remembrance and social justice, as well as forgiveness and reconciliation. (Senehi)

Mutual learning and collaborative problem solving can be applied in most conflicts, as can diplomacy, dialogue, and consensus (Musa).

In addition to these lessons offered, contributors stress the importance of persistence, commitment, and caring. History and stories in this volume reveal how "hard, long-lasting, and unsuccessful reconciliation work can be" (Klain). In many cases, efforts to broker peace have so far failed. Failure disillusions citizens and increases fears of renewed political violence. Violence resulting from failed efforts compounds victims' trauma (Byrne; Klain). In contrast, Norwegians' patience and persistence helped Sri Lanka move toward peace. Similarly, persistence paid off in Northern Ireland. At the same time, intervenors and disputing parties must have realistic expectations (Ifantis). Sometimes it is necessary to move slowly so that adversaries can redefine their identities and goals. It takes time for new ideas to emerge and take root. Perceptions change gradually. Trust must be built. Citizens and institutions must have time to prepare for change. Carefully managing expectations will reduce the risk of disappointment and disillusionment (Ifantis).

In addition to being committed to peace-building, intervenors and disputing parties must make a commitment to effect structural change. To truly resolve ethnopolitical conflict, Senehi stresses, both its psychocultural and structural causes must be addressed. If structural causes of conflict are not addressed, conflict will recur. Global wealth and power imbalances must be redressed. Comprehensive, integrated, holistic plans that take political, economic, ecological, and social imperatives into account are required for two reasons. First, if the underlying forces and factors causing and exacerbating ethnopolitical conflict are not addressed, spats and skirmishes will keep flaring up. Second, conflicts in one region can readily spill over and devastate other nations. An increase in hostilities in any one of the ethnopolitical conflicts in the Middle East or Balkans, for example, would undermine stability on a transregional scale, shatter fragile peace-making efforts in neighboring nations, compromise NATO's ability to manage post–Cold War challenges, and derail the EU's enlargement strategy and plans to create a regional security and defense coalition (Ifantis). The Israeli–Palestinian conflict has regional and global implications because radical Islamist groups are using it as a rallying point to recruit followers. Likewise, the Greece–Turkey and Cyprus conflicts are entwined and threaten regional stability.

Disputing parties and international intervenors need to fully fathom the extremes to which people will go to defend their beliefs and values or achieve their goals. Given the destructive capability and inclinations of groups embroiled in ethnopolitical conflict, even seemingly small, isolated conflicts in distant lands are, or should be, of concern to the rest of the world. Consider Kashmir: "It is a threat to itself and the world" (Hussain). Both India and Pakistan are nuclear capable. With the extremism swirling in and around the region, "radiating radical impulses" threaten regional stability and international security, explains Hussain. Add to this the illegal ceding of land to China and its strategic interest in the region, plus strained relations between India, Pakistan, and China, and an escalation in animosities could draw the United States and China into the Kashmiri conflict (Banerjee; Hussain). The way in which nations and their fates are interconnected is made plain by Batsinduka, who explains that an end to animosities in Rwanda will be "meaningless" unless all nations in the Great Lakes region of

Africa are at peace: "Once your neighbor's house is on fire, yours is surely next, and if you are accused of being a fire raiser, you better be prepared for the backfire, sooner or later."

In much the same way that military insecurity can adversely affect global security, so too can economic, ecological, and social problems. The issues are interconnected (Ifantis).[42] Ethnopolitical conflict is causally linked to and most violent in regions afflicted with acute poverty and resultant hopelessness.[43] Ethnopolitical conflict is also found in regions where degradation is a environmental problem. In many cases, people are forced to mine the environment on which they depend. When the resources on which they depend are depleted, they become environmental refugees and are forced to move on, often into regions upon which other people depend.[44] When analyzing ethnopolitical conflicts and attempting to mitigate them, economic, ecological, and social factors must be taken into account. Turkey and Greece, India and Pakistan, Serbia, Macedonia, Sri Lanka, Rwanda, and other countries discussed in this text would be more likely to achieve sustainable peace if structural challenges were addressed. To be effective, peace-building efforts must be comprehensive and address all imperatives.[45]

New, integrated approaches, capable of effecting structural change, need to be developed. Disputing parties and international intervenors need to reframe their situations, let go of old, destructive disputes, and develop new ways of interacting and problem solving. Where possible, past mistakes should be corrected (Musa). Agreements, such as those made between Israelis and Palestinians and the Ohrid Framework Agreement, should be honored and implemented. Disputing parties should forgive each other and turn their attention to the future, advises Musa. "Acknowledging history is not enough," agree Kaufman and Hassassian. Ancient adversaries "must look toward the future" and develop a shared vision on what needs to be done. Seeking peace does not entail giving up one's ethnonational identity. Rather, it entails seeking peace in an effort to preserve what people value most. As Ifantis notes, countries with "advanced, interdependent economies and consolidated democracies sustained by civil societies" are better off than those choosing to remain in a state of chronic conflict. Warring states should choose cooperation over conflict and make the former and a better future their goals, he advises.

All nations have a vested interest in eradicating violent ethnopolitical conflict. Without cooperation and peace, all Earth's inhabitants are at risk. Inventive outside-the-box ideas aimed at conflict transformation are required, emphasize Kaufman and Hassassian. Conflicting claims and old grudges need to be dealt with, so that other, more pressing economic, ecological, and social imperatives can be attended to. Global security is a superordinate challenge that confronts all nations. Achieving global security will require innovative thinking and new, holistic, triple-bottom-line approaches to the management, mitigation, and prevention of ethnopolitical violence.

The precariousness of the planet calls on people in all sectors and at all levels of society to think and act locally and globally. People need to look in their mirrors and backyards, says Musa. They need to carefully evaluate their choices and take responsibility for the ways in which they are contributing, especially indirectly, to ethnopolitical violence around the world. To effect genuine, enduring structural change, people need to see the connections between the choices that they and their chosen leaders make and the ethnopolitical conflicts in distant developing nations. They need to see how rampant consumerism, amoral secularism, and capitalistic exploitation threaten others—and themselves. Economic, ecological, and social imbalances must be addressed and corrected.

At the same time, others' values must be respected. As Musa explains, respecting others' values is like opening a heavy door (Musa). Anyone can take the first step anytime, but doing so takes effort. Only by exerting the required effort can the "treasures" behind the door be reached.

Achieving enduring peace requires understanding and commitment. This book explains the many complex factors and forces influencing ethnopolitical conflict. By sharing their stories from the front lines, contributors have shed light on the complexities of ethnopolitical conflict. They have answered questions about why ethnopolitical conflicts occur and keep recurring. Through their stories, contributors have added new voices and perspectives to the study of ethnopolitical conflict. They have shared insights that promise to help students and others more wisely weigh their opinions, choices, and actions. They have provided advice on proactive steps that members of the international community and individual citizens wanting to advance and achieve sustained peace can take. Especially thought provoking are their ideas on respect and responsibility. Suggestions they make regarding the need for new intervention approaches and the priority that should be given to prevention, mitigation and post-conflict peace-building warrant contemplation and action. So do their calls for developed countries to think and act differently. As Kaufman and Hassassian emphasize, vision and leadership are needed. Economic, environmental, and social challenges must be addressed and global structural changes effected to attain the treasures sustainable peace offers.

ENDNOTES

1. Guy Olivier Faure and Jeffrey Rubin, eds., *Culture and Negotiation: The Resolution of Water Disputes* (Thousand Oaks, CA: Sage Publications, 1993).

2. Abraham Maslow, *Motivation and Personality* (New York: Harper & Row, 1954)

3. R. Scott Appleby, *The Ambivalence of the Sacred: Religion, Violence, and Reconciliation* (Lanham, MD: Rowman & Littlefield, 2000); Judy Carter, "Believing in Peace: The Potential of Religious Beliefs and Actors to Contribute to Conflict Prevention, Management, Resolution and Post-Conflict Peacebuilding (unpublished master's thesis, Royal Roads University, Victoria, British Columbia, Canada, 2001); Ted Robert Gurr, "Minorities, Nationalists, and Ethnopolitical Conflict," in *Managing Global Chaos: Sources of and Responses to International Conflict,* eds. Chester A. Crocker, Fen Osler Hampson, and Pamela Aull (Washington, DC: United States Institute of Peace, 1996); and Gurr, Ted Robert. (1999). Why Minorities Rebel: Explaining Ethnopolitical Protest and Rebellion. In *Minorities at Risk: A Global View of Ethnopolitical Conflicts.* Washington, DC: United States Institute of Peace.

4. Carter, "Believing in Peace."

5. Jeffrey Z. Rubin, Dean G. Pruitt, and Sung Hee Kim, *Social Conflict: Escalation, Stalemate and Settlement* (New York: McGraw-Hill), 1994.

6. Volkan, Vamik D., Ast, Gabriele, & Greer, Jr., William F. (2002). *Third Reich in the Unconscious: A Study of Transgenerational Transmissions of Shared Trauma and Its Consequences for Identity Formation.* Philadelphia: Brunner-Routledge.

7. Vamik D. Volkan, *Blind Trust: Large Groups and Their Leaders in Times of Crises and Terror* (Charlottesville, VA: Pitchstone Publishing, 2004).

8. Vamik D. Volkan, on "Chosen Trauma," *Mind and Human Interaction,* vol. 3 (1991): 13; Vamik D. Volkan, *Bloodlines: From Ethnic Pride to Ethnic Terrorism* (New York: Farrar, Straus & Giroux, 1997).

9. Vamik D. Volkan, *Bloodlines.*

10. Volkan, *Blind Trust.*

11. Douglas Johnston and Cynthia Sampson, eds., *Religion: The Missing Dimension of Statecraft* (New York: Oxford University Press, 1994).

12. Nik Gowing, "Dispatches from Disaster Zones: The Reporting of Humanitarain Emergencies" (paper presented at the conference on New Challenges and Problems for Information Management in Complex Emergencies, London, England, May 1998).

13. Volkan, *Bloodlines.*

14. Carter, "Believing in Peace"; Samuel P. Huntington, "The Clash of Civilizations?" *Foreign Affairs,* vol. 72 (1993); Johnston and Sampson, *Religion;* Mark Juergensmeyer, *Terror in the Mind of God* (Berkeley: University of California Press, 2000); and Martin E. Marty and R. Scott Appleby, *The Glory and the Power: The Fundamentalist Challenge to the Modern World* (Boston: Beacon Press, 1992).

15. Juergensmeyer, *Terror in the Mind of God.*

16. Marty and Appleby, *The Glory and the Power;* Martin E. Marty and R. Scott Appleby, eds. *Fundamentalisms and Society: Reclaiming the Sciences, the Family, and Education,* vol. 2 (Chicago: University of Chicago Press, 1993); Martin E. Marty and R. Scott Appleby, eds., *Fundamentalisms and the State: Remaking Polities, Economies, and Militance,* vol. 3 (Chicago: University of Chicago Press, 1993).

17. Juergensmeyer, *Terror in the Mind of God.*

18. Benjamin R. Barber, *Jihad vs McWorld: How Globalism and Tribalism Are Reshaping the World* (New York: Ballantine Books, 1996); Juergensmeyer, *Terror in the Mind of God;* Marty and Appleby, *Fundamentalisms and Society;* Marty and Appleby, *Fundamentalisms and the State;* Martin E. Marty and R. Scott Appleby, eds., *Accounting for Fundamentalisms: The Dynamic Character of Movements,* vol. 4. (Chicago: University of Chicago Press, 1994); Martin E. Marty and R. Scott Appleby, eds., *Fundamentalism Comprehended,* vol. 5 (Chicago: University of Chicago Press, 1995); and Emile Sahliyeh, "Religious Resurgence and Political Modernization," in ed. Emile Sahliyeh, *Religious Resurgence and Politics in the Contemporary World* (Albany, NY: SUNY Press, 1990).

19. Carnegie Commission on Preventing Deadly Conflict, *Final Report* (Washington, DC: Carnegie Corporation of New York, 1997); and International Commission on Intervention and State Sovereignty, *Responsibility to Protect* (Ottawa, Ontario: International Development Research Centre, 2001).

20. Ibid.

21. Ann Dale, *At the Edge: Sustainable Development in the 21st Century* (Vancouver, British Columbia: UBC Press, 2001).

22. Frank Dukes, *Resolving Public Conflict* (Manchester, England: Manchester University Press, 1996); Wallace Warfield, "Public-Policy Conflict Resolution: The Nexus Between Culture and Process," in *Conflict Resolution Theory and Practice: Integration and Application,* eds. Dennis J. D. Sandole and Hugo van der Merwe (Manchester, England: Manchester University Press, 1993).

23. Michael Lund, *Preventing Violent Conflicts: A Stragetgy for Preventive Diplomacy* (Washington, DC: United States Institute of Peace, 1996); John Paul Lederach, *Building Peace: Sustainable Reconciliation in Divided Societies* (Washington, DC: United States Institute of Peace, 1996); John Paul Lederach, *The Journey Toward Reconciliation* (Scottsdale, PA: Herald Press, 1999); and Harold H. Saunders, *A Public Peace Process: Sustained Dialogue to Transform Racial and Ethnic Conflicts* (New York: St. Martin's Press, 1999).

24. Lewis J. Rasmussen, "Peacemaking in the Twenty-First Century," in *Peacemaking in International Conflict: Methods and Techniques,* eds. Willam I. Zartman and J. Lewis Rasmussen (Washington, DC: United States Institute of Peace, 1997).

25. William. I. Zartman, "Toward the Resolution of International Conflicts," in *Peacemaking in International Conflict: Methods and Techniques,* eds. William I. Zartman and J. Lewis Rasmussen (Washington, DC: United States Institute of Peace, 1997).

26. George Emile Irani, "Apologies and Reconciliation: Middle-Eastern Rituals," in *Taking Wrongs Seriously: Apologies and Reconciliation,* eds. Eleazar Barkan and Alexander Karn (Palo Alto, CA: Stanford University Press, 2005).

27. Judy Carter and Gordon S. Smith, "Religious Peacebuilding: From Potential to Action," in *Religion and Peacebuilding,* eds. Harold Coward and Gordon S. Smith (New York: SUNY Press, 2004).

28. George Emile Irani and Laurie Elizabeth King-Irani, *Acknowledgment, Forgiveness and Reconciliation: Lessons from Lebanon* (Beruit: Lebanese American University Press, 1996).

29. Rasmussen, "Peacemaking in the Twenty-First Century."

30. Ronald J. Fisher, *Interactive Conflict Resolution* (Syracuse, NY: Syracuse University Press, 1997); and Vamik D. Volkan, "The Tree Model: A Comprehensive Psychopolitical Approach to Unofficial Diplomacy and the Reduction of Ethnic Tension, *Mind and Human Interaction,* vol. 10 (1999): 142–210.

31. Carter, "Believing in Peace"; and Vamik D. Volkan, *The Failure of Diplomacy: The Psychoanalysis of National, Ethnic and Religious Conflicts* (Giessen, West Germany: Psychosocial-Verlag, 1999).

32. Lederach, *Building Peace.*

33. Saunders, *A Public Peace Process.*

34. Rasmussen, "Peacemaking in the Twenty-First Century."

35. Louise Diamond and John McDonald, *Multi-Track Diplomacy: A Systems Approach to Peace,* 3rd ed. (West Hartford, CT: Kumarian Press, 1996); and Fisher, *Interactive Conflict Resolution.*

36. Saunders, *A Public Peace Process.*

37. Hans Bleiker and Annemarie Bleiker, *Citizen Participation Handbook for Public Officials and Other Professionals Serving the Public,* 10th ed. (Monterey, CA: Institute for Participatory Management and Planning, 1997).

38. Robert D. Putnam, "The Prosperous Community: Social Capital and Public Life," *The American Prospect,* no. 13 (Spring 1998).

39. Fisher, *Interactive Conflict Resolution;* George E. Irani, "The Maryland Problem-Solving Forums: Edward Azar's Lebanon," in *Contributions of Interactive Conflict Resolution to Peacemaking in Protracted Ethnopolitical Conflicts,* ed. Ronald J. Fisher, (Lexington, MA: Lexington Press, 2005); Lund, *Preventing Violent Conflicts;* and Saunders, *A Public Peace Process.*

40. Rasmussen, "Peacemaking in the Twenty-First Century."

41. George E. Irani and Nathan C. Funk, "Rituals of Reconciliation: Arab-Islamic Perspectives," in eds. Said Abdul Aziz, et al., *Peace and Conflict Resolution in Islam: Precept and Practice* (Lanham, MD: University Press of America, 2001).

42. Dale, *At the Edge;* and World Commission on Environment and Development, *Our Common Future* (Oxford, England: Oxford University Press, 1987).

43. Rasmussen, "Peacemaking in the Twenty-First Century."

44. Carter, "Believing in Peace."

45. Carter and Gordon S. Smith, "Religious Peacebuilding"; Dale, *At the Edge;* Lund, *Preventing Violent Conflicts;* and Rasmussen, "Peacemaking in the Twenty-First Century."